An Applied Approach to
MICROECONOMICS
THIRD EDITION

Jack A. Chambless

Regular

Plus

Premium

Diesel

Regular $409\frac{9}{10}$

$419\frac{9}{10}$

$459\frac{9}{10}$

FORECLOSURE

FOR SALE

Market in worst free fall since '87

Kendall Hunt
publishing company

Cover image © Shutterstock, Inc.

Kendall Hunt
publishing company

www.kendallhunt.com
Send all inquiries to:
4050 Westmark Drive
Dubuque, IA 52004-1840

Copyright © 2007, 2009, 2011 by Kendall Hunt Publishing Company

ISBN 978-0-7575-9033-7

Printed in the United States of America
10 9 8 7 6 5 4 3 2 1

Contents

Preface

A Message to the Student

The problem with economics is that economists teach it. Like all economists, I must endure endless diatribes from people who feel compelled to tell me that they would rather perform root canal surgery on a rabid wolverine than sit through a discussion of bank bailouts, quantitative easing, the multiplier effect, or pretty much any other economics topic. This is unfortunate, because in reality economics need not be boring, difficult, or abstract. In fact, this social science can be among the most enlightening - and possibly, entertaining classes a student could ever take – when it is presented in a manner that is relevant to the lives of the people in the classroom.

It is my goal to help prepare you to become an economically-literate human being, by presenting real world issues to you in a controversial, timely, and (hopefully) humorous manner. It is a statistical impossibility that you will find every page of this book to be engaging and enjoyable. I can only hope that by the end of the semester, you will know a great deal more – and perhaps care a lot more – about the world around you than you did when you started the class.

As a first-time economics student in the spring of 1986, I was bewildered by how boring and mundane the author of my book made this valuable subject. It seemed that he went out of his way to write a book that would impress his colleagues but totally forgot that his audience was made up largely of novices in the field.

I have tried to give every sentence of this text careful consideration to help you gain the most from your reading. I have no desire to waste your time or talk over your head. Every part of this book was written with the understanding that students of today are more likely to insist on real world application, rather than theoretical examples. In a world of immediate access to information, any author better be prepared to offer up something that is of instant value to the reader. Of course, to get the most out of this book, you need to actually read each chapter – more than once – and ask your professor questions about anything that is unclear. Use the concept checks, classroom debates, and chapter reviews to facilitate your learning.

Concept Checks

Each concept check is designed for you to stop your reading and think about a subject that has just been covered or will be covered in the next few pages. The questions were created to make you think critically about issues that are central to the study of economics. You can find answers to these questions by emailing me by logging on to the book's website – www.jackchambless.com – where many of the answers can be found in various websites, essays, and newspaper editorials. The course website also provides my email address, physical mailing address, and phone number if you want to discuss any part of this book.

Suggested Classroom Debates

What would a college classroom be like if no one ever argued? It would be no fun. I realize it is hard to have debates in algebra or meteorology classes, but economics is a subject filled with thousands of debated issues. Economists disagree often on economic policy proposals and do so in a very spirited manner. This text will therefore give you the chance (assuming your professor is willing to go along) to debate controversial issues of our time.

Make sure you rely on the geniuses who gave us the Internet to help with your answers. It will also serve you well to suspend your emotional reactions in order to respond to some of these controversial questions in an enlightened, mature manner.

You will notice that virtually every chapter of this book has one or more topics devoted to current events like the 2007-2009 Recession, global warming, the controversial health care legislation, global financial turmoil, oil prices (and spills), and the economic policies of the Obama Administration. Please use these topics to add to your list of classroom discussions. I hope you enjoy this added feature and will take the opportunity to use it to enhance your analytical tools.

You should also feel free to follow my blog at http://jackchambless.blogspot.com/. I welcome your opinion in any of my postings.

CHAPTER REVIEWS

One thing you will notice about this book, is that it takes sort of an "old-school" approach to things. I have decided not to add PowerPoint slides, interactive software, electronic test banks, and so forth. I seem to recall when I was a student we had a book, a professor, and some chalk. That was it. We did not need all of the "bells and whistles" in order to get a great economics education. My comparative advantage does not lie within the realm of technology. Therefore, at the end of every chapter you will have a few questions that will allow you to apply what you have learned to some hypothetical or real-world issue. The pages can be removed so that you can submit your work to your professor.

RECOMMENDED BOOKS

As much as I would like to believe that the only economics book a student ever needs to read is this one, I must acknowledge that there are some other books out there you might find incredibly helpful. I highly recommend the following:

The Law by Frederic Bastiat
The Road to Serfdom by F.A. Hayek
The Wealth of Nations by Adam Smith
The Forgotten Man by Amith Shlaes
The FairTax Book by Neal Boortz and John Linder
The Making of Modern Economics by Mark Skousen
Vindicating the Founders by Thomas G. West
Give me a Break by John Stossel
Myths, Lies and Downright Stupidity by John Stossel
The Commanding Heights by Daniel Yergin and
    Joseph Stanislaw
Your Money or Your Life by Sheldon Richman
The Triumph of Liberty by Jim Powell
FDR's Folly by Jim Powell
The Libertarian Reader by David Boaz
Free to Choose by Milton and Rose Friedman
Locke, Jefferson and the Justices by George M. Stephens
Empire Builders by Burton Fulsom
The Myth of the Robber Barrons by Burton Fulsom
Eat the Rich by P.J. O'Rourke

The Farm Fiasco by James Bovard
Freakonomics by Steven D. Levitt and
    Stephen J. Dubner
Lost Rights by James Bovard
Terrorism and Tyranny by James Bovard
An American Life by Ronald Reagan
Reagan's War by Peter Schweizer
The Vision of the Anointed by Thomas Sowell
Black Rednecks and White Liberals by Thomas Sowell
The City on a Hill by Michael Reagan
The Ten Things You Can't Say in America by Larry Elder
*More Liberty Means Less Government, Our Founders
    Knew this Well* by Walter E. Williams
Up From Slavery by Booker T. Washington
Education and Capitalism by Herbert J. Walberg and
    Joseph L. Bast
Eco-nomics by Richard L. Stroup
Atlas Shrugged by Ayn Rand
The End of Prosperity by Arthur Laffer

A MESSAGE TO THE PROFESSOR

> The phenomenon of economic ignorance is so widespread, and its consequences so frightening, that the objective of reducing that ignorance becomes a goal invested with independent moral worth.
>
> Israel Kirzner

A great deal of thought was put into this book from the standpoint of what the professor needs to make economics enjoyable, without compromising the depth and structure that our discipline requires of us in the classroom.

I must first caution the professor by openly acknowledging that this textbook fills a niche in the economics textbook market by openly promoting the concept of free markets, economic liberty, and limited government. If you are inclined to disagree with these notions, this book is not for you. There are several books on the market that dance around these concepts in fear of seeming unbalanced.

I submit that world economic history has vindicated the concept that economic liberty and limited government involvement in economic systems is the most efficient model. It is for that reason that the book comes from a free market approach to economic reasoning. This does not mean that the book fails to point out the shortcomings and costs of free markets. Far from it. You will find ample material that examines the risks associated with economic liberty. I hope you will find this approach to be a welcome and refreshing departure from standard economics textbooks.

This book also relies far less on mathematics and graphs than some other books do. In my more than 20 years in the college classroom, I have come to realize that many students hate economics because we don't make it relevant enough. I contend that students will love our classes if we focus on making them lifetime users of economic concepts. One way we can do this is to get them exited about the applications of our wonderful discipline without "graphing them to death."

I hope you will join me in my attempt to make our valuable discipline one that is no longer viewed as one of the worst subjects a student can take. With any success, we can make economics rank at or near the top of everyone's list of the best classes they could ever take.

RECOMMENDED VIEWING

I have found that videotapes are very useful for learning about the science of economics.

One series stands out in particular as an outstanding supplement to the material you will read in this text. It is the "Stossel in the Classroom" series.

John Stossel is a television correspondent who has gained worldwide acclaim for his pro-liberty, pro-free-market approach to economic issues. According to Mr. Stossel, "I started out by viewing the marketplace as a cruel place, where you need intervention by government and lawyers to protect people. But after watching the regulators work, I have come to believe that markets are magical and the best protectors of the consumer. It is my job to explain the beauties of the free market." (*Oregonian,* 10/26/94)

Stossel has put together several segments, averaging 45 minutes in length, that educators around the nation have found to be very valuable. In particular, I recommend the following segments to coincide with the reading material.

Is America Number One?
Greed
John Stossel Goes to Washington
The War on Drugs: A War on Ourselves?
The Blame Game
Freeloaders
Stupid in America
Sick in America
Freakonomics

I also recommend the PBS series, *The Commanding Heights,* for an in-depth examination of 20th Century economic history and the economics of globalization.

On the course website you can also find many movies that have direct economic applications that your students might enjoy. On the SPEECHES link of the course website, you can find several audio and video links that may be of some use to you. I welcome any recommendations you might have with respect to videos, websites, books, or other materials that you believe would add to the quality of our efforts.

Jack A. Chambless is a professor of economics and professional speaker. He has taught since 1991 at Valencia College in Orlando, Florida where he served as the Patricia Whalen Chair in Social Science in 1999 and 2004, and has received numerous teaching awards from Valencia College, The University of Texas, and North Carolina State University. In addition to teaching Principles of Microeconomcis and Macroeconomics, he has also taught honors courses in economics, two online courses, and special topics courses entitled "Applied Microeconomics" and "Oil, Economics and Terrorism." He has also worked as a professional sports agent and as an energy economist for the Sarkeys Energy Center at The University of Oklahoma and the Research Triangle Institute in Raleigh, North Carolina.

A graduate of The University of Oklahoma and North Carolina State University, his fields of specialization include the political economy, labor economics, energy economics, and industrial organization.

He is a frequent contributor to *The Orlando Sentinel* and has had his work published in *The Wall Street Journal*, *The University of Miami Law Review*, *The Public Utilities Fortnightly*, *Structural Movers*, *Orlando Magazine*, and many other domestic publications. His work has been cited in *The Wall Street Journal*, *USA Today*, *U.S. News & World Report*, *Reason Magazine*, *The Foreign Press Review*, *The Atlanta Journal & Constitution*, *The Detroit News*, *The British Caledonian Press*, and many other foreign and domestic publications.

In addition to teaching, Professor Chambless speaks frequently around the United States on the Economics of Liberty. He has lectured at the Foundation for Economic Education in New York, The Young America's Foundation Freedom Fest in Las Vegas, The Florida Libertarian Convention, and Georgia State University, and has appeared on national television and radio broadcasts including *CNBC's Inside Opinion*, *FoxNews Europe* and *Your World with Neal Cavuto (FoxNews)*, *The Neal*

Photo by Sarah Chambless

Boortz Show, the *BBC*, *National Public Radio*, and *The Jim Hightower Show*. He is also currently serving as a policy advisor for The Heartland Institute – a think tank in Chicago, Illinois.

Professor Chambless enjoys hiking and canoeing in the Northwestern United States, Minnesota, and Canada, photography, and watching his favorite sports teams in his spare time.

Acknowledgements

I would like to extend my sincerest thanks to Walter Williams, Armen Alchian, Paul White, Randall K. Russell, Tarteashia Williams, Ron Brandolini, Mark Skousen, and Stephen Margolis for their forthright and constructive comments regarding past editions of this book. I also want to thank Adam Gifford and Joseph Brignone for providing valuable ideas for this edition. I am forever indebted to Michael Murphy, the long time editor of *The Orlando Sentinel's* Op-Ed page. His assistance in launching my career as a writer dates back to 1992 and persisted for 16 years. Without him, it is highly unlikely that I would have ever undertaken the risk of putting my controversial writing in the public domain.

It is difficult to put into words how grateful I am to Jessica Cannavo, Stephanie Moffett, Linda Chapman, and Jennifer Wreisner. Ms. Wreisner and Ms. Chapman are responsible for the organizational structure, copyediting, and beautiful typesetting which makes the book easy to read. Jessica Cannavo – for her work in the early stages of this process – and Stephanie Moffett for her wonderful work in completing this book, deserve a medal for putting up with my personality. I could not have asked for more professional and personable persons to work with.

Any final errors – in writing or judgment – omissions or sarcastic remarks are the sole responsibility of the author.

Dedication

For my wife, Sarah – a true believer in the cause of liberty – and the most wonderful person on Earth.

Chapter One

INTRODUCTION *to* ECONOMICS

Shutterstock © Kevin H. Knuth, 2011.

*Wh*oever loves money never has money enough; whoever loves

wealth is never satisfied with his income. This too is meaningless.

As goods increase, so do those who consume them. And what

benefit are they to the owner except to feast his eyes upon them?

ECCLESIASTES 5:10–11, NEW INTERNATIONAL VERSION

You are in the Right Place at the Right - and Wrong - Time...

I sometimes joke with my students that they picked a good time to take an economics class and a bad time to be born.

For the more than 23 years I have been an economist, my life has been pretty easy in the classroom. With the exception of two very brief disruptions in the rate at which our nation accumulated wealth, I have had the opportunity to teach students who were largely enjoying an unprecedented run of prosperity and abundance. My, how times can change.

As you begin to read this book it is somewhere between August 2011 and the summer of 2013. The closer you are to 2011, the more you have heard about, or felt, the pressure of $4 per gallon gasoline, a housing market that has seen a historic decline, price increases for food and other consumer goods that have accelerated faster than most of our paychecks, investment bank failures, health care mandates, stubbornly high unemployment rates, and constant fighting in Washington D.C. – along with every state capitol in America over what to do about soaring budget deficits.

To some, the previous paragraph is perfect evidence as to why economics is called the "dismal science."

After all, economics, as you will discover, is an examination of the perpetually dissatisfied human being. History reveals a fundamental truth about our species. No matter how much we have, we always want more. The problem is that more is not always available – and sometimes, as our recent times have shown, less and less is all that is available.

What will follow is a lengthy examination of how the science of economics can give all of us a better understanding of the forces that shape our daily lives and an appreciation (hopefully) for how economics can increase our chances of achieving a greater measure of happiness.

It's Not About the Money

Many years ago, I was having dinner with some of my relatives in North Carolina. When the check arrived, my cousin (a really smart psychologist) handed me the check and said, "Here, Jack. You're an economist. You figure out the tip."

This is a pretty typical way people talk to economists.

Sometimes while at social gatherings, I have people walk up to me and ask for my predictions on what will happen in the real estate/gold/oil/stock/bond (you get the idea) markets.

I tell them that if I knew the answers to their questions, I would be in a large cabin up in the North Woods near my private lake in the middle of my 1,000 acres of land rather than at the gathering we are at.

The point is that economics is not all about money – and what to do with money. Sure, economists are pretty good at talking about money and even get some predictions correct from time to time, but ostensibly, economics is about much more than our day-to-day finances.

What Economics is All About

When you were a newborn, what was your primary focus? Why did you yell at everyone to let them know what your focus was? When you were a toddler, did sharing your toys come naturally, or were you inclined to bite other kids who took away your stuff?

Now that you are in college, how did you go about picking your major, or the number of hours you would work at a job? How did your friends and family go about deciding where they would live or what they would eat during the 2007-2009 recession? What determines whether or not you will accept a new friend – online, or in person?

Do you ever wonder what the ideal spouse for you would be like? Do you stop to think about why people text while they are driving?

How do you go about deciding whom to vote for? Do you pick the candidates that promise to send you money? Are you inclined to vote for the one who promises to let you keep your money?

These, and other questions, often have to do with money, but not always. This semester you will discover that the social science of economics is one of the most powerful disciplines you can ever master in your quest to make good decisions. In order to unlock the secrets to this wonderfully complex, and simple, subject, we need to start by examining what economics really is.

> ➤ **Economics is the scientific study of how people make decisions in a world where wants and needs are unlimited but resources to meet our wants and needs are scarce.**

The word "economics" is based on Greek roots, but the Greeks didn't have a field of study anything like economics. The two Greek roots of the word "economics" are *oikos* – meaning the household or family estate – and *nomos*, which can mean rules, natural laws, or laws made by the government. In essence, the meaning of this word hangs on the concept of people choosing how they will manage their homes and businesses with the available resources at their disposal.

Economics is called a *decision science* because we all have to decide, each and every day, how we will utilize the resources at our disposal to meet our wants and needs.

What are resources? For economists, resources are typically divided up into four categories: Land, labor, capital, and entrepreneurship.

> ➤ **Land** encompasses all *naturally occurring resources* like water, timber, minerals, plant and animal life, and so forth.
> ➤ **Labor** is the *human effort* in the process of producing goods and services.
> ➤ **Capital** takes two forms. The first type of capital is *physical* capital. This is made up of the equipment and tools used to produce goods and services. The other type of capital is *human* capital – the knowledge, education, training, and skills we bring to the process of production.
> ➤ **Entrepreneurship** – based on the French word for *one who assumes risk* – is made up of the men and women who use their resources to invent new products and start new business ventures.

The final key word in the definition of economics – and, in fact, the most important one is the word, *scarce*.

Simply put, the resources we have at our disposal are limited – sometimes severely. This means that the problem of *scarcity* is omnipresent.

> ➤ **Scarcity is the ongoing imbalance between our wants and needs and the resources available to meet those wants and needs.**

Here is the dilemma we face. When we were born, there was an *imbalance* between the amount of food or warmth we had and the amount we desired. In essence, we all faced the problem of scarcity. When we realized we were dealing with scarcity, we started screaming. Screaming was a way of using the resources we had at our disposal (think of your lungs as capital) to let everyone know about our imbalances. Once we were fed or comforted, or given a blanket, we probably quieted down, for the time being. This period of quiet was an indication that we were satisfied with how our imbalances were dealt with…for a while.

Flash forward to today. What imbalances are you dealing with at this time? Let's see. First, there is an imbalance between the number of credit hours you have and the number of credit hours you need to complete your degree. There is the imbalance between the amount of money you are currently making and the amount of money you would like to make. So, what are you doing about those two (out of the list of thousands of imbalances you might be dealing with) imbalances?

You are making decisions with the resources you have. By using physical capital (computers, MP3 technology, calculators, and so forth) as well as your human capital, you are attempting to close the credit hour imbalance. This will occur when you get your degree. Once that imbalance is closed, you will be in a better position to close, or more likely, narrow the financial imbalances in your life.

So, how much money will close that imbalance? $70,000? $127,000? $4.32 million?

I have some bad news for many of you. If you believe, at this time, that $127,000 would satisfy you, just wait until you get there. Chances are, once you make $127,000 you will start thinking that $200,000 would be better. Then you will allocate your resources toward that goal. Mark Zuckerberg (the founder of Facebook) probably never dreamed of being a billionaire, but a funny thing happened once his net worth hit $1 billion. He kept going to work. That is because human beings are perpetually dissatisfied with their current situation.

Recessions, of course, make the problem of scarcity even worse as people lose their jobs or face reduction in their work hours or take-home pay. We know how much money we need to eat and pay our other bills but when the economy falters, we must face up to the fact

that scarcity will be a more pressing issue than when jobs are plentiful. The 2007-2009 Recession was the longest experienced by the United States since the 1930s. During the most recent downturn, incomes fell by an average of 4.2% and the number of Americans living in poverty rose to 14.3% of the population.[1]

HOW ECONOMISTS DEAL WITH SCARCITY

Contrary to the belief of many, economists are humans and we feel pain. So when the most recent economic calamity swept the planet, economists felt the impact, too. It's just that we did not feel it as much, on average, as the average person.

This is not because all economists make so much money that we do not have to worry about downturns in the economy. It is because most economists are colossal skinflints (translation: really, really cheap) when it comes to the use of our scarce dollars. Consider this excerpt from *The Wall Street Journal*:

> Academic economists gather in Atlanta this weekend for their annual meetings, always held the first weekend after New Year's Day. That's not only because it coincides with holidays at most universities. A post-holiday lull in business travel also puts hotel rates near the lowest point of the year. Economists are often cheapskates.
>
> The economists make cities bid against each other to hold their convention, and don't care so much about beaches, golf courses or other frills. It's like buying a car, explains the American Economic Association's secretary-treasurer, John Siegfried, an economist at Vanderbilt University.

"When my wife buys a car, she seems to care what color it is," he says. "I always tell her, don't care about the color." He initially wanted a gray 2007 Mercury Grand Marquis, but a black one cost about $100 less. He got black.

Some of the world's most famous economists were famously frugal. After a dinner thrown by the British economic giant John Maynard Keynes, writer Virginia Woolf complained that the guests had to pick "the bones of Maynard's grouse of which there were three to eleven people." Milton Friedman, the late Nobel laureate, routinely returned reporters' calls collect.

Children of economists recall how tightfisted their parents were. Lauren Weber, author of a recent book titled, "In Cheap We Trust," says her economist father kept the thermostat so low that her mother threatened at one point to take the family to a motel. "My father gave in because it would have been more expensive," she says.

"Where do I begin?" says Marisa Kasriel when asked about the lengths to which her father, Northern Trust Co. economist Paul Kasriel, will go to save a buck: private-label groceries, off-brand tennis shoes and his 1995 Subaru, with a piece of electrical tape covering the "check engine" light. Mr. Kasriel says he buys off-brand shoes "so that my lovely children could have Nikes."

David Colander, an economist at Middlebury College in Vermont, says his wife – his first one, that is – was miffed when he went shopping for the cheapest diamond. Economist Robert Gordon, of Northwestern University, says he drives out of his way to go to a grocery store where prices are cheaper than at the nearby Whole Foods, even though it takes him an extra half hour to save no more than $5.

Mr. Gordon, however, is no ascetic. He, his wife and their two dogs live in a 11,000-square-foot, 21-room 1889 mansion on the largest residential lot in Evanston, Ill., outside Chicago.

"The house is full, every room is furnished, there are 72 oriental rugs and vast collections of oriental art, 1930s art deco Czech perfume bottles and other nice stuff," he says.

Some economists may be cheap, at least by the standards of other people, because of their training or a fascination with money and choices that drives them to the field.

Wharton School professor Justin Wolfers and a colleague gave a friend $150 to hire movers instead of helping him to move themselves.

In recent research, University of Washington economists Yoram Bauman and Elaina Rose found that economics majors were less likely to donate money to charity than students who majored in other fields. After majors in other fields took an introductory economics course, their propensity to give also fell.

"The economics students seem to be born guilty, and the other students seem to lose their innocence when they take an economics class," says Mr. Bauman, who has a stand-up comedy act he'll be doing at the economists' Atlanta conference Sunday night. Among his one-liners: "You might be an economist if you refuse to sell your children because they might be worth more later."[2]

If you find yourself thinking that economists are a bit odd, consider this…

I once cut down a Christmas tree in a field next to my parent's house in Oklahoma, borrowed rope from my Dad, tied the tree to the roof of my vehicle, and drove 1,178 miles back to Florida with my almost free tree – in October. Okay, the tree turned brown by Thanksgiving and people laughed at me and took pictures the entire trip, but I cannot bear the thought of having to buy a tree that will only be in my house for a few weeks.

I buy almost all of my clothes at thrift stores and garage sales; only drive used cars; cut my own firewood so that I can avoid turning on the heat in the winter; purchase gifts for family members at the same garage sales I buy my clothes; use eBay to sell their gifts once they have stopped using them and never, ever pay interest to a credit card provider.

I should also mention that all of our family vacations involve sleeping in the woods in a tent. I just think anything more than $19 is too much to pay for sleeping.

The point that this is designed to make is simple. Economists are often bewildered by the spending patterns of people. We all face monetary scarcity, but using credit cards to purchase brand-new items, all of the time, even when our debts pile up before our eyes, is a recipe for magnifying the financial scarcity that is already there. We simply think it makes sense to spend as little as possible in many areas of our lives, so that we have the ability to allocate the savings to other areas of our lives where we are not that frugal (I like nice restaurants) or where we believe the payoff will be greater (investing in a business or retirement fund, for example).

OTHER PLACES IMBALANCES EXIST

Money is not the only place where scarcity shows up. For example, how many of you wish that your fellow man would turn off their phone in the movie theater and drive more carefully after the movie? If you are like many other folks out there, you are facing the problem of "common courtesy imbalances." You want it quiet in the movies and calm on the roads, but you don't get what you want. That is because the resources needed to get what you want (one really mean movie usher per movie watcher and tickets of $40,000 for every driver who acts stupid) are currently not available.

Our lives are spent dealing with the process of using our resources, or attempting to acquire resources to meet our various wants and needs. Whether it is spiritual ful-

CONCEPT CHECK

In 2010, President Obama signed legislation that required every business in America to file a 1099 tax form every time the business buys anything from a contractor that costs $600 or more.[3] For small businesses, how could this legislation ultimately impact the problem of scarcity?

fillment, finding a mate, getting your children to behave, or creating a cleaner environment, we never run out of imbalances to deal with. Economics is about the eternal quest for the *most rational use* of those resources, so that we can be happy or satisfied with our standing. As you will see, even terrorists with degrees in economics struggle with the problem of scarcity.

TERRORISM AND THE PROBLEM OF SCARCITY

"I concentrate on the importance of continuing holy war actions against America, militarily and economically. This economic hemorrhaging continues until today, but requires more blows. And the youth should try to find the joints of the American economy and hit the enemy in these joints, with God's permission."

Osama bin Laden
December 27, 2001

Considered the world's foremost terrorist, Osama bin Laden shocked millions with the glee he expressed on worldwide television broadcasts following the terrorist strikes against the United States. With his account of how his plan was carried out with far greater success than even he could have imagined, Mr. bin Laden illustrated to the entire world that terrorism is not a random act of violence, but rather an exercise in economics.

Born in Saudi Arabia around 1957, Osama was not raised in a life of poverty. His father, Mohammed bin Laden founded a construction company, and with royal patronage, became a billionaire. However, as the seventeenth son, born in a society where family status is highly important, Osama would have been deemed "less important" than his older brothers.

As a student at King Abdul Aziz University in Jedda, Saudi Arabia, Osama studied management and *economics*, coming under the influence of religious teachers who introduced him to the wider world of Islamic politics. Perhaps the first major instance where scarcity entered his adult life was during the Soviet invasion of Afghanistan in 1979. Osama supported the Afghan resistance (as did the United States), which became a jihad, or holy war. In this instance, Osama worked toward closing the imbalance between the number of Soviet troops he wanted in Afghanistan (zero) and the number that actually existed at this time.

By the mid-1980s, bin Laden had moved to Afghanistan, where he established an organization, Maktab al-Khidimat (MAK), to recruit Islamic soldiers from around the world who later formed the basis of an international network. The MAK maintained recruiting offices in Detroit and Brooklyn in the 1980s.[4]

The Taliban arose from the religious schools set up during the war against the Soviet invasion. After the Soviet Army withdrew in 1989, fighting erupted among various factions who sought control over the Afghan government. In response to the chaos, the fundamentalist Taliban was formed and within two years had captured most of the country.

After the Soviet withdrawal, bin Laden returned to Saudi Arabia and worked in his family's construction business. In 1990, in response to the Iraqi invasion of Kuwait, the Saudi government allowed American troops to be stationed in Saudi Arabia. Bin Laden was incensed that non-believers (American soldiers) were stationed in the birthplace of Islam. He also charged the Saudi regime with deviating from true Islam.

Bin Laden was expelled from Saudi Arabia in 1991 because of his anti-government activities. He eventually wound up in Sudan, where he worked with Egyptian radical groups in exile. When the United States set up military operations in Saudi Arabia to remove Iraq from Kuwait, bin Laden protested to the Saudi royal family, arguing that the U.S. was only in Saudi Arabia to secure oil supplies and, if allowed to, would never leave.

In 1992 bin Laden claimed responsibility for attempting to bomb U.S. soldiers in Yemen and for attacking U.S. troops in Somalia the following year. In 1994 pressure from the U.S. and Saudi Arabia prompted Sudan to expel bin Laden, and he returned to Afghanistan.

In 1998, bin Laden called for all Americans and Jews, including children, to be killed. He had since been connected to terrorist bombings at the U.S. embassies in Kenya and Tanzania, the attack against the USS Cole and the September 11, 2001 attacks in New York City, Pennsylvania and Washington, D.C. and others around the globe in 2003 and 2004.

The problem of scarcity, for Osama bin Laden, was straightforward. There was an imbalance between the number of Americans and Jews who are currently dead and the number he wanted dead. There was an imbalance between the number of weapons he needed to accomplish this goal and the number of weapons he had. Even with a fortune estimated at $250 million, there was an imbalance between the amount of money he needed to carry out his goal and the amount of money he had.

With the United States actively bombing his al-Qaeda network and arresting key leaders, there was a growing imbalance between the amount of resources and people he had to work with (now that he is dead) and the resources and people he needed to work with. With increased security measures in the United States, and inevitable changes to U.S. immigration policy, there will most likely be a growing imbalance between the number of terrorists al-Qaeda needs to get into the United States and the number of terrorists that will make it into the U.S. Losing the war in Iraq could create scarcity for al-Qaeda, too. If Iraq becomes a relatively free nation, this will be one less place for terrorists to flourish.

However, the astute economics student should be aware of the fact that the United States faces the problem of scarcity in this ongoing war on terrorism. Imagine the resources we need as a nation in order to eliminate every terrorist cell in the world. How much money would that cost? If we have enough money, do we have enough technology, and surveillance, and people, to pull off this task?

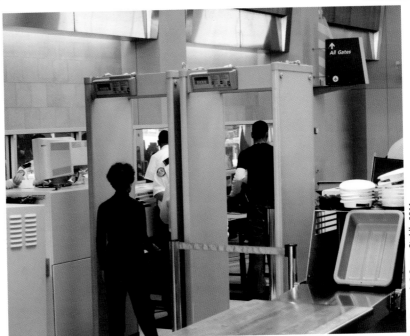

Shutterstock © James Steidl, 2011.

Since September 11th, there has also been a marked decline in the overall liberty enjoyed by Americans. The federal government has increased its presence in our mail, email, phone conversations, Internet searches and travel plans.[5] Many wonder how much more civil liberty can be given up in order to impose scarcity on the global terrorist network.

If we get rid of every terrorist by 2014, are there children who will grow up to become terrorists by 2028? Can we stop every person who enters the U.S. and accurately gauge his or her intentions? Do we have the patience that a prolonged war requires? Could we prevent a nuclear or biological attack for the remaining years of this republic?

These questions were a central part of the 2008 presidential campaign. President Obama repeatedly argued that the nation's resources would be put to the best use by removing troops and money from Iraq and diverting those resources towards an expansion of the war on terror in Afghanistan.

John McCain contended that leaving Iraq prematurely could promote civil unrest and lead to an even greater threat of terrorism coming from an unguarded Middle East.

The fact that both men even addressed this issue is one more bit of evidence that we have to make choices because our tax dollars – and the lives and health of our troops – are not available in unlimited quantities.

As you can see, the probability of eliminating the imbalance between the amount of safety and security we want and the amount we have is very, very low. We may never eliminate the imbalance. In economics, you learn that sometimes the best we can do is to narrow the imbalances in our lives.

MAKING "GOOD" DECISIONS

Have you known someone who makes really bad decisions almost all the time? On the flipside, do you know anyone that seems to have their life together when it comes to dating, money, school, and just about everything else? It could be that luck floats around and lands on some people while it misses others. Or, it could be that some people make better decisions than others with their scarce resources. In this section, you will learn how economists evaluate human behavior and how to be one of those people who seem to get things right more often than not.

During the summer of 2010, one of the greatest athletes in the world – a young man from Akron, Ohio – decided to have a one-hour television special to announce to the world where he would be working for the next few years.

His decision was not unlike the decision millions of people make every year. After all, how many of you have loaded the boxes in a van to leave for some other destination? What made his decision unique, when compared to the rest of us, is that people were willing to watch him talk about it on television. If you or I contacted a television network to sell our next moving decision to potential sponsors, the network would hang up the phone – after laughing at us for 45 minutes.

For Mr. James there was a problem of scarcity that seemed to center around the number zero – as in the number of championship rings he owned while working for the Cleveland Cavaliers of the National Basketball Association.

To deal with this problem, he announced that he would be moving to south Florida to work for the Miami Heat. When he made the announcement, a lot of people were very upset. Perhaps he could have kept the anger to a minimum if he would have held up a piece of paper with three columns – one with the heading, "BENEFITS"; one with the heading, "DIRECT COSTS"; and a final column marked, "OPPORTUNITY COST".

What do these columns mean? It means that he was attempting to engage in *rational behavior.*

> ➤ **Rational behavior is said to exist when human beings engage in a decision-making process where, at the time the decision is made, the expected direct benefits of the decision equal, or exceed, the expected direct cost, plus the opportunity cost of their decision.**
> ➤ **Benefits are the monetary and/or nonmonetary gain expected from any decision.**
> ➤ **Direct costs are the known, or expected out of pocket costs and the probability of something negative occurring as a result of the decision.**
> ➤ **Opportunity cost is the cost of choosing to use resources for one purpose, measured by the value of the next best alternative for using those resources.**

The concept of opportunity cost teaches us that when you use your time, money, energy, or any other economic resource for one purpose you have to forgo the *second best* alternative for using those resources. This means that we constantly face tradeoffs that must be made in the game of resource allocation.[6]

A simple way of grasping the idea of rational economic behavior is to consider how many of you shop for clothes.

Suppose you are at the mall looking for a new pair of pants. You spot the pair that you like, try them on and they fit great. Without looking at the price tag you decide that if they cost $50 or less you will buy them. That means that you think you will get at least $50 in *benefits* from these pants.

You look at the price tag and find that they were originally $79 but have been marked down to $39.

$39 is the *direct cost* of the pants.

Then you ponder what else you could spend $39 on. Perhaps your car needs an oil change. Maybe your iron is broken. There could be any number of 'second best' things you could spend $39 on.

If, in your mind, the benefit of the pants is greater than the direct costs plus the *opportunity cost* of replacing your iron that day, then you are rational to buy the pants.

If, on the other hand, you look at the price tag that day and see that the pants are $79 then you would be *irrational* to buy them since you believe they are only worth $50.

> ➤ **An irrational decision is one where an individual makes a decision knowing that the costs exceed the benefits.**

You can try this procedure the next time you are trying to decide where to go to school, or what to major in, or whom to vote for in a presidential election. It also can work well in deciding whether you should accept a marriage proposal or when you are contemplating a change in some other lifestyle choice.

While you are at it, there are a few things to keep in mind about the economics of rational behavior.

First, *your benefits and costs are unique to you* – as are the benefits and costs to some other person. If you decide that buying a brand new car for $27,000 will confer greater benefits than the sum total of all of the monetary costs *plus* the opportunity cost of the next best thing you could have done with $27,000 (a used car; a lot of nice clothes and your rent payment for six months, for example) then you have made a rational choice – even if everyone you know tells you that you are an economic moron.

Of course, this concept presupposes that if you see someone smoking crack behind a dumpster, you cannot assume they are irrational. You would need to ask them to explain the benefits of crack smoking, along with how much the crack cost and what else they could be doing with their time. It could be that there are many rational crack smokers out there behind the dumpsters.

Second, it is important to understand that *economists assume that people are inherently rational.* That means that we are born with an internal drive to do things that benefit us more than it costs us. Many students have trouble with this assumption, which is understandable. After all, given the average age of the person reading this book, one could assume that most students have seen their friends do so many outrageous things that it would be a safer bet to argue that we are inherently irrational and simply get lucky with good decisions from time to time.

This is not the case. Consider this: When your friend – whom you think is irrational – is driving their modified Honda Civic 112 miles per hour, on the shoulder, while listening to their music so loud that the windows shake, what do they do when they come over the top of a hill and see a highway patrol officer? How long does it take for them to slow down?

If your answer is "somewhere around .001 seconds," then you have confirmed that biologically we all have a desire for self-preservation. We eat, sleep, avoid death as much as we can and make other decisions that get most of us into old age.

Sometimes, as we will see later on, people do make arguably irrational choices, but it is not as often as you might think.

Finally, *economists tend not to evaluate the rationality of a decision ex post facto, or "after the fact."* We are most interested in the cost-benefit calculation leading up to the decision that is being made, in order to accurately assess the rationality of the choices people make.

So, with all of this in mind, one can easily see what Mr. James was thinking:

Benefits – a perceived greater probability of winning an NBA Championship, along with no state income tax in Florida and warmer weather (assuming he prefers warmer weather).

Direct Cost – Dealing with the anger and wrath of jilted Cleveland fans, as well as the pressure that would come from co-existing with other NBA stars playing for the Heat.

Opportunity Cost – The value that would have come from staying in Cleveland (assuming it was his second best choice).

Verdict? He was rational. Proof? He left Cleveland.

APPLICATIONS OF COST-BENEFIT ANALYSIS

WHY INCENTIVES MATTER...

When you were young your parents may have used incentives to get you to do things that they wanted you to do. Sometimes those incentives might have come in the form of an award and sometimes in the form of a threat.

> ➤ **Incentives are anything that changes the costs and benefits of a decision.**

Some of you might have had some trouble ending the habit of having "accidents" in your diaper while you were playing with your friends outside. Perhaps while you were playing the benefits of interrupting your fun to run to the bathroom were too low, while your diaper seemed to work well and the opportunity cost of missing play time made the costs of going inside too high.

If your parents offered you candy, or money, or extra time playing video games for every time you successfully used the bathroom then this was their way of raising the benefits of going to the bathroom to a level they hoped would exceed your costs. This is an example of a *positive incentive.*

Some of you might have had parents that told you that for every time you did not go to the bathroom you would have to spend 30 more minutes cleaning your room. This *negative incentive* was designed to increase the costs of having accidents to the point where it would be more rational to run inside.

Sometimes the government acts like parents in order to change behavior that is deemed unacceptable.

One recent example that comes to mind is the threat by President Obama to push for something called a "windfall profits tax" on America's oil companies.

According to Mr. Obama – and others who supported this idea – the oil companies made too much profit in 2007 and 2008 from the historic increase in crude oil prices. These critics charged that rather than earning increasing profits by providing better and more reliable petroleum-based products, the oil companies were simply raking in billion of dollars in extra cash as a result of nothing more than rising prices.

Exxon-Mobil, for example, reported net after-tax earnings of $40.6 billion in 2007, which amounted to $1,400 in profits *every second*.[8]

What is not often mentioned, however, is the fact that over the past several years the oil industry's net income was 5.7 cents per dollar of revenue (translation – out of every dollar earned, 94.3 cents went to operating costs), while the average for all other industries was 5.5 cents.

SUGGESTED CLASSROOM DEBATE

Economists have observed that many Americans have decided to default on their home loans – even when they can afford to make the monthly mortgage payment – because their homes are worth less than the total amount owed.[7] Is this rational or irrational behavior? Why?

The reason oil companies have been cited for "excessive greed" is simple. First, since we have all been impacted by rapidly rising gasoline prices, we are more likely to get angry with the companies who sell us gasoline. Politicians therefore can gain votes by turning our anger into political persecution of those companies without mentioning the fact that Exxon-Mobil paid $30 billion in corporate taxes in 2007.

Nevertheless, as he campaigned in 2008, Barack Obama promised to tax the profits of oil companies at a higher level and send part of the money to the American people.

When economists talk about how we make decisions we often refer to the phrase "marginal analysis."

> ➤ **Marginal analysis is the examination of incremental changes in the benefits and costs of any decision.**

Think of it this way...

If you are buying pants, there is a *marginal* (extra) *benefit* that can be derived from every pair you buy. The first pair might be worth $50 to you, the second might be worth $40, the third $25, and so forth.

The *marginal cost* is the extra cost you incur from each pair of pants you purchase. Sometimes marginal costs remain constant, sometimes costs change.

In the graph that follows, we examine the marginal benefits and marginal costs of exploring for oil for any given oil company.

Notice that we have established the marginal benefit at a constant amount of $125 per barrel. If oil prices are $125 per barrel at the time you are reading this book, then it would benefit an oil company by that figure ($125) to produce each barrel of oil.

However, the marginal cost curve is upward-sloping. This illustrates that finding and eventually producing oil comes at a higher and higher cost. Typically, the oil fields that have the most accessible oil – and therefore the cheapest oil to obtain – are utilized first. Yet as more and more oil is produced, companies have to drill in places that are more remote (offshore, for example), or in places that might be more politically unstable or that have smaller reserves of oil. All of this translates into higher production costs over time.

In this particular example, we can see that the optimum level of oil production, at $125, is 1 million barrels per day. This is where *the marginal benefit equals the marginal cost*. If the company produced only 900,000 barrels the marginal cost would equal $110. Since the marginal benefit is constant at $125, the company can earn even more profit by expanding production toward 1 million barrels.

If the company produces 1.1 million barrels the marginal cost is now $135 – causing the firm to lose $10 per barrel – and creating incentives to cut back on production.

So, where does a windfall profits tax enter the picture?

In 1980 the Jimmy Carter Administration passed a law creating the same type of tax Mr. Obama campaigned for in 2008. The tax ranged from 30 – 70% depending on when the oil had been discovered.[9]

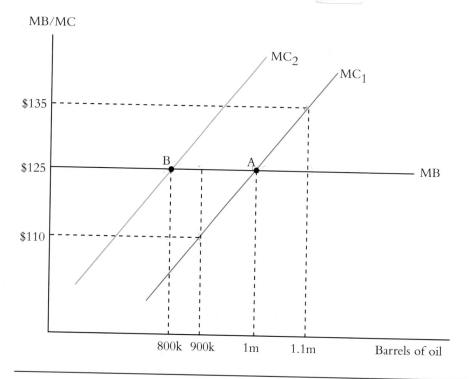

GRAPH 1.1

The result of this new tax – as you might expect – was a significant increase in the marginal cost of producing and delivering oil.

Mr. Carter's *negative incentive* of higher taxes predictably led to a drop in oil exploration as companies scrambled to use their scarce – and declining financial resources – to maintain other business operations.[10]

In the preceding diagram we see that a windfall profits tax would push the marginal cost curve from MC1 to MC2. Thus a new intersection would occur at point B, where less oil is produced than before.

What does this mean for those of us who still buy gas? The answer is pretty straightforward. If oil companies are hampered by significant increases in taxes, in order to maintain profitability the companies will have to cut back on production. Less production means less supply and, as we will clearly see in chapter 7, less supply would lead to higher prices over time.

This is one reason why many economists not only oppose windfall profits taxes but instead favor making it easier for oil companies to drill for oil in – and around the United States, where significant reserves are now protected from drilling. Those in favor of greater drilling point out that off the coast of Florida, California and in Alaska exists reserves in the billions of barrels. If oil companies were given the positive incentives of less regulation over where drilling can occur, the marginal cost of drilling would fall (since many of the reserves are readily accessible) greater production would occur and downward pressure on prices would naturally follow.[11]

This suggestion has been a politically unpopular one for many years. It is only recently that more and more Americans have become receptive to it. $3-4 per gallon has a way of doing that…

But What about BP? Didn't That Prove that Offshore Drilling is Terrible?

Good question.

According to the journal *Science*, during the summer of 2010 a total of 4.4 million barrels (185 million gallons) of crude oil spilled into the Gulf of Mexico when BP's offshore oil rig exploded.

During much of that summer, the price of crude oil hovered around $80 per barrel. That means that BP lost $352 million – before any government fines, lawsuit settlements, or cleanup costs – when the rig failed.

Do you suppose BP executives, when overseeing the construction of the Horizon rig, sat in a meeting and said, "Gee, let's see if we can have a rig that will someday leak

$352 million of our product into the ocean, cause everyone to hate us, get the government crawling into our lives, lawyers salivating with glee over all of the money they will make from us – AND have the television networks showing dead birds and fish with our product all over them!" "That would be a great business idea!!"

Pardon the sarcasm, but one necessary condition for learning economics is to be able to suspend emotion when analyzing economic events, so that you can clearly assess the cost-benefit calculations that led to an event and therefore rationally respond to that event.

The BP oil spill was simply the predictable result of a series of rational decisions made by politicians, oil company executives, consumers, and engineers. Let's look at it.

Ever since the creation of the internal combustion engine, human beings have traveled from point A to point B via the burning of dead dinosaurs. The petroleum derived from organic matter has always been sold at a price, rather than given away to the nicest drivers free of charge.

Rational drivers have always thought that they would rather pay low prices than high prices for fuel, so rational oil companies have spent decades trying to locate the lowest cost petroleum so that consumers would see an acceptable price and use more of the product over time.

From east Texas in the 1920s to the Middle East after that, to Alaska in the 1970s and eventually into the ocean, the quest for large quantities of oil to meet the demands of a growing world economy has always led to new exploration.

When the Organization of Petroleum Exporting Countries (OPEC to you and I) was formed in 1960, the world was suddenly faced with the prospect of buying oil from a region that controlled the largest reserves of petroleum – and large reserves of anger toward the United States.

A series of political events (to be covered in later chapters) led to dramatic reductions in the supply of oil flowing from the Middle East to the U.S. during the 1970s. The result was skyrocketing prices and a political push from voters to find oil in places that were not located in countries that did not like us much.

In 1989, Shell Oil announced that it had discovered the Auger oil field nearly 3,000 feet below the surface of the Gulf of Mexico. This set off a mad rush by other oil companies to explore for oil in this region.[12] This was a rational move. The cost of dealing with hostile nations as our primary supplier had grown too high. The prospect of extracting oil from U.S. waters was too good to pass up and the cost of drilling for oil in the ocean was falling as technology continued to improve.

On November 28, 1995, President Bill Clinton signed the Deepwater Royalty Relief Act – an act that dramatically lowered the royalties that oil companies had to pay the federal government for oil pumped out of the ocean floor. Mr. Clinton felt that the benefits of this act would be twofold – first, it would lower the cost of U.S. oil production, leading to greater supplies and lower consumer prices, and second, low consumer prices would keep the economy strong which tends to help politicians stay in office.

Of course, the cost of this act, one could argue, was a higher chance of something going wrong as more and more rigs would ultimately be constructed.

Any rational business, when constructing a new facility, is going to seek to keep costs down in order to enhance the chances of earning profit. An investigation by the U.S. Minerals Management Service found that the Deepwater Horizon rig

A bad idea?

was a "risky" and less expensive design that was used by BP in 42% of its rigs – far more than was used by other oil companies.[13] Economically, this may have seemed like an appropriate risk to take. After all, before 2010 exactly zero oil rigs had exploded with this design. This could have led BP officials to assume that the probability of a major spill was extremely low, justifying the use of a less expensive system for pumping oil.

Compounding matters was the fact that BP relied on federal government models that simulated what would occur if an oil spill ever became a reality. According to the U.S. government models, an oil spill would have a very low likelihood of reaching U.S. soil and would rapidly evaporate or be dissipated by waves in the ocean. The models used by the government had not been updated since 2004.[14] Four months after he took office, President Obama was warned by a federal court in Washington, D.C. that the government was unprepared for a major spill at sea and was too reliant on "irrational" environmental analysis of the risks of offshore drilling. Facing losses in federal royalties of over $10 billion, the Obama Administration supported greater offshore drilling activity.[15]

One can easily see where BP – and the federal government – thought the Deepwater Horizon rig was an economically rational rig to employ in this region. The perceived cost of something going wrong was low. The probability of an oil spill creating an environmental disaster appeared to be low as well. The desire to make profit from oil was – and is – a huge reason to build a rig that is effective, so that the oil can be claimed and sold off to those who refine it into gasoline and other products.

Now that that "low probability event" has taken place, students in an economics class should ask, "What is the most rational response to the BP oil spill?" The answer to that question really depends on how you define benefits and costs in this case. Some of you might argue that the costs associated with the damage done to the environ-

ment, the jobs destroyed in fishing and tourism-related industries, and the risks of another spill happening in the future is greater than any benefits associated with oil from the Gulf of Mexico.

Others could argue that too many jobs would be lost in the oil industry and too many people would be hurt by rising gasoline prices, to justify any curtailment of oil production in the Gulf. They might also add that many scientists have been astonished by how quickly the oil seems to have dissipated and how wildlife in this area has rebounded at a faster rate than predicted.[16]

For your purposes in this class, what is most important is to understand how the use of cost-benefit analysis can help all of us assess any situation in a practical, rather than emotional, manner. This can lead to better decision making for you, our businesses, and our government officials.

THE ECONOMICS OF TEXTING WHILE DRIVING – USING PROBABILITY THEORY

Do you text message people while you are driving? If you answered, "yes," is there something wrong with you? Individuals involved in the practice of texting while driving are 23% more likely to meet with an accident compared to their counterparts who follow the norms of safe driving. A truck driver who indulges in texting while driving is 23.2 times more likely to meet with an accident.[17]

Studies also reveal that the dangers of texting while driving are more than those associated with drunk driving. Texting while driving increases your chances of getting involved in a car crash by six times compared to driving under the influence of alcohol.

On the surface, the decision to text while operating 2,000 lbs. of machinery in the near proximity of innocent people, might have no obvious economic properties. When we dig below the surface, though, we will see that economics explains this problem beautifully.

For the economist, explaining texting while driving begins with the issue of scarcity. People text in their cars because there is an imbalance between the amount of information they have received from people they know and the amount of information they want or need at any given minute from people they know. Therefore, sending a text message is a way of attempting to close that imbalance.

Once you start texting on the highway, economists want to know what type of cost-benefit analysis you used. In other words, we attempt to discern whether or not the driver is rational to text.

The expected benefit to the text messenger is the *probability* that they will safely send and/or receive the desired information. The self-interested text messenger is not sending a text message in order to help his or her fellow man, they are doing it to help themselves.

The *direct cost* of texting while driving is measured by the probability of having an accident; the probability of getting injured, dying, or injuring/killing someone else, as well as (in states where this is illegal) the probability of getting caught, the probability of getting punished, and the expected or known penalty if you are charged.

Suppose the probability of getting into an accident is .023 (this means that 2.3% of text messengers, under similar circumstances, crash their vehicle).

Suppose if you are in an accident you have a 47% chance of being injured. Finally, suppose the average injury costs $3,250 in medical bills. Mathematically, you then have a 1.08% chance of getting an injury from texting while driving (.023 x .47 = .0108). So, is escaping injury just over 99% of the time worth a 1.08% chance of an injury?

Shutterstock © Yehuda Boltshauser, 2011.

If you have a 1.08% chance of an injury and the average injury costs $3,250, then each time you text while driving costs you $35.13. Remember, if you don't have a wreck with injuries 99% of the time you are texting, then 99% of the time your medical bill is zero dollars. The ONE TIME you have a wreck and get hurt you pay $3,250, so the average cost per texting incident is only $35.13.

The second cost associated with texting or any other behavior for that matter, is the *opportunity cost*.

If you decide to text while driving, you forgo whatever good would have come out of driving with two hands on the wheel.

As absurd as it may seem, texting while driving, while more dangerous than being drunk and arguably more selfish than many other activities, is not necessarily an irrational act. That is why people keep doing it. It is also why economists know that asking people to be courteous is laughable. You don't change behavior by asking people to care about other humans. You change behavior by changing the benefit-cost calculation.

Suppose every state had the negative incentive of $10,000 tickets for texting while driving and the positive incentive where police officers got a 10% cut from every ticket issued where texting while driving could be proven. *Then* you would see a huge change in behavior.

No economist I know has suggested such a drastic measure – yet. However, all economists know that texting while driving is not going to go away under the current laws and national begging campaign.

THE ECONOMICS OF GLOBAL WARMING – IS THERE A RATIONAL SOLUTION?

Unless you have been living under a rock the last few years, you are well aware of the raging debate that goes on day after day, concerning the degree to which human beings have put our planet in danger of dying some day.

On one side of the argument you will find those who believe that they have concrete data that the planet is warming at a rate that cannot be due to normal cyclical changes in temperature patterns, but rather due to the fact that human beings create horrific levels of pollution from the burning of oil, coal, wood, and many other resources. According to the Intergovernmental Panel on Climate Change (IPCC), an agency of the United Nations, during the 1980s and 1990s global warming appeared to be occurring at a rate of between 0.15 and 0.17 degrees Celsius per decade, for a possible increase over the next century of 1.5 to 1.7 degrees C.[18]

For people like former Vice President, Albert Gore, the Earth cannot sustain our current pace that sees 86 million barrels of oil burned *every day*. If we continue, Gore and others charge, the planet will warm to the point where critical ice formations will melt, sea levels will rise and hundreds of millions of people – and other living creatures – will be dead, or impoverished or crowded into smaller and smaller places.

On the other side we have people – scientists and non-scientists alike – who cast a very skeptical eye toward the notion that humans are the main cause of global warming and whether global warming is occurring at all. Critics point out that it is impossible to tell how much of the recent warming trend is natural or manmade. According to NASA's Goddard Institute, six of the ten warmest years on record were in the 1930s and 1940s – well before carbon dioxide emissions began to accelerate to present day levels.[19]

It is also worth noting that in November of 2009, a file appeared on the Internet that contained thousands of emails and other documents from the Climatic Research Unit at the University of East Anglia in Great Britain. The emails and documents, which became known as "Climategate," showed that scientists from all over the world had suppressed and even falsified climate data in order to magnify the threat of global warming.[20]

Of course, any of you reading this section of the book could go online and find thousands of articles that side with one group or the other. The point of this part of the chapter is not to prove who is right. The point is to bring some economic clarity into this debate so that we can be poised to tell our elected representatives how much, if any, of our scarce tax dollars should be devoted to the goal of cooling off the Earth.

While he was campaigning for the presidency, Barack Obama put forth an ambitious plan to combat global warming. Specifically, Obama said he would:

- Help create five million new jobs by strategically investing $150 billion over the next 10 years to catalyze private efforts to build a clean energy future.
- Put 1 million Plug-In Hybrid cars -- cars that can get up to 150 miles per gallon -- on the road by 2015.
- Ensure 10% of our electricity comes from renewable sources by 2012, and 25% by 2025.[21]

On the surface, you would be hard-pressed to find many Americans who would not be thrilled to see five million new jobs, 150 miles per gallon cars, and greater use of renewable energy systems like solar, wind, and ocean-generated electricity.

It is when you dig a little beneath the surface that some very questionable economics appear – as is usually the case.

First, the government's track record in creating reliable, clean energy is not impressive. Part of the problem is associated with the first law of thermodynamics – "Energy is neither created, nor destroyed." That means that in order to create energy, you must use energy and that energy does not come with zero pollution. Second, the last time the country got serious about moving away from dirty energy like coal and petroleum was in the late 1970s and early 1980s – and the government failed miserably.

| The Cost of producing energy before subsidies, per megawatt hour* | $50 | 100 | 150 | 200 | 250 | 300 | 350 | 400 | 450 | 500 |

WAVE POWER

←Cost range
Likeliest cost →

CRYSTALLINE SILICON PANELS SOLAR

THIN-FILM PANELS SOLAR

OFFSHORE WIND

BIOMASS

ONSHORE WIND

GEOTHERMAL

LANDFILL GAS

NATURAL GAS

COAL

*As of third quarter 2009

Source: Bloomberg New Energy Finance

Source: Bloomberg New Energy Finance. Reprinted by permission.

From 1973 until the early 1980s the U.S. faced an "energy crisis" that led to dramatic increases in government-funded projects to reduce our reliance on foreign oil (sound familiar) and create less air pollution.

Repeatedly, tens of billions of dollars in expenditures for everything from synthetic fuels from shale to coal gasification, biomass, wind, solar, and other projects, failed to deliver energy at anywhere near the cost of oil and coal.[22] The inherent problem that government planners could not overcome was the fact that petroleum (especially low-cost Middle East petroleum), even at historically high prices, was much cheaper to use than other forms of energy to power our cars.

The same is true today. Even though hybrid cars often deliver vastly greater fuel efficiency than standard gasoline models, the cost of purchasing a hybrid car makes it an uneconomical choice for millions of Americans. For example, the popular Toyota Prius carried a price tag of just over $29,000 for much of 2007 and 2008. At 46 miles per gallon, it would take 17.9 years for the Prius to be as economical to buy as a Toyota Corolla that cost $15,000 and got 32 miles per gallon.[23]

For many economists, spending $150 billion of the taxpayers' money to continue to look for energy sources that are *more expensive* and often less efficient than what we currently have, is a waste of money.[24] After all, if we are going to fight global warming, the consumers will ultimately be the ones who will have to be willing and able to purchase the new alternative energy technologies – assuming those technologies even appear. As the table clearly illustrates, "cleaner sources" of energy would quickly clean out the wallets of even the most well-intentioned consumer.

Surveys do show that a large majority of Americans (the world's largest energy consumer) have a desire to "go green" as long as the cost is not too great.[25]

Therein lays a major dilemma. If the government spends hundreds of billions of dollars and does not deliver a cheap alternative to oil, how will we ever get enough alternative energy usage to fight global warming – assuming global warming can and should be fought?

Furthermore, if elected officials pass legislation that is inefficient (meaning it does not pass the cost-benefit test) we could not only fail to achieve major reductions in the temperature of the planet, but we would see major economic disruptions that could, at the minimum, inconvenience people, and at the maximum, harm more people than rising temperatures have. Consider this…

In 2009 the U.S. House of Representatives passed climate legislation that would impose an 80% reduction in carbon emissions by the year 2050. This legislation (which has not been signed by the President when this book went to press) would reduce the level of overall emissions to the same amount the U.S. produced in the year 1875, when we had no cars and only 40 million people.[26] How many jobs would be destroyed – and how many families would thus be negatively impacted – by such a law? Since the legislation calls for massive taxes on coal and oil, we would have to face far higher prices for electricity, gasoline, and all products that rely on fuel and electricity.

You may also recall the government's "Cash for Clunkers" program, which took taxpayer dollars and doled out payments up to $4,500 to anyone willing to turn in a gas-guzzling used vehicle for one that got marginally better gas mileage. We were told that this program would contribute to less pollution and help the economy grow. Yet this $2.85 billion initiative had the unexpected effect of dramatically lowering the supply of functioning used cars, which led to higher car prices in the middle of a recession.[27]

It also hurt new car sales in the months following the end of the program, since many people simply bought the car they were going to buy anyway a few months ahead of schedule – lowering the demand later on.

Finally, do you remember when the federal government told us that our gasoline would now have corn-based ethanol added to it? We were told that burning a key ingredient in popcorn would reduce fossil fuel usage and thus help save polar bears from having to stand on floating ice cubes.

Well, it hasn't worked out that way. In fact, even Albert Gore, the Nobel Prize winner who has spent his political career warning all of us about the dangers of global warming, recently acknowledged what scientists have been saying the past few years. Biofuels made from corn actually *increase* carbon emissions at a faster rate than simply burning fossil fuels.[28] Billions of dollars of taxpayer money has been artificially reallocated to corn-growing states and corn-supporting politicians only to see a net increase in the very pollution we were supposed to be fighting.

Moreover, in 2011, crop prices – led by corn – increased dramatically, leading to higher rates of food scarcity for hundreds of millions of poor people around the globe.[29] By forcing up the demand for corn used to make ethanol, the amount of corn left for human consumption has fallen. This has naturally led to higher prices for corn, and products with corn and corn byproducts. Ranchers feed their cattle with products that contain corn. With higher prices for feed, they must raise prices for beef and other meat products. This leads to a reduction in the ability of financially-challenged families to buy as much food as they otherwise would. Higher corn prices have also led more and more farmers to grow corn rather than wheat, soybeans, and other crops. This trend has caused a decrease in the supply of wheat and soybeans, and higher prices for those crops, too.

OPPORTUNITY COST AND THE PRINCIPLE OF COMPARATIVE ADVANTAGE

Virtually every year I take my family on a camping vacation somewhere in North America. While we are away, I don't think about my job much, but I do apply at least one part of my profession to our trips in order to assure peace and harmony. That is the concept of comparative advantage.

> ➤ **The principle of comparative advantage states that a person, or business or nation can gain production and consumption possibilities by specializing in the production of goods and services that can be produced at a lower opportunity cost than the next best competitor can.**

How does this apply to my camping trips, or to your life, or to the trade policies of the United States? Here's how…

Photo courtesy Jack Chambless

SUGGESTED CLASSROOM DEBATE

If a warming planet threatens the food supply for wolves – that thrive on very cold weather – how much would you be willing to pay in gasoline taxes, per gallon of gasoline, in order to increase the probability that wolves and other species do not become extinct over time?

I absolutely hate putting up a tent. I made a 'D' in high school geometry, so I am not even sure I could manage to understand how all of the tent poles are supposed to cross in order to keep the tent from collapsing. Mrs. Chambless, on the other hand, is a geometric genius.

However, she does not really enjoy gathering firewood, cleaning fish, or cooking outdoors. I love to cut up dead trees, filet fish, and cook over a fire. Bingo!

Since she has a comparative advantage in putting up tents and I have a comparative advantage with axes and fire, we each specialize in what we are best at. This does not mean that if push came to shove I could not put up a tent. It also does not mean that she doesn't know how to cook or burn wood. If that were the case we would both have an *absolute advantage* over one another.

What comparative advantage means is that while each of us could do everything that needs to be done, neither of us should focus on what the other is best at. This *trade* we have with one another leads to an optimum condition for both, without incurring the high opportunity cost of attempting something we are not really best suited for.

So, if my wife and I can use this concept for our benefit, could it be rational for entire countries follow our lead?

NUCLEAR INTELLIGENCE FOR......MANGOS?

In March of 2006, former President Bush met with Indian Prime Minister Manmohan Singh to hammer out a new trade agreement.[30] The agreement called for the U.S. to sell nuclear fuel and reactor components to India, so that India could expand its supply of energy over time. This agreement ended a decades-long moratorium on sales of these products to the world's largest democracy.

On that same day, India agreed to begin selling mangos to the United States. In fact, Mr. Bush said, "And oh, by the way, Mr. Prime Minister, the United States is looking forward to eating Indian mangos."

We should be. According to many fruit connoisseurs, India produces some of the greatest mangos in the world.

The bottom line from this agreement is simple. If the United States decided to become self-sufficient in the mango growing business, we would incur a huge opportunity cost associated with all of the resources we would have to divert from more productive areas and into mangoes. Our American mangos, since we do not have a comparative advantage, would be more expensive and would not taste as good as what the Indians can grow.

Moreover, while no one questions the fact that India has enough bright people to produce products for nuclear

power, it makes more sense for India to use the money it makes from selling what it is good at to buy what it is not as good at. In this case, it makes sense to turn profits from mangos into American nuclear reactor parts. The end result is that such voluntary trade leads to greater wealth for both countries.

Later in the book we will examine international trade and comparative advantage in more detail. We will see that trade is one area where economists tend to agree. What we agree on is the fact that when we trade with one another there are benefits conferred on both parties – despite all of the claims that free trade is an irrational thing to pursue.

THE ECONOMICS OF IRRATIONAL BEHAVIOR

Once upon a time, economics was pretty easy for economists. We simply told our students that inherently people are rational, and that was that. After all, you recall the scenario where your friend is speeding and then instinctively slows down, right?

But what about people who speed up when they see a police officer turn on the blinking lights? What about people who know they are in big trouble but proceed to engage in a high-speed chase where they run other drivers off the road, plow over an unsuspecting armadillo or two, and then pull out a gun and start shooting at the pursuing officer? Is that kind of behavior rational? It seems that cable television is filled with programs dedicated to the irrational man.

Traditional economics would suggest that the person who is in the high-speed chase simply decided that the benefits of the chase, measured by some probability of escape, were greater than the potential costs of death or incarceration. Vernon L. Smith and Daniel Kahneman might vigorously disagree. These guys – one an economist from George Mason University, the other a professor of psychology from Princeton – won the 2002 Nobel Prize in Economics by essentially "proving" that people act in an irrational manner more than we think.

Mr. Kahneman is the first psychologist to share in the Nobel Prize. He and Professor Smith took economics into the laboratory and, through repeated tests – using students as guinea pigs – the researchers found that the assumption that self-interested individuals will consider the benefits and costs of their actions in a systematic manner that yields rational outcomes is not always true.[31]

Instead, they found that people repeatedly make errors in judgment that can be predicted and categorized. One important discovery was that people are averse to recognizing their losses. This is another way of saying that we irrationally tend to live in denial.

For example, suppose you were holding on to a brief case with an unknown amount of cash in it. In front of you is another brief case, also containing an unknown amount of cash. You are told that one of the brief cases has $1,000 in it, while the other one has $1 million in it. You are given the choice of opening the brief case on the table – and keeping whatever is in it – or you can take $600,000 to not open either one. If this sounds familiar, it should because it is the basis for a game show called *Deal or No Deal.*

It is also a game show where the traditional assumption of the rational man is getting clobbered.

In the preceding example, you have a fifty percent chance of getting $1 million. .50 x $1 million = $500,000. That means you *should* take the guaranteed $600,000, right? Yes, if you are *rational.* No, if you are like many of the contestants, who, facing even lower odds of getting the million bucks routinely keep playing rather than taking the offers of guaranteed money.[32]

One of the dilemmas for traditional economic theory is that it can't explain why people do generous things with their money, such as leaving large tips for waitresses in restaurants they'll never visit again. Behavioral economists reason that it's because people have an emotional preference for fairness that competes with the desire to maximize wealth.

This new field of study could help us understand why some Latin American and European cultures are prone to accept high taxes and burdensome government rules – yet don't always seem mind,[33] while others seem to revolt at the very mention of greater government intrusion. We could also learn more about why people refuse to leave their homes as hurricanes approach,[34] why Brett Favre kept retiring and un-retiring[35], how people can overcome racism[36] and much more by considering the role that *emotions* play in the decision making process.[37]

WAS JESUS IRRATIONAL?

On February 25, 2004, Mel Gibson's movie – *The Passion of the Christ* debuted in over 4,000 theaters across the country. This extremely controversial and violent movie depicted Mr. Gibson's view – and the view of others – of what the last 12 hours of Jesus' life may have been like. Christians and non-Christians alike had widely divergent opinions on the degree to which Gibson's portrayal of these historical events was accurate. However, what seems to be almost universally agreed upon is that Jesus was a real being who lived and was crucified approximately 2,000 years ago. It is also considered a universal truth that crucifixion was one of the most horrific forms of punishment human beings have ever used.

A question that might be an interesting one for economists to tackle is whether or not Jesus was a rational man. Specifically, if history is accurate in that Jesus spent approximately three years of his life as the self-proclaimed son of God, knowing the penalty for such a claim, what possible benefits could he have received from going through with his crucifixion?

To an economist, we would want to know what Jesus believed to be the benefits of being crucified. What were the direct costs of his crucifixion – for him? What was the opportunity cost of being crucified?

History records that Jesus argued that only by his crucifixion could the world be saved from sin. That seems to suggest that he believed the benefits of his death to be great and was willing to give up his life (the direct cost) as well as the value of the next best choice, which to Jesus seemed to be the lost salvation of mankind.

So, was he rational, or irrational?

THE QUESTIONS EVERY ECONOMY MUST ANSWER

An *economy* is the mechanism through which resources are organized to meet the wants and needs of those who live in society. An economy can be as small as an individual – after all, you are attempting to use resources to meet your own needs – or it can mean the economy of a neighborhood, city, county, state, region of a state, region of a country, country, continent, or planet!

SUGGESTED CLASSROOM DEBATE

On December 25, 2009 Umar Farouk Abdulmutallab attempted to bring down a Detroit-bound jet by using a bomb hidden in his underwear. Now when we go to the airport we often face a full-body scan or full body pat-down before we can fly. Is this a rational response to an attempted underwear bombing? Why or why not?

Typically, the mechanism (more on this in chapters 2 & 3) for "organizing" resources is one that combines profit-seeking businesses and individuals with government agencies. Rarely do we see only the government making all of the choices and rarer yet do we see anarchy – only individuals making the decisions.

No matter what mechanism that is selected, there is no guarantee that poverty will disappear or that everyone will have the same access to goods and services. The economy of any area is a dynamic force made up of one, or perhaps billions of people, all striving to survive and prosper. The degree to which the people will achieve this goal depends on how participants choose to manage resources and allocate goods and services. In essence, every economy must answer three questions:

- What to produce?
- How to produce it?
- For whom to produce?

A big part of the answer to the first two questions entails an examination of the resources that an economy has to work with. The state of Utah has a large number of highly educated individuals and wonderful natural tourist attractions. Combined with an entrepreneur-friendly business environment, Utah enjoys the designation as one of the best states to seek a job in.[38] West Virginia, on the other hand, while rich in coal resources, is poor in terms of its policies toward new businesses and poor in terms of human capital. Thus, West Virginia continually ranks near, or at the bottom of the United States in terms of wealth creation.[39]

One of the reasons the United States is relatively rich is because of our abundant natural resources. After all, when compared to most nations, the U.S. has much more farming land, fresh water, timber, minerals, and natural gas. However, bountiful natural resources are not the ticket to prosperity. In Congo, a nation rich in diamonds, tyrannical rulers have kept the Congolese people from participating in free trade.[40] On the other hand, Hong Kong is extremely poor in natural resources but extremely rich in terms of per capita income (income per man, woman and child) because – as we will see in the next chapter – the government there largely leaves people alone.

Having a lot of labor is also a nice thing to have. One of the reasons China's economy is growing so rapidly is because China has hundreds of millions of adults who are available for work. The same is true for India. Yet, having a lot of people is also not sufficient to satisfy the needs of an economy. India and China are still poor countries compared with much of Europe and America.

What about capital? Is that the magic solution to the problem of scarcity? While it is true that having tremendous technology, large amounts of equipment and other physical tools helps, one only needs to look at the former Soviet Union to find out how useless capital is as a primary creator of wealth. Not only did the Soviet Union rank near the top of the world in military and space technology, but in terms of human capital, this country had some of the brightest engineers and scientists on the planet. Yet, it was not enough to take care of the average Soviet citizen.

As it turns out, in answering the first two questions of "What?" and "How?", the key resource seems to be the number of entrepreneurs an economy has. That's right. Those nations that tell people to take risks creating new products and services – and then allow the risk takers to reap, and keep, the rewards stemming from those risks, tend to be the richest countries in the world.

ANSWERING THE QUESTION OF "FOR WHOM?"

Perhaps the most difficult question facing the participants in any economic system is the question of who will get the goods and services that are produced. The answer to this question has contributed to revolutions, wars, and wide-ranging government intrusions into people's lives. In many respects, this seems to be a fairly simple question. In the United States, this question is answered largely by the concept of *ability to pay*.

Ability to pay means that if you want a ticket to see the Boston Red Sox play baseball or a new iPod or three pounds of Alaskan king crab, all you have to do is look at the price of each of these items. Then look at how much money you possess. If you have enough money and you agree with the price that is required, congratulations! You will have your ticket, your iPod, and your crab.

CONCEPT CHECK

Log onto www.jackchambless.com. Find the MISC. link and scroll down until you find the Heritage Foundation findings on global economic freedom by country. You should take a detailed look at a variety of nations and the factors used to evaluate their level of entrepreneurship to gain a clearer picture of why some resource-rich countries are relatively poor, while other resource-poor countries are rich.

There are some goods and services, however, where the concept of ability to pay creates a dilemma for our country. Should police and fire protection be based on the ability to pay? Can you imagine calling 911 one night to report a serial killer walking around in your house only to have the operator ask you if you have the requisite $49.95 to capture killers, plus a $500 surcharge for serial killers? What about fire protection? You can see the problems there.

The fire department announces that from now on you have to pay $15 per month for fire department insurance. If you pay and your apartment catches on fire, you are covered. What if you pay but your neighbor decides to use his $15 to buy crack? You wake up one night with your hair on fire because your neighbor's crack pipe fell off his bed and set the entire complex ablaze.

What about education? Should K–12 and college be based on ability to pay? Former presidential candidate, John Edwards once argued:

> Providing a free year of college tuition will eliminate the sticker shock that scares off so many kids. It will simplify a financial aid process now so complex that getting a student loan can be tougher than getting a small business loan. After students get through that first year, which is the toughest, they'll know financial aid is available, they'll know education is an investment worth making, and they'll have access to people who can help them pursue both. Maybe more important, if they work hard, they'll know they can succeed in college.[41]

Mr. Edwards seems to understand that resources are scarce for many people who aspire to receive an education. He also seems to understand that an educated society is vital to the long-term economic progress of the United States. However, not everyone would agree that education should get an exemption from the ability to pay doctrine.

Frederic Bastiat, a renowned economist of the nineteenth century, once argued that public education is a form of *plunder*, where government steals from the taxpayers (some of whom are childless) to provide for government education.[42] To Bastiat and other lovers of economic liberty, education is best left to the private sector (i.e. pay for your own kid to go to school) if society desires a high-quality education for our children and minimal plunder of the taxpayer.

Who's right? It depends on whether you are prone to use normative or positive analysis.

> ➤ **Normative analysis is a way of looking at economic policies that rely on our value judgments about "what ought to be."**

If you believe that education is fundamentally a right of our existence, you would probably argue that every person, regardless of ability to pay, should be entitled to some basic level of education.

> ➤ **Positive analysis is a way of looking at economic policies without the use of one's value judgments. With positive analysis, statements such as "If, then" are common.**

If you are in the camp that argues that "if" we provide education for all, "then" we must be willing to face higher taxes, educational bureaucracy, lack of school choice, and so forth, you are making a statement based on fact rather than feelings. The "then" part of the equation is often referred to as the *law of unintended consequences*.

> ➤ **The law of unintended consequences is the principle that for every law, or policy that is implemented with one set of objectives or goals in mind, there is always one or more unintended consequences that will stem from that law or policy.[43]**

If you tend to view the world from a more normative standpoint, it should be pointed out that a very real danger of that way of thinking is that you lose sight of the economic costs and unintended consequences of your value judgments. Saying education should be a right begs the question as to what cost we should incur to guarantee this right. You must live in reality, and reality has clearly shown us that the unintended consequences of government education for all is that poor people in America often receive the worst education in government schools (more on this in chapter 5).

America spends more on public education than any other nation in the world. Yet our K–12 school system is universally regarded as one of the worst.[44] In standard math and science tests, U.S. kids routinely score at or near the bottom of the international list. Using positive analysis, we could say that if spending on education increases, there is no guarantee that educational quality will improve. However, positive analysis would also say that if we had a totally private model, then some students with bad parents might be left behind with no education at all. After all, does the free market provide a car or home to everyone?

John Edwards seems to have good intentions. Unfortunately, Mr. Edwards has failed to acknowledge the first fallacy of economics. That is the belief that there is, indeed, such a thing as a "free lunch."

CONCEPT CHECK

The following photo was taken in Canada's Jasper National Park. In order to reduce air pollution caused by the burning of firewood, the Canadian government required every camper to pay $8.80 per day (Canadian) during the summer of 2008 in order to burn firewood in this park. However, the firewood is provided, "free of charge" to the camper. In America's national parks, campers do not have to purchase a fire permit, but do have to pay for firewood acquired in the parks. In which country is the law of unintended consequences most likely appearing? Why?

Photo courtesy Jack Chambless

ENDNOTES

1 See "Slump Over, Pain Persists" by Sara Murray, *The Wall Street Journal*, September 21, 2010; and "Lost Decade for Family Income" by Conor Dougherty & Sara Murray, *The Wall Street Journal*, September 17, 2010.

2 See "Secrets of the Economist's Trade: First, Purchase a Piggy Bank" by Justin Lahart, *The Wall Street Journal*, January 2-3, 2010. *The Wall Street Journal* by Dow Jones & Co. Copyright © 2010. Reproduced with permission of Dow Jones & Company, Inc. in the format Textbook via Copyright Clearance Center.

3 See, "The 1099 Stonewall," *The Wall Street Journal*, September 18-19, 2010; and "Small business gets help, hindrance from Congress" by Noam N. Levey & Lisa Mascaro, *The Orlando Sentinel*, September 15, 2010, p. A12.

4 See http://www.infoplease.com/spot/osamabinladen.html

5 See "Repeal the Patriot Act" by Andrew P. Napolitano, *The Wall Street Journal*, March 5, 2004.

6 Increasingly, states are finding out how opportunity cost comes into play in determining whether land will be used for development of homes and businesses or will be set aside in the name of preserving the environment. See "No More Room?" by John Myers, *The Duluth News-Tribune*, February 23, 2006, and "Clogged Rockies Highway Divides Coloradoans" by Kirk Johnson, *The New York Times*, January 25, 2006.

7 See "Emotion Drives Many Defaults" by James R. Hagerty, *The Wall Street Journal*, May 11, 2010, p. A4.

8 See "The Mystery of Energy Independence" by Joseph Bast, *The Heartlander*, June-July 2008; and "What Obama doesn't say tonight might speak volumes" by George Will, *The Orlando Sentinel*, August 28, 2008.

9 See *Energy Economics and Policy* by James M. Griffin and Henry B. Steele, Academic Press Inc., 1986, pp. 293-297.

10 See "Blame Congress for High Oil Prices" by Mackubin Thomas Owens, *The Wall Street Journal*, May 29, 2008, pg. A17.

11 See "Why drill for oil? Well, it's a way to avoid future wars" by Peter Schweizer, *USA Today*, August 13, 2008, pg. 11A.

12 See "An Oil Thirsty America Barreled into 'Dead Sea'" by Neil King Jr. & Keith Johnson, *The Wall Street Journal*, October 9-10, 2010.

13 See "BP relied on Cheaper Wells" by Russell Gold & Tom McGinty, *The Wall Street Journal*, June 19-20, 2010.

14 See "BP Relied on Faulty U.S. Data" by Neil King Jr. & Keith Johnson, *The Wall Street Journal*, June 24, 2010; and "Drilling for Better Information" by L. Gordon Croviz, *The Wall Street Journal*, June 28, 2010.

15 See "Obama Decried, Then Used Some Bush Drilling Policies" by Neil King Jr. and Keith Johnson, *The Wall Street Journal*, July 6, 2010.

16 See "Global-warming predictions hurt cause" by Mike Thomas, *The Orlando Sentinel*, January 13, 2011.

17 http://www.buzzle.com/articles/dangers-of-texting-while-driving.html

18 See "Ten Principles of Energy Policy" by Joseph Bast, The Heartland Institute, 2008, pg. 9.

19 See "Not So Hot" *The Wall Street Journal*, August 29, 2007.

20 See "Climate Science in Denial" by Richard S. Lindzen, *The Wall Street Journal*, April 22, 2010, p. A23.

21 See http://my.barackobama.com/page/content/newenergy

22 See *Energy Economics and Policy* by James M. Griffin and Henry B. Steele, Academic Press Inc., 1986.

23 See "The Economics of Hybrids" by Mike Spector, *The Wall Street Journal*, October 29, 2007, pg. R5.

24 See "The Mystery of Energy Independence" by Joseph Bast, *The Heartlander*, June-July 2008.

25 See "What Price Green?" by Anjali Athavaley, *The Wall Street Journal*, October 29, 2007, pg. R6.

26 See "The Carbon Recession" *The Wall Street Journal*, May 12, 2010.

27 See "Ou Est Le 'Cash for Clunkers'?" By Victor Dial, *The Wall Street Journal*, January 7, 2011.

28 See "Al Gore's Ethanol Epiphany" *The Wall Street Journal*, November 27-28, 2010.

29 See "Prices Soar on Crop Woes" by Scott Kilman & Liam Pleven, *The Wall Street Journal*, January 13, 2011.

30 See "Bush and India Reach Pact That Allows Nuclear Sales" by Elisabeth Bumiller and Somini Sengupta, *The New York Times*, March 3, 2006.

31 See "Nobel Winners for Economics are a New Breed" by Jon E. Hilsenrath, *The Wall Street Journal*, October 10, 2002, pg. B1.

32 See "Why Game Shows Have Economists Glued to Their TVs" by Charles Forelle, *The Wall Street Journal*, January 12, 2006.

33 See "Inequality and Happiness: Are Europeans and Americans Different?" by Alberto Alesina, Rafael Di Tella and Robert MacCulloch, Unpublished paper, June 2002; and "Anger over free-market reforms fuels leftward swing in Latin America" by David J. Lynch, *The USA Today*, February 9, 2006.

34 See "Riding it Out" by Linda Shrieves, *The Orlando Sentinel*, September 1, 2005; and "Excuses for braving Katrina are fatal" by Joshua Norman, *The Orlando Sentinel*, February 19, 2006.

35 See "He Missed the Guys" by Brian Murphy, *The St. Paul Pioneer Press*, August 19, 2010.

36 See "Racism Studies Find Rational Part of Brain Can Override Prejudice" by Sharon Begley, *The Wall Street Journal*, November 19, 2004, page B1.

37 Economist Ulrike Malmendier has found that buyers on eBay – an online auction site – are given the chance of bidding on an item or using a feature called Buy it Now, where the shopper can buy immediately, 43% of the time, buyers ended up bidding up the item to a higher price than the original Buy it Now price. For some buyers, the research found a greater desire to win the auction than to save money using the Buy it Now feature.

38 See "Incentives Spur Utah's Growth" by Jim Carlton, *The Wall Street Journal*, November 27-28, 2010.

39 See "Robert Byrd's Highways to Nowhere" by Brian Bolduc, *The Wall Street Journal*, July 10, 2010.

40 See "Piles of Diamonds Fail to Enrich Congo" *The Orlando Sentinel*, May 20, 2001.

41 See http://www.johnedwards2004.com/education.asp.

42 See *The Law*, by Frederic Bastiat, pg. 18.

43 For example, laws passed to force car manufacturers to increase the fuel efficiency of automobiles has led to more people dying in traffic accidents. Congress wanted to help people save gas and money, but the car companies, to comply with the law, used lighter materials that do not offer a much protection. See "CAFÉ is Bad for Your Health" by Sam Kazman, *The Wall Street Journal*, November 14, 2005, pg. A23; and "Burn, Baby, Burn" by John Tierney, *The New York Times*, February 7, 2006, pg. A25.

44 See http://abcnews.go.com/2020/Stossel/story?id=1500338; "Basic Instincts" by Chester E. Finn Jr. and Diane Ravitch, *The Wall Street Journal*, February 27, 2006; and www.independent.org/tii/content/pubs/review/tir52_payne.html for more on the quality of education in the United States and other countries.

CHAPTER REVIEW

1. Where does the issue of scarcity enter in to the decision to attend college?

2. What is the opportunity cost of marriage? How does the opportunity cost differ from the direct cost?

3. Under what conditions would it be rational for a student to attempt to cheat on an examination? How could this decision be irrational?

4. Compare and contrast normative and positive analysis in the issue of providing health care benefits to people who live in poverty.

Chapter Two

THE ECONOMICS of LIBERTY

Photo courtesy Jack Chambless

History demonstrates that time and again, in place after place, economic growth and human progress make the greatest strides in countries that encourage economic freedom. Government has an important role in helping to develop a country's economic foundation. But the critical test is whether government is genuinely working to liberate individuals by creating incentives to work, save, invest, and succeed.

RONALD REAGAN

MUCH ADO ABOUT SOMETHING

> All people, however fanatical they may be in their zeal to disparage and to fight capitalism, implicitly pay homage to it by passionately clamoring for the products it turns out.
>
> Ludwig von Mises

A few years ago, Mark Skousen – a world-renowned economist – visited Mongolia to present a series of lectures on economic history. While he was there, he was treated like a rock star. His lectures on the merits of capitalism were met with standing-room-only crowds of people who hung on his every word as he regaled the audience with the story of how capitalism triumphed over communism.

When Professor Skousen shared his experience with me upon his return, I must admit I was pretty jealous. Maybe I felt that way because he is just better at what he does than I am. On the other hand, my jealousy may have come from hearing that his audience received the concept of economic liberty with such attentiveness and appreciation. I actually found myself daydreaming of having students standing on their chairs in wild applause as I lectured on self-interest and private property rights. Then I woke up. What a shame.

Back in the reality of the American college classroom, economists are generally greeted with a heightened sense of apathy and indifference when we lecture on economic freedom. Maybe it is because American college students don't care about such things. Or, could it be that those of us born in a free and prosperous nation simply take liberty as a given? That might be it.

By the end of this chapter you might never take economic liberty for granted again.

WHEN LIBERTY DID NOT EXIST

It is probably hard for you to imagine a world where your chances of being a slave or servant to some king are higher than your chances of being free. However, not so long ago this was precisely the fate that the majority of the world faced, from birth. Today, most people in the world who are wealthy, accumulated their wealth by serving their fellow man. A thousand years ago, most of the world's richest people got rich by plundering and enslaving their fellow man.

In the year 1000, the richest man in Moorish Spain, one of the richest countries in that year, took the name Al-Mansur (Arabic for "The Conqueror"). His name was appropriate, inasmuch as he successfully accumulated more than six million pieces of gold from the raids against Christian Spain.

Bill Gates is rich, but Mr. Gates would be embarrassed to discuss his bank account with Machmud of Ghazni. The ruler of a kingdom of central Asia at the beginning of the second millennium, Machmud resided in an opulent palace with more than 400 poets hired to entertain him.

Machmud maintained his lifestyle by invading India annually for more than 25 years, looting temples for gold and jewels. In 1019, it is recorded, he took so many captives that the price of slaves plummeted for several years. Of course, before Machmud and Al-Mansur, the world had the Egyptian empire that enslaved Jewish people.

After Machmud and Al-Mansur, Britain ruled over much of the world – which did not make the various kings of England many friends in much of Europe, Asia, and Africa. In each instance, ransom, murder, theft, plunder, and slavery were common practices in the process of wealth accumulation.[1]

FROM JOHN LOCKE TO THE "GREAT EXPERIMENT"

John Locke (1632-1704) was an Englishman who lived under the rule of Charles II. He became famous with the publication of two treatises on government in 1690.

From the time the first governments existed until 1690, the world's inhabitants believed (or had accepted the fact) that men derived their rights from government and that any expansion in human, civil, religious, political, or economic rights must therefore come from the hand of government.

Locke's treatises challenged this view. According to Locke, the state of nature was one in which "all men are by nature free, equal and independent" and all enjoy "the rights of life, liberty and property."[2]

Locke argued that people "consent" to enter into social contract – such as offering their labor services to an employer – and "accept the bonds of government" in order to better protect their rights. He argued that government is based on the consent of the people and that an "absolute monarch" is "inconsistent with civil society."

It was Locke's contention that, in its natural state, property is not owned by anyone and that people come to own property by combining their labor with it. In other words, you and I use our skills, education, and training to earn money, and with that money we buy homes, cars, DVD players, and other things. Locke's historically unique position was that government did not own property. He felt that people owned property and that the primary function of government was to protect property rights.

This "natural law" theory of the relationship between government and the people was quite unsettling for the British monarchy – and for good reason. After all, what ruler wants to wake up one morning to realize that a revolutionary groundswell is taking place, and that the basis for the revolt is the idea that government is too big, too oppressive, and too limiting, and that the desired government for the future would be one where the people, rather than some king, would rule?

Government gains power by subjecting people to rules and regulations that limit freedom. The monarchy saw Locke – and his contention that the people have the right to "resume their original liberty" by dissolving their bonds with government – as a direct threat to the king's power.

Locke's work was the basis for the call to revolution within the colonies in the 1700s. Thomas Jefferson ranked Locke as one of the most important thinkers on liberty. In fact, a quick reading of the Declaration of Independence illustrates how heavily Jefferson borrowed from Locke in his defense of the American Revolution[3]:

We hold these Truths to be self-evident, that all men are created equal, that they are endowed by their Creator with certain unalienable Rights, that among these are Life, Liberty, and the Pursuit of Happiness--That to secure these Rights, Governments are instituted among Men, deriving their just Powers from the Consent of the Governed, and whenever any Form of Government becomes destructive of these Ends, it is the Right of the People to alter or abolish it, when a long Train of Abuses and Usurpations, pursuing invariably the same Object, evinces a Design to reduce them under absolute Despotism, it is their Right, it is their Duty, to throw off such Government.

The birth of the United States was the world's first major experiment with government based on the protection of life, liberty and property. Nowhere else on Earth was liberty celebrated as it was in the United States, and yet even our own nation has not enjoyed a history devoid of the zero-sum exploitation of human beings. The institution of slavery lasted until 1865. Even after slavery ended, segregation and discrimination remained.

The taking of the lands that American Indians had lived on for generations, along with the forced movement of these indigenous people and even the slaughter of those who resisted, is a testament to the fact that any government – even one with liberty as the basis of its creation – can selectively ignore the "natural rights" of mankind, when government's goals are blocked by the liberty of the individual.

Today, more and more nations are experimenting with the concepts born out of the writings of John Locke. Dictators and despotic governments are becoming increasingly rare – and the people of the world happier[4] – as more nations discover the merits of free markets and free people.

LIBERTY AND CAPITALISM

In the last chapter we examined the types of resources every economy uses to determine what goods and services to produce and how to produce them. You may recall that the first three resources – land, labor, and capital – are important, but woefully insufficient in explaining the vast differences that exist in the level of wealth enjoyed by the nations of the world.

World history has shown that those nations that pursue capitalism to the greatest extent possible are the nations that generate the highest standards of living for people up and down the economic spectrum. Capitalism, in its purest form, has delivered more people from starvation and homelessness than any other economic system ever experimented with.[5] In order to better understand how this could be so, we should begin with a definition of capitalism.

> ➤ **Capitalism is an economic system that is based on free exchange, contracts, and self-interested activities that do not violate the right to life, liberty, and private property.**

How many of you have heard that capitalism is an economic system based on greed, lies, stealing, corruption, fraud, exploitation, environmental degradation, and other forms of mean behavior? If this is what you have heard, you are not alone. The media is filled with examples of how much people hate capitalists. How many movies have you seen where some profit-seeking businessperson is the villain? The list is endless.[6]

If you turn on the television, or read the newspaper, you will find many articles on the "absurd" profit being earned by oil executives,[7] or corporate scandals or "heartless" companies charging "outrageous" prices for medicine, homes, or food.

By contrast, books like *Atlas Shrugged* (by Ayn Rand) celebrate the capitalist as a hero of society – an uncommon sentiment these days.[8]

Looking at the definition of capitalism, it might seem a bit odd that people would find this economic system offensive. After all, don't we all pursue our self-interest to make more money? Don't we all have some – and seek more – private property? Isn't trade and voluntary exchange something we naturally pursue?

DILBERT: © Scott Adams/Dist. by United Feature Syndicate, Inc.

HOW THINGS GET DONE

> Here are a million human beings who would all die in a few days if supplies of all sorts did not flow into Paris. It staggers the imagination to try to comprehend the vast multiplicity of objects that must pass through its gates tomorrow, if its inhabitants are to be preserved from the horrors of famine, insurrection, and pillage. And yet, all are sleeping peacefully at this moment, without being disturbed for a single instant by the idea of so frightful a prospect. What then, is the resourceful secret power that governs the amazing regularity of such complicated movements, a regularity in which everyone has such implicit faith, although his prosperity and his very life depend upon it? The power is an absolute principle, the principle of free exchange. We put our faith in that inner light which Providence has placed in the hearts of all men, and to which has been entrusted the preservation and the unlimited improvement of our species, a light we term self-interest, which is so illuminating, so constant, and so penetrating, which it is left free of every hindrance.
>
> Frederic Bastiat

Think back for a moment to when you were a child. How did you learn to share your toys with other children? Did it come naturally, or was it more comfortable being selfish? Now think about your reason for being in this class. Did you decide to take economics because you wanted to make sure your professor had a full class? Perhaps you are in college because you read somewhere that college graduates are less likely to become criminals, and out of your desire to reduce your neighbor's chances of being robbed you began your college career?

If you have a job, why do you work? Is it so the customers of your company will be happy? Is it so your company will make profit? You know darn well what the answer to every one of these questions is. In every instance, your *self-interest* is the driving force.

Should you feel guilty? After all, shouldn't human beings do things for one another because we love one another and have risen above the Darwinian pursuit of self-preservation? Maybe you do feel guilty, but perhaps you shouldn't.

It is important to acknowledge that there are a lot of things we do out of *benevolence* and *love* for our fellow man. Opening a door for an elderly person or helping a child who has fallen down qualify as examples. Giving our time or money to charity and being faithful to our loved ones is also a good thing to do.

While doing things in a selfless manner is laudable, when we consider most human acts we reach one immutable conclusion: that, inherently, people do things out of self-love.

HOW THIS BOOK REACHED YOUR HANDS

I would like to be able to say that I spent long hours researching and writing this book because I care so much about America's economics students, that I felt compelled to educate them with my words of wisdom. I would like to say that, but it would be a lie. In reality, I wrote this book because I care very deeply about my wife, my children, and myself. I am guilty of being self-interested.

As it turns out, the lumberjack who cut down the tree to make the paper that is in this book is also self-interested. So is the engineer who designed his saw. So is the factory worker who built the saw. The truck driver who hauled the lumber to the paper plant is self-interested. The oil company that made the diesel fuel for the trucker is self-interested, as is the tire maker, the truck manufacturer, and the people who put asphalt on the road from the forests of Oregon to the paper mill in Idaho. Come to think of it, so are the people who made the road signs in Idaho.

Why isn't love of our fellow man enough to provide us with paper?

Shutterstock © Jessie Eldora Robertson, 2011.

I am pretty sure the person who created the software I used to word-process this book probably does not care too much about the economic necessities of some college professor in Florida. I'll bet Bill Gates cares about Bill Gates. I think Fred Smith is self-interested, too. He's the guy who runs Federal Express — the company I used to ship book materials to my publisher in Dubuque, Iowa.

Speaking of the publishing company, I know the folks who work there and they are very nice. But there's something funny: They did not offer to publish my book without earning any money from it. How stingy. Kendall-Hunt has a motivation known as self-love that leads its employees to desire food, vacations, clothing, and other things that my book helps create. This keeps the company from publishing this book for nothing. After the copy editor put the finishing touches on the book, she sent it to a printing company. Those greedy people actually charged Kendall-Hunt money to print the book! The nerve!

Then the book was shipped (free of charge?) to your bookstore that gave you the book for free because you have a nice face, right? No. The bookstore, depending on the level of competition it faced in the textbook market, decided what price to charge you. After all, if they gave books away for free, where would their wages and salaries come from – the tooth fairy?

Then you showed up at the store. Where did you get your money? If you are like most college students, you had to work very hard at a job to earn the money for this book. Did you go to work out of love for your fellow man? Well, did you? You probably went to work out of a love for yourself. The company hired you because they love to make money and you were needed to help them do that.

Once you had your hard-earned money in your hand, you handed it over to the bookstore that sold you the book. Of course, we haven't even touched on the cash register company that helped create your receipt, the corrugated box company that made the boxes your book was shipped in, or the shoe company that made the shoes you wore to walk into the bookstore.

It is quite possible that thousands of people, all working to provide for their own lives, worked together to bring this book to you. Out of the spontaneous behavior of self-loving individuals came the orderly production and distribution of this product.

This idea of "spontaneous order" was championed by the economist, Friedrich Hayek.[10] According to Hayek, the idea that a harmonious, evolving order arises from the interaction of a decentralized, heterogeneous group of self-seeking individuals with limited knowledge. This order, he claimed, was not "designed" nor could be "designed" by a social planner, even a very wise one, but merely "emerged" or evolved spontaneously from a seemingly complex network of interaction among people with limited knowledge.[11] This means that no one person really knows how to create a book. It takes many self-interested people to work together to create this book. As we all act on our self-love, we inevitably serve one another. Therefore, the money we earn could be called "certificates of performance."[12]

With these certificates of performance we earn the right to file a claim on goods and services our fellow man produces. I did not have to care about you to write the book. I only had to care about myself. But out of this self-love, you got your book, I get my royalty checks, and my local grocer, the cable television provider, and many, many others get to acquire my certificates as I patronize their establishments. Adam Smith would be proud of all of us.

THE FATHER OF ECONOMIC THOUGHT

1776 was a watershed year for the United States. In that year our forefathers informed the King of England that they were tired of paying high taxes with little or no say in how their lives would be run. With the signing of the Declaration of Independence came an era in which individuals would be allowed to experiment with newfound freedom to chart the course of their lives.

Across the ocean another document was published that did not create as much controversy as the nasty letter the colonies sent to England, but it would eventually be almost as significant in shaping the lives of people in the United States and around the world.

Adam Smith was a Scottish professor of logic and moral philosophy who, in 1776, published a landmark book titled *An Inquiry into the Nature and Causes of the Wealth of Nations*. The book, originally delivered in lecture form at Glasgow University, was the most comprehensive treatment of economics, and its ramifications for politics, that had ever been attempted. It was in this book that Smith beautifully articulated the proposition that man, by his very nature is driven to make decisions based on the overriding feeling of self-interest. Specifically, Smith said:

CONCEPT CHECK

In the fall of 2010, a group of miners in Chile were rescued after spending 69 days trapped underground. Go online to read Leonard Read's classic essay, "I, Pencil," then explain how this essay illustrates the argument that capitalism saved the life of those miners.

In almost every other race of animals, each individual, when it is grown up to maturity is entirely independent, and in its natural state has occasion for the assistance of no other living creature. But man has almost constant occasion for the help of his brethren, and it is in vain for him to expect it from their benevolence only. He will be more likely to prevail if he can interest their self-love in his favor, and show him that it is for their own advantage to do for him what he requires of them.[13]

Let's ponder the enormity of Smith's statement for a moment and consider its implications. Many of you might be under the impression that Smith is prescribing a recipe for a greedy society, where people care only about their own well-being and do nothing to help their fellow man. In reality Smith is arguing that enlightened self-interest – the type of behavior where both parties end up better off than before, is what gets things done in our world – even when it comes to miracles….

Photo courtesy Library of Congress

HOW ADAM SMITH HELPED WITH THE "MIRACLE ON ICE"

On February 22, 1980, I was sitting in the living room of my best friend when, at 13 years of age, I witnessed one of the great moments in the history of the United States – and in the history of self-interested pursuits.

While I did not think of it that way at the time, the victory by the United States Olympic hockey team over the Soviet Union was indeed the triumph of capitalism. In fact, for the 20 men and the coach that led them to the greatest moment in U.S. sports history, the name Adam Smith could have been evoked during the aftermath of this stunning win and it would not have been too far-fetched to do so.

The American economy – and America itself – was in deep trouble in 1980. Prices were rising rapidly, unemployment was over 10% and a terrible sense of hopelessness had gripped the American people. It was also during that time that the Soviet Union was expanding its doctrine of tyranny in Asia, Africa, and Latin America. In many ways it seemed America's best days were behind us, while the Soviet Union was on the way to the terrible Cold War victory its government had predicted.

That is when 20 college age men and a hockey coach from The University of Minnesota proceeded to save our country from the pits of economic despair.

Most of you reading this book do not recall when the Olympics relied on amateur athletes. That means you also don't recall that the Olympics used to have a whole lot more to do with geopolitics than it does today.

During the Cold War (1947-1991) the United States and the Soviet Union never fired a missile or a bullet at one another. The Olympics turned out to be a political battlefield, where athletes from both nations competed for the implicit right to claim superiority over one another.

In 1980, the U.S. faced a daunting task. The USSR had won the gold medal in hockey in 1964, 1968, 1972, and 1976 and was considered by far, the best team in the world – including the National Hockey League. In fact, the Soviets humiliated a team of NHL All-Stars by a score of 6-0 before the winter games began.

Most of the Soviet players like Vladislav Trediak, Sergei Makarov, and Valery Kharlamov had played together for a decade or more. Many Soviet players, while not allowed to play for money, were handsomely subsidized by their government and were afforded luxuries that the average Soviet citizen could only dream about. In essence, while the Olympic rules stated that no professionals could compete, the Soviet Union had its own professional players.

On the other hand, the United States could only use players that had never earned money as real professionals. This meant that the team was totally comprised of players that were either in college, or had recently finished college. Most of the players had never played together only seven months before the Lake Placid games. Many of the players despised one another, as a result of heated rivalries between Minnesota and Boston-area athletes.[14]

It was this hand that was dealt to Herb Brooks, the man in charge of putting a team together.

The day before the 26th anniversary of the "Miracle on Ice," I spoke with Jack O' Callahan, one of the more famous players from this team. I asked Mr. O' Callahan to look back on this team and assess the extent to which self-interest played a role in its success. What follows are the questions I asked and Mr. O' Callahan's answers. This should help you see that Adam Smith was never far off from the events that unfolded.

To what extent did self-interest play a role in your willingness to make the sacrifices Coach Brooks demanded of you?

Answer: I can't really look at it as pure self-interest as that implies that all I cared about was myself. However, there was an element of self-interest. I was definitely interested in furthering my development as a hockey player and learning more about myself as an athlete and competitor. I was excited to play for a new coach with new ideas and philosophies and I was determined to play on that team.

My view at the time was that I would not have much of a professional hockey career after the Olympics and I was very excited about being at the Olympic Games, representing my country, sharing that experience with my family and teammates, etc. I totally understood the beauty of being an Olympic athlete, win or lose. I viewed myself as a total team player, but if I try to boil down how much of my efforts were selfish or individual based, it all disconnects. I was interested in challenging myself on whatever level necessary to be a better player and to help make my team a better team so we could reach our potential and compete at the highest level during the games. Is that self-centered? Maybe, but also, maybe not; perhaps, without realizing it, a little of both.

Did the fact that you were an amateur in 1980 make a difference in the effort you put forth?

Answer: Not really, we viewed ourselves as the U.S. Olympic Hockey team and as much as that implied amateurism, we didn't really dwell on that aspect. In a more clear sense, there were no NHL players in those Olympics and therefore everyone was "amateur." We didn't really think about it, that was just what the Olympics were at that time. We were just playing hockey. I don't think any hockey player in an Olympic event or in any important competition would give anything less than their absolute best effort.

The Olympics, the nationalism aspect, the environment, and the code of competitive athletes all demands that. The difference for us is that we spent seven months together growing as a team, learning about one another in a team environment. That aspect made us much, much stronger than had we been 20 quality players thrown together and given 2 days to prepare. Given our preparation experiences, our team was much stronger than 20 individuals taken separately.

Did you and your teammates consider the goal of winning a gold medal to be something that would help your personal careers or were you more interested in the accomplishment of the team as a whole?

Answer: I can only speak to my feelings, but I can probably speak for the team when I say that my thoughts of winning the gold (when I allowed myself to think about it) was only that it would be fun and tremendously rewarding on a team accomplishment level. The part about how this could benefit us as individuals only may have entered our thoughts when the agents started talking to us after we had won.

Also, winning gold did not exactly create a greased skid into the NHL. I spent the next two years playing for the Blackhawks farm team in Moncton, New Brunswick and many guys ended up in the minors for at least a little while, some guys forever. We mostly viewed our Olympic experience as something separate and special, rather than a means to an end. It was all about setting a goal and through a lot of sweat and personal challenges, having an opportunity to reach that goal. The most fun is always in the pursuit, not necessarily the result.

Do you believe that professional hockey players should be used in the Winter Olympics? Why, or why not?

Answer: I like seeing the best players in the Olympics, at every level. If they are professionals, fine, if not, fine also. When there were amateurs, everyone was always saying that the eastern bloc countries were getting paid and there was all this grousing about that. People whine about anything, and if we went back to the way it used to be, they would complain and if we stay the way we are, they'll complain. At least with the only rule being that the best players make the team, the playing field is level. It's the same in the other sports, how do you legislate out athletes that are compensated to compete?[15]

How do you hold other nations accountable to what the US considers professional? Why do we get to make the rules? What we have to accept is that there are great athletes in the world and not all of them are from the US. We need to cherish great athletic feats and accomplishments even when those athletes are not Americans. We also need to look at the positives, not the negatives.

Could part of the reason the Soviet Union lost in 1980 be due to the fact that their players grew up in a Communist system that denied them the opportunity to seek out their self-interest?

Answer: I really don't think any of that mattered. They were just hockey players, like us. In those times of the Soviet Union, their self interest was all about the safety of their families and extended families. Believe me, they were plenty self-motivated. It is all relative. There were many reasons why they lost and one of the main reasons is that the U.S. hockey team in 1980 was highly talented and tremendously prepared. You have to add to that, the fact that the USSR may have been a little over-confident given that they had just beaten us 10-3 and basically were beating everyone else pretty handily.

The confluence of these facts leads me to believe that the reason we had a chance to win was, for that one game, we were better prepared than our opponents who, typically, were the most prepared team in the world. They may have let their guard down. We were definitely better prepared mentally but also, we were much better prepared physically and emotionally than our opponents realized. During those Olympics, we surprised a lot of good teams with our physicality, our raw emotional intensity, our passion, our talents, our abilities, and our overall commitment to one another. It was very special and that is why people continue to talk about it, [26] years later.

In the years following the 1980 games two interesting things have occurred. First, if you watch the Disney movie, *Miracle*, you will notice at the end of the movie, an update on where all of the players from the American team are now. You will undoubtedly notice that the vast majority of them are capitalists. Many, like Jack O' Callahan, are involved in financial markets. Others are real estate developers, NHL coaches, doctors and public speakers.

The second fact is that since the United States began using professional athletes in the winter games, we have never won another gold medal.

Does this mean that the professional athletes are not self-interested? No. It most likely means that since they are already making hundreds of thousands, if not millions of dollars per year, their individual self-interest has already been attained, making it much more difficult to get excited about playing for free. It also makes it unrealistic that the professionals would give up seven months of pay to train with one another for the Olympics. When combined with the fact that the Cold War is over, it is unlikely we will ever see 20 young men pull off something of this magnitude again – even if it is in our self-interest to see another 'miracle' on ice.

PROFIT VS. NOT-FOR-PROFIT: WHICH MOTIVATION SAVES MORE PEOPLE?

Bettmann/CORBIS

"Our logistics capability in Katrina was woefully inadequate. I was astonished to see we didn't have the capability most 21st-century corporations have to track the flow of goods and services."

Michael Chertoff, Secretary,
Department of Homeland Security

While we are undertaking this thorough investigation of enlightened self-interest, it might be a good time to compare self-interested businesses and individuals to

Photo courtesy Jack Chambless

Can capitalism clean up this mess?

government agencies in order to see why people tend to be more frustrated with one than with the other. Can you guess which one? If you yelled, "Government!!" then you are not alone.

Do you remember hurricane Katrina? Do you remember what happened before and after Katrina? If you are not sure, let's refresh your memory.

On March 1, 2006 the Associated Press released video footage of a meeting of federal officials that took place days before Katrina devastated the Gulf Coast. In the video,[17] federal disaster officials warned President Bush that Katrina could breech the levees and flood New Orleans and overwhelm rescuers.[18]

Critics of the Bush Administration point out the Mr. Bush did not ask the federal officials a single question during this meeting. In fairness to Mr. Bush, it really wouldn't have mattered how many questions he asked. The chances of the federal government effectively managing the preparation before the hurricane hit, the response after it hit, the rebuilding years after it hit, or the next time a hurricane hits was – and is still – very small.

This reality is not because storms are unpredictable in their path, size and damage. No, the reason government failed then – and will fail again – is because government does not have the same motivation for doing things as the private sector. The private sector is motivated by profit. When you buy food, do you rely on some government office to supply it, or do you go to the for-profit grocery store? Did the Bureau of Nice Garments make your clothes? Was your car built by the Department of Transportation? You get the idea.

Government agencies, by their very nature, are more likely to be unproductive at solving problems because those agencies are *not-for-profit*. Since profit is not a motive – or even allowed – in the public or government sector, the incentive to find the most economical solution to any given problem is generally lacking without the forced help from taxpayers.[19] The lack of *consequences* also hurts the chances that government will serve us well. When a business operates with a high level of inefficiency and/or incompetence, people can refuse to give their money to that business. Government is the only institution allowed to use force to make you pay for its services. Therefore, if lousy service is offered, you cannot refuse to send your taxes to the agency you are upset with.

Think about Federal Express and the post office. With whom would you trust a life-critical package? What about government (public) schools versus private schools? Why do private school kids perform better, on average? Why do we see so many reports about the number of foster children whom various state governments have lost?[20] What if a private day care facility lost kids or let them die? How long would it take for bankruptcy proceedings to begin?

When Enron, WorldCom, Global Crossings, and other corporations were found to be lying and stealing, we saw many headlines on how corporations could not be trusted. One headline read, "Corporate greed is striking at the heart of the economy."[21] However, when mounting evidence shows up that various government agencies like the Bureau of Indian Affairs or the Bureau of Land Management have either lost billions of taxpayer dollars,[22] or have helped burn down forests and homes

The Cruisers and Convoys Act of 1708 established a prize court that awarded British naval crews with cash from the sale of enemy ships they seized.[26] What would happen if the U.S. government established a prize court that awarded military personnel and law enforcement officials with cash for capturing terrorists?

through careless oversight,[23] do we get to bankrupt that ineffective government agency, or do they simply get more money to try to fix their mistakes?

Everywhere we see people pursuing profit, we tend to be satisfied. Virtually everywhere government is in charge (have you been to the driver's license office lately?) we see bureaucracy, waste,[24] mismanagement, and apathy.[25]

So, what if we privatized FEMA and turned over its operations to Wal-Mart? Why Wal-Mart? Well, for starters it could be argued, rather easily, that Wal-Mart did a far better job before and after Katrina than FEMA did. Before the storm hit, Wal-Mart began stocking the shelves of stores in the Gulf region with goods that would be in great demand before and after the storm. Trucks were lined up in the outlying areas of the devastated areas waiting with even more water, food, and other necessities.

Even though Katrina damaged 89 Wal-Mart stores, the company moved quickly to reopen most of them and provided over $4 million in housing aid for its workers. In total, 2,500 trailer-loads of water and emergency supplies arrived to assist the Red Cross and other charities while FEMA officials were still arguing about how bad the hurricane really was.[27]

Meanwhile, by every measurable account, FEMA, along with local politicians in New Orleans and Louisiana, blew it.

Not only was there the colossally slow response to the disaster before and after it struck,[28] but as it turns out, FEMA used our hard-earned tax dollars in a way that would get every executive at Wal-Mart arrested and sent to prison.

Six months after the storm, records indicated that many residents of the Gulf Coast had taken advantage of FEMA's lax oversight to bilk taxpayers out of tens of millions of dollars. Residents impacted by the storm were supposed to get $2,000 per household. They were told to provide a name, social security number, and address.

Some people were able to get payments of $2,000 up to *18 times* by using fake names, fake social security numbers, social security numbers of dead people, and addresses that often were nothing more than vacant lots.[29] In addition, you may recall hearing about all of the

blue tarps that the government bought with our money at prices far greater than what we would pay at Home Depot. You might also remember all of the trailers you bought for victims of Katrina that were never delivered or the hotel rooms and cruise ship cabins people stayed in for months with no regard to the cost. In fact, when hurricane Gustav hit in September of 2008, people had to be evacuated from trailers that the taxpayers were still subsidizing three years after Katrina.

This is not new for FEMA. In the past, FEMA has used your money to pay for floods in areas that did not flood, hurricane damage in areas where hurricanes did not strike, and fires in areas that did not burn.[30]

What if Wal-Mart, or Lowes, or Home Depot did that? Can you imagine how far the stock price of each company would fall? Profits would decline, the corporate bond rating would fall and the stockholders would demand a government investigation of the fraud and mismanagement of their resources.

Fortunately, we don't see corporations engaging in consistently stupid and wasteful behavior. The free market has a way of finding companies – and punishing them – for behaving wastefully. It is called losses, bankruptcy, and unemployment.

Of course, this does not mean that capitalists never do bad things. We sometimes see that people who call themselves capitalists really don't know Adam Smith at all.

WHEN "CAPITALISTS" GIVE CAPITALISM A BAD NAME

Because of capitalism, we have endless varieties of toothpaste, bread, clothes, cars, music, and more. Because of capitalism, we have almost immediate responses to consumer demand for faster computers, picture-taking cell phones[31] and portable Blu-Ray players. Capitalists like Bill Gates have given away billions of dollars in profits to help with vaccines around the world and other causes.[32]

Yet, the men and women who have created all of these incredible goods and services have simultaneously proven that they often suffer from *socio-political myopia* – a shortsighted view of how society and political systems shape our desires within the economic system.

In effect, businesses and individuals often succumb to the age-old temptation to be greedy. It can also cause people who claim to be supporters of capitalism to lobby for special rules and regulations designed to favor their companies and harm their competitors. The lobbying leads to a great deal of money flowing to the politicians willing to assist in this game of "crony-capitalism."[33] Television journalist, John Stossel, has championed the cause of enlightening people of the dangers of subsidies, bailouts, and special favors for businesses.[34]

The recent recession of 2007-2009 has helped shed a great deal of light on how far away we are from the ideas of Adam Smith. Under Adam Smith's view of capitalism, we would have not had our government take trillions of dollars away from current and future taxpayers to rescue General Motors, the banking and insurance industries, or homeowners who bought houses that they ultimately could not afford.

A key function of capitalism is that people are allowed to pursue whatever peaceful exchanges they desire, as long as they understand that they will bear the responsibility for their choices. Under capitalism, we see rappers, dancers, software engineers, chefs, musicians, and mechanics all seeking ways to make more money by doing something better, faster, or cheaper. When capitalism works well, we end up with folks like Eminem and Steve Jobs – millionaires who gave us what we wanted. Capitalism does not pass judgment on how wealthy we should be allowed to be or whether what we offer to society is really important. The system simply tells us to proceed to take risks but not to expect the forced taking of our fellow man's money if we do not succeed.[35]

Corporate leaders hate the fact that union workers make so much money and that government bosses them around with respect to the pay of lower-level workers. Yet, it was corporate leaders who should have noticed that disgruntled individual workers might someday become disgruntled *groups* of workers. Now many labor unions have pushed wages to levels that are arguably not commensurate with productivity gains (see the airlines), and profits have suffered.

Shutterstock © tlorna, 2011.

Minimum-wage laws impact profits for small business owners unfavorably. Owners and managers contend that they should be allowed to freely contract with labor for a wage that equals the prevailing equilibrium pay rate. The right to freely enter into contracts with one another over pay is a major part of what makes capitalism work. Without contracts – and the enforcement of them – we see nations collapse into poverty as people become increasingly mistrustful of one another.

However, pragmatic capitalists must understand that human beings do not always like the wage that is created in a contractual agreement. If people believe they "deserve" more money, they will use the arm of government to alter contracts where they can. This was the case in the 1930s when people – increasingly distrustful of businesses – pushed for the establishment of the minimum wage.[36] We will see in chapter 8 the minimum wage laws have been a disaster for poor and unskilled Americans. Yet, people at the bottom of the economic ladder continue to support the forced increases in compensation under the guise of "fairness" and "justice."

Lawsuits concerning employee discrimination, sexual harassment, and product liability are increasing in number every year. One wonders how litigious our nation would be if fast-food restaurants – seeing the lawsuit trend – would have rushed in with healthier foods or nutrition facts *before* the lawyers smelled money. One wonders if corporations would face as many discrimination suits if they would have seen the growing social intolerance for economic injustice toward minorities and women. How could any rational business not see the demonstrations of the 1960s leading to new laws for the disabled, the elderly, and women? Yet, we still have businesses losing millions because of the myopic way they see societal evolution.

Speaking of societal evolution, the election of President Obama was a culmination in a series of events that mirrored the election of Franklin D. Roosevelt in 1932. Voters in 1932 and 2008 were convinced that capitalism had failed and that something had to be done to rein in greedy businesses. Fear has a way of causing human beings to vote for drastic changes. Roosevelt convinced voters that Wall Street had ruined their lives and that government had to step in and pass massive new regulations and taxes in order to restore the economy. Mr. Obama repeatedly argued that the economy had been driven into a ditch by the failed practice of unfettered capitalism.

In a 2010 speech, he had this to say about the basic construct of capitalism:

"The basic idea is that if we put our blind faith in the market and we let corporations do whatever they want and we leave everybody else to fend for themselves, then America somehow automatically is going to grow and prosper." [37]

President Obama, echoing the sentiments of millions of Americans, embarked on a campaign to re-regulate capitalism. In the next chapter, we will take an extensive look at the new laws and regulations passed during his first term in office.

It is important to note that economists are frequently asked, "Was the housing crisis and subsequent recession proof that capitalism failed?"

Economics students must understand that recessions and financial crises are a natural part of capitalism. No economy ever grows uninterrupted. Whether it is from floods, drought, wars, disease, sudden drops in consumer spending, changes in government policies, or any number of other events, we always experience economic downturns. We will see throughout the rest of the book that the housing crisis was a predictable event – as was the recession that followed. Capitalism provides no guarantees of constant wealth, just the guarantee that you will be allowed to pursue wealth.

CAPITALISM AND TOLERANCE

One of the primary reasons why there are no nations practicing pure capitalism is due to the fact that under capitalism, there are many areas where we would all have to restrain our own moral convictions in order to preserve the freedoms of our fellow citizens.

If you have ever thought that you are an Adam Smith capitalist, consider these questions:

Would you be willing to live in a country where gambling, drugs, and consensual prostitution between adults is legal? What are your views on social security, Medicare, unemployment compensation, farm support payments, foreclosure relief, and Aid to Families with Dependent Children?

What about income and property taxes? What should the law be in those areas?

Capitalism – in its purest form – requires a great deal of tolerance on your part and on the part of your fellow man. In a capitalistic society, the aforementioned markets where drugs are bought and sold, gambling occurs, and adults agree to exchange money for sexual favors, would all be legal. If someone uses the money that they peacefully earned to engage in any of these activities, liberty demands that we not interfere so long as our rights are not infringed upon. In capitalism, there would be exactly zero pennies allocated to fix the troubles of your fellow man, courtesy of taking the tax dollars (private property) away from some other party. Doing so would constitute theft (more on this in the next chapter). In capitalism, income and property taxes would not exist – these constitute a confiscation of property. The entire country, your state, county, and city would be run on voluntary (sales) taxes.

So, are you a capitalist?

Would anything be illegal under capitalism? Of course. Arson, child pornography, slavery, murder-for-hire, and any other market where someone's life, liberty, or property is threatened or taken away, would be against the law. Capitalism does not mean "anything goes." It means that you have the liberty to pursue your self-interest in a peaceful manner.

It also means your private property is protected.

Photo courtesy Jack Chambless

SUGGESTED CLASSROOM DEBATE

This man is an immigrant worker who works loading carcasses of peeled shrimp into a truck on the coast of Oregon. What protection does capitalism afford him? What, if anything, is the government's obligation to him?

CAPITALISM AND PRIVATE PROPERTY

After such an extensive look at the importance of self-interest, you might be inclined to think that all an economy needs to be healthy is a bunch of money-pursuing individuals running around inventing new things and showing up for work on time. While that helps, it is only half the root structure of a healthy economic system. The other half of the equation is what happens to your money and your property once you have worked so hard to earn it.

According to the United States Constitution, you have: A legal right to your life, liberty, and property.

Many people might argue that the Founding Fathers believed you have a right to life and liberty, but the last part of the phrase is "pursuit of happiness." Let's take a deeper look.

The 1776 Virginia Declaration of Rights reads:

> That all men are by nature free and independent, and have certain inherent rights, of which when they enter into a state of society, they cannot by any compact, deprive or divest their posterity; namely, the enjoyment of life and liberty, with the means of acquiring and possessing property, and pursuing and obtaining happiness and safety.

In 1795 the Supreme Court declared:

> The right of acquiring and possessing property, and having it protected, is one of the natural, inherent, and unalienable rights of man. No man would become a member of a community, in which he could not enjoy the fruits of his honest labor and industry. The preservation of property then is the primary object of the social compact.[38]

Finally, in Thomas Jefferson's First Inaugural Address, he stated:

> A wise and frugal government shall restrain men from injuring one another, shall leave them otherwise free to regulate their own pursuits of industry and improvement, and shall not take from the

mouth of labor the bread it has earned. This is the sum of good government.[39]

When the Founding Fathers declared that we all have a right to life that means that government has an obligation to protect us from people who try to end our lives. No one should be allowed – they argued – to take your life if you are not trying to violate the rights of that person.

Liberty, to the Founders, meant your right to do *anything that is peaceful*. Thomas Jefferson would have never had a Constitutional problem with your selection of belly rings, tattoos, cigarettes, or rap music. He and the other Founders supported your right to independent thoughts and even offensive words – so long as your words do not take away the life, liberty, or property of others.

Finally, the Founders believed that if you pursue your self-interest in a peaceful manner, you should be allowed to keep the money you earn and peacefully spend it as you wish, again, as long as you are not violating the rights of others. Your *property rights* are thus the right to pursue, and keep, the money and goods you acquire.

YOUR INTERESTS

> "Capitalism has become more responsive to what we want as individual purchasers of goods, but democracy has grown less responsive to what we want together as citizens."[41]
>
> Robert Reich

Once something is called a right, the government has a legal obligation to secure our rights. We don't have to prove we deserve our rights; they are part of the contract we have with our elected officials. What can be confusing for some people is the distinction between rights and interests. Simply put, you have an interest in anything that is not a right. Confused? Consider this example:

A man walks into a store hoping to get change for a dollar. He asks the shop owner for change so he can make

SUGGESTED CLASSROOM DEBATE

In 2010, a judge in Minnesota ordered a woman to pay $1.5 million in fines for sharing 24 digital songs. Do you believe that sharing music, books, movies, and other files over the Internet constitutes a violation of someone's private property rights[40]? Why or why not?

a phone call. The shop owner tells him that he will give change only if the man buys something.

The man brings a canned soft drink back to the counter. The shop owner tells him the drink costs 85 cents. The potential customer claims that if he pays 85 cents, he will not have enough money left to make the phone call.

Does the customer have a right to change? Does he have a right to a soft drink for 85 cents? For that matter, does he have a right to be in the store at all?

Clearly, the customer has the right to not be killed for peacefully entering the store. The law is also pretty clear that if a store is "open to the public," the public can shop around without fearing that forced transactions will take place. If the man buys the drink for 85 cents, he has the right to the remaining 15 cents of his private property. He also has the right to 12 ounces of soft drink if that is what the soft drink company indicates is in the can.

However, he has no right to the price he desires or to be in the store under any circumstances he deems correct. The key here is that people must consent to exchange private property. Until the terms of exchange are agreed upon, he simply has interests he wants met.

With that in mind, what if we simply expanded the list of rights, to include a house?

WHY WE HAVE ONLY THREE RIGHTS

Valentines Day 2001 was a day of tremendous love in Washington, D.C. That was the day that Representative Charles Rangell (D) from New York stood before the U.S. Congress and proposed an amendment to the United States Constitution that read:

> Constitutional Amendment--States that all U.S. citizens shall have a right to a home, which shall not be denied or abridged by the United States or any State.

Representative Rangell was joined by co-sponsors, Donna Christensen, Carolyn Kilpatrick, Dennis Kucinich, and Barbara Lee. Not joining Mr. Rangell were Thomas Jefferson, James Madison, Ben Franklin, George Washington, and the other Founding Fathers who were spinning in their graves that day.

Using normative analysis, it is easy to see why one might argue that such an amendment is a kind and decent thing to do. After all, who among us derives any joy from seeing a homeless person? No one I know.

However, if we apply positive analysis we would ask, "If housing is a right, then how would government secure this right?"

Think about it for a minute. Does the government have to steal from your neighbor to secure your property? Does the government have to kill someone to secure your right to life? Does the government have to tell people who like rap music not to listen to it so you can enjoy jazz? The answer is pretty obvious. To secure our rights the government has to use force only if someone is violating our rights.

If the government says we have the right to life, liberty, property, and a home; that means you no longer have to do anything to have a home. It is automatically yours. But how do we give you a home if you do not currently have one? If you guessed that the government would have to take away the homes and/or money of other people, then congratulations! You are on your way to becoming an economically literate member of the human race.

Maybe the government would have to go around and find out how many people have more than one home and force them to give away all but one. Maybe the government could force people to work for Habitat for Humanity, to build homes for everyone who does not have one. Maybe the government could ask for donations to the IRS for the "Right to a Home Fund." Oh, for a minute there I forgot that the government rarely asks for donations. Instead, the government would most likely raise taxes to pay for all the new homes that would have to be built.

I wonder: If we would have the right to a home, would we have the right to say what kind of home? Could really nice people who have no home get a mansion? Could people with big families and no home get a four-car garage? Would the disabled be guaranteed the right to a home that accommodates their disabilities? Would the elderly be guaranteed the right to a home with free heating? Would the lazy get free maids to clean their homes?

As you can see, when we evaluate the economic effects of adding to the list of rights we find many hidden costs that would have dire consequences. This is precisely what is occurring in Zimbabwe, where President Robert Mugabe has unilaterally taken property away from farmers who have owned land for years and has transferred it, by force, to people who had an interest in having the land. As a result, widespread famine and disease has broken out as the new owners, ill-equipped to farm the land, have been unable to feed Zimbabwe's people.[42]

Perhaps that is why the Founders realized that life, liberty, and property were all that could be guaranteed as rights. The rest of the list – our interests – would have to be earned.

CAN CAPITALISM SAVE THE MANATEE?

"If your culture is based on free enterprise, anything-goes capitalism, then everything's going [extinct] sooner or later."

James Lloyd, professor, University of Florida[44]

When the Pilgrims arrived in America they learned a powerful and almost fatal lesson during their first years in our country. Initially, they intended to establish a system of common ownership of property with everyone working for the common good and taking from the general store-house what they needed. They nearly starved to death.[45]

The next harvest, however, was plentiful.[46] It was during the third winter that Governor Bradford told the remaining colonists that, in the spring, people would be allowed to grow food on their own property and trade with one another. No longer would *common property* – property owned by all, and therefore owned by no one – would be used.

At the dawn of the 21st century, the West Indian Manatee is severely endangered, with approximately 2,900 manatees left in the world. What do the pilgrims and endangered animals have in common? They each teach a valuable lesson of the problem of common property and the role of private property, self-interest, and entrepreneurship.

Whenever something is common property it tends not to be taken care of very effectively. All you have to do to prove this statement is look out your window the next time you are at a stop sign. On the ground you will see enough cigarette butts to cover half of North Carolina. Since no one owns the street, no one has an explicit interest in making sure the street is taken care of. How

many smokers do you suppose throw cigarette butts on their driveway? A driveway is private property, which means ruining it would exact an economic price on the person who owns it. This is the *Tragedy of the Commons.* Common property is not treated in an efficient manner because no one individual has an incentive to preserve the good.

Manatees are an example of the common property problem. No one owns the waterways where they travel. No one owns the manatees. Therefore boaters have little express interest, beyond avoiding fines, to take care of manatees. You can see several examples of this fact by the number of boat motor scars that are pervasive on the manatees in Florida.

However, since many people have a desire to see, and interact with manatees, some entrepreneurs near Crystal River, Florida have opened businesses that take people out in wetsuits to swim with the manatees.

The manatee tour operators that have joined this market have a vested interest in making sure that people proceed through these waters at a safe speed. The vested interest is the potential for lost profit if manatees continue to be killed and eventually become extinct. By selling the rights to swim with manatees, they make sure that their

Photo courtesy Jack Chambless

boats are not intrusive to this animal and that customers obey the very strict regulations on approaching them.

If we simply asked people to be careful and left it at that, how many people – with no financial stake at all in the manatee population – would make sure they preserved this species? Asking our fellow man to be careful near the manatees might persuade some to heed the rules or do the morally right thing. However, our chances of seeing the manatees survive increase with private property rights being established in these waterways. With private property comes the right to put a price on that property. The moment that happens people are much more judicious in their use of the resource and measurable positive externalities are created.

> ➤ **A positive externality exists when a transaction between two parties leads to spillover benefits to individuals who were not part of the original transaction.**

Economists argue that when a transaction between two parties leads to each party being made better off and third parties benefiting as well, the most prudent thing the government can do is encourage this activity so that we will all be better off.

The manatee tour business is not alone in injecting capitalism into environmental protection. Anheuser-Busch, owner of the Sea World theme parks, has an active manatee rescue program that has saved 275 manatees from dying from 1976-2002.[47]

In Mongolia, wild goat herders are given training on alternative ways to earn income in the global economy in exchange for not killing the endangered snow leopard that often threatens their goats. This program has helped move people out of a relatively low paying occupation into a higher paying one, all while helping save the remaining 1,000 or so leopards.[48] In China, tiger farms are being used to raise tigers for sale to people who believe in the medicinal value of these animals. This has helped ease pressure brought by poaching wild tigers.[49]

Finally, environmental groups are learning about Adam Smith as they try to protect pristine lands. One San Francisco-based group recently purchased 600,000 acres from a timber company in order to keep northern Idaho's St. Joe River from being developed by home and hotel-building companies.

Increasingly, environmental protection groups are learning that a very effective way of preserving land, plants and animals is to rely more on the exchange of private property through conservation banks, private property trades, and purchases of vital ecosystems rather than through waiting on government or mass pleas for people to "work together for the common good."[50] In places where common property rights abound, fishing grounds become depleted and rare species face extinction.[51]

These examples – and many more that can be found with research on your part – illustrate the powerful role that incentives play in an economy where private property rights and self-interest are combined. When used properly, self-interested behavior can accomplish both economically desirable outcomes as well as morally, or socially-desirable outcomes.

CAPITALISM AND EMINENT DOMAIN

"You look at it and think, Gosh almighty, we've got to get this stuff out of here. I mean, it's so bad looking. Those houses are in horrible condition."

Boone Pickens

Who is Boone Pickens and what is he talking about? Well, he is a billionaire oilman and graduate of Oklahoma State University. Not long ago, he donated $165 million to his alma mater to build a sports complex. The problem is that many people in the neighborhood where OSU wanted to build the complex did not want to accept OSU's offer of 70% of the value of their homes to move.[52] In the opinion of Mr. Pickens and OSU, it was time for the government to kick the homeowners out so OSU athletes can have enough room to stretch…

We close this chapter with a recent development that every man, woman and child in the United States should be aware of. While it has been years in the making – and was addressed by the Founders – the issue of what *eminent domain* really means has only recently been settled in the United States Supreme Court. The ramifications of this

CONCEPT CHECK

In 2010, a massive earthquake devastated Haiti. Why is it far more likely that recovery will be slower in Haiti than it will be for the victims of the March 2011 earthquake in Japan? Visit http://www.heritage.org/index/ to assist your answer.

decision continue to reverberate around the U.S. and cast a long shadow over the future of liberty-based capitalism.

If you take a quick look at the fifth amendment to the Constitution you will see that the Founding Fathers gave the government the power to take your home or business away from you, as long as it was for the purpose of serving the public (military bases, highways, bridges and so forth) and as long as the government provided you with a just price for your property. Thus, the phrase "eminent domain" means "superior ownership."[53]

For the bulk of the life of the United States, eminent domain cases revolved around projects that largely served the common good of the citizens of the U.S. However, in the past couple of decades, more and more cases have cropped up where the government has taken away private property from one person only to ostensibly hand it over to another *private* entity.[54] Clearly, you did not read anything in the Constitution that provides for any person or company taking away your property, so what gives?

Suppose you live in a city that has a professional sports team. One day the owner of the team decides that he would like to build a new stadium – in your neighborhood, and the ones next to your neighborhood. He shows up at a meeting of all the homeowners and offers to pay all of you 10% more than the assessed value of your homes; 80% of the residents agree, 20% – including you, disagree.

He buys out most of your neighbors and then offers you and the remaining holdouts 30% more than the market value. More people agree to sell, but you and many others refuse to sell at that, or any price.

The owner then goes to the city council and tells them of his dilemma. After all, he can't have your house in the middle of the field, can he?

The city council tells him that he will just have to find another spot. Since a football stadium is a private business (does he give away tickets and food for free?), there is no Constitutional provision for taking your home.

Then he tells the city council that you and your neighbors collectively pay $147,331.09 per year in property taxes and, if he is allowed to move in, he will pay over $2 million in property and sales taxes to the city.

"So what," says the city council.

Then he leans forward and asks them, "What do you use taxes for?"

"Well, taxes are put toward public use projects," replies the council.

"Precisely," says the owner. "If you kick these people out, I will pay more than them in taxes and thus, you will have more money to put toward expanding projects that benefit the public!"

The next thing you see is a bulldozer crushing your house.

KELO V. NEW LONDON, CONNECTICUT

> "The beneficiaries are likely to be those citizens with disproportionate influence and power in the political process, including large corporations and development firms. As for the victims, the government now has license to transfer property from those with fewer resources to those with more. The Founders cannot have intended this perverse result."
>
> Sandra Day O' Conner, former Supreme Court Justice in her dissenting opinion in *Kelo v. New London, Connecticut*

On June 24, 2005 I was standing in a bait shop in Tyler, Texas preparing for a day of fishing with one of my old friends from high school. I had promised my wife that while we were on vacation I would avoid reading newspapers, inasmuch as the stories in them make me even more pessimistic than I naturally am.

I happened to glance over at the newspaper rack when I noticed that the *Dallas Morning News* had a headline about eminent domain.

As much as I wanted to resist, I couldn't. I picked up the paper and there in front of me was the news that private property rights – and capitalism itself – had been dealt a horrible blow.

Susette Kelo and her friends put up an incredibly laudable fight. When the city of New London told her to get out so developers could put up something "superior"

SUGGESTED CLASSROOM DEBATE

Did the Founding Fathers make a mistake by ever allowing the taking of private property for any reason? Is it possible to achieve the greater good without ever having to resort to forced confiscation of private property? Why, or why not? Does pure capitalism have room for eminent domain? How is movie piracy similar to eminent domain?

Did they make a mistake?

to her home, she took her government to court. The case worked its way through the system where it was inevitably decided – by one vote – that she, and the rest of us, were simply occupying a space rather than enjoying the rights we were intended to have.

Writing for the majority in this 5-4 decision, Justice John Paul Stevens argued that, "promoting economic development is a traditional and long accepted function of government" and that local officials are better positioned than federal judges to decide what's best for a community.[55] Immediately following the ruling, the mayor of Arlington, Texas declared, "This is the final decision, the final appeal. I don't think there is anything out there that is a danger to us now."[56]

What was the mayor talking about? If you guessed a new football stadium for the Dallas Cowboys, congratulations.

The Cowboy's owner, Jerry Jones wanted a new stadium. Standing in his way were 15 homes, or lots, and 4 apartment complexes. Not any more. The new stadium opened in 2009.[57]

ADDING IT ALL UP

Not surprisingly, we have never witnessed a nation at any time in history that has been completely capitalistic. Capitalism as an economic system is based on *maximum liberty* and *minimum security*. That means that if a nation pursues pure capitalism, its citizens and businesses must understand that self-interested behavior that created positive outcomes will be allowed and the private property that is accumulated from those efforts will not be taken away.

This also means that businesses who assume risks will not be given subsidies, bailouts, protective tariffs, or laws that stifle competition. Individuals will not receive the tax dollars of their fellow man if they make bad decisions or fall on hard times.[58] Charity, however, is a common feature of capitalism. Rich countries tend to have the most giving people. In fact, charitable contributions by U.S. citizens top $300 billion per year – more than the GDP of many western European nations.

SUGGESTED CLASSROOM DEBATE

Many of the poorest nations in the world are in Africa – a continent that is rich in natural resources. Many economists who study Africa have found that higher levels of foreign aid have actually caused poverty to increase in Africa.[59] Yet, Bill Gates has argued that Africa needs more – and better aid.[60] Use the footnotes provided to research poverty in Africa, then discuss with your classmates whether or not capitalism would work better than aid.

ENDNOTES

1 This is still the case for many nations today. North Korea's Kim Jong il, Burma's Than Shwe and Sudan's Omar al-Bashir are but a few of the tyrants that ruin the lives of their people with the denial of liberty.

2 For more on Locke, see http://plato.stanford.edu/entries/locke/ as well as *Locke, Jefferson and the Justices: Foundations and Failures of the U.S. Government* by George M. Stephens, Algora Publishing, New York, 2002.

3 It is also important to note that the founders borrowed from the Iroquois Indians in creating a nation based on liberty and property rights. See "The Founding Sachems" by Charles C. Mann, *The New York Times,* July 4, 2005.

4 See "Survey Says: People are Happier" by Matt Mabe, *BusinessWeek,* August 20, 2008.

5 See *The Making of Modern Economics* by Mark Skousen, M.E. Sharpe, 2002; *How Capitalism Saved America* by Thomas J. DiLorenzo, Crown Forum, 2004; *The Triumph of Liberty,* by Jim Powell, The Free Press, 2000; *The Commanding Heights* by Daniel Yergin and Joseph Stanislaw, Simon & Schuster, 1998; and *Give me a Break* by John Stossel, Harper Collins, 2004.

6 See "Hollywood has a New Villain," by Deborah Hornblow, *The Orlando Sentinel,* August 13, 2004.

7 See "Backlash Spreads as Profit Surges at Oil Companies" by Jeffrey Ball, John J. Fialka and Russell Gold, *The Wall Street Journal,* October 28, 2005.

7 See *The Triumph of Liberty,* by Jim Powell, The Free Press, 2000, p. 19.

8 See "Capitalist Heroes" by David Kelley, *The Wall Street Journal,* October 10, 2007.

9 See "Scapegoating For-Profit Colleges," *The Wall Street Journal,* August 27, 2010, p. A16.

10 For more on Hayek see *Friedrich Hayek: A Biography* by Alan Evenstein, Palgrave Publishers Ltd., New York 2001.

11 See the essay entitled, "I, Pencil" by Leonard Read at http://www.econlib.org/LIBRARY/Essays/rdPncl1.html and http://cepa.newschool.edu/het/profiles/hayek.htm for more on Hayek.

12 See "Giving Back" by Walter Williams at www.jewishworldreview.com.

13 See *An Inquiry into the Nature and Causes of the Wealth of Nations,* Adam Smith, the Modern Library, New York, p. 15.

14 See *The Boys of Winter,* by Wayne Coffey, Crown Publishers, 2005.

15 Mr. O'Callahan has hit on an interesting idea here. While many people believe that Olympians were amateurs up until the last couple of decades, in reality there were many professional athletes centuries ago that competed in the Olympics. See "UF Scholar Shakes Up History of Olympics" by Jack Stripling, *The Gainesville Sun,* February 18, 2006.

16 See "Candidates Join to Tout Their Faith" by Charles Babington and Beth Fouhy (AP), *The Orlando Sentinel,* August 17, 2008.

17 Log onto OrlandoSentinel.com/news then click on Nation/World for the video.

18 See "In Tape, Bush Warned on Katrina" by Margaret Ebrahim and John Soloman, *The Orlando Sentinel,* March 2, 2006.

19 See "Clean Energy Sources: Sun, Wind and Subsidies" by Jeffrey Ball, *The Wall Street Journal,* January 8, 2010, p. A13.

20 See "Foster-care Abuse Rises Sharply" by Rene Stutzman, *The Orlando Sentinel,* June 22, 2002.

21 See "Scandal's Cost" by Susan Strother Clarke, *The Orlando Sentinel,* June 30, 2002.

22 See www.earthportals.com/Portal_Messenger/bia.html

23 See www.naiaonline.org/body/articles/archives/forest_burn.htm

24 See "Why did the National Road Fail?" by Burton Folsom, Jr., *The Freeman* (The Foundation for Economic Education), July/August 2004.

25 Even for-profit airport screeners do a better job than the ones hired by the government. See, "Private Airport Screeners Outperform Their Government Counterparts" by Robert W. Poole, Jr., *Budget & Tax News* (The Heartland Institute), July 2005, pg. 6.

26 See "Incentives vs. Government Waste" by John Steele Gordon, *The Wall Street Journal,* May 14, 2010, p. A19.

27 See "How Wal-Mart Responded to Katrina" by Beth Hoffman, *The Freeman,* October 2005, pg. 10.

28 See "Officials Standoff Stymied Response" *The Orlando Sentinel,* September 11, 2005; "Behind Poor Katrina Response, A Long Chain of Weak Links" by Robert Black, Amy Schatz, Gary Fields and Christopher Cooper, *The Wall Street Journal,* September 6, 2005.

29 See "Audit Finds FEMA Bilked of Millions" by Megan O'Matz, *Orlando Sentinel,* February 14, 2006.

30 See "FEMA Says it Overpaid" by Megan O'Matz and Sally Kestin, *The Orlando Sentinel,* January 11, 2006; "Wildfires Sparked Furry of Claims" by Sally Kestin, *The Orlando Sentinel,* September 18, 2005; and "Cheaters Get 'Easy Money' from FEMA" by Sally Kestin, Megan O'Matz, John Maines and Jon Burstein, *South Florida Sun-Sentinel,* September 18, 2005.

31 For example, in Africa, capitalism has led to millions of people being connected to family members for the first time in years as cell phone makers continue to lower prices and offer more towers. See "Cell Phones Catapult Rural Africa to 21st Century" by Sharon LaFraniere, *The New York Times,* August 25, 2005.

32 See "Yes, Bill Gates really does think he can cure the world," *The Economist,* January 25-February 4, 2005.

33 See "An Economy of Liars" by Gerald P. O'Driscoll Jr., *The Wall Street Journal,* April 20, 2010, p. A21.

34 For an extensive look at this issue see http://stossel.blogs.foxbusiness.com/2010/01/14/crony-capitalism-v/

35 One company, Southwest Airlines, was the only airline to refuse a taxpayer-financed bailout after the attacks of September 11th. Now, Southwest is routinely the only airline turning a profit. See "Southwest's Earnings Soar" *The Orlando Sentinel,* April 15, 2005; and "Orlando's New No. 1" by Beth Kassab, *The Orlando Sentinel,* January 19, 2006.

36 See "Paul Remarks Have Deep Roots" by Jonathan Weisman, *The Wall Street Journal,* May 22-23, 2010, p. A3.

37 See "Capitalism Saved the Miners" by Daniel Henninger, *The Wall Street Journal*, October 14, 2010.

38 See the Virginia Declaration of Rights (1776), in *Founders Constitution*, ed. Kurland and Lerner, 1:6.

39 See Vindicating the Founders: Race, Sex, Class and Justice in the Origins of America, by Thomas G. West, Rowman & Littlefield Publishers, Inc., 1997, p. 38; and Thomas Jefferson, First Inaugural Address (1801) in *Writings*, 494.

40 For more on this issue, see "Don't Stop Believing in Risk of Song Sharing" by Joe Barrett, *The Wall Street Journal*, November 5, 2010.

41 See "Supercapitalism is good for consumer, bad for the citizen" by Robyn Blumner, *St. Petersburg Times*, September 23, 2007, pg. 5P.

42 See "Zimbabwe's economic fall unprecedented 'in peacetime'," by Lesley Wroughton, *The Globe and Mail*, July 27, 2005.

43 Source: The Royal Alberta Museum; Edmonton, Alberta, Canada.

44 See "Lovable But Not Flashy" by Linda Shrieves, *The Orlando Sentinel*, September 28, 2005.

45 See "The Tragedy of the Commons" at http://www.srmason-sj.org/council/journal/oct99/gcmesoct.html and www.americanheritage.com/98/oct/022.htm. "Property Rights: Basis of Prosperity" by Carol Saviak, *The Orlando Sentinel*, November 22, 2007.

46 See "The Essence of Americanism" by Leonard Read, from a 1961 lecture at the Foundation for Economic Education.

47 See *Horizons*, First Quarter 2002, pg. 5.

48 See "In Mongolia, Incentives to Keep Leopards Alive" by Leslie Chang, *The Wall Street Journal*, June 17, 2002, pg. A17.

49 See "China's Tiger Farms Spark a Standoff" by Shai Oster, *The Wall Street Journal*, February 13-14, 2010.

50 See "Saving the Environment: Money Talks" by Malcolm G. Scully, *The Chronicle of Higher Education*, November 23, 2001; "Green Groups See Potent Tool in Economics" by Jessica E. Vascellaro, *The Wall Street Journal*, August 23, 2005; "A Fish Story" *The Wall Street Journal*, November 6, 2003; and "Conservation Banks Catch On, Aiding Wildlife and Builders" by John J. Fialka, *The Wall Street Journal*, February 22, 2006.

51 See "Global Fishing Trade Depletes African Waters" by John W. Miller, *The Wall Street Journal*, July 18, 2007; and "Sad Truth About Tigers in India" by Mehul P. Dixit, *The Orlando Sentinel*, August 9, 2007.

52 See "Boone Picken's Gift to Oklahoma State Sparks Local Rivalry" by Ryan Chittum, *The Wall Street Journal*, March 30, 2006.

53 See http://www.fff.org/freedom/fd0412a.asp for more on the history of eminent domain.

54 There are thousands of such cases. See, for example, "Eminent Domain Takes Center Stage in Redevelopment Debates" by Samuel R. Staley, *Budget & Tax News* (The Heartland Institute), April 2005; "Daytona wins right to force Boardwalk sale" by Ludmilla Lelis, *The Orlando Sentinel*, August 20, 2005; Eminent Domain: Is It Only Hope for Inner Cities?" by Ryan Chittum, *The Wall Street Journal*, October 5, 2005; "Chicago May Seize Homes, Businesses for Airport" by Steve Stanek, *Budget & Tax News* (The Heartland Institute), December 2005.

55 See "Eminent Domain Upheld" by Hope Yen, *The Dallas Morning News*, June 24, 2005; and "Court Says Public Purpose Trumps Private Property Rights" by Steve Sanek, *Budget & Tax News* (The Heartland Institute), August 2005.

56 See "In light of stadium, ruling pleases Arlington" by Jeff Mosier and Jim Getz, *The Dallas Morning News*, June 24, 2005.

57 There is some good news. After this ruling, many states began enacting legislation that would make it more difficult for private property owners to lose their homes. One bank (BB&T) even adopted a policy of refusing to loan money to any business that was seeking to use eminent domain over another private party. See "Utah Bans Eminent Domain Use by Redevelopment Agencies" by Henry Lamb, *Environment & Climate News* (The Heartland Institute), June 2005; "States move to protect property" By Emily Bazar, *USA Today*, August 3, 2005; "Bill puts a rein on controversial view of eminent domain" by Kenneth R. Harney, *The Orlando Sentinel*, November 6, 2005; and "Financial giant takes a stand on eminent domain" by Brooke A. Masters, *The Orlando Sentinel*, January 26, 2006.

58 See "Wielding charity in tsunami land" by Kathleen Parker, *The Orlando Sentinel*, January 9, 2005, pg. G3; and "Americans are definitely not stingy" by Peter Brown, *The Orlando Sentinel*, December 31, 2004.

59 See "Why Foreign Aid is Hurting Africa" by Dambisa Moyo, *The Wall Street Journal*, March 21-22, 2009; "Africa Needs Growth, Not Pity and Big Plans" by Matt Ridley, *The Wall Street Journal*, November 27-28, 2010; and "A Continent of New Consumers Beckons" by Peter Wonacott, *The Wall Street Journal*, January 13, 2011.

60 See "Africa Needs Aid, Not Flawed Theories" by Bill Gates, *The Wall Street Journal*, November 27-28, 2010.

CHAPTER REVIEW

1. What would capitalism, in its purest form, say about the institution of slavery?

2. From the perspective of Adam Smith, would it be legal for gas stations to raise prices during a hurricane? Why, or why not?

3. What is the difference between an interest and a right? Give some examples.

4. Where do hockey sticks come from? Be specific.

Chapter Three

THE ECONOMICS *of* SECURITY

Photo courtesy Jack Chambless

We all declare for liberty; but in using the same word we do not all mean the same thing. With some the word liberty may mean for each man to do as he pleases with himself, and the product of his labor; while with others, the same word may mean for some men to do as they please with other men, and the product of other men's labor. Here are two, not only different, but incompatible things, called by the same name – liberty. And it follows that each of these things is, by the respective parties, called by two different and incompatible names – liberty and tyranny.

ABRAHAM LINCOLN

THE SEARCH FOR SECURITY

As the proud father of three children, I know all too well how important it is for them to feel safe and secure. Sometimes my kids ask me to lie next to them when a late-night thunderstorm rolls through our town. They used to ask me to go upstairs before them, to turn on the lights because the darkness was a little unsettling. By providing them with the security they desire, I make them feel comfortable at those particular moments. What they may not realize is that there is a trade-off between security and freedom. Every time I go upstairs ahead of them to secure them, they lose the freedom to be upstairs alone to play and/or get into mischief without Daddy bothering them.

The same is true with respect to the relationship between government and our economic system. For many people capitalism is undesirable because this system inherently requires *personal responsibility*. In our natural state, we seek to avoid pain. As a result, we humans will seek to have someone else shoulder the responsibility for our choices if we can. The moment we ask government to bear responsibility for our shortcomings we invite government into our lives to guide our behavior and restrain our liberty.

As we saw in chapter two, individuals often reject the choice of maximum liberty and personal responsibility, as they call themselves capitalists! The examples are endless. After September 11th, the airline "capitalists" ran to Washington, D.C., to beg Congress for a $15 billion bailout to help cover the inevitable losses that were going to accrue from fewer people flying. The steel industry recently asked for – and got – higher taxes placed on foreign makers of steel. The steel "capitalists" did not want to face the competition that comes from Russia and other countries. Farm "capitalists" get billions of dollars every year in tax money to keep them in farming. Artists get more than $100 million of your money each year because they feel they could not make enough money on their own in the capitalistic art market. And so on and so on.

Of course, private citizens also want protection from the normal pitfalls of life. We tell government to give us social "security" because we are afraid to fund our own retirement. We ask for unemployment checks because we don't want to take the risks of saving our own money for times we don't have a job. And sometimes we ask for the government to secure the value of our homes.

THE FANNIE MAE & FREDDIE MAC STORY...

When home values began to collapse and foreclosures accelerated in 2007-2010, many Americans – who would have been furious if the government limited how much profit they could earn on their home – begged the government to provide assistance when prices moved the other direction.[1]

The monumental downturn in this market culminated with the U.S. Treasury Department announcing the government takeover of the mortgage companies Fannie Mae and Freddie Mac in September 2008.

Each of these companies were chartered by the government but operated as private firms with shareholders and private sector relationships with businesses and individuals.

For years when a person would take out a mortgage on a home, the bank that processed and provided the initial loan would sell the note on the house to one of these two giant firms. But the bank would not simply sell one loan at a time. Banks all over America would bundle together thousands and thousands of loans and sell the package as "pooled mortgages," that allowed investors in Freddie Mac and Fannie Mae to earn profits from the loans that were bought from the banks.[2]

The problem is that those profits turned into enormous losses when the housing market began to see a collapse in prices, foreclosures, and lost equity. One of the principle causes (but not the only cause) of this downturn can be traced back to 2002.[3]

On June 18, 2002, President Bush gave a speech on, among other things, the state of home ownership in America. Mr. Bush said,

The goal is, everybody who wants to own a home has got a shot at doing so. The problem is we have what we call a homeownership gap in America. Three-quarters of Anglos own their homes, and yet less than 50% of African Americans and Hispanics own homes. That ownership gap signals that something might be wrong in the land of plenty. And we need to do something about it.

We are here in Washington, D.C. to address problems. So I've set this goal for the country. We want 5.5 million more homeowners by 2010 – million more minority homeowners by 2010. Five-and-a-half million families by 2010 will own a home. That is our goal. It is a realistic goal. But it's going to mean we're going to have to work hard to achieve the goal, all of us. And by all of us, I mean not only the federal government, but the private sector, as well.

I'm going to do my part by setting the goal, by reminding people of the goal, by heralding the goal, and by calling people into action, both the federal level, state level, local level, and in the private sector.

And so what are the barriers that we can deal with here in Washington? Well, probably the single barrier to first-time homeownership is high down payments. People take a look at the down payment, they say, 'that's too high, I'm not buying.' They may have the desire to buy, but they don't have the wherewithal to handle the down payment. We can deal with that. And so I've asked Congress to fully fund an American Dream down payment fund which will help a low-income family to qualify to buy.

We believe when this fund is fully funded and properly administered, which it will be under the Bush administration, that over 40,000 families a year – 40,000 families a year – will be able to realize the dream we want them to be able to realize, and that's owning their own home.

The second barrier to ownership is the lack of affordable housing. There are neighborhoods in America where you just can't find a house that's affordable to purchase, and we need to deal with that problem. The best way to do so, I think, is to

Shutterstock © ARENA Creative, 2011.

set up a single family affordable housing tax credit to the tune of $2.4 billion over the next five years to encourage affordable single family housing in inner-city America.

The third problem is the fact that the rules are too complex. People get discouraged by the fine print on the contracts. They take a look and say, 'well, I'm not so sure I want to sign this. There's too many words. There's too many pitfalls.' So one of the things that the Secretary is going to do is he's going to simplify the closing documents and all the documents that have to deal with homeownership. It is essential that we make it easier for people to buy a home, not harder. And in order to do so, we've got to educate folks. Some of us take homeownership for granted, but there are people – obviously, the home purchase is a significant, significant decision by our fellow Americans. We've got people who have newly arrived to our country, don't know the customs. We've got people in certain neighborhoods that just aren't really sure what it means to buy a home. And it seems like to us that it makes sense to have a outreach program, an education program that explains the whys and wherefores of buying a house, to make it easier for people to not only understand the legal implications and ramifications, but to make it easier to understand how to get a good loan.

There's some people out there that can fall prey to unscrupulous lenders, and we have an obligation to educate and to use our resource base to help people understand how to purchase a home and what – where the good opportunities might exist for home purchasing.

Finally, we want to make sure the Section 8 homeownership program is fully implemented. This is a program that provides vouchers for first-time homebuyers which they can use for down payments and/or mortgage payments.

So this is an ambitious start here at the federal level. And, again, I repeat, you all need to help us every way you can. But the private sector needs to help, too. They need to help, too. Of course, it's in their interest. If you're a realtor, it's in your interest that somebody be interested in buying a home. If you're a homebuilder, it's in your interest that somebody be interested in buying a home.

> And so, therefore, I've called – yesterday, I called upon the private sector to help us and help the homebuyers. We need more capital in the private markets for first-time, low-income buyers. And I'm proud to report that Fannie Mae has heard the call and, as I understand, it's about $440 billion over a period of time. They've used their influence to create that much capital available for the type of homebuyer we're talking about here. It's in their charter; it now needs to be implemented. Freddie Mac is interested in helping. I appreciate both of those agencies providing the underpinnings of good capital.[4]

If we look at the long history of home ownership in America, it was a simple reality of life that if you wanted a home you had to have good credit, stable employment, and normally a down payment of 20% of the value of the home or banks would turn you away.

Mr. Bush – and the federal government – put pressure on the banking sector to loosen those rules in order to provide more security to prospective homebuyers.

From 2002 through much of 2006 millions of Americans with shaky credit, an unstable employment picture and little or often no money down, were able to qualify for loans as a result of this pressure to extend capital to more people.

As we will see in chapter seven, the demand for homes was artificially inflated to the point where prices skyrocketed and people began pouring money into new subdivisions and investment properties that could be easily "flipped" for a profit.

In Florida, Nevada, Texas, California and other pockets of the country, there seemed to be no end to the increase in home values.

When the end came – and it always does – the very same banks, investors and homeowners who so jubilantly jumped into the housing market – even when it was not financially sound to do so – were now left with rapidly declining values and an inability to make payments, whether it was to investors or to other banks.

Rather than allow the market to punish those who were financially reckless – and therefore set the stage for a more efficient and economically sound housing and banking market in the future – the federal government opted to takeover Fannie Mae and Freddie Mac and infuse $200 billion of the taxpayers' money into these newly nationalized entities.[5]

Will $200 billion be the final cost of the federal bailout? Will the federal government operate Fannie Mae and Freddie Mac more efficiently than the private sector could? Will the government require that future homebuyers come up with 20% down or will political pressure to be "fair" to people lead to an ongoing cycle of bailouts and more turmoil in the housing market?

Only time will tell, but any of you reading this section of the book should not be optimistic that the government will never come to you again to bail out millionaire bankers or your fellow citizen who believes that they are entitled to your money in order to maintain their residence.

The mortgage bailout is not the end of the story. It would take a thousand pages to cover the hundreds of thousands of security-based programs that have evolved over the last several decades. In this chapter, we will look at how the economic systems of communism, socialism, and the mixed economy seek to create – or impose – security in order to humanely battle the problem of scarcity. The results range from horrific human suffering to mere inconvenience and annoyance.

COMMUNISM – THE ULTIMATE SECURITY BLANKET?

I was once at an Irish bar having a beer with a few economists – most of whom were devout followers of Karl Marx. When one of them asked me how many classes I teach in a typical semester, I said, "Seven."

"Seven!?!" He shrieked. "You're exploited!"

I tried to explain to him that it was my choice to teach seven classes, but he insisted that I only thought I wanted to teach seven classes. In reality, he argued, my employer was simply taking advantage of me instead of paying me a decent enough salary to teach only two or three classes. I am not sure what the word "decent" means, but I do know that Karl Marx would have been proud of my fellow economist for recognizing my "suffering."

Karl Marx was a German philosopher who, after 18 years of reflection, angst, and deliberation, produced one of the most influential books in the history of economic thought. *Das Capital* (German for the Capital) was a 2,500 *page*, four-volume treatise on markets, capitalism, and the perceived exploitation of human beings. In this breathtakingly complex document was a recurring theme: that enlightened self-interest, contrary to the writings of Adam Smith, is a destructive, exploitative force, rather than the force of good. Marx went so far as to argue that:

> Capital is dead labour, that vampire-like, only lives by sucking living labour.

Marx was not oblivious to the inner workings of free markets. His fundamental understanding of labor as an input in the production process was sound. He is the person who created the word capitalism and he even bought and sold American and English stocks, earning enough money to write his colleague, Friedrick Engels in 1864 and brag, "The time has now come when with wit and very little money one can really make a killing in London."[6]

Where Marx severely departed from Adam Smith was in his argument that the nature of capitalism is to monopolize labor resources and, in turn, exploit workers by earning profit on the surplus value that they generated.[7] By surplus value, Marx meant the difference between the wages labor is paid and the price charged for a good or service. For Marx, labor was the sole determinant of value therefore there should be no profit for any business – only returns to labor for their efforts.

Along with Frederick Engels, Marx went on to publish *Manifesto of the Communist Party* that provided a detailed prescription for saving the world from the clutches of capitalism. Among the items included in their recommendations were:

1. Abolition of property in land and application of all rents of land for public purposes
2. A heavy progressive or graduated income tax
3. Abolition of all right to inheritance
4. Confiscation of all the property of all emigrants and rebels
5. Centralization of credit, the means of communication and transport in the hands of the state.[8]

As it is easy to see, Marx reviled the concept of economic liberty and believed that the government should take away money and property to provide for the equality and security of the masses. Marx also subscribed to the belief that the employee-employer relationship generates a zero-sum game where the capitalists become better and better off at the expense of helpless workers. Marx believed that at some point, this system would not survive and would be thrown out by revolutionary forces.

Marxian ideology got its day in the sun on November 7, 1917, when Russia fell under the weight of revolution to Vladimir Lenin and the Council of People's Commissars. On December 30, 1922, the Union of Socialist Soviet Republics (USSR) came into being.

APPLYING THE THEORY OF COMMUNISM

> Sixteen men in Moscow today are attempting one of the most audacious economic experiments in history…they are laying down the industrial future of 146 million people and one-sixth of the land of the area of the world for fifteen years. These sixteen men salt down the whole economic life of 146 million people for a year in advance as calmly as a Gloucester man salts down his fish.
>
> Stuart Chase

Lenin faced an immediate economic crisis in the Soviet Union. Industrial production had fallen to levels not seen since 1913, and internal dissent was mounting. With his attempts at nationalizing the economy and regulating production faltering, Lenin created his New Economic Policy (NEP) that allowed peasants to sell their surpluses at free-market prices, and some small-scale industries were returned to private ownership. As a result, by 1926, production levels and the overall health of the economy began to improve, but Lenin, who died in 1924, did not live to see this change.

> One death is a tragedy. A million deaths is a statistic.
>
> Josef Stalin

His successor, Josef Stalin, had a very different perspective on managing the economy of the Soviet Union. Stalin believed that his country would be best served by a massive campaign to build up Russian industry by making the country more self-reliant and more centrally planned.

In 1929, he began his first "Gos-Plan" – a series of five-year plans designed to control output, employment,

1818
1883

Shutterstock © Dariush M, 2011.

and prices. Under central planning the Soviet Union assigned production quotas to all state-run factories, farms, and other production facilities.

In a capitalist system, there is no central planning of markets. Markets are dynamic and ever-changing. Imagine trying to plan exactly what the output level of Internet services needs to be in five years or even five weeks from now. It would be a daunting task to say the least. However, you must bear in mind that Stalin perceived a day when planning would satisfy all of the wants and needs of his people. By assigning production quotas, he hoped to meet those needs without allowing profit to occur. Ironically, millions of Soviet citizens died of starvation or were executed during this attempt to meet what were often unrealistic quotas.

> Stalin was personally responsible for the murder of more people than any other human being in the 20th century—and probably any other century. Stalin took Lenin's system of slave labor camps and turned it into a vast secret empire in the depths of Siberia. Lenin chose to let millions starve to death in order to sustain his war effort, but Stalin went further by deliberately engineering famines on an even greater scale. Finally, Stalin crossed the one line that Lenin would not, by ordering the executions of fellow Communists on a massive scale.[9]

Under communism, the government helps "secure" people from the "exploitative" prices of the free market by making it illegal to charge prices above the government-set level. Rampant shortages persisted in Russia and other Eastern European nations as a result of this policy. In many cases, getting a new apartment, car, or television set took years of waiting. Shortages of food, electric power, and medicine were also severe. In some years, the average Soviet citizen spent an average of four out of every five working days standing in lines, hoping that a stick of butter or loaf of bread would be available.

Marx did not call for leaders to use the type of brute force that Stalin, Kim Jong-il or Fidel Castro have used in the name of communism. In fact, just like we have never seen a purely capitalistic economy, we have also never witnessed pure communism. What we see in Cuba and North Korea – and what was used in the former Soviet Union – was a 'command and control' system, rather then the voluntary pursuit of the betterment of mankind. Then again, Marx should have been able to recognize that it is

biologically unnatural for people to deny their self interest or avoid the pursuit of private property. Indirectly, Marx helped cause the rise of Stalin by advocating naïve economic policies.[10]

IS SOCIALISM ANY BETTER?

> The inherent vice of capitalism is the unequal sharing of the blessings. The inherent vice of socialism is the equal sharing of misery.
>
> Winston Churchill

In the fall of 2003, I had the opportunity to publicly debate a Marxist economics professor from one of the country's top private universities.[11] During the three hours we argued with each other, he offered up a grand vision of what a more economically kind country would look like. To his credit, he never mentioned North Korea or Cuba, but he did point out that many European nations have done a much better job of providing economic security without resorting to firing squads and slave labor camps. Let's look at it.

IS SWEDEN PARADISE?

If concern for the quality of human life were part of the Winter Olympics, Sweden—along with strong performances in skiing, the biathlon and hockey—would rout the rest of the world on the way to a gold-medal performance. Located in northern Europe, this home to just over nine million people can lay claim to an honest-to-goodness push for the utopian society.

Most of us are very familiar with at least one company that comes from this picturesque nation: IKEA furniture. Let's consider how different our lives would be if we left the U.S. to go to work for this popular company.

As a new employee you might first want to know what benefits you would be entitled to. If entitlements are your concern, you have come to the right country

CONCEPT CHECK

Who is Hugo Chavez and what is he doing in his country? Why do you suppose he was able to get elected to begin with?

– because the Swedish government has apparently adopted the mindset that workers must be protected from virtually every possible economic crisis that might befall them.

For starters, to deal with the possibility that you might be overworked, the government passed the Working Hours Act of 1982 that provides for a statutory maximum of 40 hours on average, per week, over a period of four weeks. The law also prohibits night work and stipulates that the employee must have, per week, at least 36 hours of continuous time off.

Should you ever ask to work overtime to make some extra money for cross-country skiing lessons, you will be informed that you may not work more than 48 hours in four weeks or 50 hours over a calendar month.[12] The Working Hours Act also prohibits putting in more than 200 hours per year in overtime.

Shutterstock © Oleksiy Mark, 2011.

Suppose you are hired as a part-time worker at IKEA, but you really want to work full-time. In Sweden, part-timers qualify for a subsidy – paid for by the taxpayers, where, "in case of involuntary part-time the wage earner can be compensated for the difference between full-time and part time through the unemployment insurance system if the qualification rules are fulfilled."[13]

For those of you who have fainted, when you wake up and continue reading, you should bear in mind that part-timers qualify for this form of underemployment insurance for only 300 days.

Should you happen to get married and end up with a little Swedish-American bundle of joy a year later, do not worry about day care, or health care costs. Child care and health care benefits are ostensibly "free" (i.e. the tab is picked up by taxpayers) in Sweden. Should you choose to stay home with your child, you are covered by the Child Care Leave Act of 1978 that – hold onto your seats – allow you *and your companion* to take up to ten months of leave from your job, at 80% of your previous pay rate! In addition, one of you will be given the right to stay away from the job for an additional month, at 90% of your prior pay.

If you think ten months is not enough bonding time between you and little Bjorn, you can opt for the plan that allows for 15 months, at 60% of your pay, to stay at home. It gets even better.

One parent maintains the right to reduce his or her work hours until the child is eight years old, while leave for temporary care of a child totals 60 days per year. All of this comes at a guarantee that your job will be there for you when you return, with the mere requirement that you and/or your companion have been employed for at least six months consecutively or 12 months during the last two years, prior to the child's birth.

Suppose when you come back to work, you lose your job because of a new global financial crisis. Don't fret, because in Sweden, workers who have worked for at least five months during the 12 months prior to unemployment, qualify for 300 days of unemployment insurance at 80% of previous income if they are under 55 years of age and 450 days if they are over 55.

By now, many of you may have your bags packed and are on hold with a major airline trying to find out ticket prices to Stockholm. Before you go, perhaps a couple of minor details should be provided.

First, in order to pay for all of these "free" programs, the top tax rate on the most successful Swedish workers is 60%. This tax rate does not include property, sales, and other taxes Swedish citizens have to pay. By contrast, the top tax rate in the U.S. was 35% at the time of this writing.[14] In Hong Kong it is 16%. Not surprisingly, many times the free services end up costing the most.

A recent study found that the average Swedish household has a median income that is lower than the median income of African-Americans. If Sweden was a U.S. state, its income would make it the poorest of all the states.[15] This might be why more and more Swedish voters have begun to push for less taxation and social services. After all, when accounting for the people who do not have jobs, plus those who are taking advantage of Sweden's generous sick leave policies, the effective unemployment rate was between 20% and 25% for much of the last decade.[16]

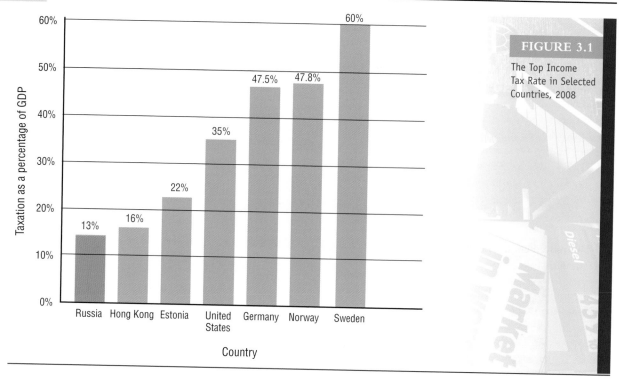

FIGURE 3.1

The Top Income
Tax Rate in Selected
Countries, 2008

THE PROBLEM WITH FRANCE AND GREECE AND VENEZUELA AND....

> Government is a broker in pillage and every election is an advanced auction on stolen goods.
>
> H.L. Mencken

Sweden is not alone in its security-induced economic struggles. In France, restaurant owners face labor laws that limit workers to 43 hours per week – unless the restaurant owner pays overtime of up to 150% of the basic wage rate plus money for "compensatory time off." That probably doesn't matter much because France's 19.6% tax on all restaurant meals helps hold down the number of customers.[17]

The French government also collects roughly 45% of France's output in the form of taxes. The top tax rate in France is almost 50%.[18] Moreover, if an employee takes maternity leave in France, the employer must keep the job open for the worker for three years. France even pays couples $850 and $1,215 per month if the parents of two kids will agree to have a third.[19] After all, with so many retirees and other people to support, the French government is going to need plenty of tax payers in the future.

French labor law keeps most stores closed all day Sunday and they can only be open for 10 hours on other days because French workers are not permitted to work more than 35 hours per week.[20] French courts recently ruled that after an employee has been with a company for at least "two paychecks," it will cost the company 3 to 12 months of pay to get rid of that worker, should they want to dismiss him or her.

Not surprisingly, France has a struggling economy that produces very few new products or jobs. The tension that high unemployment and poverty brings is the primary cause for the recent wave of riots that France's immigrants participated in.[21]

On the other hand, even when the French government attempts to interject the free market into its system, riots break out. In March of 2006, the government proposed rules that would make it easier for French employers to fire younger workers. Demonstrators took to the streets protesting this change to a more competitive economy.

Such a result is not surprising. According to a recent poll, out of 20 countries surveyed, French citizens expressed the lowest level of faith in the free market. Only 36% of French citizens agreed that the free market is the "best system on which to base the future of the world." – This is compared to 71% in the U.S., 66% in Great Britain, and 74% in *China*.[22]

This has not prevented French president, Nicolas Sarkozy from unveiling an ambitious plan to reduce taxes and welfare spending in France. Calling the social welfare system "unjust" and "financially untenable," Mr. Sarkozy has pushed for legislation that would end France's 35-hour work week; a reduction in wealth and income taxes and the abolishment of inheritance taxes.[23]

CONCEPT CHECK

In 2010, Ireland succumbed to the global financial crisis and accepted a European Union loan of $110 billion.[25] Many within the EU called for Ireland to raise its corporate income tax (the rate is 12.5%) in order to restore financial solvency.[26] Instead, Ireland has embarked on a massive campaign to cut social welfare spending.[27] Which plan – tax hikes or spending cuts – has the highest probability of restoring Ireland's economy? Why?

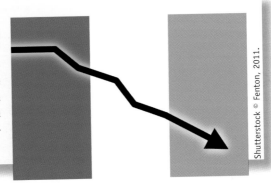

Shutterstock © Fenton, 2011.

This movement in France is not isolated. Denmark and other western European nations are going through similar capitalistic reforms, largely in response to the rapid rise of Estonia, Poland and other eastern European nations.[24] As these former Communist countries continue to push for free market reforms, the rising standard of living has led to more jobs and opportunities for eastern and western Europeans alike. As more companies flee the high-tax, heavy welfare states of the West, more pressure has been put on France and other nations to pursue reforms that will keep jobs and tax revenue from fleeing entirely.

This was one of the reasons for the recent election of Angela Merkel as Chancellor of Germany. Ms. Merkel was elected largely on a platform that reminded people of Margaret Thatcher.[28] Ms. Thatcher cut taxes and subsidies to businesses and fought Britain's powerful labor unions in a successful push to move England away from socialism. Now German voters seem to have warmed to the idea of becoming more competitive on the world stage.[29]

Recently, Germany relaxed regulations that used to force businesses to close at 6 p.m. each evening. Led by Finance Minister Wolfgang Schauble, Germany has also managed to lower taxes and cut government spending over the past few years. The result has been a sharp increase in Germany's level of production, income, and exports, and one of the strongest economic recoveries in the world.[30] Ironically, this long-time supporter of generous government payouts in the name of economic security, has now begun a campaign to encourage the United States to reduce our level of deficit spending in order to avoid runaway debt and higher taxes in the future.[31]

In Spain, Portugal, Sudan, Venezuela, Bolivia, Greece, and other parts of the world, governments continue to expand their power – all in the name of fairness and the social good – only to see hundreds of thousands of bright, highly motivated people leave these nations for places like Hong Kong, Ireland, Brazil, and Australia.[32] Greece, in particular, has fallen on hard times. According to the World Bank, Greece ranks 109th out of 183 nations in the ease of doing business; 140th in the amount of time it takes to start a business; 154th in protecting investors and equally low in everything from enforcing contracts to flexibility in labor relations.[33]

Not surprisingly, Greece suffers from high levels of tax evasion,[34] heavy debt, rising unemployment, riots, and a condition of near bankruptcy that required a bailout by the European Union in 2010.[35]

This trend is all because increased taxes and excessive regulations have drastically reduced the

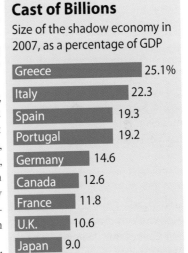

Cast of Billions

Size of the shadow economy in 2007, as a percentage of GDP

Greece	25.1%
Italy	22.3
Spain	19.3
Portugal	19.2
Germany	14.6
Canada	12.6
France	11.8
U.K.	10.6
Japan	9.0
U.S.	7.2

Lars P. Feld, University of Heidelberg, Friedrich Schneider Johannes Kepler University Linz

CONCEPT CHECK

Cuba's government has a list of 124 "authorized" activities for people who want to employ themselves. Carpenters are on the list but they are only allowed to "repair existing furniture upon the request of a customer."[36] They cannot make furniture to sell to the general public. What Marxian principle is the basis for this law?

incentives that entrepreneurs need to serve their fellow man.

CAN SOCIALISM MAKE YOU HAPPY?

Not all people are unhappy with socialism. It is critical to your understanding of socialism that you consider the fact that people in Europe and Latin American have freely elected socialist leaders. The leaders – while campaigning for office – told them that they would receive certain taxpayer-financed benefits. The politicians also told them that the benefits would come at the cost of much higher tax rates than capitalistic nations have. Venezuelan voters – who have seen Hugo Chavez seize more than 2.5 million acres of private property – were well aware that he was not going to push for Venezuela to become the next Hong Kong.

Those politicians keep winning elections and we *do not see* a massive migration of people away from Europe to America. This means that socialism can be, for many people, the system that delivers the most happiness – even if half their money leaves them by force. In fact, many studies show that some of the most socialistic nations in the world have some of the happiest people.[37]

Economists who have investigated this paradox have found that one of the primary differences between nations that embrace socialism and those that pursue capitalism is the divergent *cultural influences* that are found around the world. Simply put, what makes some people happy – more money and more stuff – does not make others happy.[38] It has been empirically shown that Europeans tend to be much happier when they perceive that their government is actively correcting for inequality in earnings.[39]

There is some evidence that certain places in the United States also desire European-style socialism. Many organizations rank states by economic freedom. Some states like New Hampshire with an openly Libertarian history[40] tend to embrace lawmakers that advocate zero state income and sales taxes and limited regulations. Other states like New York, California, Minnesota, Illinois,[41] and Michigan have much higher tax and regulatory burdens, and actively assist the poor with generous social welfare programs.[42]

Over the past decade, New York has lost 409,000 people while California has lost 1.32 million. Michigan – once the bastion of industrial activity had an unemployment rate of 12.4% - three full percentage points higher than the U.S. average in 2010.[43] Moreover, each of these states have seen rising state income tax burdens (Californians pay the highest state income tax rate of 10.3%) and soaring budget deficits as more businesses flee to places like Texas[44] and Florida.[45]

Yet, for many people, the quality of life in New York, Minnesota, and California is still far greater than it is in states where people are expected to be more self-reliant.[46]

Yet, not everyone living in socialistic places is happy….

HOW UNHAPPY EUROPEANS – AND AMERICANS – COULD USE FREDERIC BASTIAT

In 1849, French economist Frederic Bastiat penned a short book entitled, *The Law*. It was in this book that he prescribed a recipe for any society that wishes to support justice, economic progress, and happiness for the largest part of society. The problem with socialism, according to Bastiat, is that the socialist sees human beings as mounds of clay to be molded in the manner the government official deems necessary to bring about the "greater good" of society. This compels government to use force and coercion to carry out the grand vision of greater security for mankind.

The great flaw with the current European model, Bastiat argued, is that the socialists are so eager to do good that they are willing to resort to theft to accomplish their benevolent goals. He argued that, in a civilized society, none of us has the right to use force to plunder the property of our fellow man.

Even if we intend to charitably give our neighbors' property to the poor, we will be arrested if we rob him to do so. By what right then, Bastiat asked, do we have to use our votes to take away the money (through taxation) of our fellow man in order to give it to someone who has no legal claim to it? Isn't this simply *legalized plunder*?

Socialists believe that people aren't charitable and that businesses are corrupt. As Warren Sapp – a millionaire former football player – once argued, "We've designed a system for people to cheat and steal and pillage, so that the rich get richer and the poor don't get a damn thing."

People with socialist leanings see government as a sort of savior, a healer of all that ails us. This means that in much of Europe and America, voters eagerly support increasing taxes on the most successful citizens. This in turn, is called things like "justice," "fairness," or "equitable."

In 2009, Americans gave $303.75 billion to charity.[47] This was down from a high of $315 billion the year before, but still higher than the entire Gross Domestic Product of 157 countries – including Norway, the Czech Republic, Portugal, Denmark and Finland.[48] Adjusting for inflation and population changes, GDP per person in America has risen over the past 50 years by about 150%, while charitable giving per person has risen by about 190%.[49]

In summary, socialism does not confer the type of evil and oppression we see in the command and control economies. Nor does socialism create the rampant poverty we see where communism is experimented with. Yet, as Bastiat so accurately pointed out, there is still an element of force that all socialistic nations must use in order to create the "fair" society they desire. That is perhaps why people in China and India are moving from socialism to capitalism.[50]

THE 33% DILEMMA

In 2005, prime ministers of India and China agreed to an economic "strategic partnership" that represents an important and natural step in the continued globalization of the world economy, and one that could have a dramatic effect on Americans in the 21st century.

With about one-third of the world's people, the agreement between China's Wen Jiabao and India's Manmohan Singh could, in the estimation of many economists, spell significant and far-reaching problems for the United States.

It is important for Americans to understand that this warming of relations between Asia's growing economic powers is rooted in their perception of shared self-interests in selling their goods and service to the West, most importantly, the United States and European Union countries.

Their emergence as key players in the international economy, stems from a rejection of the centrally planned economies of the previous half-century that had led them further down the road to poverty.

It also stems from the growing premium on the value of human capital in the world economy – both in the global-technology sector where India has excelled and in manufacturing where China has been taking market share from western companies.[51]

In 1947, India gained its independence from Great Britain and immediately charted a course born out of a belief in the power of technically planned socialism. Prime Minister Jawaharlal Nehru nationalized the coal, steel and machine-tool industries and launched a massive government campaign to create the technological infrastructure that would be necessary to bring Indians out of poverty.

Led by the economist P.C. Mahalanobis, the Indian Statistical Institute created a mathematical model designed to plan every facet of the economy.

Two years later, the communist takeover of China created the experiment known as the Great Leap Forward. The Maoist plan to modernize the Chinese economy by abolishing private-property rights and forcibly organizing farmers into industrial production led to the starvation of

millions of Chinese citizens and decades of unprecedented poverty.

Today, an economic miracle is under way in both countries as they have turned their backs on socialism and discovered capitalism with a vengeance.

From 2007-2010, India's economy grew at an astounding rate of 7.4-9.2%,[52] surpassing China for the first time as the country with the fastest rate of economic growth.[53] China has also averaged nearly double-digit increases in its gross domestic product during the past several years. During the same time frame, the U.S. actually shank under the weight of the "Great Recession."

Literacy rates in both China and India have risen sharply. China now produces four times more engineers than the United States. Moreover, fully 30% of the world's computer-software engineers are now from India.

Another telltale sign of economic growth is the fact that in both nations the population is rising at a decreasing rate – an indication the economy has entered a sustained period of rising wealth and opportunity.

At the current rate of economic growth, China will produce a GDP larger than the United States within the next two decades, while India will have a per-capita income equal to the United States' by 2066 or earlier.[54]

Precisely how India and China reversed decades of poverty and despair is fairly straightforward.

In 1991, the Indian government took a momentous decision when it began dismantling state control over the economy. Under the leadership of Rajiv Gandhi and Narasimha Rao, the government lowered tariffs and taxes, did away with public-sector monopolies and liberalized rules and regulations for willing entrepreneurs.[55]

The result was 170 million fewer Indians living in poverty than in 1980.[56] In 2004, the Indian government pushed through further reductions in tariffs on machinery items, computers, cellular phones, and power-transmission equipment.

China began its economic reforms during the 1980s with liberalization of profit-seeking in the agricultural sector. The 1990s and this decade have brought an acceleration of the free- market rejection of Marxian economics.

The Clinton administration bolstered China's attempts to trade internationally when it relaxed the human-rights test that China had been forced to pass to gain most-favored nation status.

As a result, artificial and inflationary barriers to Chinese goods fell sharply. Consequently, the high productivity in Chinese factories carried over into much lower prices for Americans shopping at Wal-Mart and other retail stores and created China's current purchasing power of over $9.85 trillion – second only to that of the United States.[57]

In 2004, China, borrowing heavily from the supply-side policies of Ronald Reagan, reduced the marginal tax rate on businesses from 28% to 24%.[58] In addition, the value-added tax was cut and, for the first time since 1949, China amended its constitution to guarantee all citizens the right to own private property.

In the past, students from India and China would come to America to study engineering and then stay here – most of the jobs in Silicon Valley were created by immigrant entrepreneurs. Today, a reverse brain drain is occurring in which Indian and Chinese students, buoyed by rising standards of living in their homeland, are leaving the United States to start businesses in their native land.[59] U.S. companies like Starbucks, Ford, and General Electric have also noticed that India, in particular, has become a very productive nation to invest in[60] – whether the investment is in human or physical capital.

On November 16, 2010, *The Wall Street Journal* published a long article entitled, "China's 'State Capitalism' Sparks a Global Backlash." I would like to strongly suggest that at this time you put down the book, go online to find this article and read every ominous word of it....

China, with a projected 2054 GDP of $70 trillion (U.S. projected GDP is less than $40 trillion for that year) has recently undergone yet another economic transformation that is taking this nation from a net copier of technology to a net creator of technology, with a fascinating blend of free market capitalism and government planning.[61] This form of "state capitalism" is being watched very carefully by economists all over the world in an attempt to ascertain the degree to which other nations might find it tempting to move in this relatively unique direction.

In a nutshell, China's government has fostered an environment from which entrepreneurs in key selected industries such as alternative energy technology and rare earth minerals, can freely pursue profits with government support in everything from currency markets to access to financial capital. As this article clearly illustrates, this is not a command and control type of economy. Nor is it capitalism or socialism. It has elements of all of these systems and thus far, the elements are working well.

It remains to be seen whether China can maintain the type of state capitalism that it has fostered. We could end up seeing China fall victim to the same political pressure that other nations do when planning is a key feature of an economy. Eventually, the pressures of capitalism and planning collide and either the nation moves toward freer markets or reverts back to state control.

One thing is certain however. The United States – and the rest of the world – had better not take China lightly. As world history has repeatedly shown, nations don't stay on the top of the economic heap forever – or for very long. This century may well be the one where the United States answers to one, or more nations, rather than being the dominant country that we have been for more than one hundred years.[62]

This man makes money by advertising large airline seats on the sidewalks of New York City. Would pure capitalism ever create jobs like this – at a wage that helps this man take care of his family – or do we have to have government regulate what American Airlines pays him to make sure he is treated fairly?

Photo courtesy Jack Chambless

IS THE MIXED ECONOMY THE PERFECT MIX?

So far it is unlikely that many of you have decided to move to North Korea or France. Still, you might find yourself disinclined to argue that capitalism is the ideal system. After all, shouldn't there be at least some minimal economic security provided by government? Wouldn't an economic system that allows us a great deal of freedom, while restraining greed and securing us from random unfortunate events, be ideal? Let's look at what that system would do. To see it, just open your eyes, because the United States is a good example of a mixed economy.

In America, you are allowed to pick your major; open a business; move to another state; keep most of your money (most people get to anyway); buy the house, cars, and foods you can afford; and run your life largely in a manner that you see fit. Our economy produces over $14.8 trillion in output each year, which is equal to every nation in Europe *combined* and higher than Japan ($4.3 trillion).[64]

When we look around the stores and malls of the United States, we see billions of goods and services that fit both our wants and needs. Poor people in America are some of the richest poor people in the world and often own cars, homes, cell phones and luxury goods. Having a blend of capitalism without letting the government turn its back on people who struggle economically seems to be the system we have worked toward. As a result, we

Shutterstock © baur, 2011.

CONCEPT CHECK

In the past few years the Brazilian economy has become one of the largest in the world. Go online, find out why and compare the economic policies of the Brazilian government to that of the United States.[63] In which areas does it appear that Brazil is less socialistic than the U.S.?

have a country with social security, welfare for the poor, aid to college students and farmers and struggling businesses, regulations that rein in corporate scandals, and laws fighting the degradation of the environment and human rights.

IS AMERICA BECOMING A SOCIALIST COUNTRY?

> Experience should teach us to be most on our guard to protect liberty when the government's purposes are beneficial. Men born to freedom are naturally alert to repel invasion of their liberty by evil-minded rulers. The greater dangers to liberty lurk in insidious encroachment by men of zeal, well-meaning but without understanding.
>
> Justice Louis Brandeis, Olmstead v. United States 277 U.S. 479 (1928)

At first glance, the question of America becoming less free seems absurd. However, decades ago, in a landmark book entitled, *The Road to Serfdom*, Friedrich Hayek, an Austrian economist sounded a warning to the United States and other nations. The warning, largely dismissed during the past 60 years, is now getting a fresh look, and Hayek, once dismissed by the intellectual elite, has come to the forefront of the battle over economic liberty.[65] Hayek's message is simple: Over time, countries that pursue a mixed economy allow government to increase its power to tax, spend, and regulate. The result is an incremental slide from the good intentions of government security to the oppressive hand of government force.

It would seem, by most objective standards that America – recessions notwithstanding – is still a great place to live today. After all, economists point out that geographic mobility is a good indicator of which economies are working well. Have you noticed how many people from around the world want to move here?

However, there is a growing body of evidence to suggest that America is indeed moving further and further away from the ideas of Adam Smith and John Locke. In 2011, the United States fell to ninth place in the rankings of global economic freedom.[66] 2010 saw the first drop from a standing of "economically free" to "mostly free." In 2011, the U.S. fell behind Denmark[67] and stayed behind Canada on the list. Canada – long a nation that the U.S. pointed to as an example of North American socialism – has risen up the rankings with a combination of business-friendly tax and regulatory policies and modest growth in government spending.[68]

THE EVIDENCE

> The inevitable progression of things is for government to gain ground and for liberty to yield.
>
> Thomas Jefferson

Most economists would agree that the evidence from centuries of economic activity indicates that the more freedom a nation enjoys, the greater will be that nation's economic and social progress. By freedom we mean the freedoms outlined in the Fifth Amendment of the U.S. Constitution.

Freedom also applies to how the government takes and uses our money. Article one, section eight of the Constitution reads:

> The Congress shall have power to lay and collect taxes, duties, imposts and excises, to pay the debts and provide for the common defense and general welfare of the United States; but all duties, imposts and excises shall be uniform throughout the United States.

If we look at four issues – taxes, government spending, government regulation, and civil liberties – we find that America is moving away from the idea of economic liberty and toward economic security.

THE HISTORY OF INCOME TAXES IN AMERICA

> We must make our election between economy and liberty or profusion and servitude. If we run into such debts as that we must be taxed in our meat and in our drink, in our necessities and our comforts, in our labors and our amusements, for our callings and our creeds, as the people of England are, our people, like them must come to labor 16 hours in the 24, and give the earnings of 15 of these to the government for their debts and daily expenses; and the 16th being insufficient to afford us bread, we must live as they now do, on oatmeal and potatoes; have no time to think, no means of calling the mismanagers to account; but be glad to obtain the subsistence by hiring ourselves to rivet their chains on the necks of our fellow sufferers.
>
> Thomas Jefferson

As you can see, Mr. Jefferson had very definitive ideas on the consequences of taxes on liberty. For that reason, from the ratification of the U.S. Constitution in 1787 until 1913, there was no such thing as the federal income tax. Now that you have fallen off your chair, it is time to get back up and read on.

From 1791 through 1802, the U.S. government was supported by internal taxes on distilled spirits, carriages, refined sugar, tobacco and snuff, property sold at auction, corporate bonds, and slaves. The War of 1812 brought about the nation's first sales taxes on gold, silverware, jewelry, and watches. In 1817, however, Congress did away with all internal taxes, relying on tariffs on imported goods to provide funds for running the government.

In 1862, in order to support the Civil War effort, Congress enacted the nation's first income tax law. During the Civil War, a citizen from a northern state earning $600–$1,000 per year paid at the rate of 3%. This was also the year that inheritance taxes debuted. By 1866 the Internal Revenue Service was collecting more than $310 million, the highest amount in the 90-year history of the U.S. The Act of 1862 established the office of the Commissioner of Internal Revenue.

The Commissioner was given power to assess, levy, and collect taxes and the right to enforce the tax laws through seizure of property and income and through prosecution. This mechanism is still with us today.

In 1872, the income tax was eliminated in favor of taxes on tobacco and distilled spirits (booze) but had a short revival in 1894–1895. In 1895, the U.S. Supreme Court decided that the income tax was unconstitutional because it was not apportioned among the states in conformity with the Constitution.

1913

For the first 45,438 days of America's life, the people did not have "the fruits of their labor" touched with a comprehensive federal income tax. That all changed on February 12, 1913 when Congress ratified the Sixteenth Amendment to the U.S. Constitution which reads:

> The Congress shall have power to lay and collect taxes on incomes, from whatever source derived, without apportionment among the several States, and without regard to any census or enumeration.

As the table following illustrates, the first income tax was applied to the highest incomes in America ($20,000 in 1914 translates to well over $250,000 in today's money) and was relatively modest in terms of the percentage of income taken.[69]

INCOME RANGE	MARGINAL TAX RATE[39]
$20,000–$50,000	1%
$50,001–75,000	2%
$75,001–$100,000	3%
$100,001–$250,000	4%
$250,001–$500,000	5%
$500,001 and above	7%

By the end of World War I, the top income tax rate had risen from 7% to 77%. In fiscal year 1918, annual internal revenue collections passed the billion-dollar mark for the first time, rising to $5.4 billion by 1920. By World War II, tax collections had increased to $7.3 billion. Yet it was a little-publicized change in the way taxes are collected that caused the explosion of revenue to $43 billion by 1943.

In 1942, Congress raised income taxes dramatically – ostensibly to pay for the mounting war effort and Franklin Roosevelt's "New Deal" social programs. For the first time, income taxes were to be collected from tens of millions of people who previously had been exempt from income taxation. The "class tax (tax on the rich)" became known as the "mass tax." In those days, people had to pay their taxes all at once – in the spring. As the spring of 1943 rolled around, Congress feared that even with a war raging, the voting public would not stand for this massive tax increase. Enter Mr. Beardsley Ruml.

Mr. Ruml was, at that time, chairman of the board of directors of the New York Federal Reserve Bank and treasurer at R.H. Macy & Co. When approached by Henry Morgenthau, the Treasury Secretary at the time, Mr. Ruml heard Mr. Morgenthau lament, "Suppose we have to go out and arrest five million people?" Fearing mass tax evasion, Mr. Ruml suggested that the government change the way we pay our taxes. Mr. Ruml suggested that the government get businesses to collect taxes for it.

The idea was simple. Have businesses deduct a percentage of a worker's gross pay every week and send the money to Washington, D.C. This "pay as you go" plan was argued to be much simpler and kinder, since workers would no longer be asked to worry about one tax bill once a year. The government would simply take a little from each paycheck, and the problem would be solved. This was the birth of the federal income tax withholding that is still with us to this day.

DILBERT: © Scott Adams/Dist. by United Feature Syndicate, Inc.

You can imagine what happened to federal income taxes after that point. The top tax rate hit 88.9% during the war.[70] This was not the highest proposed tax rate, however. In a message to Congress on April 27, 1942, FDR stated:

> Discrepancies between low personal incomes and very high personal incomes should be lessened; and I therefore believe that in time of this grave national danger, when all excess income should go to win the war, no American citizen ought to have a net income, after he has paid his taxes, of more than $25,000 a year.[71]

The Treasury then advised Congress:

> To implement the President's proposal, the Treasury now recommends the enactment of a 100 percent war supertax on that part of income after regular income tax which exceeds a personal exemption of $25,000.[72]

With the war supertax in place for the 1943 taxable year, Congress soon discovered that even in a time of war people care about incentives.

For that year, the IRS reported that a grand total of zero Americans had filed returns showing earnings of more than $25,000! The 100% tax had led to 100% tax evasion, and soon Congress repealed FDR's supertax.[73]

THREE MEN AND YOUR MONEY

In 1962, the federal budget deficit stood at $7.1 billion – the third largest shortfall since World War II. The U.S. was on the precipice of even greater funding shortfalls as the combined effects of the space race, Cold War outlays and the Vietnam conflict loomed.

Faced with the reality that the economy would not be able to sustain the tax revenues necessary to fund these endeavors, John F. Kennedy stood before the Economic Club in New York in December of 1962 and said, "It is increasingly clear that…an economy hampered by restrictive tax rates will never produce enough revenues to balance our budget just as it will never produce enough jobs or enough profits. In short, it is a paradoxical truth that tax rates are too high and tax revenues are too low and the soundest way to raise the revenues in the long run is to cut the rates now."

The following year, President Kennedy was successful in producing legislation that would lower the top income tax rate from a staggering 91% to 70%.

This was the top rate until 1981. In that year, the number of tax brackets was 14, to go along with the rate of 70%, on the most successful Americans. By 1986, the number of income tax brackets was down to two, and the top rate was 28%. What happened?

> At the peak of my career at Warner Bros., I was in the ninety-four percent tax bracket; that meant that after a certain point, I received only six cents of each dollar I earned and the government got the rest. The IRS took such a big chunk of my earnings that after a while I began asking myself whether it was worth it to keep on taking work. Something was wrong with a system like that. When you have to give up such a large percentage of your income in taxes incentive to work goes down.

> When government confiscates half or more of a corporation's profit, the motivation to maximize

profits goes down, and owners and managers make decisions based disproportionately on a desire to avoid taxes, they begin looking for tax shelters and loopholes that contribute nothing to the growth of our economy. Their companies don't grow as fast, they invest less in new plants and equipment, and they hire fewer people.

Any system that penalizes success and accomplishment is wrong. Any system that discourages work, discourages productivity, discourages economic progress is wrong. If on the other hand, you reduce taxes and allow people to spend or save more of what they earn, they'll be more industrious; they'll have more incentive to work hard, and money they earn will add fuel to the great economic machine that energizes our national progress. The result is more prosperity for all—and more revenue for government. A few economists call this principle supply-side economics. I just call it common sense."

Ronald Reagan

Photo courtesy Jack Chambless

Photo courtesy Chuck Bigger

John F. Kennedy and Ronald Reagan were of the mindset that our Founding Fathers did not intend for such a large percentage of our income to be paid to the government. As a matter of fact, a quick reading of Article 1, Section 8, illustrates that the Founders thought that taxes should be "uniform" across the nation.

What does this word mean? Does uniform mean one tax rate – a flat rate – for all, or does it mean that it is acceptable for the government to have a uniform tax code for all citizens – even if one group pays more than another?

In 1981, Reagan signed into law the largest tax cut in the history of the United States – a $750 billion reduction over six years. The Tax Reform Act of 1986 lowered individual income tax rates over a five-year period and helped create an estimated 43 million jobs.[74] It would seem that having seen tax brackets fall from 14 to 2 and the top rate fall from 70% to 28%, would suggest that increased economic freedom was launched in 1986. Launched? Yes. Sustained? No.

In 1990, President Bush passed the Revenue Collection Act, which added the 31% bracket to income taxes as well as higher gas taxes. Later, taxes were increased for boats, planes, jewelry, and expensive cars. President Clinton topped the Bush tax hike with the 1993 Revenue Reconciliation Act, which raised taxes by the largest amount ($250 billion) in the history of any nation on Earth. The Clinton tax hike added the 36% and 39.6% brackets to the federal income tax code that was with us until 2001.

Fortunately for Mr. Clinton, the combination of low interest rates and a surging technology sector eased the burden of his tax increase, and the economy continued to grow, although studies show that the economy did not grow as much as it could have had his tax hike not been enacted.[75] Mr. Bush Sr. was not so fortunate. His tax increase at the outset of the 1990–91 Recession helped worsen the economic downturn and led to his defeat in the 1992 election.

By 2008, the percentage of the gross domestic product (the total value of production in the U.S.) collected in taxes was higher than at any time since 1944. In 2010, the government took approximately 28% of the GDP in the form of income, property,[76] social security, and other taxes.[77] America now has the second highest corporate income tax burden in the world.[78] This, of course, means that individuals in America face one of the highest tax burdens in the developed world.[79] Corporations are not monolithic entities. Rather, they are legally recognized persons. Since corporations are owned by individuals – either privately, or in the form of stock ownership, it is literally impossible for a corporation to pay corporate taxes. Instead, the individuals who make up the ownership pay the taxes, along with the consumers of the corporation's goods and services in the form of imbedded taxes – taxes that show up in the price of what we buy.

This does not include debates that have been taking place in Congress on how pay for the massive increase in the demand for social security, Medicare, and prescription drug coverage for the 76 million baby-boomers (people born between 1946–1964) now that they have begun to retire.

By many estimates, the unfunded liability of Social Security and Medicare (the tax dollars that have not yet been collected but that will have to be paid to the elderly in the future), totals more than $107 *trillion* dollars.[80] Without cuts in government spending in many other areas of the budget, Congress will most likely push for enormous increases in taxes over the next 20 years in order to meet the legal obligation to our parents and grandparents. This is a common situation not only in America, but in Europe as well. If we look at other nations that are considered socialistic, a common pattern appears – high marginal tax rates and rising taxes as a percentage of GDP over time.

In 2011, the average American worked until April 9 just to meet his or her federal tax obligation. That date is expected to increase to May 1 by 2013 – just about the time most of you will be making real money.[81]

Shutterstock © Kames Steidl, 2011.

PRESIDENT OBAMA'S PERSPECTIVE ON TAXES

"Probably the least efficient way of giving the economy a boost, is to give large tax cuts to millionaires and billionaires."

Barack Obama

"Anyone who thinks we can move this economy forward with a few doing well at the top, hoping it'll trickle down to working folks running faster and faster just to keep up – they just haven't studied our history."

Barack Obama

In 2001 and 2003, President Bush signed legislation that brought our tax code to the numbers on the table that follows. These tax cuts included a reduction in marginal tax rates and a variety of other cuts to assist married couples, families with children, single mothers, and seniors. Some hailed the tax cuts – to be phased in over 10 years – as the beginning of a long battle to reduce the tax burden of working Americans. Economists who liked the idea of the cuts were concerned that they were too small and would take too long to implement to be fully effective.

Federal income tax rates for 2011

SINGLE	MARRIED FILING JOINTLY	Marginal Rate
Taxable income		
Up to $8,500	Up to $17,000	10%
34,500	69,000	15
83,600	139,350	25
174,400	212,300	28
379,150	379,150	33
Above 379,150	Above 379,150	35

Source: IRS

Whatever the opinion of economists, the Bush tax cuts were given an expiration date of January 1, 2011.

In December 2010, President Obama signed legislation that extended the tax rates created in the Bush years through 2012. In addition, Mr. Obama agreed to lower the employee's portion of the payroll (FICA) tax from 6.2% to 4.2% for 2011 only.[82] His decision to extend, and even slightly reduce our tax burdens stemmed from the 2010 midterm elections that saw a huge increase in the number of tax-cutting candidates who won their elections.

It is important to note that Mr. Obama made no promises for what the tax code would look like starting in 2013. He is on record arguing for increases in capital gains taxes (the taxes paid on investment income). He signed legislation requiring businesses to file more tax paperwork on transactions of $600 or more and has sought tax hikes for his health care legislation.[83]

WHY SOME RICH PEOPLE DESIRE HIGHER TAXES

While he was running for president, Mr. Obama was asked by Charles Gibson (you can watch this exchange on YouTube) why he supported raising capital gains taxes when there was ample evidence that when Bill Clinton lowered capital gains taxes, the government earned more revenue. In response, Mr. Obama said, "Well Charlie, what I've said is that I would look at raising the capital gains tax for purposes of fairness."

While some of you would recoil at such an answer, you need to understand that there are many rich Americans who actually support the idea of higher taxes on themselves and their wealthy brethren. Bill Gates Sr. once said, "I am a fan of progressive taxation. I would say our country has prospered from using such a system – even at 70% rates to say nothing of 90%."[84]

You will not be hard-pressed to find many actors, actresses, athletes, academics, and even business owners who vote for politicians who argue that rich folks should pay more.

Part of the reason for this seemingly odd desire is because of a theory that beyond a certain level of income, rich people do not get as much use from each dollar earned than a poor person would from obtaining an extra dollar. This makes intuitive sense. After all, if you make $10 million per year, how will your life be transformed if you suddenly make an extra $100? On the other hand, if you make $8,000 per year, that $100 is a much bigger percentage boost to your standard of living.

Thus, often politicians – and voters – ignore the deleterious effects that higher taxes have on economic progress, job creation, and wealth – and line up behind the "fairness" argument to support a more socialistic transformation of the income tax code. This has led to changes in the income tax code over time that now has only 53% of all Americans who actually pay taxes. 47% of us – through the proper deductions, the Earned Income Tax Credit and other means – have managed to no longer owe the federal government a dime.[85] For many economists, this creates an important question:

If the United States ever gets to the point where 51% of the people no longer pay taxes, what tax rate will those people vote for the other 49% to pay?

GOVERNMENT SPENDING

> I do not believe that Washington should do for the people what they can do for themselves through local and private effort.
>
> John F. Kennedy

High taxes are not the only measure of socialism. The amount of and type of government spending is also part of the equation. In this regard there is either good news or bad news depending on your personal beliefs about the role and size of government. If you are in favor of increased government spending in the name of making our country more "secure," then you should be very, very pleased with the following information. As the next few pages clearly illustrate, the federal government feels your pain and is all too happy to use your money to help ease it.

SUGGESTED CLASSROOM DEBATE

There is currently legislation in the U.S. Congress that seeks to abolish the IRS, eliminate income taxes, and replace the current tax system with a national sales tax.[86] Should the United States pursue this course of action? Why, or why not? Many nations, including Iraq, Romania, Russia, and Estonia have adopted a flat income tax.[87] Would this make more sense? To learn more about the "Fair Tax" proposal log onto www.fairtax.org.

Table 1.1—SUMMARY OF RECEIPTS, OUTLAYS, AND SURPLUSES OR DEFICITS (–): 1789–2013

(in millions of dollars)

Year	Total			On-Budget			Off-Budget		
	Receipts	Outlays	Surplus or Deficit(−)	Receipts	Outlays	Surplus or Deficit(−)	Receipts	Outlays	Surplus or Deficit(−)
1789–1849	1,160	1,090	70	1,160	1,090	70	....	....	....
1850–1900	14,462	15,453	−991	14,462	15,453	−991	....	....	....
1901	588	525	63	588	525	63	....	....	....
1902	562	485	77	562	485	77	....	....	....
1903	562	517	45	562	517	45	....	....	....
1904	541	584	−43	541	584	−43	....	....	....
1905	544	567	−23	544	567	−23	....	....	....
1906	595	570	25	595	570	25	....	....	....
1907	666	579	87	666	579	87	....	....	....
1908	602	659	−57	602	659	−57	....	....	....
1909	604	694	−89	604	694	−89	....	....	....
1910	676	694	−18	676	694	−18	....	....	....
1911	702	691	11	702	691	11	....	....	....
1912	693	690	3	693	690	3	....	....	....
1913	714	715	−★	714	715	−★	....	....	....
1914	725	726	−★	725	726	−★	....	....	....
1915	683	746	−63	683	746	−63	....	....	....
1916	761	713	48	761	713	48	....	....	....
1917	1,101	1,954	−853	1,101	1,954	−853	....	....	....
1918	3,645	12,677	−9,032	3,645	12,677	−9,032	....	....	....
1919	5,130	18,493	−13,363	5,130	18,493	−13,363	....	....	....
1920	6,649	6,358	291	6,649	6,358	291	....	....	....
1921	5,571	5,062	509	5,571	5,062	509	....	....	....
1922	4,026	3,289	736	4,026	3,289	736	....	....	....
1923	3,853	3,140	713	3,853	3,140	713	....	....	....
1924	3,871	2,908	963	3,871	2,908	963	....	....	....
1925	3,641	2,924	717	3,641	2,924	717	....	....	....
1926	3,795	2,930	865	3,795	2,930	865	....	....	....
1927	4,013	2,857	1,155	4,013	2,857	1,155	....	....	....
1928	3,900	2,961	939	3,900	2,961	939	....	....	....
1929	3,862	3,127	734	3,862	3,127	734	....	....	....
1930	4,058	3,320	738	4,058	3,320	738	....	....	....
1931	3,116	3,577	−462	3,116	3,577	−462	....	....	....
1932	1,924	4,659	−2,735	1,924	4,659	−2,735	....	....	....
1933	1,997	4,598	−2,602	1,997	4,598	−2,602	....	....	....
1934	2,955	6,541	−3,586	2,955	6,541	−3,586	....	....	....
1935	3,609	6,412	−2,803	3,609	6,412	−2,803	....	....	....
1936	3,923	8,228	−4,304	3,923	8,228	−4,304	....	....	....
1937	5,387	7,580	−2,193	5,122	7,582	−2,460	265	−2	267
1938	6,751	6,840	−89	6,364	6,850	−486	387	−10	397
1939	6,295	9,141	−2,846	5,792	9,154	−3,362	503	−13	516
1940	6,548	9,468	−2,920	5,998	9,482	−3,484	550	−14	564
1941	8,712	13,653	−4,941	8,024	13,618	−5,594	688	35	653
1942	14,634	35,137	−20,503	13,738	35,071	−21,333	896	66	830
1943	24,001	78,555	−54,554	22,871	78,466	−55,595	1,130	89	1,041
1944	43,747	91,304	−47,557	42,455	91,190	−48,735	1,292	114	1,178
1945	45,159	92,712	−47,553	43,849	92,569	−48,720	1,310	143	1,167
1946	39,296	55,232	−15,936	38,057	55,022	−16,964	1,238	210	1,028
1947	38,514	34,496	4,018	37,055	34,193	2,861	1,459	303	1,157
1948	41,560	29,764	11,796	39,944	29,396	10,548	1,616	368	1,248
1949	39,415	38,835	580	37,724	38,408	−684	1,690	427	1,263
1950	39,443	42,562	−3,119	37,336	42,038	−4,702	2,106	524	1,583
1951	51,616	45,514	6,102	48,496	44,237	4,259	3,120	1,277	1,843
1952	66,167	67,686	−1,519	62,573	65,956	−3,383	3,594	1,730	1,864
1953	69,608	76,101	−6,493	65,511	73,771	−8,259	4,097	2,330	1,766
1954	69,701	70,855	−1,154	65,112	67,943	−2,831	4,589	2,912	1,677

1955	65,451	68,444	-2,993	60,370	64,461	-4,091	5,081	3,983	1,098
1956	74,587	70,640	3,947	68,162	65,668	2,494	6,425	4,972	1,452
1957	79,990	76,578	3,412	73,201	70,562	2,639	6,789	6,016	773
1958	79,636	82,405	-2,769	71,587	74,902	-3,315	8,049	7,503	546
1959	79,249	92,098	-12,849	70,953	83,102	-12,149	8,296	8,996	-700
1960	92,492	92,191	301	81,851	81,341	510	10,641	10,850	-209
1961	94,388	97,723	-3,335	82,279	86,046	-3,766	12,109	11,677	431
1962	99,676	106,821	-7,146	87,405	93,286	-5,881	12,271	13,535	-1,265
1963	106,560	111,316	-4,756	92,385	96,352	-3,966	14,175	14,964	-789
1964	112,613	118,528	-5,915	96,248	102,794	-6,546	16,366	15,734	632
1965	116,817	118,228	-1,411	100,094	101,699	-1,605	16,723	16,529	194
1966	130,835	134,532	-3,698	111,749	114,817	-3,068	19,085	19,715	-630
1967	148,822	157,464	-8,643	124,420	137,040	-12,620	24,401	20,424	3,978
1968	152,973	178,134	-25,161	128,056	155,798	-27,742	24,917	22,336	2,581
1969	186,882	183,640	3,242	157,928	158,436	-507	28,953	25,204	3,749
1970	192,807	195,649	-2,842	159,348	168,042	-8,694	33,459	27,607	5,852
1971	187,139	210,172	-23,033	151,294	177,346	-26,052	35,845	32,826	3,019
1972	207,309	230,681	-23,373	167,402	193,470	-26,068	39,907	37,212	2,695
1973	230,799	245,707	-14,908	184,715	199,961	-15,246	46,084	45,746	338
1974	263,224	269,359	-6,135	209,299	216,496	-7,198	53,925	52,862	1,063
1975	279,090	332,332	-53,242	216,633	270,780	-54,148	62,458	61,552	906
1976	298,060	371,792	-73,732	231,671	301,098	-69,427	66,389	70,695	-4,306
TQ	81,232	95,975	-14,744	63,216	77,281	-14,065	18,016	18,695	-679
1977	355,559	409,218	-53,659	278,741	328,675	-49,933	76,817	80,543	-3,726
1978	399,561	458,746	-59,185	314,169	369,585	-55,416	85,391	89,161	-3,770
1979	463,302	504,028	-40,726	365,309	404,941	-39,633	97,994	99,087	-1,093
1980	517,112	590,941	-73,830	403,903	477,044	-73,141	113,209	113,898	-689
1981	599,272	678,241	-78,968	469,097	542,956	-73,859	130,176	135,285	-5,109
1982	617,766	745,743	-127,977	474,299	594,892	-120,593	143,467	150,851	-7,384
1983	600,562	808,364	-207,802	453,242	660,934	-207,692	147,320	147,430	-110
1984	666,486	851,853	-185,367	500,411	685,680	-185,269	166,075	166,174	-98
1985	734,088	946,396	-212,308	547,918	769,447	-221,529	186,171	176,949	9,222
1986	769,215	990,441	-221,227	568,986	806,901	-237,915	200,228	183,540	16,688
1987	854,353	1,004,083	-149,730	640,951	809,308	-168,357	213,402	194,775	18,627
1988	909,303	1,064,481	-155,178	667,812	860,077	-192,265	241,491	204,404	37,087
1989	991,190	1,143,829	-152,639	727,525	932,918	-205,393	263,666	210,911	52,754
1990	1,032,094	1,253,130	-221,036	750,439	1,028,065	-277,626	281,656	225,065	56,590
1991	1,055,093	1,324,331	-269,238	761,209	1,082,644	-321,435	293,885	241,687	52,198
1992	1,091,328	1,381,649	-290,321	788,902	1,129,310	-340,408	302,426	252,339	50,087
1993	1,154,471	1,409,522	-255,051	842,537	1,142,935	-300,398	311,934	266,587	45,347
1994	1,258,721	1,461,907	-203,186	923,695	1,182,535	-258,840	335,026	279,372	55,654
1995	1,351,932	1,515,884	-163,952	1,000,853	1,227,220	-226,367	351,079	288,664	62,415
1996	1,453,177	1,560,608	-107,431	1,085,685	1,259,704	-174,019	367,492	300,904	66,588
1997	1,579,423	1,601,307	-21,884	1,187,433	1,290,681	-103,248	391,990	310,626	81,364
1998	1,721,955	1,652,685	69,270	1,306,156	1,336,081	-29,925	415,799	316,604	99,195
1999	1,827,645	1,702,035	125,610	1,383,177	1,381,257	1,920	444,468	320,778	123,690
2000	2,025,457	1,789,216	236,241	1,544,873	1,458,451	86,422	480,584	330,765	149,819
2001	1,991,426	1,863,190	128,236	1,483,907	1,516,352	-32,445	507,519	346,838	160,681
2002	1,853,395	2,011,153	-157,758	1,338,074	1,655,491	-317,417	515,321	355,662	159,659
2003	1,782,532	2,160,117	-377,585	1,258,690	1,797,108	-538,418	523,842	363,009	160,833
2004	1,880,279	2,293,006	-412,727	1,345,534	1,913,495	-567,961	534,745	379,511	155,234
2005	2,153,859	2,472,205	-318,346	1,576,383	2,069,994	-493,611	577,476	402,211	175,265
2006	2,407,254	2,655,435	-248,181	1,798,872	2,233,366	-434,494	608,382	422,069	186,313
2007	2,568,239	2,730,241	-162,002	1,933,150	2,276,604	-343,454	635,089	453,637	181,452
2008	2,521,175	2,931,222	-410,047	1,858,960	2,461,157	-602,197	662,215	470,065	192,150
2009	2,104,995	3,517,681	-1,412,686	1,450,986	3,000,665	-1,549,679	654,009	517,016	136,993
2010 est.	2,165,119	3,720,701	-1,555,582	1,529,936	3,163,742	-1,633,806	635,183	556,959	78,224
2011 est.	2,567,181	3,833,861	-1,266,680	1,893,113	3,255,668	-1,362,555	674,068	578,193	95,875
2012 est.	2,926,400	3,754,852	-828,452	2,205,925	3,154,610	-948,685	720,475	600,242	120,333

★ $500 thousand or less.

Note: Budget figures prior to 1933 are based on the "Administrative Budget" concepts rather than the "Unified Budget" concepts.

Source: Office of the President of the United States. See http://www.whitehouse.gov/omb/budget/fy2009/sheets/hist01z1.xls

If we add up total federal spending during the entire eight years of the Reagan administration and the first two years of the first Bush administration, we see that total federal outlays amounted to $9.486 trillion.

This period covers the massive military buildup to end the Cold War and the cost of Operation Desert Shield in 1990. Federal spending during the last two years of the Bush administration and the entire eight years of the Clinton administration totaled $15.400 trillion. This was in spite of the fact that military spending either grew slowly or was cut (the only area of spending that ever fell) during this time.

COMPASSIONATE CONSERVATISM AT WORK

> "We will insist on a budget that limits and tames the spending appetite of the federal government. A taxpayer dollar ought to be spent wisely, or not spent at all."
>
> George W. Bush

When George Bush ran for president in 2000, he campaigned as a "compassionate conservative."

When President Bush unveiled his first budget in 2001, it called for $28 trillion in new spending over 10 years.[88] To get a visual idea of that figure, imagine 28,000,000,000,000 one-dollar bills placed end-to-end. They would circle the orbit of the Earth around the sun approximately 30 times. By the time Mr. Bush unveiled his budget for fiscal year 2009, government spending under his watch had grown by 57% – and this does not include spending for the war on terror or the invasion of Iraq.[89] This figure is compared to a decrease in government spending (after adjusting for inflation) by 0.7% during Bill Clinton's first term in office.[90]

In 2009 – the last year where complete data was available for this book – federal spending totaled $3.517 trillion. Of that figure, $654.57 billion was allocated to social security; $436.99 billion for Medicare; $610.57 billion for income security (social welfare payments) and $425 billion for Medicaid. These figures mean that $2.127 trillion, or 60.47% of the entire federal budget was a transfer of income from one citizen to another in just these areas.[91] The preliminary budget tally for 2010 showed an increase in federal spending by 21.4% compared to 2008 with a 240.4% increase in unemployment benefits leading the way.[92]

On September 14, 2010 *The Wall Street Journal* ran an article entitled, "Obstacle to Deficit Cutting: A Nation on Entitlements" with the following chart:

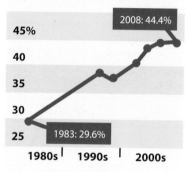

Expanding Net
Percentage of U.S. population living in a household receiving some government benefits

Source: U.S. Census Bureau

You may recall that as of 2010, 47% of Americans were no longer paying income taxes. With over 44% of our population of over 308 million people receiving assistance from the forced taking of their fellow man's money, it is readily apparent that the United States is extremely close to what economists call the tax and entitlement "tipping point" – the point at which more Americans are net recipients of taxpayer aid rather than net contributors to the economy, and hence, the tax system. This trend has virtually every economist you meet fretting about the possibility of a bankrupt America.[93]

THE FOUNDERS' VIEW OF GOVERNMENT SPENDING

Article 1, Section 8 of the Constitution, gives Congress the authority to spend our tax money on national defense, federal debt, and items that promote the general welfare of U.S. citizens.

Perhaps it would help if we could explain what the Founders meant by the term, *general welfare.*

> The powers of the federal government are enumerated; it can only operate in certain cases; it has legislative powers on defined and limited objects, beyond which it cannot extend its jurisdiction.
>
> James Madison 1788

They are not to do anything they please to provide for the general welfare, but only to lay taxes for that purpose. To consider [Otherwise], would render all the preceding and subsequent enumerations of power completely useless. It would reduce the whole instrument to a single phrase, that of instituting a Congress with power do to whatever would be for the good of the United States; and, as they would be the sole judges of the good or evil, it would be also a power to do whatever evil they please. Certainly no such universal power was meant to be given them. It was intended to lace them up straightly within the enumerated powers and those without which, as means, these powers could not be carried into effect.

Thomas Jefferson 1791

If Congress can do whatever in their discretion can be done by money, and will promote the General Welfare, the Government is no longer a limited one, possessing enumerated powers, but an indefinite one, subject to particular exceptions.

Thomas Jefferson 1791

I hope our courts will never countenance the sweeping pretensions which have been set up under the words 'general defense and public welfare.' These words only express the motives which induced the Convention to give to the ordinary legislature certain specified powers which they enumerate, and which they thought might be trusted to the ordinary legislature, and not to give them the unspecified also; or why any specifications? They could not be so awkward in language as to mean, as we say, 'all and some.' And should this construction prevail, all limits to the federal government are done away.

Thomas Jefferson 1815

Our tenet ever was that Congress had not unlimited powers to provide for the general welfare, but were restrained to those specifically enumerated, and that, as it was never meant that they should provide for that welfare but by the exercise of the enumerated powers, so it could not have been meant they should raise money for purposes which the enumeration did not place under their action; consequently, that the specification of powers is a limitation of the purposes for which they may raise money.

Thomas Jefferson 1817

The federal government is acknowledged by all to be one of enumerated powers. The principle, that it can exercise only the powers granted to it....is now universally admitted.

Chief Justice John Marshall 1819

With respect to the words 'general welfare,' I have always regarded them as qualified by the detail of powers connected with them. To take them in a literal and unlimited sense would be a metamorphosis of the Constitution into a character which there is a host of proofs was not contemplated by its creators.

James Madison 1831

I cannot undertake to lay my finger on that article of the Constitution which granted a right to Congress of expending, on objects of benevolence, the money of their constituents.

James Madison 1794

THE LEGACY OF ALEXANDER HAMILTON

From the preceding analysis it should be relatively clear that the Founding Fathers believed that general welfare meant spending money only to protect our rights and spending on only those categories specifically enumerated in Article 1, Section 8. (For the complete list, see the back of the book where the entire U.S. Constitution can be found.)

If the Founders had their way, the federal budget for this fiscal year would be hundreds of billions of dollars, lower than it is. How did we get to the point where out of every $100 you pay in taxes, over $60 is simply given to someone else? The blame, or credit, depending on your perspective, falls largely on Alexander Hamilton.

You may recall from your history studies that Alexander Hamilton was a brilliant man. At 18 years of age he was writing editorials. George Washington thought enough of him to make him an aide. Hamilton went on to become the country's first Treasury Secretary and is largely responsible for helping to establish the good credit of the United States' early government.[94] Yet it was his work during the Constitutional Convention that has helped lead America down the road toward socialism.

During the convention, Hamilton – who once told Washington that he "long since learned to hold public

justice for every sitting justice over the age of 70.[96] That would have pushed the total number of justices from 9 to 15. Surely anyone can see the political windfall that would have been bestowed upon FDR. With six extra justices – all appointed by FDR – the Supreme Court would have been packed with people more sensitive to his political agenda.

As part of the 1933 Agricultural Adjustment Act, Congress implemented a processing tax on agricultural commodities, from which funds would be redistributed to farmers who promised to reduce their acreage. The Act intended to solve the crisis in agricultural commodity prices that was causing many farmers to go under.

The Court found the Act unconstitutional because it attempted to regulate and control agricultural production, an arena reserved to the states. Even though Congress does have the power to tax and appropriate funds, argued Justice Roberts, in this case those activities were "but means to an unconstitutional end," and violated the Tenth Amendment.

However, the court unwittingly sowed the seeds of a socialist forest by going on to say:

> ..the grant is that public funds my be appropriated to provide for the General Welfare of the United States....Since the foundation of the Nation, sharp differences of opinion have persisted as to the true interpretation of that phrase. Madison asserted that it amounted to no more than a reference to the other powers enumerated in the subsequent clauses of the same section; that, as the United States is a government of limited and enumerated powers, the grant of power to tax and spend for the general welfare must be confined to the enumerated legislative fields committed to the Congress. Hamilton, on the other hand, maintained the clause confers a power separate and distinct from those later enumerated, is not restricted in meaning by the grant of them and Congress consequently has a substantive power to tax and to appropriate, limited only by the requirement that it shall be exercised to provide for the General Welfare of the United States. Each contention has had the support of those whose views are entitled to weight. Study of all these leads us to conclude that the reading by Mr. Justice Story (the Hamiltonian position) is the correct one. It results that the power of Congress to authorize expenditure of public moneys for public purposes is not limited by the direct grants of legislative power found in the Constitution.[97]

opinion of no value" – delivered a five-hour speech. During his speech he proposed election of a president and senators for life by electors with property. Hamilton argued for the abolishment of state governments. The president was to have the veto and be able to enforce – or ignore – any law.[95]

Moreover, and perhaps most damagingly, Hamilton argued that the general welfare clause of the Constitution should not be confined to the enumerated powers of Congress, but rather Congress should be able to apply government spending in a more liberal manner so long as Congress could argue that the spending was for the "general welfare." Hamilton's proposals were rejected flatly. In fact, not one member of the convention seconded any of his ideas. Yet in 1936, Hamilton's views on government spending became the law of the land.

THE UNITED STATES V. BUTLER

When Franklin D. Roosevelt was elected president in 1932, he came into office promising America a "New Deal." The "old deal" was that government had limited powers to tax and spend and Americans had to rely on their own creative energies for their well-being. Roosevelt immediately began changing the relationship between government and the people. It was under his direction that a whole host of welfare and public works projects were created. The only problem was that the Supreme Court kept ruling his new programs unconstitutional – that is, until 1936.

Frustrated with the Supreme Court, Roosevelt began discussing the idea of adding one new Supreme Court

Since January 6, 1936, the United States Congress has had the authority to spend your money as it sees fit. Republicans and Democrats alike now use your money to fund everything from rainforest museums in Iowa to bailouts for banks, insurance companies and automobile manufacturers to "victims" of natural disasters who built houses six feet under the ocean.....

HOW TO GET PEOPLE
TO HATE YOU

> We have the right, as individuals, to give away as much of our own money as we please to charity; but as members of Congress we have no right so to appropriate a dollar of the public money.[98]
>
> David Crockett

I sure wish Mr. Crockett would have been around to come to my aid in September of 2005. I needed him because it was during that time that I was invited to appear on *Your World with Cavuto* – a *Fox News* program devoted to economics and politics.

I had appeared on Neal Cavutos' show a couple of times in 2004 to talk about the economics and constitutionality of rebuilding homes in Florida in the wake of the hurricanes that came through that summer. So, when *Fox News* called me to talk about the same topic as it applied to residents of New Orleans, I thought it might be a good idea to help educate taxpayers about Article 1, Section 8 of our rulebook. Apparently, the people of Louisiana – and seemingly millions of others around the country – did not really like hearing about James Madison's view of plunder. As one person put it:

"I just saw your disgraceful interview as was rotating from *Fox News* to CNN. Do you truly believe that taxpayers' money should not be used to help New Orleans and surrounding areas? If so, WHAT IS TAX MONEY FOR???

"You are borderline evil for even suggesting that our government, which ideally should function primarily to protect us, do NOTHING to aide a state which is not capable of covering the totality of this natural disaster.

"I am from New Orleans, but currently live in Los Angeles. You are in effect, suggesting that I, my family, friends and everyone from New Orleans suffer because of something we had no control over.

"No amount of logic could justify your ridiculous comments in front of the nation tonight. You're abandoning fellow human beings because you are too selfish to let your tax dollars go to a human cause.

"You made yourself seem like a callous, heartless beast in front of many, many people – despite any good intentions you may have thought you had."

This email was one of the more polite ones I received. The death threats over the phone were even less fun.

The question of what to do about the Gulf Coast in the wake of Hurricane Katrina was an interesting one. The type of normative analysis that is so often connected with socialism would call for taxpayer dollars – of whatever amount necessary – to be used to rebuild New Orleans. This is certainly the Hamiltonian approach the

Bush Administration took and one that both Barack Obama and George Bush supported.

But does the rebuilding of New Orleans, with taxpayer dollars, satisfy the "general welfare" test?[99] Does it line up with capitalism?

It is inarguable that the people of New Orleans have every right to go home and rebuild their lives. They can use their money, their insurance, the charity of their neighbor and whatever other resource they can peacefully procure.

However, if we say that a person in New Orleans should be able to get the tax dollars of a person in Maine, are we not calling for the legal plunder that Bastiat talked about?[100] Moreover, if we allow people to rebuild with taxpayer dollars, are we not artificially lowering the cost of living in an area that will get hit again someday?[101]

Is this type of charity enough?

By doing that, are we not going to end up causing the death of even more people who would not have come back, if not for the taxpayer aid? Two years after Katrina hit, there were still 87,000 households living in travel trailers within the same path that the storm took.[102]

If rebuilding New Orleans does pass the general welfare test – after all, it is a major port – wouldn't the corporations who stand to profit from having this city intact rebuild it on their own, in order to keep making profit from jazz, good food and access to the Gulf of Mexico? Wouldn't homeowners who prefer to live in New Orleans do the same thing? Does taxpayer-financed "charity" lead to the problem of moral hazard?[103]

> ➤ **Moral hazard – The prospect that a person, or institution insulated from risk may behave differently from the way it would behave if it were fully exposed to the risk. Moral hazard arises because an individual or institution does not bear the full consequences of its actions, and therefore has a tendency to act less carefully than it otherwise would, leaving another party to bear some responsibility for the consequences of those actions.**

CONCEPT CHECK

In 2010, President Obama announced a $1.5 billion program designed to assist homeowners facing foreclosure. Mr. Obama, in defense of this plan said, "The money will go to homeowners who have lost their jobs, owe more than their houses are worth, and cannot afford to make monthly payments."[104]Give some specific ways in which this program could lead to the problem of moral hazard for banks, taxpayers, and homeowners who are not facing foreclosure.

SOCIAL INSECURITY?

The following is a direct quote from a friend who works for the Social Security Administration. The quote is in response to my question as to whether we as individuals should have the right to keep even some of our social security taxes to make private investment decisions:

> As an SSA employee, and as a private Joe Citizen, I think it's a huge mistake to allow anyone to take any money from their SSA taxes to invest themselves. A huge mistake! If it were not for the social security system, we would have countless elderly people living on the street, in the back room of their kids' houses, etc. Most people need every penny they can get their hands on just to survive. If the system allows them to keep any of it or invest themselves, they won't invest it. They'll spend it on kid's clothes, rent, food, utilities, G.I. Joe with the Kung Fu grip, etc. Then, when they're 62 or whatever, they'll come up to one of the SSA offices and we'll tell them, Sorry, we gave you yours. You are due no more from this agency. Then what? Homeless, back room of their kids' houses, or worse. There probably are quite a few people who could make their money work for them lots better than the government can. But how do you determine who those people are? Do you let some have their taxes back, and some not? And what happens when those so-called smart people invest in some no-account company and lose their a-----? They'll be back at the SSA office, and we'll say, Sorry, we gave you yours. You are due no more.

From 1776 to 1935 the government's relationship to the citizenry – as it applied to retirement – was pretty straightforward. "Save money if you want to quit working some day," was the message.

During the Great Depression, with hardship hitting elderly Americans in a particularly harsh way, the Roosevelt Administration created our nation's first *forced* retirement plan.[105]

The plan was quite simple. Workers would have part of their paychecks taken (matched by their employers) in the form of a payroll tax. This tax would finance the Social Security Trust Fund – a fund made up of government securities (Treasury bonds, for example) that retirees could draw upon once they met the legal age requirements.

In 2010 the first $106,800 of income was taxed at a rate of 12.4% - 6.2% paid by the employee, and, in theory, 6.2% paid by the employer.[106] We use the phrase "in theory" because empirical analysis suggests that much of the payroll tax paid by employers shows up in the form of lower earnings for the worker, higher prices for consumers and less profit for shareholders.

Of course, all of the money you pay in payroll taxes is set aside in a fund, under your name, earning interest – just for you – until you let the Social Security Administration know that you have retired, right?

Yes, if you believe in Santa Claus and the Easter Bunny.

Starting somewhere around .01 seconds after FDR signed the legislation, Social Security became an intergenerational transfer of money from taxpayers to retirees.

In 1950 – when there was a lower population and people did not live very long – there were 16 people paying into Social Security for every person receiving benefits. Today, for every 3.3 workers there is a retired person getting their money. By 2050, it will be 2 workers for every retiree. Who knows, with medical breakthroughs and a slowdown in population growth, there might come a day where every retiree in America has their own personal taxpayer!

In 2018 it is anticipated that more money will be paid out in benefits than is available in the trust fund. Thus, the government will have to use tax revenues from income taxes to help support Social Security. This is part of the reason why many economists believe that several things will have to happen to "save" Social Security. Among the possibilities include raising the payroll tax and/or payroll tax threshold, raising the retirement age, lowering the benefits paid, or seeking some private sector remedy.

In 2003, former President Bush proposed letting taxpayers keep a portion (less than 3%) of their payroll taxes to invest in funds other than the Social Security Trust Fund. Mr. Bush said, "We must offer younger workers a chance to invest in retirement accounts that they will control and they will own."

In December 2010, Congress approved a $4.3 billion bill that would provide expanded health care benefits for people who became sick after working at the toxic debris pile of the collapsed World Trade Center.[107] Should these people get this money? Why, or why not?

David Crockett, James Madison, and Frederic Bastiat may have been applauding Mr. Bush somewhere, but back in America where senior citizens vote and young people do not, his proposal was wiped out by lobbyists representing the interests of older Americans who have the most to lose if taxpayers are ever allowed to invest their own income in accounts that they freely choose.

GOVERNMENT REGULATION

"Businesses should live up to their responsibilities to create American jobs, look out for American workers, and play by the rules of the road."

Barack Obama

I am almost ashamed to admit this, but on the day I sat down to write this section, I found myself staring blankly at the computer screen for what seemed like hours. I kept asking myself, "Where do I begin?" Writing about the monumental growth of government regulations is a lot like trying to write about the universe. You can see the universe is out there, but since you don't see where it ends, how do you explain it?

Since most of you do not currently run a business, it might be wise to start out with a definition of the word, *regulation*.

> ➤ **A regulation is a rule or law imposed by government on business firms.**

None of us want to see seven-year-old children working in sweat shops any more than we want to eat poisoned meat, breathe black air, or fly in planes with a 50/50 chance of crashing into the side of a mountain. A large majority of Americans are in agreement that government is needed to regulate business and industry to keep us safe from "evil" business people. As a consequence, the government's reach into our lives has expanded every year.

Depending on where you live, you may or may not be allowed to smoke in a bar. You might not be allowed to have your body pierced or lie down in a tanning bed.[108] You might not be allowed to drive without wearing a seat belt. You might not be able to hire whomever you want at the price you and the other person agree to. You might not be able to buy light beer on Sunday. These are some of, as Mr. Obama might say, "rules of the road." One might ask, "How many rules does the road need?" When do the rules of the road do more harm to businesses and individuals than good?

Ironically, these are precisely the questions President Obama sought to address in a surprising editorial in the January 18, 2011 edition of *The Wall Street Journal.*

In his editorial, Mr. Obama explained his rationale for issuing an executive order requiring all federal agencies to "ensure that regulations protect our safety, health, and environment while promoting economic growth."[109] President Obama argued that the federal government needed to examine all regulations with an eye toward throwing out any rules that had become outdated or were stifling job creation.

What is interesting about his editorial, is that it came on the heels of two straight years of massive increases in the number of regulations businesses were forced to adhere to under Mr. Obama's watch. Consider this:

A September 2010 study for the Small Business Administration found that complying with federal regulations cost companies with fewer than 20 employees an average of $10,585 per worker, compared with $7,755 an employee for large companies.[110]

The Competitive Enterprise Institute estimates that America's regulatory burden reached $1.17 trillion in costs to businesses on an annual basis by 2010. This figure is almost as much as Canada's entire Gross Domestic Product. That $1.17 trillion in costs gets passed on to all of us in the form of higher prices, lower wages and salaries, and fewer job opportunities. After all, what would you do if you ran a business that was saddled with over $10,000 in costs, per worker? Would you just say, "Oh well, that's fine, I will just earn a lot less profit?"

In December 2010, the total number of pages of new regulations passed during the first 22 months President

Obama was in office, reached 75,000 with an average of 327 new pages of rules created every day.

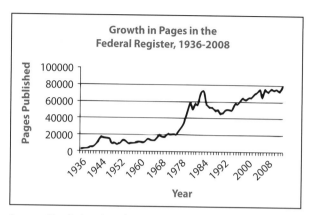

Growth in Pages in the Federal Register, 1936-2008

Source: The University of Pennsylvania Law School

In fairness to the Obama Administration, the Bush years were not lacking in government intrusion into the lives of those men and women who produce the goods and services we all enjoy. Under Mr. Bush, the federal government added almost $30 billion in new costs while the number of new federal workers employed to enforce those rules rose by 41%.[111]

It would be a huge oversight to leave out some of the examples of the types of rules businesses face these days. There are not enough trees in the Pacific Northwest that could be turned into the amount of paper needed to cover all of the rules, so I have selected some of the more recent highlights.

The government desires many things for our health. Among them is the safety of the clothes our children wear and the toys they play with. Toward that end, the regulators have really clamped down on the amount of lead our kids are allowed to be near. Of course, everyone knows that exposure to large quantities of lead can impede the cognitive development of little folks, but the rules that are now in place ban products with more than three one-hundredths of 1% lead.

This means that items like zippers, buttons, belts, hinges on a child's dresser, certain bicycles parts, and more, are banned. Even though laboratory tests run by scientists show that lead in these items is not "bioavailable" (cannot be absorbed in the blood no matter how much a toddler chews on it) and is of too small a quantity to do any damage even if swallowed, the regulators have still said, "No."

In the toy industry alone, this irrational regulation led to $2 billion in losses in 2008. The motorcycle industry lost $1 billion in sales from the ban, and major charities like Goodwill and The Salvation Army had to throw away between $100 million and $170 million in used clothes that did not meet the federal government's safety tests.[112]

The Environmental Protection Agency worries about us, too. Businesses that work on older construction sites are required to invest in lead-testing kits, plastic sheeting, respirators, protective clothing, and worker certification programs to deal with the possibility of lead exposure. For a typical mold-removal business, the lead rules add $160,000-$300,000 per year in costs – even though many of the homes they work in were built after 1978 – when no lead paint was sold.[113]

The EPA recently proposed a reduction in the "acceptable ozone level in the air" from .075 parts per million to between .06-.07 parts per million. This might seem like a fairly benign proposal. The EPA estimated that the new rules, which would force every business in America that uses energy (translation: 100% of businesses) to comply, would cost between $19 billion and $90 billion annually. The benefits, according to the EPA would be $13 billion in lower health care costs associated with respiratory illnesses.[114]

When have you ever bought a shirt that was worth $13 to you but cost you between $19 and $90?

Do you drive a car? Do you use the Internet? Do you have a bank account? If you answered "Yes" to any of these questions, government protectors are looking out for your well-being, too.

How much is enough?

In 2009, President Obama ordered car manufacturers to increase the average fuel economy from 27.5 miles per gallon to 39 miles per gallon by 2016.

It would be really nice if General Motors and all the rest could achieve this goal as quickly as politicians can order it to happen, but two things stand in the way: consumers, overall, still prefer larger vehicles and the cost of meeting the new regulation would not be low.

On average, the price of new cars would rise by $1,300 after the carmakers folded in the costs of the new technologies needed to meet this requirement.[115]

Moreover, many economists have pointed out that in the past when fuel efficiency standards are forced up, the level of pollution-reduction achieved is far lower than government officials predict. This is because higher car prices encourage millions to hang on to their older, less-efficient cars for a longer period of time. Furthermore, every time we are forced to buy cars that are lighter and more environmentally friendly, the number of traffic fatalities increases.[116]

While you are shopping for your next light car online, bear in mind the new regulatory push that is taking place here, too.

In 2010, the Federal Communications Commission proposed a plan that would force Internet service providers to operate under the same decades – old rules that phone providers adhere to. In a nutshell, the "net-neutrality" rule would require Internet providers to treat all traffic equally, and not slow or block access to websites.[117]

While this might seem, on the surface, to be a consumer-friendly proposal, Internet service providers point out that allowing government to force companies to treat all traffic equally, when some traffic requires far greater technological requirements than others, could force providers to cut back on more expensive services, leaving many of you who watch a lot of videos or play online games with less service over time.

If net-neutrality passes and our online searches begin to resemble a race between two turtles, you might find yourself reluctant to engage in as much online banking as you used to. You might find yourself actually going to a bank to conduct business. Well, that industry has changed, too.

In the wake of the financial panic that gripped the country in 2008-2009, the Obama Administration moved at lightning speed to change the rules of the banking road.

Among the new regulations passed in 2010 were restrictions on investments banks could make (to prevent the type of hyper-investing in complicated home-mortgage portfolios), requirements that banks hold more cash in reserve, shareholder rights to set executive compensation, and government authority to seize and dismantle financially struggling firms that would pose a danger to the economy.[118]

All together, the 2,300 page law created 243 new rules for the financial industry – including investment and accounting firms[119] – prompting some banking executives to contend that all of the new rules would lead to an end to small community banks.[120]

You will notice that the preceding analysis has not even delved into the laws that make it illegal to summarily fire drug addicts working at your company, or the laws that end secret ballots in union elections, or the laws that do not allow you to shop for health insurance across state lines, or the FDA rules that have led to upwards of 4.7 *million* people who have died prematurely from 1963-1999 while waiting for government permission to use certain medicines.[121]

We have also not mentioned mandatory health care coverage that led the founder of Home Depot to argue that his company could have never gotten off the ground under today's regulatory climate,[122] food safety regulations (where regulators keep failing to keep food safe), airport security, state and local rules, or most of the other regulations that the average family pays $10,000 per year for.[123]

What is clear is that Mr. Obama's call for an examination of government regulations is warranted. To the casual reader of this chapter, economists seem to want no rules for the suppliers of goods and services. That is not the case at all. Economists simply call for a cost-benefit test applied to all rules. We also want the cost-benefit test to rely on measurable data so as to make the most rational

SUGGESTED CLASSROOM DEBATE

In January 2011, the Environmental Protection Agency extended regulations over how companies must deal with oil spills to include dairy farmers. Under the new regulations, farmers and places that make yogurt, ice cream, and butter, must prepare and implement an emergency management plan that includes the construction of "containment facilities" such as dikes or berms, to mitigate the effects of a milk spill. The EPA justified the regulation by saying that milk has "a percentage of animal fat, which is a non-petroleum oil."[126] Does this regulation, in your opinion, pass the cost-benefit test? Why, or why not?

determination over what the rules should be. In 1981, President Reagan issued an executive order that called for a measure of benefits and costs behind new regulations. President Obama expanded this order by allowing agencies to consider "equity, human dignity, fairness, and distributive impacts."[124]

The inherent difficulty with this amendment to the Reagan order is the difficulty in measuring equity, fairness, or possible violations of human dignity.

Therefore, when Mr. Obama said, "America's free market has not only been the source of dazzling ideas and path-breaking products, it has also been the greatest force for prosperity the world has ever known," America's business leaders were probably appreciative for the change in his tone,[125] but remained skeptical that the right calculations would be used to determine the laws that would govern business going forward.

REGULATIONS, CIVIL LIBERTY, AND SOCIALISM

Since September 11th, there has been a shift in the mindset of many Americans, and, as a result of that shift, there has been a shift in the priorities of politicians elected by those Americans.

Of course, the changes we are speaking of center around the civil liberties we have enjoyed – to varying degrees – since our country's inception. Those civil liberties – the right to free speech and privacy – are now being challenged in an era where the perceived terrorist threat has many people willing to trade in some liberty for added security. After all, if we don't actively search for terrorists here, the argument goes, how can we maintain our mixed economy in the long run?

THE PATRIOT ACT

Shortly after the World Trade Center was reduced to rubble, the U.S. Congress passed a sweeping anti-terrorism law called the Patriot Act. This Act, critics charge, has ostensibly altered, if not severely damaged, the Fourth Amendment to the U.S. Constitution (see the back of the book).

Under the Patriot Act, a secret court can order you to turn over documents, records and other tangible items to the FBI and force you to remain silent about both the seizure and the court order. You cannot challenge the

order by appearing before the court prior to the order being issued. And after the order is issued, your attorney – if you have one – will not be successful in stopping it.[127]

The Patriot Act expands the definition of terrorism to include any "acts dangerous to human life that are a violation of the criminal laws of the United States or of any State" or acts that "appear to be intended to intimidate or coerce a civilian population or to influence the policy of a government...."

Under this definition, any demonstrators or protesters involved in a march that turns violent could be classified as terrorists. A Rutherford Institute study points out that "diverse domestic political groups which have been accused of acts of intimidation or property damage, such as Act Up, PETA, and Operation Rescue, could be targeted as terrorist organizations."

The definition of terrorism as "acts that appear to be intended to...coerce a civilian population or influence the policy of a government" could certainly include writing a book, making speeches, teaching, or even buying or reading a book with the intent to spread its ideas to the public.

The Act also gives the government the authority to, without you knowing it, read your mail before you open it and prosecute you on the basis of what it reads; find out where you travel, what you confide to your lawyer and what periodicals you read.[128]

The Bush Administration was also successful in compelling Internet search providers to give the government samples of searches that Americans had gone through on the Internet. Google executives refused to turn over the documents, citing the rights to privacy that their customers have (had, depending on when you might be reading this...).[129]

HAS THE GOVERNMENT MADE IT DANGEROUS TO FLY?

On September 27, 2001, Netscape ran a poll over the Internet that asked, "Are you willing to trade some civil liberties for heightened security?" Of the 137,499 people who answered, 67% said "yes." This answer must have been just what Congress wanted to hear, because later that year the House of Representatives and Senate voted to turn over all airport security to the federal government. In fact, the vote in the Senate was 100-0 in favor of having the same group that runs our public schools and post offices provide safety in the skies. "If you don't have federalism, it doesn't work," said Sen. John D. Rockefeller, D-West Virginia. "You can't professionalize, unless you federalize," agreed Senate Majority Leader Tom Daschle, D-South Dakota.

On February 19, 2002, the federal government took over the supervisory role for the 28,000 screeners who work for private contractors.

In April of 2002, The Transportation Security Administration announced that 60,000 screeners were needed to meet the needs of the nation's airports. The screeners, who will make between $23,600 and $35,400 annually, must have a high-school diploma, GED or equivalent, or at least one year of full-time experience in security work, aviation screener work, or X-ray technician work – and must be a U.S. citizen.

The government's contention has been that if it had been in charge of supervising airport screeners on September 11th, the probability of an attack would have been much lower. Let's look at it. The government runs the United States Customs Department and the Immigration and Naturalization Services. These are the agencies that let the hijackers into the country even though three had expired visas and six had no records at all.

In March of 2002, the INS sent out approved student visas for hijackers Mohamed Atta and Marwan Al-Shehhi, six months after they were already dead from blowing up the World Trade Center! When asked about such a horrific oversight, the head of the INS, James Ziglar, said that INS rules are so complicated that he wasn't sure whether it was illegal for Atta to come back into the country with an expired tourist visa and an application for a student visa.

Atta applied for a student visa on September 19, 2000, and was notified he was approved ten months later. Ziglar said the INS system was so low-tech that forms were tossed into a box and mailed when the box was full.

When asked about his personal qualifications to head the INS, Mr. Ziglar replied, "Well, I have some friends who are immigrants."[130] Yes, that is exactly what he told Congress. Now you can sleep well.

Economist Walter Williams recently joined a legion of critics who would agree with his assessment of airport security.

"Americans have been bamboozled into believing that with federalization of airport security, we'd be safer. After all, according to media reports, Europeans who have a much longer history of dealing with terrorists have government-controlled airport security. Nothing can be further from the truth."

According to Robert Poole, a Reason Foundation air transportation expert (reason.org), 33 out of 35 European airports use private companies for passenger and baggage screening, and that includes high-risk airports such as: Amsterdam, Belfast, Copenhagen, Frankfurt, Hamburg, Paris, and even Tel Aviv's Ben Gurion Airport. At these airports, the government sets security standards. A private for-profit contractor performs the security screening. There're strong oversight and penalties exacted for not meeting the standards.

Should the safety of this jet be left in the hands of a non-profit agency?

So what has the new Transportation Security Act (TSA) mandated, and even if the mandates made complete sense, will they be achieved? TSA mandated 100% baggage screening by January 18, 2002. That was not achieved. TSA mandated federal takeover of existing security contracts by February 17, 2002. Again, failure. TSA mandated that 30,000-plus passenger and baggage screeners be federalized and trained by November 19, 2002.[131]

That deadline wasn't met either.

ADDING IT ALL UP

Over the last two chapters you have become an expert in the costs and benefits of every major economic system available to you today. As an economics student, it is up to you to decide which one is the most rational one for you. Somewhere between the mixed economy and capitalism might prompt you to move to New Zealand or New Hampshire. Maybe you would be happier in Norway, or Northern California, where a more socialistic system is in place.

The most important thing to remember is that every choice comes with a cost. If you trust government to take care of you, there will be the cost of reduced economic and civil liberty. If you trust yourself and free markets, there will be the cost of greater personal responsibility. Perhaps it would serve us all well to remember the words of Ronald Reagan, who once said:

"We who live in free market societies believe that growth, prosperity and ultimately human fulfillment, are created from the bottom up, not the government down. Only when the human spirit is allowed to invent and create, only when individuals are given a personal stake in deciding economic policies and benefiting from their success – only then can societies remain economically alive, dynamic, progressive and free. Trust the people."

ENDNOTES

1 See "No Bailouts for Borrowers" by Andy Laperriere, *The Wall Street Journal*, December 4, 2007, pg. A21.

2 See "How Fed's Bailout Can Affect You" by Kevin G. Hall, *The Orlando Sentinel*, September 8, 2008.

3 It is important to point out that there are many causes – artificial and natural – that contributed to the collapse in housing prices. In 1977, the Community Reinvestment Act forced banks to extend credit to people with less than desirable credit and employment histories. In 1995, President Clinton signed the Gramm–Leach–Bliley Act which allowed commercial banks, investment banks, securities firms, and insurance companies to consolidate. This legislation contributed to the massive bundling of home mortgages into complicated investment packages. Each of these acts led to an artificial increase in home prices and eventually the meltdown in housing prices.

4 For the complete text of the speech, go online to http://www.hud.gov/news/speeches/presremarks.cfm.

5 See "U.S. Seizes Mortgage Giants" by James R. Hagerty, Ruth Simon and Damian Paletta, *The Wall Street Journal*, September 8, 2008; and "Mortgage Bailout is Greeted with Relief, Fresh Questions" by Deborah Soloman, Michael Corkery and Liz Rappaport, *The Wall Street Journal*, September 9, 2008.

6 For a detailed examination of Marx, see *The Making of Modern Economics* by Mark Skousen, M.E. Sharpe, publisher, 2001, pp. 131–164; See *The Worldly Philosophers,* by Robert Heilbroner, Simon & Schuster, 1968.

7 For the rest of the list, see www.anu.edu.au/polsci/marx/classics/manifesto.html.

8 See *A Concise History of the World,* by Rondo Cameron, Oxford University Press, 1997.

9 See www.gmu.edu/departments/economics/bcaplan/museum/musframe.htm.

10 See "The Wealth of Nations" by Leszek Balcerowicz, *The Wall Street Journal*, October 6, 2005.

11 To watch the debate, log on to www.jackchambless.com. Click on the SPEECHES link then scroll down to the "Debate with a Marxist Economist." I welcome your comments and criticisms.

12 See "Working Time Transitions in Sweden" by Dominique Anxo and Donald Storrie of The Centre for European Labour Market Studies, Goteborg, Sweden.

13 Fulfillment requires that the worker puts in 1–34 hours of work per week.

14 As this book went to print, the 2012 Presidential election had not been conducted. The 35% rate was extended for 2011-2012 but was scheduled to rise to 39.6% in 2013.

15 See "Swedes less well off than African-Americans," *Reuters,* May 6, 2002.

16 See "Sweden's Moderates Now Look Electable" by Terence Roth and Louise Nordstrom, *The Wall Street Journal,* September 14, 2005.

17 See "France Fails in Bid to Cut Restaurant Tax," *The Wall Street Journal,* February 11, 2004.

18 See "Even the chefs are leaving France" by Richard C. Morris, *Forbes,* November 30, 1998, pp. 84–94 and http://www.businesspundit.com/12-countries-with-the-highest-lowest-tax-rates/

19 See "Have more children, France urges citizens" by John Leicester, *The Orlando Sentinel*, September 22, 2005.

20 See "Behind Slow Growth in Europe: Citizen's Tight Grip on Wallets" by Marcus Walker, *The Wall Street Journal,* December 10, 2004; and "In France, Working Long Hours Becomes a Crime" by David Woodruff, *The Wall Street Journal*, June 15, 1999.

21 See "Bonfire of the Vanities" by Theodore Dalrymple, *The Wall Street Journal,* November 7, 2005; "Our Immigrants, Their Immigrants" by Joel Kotkin, *The Wall Street Journal*, November 8, 2005; Les Miserables, *The Wall Street Journal*, November 5-6, 2005; "France needs freedom, not welfare" by Jack A. Chambless, *The USA Today*, November 10, 2005.

22 See "Liberte', Precarite: Labor Law Ignites Anxiety in France" by Andrew Higgins, *The Wall Street Journal*, March 29, 2006.

23 See "French Revolution," *The Wall Street Journal*, September 20, 2007.

24 See "Lazy Europe?" by Daniel Schwammenthal, *The Wall Street Journal*, April 25, 2007.

25 See "Ailing Ireland Accepts Bailout" by Marcus Walker, Charles Forelle and David Enrich, *The Wall Street Journal*, November 22, 2010.

26 See "In Ireland, Bailout Triggers a Wave of Anger" by Guy Chazan & Neil Shah, *The Wall Street Journal*, November 24, 2010.

27 See "Irish Cutbacks Pile It On for 'New Poor'" by Guy Chazan, *The Wall Street Journal*, November 27-28, 2010; and "Ireland's Low-Tax Path to Fiscal Health" by Brian Cowen, *The Wall Street Journal*, December 8, 2010.

28 For more on Lady Thatcher, see http://www.youtube.com/watch?v=40NVkfbaMo4

29 See "Europeans discover the value of work" by Peter Brown, *The Orlando Sentinel*, August 27, 2004.

30 See "The Wirtschaftswunder: Another Look" by Lawrence H. White, *The Wall Street Journal*, September 8, 2010; and "German Economy Steams Ahead" by Brian Blackstone, *The Wall Street Journal*, January 13, 2011.

31 See "Germany Criticizes Fed Move" by Patrick McGroarty, *The Wall Street Journal*, November 8, 2010.

32 See "Is America Number One" ABC News Special with John Stossel, September 19, 1999; "Something's cushy in Denmark" by Mark Landler, *The Orlando Sentinel*, November 20, 2005; "Thousands back land reform in Venezuela" by Christopher Toothaker, *The Orlando Sentinel*, October 9, 2005; "Bolivia sets sights on 10 companies" by Fiona Smith, *The Orlando Sentinel*, March 7, 2006, pg. A5; "Betrayal: Why Socialism Failed in Africa" speech by George B.N. Ayittey at The Foundation for Economic Education, April 2005; "Latin America is skeptical" by Andres Oppenheimer, *The Orlando Sentinel*, February 20, 2006; and "More U.S. Job-Hunters Try Australia" by Geoffrey Rogow, *The Wall Street Journal*, December 27, 2010, p. A11.

33 See "The Greek Economy Explained," *The Wall Street Journal*, May 7, 2010.

34 See "Tax Evasion Dogs Greece" by Sebastian Moffett & Alkman Granitsas, *The Wall Street Journal*, February 10, 2010, p. A13.

35 See "Europe Bankrolls Greece" by Charles Forelle & Marcus Walker, *The Wall Street Journal*, April 12, 2010; "Greek Red Tape Hamstrings Growth, Entrepreneurs Say" by Sebastion Moffett & Alkman Granitsas, *The Wall Street Journal*, May 20, 2010; and "Privatization Can Help Greece" by Allan H. Meltzer, *The Wall Street Journal*, May 21, 2010.

36 See "Cuba Unveils Huge Layoffs in Tilt Toward Free Market" by Jose' de Cordoba & Nicholas Casey, *The Wall Street Journal*, September 14, 2010.

37 See "Survey Says: People are Happier" by Matt Mabe, *BusinessWeek*, August 20, 2008.

38 See "Whether People Define Themselves as Happy Depends on the Era" by Cynthia Crossen, *The Wall Street Journal*, March 6, 2006.

39 See "Culture matters the most, some say" by Alexander Stille, *The New York Times*, February 18, 2001 (date published in *The Orlando Sentinel*).

40 See New Hampshire's Free State Project at http://www.freestateproject.org/

41 In 2011 Illinois dramatically increased personal and corporate income taxes. See "Tax Hikes in Illinois; Wisconsin 'Open for Business'" by Daniel Halper, *The Weekly Standard*, January 18, 2011.

42 See "Economic Freedom Greatest in Middle America, Study Says" by Lawrence J. McQuillan, Robert E. McCormick and Ying Huang, *Budget & Tax News* (The Heartland Institute) January 2005, pg. 9.

43 See "If You Like Michigan's Economy, You'll Love Obama's" by Phil Gramm and Mike Solon, *The Wall Street Journal*, September 13-14, 2008, pg. A12 and http://www.bls.gov/news.release/laus.nr0.htm

44 See "The Great Lone Star Migration" by Michael Barone, *The Wall Street Journal*, January 8-9, 2011.

45 See "How Not to Balance a Budget" *The Wall Street Journal*, September 13-14, 2008, pg. A12.

46 Minnesota's generous welfare benefits are one reason why immigrants are now pouring into the state, costing taxpayers upwards of $188 million per year in benefits. See "Far from Mexico, immigration an issue" by Martiga Lohn, *The Orlando Sentinel*, February 4, 2006.

47 Source: The Center for Philanthropy at Indiana University.

48 Source: CIA World Fact Book.

49 See "A Nation of Givers" by Arthur C. Brooks, *The American*, March/April 2008.

50 See "India's Surging Economy Lifts Hopes and Ambitions" by Paul Beckett, Krishna Pokharel & Eric Bellman, *The Wall Street Journal*, November 28, 2007.

51 See "They're Rounding the First Turn! And the Favorite Is....." by Nicholas D. Kristof, *The New York Times*, January 17, 2006.

52 See http://www.indexmundi.com/india/gdp_real_growth_rate.html

53 See http://timesofindia.indiatimes.com/articleshow/2090174.cms

54 See "Sizzling Economy Revitalizes India" by Amy Waldman, *The New York Times*, October 20, 2003; and "India Everywhere in the Alps" by Mark Landler, *The New York Times*, January 26, 2006.

55 See "There's More to Growth than China…" by Martin Feldstein, *The Wall Street Journal*, February 16, 2006; and "A Passage to Prosperity" by Arvind Panagariya, *The Wall Street Journal*, July 14, 2005.

56 Yet, millions of Indians who live in poverty still have little chance of gaining wealth within India due the Hindu caste system that labels many Indians as ostensibly inferior, from birth. For more, see "Untouchable" by Tom O'Neill, *National Geographic*, June 2003, pp. 2-31.

57 Source: CIA World Fact Book.

58 See "Beijing Sets Tax Plan to Aid Growth" by Matt Pottinger, Kathy Chen and Karen Elliot House, *The Wall Street Journal*, February 6, 2004.

59 See "Global Playing Field: More Level, but it Still Has Bumps" by Joseph Stiglitz, *The New York Times*, April 30, 2005; "Revolutionary China, Complacent America" by Charlene Barshefsky and Edward Gresser, *The Wall Street Journal*, September 15, 2005; and "U.S. Dozes as China Roars" by Peter Morici, *The Orlando Sentinel*, November 13, 2005.

60 See "Starbucks Brews Coffee Plan for India" by Paul Beckett, Vibhuti Agarwal & Julie Jargon, *The Wall Street Journal*, January 14, 2011; "A New Detroit Rises in India's South" by Eric Bellman, *The Wall Street Journal*, July 9, 2010; and "A Glimpse at India, Minus the Red Tape" by Geeta Anand & Amol Sharma, *The Wall Street Journal*, January 14, 2011, p. A16.

61 See "In China's Orbit" *The Wall Street Journal*, November 20-21, 2010, p. C1.

62 See "The Global Jobs Competition Heats Up" by Martin Neil Baily, Matthew J. Slaughter & Laura D'Andrea Tyson, *The Wall Street Journal*, July 1, 2010.

63 You can also find answers by reading "Hillary Clinton: Accidental Supply-Sider" by Steve Forbes, *The Wall Street Journal*, June 28, 2010.

64 Source: CIA World Fact Book.

65 See "Why Friedrich Hayek is Making a Comeback" by Russ Roberts, *The Wall Street Journal*, June 28, 2010.

66 See "The U.S. Loses Ground on Economic Freedom" by Terry Miller, *The Wall Street Journal*, January 12, 2011.

67 See "The Best Country to Start a Business" by Jeff May, *The Wall Street Journal*, November 15, 2010, p. R4.

68 See "Canada: Land of the Free" by Mary Anastasia O'Grady, *The Wall Street Journal*, June 26-27, 2010 pl. A11; and "Target is Going Abroad – to Canada" by Ann Zimmerman & Karen Talley, *The Wall Street Journal*, January 14, 2011.

69 Source: National Constitution Center, Philadelphia, PA. See www.constitutioncenter.org.

70 See "Uncle Sam—50 years in withdrawal" by John Leyden, *The Orlando Sentinel*, July 4, 1993.

71 See The Public Papers and Addresses of Franklin D. Roosevelt, 12 (New York: Harper & Brothers, 1950), p. 90.

72 IBID.

73 See *The Limits of Symbolic Reform: The New Deal and Taxation* by Mark Leff (London and New York: Cambridge University Press, 1984) pp. 290–291.

74 See "Still Morning in America" *The Wall Street Journal*, January 20, 2006; *The Seven Fat Years* by Robert L. Bartley, The Free Press, 1995; and *Reaganomics* by William A. Niskanen, Oxford University Press, 1988.

75 See "Higher Retroactive Tax on Wealthy Is Blamed, in Part, for Slowing Growth" by Fred R. Bleakley, *The Wall Street Journal*, July 6, 1994.

76 See "Paradise's cost: Land boom taxes Montanans" by Kim Murphy, *The Orlando Sentinel*, January 6, 2010.

77 See "It's Their Money," *The Wall Street Journal*, April 10, 2001; "Taxed into submission" by Tom Zucco and Letitia Stein, *The St. Petersburg Times*, March 12, 2006; and "Federal Income Tax Hike Looms for Millions of Middle-Income Americans" by Steve Stanek, *Budget & Tax News* (The Heartland Institute), June 2005.

78 See "International Tax Competition – A 21st Century Restraint on Government, *Policy Analysis*, The CATO Institute, April 12, 2002; "Time to End the Corporate Income Tax" by Richard W. Rahn, *Budget & Tax News* (The Heartland Institute), January 2005; "Irish Subsidiary Lets Microsoft Slash Taxes in U.S. and Europe" by Glenn R. Simpson, *The Wall Street Journal*, November 7, 2005; and "Our Broken Corporate Tax Code" by Henry M. Paulson, Jr., *The Wall Street Journal*, July 19, 2007.

79 See "Time to Junk the Corporate Tax" by Michael J. Boskin, *The Wall Street Journal*, May 6, 2010, p. A19.

80 Source: The National Center for Policy Analysis, June 11, 2009.

81 Source: The Tax Foundation.

82 See "White House Sees Template in Tax Deal" by Laura Meckler & Jonathan Weisman, *The Wall Street Journal*, December 18-19, 2010, p. A5.

83 See "The Small Beer Bill," *The Wall Street Journal*, September 11-12, 2010, p. A12; "Tax Hikes and the Small Business Job Machine" by John Engler and Jerry Howard, *The Wall Street Journal*, November 17, 2010; "The 1099 Democrats" by Daniel Henninger, *The Wall Street Journal*, November 11, 2010; and "The Economics of Capital Gains Taxes is Well Known" Letters to the Editor, *The Wall Street Journal*, September 25-26, 2010.

84 See "The Bill Gates Income Tax" by Arthur Laffer, *The Wall Street Journal*, October 5, 2010, p. A23.

85 See "Nearly half in U.S. escape income tax" by Stephen Ohlemacher, *The Orlando Sentinel*, April 8, 2010.

86 See *The Fair Tax Book by Neal Boortz* and John Linder, Regan Books, 2005; "Economists Back 'Fair Tax' Proposal" by Merrill Bender, *Budget & Tax News* (The Heartland Institute), June 2005; and "How to Tax Fairly" by Jack A. Chambless, *The Orlando Sentinel*, April 10, 2005.

87 See "Flat Tax Club," *The Wall Street Journal*, January 6, 2005; and "Do We Want a Free Market in Iraq?" *Forbes*, February 16, 2004, p. 37.

88 See "A Budget for Taxpayers, Not Tax Consumers" by Stephen Moore, *The Wall Street Journal*, April 12, 2001.

89 See "The Spending Explosion" *The Wall Street Journal*, September 10, 2008, pg. A14.

90 See "Federal Spending soars in Bush's White House" by Ron Hutcheson, *Knight Ridder Newspapers* (appearing in *The Orlando Sentinel*), December 7, 2003, p. A13; "Conservative Republicans Push for Slowdown in U.S. Spending" by Richard W. Stevenson, *The New York Times*, January 22, 2004; "Riding the Omnibus," *The Wall Street Journal*, January 26, 2004; "Promises, Promises But Who's Minding the Budget?" by George Melloan, *The Wall Street Journal*, January 20, 2004; and "President Signs Budget Busting Medicare Reform" by John Skorburg, *Budget & Tax News* (The Heartland Institute), January 2004.

91 Source: The White House Office of Management and Budget http://www.whitehouse.gov/omb/budget/Historicals

92 See "The 2010 Spending Record," *The Wall Street Journal*, October 12, 2010, p. A20.

93 See "The Bankrupting of America" by Mortimer Zuckerman, *The Wall Street Journal*, May 21, 2010.

94 For a detailed account of his life and influence on the economy, see *Alexander Hamilton* by Ron Chernow, The Penguin Press, 2004.

95 See *Locke, Jefferson and the Justices: Foundations and Failure of the U.S. Government,* by George M. Stephens, Algora Publishing, 2002.

96 See "Congress Rediscovers the Constitution" by Roger Pilon, *The Wall Street Journal*, January 4, 2011.

97 United States v. Butler, 297 U.S. 1 (1936).

98 See "Not Yours to Give" from *The Life of Colonel David Crockett*, compiled by Edward S. Ellis (Philadelphia; Porter & Coates, 1884).

99 See "Taxpayers May Face Hurricane Tab" by Elizabeth Williamson, *The Wall Street Journal*, May 31-June 1, 2008.

100 Recent reports do indicate that rich people usually get more money from FEMA than poor people do. See "FEMA refunds assist higher earners most" by Sally Kestin, Megan O'Matz and John Maines, *The Orlando Sentinel*, December 11, 2005.

101 See "Building on the Edge" by Joe Newman, *The Orlando Sentinel*, December 14, 2005.

102 See "Storm victims' housing aid, set to end in August, extended into '09" by Cain Burdeau, *The Orlando Sentinel*, April 27, 2007, pg. A9.

103 For more analysis of moral hazard, see "The gospel according to moral hazard" by Ellen Goodman, *The Orlando Sentinel*, March 24, 2008, pg. A21.

104 See "$1.5B foreclosure help" by Peter Nicholas & Ashley Powers, *The Orlando Sentinel*, February 20, 2010.

105 The initial tax for this plan was 2% - equally divided between employer and employee. See "Meaning of freedom – a process or a result?" by David Moreland, *The Orlando Sentinel*, February 27, 2010.

106 The employee rate fell to 4.2% for 2011 only.

107 See "Health Bill for 9/11 Responders is Approved" by Delvin Barrett, *The Wall Street Journal*, December 23, 2010, p. A7.

108 See "Van drives around Daytona's ban on body piercing" by Ludmilla Lelis, *The Orlando Sentinel;* and "States Crack Down on Indoor Tanning" by Jennifer Saranow, *The Wall Street Journal*, January 26, 2005.

109 See "Toward a 21st Century Regulatory System" by Barack Obama, *The Wall Street Journal*, January 18, 2011, p. A17.

110 See "Obama Courts Business Support" by Elizabeth Williamson and Jonathan Weisman, *The Wall Street Journal*, January 19, 2011.

111 See "Red Tape Rising: Regulatory Trends in the Bush Years" by James L. Gattuso, *Backgrounder* (The Heritage Foundation), March 25, 2008.

112 See "There is No Joy in Toyland" by Anne M. Northup, *The Wall Street Journal*, December 24, 2009.

113 See "New Lead-Paint Law Heavy on Budgets" by Sarah E. Needleman, *The Wall Street Journal*, May 18, 2010.

114 See "EPA Proposes Tighter, Costlier Smog Limits" by Mark W. Peters and Stephen Power, *The Wall Street Journal*, January 8, 2010.

115 See "Light Cars are Dangerous Cars" by Robert E. Grady, *The Wall Street Journal,* May 22, 2009.

116 IBID.

117 See "New U.S. Push to Regulate Internet" by Amy Schatz, *The Wall Street Journal*, May 6, 2010.

118 See "Senate OKs financial overhaul measure" by Janet Hook and Jim Puzzanghera, *The Orlando Sentinel*, May 21, 2010.

119 See "The Uncertainty Principle" *The Wall Street Journal*, July 14, 2010, p. A18.

120 See "The End of Community Banking" by Sarah Wallace, *The Wall Street Journal*, June 29, 2010.

121 See "Drug Regulations Cause Millions of Deaths Each Year, Study Finds" by Susan Konig, *Health Care News* (The Heartland Institute), January 2005.

122 See "Stop Bashing Business, Mr. President" by Ken Langone, *The Wall Street Journal*, October 15, 2010.

123 See "Principles for Economic Revival" by George P. Shultz, Michael J. Boskin, John F. Cogan, Allan Meltzer, and John B. Taylor, *The Wall Street Journal*, September 16, 2010, p. A23.

124 See "Move Reflects Shift in President's Tone" by David Wessel, *The Wall Street Journal*, January 19, 2011.

125 For more on businesses perspective of Mr. Obama's relationship with them, see "Business Groups Slams 'Hostile' Policies on Jobs" by Elizabeth Williamson and Darrell A. Hughes, *The Wall Street Journal*, June 23, 2010; and "Revisiting the Regulations Affecting Business" by Elizabeth Williamson, *The Wall Street Journal,* July 12, 2010, p. A4.

126 See "Land of Milk and Regulation" *The Wall Street Journal*, January 27, 2011.

127 See "Here's a U.S. Secret Revealed: The Fourth Amendment is Dead" by Charles Levendosky, Editorial page editor, *Casper (Wyoming) Star-Tribune*, April 28, 2002.

128 See "Repeal the Patriot Act" by Andrew P. Napolitano, *The Wall Street Journal*, March 5, 2004; and *Terrorism and Tyranny* by James Bovard, Palgrave MacMillan, 2003.

129 See "In Google case, activists see privacy eroding" by Douglas Birch, *The Orlando Sentinel*, January 22, 2006; "Internet Users Thinking Twice Before a Search" by Katie Hafner, *The New York Times*, January 25, 2006.

130 See "Congress lambastes INS Chief" by Tamara Lytle, *The Orlando Sentinel,* March 20, 2002.

131 www.jewishworldreview.com/cols/williams.html

CHAPTER REVIEW

1. What are some of the major differences between socialism and the mixed economy? Give specific examples.

2. What would Frederic Bastiat, Alexander Hamilton, and James Madison say about government bailouts of banks and automotive companies? Fully explain.

3. What were the major differences between Franklin D. Roosevelt and John F. Kennedy with respect to the role of government in the life of American workers?

4. How do regulations impact the overall level of poverty and employment?

Chapter Four

ECONOMICS *as a* SCIENCE

Shutterstock © Dwight Smith, 2011.

*A*ny man of energy and initiative in this country can get what he wants out of life. But when initiative is crippled by legislation or by a tax system which denies him the right to receive a reasonable share of his earnings, then he will no longer exert himself and the country will be deprived of the energy on which its continued greatness depends.

ANDREW MELLON

THE SCIENCE OF ECONOMICS

> Facts do not cease to exist because they are ignored.
>
> Aldous Huxley

We spent the first three chapters laying out the argument that economics can explain the sources of wealth and happiness all over the world. But how do you know whether economists simply think we are right, or whether we can prove we are right?

One of the most significant obstacles economics professors have to overcome each semester is the perception by students that economics is steeped in intellectual guesswork. After all, who among us has not seen economists on CNN, or some other network, debating issues, disagreeing with other scholars, and generally using terminology that the majority of human beings do not understand or even remotely comprehend? In this chapter, we will uncover the scientific processes that form the foundation of economics as a social science. It is here that you will discover that there is virtually no type of human behavior that cannot be explained – to an extent – with the use of logic, economic theory, and mathematics.

This does not mean economists know everything about the causes of human behavior. After all, if we (economists) are so smart, why did we fail to accurately predict the biggest recession to hit the United States in over 70 years? Increasingly, economists are recognizing that the mathematical models we use to explain human decisions, cannot possibly capture all of the variables behind our decisions.[1] As one famous economics professor once said, "Economics is a powerful tool, a lens for organizing one's thinking about the complexity of the world around us. That should be enough. We should be honest about what we know, and what we don't know, and what we may never know. Admitting that publicly is the first step toward respectability."[2]

THE SCIENTIFIC PROCESS

How often has a professor told you that skipping class or working too many hours is bad for your grade? What makes them say this? Isn't it simply common sense that not attending classes you've signed up for raises the probability of working at a terrible job someday? Common sense is nice to have, but wouldn't it be nicer if you knew exactly how many classes you could miss before you end up hurting your grade? How could we help students make definitive judgments about what type of behavior they should pursue while in college? As it turns out, the use of statistics, algebra, and calculus is a good start.

Before you run for the admissions office to drop this class, please be aware that your professor does not expect you to be an expert in matrix algebra or to know the difference between a first order and second order derivative. In this course it is generally assumed that students have limited mathematical expertise, so this chapter will walk you through the basic mathematical process that economists use to explain the causes and consequences of human decisions. To do that, we rely on the concept of an economic model.

> ➤ **An economic model is a way of explaining how some sector of the economy functions.**

The behavior of students in a classroom can be modeled. That means we can show you the mathematical link between certain behaviors and the outcomes you will attain in your classes. To do so involves four distinct steps that makes up the scientific process:

1. The selection of the dependent and independent variables
2. Making assumptions concerning the relationship between the independent and dependent variables
3. Assessing the implications of our assumptions
4. Testing our hypothesis

Step One — Variable Selection

In virtually every economics class, there will be a wide range of test scores on any given test. This is interesting, because each student has the same book, the same access to the professor, the same lecture material, and so forth. How can a range of grades from 11–97 be explained? If an economist were asked to provide this explanation, she would first assign a dependent variable to the question at hand.

> ➤ **A dependent variable is a variable whose value depends on some other variable.**

In this case, the dependent variable would be test scores. That is what we are trying to explain, and of course, test scores depend on several independent variables.

> ➤ **An independent variable is a variable whose value is independent of other variables.**

Before we begin picking our independent variables, we should note some rules that apply to model building. First, any variable we pick *must be measurable*. That means we must be able to assign a quantity or dollar amount to that variable. For example, the attitude of a student toward the professor might have an impact on the test grade, but attitude is not measurable; therefore, we would not include it in our list of independent variables. An exception to this rule is when we have situations where there is an "either-or" situation that needs to be addressed.

Suppose a professor wanted to find out if there is a gender-based explanation for test scores. The economist in charge of this model could create a "dummy variable" – a variable that has no numerical value but is still measurable – to incorporate gender. We will see later on how the dummy variable issue is handled.

The second rule is that the variables selected *must make some intuitive sense*. While it is logical to include the number of hours students work each week in this model, it does not make sense to include as a variable the number of times they visited their grandparents when they were six years old. While it is readily apparent that the latter variable is ridiculous, there may be variables that you think should be included but in reality should not be, because they occur with such infrequency or are so hard to get data for that the variable is best left out of the model. Keep in mind that usually someone is paying the economist to model some problem. The accountants are going to want the economist to be able to justify why any variable should be picked. The more variables that are selected, the more money the research will cost, and we all know how picky accountants can be about what things cost.

Now that we have some basic understanding of where to begin, let's look at five different variables we might want to consider in a model explaining test scores:

1. Number of classes attended
2. Number of hours spent at work each week
3. Number of study hours per week
4. Gender
5. Number of times the student cheated

Notice that each variable is measurable (survey data would help greatly here) and makes intuitive sense. There are many other variables that could be picked, but for our purposes, these five will be sufficient in understanding the second step in the scientific process.

Step Two — Making Assumptions

Assumptions are made to establish the *cause-and-effect relationship* between our independent variables and our dependent variable. We should stop here for a moment to look at the term "cause and effect." In the world around us, there are three ways to look at the interconnectedness of events. We can say that two events have taken place through coincidence, because they are correlated, or because one event caused the other.

As you might imagine, *coincidence* is the weakest form of connection between two events. For example, suppose the night before your first economics test, your roommate prepares your favorite meal. The next day you score a 96 on the exam. You reach the conclusion that as long as you get your favorite meal the night before a test, you will make a 96, so you stop going to class or studying and simply wait for this lucky meal. The two events happened around the same time, but there is no scientific relationship between the two events.

It has been observed that in most years that a team from the American Football Conference of the National Football League wins the Super Bowl, the U.S. economy is fairly weak. In years a team from the National Football Conference wins, the economy has been strong. Does this mean that if the San Diego Chargers (an AFC team) win the Super Bowl in 2014 that the stock market will fall and unemployment will rise?

Correlation is stronger than coincidence. When two events are correlated, it means that one event has been shown to have some relationship to another event. But that relationship is not strong enough for the scientist to say that the one event will repeatedly cause the second event. For example, there appears to be a correlation between the height of the person running for president and the likelihood of their election. There could also be a correlation between facial symmetry and the odds of winning. This means that if a person is considered homely

CONCEPT CHECK

The National Hockey League's Minnesota Wild is made up of an almost entirely white roster, while the National Basketball Association's Minnesota Timberwolves has mostly black players. Is this a coincidence? Are there variables that could accurately explain the racial composition of professional sports?

Photo courtesy Jack Chambless

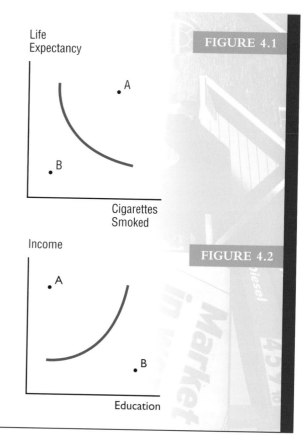

FIGURE 4.1

FIGURE 4.2

or is short, his or her odds of winning are lower, but being homely or short does not guarantee losing. Correlation simply means that it is not a coincidence that people opt for taller, better-looking politicians, but it is not a scientific fact that only those people with those characteristics will be elected.

Causation is the strongest form of connection between an independent variable and a dependent variable. When economists discover a causal relationship between two variables, it means that over and over again the occurrence of one event will cause the occurrence of another event. For example, there is a causal negative relationship between the number of cigarettes smoked and the number of years a person will live. There is a proven positive relationship between the number of years of education a person receives and that person's lifetime income. Figures 4.1 and 4.2 illustrate the concept of causal relationships. What does point A and B on each diagram mean?

In 4.1 we see that, as the number of cigarettes smoked increases over an average person's lifetime, the fewer years that person can expect to live. Point A on 4.1 shows a person who smoked a great deal but lived a long time. Point B shows a person who never smoked and died very young. These are called *statistical outliers*.

CONCEPT CHECK

Does Wal-Mart *cause* towns like Paris, Texas to lose small businesses? Why or why not?

Photo courtesy Jack Chambless

Outliers are observed points that are several deviations away from the normal observed data points. When economists see outliers, we largely ignore them. We ignore them because for every person who lives to be 104 while smoking like a chimney, there are far more people who end up dead from this behavior.

Now that we have a basic idea of what the term, *causation* means, let's go back to our model of your behavior and test scores to look at the assumptions we should make concerning the relationship between the independent and dependent variables. There are five possible assumptions we can make.

THE POSITIVE RELATIONSHIP

Of the five variables we selected, the only one that should have a clear positive causal relationship with test scores is the number of classes attended. As Figure 4.3 illustrates, as the number of classes attended increases, the student can expect his grades to increase. This assumption is made *ceteris paribus,* meaning "everything else being equal."

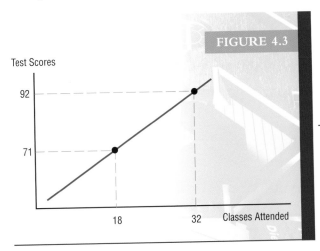

FIGURE 4.3

In other words, assuming normal behavior with respect to studying, alcohol consumption, sleep, and so forth, the typical student can expect to be helped from attending all classes. However, there are many instances where students miss class frequently and still survive, just as there are students who never miss and do poorly. The number of times you go to class is just one variable in this model. It would be wise to assume that other things matter as well.

THE NEGATIVE RELATIONSHIP

If you are like other college students, you have mastered the art of living in denial when it comes to the relationship between your work hours and your grades. Professors realize many of you are working to support your life, but some of you are working to support your *lifestyle*. You have rationally decided that the benefits of working – a nice car, stylish clothes, etc. – outweigh the opportunity cost of studying and making better grades. Figure 4.4 calls into question whether your priorities are in order.

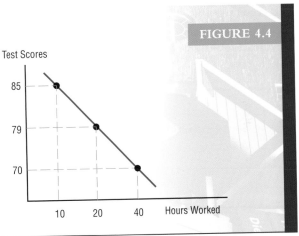

FIGURE 4.4

Notice that if you worked ten hours per week, ceteris paribus, you might average an 85 on your exams. Twenty hours per week might lead to an average of 79. Working 40 hours might mean a 70 average. All students are different, of course, and some can overcome huge workloads,

Shutterstock © HelleM, 2011.

CONCEPT CHECK

Recent studies show that college-age Americans spend an average of 53 hours per week on entertainment-related activities like social networking, video games, music, sending text messages, and more.[3] What is the most likely relationship between the hours spent on these activities and a student's grade point average? If students in China and India spend far less time on these activities, what are the implications for wages and salaries for Americans over time?

but for the average student there is a negative relationship between work hours and test scores, whether you want to admit it or not.

ZERO RELATIONSHIP

Why would a scientist load into any model an independent variable that is assumed to have no impact on the dependent variable? In some cases we would not do this. For example, including a variable measuring the impact of the average winnings of an *American Idol* contestant on test scores would not be a wise use of our resources. However, including gender or race might be interesting.

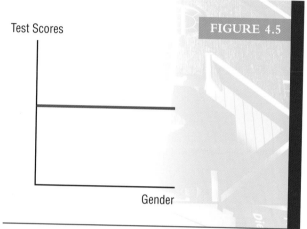

When is enough, enough?

If a professor was concerned that his or her classes were gender or racially biased, including a dummy variable to account for this possibility would be appropriate. The social scientist could simply assign a one to every male in the class and a zero to every woman. In the section on hypothesis testing, we will show how this would help uncover any statistically significant relationship between gender and test scores. Figure 4.5 illustrates the assumption that there is no relationship between the two.

THE CONVEX RELATIONSHIP

Have you ever over-studied for a test? Most students don't suffer from having a hyperactive work ethic, but, if you do, it could come back to bite you. Consider this scenario:

You have attended all classes, taken perfect notes, sought out advice and answers to your questions, and generally conducted yourself as the model college student. Then it comes time to prepare for your first test. Figure 4.6 shows that, as your study hours increase from 5 to 35, your grade will rise from a 60 to 98.[4]

However, notice that with every hour after 35, your grade begins to fall. How could this happen? It is possible that studying more than the optimal number of hours could lead to fatigue, stress over minute details, significant ideas becoming blurred, and other problems arise.

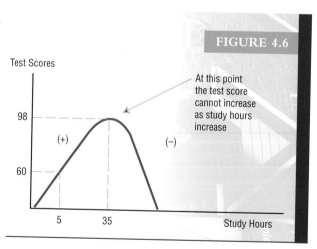

This means that there are diminishing returns from studying – i.e., studying can be too much of a good thing. When should you stop? It depends on many variables beyond the scope of this chapter, but a good rule of thumb would be to pay close attention to the incremental gains you are making in retention from each hour you study. When those gains come at a slower and slower rate, you are getting close to the best you can do.

THE CONCAVE RELATIONSHIP

Like anything else, the first time a person cheats on a test, they are probably not very good at it. However, with practice, you, too, could become a good cheater! Figure 4.7 illustrates this idea.

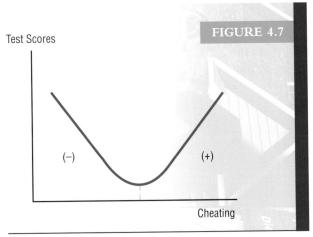

FIGURE 4.7

Notice that the first several times the student is cheating, there is a negative relationship between cheating and the test score. Perhaps the student is trying to figure out the most efficient way to go about stealing answers and initially gets caught with great enough frequency, or is cheating off the wrong people and test scores suffer. However, beyond the global minimum (the low point on the function), as students continue to improve their cheating skills, their test grades — and chances of becoming a politician — increase.

STEP THREE — THE IMPLICATIONS

In this step we use logic to analyze the implications of the assumptions concerning the relationship among the economic variables. This is an important step to help those who might be paying for, or affected by the research, to understand what we might expect to see occur in the real world if our assumptions are proven right.

Suppose we find that for every increase in work hours by ten hours per week, a student can expect to lose one full letter grade in any given class. The implications of losing one full letter grade could be fewer scholarships, internships, and eventually fewer job opportunities.

With fewer job opportunities would come lower lifetime earnings, more stress, a smaller home, less choices in who the student would be able to marry, a lower retirement income, and so forth. You might find yourself doubting that working too many hours could lead to so many bad things, or you could ask yourself why it is that the students with the best grades in the most difficult majors seem to enjoy a higher probability of lifetime success.

STEP FOUR — TESTING THE HYPOTHESIS

In the first and second steps of our model, we hypothesized that there was a relationship between several different variables and test scores for the typical college student. Step four is where we find out if we were right.

In this step we mathematically verify the interconnectedness between each independent variable and the dependent variable. To do this, the economist first gathers data on each variable in the following equation:

Test scores = b0 + b1 classes attended + b2 work hours + b3 gender + b4 study hours + b5 study hours2 + b6 number of times cheated + number of times cheated2

If you recall basic algebra, test scores are our 'Y' variable, b0 is our intercept term, and the other "bs" represent our *coefficients* on the independent variables. Squaring the study hours variable and number of times cheated variable allows us to find out if there is a convex or concave relationship between those variables and test scores.

Photo courtesy Jack Chambless

CONCEPT CHECK

In a survey of teenage drivers, Allstate Insurance Co. found that girls are reportedly driving more aggressively than boys, with 16% of girls reporting that they drive aggressively (up from 9% in 2005).[5] If this is a new trend for America's roads, what are the implications for insurance rates and consumer prices? Why?

> A coefficient is the mathematical connection between the independent and dependent variable that is discovered in the algebraic process known as multiple regression analysis.

At this time, none of you would be expected to know what multiple regression analysis (sometimes called matrix algebra) is. This will be discovered later on in your college careers if you take more statistics and econometrics classes. The reason it is even mentioned here is because it is important to show that all of the lines you encounter on all of those diagrams are not just lines, but rather actual relationships that have been empirically proven over time. If you can have at least some surface understanding of where the lines come from, you will gain a deeper appreciation for the concepts of supply and demand and many other economic principles.

Economists studying test scores would load all of the data they uncovered into a statistical software package on their computer and set test scores equal to all of the data uncovered. The computer would then be instructed to compute the coefficients for each variable and do a test to determine if each variable is "statistically significant" in explaining test scores.

HOW TO INTERPRET DATA

Suppose the computer spits out the following data for each of the variables selected:

$$B0 = 29$$
$$B1 = 3.11$$
$$B2 = -4.05$$
$$B3 = 2.77$$
$$B4 = 4.53$$
$$B5 = -1.37$$
$$B6 = -7.31$$
$$B7 = 2.08$$

CONCEPT CHECK

Extensive research seems to suggest that beer, in moderation, is good for us.[7] Does this mean that keg parties can help you live a longer life?

What do these numbers mean? Very simply, the results indicate that, if every other variable equaled zero, the average student could expect to earn at least a 29 on any given exam. For every class attended, their test grade increased by 3.11 points.

Every hour of work (measured in increments of ten hours per week, for example) led to a drop in test scores by 4.05 points.

For the dummy variable on gender, since we assigned a one to every male and a zero for every female, the algebraic equation dropped women from the model when it came to this variable. Since the coefficient on gender equals 2.77, it means that being male helped test scores by 2.77 points.

Initially, every hour a student studied raised that student's grades by 4.53 points. After some point (in calculus you will learn how to solve for this "global maximum"), each hour of studying led to a drop of 1.37 points. Cheating hurt the average student by 7.31 points per test initially, but led to improved test scores of 2.08 points after the bottom of the function was reached.

Remember that these numbers were simply created to help shed light on how to interpret the data. The numbers are not as important as the relationships the numbers suggest and the implications that can be drawn from them. Assume for a moment that each coefficient has been proven to be statistically significant – in other words, we can say with 95% certainty that each independent variable has the mathematical relationship to the dependent variable that the coefficients indicate.[6] What would the implications be?

Photo courtesy Jack Chambless

Is ratemyprofessor.com a statistically reliable predictor of professor quality? Why, or why not?

For the professor and the student, the data would provide some empirical support of the assumptions that were made and would help each of them to determine the proper course of action. Students might decide to work less, manage their study hours more effectively, and not miss class. Professors might try to learn ways to account for different learning styles between males and females and how to catch the cheaters! On the other hand, students and professors can ignore the data and run the risk of repeating destructive behavior.

APPLYING MODELS TO THE "REAL WORLD"

What fun would the study of economics be if we couldn't apply economic models to everyday life? Most of us are going to spend 80 or more years as living beings on Earth. While we are here, it seems the least we could do is to understand how the world around us works. In this section of the chapter, we will use economic models to more fully understand what Alfred Marshall once called "the ordinary business of life."

CASE STUDY #1 — SHOULD THE ELDERLY BE ALLOWED TO DRIVE? SHOULD YOU?

I know that this is a terrible question to ask. Maybe it is because I only had one grandparent – and I only saw her for a week of my life – that I am not ashamed to ask it. Another reason the question might occur is the number of personal experiences I have had with senior citizens driving 37 miles per hour in the left-hand lane of the interstate. Then again, there is data showing that the relationship between driver age and the fatal crash rate is concave.

As the table above clearly illustrates, your grandparents might be hazardous to our health. Notice that for Florida drivers who are 85 and older, the fatal crash rate is 2.92 per 10,000 licensed drivers. That figure is higher than for drivers 75–84 as well as drivers who are 65–74.

It appears that drivers in the 65–74 age group are at the lowest risk for being in a fatal car crash. People in this group have been driving, on average, for more than 40 years. That experience behind the wheel, combined with the fact that more mature drivers have not yet begun experiencing deterioration of visual acuity, reflexes, and muscle coordination, makes them better drivers than very old senior citizens, on average.

Before we get too worried about seeing a centenarian on the highway, perhaps we should look at the other part of this concave function. You might not be too happy to see that you are in the age group of the people most likely to get wiped out on the roads. If you are 15–24 years of age, the data show a higher fatality rate for you than for your great-grandparents! This makes intuitive sense. Younger drivers are not only less experienced, but are more inclined to drink and drive, speed, send text messages and drive recklessly.[8]

The data seems to suggest that the very young and very old should be of paramount concern.

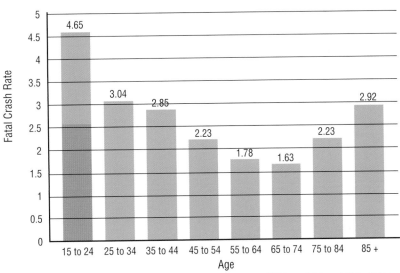

Source: Florida Highway Patrol, 2002 statistics; Florida Department of Highway Safety and Motor Vehicles

SUGGESTED CLASSROOM DEBATE

Should the U.S. model itself after Germany and require people to be 18 years old to drive? Why or why not?

CASE STUDY #2 — WHAT IS YOUR FAVORITE TEAM WORTH TO YOU?

WHAT PRICE VIKINGS FANDOM? FUNNY YOU SHOULD ASK

By Conor Dougherty

MINNEAPOLIS—Christopher Slinde, a lifetime Minnesota Vikings fan who has endured decades of heartbreak and lots of overpriced beer in supporting his team, believes Vikings fandom is priceless. According to economists, it's worth $530.65.

WSJ's Conor Doughtery speaks with colleague Adam Najberg about the Minnesota Viking's value to the Twin Cities as the team threatens to leave the area if it doesn't get a new stadium to replace the Metrodome.

"This is deep," said Mr. Slinde, a 33-year-old X-ray technician, outside the Park Tavern near Minneapolis on Sunday. He had been handed a recent economics paper that is tattooed with equations and attempts to value, in dollars, the joy and pain Minnesotans get from the Vikings.

"Don't economists spend their time on more serious stuff?" he asked, after thumbing through the paper in the cold.

As fans pack stadiums and couches to watch the National Football League's divisional playoffs this weekend, they care about victory. Economists are tackling a more abstract challenge: putting a price on the emotional benefits of having a pro sports team in town.

The worth of fandom may seem theoretical, or even silly. But it's serious business for teams like the Vikings, who want Minnesotans to help them pay for an $870 million stadium to replace the Hubert H. Humphrey Metrodome in downtown Minneapolis. The Vikings' Metrodome lease runs out in 2011 and the team says it won't sign an extension without a deal for a new stadium.

The team hasn't explicitly said it will bolt without a deal. But it insists the Metrodome cannot support a modern NFL franchise. So, many fans are convinced that without a new stadium, the Vikings will take their quest for football greatness to a warmer state with no Nordic heritage.

Sports teams sell their facilities as economic-development projects that create jobs and generate tax revenue. But a slew of studies have shown that publicly subsidized stadiums—usually paid for by selling bonds and paying the cost and interest with tax revenue—rarely return the money governments put into them. Teams continue to argue, often successfully, that they are worthy of subsidies because they are a source of civic pride and purpose.

But what is that worth? Economists Aju Fenn and John Crooker tried to answer the question in a study published in July 2009 in the Southern Economic Journal.

The two used "contingent valuation methodology," which is a nerdy way of saying they surveyed people and used statistical models to turn the answers into an average price Minnesotans place on the Vikings.

The study was conducted in 2002, and the figures are not adjusted for inflation (or for the recent acquisition of quarterback Brett Favre).

You couldn't touch that money. It's an abstract figure meant to catch everything from the joy of donning blond braids and Vikings horns to the feeling of pride that even nonfans get from living in a "major league" city. In the broadest sense, Mr. Crooker says, "welfare value" represents the worth Minnesotans place on having the Vikings in Minnesota.

It's tough putting a price on feelings, which is why some economists are skeptical of contingent value studies.

"It's not that this is capturing nothing, it's just that it's not legitimate to interpret people's answers as if folks were spending their own money," says Peter Diamond, an MIT economist. He co-authored a 1994 paper titled: "Contingent Valuation: Is Some Number Better Than No Number?"

Mr. Fenn, chair of the department of economics and business at Colorado College, got the idea for his Vikings study 10 years ago, while teaching a sports economics class at the University of St. Thomas in St. Paul. The Vikings had a new owner so then, as now, fans were worried the team would leave.

Other economists have used contingent valuation to measure the social benefits of professional teams. But Mr. Fenn believed fears of a Vikings departure would produce a more accurate tally of the value Minnesotans get from their purple and gold team.

Brian Sand, an ardent Minnesota Vikings fan, in the basement lair where he watches games with his friends.

Minnesotans are no strangers to sports abandonment. In 1960, the Minneapolis Lakers basketball team moved to Los Angeles, a city not known for its lakes. The Minnesota North Stars hockey team became the Dallas Stars in 1993.

So, on a fall evening before a 1999 Monday Night Football game, Mr. Fenn and some students went to a Metrodome parking lot to survey tailgaters. Some fans whipped out their checkbooks to make the point that they would pay on the spot to keep the Vikings in town. (No donations were collected.) The drunker fans got, the more they were willing to pay, Mr. Fenn observed.

Survey questions were fine-tuned by the Metrodome experience. In the 2002 off-season (to minimize in-season emotions), Messrs. Fenn and Crooker mailed 1,400 surveys to households across Minnesota, capturing both fans and nonfans.

The study's figures were based on the mail surveys, which had 30 questions ranging from demographic information to how much time the person discussed the Vikings at home and at work. But the so-called welfare value was generated from a single yes or no question: Would you be willing to pay $X out of your own household budget for the next year to make a new stadium possible? There was one price on each survey (it ranged from $5 to $100).

Mr. Fenn cautions that the $702 million welfare value doesn't mean that helping the Vikings with a stadium would be the best use of the state's tax dollars.

"We're not suggesting that the state of Minnesota act a certain way, or that voters support [a new stadium], or not support it," he says. "We're just point-ing out that the Vikings mean a lot to the average Minnesotan."

You don't need a doctorate in economics to discover that the Vikings mean a lot to Brian Sand, a Minneapolis police officer. He watches games in a basement lair he calls "Jerseys" for the four framed and autographed Vikings jerseys hanging on the walls.

On a recent Sunday evening, Mr. Sand was seated on the Jerseys couch with his fiancée, Emily Johnson, eating chocolate-chip cookies and chuckling as the Vikings' archrival, the Green Bay Packers, lost their championship hopes on an embarrassing fumble.

If he had to, Mr. Sand guesses he would spend up to $500 a year to keep the Vikings around. As a kid, he devoted his Sundays to church and the Vikings, and the team still helps him get through the cold Minnesota winters. "This state is a Viking state," says Mr. Sand.

Mr. Slinde, the X-ray technician, says he'd be out of a hobby if the Vikings left town. No more tailgat-ing in the cold or watching games at bars or at friends' houses. No point in listening to sports talk radio. The only benefit Mr. Slinde can see is that if Vikings left town, he'd save a lot of money.

CONCEPT CHECK

What is the relationship between the existence of professional sports teams in a city or state and the overall emotional well-being of the people in that area? Do you see any flaws with this model?

CASE STUDY #3 — DOES EDUCATION SPENDING MATTER?

If I had one dollar for every time I have heard someone say that the answer to America's education problems is to spend more money, I would have enough money to buy every failing public school in the country. There is just one sticking point: It appears that spending money on underper-forming government schools has no impact on the reading scores of our kids.

How could this be true? Don't we all know that we have to spend money to edu-cate children? Of course, we do. Books cost money. So do teachers and buildings.

The data suggests that reading scores (as the dependent variable) are impacted by multiple independent variables, but that education spending is not one of them. The variables that might matter include the

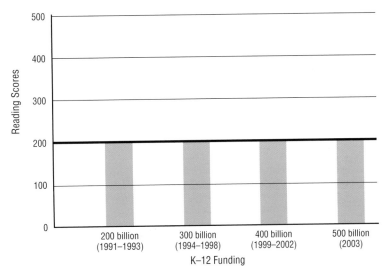

Source: U.S. Department of Education Budget Service and NEAP

amount of time parents spend reading to their children, the amount of time teachers spend teaching children to read, and the overall productivity of the school a child attends. However, simply throwing money at a school is no more likely to impact reading scores than throwing lottery money around will reduce the rate of homelessness.

This should be of paramount concern to taxpayers, parents, and politicians. In 2003, President Bush signed the No Child Left Behind Act. This Act provided for a record increase in federal education spending. In 2001, the federal government spent $35 billion on education. In 2006, federal spending hit $84 billion – a 137% increase in five years.[9] For 2009, the total was $91 billion. When we add in state and local expenditures, over $500 billion was spent on education by 2011 and in later years yet, the results (as we will see in the next chapter) are unchanged. Children are still struggling.

CASE STUDY # 4 — LOWER TAXES = MORE REVENUE

> In the early stages of the state, taxes are light in their incidence, but fetch in a large revenue...As time passes and kings succeed each other, they lose their tribal habits in favor of more civilized ones. Their needs and exigencies grow...owing to the luxury in which they have been brought up. Hence they impose fresh taxes on their subjects... [and] sharply raise the rate of old taxes to increase their yield...But the effects on business of this rise in taxation make themselves felt. For businessmen are soon discouraged by the comparison of their profits with the burden of their taxes... Consequently production falls off, and with it the yield of taxation.
>
> Ibn Khaldun

When my sons were little, I paid them for picking up oranges and acorns in our yard and on our deck. They got $.05 for every orange they picked up off the ground before I mowed and $.01 for every acorn they picked up off the deck in the winter. (Note: This may sound like I am cheap, but you should see how many oranges and acorns they could pick up...)

To teach them about taxation, I told them that on the first dollar they earn, I planned to take away $.10 and give it away to some other child. For the second dollar, I would take away $.25 and for every dollar over $2, I would make them give me $.40.

After staring at me for a moment, they both told me that they did not want to pick up oranges and acorns anymore.

You might think that they reacted this way because they are the sons of a liberty-loving economist. While I

am flattered that you might think that, the real reason they will react negatively to my plan is because they are normal human beings.

Speaking before the Economic Club in New York in December 1962, John F. Kennedy said:

> Our true choice is not between tax reduction, on the one hand, and the avoidance of large federal deficits on the other. It is increasingly clear that an economy hampered by restrictive tax rates will never produce enough revenues to balance our budget just as it will never produce enough jobs or enough profits. Surely the lesson of the last decade is that budget deficits are not caused by wild-eyed spenders but by slow economic growth and periodic recessions and any new recession would break all deficit records. In short, it is a paradoxical truth that tax rates are too high today and tax revenues are too low and the soundest way to raise the revenues in the long run is to cut the rates now.

These turned out to be very prophetic words of wisdom. In 1963, the top tax rate was 91%. It was cut to 70% by 1965 – two years after JFK was assassinated. Tax revenues increased by 33% as the economy expanded by 42%. This was not an atypical result.

During the 1920s, Secretary of Treasury Andrew Mellon persuaded Congress to implement tax cuts on income and investments. From 1921 to 1929 the federal government pushed through six separate tax cuts. In particular, the top income tax rate fell from 73% to 24%. During that time period, tax revenues increased from $719 million to over $1 billion.

In 1981 Ronald Reagan came into office promising to cut income taxes. You may recall from chapter two that President Reagan suggested that government would get more revenue from lower tax rates. From 1981 to 1986 tax rates fell dramatically and total federal revenues increased. The federal government collected just over $599 billion from taxpayers in 1981. By 1989 the amount was over $990 billion.[10]

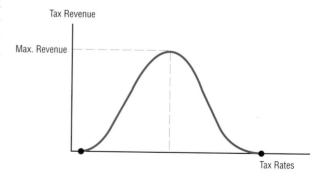

Economist Arthur Laffer became famous for the graph above that shows what Mellon, Kennedy, and Reagan proved to be true.

Notice that if the tax rate equaled 0%, the government would collect no revenue. As taxes increase, revenue begins to increase since few, if any, of us would reduce our work hours, quit our jobs, or alter our behavior in some way that hides income from the IRS.

However, there is a tax rate that will yield maximum revenue for government. What that tax rate is has been debated and empirically studied for more than two decades. Most estimates suggest a rate between 17–23%.[11]

Once the top rate is surpassed, businesses and individuals alike begin to have disincentives to work, create new products, and jobs, and they begin to hide their money by working "off the books" or sheltering their money in untaxed accounts. The result is that the economy suffers from the lack of entrepreneurial undertakings, and the government loses money.

This fact did not keep Barack Obama from campaigning for an increase in income taxes on individuals who earn more than $250,000 per year as well as capital gains taxes.[12] His plan called for using the added revenue from this tax hike to help pay for, among other things, health care for people who do not have insurance and deficit reduction.

The Tax Policy Center estimated that over ten years, Mr. Obama's tax package would *reduce* federal revenues by $2.8 *trillion*.[13] Given what we know about the Laffer Curve, many economists were left wondering what people without health insurance were going to do if a tax increase on more productive Americans lead to less revenue,[14] rather than the greater revenue Mr. Obama argued would appear.[15]

ENDNOTES

1   See "Economists' Grail: A Post-Crash Model" by Mark Whitehouse, *The Wall Street Journal*, November 30, 2010.

2   See "Is the Dismal Science Really a Science?" by Russ Roberts, *The Wall Street Journal*, February 27-28, 2010.

3   See "Kids cram more media hours into a full day" by Bonnie Miller Rubin, *The Orlando Sentinel*, January 21, 2010, p. A8.

4   You will notice on graph 4.6, that it appears that studying zero hours will create a grade of zero. Obviously, this is not so. The graph is drawn this way for exposition purposes. In reality, the intercept term will be greater than zero, meaning that if study hours equaled zero, there would be some grade above zero that would still be earned in most cases.

5   See "Do Girls Speed More Than Boys?" by Joseph B. White and Anjali Athavaley, *The Wall Street Journal*, May 5, 2010.

6   The concept of statistical significance can be reviewed in any basic statistics book.

7   See "Healthy Brew: Beer, It Seems, Is Good for You" by Ken Wells, *The Wall Street Journal,* August 13, 2002.

8   See "100 mph drivers often get just a slap on the wrist" by Scott Powers, *The Orlando Sentinel*, May 15, 2005; and "Driven to Distraction" *The Orlando Sentinel*, February 6, 2005.

9

10 See "Supply Side 'Alchemy' at Work," by Daniel J. Mitchell, *The Wall Street Journal.*

11 *The Flat Tax* by Robert E. Hall and Alvin Rabushka, Hoover Press, 1985 and www.fairtax.org/.

12 See "Cap Gains Taxation: Less Means More" by Allen Sinai, *The Wall Street Journal*, September 21, 2010.

13 See "Would you care for a spending decrease with that tax cut?" by Debra J. Saunders, *The Star Tribune*, August 6, 2008, pg. A13.

14 See "Higher Taxes Won't Reduce the Deficit" by Stephen Moore and Richard Vedder, *The Wall Street Journal*, November 22, 2010.

15 See "You Can't Soak the Rich" by David Ranson, *The Wall Street Journal*, May 20, 2008, pg. A23.

CHAPTER REVIEW

1. In constructing an economic model to explain why North Koreans earn less money each year than South Koreans, what variables would you select? Why?

2. Draw the most likely relationship between the price of gasoline and the sale of large SUVs.

3. What is the relationship between income tax rates and income tax revenue? Why?

4. Why is there a concave relationship between the productivity of workers on a farm and the cost of operating a farm?

Chapter Five

THE ECONOMICS *of* CRIME, POVERTY, *and* EDUCATION

*O*nly the educated are free.

EPICTETUS

THE ECONOMICS OF CRIME

When it comes to the issue of crime, most people would believe that the role of the economist is to explain the cost of crime in terms of the impact on health care costs, productivity, public expenditures, and so forth. For example, a study, by David Anderson of Centre College in the *Journal of Law & Economics*, placed the total annual cost of crime at $1.7 trillion, which is $4,118 per person.[1] While some economists, like Mr. Anderson focus on the direct economic consequence of crime, there are a good number of economists who have also tried to explain the causes of crime.

The decision to commit a criminal act is filled with economic properties. First there is the issue of scarcity. *The Wall Street Journal* once reported that, as bowling shoes became fashionable among teenagers, more young people are stealing bowling shoes from bowling alleys.[2]

The problem of scarcity can help explain this peculiar behavior. Obviously, there is an imbalance between the number of bowling shoes available through legal means and the number of bowling shoes these teenagers have. Stealing them is a way of closing this imbalance. The teenaged thieves are also self-interested. They are not stealing the shoes for the betterment of mankind, but rather the betterment of their wardrobe.

There is also an opportunity cost associated with this act. Instead of stealing the shoes, the teenagers could offer to buy them or wear some other type of shoe. Are the teenagers rational? If the benefits of stealing the shoes are greater than the opportunity cost, plus the direct cost, then stealing is rational. This is where the discussion of crime, as an economic act, becomes interesting.

The landmark examination of the economics of crime is set forth in a paper by Nobel laureate Gary Becker.[3] Becker argued that, for the criminal, the cost of crime could be broken up into two parts.

We have already mentioned opportunity cost as one of the costs incurred. Upon closer examination, we find that one of the major reasons why people engage in criminal activity is because the opportunity cost of doing so is very small.

Notice that you rarely read about a successful accountant who robs grocery stores on her way home from the office. For people with high levels of education and training, the opportunity cost of crime is quite large. To be criminals, they would have to be willing to run the risk of forgoing their next-best choice. If the next-best choice is accounting or engineering, it makes little sense to don a gorilla mask and start knocking off the local supermarkets.

On the other hand, the evidence indicates that the second-best choice for criminals is one that usually does not pay as well. Most criminals are unskilled and uneducated. Legal means do not pay as well or offer much of a career. To a high school drop-out with no vocational training, becoming an armed robber might seem like the most logical occupation.

CRIME AND PROBABILITY THEORY

To Becker, the second, and far larger, cost is the direct cost of criminal activity. The direct cost includes not only the cost of bullets, ski masks, and gas for the getaway car, but the probability of capture and conviction, the probability of spending time in jail, the length of the sentence, and the probability of parole.[4] Notice the world probability. You should recall from chapter one that when a person commits a criminal act, there is a probability between zero and 100% that he or she will end up in prison.[5] Let's look at burglary as an example of how probability theory works.

Edward Rubenstein found that, "Only 7% of U.S. burglaries result in an arrest. Of those arrested, 87% are prosecuted. Of those prosecuted, 79% are convicted. Of those convicted, a mere 25% are sent to prison (most are paroled)."[6] If we multiply all of these probabilities, we find that the potential burglar faces only a *1.2% chance of going to prison each time he or she creeps into a house looking for a new laptop computer.*

CONCEPT CHECK

John McCain once sponsored legislation that would outlaw gambling on college sports. Where does probability theory enter into someone's decision to violate laws like this?

Shutterstock © Daniel Padavona, 2011.

Once in prison, the average unlucky burglar will stay there about 13 months, but since the burglar will stay out of jail *over 98% of the time*, the expected cost of each act of burglary — to the burglar — is only 4.8 days.

You can see the dilemma for law enforcement officials. Incarceration for 4.8 days is a very small price to pay for the chance to pilfer thousands of dollars in goodies. One has to wonder what would happen if the average burglar was also good at probability theory. It also makes one wonder why more professional statisticians are not out looking for houses to burgle! With all this in mind, we can see how the discipline of economics can begin to explain the economic process of opting for crime as a vocation. By using economic models, we can move from observing criminal behavior to explaining the *cause* of criminal behavior.

THE CAUSES OF CRIME – AND WHY CRIME RATES HAVE FALLEN

Ask 100 people on the sidewalk what causes crime, and you will get close to 100 different answers. For every answer you get, there will probably follow some theory as to how America can reduce our out-of-control crime problem. There is only one small sticking point: America's crime rate has actually been falling for the past several years and, in 2005, reached it lowest level since 1973.[7]

This leaves us with two questions that must be answered: First, what do economists know about the causes of crime? And what do we know about why there has been less crime over time?

Numerous studies by economists, criminologists, sociologists, and other social scientists have been done with no one definitive independent variable having been discovered as the most statistically significant predictor of criminal behavior. However, many factors have been discovered to have played a causal role in the crime rate. The research indicates that drug and alcohol abuse, having

Source: Bureau of Justice

FIGURE 5.1

FIGURE 5.2

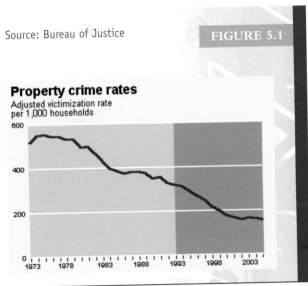

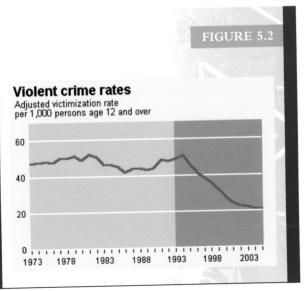

been the victim of child abuse, or residing in a decaying community and a weak economy can lead to higher incidence of crime.[8]

On the other hand, active community policing programs, and high levels of educational achievement are significant predictors of lower levels of criminal activity. Surprisingly, the research does not yet support any causal link between the crime rate and violence in the movies or on television.[9] Nor does current research support the notion that economic growth brings down the crime rate.

During the 2007-2009 Recession, many people were afraid that a rising unemployment rate would lead to a surge in property and violent crime. It did not happen. Instead, the trend toward lower crime continued unabated. According to the FBI's Uniform Crime Reports, homicide dropped 10% nationwide in the first six months of 2009; violent crime was down 4.4%, and car thefts fell by 19%.[10]

While none of the aforementioned variables – or the relationship between the variables and crime – should come as a surprise to anyone, there are some that have recently been investigated by economists that yield some interesting results.

THE ECONOMIC IMPORTANCE OF FATHERS

For years the rate of divorce and out-of-wedlock births has been a source of concern to social scientists, but only recently have we had any data to articulate why all of America should be worried about the lack of fathers in the lives of many of our children.

> The lack of a father presence in their daughter's lives has been linked to a increased risk for those teenagers of pregnancy. The U.S. Department of Justice, Bureau of Justice Statistics has reported, and Louis Sullivan, former cabinet member of former President Bush, has confirmed, that 70% of the juveniles in state reform institutions grew up in single- or no-parent situations; additionally, 72% of adolescent murderers, 60% of rapists and 70% of the long term prisoners in America grew up without a father in the home. According to a recent report of the U.S. Department of Health and Human Services, children in father-absent families have a much higher risk of drug and alcohol abuse, mental illness, suicide, poor educational performance, teen pregnancy, and criminality.[11]

These numbers – and others like them – have helped spawn a new movement in America to make fathers and

Shutterstock © Flashon Studio, 2011.

mothers more aware of the critical role dads play in the development of children.[12] Thanks to statistical evidence, the role of men has risen above sperm donor to one of paramount importance in reducing America's crime rate.

DO MORE GUNS EQUAL LESS CRIME?

> The most foolish mistake we could possibly make would be to allow the subject races to possess arms. History shows that all conquerors who have allowed their subject races to carry arms have prepared their own downfall by so doing.
>
> Adolf Hitler

Rosie O'Donnell would not like John R. Lott much. Ms. O'Donnell, a vocal anti-gun advocate, has, on many occasions, called for a ban on guns. She is not alone. Many

Americans view the existence of guns as the major cause of crime in our nation. The problem is that the research does not support this opinion.

John Lott is a professor of economics at The University of Chicago and the author of a controversial book, *More Guns, Less Crime: Understanding Crime and Gun Control Laws.*[13] Professor Lott's work amounts to the most thorough criminological study ever performed on the relationship between concealed weapons laws and the crime rate.

Throughout the nineteenth century, "the right to keep and bear arms" meant exactly what it said: The right to carry a gun was protected just as firmly as the right to own a gun. Some states, particularly in the South, enforced laws against carrying handguns concealed, but the right to openly carry was almost universally respected.

By the 1970s, however, the right to carry had been restricted in most jurisdictions. America was well on the way to treating guns like cigarettes: permissible in private, but completely banned from public spaces.

In 1988, however, Florida initiated a national trend by enacting a "shall issue" handgun permit law, allowing any adult who has a clean record and has taken safety training to obtain a permit to carry a concealed handgun for protection. Now over half the states have similar laws.

Lott collected data from every one of the 3,054 counties in the United States over an 18-year period and examined changes in the rates of nine different types of crime. He also accounted for the effects of dozens of other variables, including variations in arrest rates, in the age and racial composition of a county's population, in national crime rates, and in changes made to gun-control laws, including the adoption of waiting periods. Lott's findings show that concealed weapons laws significantly reduce violent crime. On average, the murder rate falls by 10%, that of rape by 3%, and aggravated assault by 6%.

While crime begins to fall off immediately, the benefits of concealed handgun laws take about three years to be fully felt. This is not surprising: In most states, a flood of applications occurs in the first few weeks the law is on the books, followed by a gradual rise in the percentage of the population that has acquired permits. The larger the percentage of the population with permits, the greater the drop in crime, with the percentage ranging from 1-5%.

Apparently, while concealed handgun laws do not reduce the appetite criminals have for other people's property; they do encourage the more rational subset to acquire it in ways that do not put their own lives at risk. And everyone, not just gun carriers, benefits from the reduced crime rate, since aggressors cannot know which potential victims might have a concealed weapon.[14]

In 2010, the United States Supreme Court appeared to agree with Lott's findings, in a ruling where the Court said that the Second Amendment to the Constitution extended nationwide and that federal judges could strike down state laws that prohibit the carrying of firearms.[15]

THE ABORTED CRIME WAVE?

Steven Levitt, an economics professor at the University of Chicago, and John Donohue, a Stanford University law professor, recently completed one of the most controversial studies on crime that has come along in years. Messrs. Levitt and Donohue argue that the legalization of abortion in the early 1970s played a key role – perhaps explaining as much as 50% – in the declining crime rate of the 1990s.[17]

Between 1992 and 1999, murders in the U.S. fell by 35%, robberies fell 39%, and violent crimes fell 26%. Many people speculated that the booming economy might have caused the decline. Others argued that a new "zero tolerance" approach in places like New York City was the primary cause of the lower crime rates. According to Levitt:

> The theoretical justification for our argument rests on two simple assumptions: 1) Legalized abortion leads to fewer "unwanted" babies being born, and 2) unwanted babies are more likely to suffer abuse and neglect and are, therefore, at an increased risk for criminal involvement later in life.
>
> The first assumption, that abortion reduces the number of unwanted children, is true virtually by definition.
>
> The second assumption, that unwanted children are at increased risk for criminal involvement, is supported by three decades of academic research. If one accepts these two assumptions, then a direct mechanism, by which the legalization of abortion can reduce crime, has been established. At that point, the question merely becomes: Is the magnitude of the impact large or small?
>
> Our preliminary research suggests that the effect of abortion legalization is large. According to our estimates, as much as one-half of the remarkable decline in crime in the 1990s may be attributable to the legalization of abortion. We base our conclusions on four separate data analyses. First, we demonstrate that crime rates began to fall 18 years after the landmark Supreme Court decision Roe vs. Wade legalized abortion across the nation, just the point at which babies born under legalized abortion would be reaching the peak adolescent crime years. Second, we show that the five states that legalized abortion in 1970 — three years before Roe vs. Wade — saw crime begin to decrease roughly three years earlier than the rest of the nation. This is a bit more convincing to me but still far from conclusive.
>
> Third, we demonstrate that states with high abortion rates in the mid-1970s have had much greater crime decreases in the 1990s than states that had low abortion rates in the 1970s. This relationship holds true even when we take into account changes in the size of prison populations, number of police, poverty rates, measures of the economy, changes in welfare generosity, and other changes in fertility.

> This is the evidence that really starts to be convincing, in my opinion. Fourth, we show that the abortion related drop in crime is occurring only for those who today are under the age of 25. This is exactly the age group we would expect to be affected by the legalization of abortion in the early 1970s. That is where our paper stops. Our paper is a descriptive exercise attempting to explain why crime fell.

The implications of this research cannot be understated. One look at the Internet on this subject will reveal dozens of hysterical, emotional, and biblical responses to the work of Levitt and Donohue. For public policymakers the possibility that aborting unborn children can dramatically lower crime rates presents an interesting subset of questions. Should the government offer to fund all abortions on demand? Should the government target high-crime areas and offer to pay for abortions? Should the private sector – hard hit by property crimes, shoplifting and high health care costs – offer to subsidize abortions?

From a pure cost-benefit approach, paying for abortions would make sense. After all, an abortion costs a few hundred dollars, but criminals inflict far more damage on the nation than that. On the other hand, some would argue that abortion itself is a crime and therefore the cost-benefit analysis might miss some important calculations. If we measure cost in pure dollar terms and do not include the social or moral cost (however we wish to define that), does the cost-benefit approach fall short? That is left for you and other citizens to decide.

THE ECONOMICS OF POVERTY

In chapter one, we saw that every economy must answer questions about what will be produced, how the good and services will be produced, and for whom the goods and services will be produced. The "for whom" part of the equation can present a tremendous set of difficulties for a nation, because in every country there are some people who have access to a tremendous array of goods and services while others find themselves going to bed hungry and cold on any given night. In this section of chapter five, we will utilize economic models to explain what causes poverty and what society can do about the problem of poverty.

WHO ARE THE POOR?

Before we can start a discussion of the causes of poverty, it is important that we first examine data pertaining to who is poor in America. The U.S. Census Bureau is largely responsible for providing data on poverty rates on an annual basis. The following table summarizes a recent threshold for poverty. A person or family is considered to be poor if he, she, or it falls below these thresholds. The thresholds are considered to reflect the minimum amount a person or family would have to earn each year to meet the most basic needs with respect to food, clothing, shelter, medical attention, and so forth.

For a family of four, the poverty threshold was $22,050 in 2010. It should be noted that when the Census Bureau counts income, it does not include capital gains and non-cash benefits such as public housing, Medicaid, and food stamps.[18] Over 70% of our poor people have one or more cars, a telephone, and a washing machine. Over 90% of poor people in the U.S. have a refrigerator, stove, and color television,[19] and 46% own their own homes.[20] With these figures in mind, we turn to the number of people and composition of the people who are poor in America.

The Census Bureau is not the only agency that measures poverty. The following table illustrates the "official" poverty level according to the Department of Health and Human Services.

As one might imagine if we have multiple agencies coming up with divergent poverty thresholds – and if those agencies do not count non-income wealth like private property, one can end up with a skewed view of what actually constitutes poverty in America.

In 2010 the Census Bureau concluded that 13.2% of the American population lived below the poverty line. Eighteen percent of children lived in poverty that year.

TRENDS IN THE POVERTY DATA

During the 2008 presidential campaign, Barack Obama repeatedly criticized the economic record of George Bush. Figure 5.4 illustrates why Mr. Obama felt he had a legitimate complaint. During the early part of Mr. Bush's administration, the U.S. economy was experiencing the aftermath of a recession. By the 2008 elections, the U.S. was in the middle one of the longest recessions we have ever experienced. Whenever an economy experiences an economic downturn, there is going to inevitably be an increase in factory closings, an increase in unemployment, and a natural upswing in the overall poverty rate.

There is some good news on the poverty front. People who are born poor do not have to stay poor if economic conditions are favorable to upward mobility. You will notice that for much of the 1980s and 1990s, the rate of poverty fell in America. The pro-economic growth policies of Ronald Reagan and Bill Clinton helped create this trend, which saw more and more Americans climb the economic ladder.

One 17-year study of lifetime earnings by the Federal Reserve Bank of Dallas found that a mere 5% of people who started out in the lowest 20% of income-earners stayed there over that time period.[21] As the table below illustrates, there is a great deal of positive movement in total income levels for poorer Americans.[22] This is due in large part to the economic and geographic mobility of our society and the incentives created by the quasi free-market

FIGURE 5.3

THE 2010 POVERTY GUIDELINES FOR THE 48 CONTIGUOUS STATES AND THE DISTRICT OF COLUMBIA

Persons in family	Poverty guideline
1	$10,830
2	14,570
3	18,310
4	22,050
5	25,790
6	29,530
7	33,270
8	37,010
For families with more than 8 persons, add $3,740 for each additional person.	

Source: The Federal Register

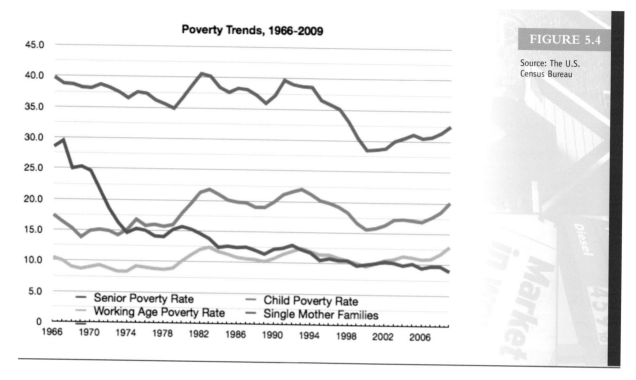

Poverty Trends, 1966-2009

FIGURE 5.4

Source: The U.S.
Census Bureau

— Senior Poverty Rate   — Child Poverty Rate
— Working Age Poverty Rate   — Single Mother Families

system. When people see that with education, training, and hard work, it is possible to move out of poverty, many people will undertake the necessary steps to attempt to strive for success. Some might move into the lower middle class. Others might become firmly middle class, while others can emerge from poverty to become rich.[23]

It is important to note that such economic mobility is fairly exclusive to the United States. In most nations around the world, poverty rates dwarf what we consider poverty in America. In Mexico, an estimated 40 million people live on less than $2 per day, while globally over 50% of the planet's more than six billion people live on less than $2 per day. In countries like Haiti, Benin, Liberia, Ethiopia, and Somalia, military dictatorships, the institution of slavery, and the lack of economic freedom have combined to create annual incomes of a few hundred dollars per year and life expectancy rates that would be appalling to the average poor American who has access to subsidized housing, and charities that provide food, Christmas gifts, and medical care.[24]

U.S. Income Mobility

Percentage change in median income from 1996 to 2005, by 1996 income quintile, in 2005 dollars:

Income level

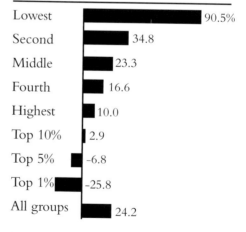

Lowest	90.5%
Second	34.8
Middle	23.3
Fourth	16.6
Highest	10.0
Top 10%	2.9
Top 5%	-6.8
Top 1%	-25.8
All groups	24.2

Source: Treasury Dept. 2007

SUGGESTED CLASSROOM DEBATE

Watch the movie entitled, *The Pursuit of Happyness*. How realistic do you think it is for someone to achieve what Chris Gardner achieved, starting from where he did? Why?

THE CAUSES OF POVERTY
IN AMERICA

If we use the concept of economic modeling to explain poverty in America, we would select annual income as our dependent variable. What independent variables should we select? This is where a tremendous debate has entered into the picture. While some variables make perfect sense – educational achievement, years of work experience, age, resource endowments, family size, labor market conditions, and immigration trends come to mind – other variables have recently been suggested that have traditionally been overlooked by economists. Some of the less obvious variables include private vs. public school education, government policies to help the poor, and the existence of slavery.

For years (centuries?) economists have known that *education* and poverty are inextricably linked. Simply put, a high school drop-out should not expect to earn a six-figure salary over his or her lifetime. Some might, but it would not be a wise use of probability theory to bank on becoming rich after leaving the ninth grade. In reality, one of the biggest components of the income gap is explained by differences in human capital acquisition.

Unfortunately for the poorest and least educated Americans, this trend is accelerating as our "new economy" continues to pick up steam. As technology and the ability to work with technology continues to be a pervasive force in our economy, those individuals – from auto mechanics to aeronautical engineers – who are best suited to utilize technology will be the individuals who earn the highest incomes.[25]

Age and work experience also play a role in explaining income differences and thus poverty rates. People who are impoverished tend to be younger and less experienced

individuals. Over time, greater work experience – especially if work experience is not frequently interrupted or truncated by prolonged periods of unemployment – is a key to rising income.[26] Poorer people tend to have longer periods between jobs, minimal work experience, and thus a lower lifetime earnings profile.

Resource endowments and *labor market conditions* in which a person operates also contribute to differences in earnings. Tiger Wood's children will probably not end up poor. The daughter of a single mother on welfare, on an American-Indian reservation in Montana, probably will be poor as an adult. This is due to differences in initial resource endowments (land, capital, and so forth) and differences in access to resources (schooling) over time. Yet, there are exceptions to this more common outcome.

A good friend of mine grew up desperately poor in our hometown of Hugo, Oklahoma. Through an incredible work ethic, he went on to graduate with a degree in economics from the University of Oklahoma in only three years and eventually Columbia Law School. Today he is a highly successful and affluent attorney in Los Angeles. He had virtually no resources to speak of as a youngster except a strong desire to emerge from poverty. While he is a statistical outlier, he is also an example that lack of resources need not be an unalterable ticket to poverty.

With respect to *labor market conditions*, the type of employment opportunities a person works toward or finds most available can also explain why some people are so poor. In the Great Plains, rural Americans face much higher rates of poverty because of unfavorable supply and demand conditions. With very few businesses moving into Nebraska, eastern Montana and the Dakotas, there is very little demand for labor just east of the Rockies.

This is where *geographic mobility* and personal choices can play a role. Where labor market conditions are creating very low annual earnings, you will see higher poverty

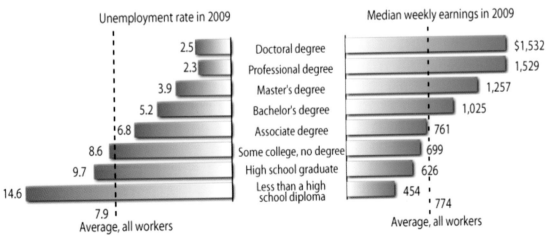

Education pays

Source: Bureau of Labor Statistics, Current Population Survey

CONCEPT CHECK

In the aftermath of Hurricane Katrina, New Orleans mayor, Ray Nagin expressed frustration with the number of Hispanic people that were coming into his city to work in the area of cleanup and construction. At one point Mr. Nagin said, "How do I ensure that New Orleans is not overrun with Mexican workers?"[29] Based on what you have learned about poverty, can you provide a more economically sensible quote that Mr. Nagin could have used?

levels. If a person cannot, or will not, seek chances to move out of a poorer area – or seek the proper education and training to move out of poverty within that region – chronic poverty can persist from one generation to the next. A child born near Silicon Valley has a better chance to see the actual gains from becoming educated than a child in the inner city of Philadelphia.

Speaking of geographic mobility and choices, for years economists and non-economists alike have wondered whether immigration plays a role in explaining poverty in America. The theory is that the more immigrants we have, the larger will be the supply of labor and the lower wage rates will be. To an extent the research bears this theory out. Recent evidence suggests that the most recent wave of undocumented immigrants did cause downward pressure on wage rates for the most unskilled and uneducated Americans.[27]

However, the overwhelming evidence indicates that most unskilled immigrants take jobs that many Americans simply won't take. These jobs include, but are not limited to, migrant work in agricultural fields, clothing production, landscaping, home construction and meat processing plants. Moreover, immigration studies have repeatedly shown that immigrants actually help reduce poverty not only by creating jobs in America but by stimulating the demand for U.S. goods. Immigrants tend to have higher savings rates, better educational achievement, and an entrepreneurial spirit that has led to more jobs and income for America rather than less.

PUBLIC SCHOOLS AND POVERTY

Today, I can't recommend in good conscience, that an African-American family send their children to the Minneapolis public schools. The facts are irrefutable: These schools are not preparing our children to compete in the world.

Louis King,
former member of the Minneapolis School Board

Over the past several years, economists have begun to cast a larger net out into the ocean of variables that might explain persistent poverty in America. In particular, we have wondered why, despite the large gains made by black Americans[30] the poverty rate (25.8% in 2009) among black people remains higher than any other demographic group.[31] Of course, high rates of poverty are not exclusive to black people in our country. American Indians, whites in the rural south and Appalachia and Hispanics also find economic hardship at higher rates than most Americans.

Economists have now begun to look at educational choices, government policies to reduce poverty, and the institution of slavery as potential explanatory variables.

EDUCATIONAL QUALITY

We may be putting millions of children into a lifetime of financial struggles because of the way our government education model has been established in America.

First, American K-12 teachers rank second in the world in annual salary – falling only behind Germany.[32] In 2007 the average salary for an American K-12 teacher is $34.06 per hour – compared to $25.08 per hour for the average white-collar worker.[33] The U.S. also ranks at the top of the world in total annual spending, per student, on education, with more than $10,000 per student, per year in expenditures.[34] Despite all of the money poured into public schools, the results are not statistically impressive.

National Geographic recently conducted a poll that uncovered the fact that half of the 18-24 year old Americans surveyed could not find New York on a map. Eleven percent *could not find the United States* on a map.[35] In the most recent international tests given to 15-year old kids from the 30 countries that make up the Organization for Economic Development and Cooperation, American kids finished 25th in math and 21st in science, prompting President Obama to say, "Incompetent teachers must be identified and weeded out."[36]

Microsoft founder, Bill Gates has gone so far as to argue that America's high schools are "ruining the lives of millions of Americans every year."[37]

Perhaps Mr. Gates will take comfort in knowing that in one school in California, *7-10 year old students* were recently given a test where they were asked to rate the following activities according to how often they experienced the thought or emotion[38]:

"Touching my private parts too much."
"Thinking about sex when I don't want to."
"Not trusting people because they might want sex."
"Having sex feelings in my body."

Then again, maybe this type of test is not what Mr. Gates needs kids to take to make them better suited to be computer software designers some day.

Mr. Gates would also most likely find it somewhat disturbing that between 2001 and 2005, approximately 2,750 teachers nationwide had their credentials revoked, denied, surrendered or sanctioned for engaging in sexual misconduct as SAT scores reached their lowest level of the decade in 2008.[39]

Another fact concerning America's government school system is that the overall quality of teachers is lower than in most other developed nations.[40] When economists look at requirements associated with receiving a degree in education; a teaching certificate and a bachelor's degree in education,[41] the U.S. pales in comparison to the much more rigorous standards expected of teachers in places like Finland, Korea, and other industrialized nations.[42] In the United States, 23% of new teachers come from the top third of their graduating class in college. Only 14% of new teachers in high-poverty schools come from the top third of their class. In Singapore, South Korea, and Finland 100% of new teachers come from the top third of their class.[43] Guess where Singapore, South Korea, and Finland rank in terms of educational quality?

When you combine the entrenched power of the teachers union with rigid rules that make it almost impossible to fire tenured teachers – and the bureaucracy that comes from the growth in administrative jobs – it is much more likely that you will see a higher degree of failure coming from government schools than you would from private schools that do not face such obstacles to effective teaching.[44]

This is not to say that some teachers in some schools aren't doing an incredibly productive job under difficult circumstances. It also does not absolve parents of the responsibility for their child's education. There are numerous outlets on the internet and in the private sector for helping children learn. Garage sales and thrift stores have books that are inexpensive – and libraries are abundant. Studies show that a parent's education achievement and involvement plays a significant role in determining the educational outcomes of children.[45]

However, in state after state "consumers" of government education are not getting the value they expect from their tax dollars – even when they participate in pre-school programs designed to give children a head start on their education.[46]

SCHOOL CHOICE

So, why don't parents – especially poorer parents whose children are more likely to be in bad schools – simply send their kids somewhere else? After all, 2,000 of America's high schools – less than 15% of the total – are responsible for producing 81% of all Native American dropouts, 73% of all African-American dropouts, and 66% of all Hispanic dropouts.[47]

Suppose you an American living in Orlando with a school-age child whom you want to see get the best education possible. In Orlando, like all other large cities in America, you have three predominant choices – private school, home school, or public school. If you are poor, the chances of your being able to afford a private school education is extraordinarily low, if not equal to zero.

Private school and home schooling – which studies show creates the highest SAT scores[48] and overall academic achievement[49] – is also probably not a viable option. As a poor person in Orlando – or just about anywhere else, you would not only be hard-pressed to afford time away from work to educate your child, but you might also be relatively uneducated, which means you might not be qualified to teach your child.

That leaves most poor Americans with one real choice – the public, or government-run, school system. If your school system ranks at or near the bottom in test scores, reading and math achievement, college placement, or graduation rates, it might lead you to consider sending your child to a public school in the suburbs where you have heard that the schools are much better. The problem is, in much of America *you do not have the right to send your child to the public school of your choice*.[50] Instead, you must send your child to the public school that is in your district – even if you don't want to. There are a few exceptions for magnet or charter schools, but by and large the public school system in your district has a functional monopoly over your child.

What if, by law, there was only one cell phone in America? Would the company provide the best product at the best prices, or would you get declining quality and higher prices over time?

In Detroit, over $11,000 in taxpayer money is spent per child each year – and the city sees only 25% of its students graduate from high school.[51] Less than half of New York City's students graduate even though spending per pupil is highest in America at over $14,000 per year. Meanwhile Catholic and other private schools spend far less in each city and often have graduation rates above 90%.[52]

Should they have a choice?

PISA 2003 Mean Scores
in Mathematics
OECD Countries

Finland	544	Germany	503
Korea	542	Ireland	503
Netherlands	538	Slovak Republic	498
Japan	534	Norway	495
Canada	532	Luxembourg	493
Belgium	529	Poland	490
Switzerland	527	Hungary	490
Australia	524	Spain	485
New Zealand	523	**United States**	483
Czech Republic	516	Portugal	466
Iceland	515	Italy	466
Denmark	514	Greece	445
France	511	Turkey	423
Sweden	509	Mexico	385
Austria	506		

Source: OECD, *Learning for Tommorow's World: First Results from PISA 2003*

Which group of people has the fewest educational choices? If you say poor people, you are correct. Now let us ask which race of people has the highest poverty rates? If you say African-Americans, you are right again. If we now ask if there is a connection between the lack of school choice for a majority of African-Americans and the poverty rate of African-Americans, we find one immutable conclusion: Many black people in America today are largely trapped by a school system that has few incentives to innovate and even fewer competitors.[52]

Without fear that black parents will pull their children out of horrible schools, why should teachers or administrators in these schools seek to improve the quality of education in Orlando?

In Florida, among the 68 schools to which the state recently gave failing grades, the vast majority were in predominantly poor neighborhoods with mostly black residents. Is it any wonder that black families from Miami, Milwaukee and Washington, D.C., recently fought to gain *vouchers* so that children in the some of the most expensive – and worst – school districts in America could leave for better schools in the private sector?[53] Is it at all surprising that minorities now make up 15% of the more than 2 million home-schooled children, or that home-schooling has seen a 77% increase from 1999 to 2007?[54]

CAN VOUCHERS REDUCE POVERTY?

In 2002, Florida governor Jeb Bush signed into law the first state-wide school voucher program in the United States.

A voucher is the assignment of a specified amount of tax dollars to a parent to use to send a child to the private school of their choice. In addition to the voucher program, Florida instituted a grading system for all government schools that assigned schools a grade of 'A' through 'F' based on the results of an annual test given to all students. Up to $3,500 of private-school tuition, plus books and transportation costs, were paid by the Florida Corporate Income Tax Credit Scholarship Program, which let businesses divert a portion of their state taxes to these school-choice vouchers.

If a school got an 'F' grade two years in a row, parents could either apply for a voucher, or send their child to another government school of their choice.

About 55,000 people applied for the scholarships, which were available to children who qualify for free or reduced-price lunches in public schools.

In 2006 the Supreme Court of Florida ruled the voucher program unconstitutional, ending, for the time being, part of Florida's experiment with greater competition in the market for education.[55] However, in 2010 the state of Florida expanded the Tax Credit Scholarship Program – a program that allows businesses to donate money to low-income families who seek private schooling.[56]

The voucher movement has gained significant momentum over the past several years. In Arizona, Utah, Georgia, Ohio and other states, parents have taken to the streets and to the voting booth to demand their right to shop around for good teachers.[57]

While this struggle has met with mixed results, economists like Harvard's Caroline Hoxby have helped lend scientific support to school choice by uncovering the statistical impact of choice on public schools.

Dr. Hoxby, and others, has found that there is a statistically significant positive relationship between school choice and the overall test scores of public school kids that *do not change schools*. This means that as more and more kids opt to use vouchers in places like Milwaukee, Wisconsin, the government schools – faced with the Darwinian choice of adapt or die off – have opted to improve the overall quality of instruction in order to keep kids from fleeing.[58] By 2008, Milwaukee Public Schools had lost almost 10,000 students whose parents opted for educational freedom.[59]

This makes intuitive sense. After all, it is the prospect of losing customers to places like Crispers and Panera Bread that prompted McDonalds to roll out healthier foods.

Not surprisingly, teachers unions all over the country have put up vehement opposition to school choice. And why not? What inferior competitor ever welcomes competition? It would be economically irrational for teachers in government schools to embrace competition unless they know they would be picked over the private schools. The current waiting list in America for enrollment in charter schools is over 350,000 as these schools continue to dramatically outperform traditional public schools.[61]

The fact that the unions fight against competition is all economists need to know about what government school teachers think about the quality of the product they put out. When Michelle Rhee was appointed chancellor of Washington, D.C.'s notoriously horrible public schools, she fired 241 teachers and put 737 more on notice for being rated "minimally effective." The result? Test scores began to improve by double-digits and the teachers in the District of Columbia lobbied for Ms. Rhee's resignation.[62]

What remains to be seen is whether poorer Americans – and in particular, black and Hispanic Americans – will continue to gain the freedom they have in all other markets. So far, African-American and Hispanic parents have been the most vocal supporters of vouchers.[63] That is because the only way their kids will be able to get out of poverty is if they can get the same educational choices that richer Americans have always enjoyed.[64]

THE WAR ON POVERTY

> To be dependent is to be degraded. Men may pity us, but they cannot respect us.
>
> Proclamation at a convention for black Americans, New York, 1848

One hundred years after Abraham Lincoln signed the Emancipation Proclamation – freeing most of the slaves in the United States, the United States Congress passed the Civil Rights Act. It was around the same time that President Lyndon Johnson accelerated the battle against poverty that began with the administration of Franklin D. Roosevelt.[66]

Roosevelt was responsible for passing legislation that created a taxpayer-funded social welfare network that included, but was not limited to, welfare checks paid to widowed mothers. Roosevelt meant for such welfare to be temporary. He was afraid that welfare would "become the subtle destroyer of the human spirit."

What he did not know is that there is nothing as permanent as a temporary government program. Since the mid-1960s the federal government has spent almost $9 trillion dollars attempting to rid our nation of poverty.[67]

In 1960 only 21% of black children grew up in female-headed households. By 2006, 65% did.[68] The number of black children born out of wedlock was 28% in 1965. Today the figure is almost 70%. By the late 1990s, the crime rate, divorce rate, high school drop-out rate, and poverty rate had increased for black Americans – and did so well into this decade as well. In the same time period, life expectancy decreased.

While no one can argue that no poor person – of any race – has benefited from social welfare spending, the question for economists centers on the role of government in creating higher poverty rates by damaging the incentives people have to work and be creative.

The Heritage Foundation's research indicates that the major underlying factors producing child poverty in the United States are welfare dependence and single parenthood. Race per se is not a factor in producing child poverty; race alone does not directly increase or decrease the probability that a child will be poor. When a black child is compared with a white child raised in identical circumstances, both children will have the same probability of living in poverty. Similarly, when whites with high levels of single parenthood and welfare dependence (matching those typical in the black community) are compared to blacks, the poverty rates for both groups are nearly identical.

In 1996 Congress created the Personal Responsibility and Work Opportunity Reconciliation Act, which President Clinton signed into law. Since 1996 studies show a direct link between setting time limits on welfare benefits and a reduction in welfare rolls and poverty rates.[69] In fact, in August 1996 12.2 million people were on the welfare rolls. By December 2006 the number was 4.1 million – a decline of 67%.[70] The results of welfare reform were particularly significant in reducing dependence among black Americans – who now make up 37.2% of all AFDC payments – compared to 38.8% of payments going to white families.

It is interesting to note that welfare reform alone does not account for the economic gains some states have made over the past several years. Taxes matter, too.

The ten states with the lowest tax burdens saw a 13.7% drop in poverty during the last decade, while the ten states with the highest tax burden saw poverty rates increase by 3%.[71]

CONCEPT CHECK

In 1920 the state of Florida spent $8.26 million on the education of white children while spending $643,701 on black children.[65] Could that partly explain the higher drop-out rates of black Floridians today? Why or why not?

It makes economic sense – in any war against poverty and welfare dependence – to not only offer negative incentives of time limits and lower aid allowances but also positive incentives of being allowed to keep more of ones earnings after they leave the welfare rolls.

SLAVERY AND POVERTY

> Every race has a soul, and the soul of that race finds expression in its institutions, and to kill those institutions is to kill the soul. No people can profit or be helped under institutions which are not the outcome of their own character.
>
> Edward Blyden (1903)

Undoubtedly you have heard or read about the recent debate concerning the causes of earnings differences between black and white Americans. This debate is poised to create one of; if not the most, controversial socio-economic battles our nation has seen in years. The issue of course is the role that institutionalized slavery might have played in exacerbating the problem of poverty for black Americans who are alive today.

For black and white Americans alike, this is an emotionally painful and philosophically charged issue.

On one side of the debate you have Americans – black and white – who argue that the existence of slavery helped build the country but that the slaves were not compensated for their efforts as a free individual would be. To proponents of reparations for slavery, the contention is that the descendents of slaves have also suffered from the legacy of slavery.

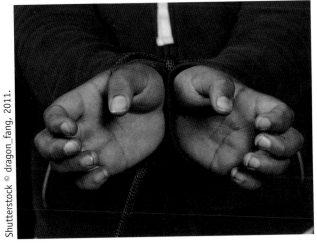

Shutterstock © dragon_fang, 2011.

Did these lead to lower earnings for African-Americans today?

This legacy, it is argued, includes Jim Crow laws, poll taxes, systemic labor market and educational discrimination, and segregation as well as the separation of the races in buses, hotels, restaurants, and other facilities. The legacy of slavery, therefore, has impacted the social, economic, and political lives of black Americans long after the Emancipation Proclamation was signed. Therefore, proponents argue, current black Americans should receive monetary compensation for the government's compliance in allowing slavery to exist until 1865 and quasi-slavery to exist from 1865 until the passage of the Civil Rights Act in 1964.[72]

On the other side of the fence, you have black and white Americans who share the view of Henry Hyde (R-Illinois) who once said, "The notion of collective guilt for what people did 200-plus years ago, that this generation should pay a debt for that generation, is an idea whose time has gone. I never owned a slave. I never oppressed anybody. I don't know that I should have to pay for someone who did own slaves generations before I was born."

Walter Williams and Thomas Sowell – two prominent African-American economists – have gone so far as to argue that today's black Americans are the indirect beneficiaries of their ancestors' enslavement. This argument is based on the fact that if we compare the economic well-being of blacks in Africa to the well-being of blacks in America, there is no question that black people in America are better off. In fact, as Dr. Williams points out, if black people in America were thought of as their own nation, the total income of the 35 million blacks that live in this nation would make black Americans the 14th largest economy in the world.[73]

If slavery had never existed, they argue, the overall population of black people would be far lower and therefore the total income of black people in America would be less than it is today. In addition, Mr. Williams asks:

> Are the millions of Europeans, Asians and Latin Americans who immigrated to the U.S. in the 20th century responsible for slavery, and should they be forced to cough up reparations money? What about descendants of Northern whites who fought and died in the name of freeing slaves?[74]

As you can see this is a thorny issue for economists to evaluate. Nonetheless, if cities like Chicago – that once passed a resolution by a vote of 46–1 to look into slave reparations – are going to continue to move on this issue, economics students should be well versed in the methodology one might use to link the existence of slavery to the current plight of impoverished black Americans.

THE HISTORY OF THE REPARATIONS MOVEMENT

Dutch traders brought the first slaves to America in 1619. From that time until 1865, millions of other Africans followed. With the abolition of slavery in 1865, came the first call for reparations. General Sherman of the Union forces set aside land along the Georgia and South Carolina coasts for black settlement. Each family was to receive 40 acres, and Sherman later offered the loan of Army mules. Within six months, 40,000 freed slaves had settled on hundreds of thousands of acres of land. Several months later, Congress passed a bill establishing the Freedman's Bureau to oversee the transition of blacks from slavery to freedom. However, shortly after that President Andrew Johnson began allowing former Confederates to reclaim their property – a trend that continued in succeeding decades.[75] In 1866 and 1867 Representative Thaddeus Stevens introduced reparations bills that did not pass. In 1915 Cornelius Jones sued the U.S. government, arguing that it had profited from slave labor through a federal tax on cotton. Since the slaves had never been paid, Jones calculated they were owed $68 million. Jones lost his suit.

In 1963 – after decades of lynching, riots, and anti-black laws and legislation, Martin Luther King wrote, "no amount of gold could ever provide adequate compensation for the exploitation of the Negro in America down through the centuries."

King did believe, however, that a price could be placed on unpaid wages. Around that same time, a Detroit activist named Ray Jenkins took up the fight for reparations. In 1963 he formed the Slave Labor Annuity organization. Jenkins' grandfather, a former slave who died in 1958, had been part of an environment where the average slave was sold for $778 ($14,428 in 2009 dollars). Jenkins' campaign did not lead to any monetary payment to the descendents of slaves.

In 1988, Congress apologized to Japanese Americans interned in camps during World War II and authorized payments of $20,000 each to roughly 60,000 survivors. By one estimate, the German government has paid $60 billion to settle claims from victims of Nazi persecution. Today, the National Coalition for Blacks for Reparations in America (N'COBRA) has over 25 chapters and is working on a reparations lawsuit.

REPARATIONS ESTIMATES

If at some point the U.S. government takes up the issue of reparations – and decides to pay reparations to African-Americans – the taxpayers will be very interested in the formula used to determine how much money should be paid.

Economist Larry Neal, adjusting for inflation, has calculated that unpaid net wages to blacks before emancipation amount to $1.4 trillion today. If we were to divide that figure by 40 million (the current population of black people in the U.S.) the per-person payout would equal $35,000. Should that be the settlement? Have current black Americans suffered to the tune of $35,000 per person?

Would Denzel Washington, Oprah Winfrey and other wealthy black Americans get a check? Would $1.4 trillion impact the government's ability to pay for social security, defense, education, and health care programs? Would black people who pay taxes get a bigger payout than those who do not? Would people with one black and one Hispanic or white parent get $17,500?

Would white Americans who can prove that their ancestors fought against slavery be exempt from paying taxes to the reparations fund? What about white people whose ancestors were not living in America during the time of slavery? Would they have to pay? Should American Indians get reparations next?

Would all programs that have helped blacks procure greater employment opportunities (affirmative action and college set-aside programs) be eliminated in response to the payout? Would black people notice higher prices being charged of them now that every black person would be financially better off?

Would the incentives of black children to do well in school be diminished with the receipt of such a huge payment? These and other questions like them are not posed lightly. They are serious questions that must be answered before any money is allocated to the reparations issue.

It is doubtful that many black people believe that they have been harmed $35,000 worth. Surely most of us would agree that the more years that pass since the end of slavery, the less likely it is that black people are victimized by slavery. Remember that Mr. Neal calculated the lost wages to slaves before emancipation. There are no black people alive today who would fit into that category.

The assignment of an economic variable that would accurately account for current damages stemming from the institution of slavery would be a monumental undertaking and perhaps an impossible one. Guessing the amount would be even more politically unsettling. Perhaps we will never know what impact slavery has had on black people today.

ENDNOTES

1 To take a look at his home page or to email Mr. Anderson about his research, go to www.centre.edu/web/academic/faculty/anderson.html or see "The Cost of Crime" for a detailed look at the various categories in this study. Log onto www.economics.about.com/money/economics/library/weekly/aa041300.htm.

2 See "Bowling Shoes Are So Hot, People Rent them to Steal a Pair" by Shirley Leung, *The Wall Street Journal,* April, 2001.

3 See Gary Becker (1968). "Crime and Punishment: An Economic Approach". *The Journal of Political Economy* 76: pp. 169-217.

4 See *The Economics of Life* by Gary and Guity Nashat Becker, McGraw-Hill, 1997, pp. 135–144.

5 In the week following the September 11th attacks, crime in New York City fell by 34%. This was partially attributed to an increased police presence in the city and thus, a higher probability of capture. See "Crime Rate in New York Fell Sharply After Attack," *The Wall Street Journal,* September 19, 2001.

6 See "The Economics of Crime" by Ed Rubenstein, Imprimis, Hillsdale College, Hillsdale, Michigan, 1995.

7 Source: United States Bureau of Justice.

8 See "Poking Holes in the Theory of 'Broken Windows'" by D.W. Miller, *The Chronicle of Higher Education,* February 9, 2001, pp. A14–A16; "On Crime As Science (A Neighbor at a Time)" by Dan Hurley, *The New York Times,* January 6, 2004, p. D1; and "The Hallmark of the Underclass" by Charles Murray, *The Wall Street Journal,* September 29, 2001.

9 See "Economists Demonstrate That Neighbors, Not Wardens, Hold Keys to Cutting Crime" by Amanda Bennett, *The Wall Street Journal,* 1994.

10 See "A Crime Theory Demolished" by Heather Mac Donald, *The Wall Street Journal,* January 5, 2010.

11 See "Best Crime Stopper: A Father at Home" by William S. Comanor and Llad Philips, *The Wall Street Journal,* May 10, 1998, and www.ncpa.org/pi/crime/aug98g.html.

12 See "Identity, love and security from parents" by Parris Baker, *The Orlando Sentinel,* August 3, 2007, pg. A19.

13 See "Both Sides in Gun War Are Armed With Numbers, But Who is Right?" by Ray Rivera, *The Salt Lake Tribune,* August 22, 1999; and "Watchful dad slays gunman" by Rich McKay, *The Orlando Sentinel,* March 20, 2002.

14 See "Weapons-on-campus push gains steam" by Zinie Chen Sampson, *The Orlando Sentinel,* August 13, 2007.

15 See "Justices Broaden Gun Rights" by Jess Bravin, *The Wall Street Journal,* June 29, 2010.

16 See "Gun foes to warn tourists on law" by Linda Kleindienst, *The Orlando Sentinel,* September 26, 2005.

17 See "In the New Economics, The Economy Has Little to Do With It" by Jon. R. Hilsenrath, *The Wall Street Journal,* April 27, 2001; *Freakonomics* by Steven D. Levitt and Stephen J. Dunbar, Harper Collins, 2005; and "The Impact of Legalized Abortion on Crime" by John Donohue and Steven Levitt, *Quarterly Journal of Economics,* 2000.

18 See http://www.census.gov/hhes/www/poverty/threshld/thresh07.html for the government's data on poverty and other poverty measures.

19 See "Income Mobility: Alive and Well" by David R. Henderson, *The Freeman,* October 2005; and *Myths of Rich and Poor* by W. Michael Cox and Richard Alm, Basic Books, 1999, pg. 15.

20 See "Poor America" by Douglas Besharov, *The Wall Street Journal,* March 24, 2006, p.A10.

21 See "Why Decry the Wealth Gap?" by W. Michael Cox and Richard Alm, *The New York Times,* January 24, 2000.

22 See "Movin' On Up" *The Wall Street Journal,* November 13, 2007.

23 See "Economic Scene" by Virginia Postrel, *The New York Times,* August 10, 2000; and "Impossible American Dream?" by Robert Samuelson, *The Orlando Sentinel,* November 29, 2007.

24 See "Haiti has it all—poverty, crime and political fraud" by Tasha C. Joseph, *The Orlando Sentinel,* April 15, 2001; and "Concern grows that kids are on slave ship", *The Orlando Sentinel* (from the *Associated Press*), April 15, 2001, page A3.

25 See "Who Wins in the New Economy?" *The Wall Street Journal,* June 27, 2000, page B1; and "White men with degrees earn the most" by Genaro C. Armas, *The Orlando Sentinel,* March 28, 2005.

26 See *Basic Economics: A Citizen's Guide to the Economy* by Thomas Sowell, Basic Books, 2001.

27 See "Clandestine population perplexed economists" *The Orlando Sentinel* (from the Los Angeles Times) March 11, 2001.

28 See "Immigration Heritage" *The Wall Street Journal,* June 8, 2007, pg. A16; "Immigration Doesn't Displace Natives" by Richard Vedder, *The Wall Street Journal,* March 28, 1994; "Immigration benefits U.S., study says" *The Orlando Sentinel,* May 18, 1997, p. A–6; "Demagoging the Immigration Issue" by Albert R. Hunt, *The Wall Street Journal,* July 7, 1994, p. A13; "Immigrant-Bashing's Latest Falsehood" by John J. Miller, *The Wall Street Journal,* March 8, 1994; "Immigrants Lead a Recovery" by Joel Kotkin, *The Wall Street Journal,* April 22, 1994; "Immigrants A Plus for Companies" by Vicki Vaughn, *The Orlando Sentinel;* and "Welcome More Immigrants" by Stephan-Gotz Richter and Daniel Bachman, *The Wall Street Journal,* July 22, 1999; and "Imagining Life Without Illegal Immigrants" by Dean E. Murphy, *The New York Times,* January 11, 2004.

29 See "Migrant workers fill Big Easy" by Peter Pae, *The Orlando Sentinel,* October 12, 2005.

30 See "Black, Successful—and Typical" by Jason L. Riley, *The Wall Street Journal,* May 13, 2002.

31 Source: United States Census Bureau and the National Poverty Center.

32 Source: U.S. Department of Education.

33 See "Teachers Are Highly Paid, Survey Shows" by Ryan Bedford, *Budget & Tax News,* May 2007.

34 Source: U.S. Census Bureau.

35 For complete survey results see http://www.nationalgeographic.com/geosurvey/download/RoperSurvey.pdf.

36 See "Obama: Schools must buckle down" by Peter Nicholas, *The Orlando Sentinel,* September 28, 2010.

37 See "What, me worry?" by Thomas Friedman, *The New York Times* (published in *The Orlando Sentinel*), April 30, 2005.

38 See "Parents take another hit in the culture wars" by Kathleen Parker, *The Orlando Sentinel,* November 6, 2005.

39 See "Teacher Sexual Misconduct Runs Rampant in U.S. Public Schools" by Karla Dial, *School Reform News,* December 2007; and "Class of '08 Fails to Lift SAT Scores" by John Hechinger, *The Wall Street Journal,* August 27, 2008, pg. D1.

40 See "Teacher Can't Teach" by Chester E. Finn Jr., *The Wall Street Journal,* March 11, 2005; and *The Conspiracy of Ignorance: The Failure of American Public Schools* by Martin Gross, Harper Collins, 1999.

41 See "Teacher Training is Panned" by Stephanie Banchero, *The Wall Street Journal,* November 16, 2010.

42 In Finland, teachers are required to have a master's degree and six years of preparation in a specific subject area before they are allowed to teach. It should also be noted that Finland's students rank first in the world in math, reading and science. See "Should U.S. try imitating Finland?" by Robert G. Kaiser, *The Washington Post,* October 2, 2005 (date published in *The Orlando Sentinel*); and "Finland tops global school table," *BBC News,* September 10, 2008.

43 See "The Education Manifesto" by Michelle Rhee and Adrian Fenty, *The Wall Street Journal,* October 30-31, 2010.

44 See "The Greatest Mistake in American History: Letting Government Educate Our Children" by Harry Browne, (speech before The Foundation for Economic Education, December 2004).

45 See "The Culture Gap" by Brink Lindsey, *The Wall Street Journal,* July 9, 2007.

46 See "Protect Our Kids from Preschool" by Shikha Dalmia and Lisa Snell, *The Wall Street Journal*, August 22, 2008, pg. A15.

47 See "If Schools Were Like 'American Idol'," by Rupert Murdoch, *The Wall Street Journal*, October 8, 2010.

48 See "Home-Schooled Kids Defy Stereotypes, Ace SAT Test" by Daniel Golden, *The Wall Street Journal*, February 11, 2000.

49 For the data on home schooling, see www.uhea.org/stats.html. For data on private school productivity, see "New Publication Documents Benefits of Private Education" by Joe McTighe, *School Reform News* (The Heartland Institute) February 2005; and *Let's Put Parents Back in Charge* by Joseph Bast and Herbert Walberg, The Heartland Institute, 2005.

50 For a detailed examination of this fact, you should watch the DVD entitled, "Stupid in America," which aired on January 13, 2006 (ABC; John Stossel as host). Log on to www.jackchambless.com, click on SPEECHES and scroll down to Stupid in America to watch this program.

51 See "Students in Failing Public Schools Need Federal Education Reform" by Dan Proft, *School Reform News*, September 2008, pg. 17.

52 See "Innovative Catholic schools target low-income students" by Jay Mathews, *The Orlando Sentinel*, April 6, 2003, from the *Washington Post*.

53 See "Blacks Support for School Choice Increases in New Orleans, Nationwide" by Jim Waters, *School Reform News*, September 2008, pg. 13.

54 See "State Flunks 68 Schools" by Lori Horvitz, *The Orlando Sentinel*, June 13, 2002; "Poorest Schools get the most F's" by Leslie Postal and Lori Horvitz, *The Orlando Sentinel*, June 23, 2002; and "DC Vouchers Approved" by Robert Holland, *School Reform News* (The Heartland Institute), March 2004.

55 See "For some black students, school is best at home," *The Orlando Sentinel*, January 16, 2011.

56 See "War Against Vouchers" by Andrew J. Coulson, *The Wall Street Journal*, January 9, 2006.

57 See "Florida's Unheralded School Revolution" by Adam R. Schaeffer, *The Wall Street Journal*, April 30, 2010.

58 For extensive analysis of what is taking place within this movement, see "School Choice Legislation is all the Rage in 2005" by Lisa Snell, *School Reform News* (The Heartland Institute) May 2005; "Federal Court Upholds Arizona Tax Credits" by George A. Clowes, *School Reform News* (The Heartland Institute) May 2005; "2,000 March for School Choice in Florida" by Jenny Rothenberg, *School Reform News*, July 2005; "Ohio Creates Nation's Largest Voucher Program" by Kate McGreevy, *School Reform News*, September 2005; "Georgia Parents Sue for Vouchers" by George A. Clowes, *School Reform News*, March 2005.

59 See "Milwaukee's model: City Schools that work" by John Tierney, *The New York Times*, March 8, 2006 (date published in *The Orlando Sentinel*).

60 See "Voucher Competition Begins to Make Inroads in Milwaukee" by George Clowes, *School Reform News*, September 2008 pg. 16

61 See "Would a School thrive if teachers made $125,000?" by Elissa Gootman, *The New York Times*, March 9, 2008

62 See "Charter Schools and Student Performance" by Paul E. Peterson, *The Wall Street Journal*, March 16, 2010

63 See "The Education Manifesto" by Michelle Rhee and Adrian Fenty, *The Wall Street Journal*, October 30-31, 2010

64 See "School Choice and the Standpoint of African-American Mothers: Considering the Power of Positionality," by Camille Wilson Cooper, *Journal of Negro Education*, Spring 2005; and see "Opportunity Scholarships: Chance for a better life" by Ed Rodriquez and Julio Fuentes, *The Orlando Sentinel*, September 15, 2005.

65 For a detailed analysis of the impact of school choice on educational quality, see *School Choice – the findings* by Herbert J. Walberg, The Cato Institute, 2007.

66 Source: Florida Center of Political History and Governance, Tallahassee, Florida.

67 See "In war on poverty, early gains and a long stalemate" by Peter Grier and Patrik Jonsson, *The Christian Science Monitor*, January 9, 2004.

68 Source: The Cato Institute http://www.cato.org/pub_display. php?pub_id=6698

69 Source: The Annie E. Casey Foundation.

70 See www.upjohninst.org/publications/titles/ecwr.html.

71 See *Welfare Reform After Ten Years* by Gary MacDougal, Kate Campaigne and Dane Wendall, The Heartland Institute, July 2008.

72 See "Low-Tax States Cut Poverty Rates" by Jessa Haugebak, *Budget & Tax News* March 2007, pg. 3.

73 For more on this argument, see *The Debt: What America Owes to Blacks* by Randall Robinson, The Penguin Group, 2001; "The Push to Pay for the Past" by Maria T. Padilla, *The Orlando Sentinel*, April 8, 2001, p. G1; "Voices of Slavery" by Maria T. Padilla, *The Orlando Sentinel,* April 29, 2001.

74 For more from Dr. Williams see http://www.youtube.com/watch?v=OUL152yGVGI

75 www.jewishworldreview.com/cols/williams.html

76 www.swagga.com/reparation.htm

CHAPTER REVIEW

1. What are some of the major economic causes of crime?

2. List and explain four factors that contribute to poverty.

3. What role does school choice play in explaining earnings differences?

4. What could help explain the rate of poverty found on American Indian reservations?

Chapter Six

The MARKET EQUILIBRIUM PROCESS

Photo courtesy Jack Chambless

*T*each a parrot the terms, supply and demand,
and you've got an economist.

THOMAS CARLYLE

THE CONFUSION ABOUT MARKETS

Former British Prime Minister Winston Churchill once asked Lady Astor if she would have sex with him for 1 million pounds. When she said, "Yes," he asked her if she would have sex with him for 100 pounds. She said, "What do you think I am – a prostitute?" He replied, "We've already established that. Now we're just haggling over the price." Mr. Churchill understood markets.

On any given day, we all, directly or indirectly, participate in some market transaction. If you have a job, you are the supplier of a labor resource to an employer, who is the demander of that resource, for a price known as the wage rate. Outside of your job, you might be the demander in any number of markets from hockey skates to sushi.

We all have some fundamental understanding of the forces of supply and demand that shape our lives. However, there is also a great deal of misunderstanding about markets. Sometimes this misunderstanding leads to emotional reactions (think gasoline) to changes in economic conditions. Sometimes misunderstanding the market leads to people dying unnecessarily. This chapter will clear up the confusion that surrounds the concepts of supply and demand.

WHAT IS A MARKET?

When studying something new – especially when preconceived ideas are abundant – it is always a good idea to start with the most basic questions. To some of you, the question, "What is a market?" might seem silly, but unless we start here, many of you are going to end up lost.

> ➤ **A market is an arrangement through which buyers and sellers meet or communicate for the purpose of exchanging goods and services at mutually agreed-upon prices.**

Let's think about the significance of this definition for a moment, starting with the phrase "buyers and sellers." A buyer is a person who is willing and able to purchase a good at a particular price at some moment in time. Some of you might be willing to buy a Ranger Rover, but you might not be able. Others of you might be able to buy a CD featuring MC Hammer's greatest hits, but you might not be willing. A market cannot exist unless there are people who can satisfy both criteria of being a buyer.

A seller is someone who is willing and able to sell some good, or service, at a particular price, at some moment in time. The "willing and able" standard prevails here, too. You can be quite certain that there are individuals out there who would be willing to sell pills that will turn water into gasoline. However, if the technology needed to deliver such a product does not exist, then no one will be able to sell us this cheaper source of fuel. There are individuals in our economy who are able to sell hypodermic needles that have been previously used by drug addicts. However, they are probably not willing to go through the trouble of opening up a used needle stand in your city.

Another point of clarification that is needed is why we say buyers *and* sellers. Can't we have a market with just one of the two? Well, no. We cannot. If there are people willing and able to purchase an apartment on the moon, but no one is currently supplying such services, then we do not yet have a market. There are probably many people from Kabul, Afghanistan who would be willing and able to rent out their homes to people who might want to live there. It does not matter what they are willing and able to supply. It takes willingness to supply – and someone's willingness to *buy* to have a market.

Next we have the words *meet* and *communicate*. In most markets, buyers and sellers meet somewhere to conduct business. Restaurants, gas stations, toll roads, and so forth are examples of markets where buyers and sellers conduct business at some physical location. For centuries, all markets were based on meetings between people willing and able to buy and sell. This is no longer the case.

HOW THE INTERNET HAS ALTERED THE MARKET

> The real price of everything is the toil and trouble of acquiring it.
>
> Adam Smith

What Mr. Smith means is that with every purchase there is a transaction cost.

> ➤ **Transaction costs are the direct and opportunity costs of engaging in market transactions.**

For many everyday items, your transaction costs would entail getting dressed, getting in your car, driving to the local bookstore, grocery store, or car dealer(s) and spending varying amounts of time finding the romance novel, cantaloupe, or car that you wanted. If you found the item, you then would have to decide if the price was right. If you concluded that it was, you would proceed to the register – or office of the salesperson – and arrange to pay for the item in question.

This song and dance might seem like a scene from a million years ago, now that the Internet has fundamentally and permanently changed the way many markets work. Now if you want a book, you can go to any number of websites, and quickly order your selection and pay for it, all without ever getting out of your pajamas or starting your car in the middle of a rainstorm. There are sites in some cities that allow you to access a menu of your local grocer, order your items, and have them delivered to your home. Cell phones now have apps that allow consumers to comparison shop while using global positioning systems to identify exactly where to buy the less expensive products that were found by the phone.[1] This reduction in transaction costs has put tremendous pressure on retailers to keep prices competitive.[2]

Car buying has also seen a power shift from the sellers to the buyers in many ways. It used to be that you never really knew how much the dealer had paid for the vehicle you wanted. You never knew how much profit they were going to make, and you certainly did not know if there was a better deal in another city.

Now you can go online and find out exactly what the invoice cost is for many dealers. You can find out where the same vehicle might be in any number of cities and what each dealer is asking. This means you can arm yourself with information that dramatically lowers the transaction costs of buying a car.

Whom do you have to thank for this dramatic change in our shopping lives? The list is endless, but it is made up of people with unquestionably large IQs, and bank accounts, who several years ago developed an information superhighway that is now serving millions of people very well.

What this all means is that the phrase "or communicate" in the definition of a market has become increasingly more important. This has lowered the search costs associated with our purchases and freed us up to pursue more pleasurable pursuits.

In fact, getting great deals over the Internet has become so common that your government has begun wondering whether some of the deals you are getting are too great. A few years ago, the U.S. Justice Department began an investigation of Orbitz – an online travel business.[3] The question at hand was whether or not the low prices (in some cases far lower than those offered by Travelocity or Expedia) were *too low*.[4] The government was worried that if consumers using Orbitz continued to get significantly lower prices compared to other online travel businesses, in the long run some higher-priced companies would go out of business, causing less competition and eventually higher prices.

Shutterstock © egd, 2011.

CONCEPT CHECK

Some economists have suggested that toll road fees should rise during peak-use hours to reduce traffic congestion.[5] Others have argued that the Internet will help reduce traffic jams over time without raising toll road prices. What logic is the latter argument based on?

The Internet will also lead to significant changes in labor markets. Millions of Americans have a home office, and more jobs are moving into the realm of "distance production." This means that over time, as technology continues to improve, we can expect to see less need for workers to commute to an office. Imagine the impact on traffic congestion, the market for day care, the environment, and our geographic mobility as we become better equipped to do our jobs from the home. This trend is particularly helpful during a time when the U.S. economy is struggling to emerge from recession. During the 2007-2009 Recession, many Americans were unable to sell their homes and move to a place offering better jobs. As online employment becomes more common, it will not be as necessary to wait for a house to sell before you can take a new job.

WHY MARKETS EXIST

Another source of confusion for many students is why we have markets to begin with. If we go back to the definition of a market, we can see part of the answer. The phrase "for the purpose of exchanging goods and services" tells you a lot about the functional purpose of markets, but it does not tell the whole story.

One reason for markets is that we are all pathetically inept at so many things but probably have a comparative advantage in at least one thing. Recall from chapter one that having a comparative advantage means that compared to someone else, you can produce some good or service at a lower opportunity cost. This situation offers you and others, a chance to specialize in something that the market might ultimately desire – like the production of eggs....

WHAT COLLEGE-AGE WOMEN KNOW ABOUT COMPARATIVE ADVANTAGE

O.K., ladies. Pay close attention, because you might be able to make a lot of money, legally, without having to find a job at this point in time.

That is because compared to men – and compared to women who are infertile – many of you have something valuable inside your body that the free market is demanding. If you guessed your eggs, you are right on the money.

Over the past several years an explosion has taken place in the number of people who are willing and able to pay healthy, intelligent, young women for their eggs. Many cash-strapped college girls with high SAT scores and good looks are making up to $35,000 for their eggs.[6] That is enough money to pay for a lot of books and tuition.

Since many couples around the U.S. struggle to have children – and since our quasi-capitalistic economy places a high economic value on looks and intelligence – there has been a natural gravitation to college campuses to find women who can help people create "desirable" children.

The comparative advantage here is pretty easy to detect. *Compared* to women who are infertile, or to women who are older, or less attractive, or who flunked out of middle school, the women with the preferred traits have an economic *advantage*. It only stands to reason that if a woman has a property right over her body, then she might decide to part with part of her private property for the right price.

This is a beautiful part of the market process. We can rest comfortably knowing that even if we are hopeless in thousands of areas of production, if we specialize in one – and if the market wants what we have to offer it – we can earn enough money to give it away to those people who have specialized in the things we are not as good at.

The second major reason for the existence of markets is *self-interest*. Once we decide what our comparative advantage is, and where we are going to offer our services, we do so in order to provide for our needs and the needs of our families, first and foremost. Without the guiding hand of self-love, markets would not work very effectively.

Finally, there is the issue of *scarcity*. We all have imbalances that we want closed. Our local grocer, eBay, and millions of other business firms help consumers with their imbalances while we help businesspeople with their desire to earn more money.

SHOULD MARKETS BE FAIR?

Often I travel with my family – and a few other families – to Tennessee to enjoy a week of camping.

One year while I was cooking breakfast for everyone, a lady from one of the families (whom I like) began fussing about a little business venture I had started with my sons. The venture involves finding things that people have for sale – that are way undervalued based on market conditions – and reselling those items on eBay.

According to her, I was simply taking advantage of people by not paying them a fair price to begin with and then I was taking advantage of other people by selling the item for far more than I paid, rather than for a "fair" price.

This argument did not sit well with me, or my sons, whom I am trying to help understand how markets work. In fact, I was tempted to jokingly (sort of) tell her that the pancakes and bacon she was about to eat were paid for by the cook (me) and that she was being unfair not to offer me a "fair" price for her breakfast.

Of course, my lovely wife would have had a heart attack if I said this; so I simply smiled, nodded and wished our friend would realize how futile it is to clearly define what the word *fair* means.

Yet, it is true that human beings have an innate sense of "fair play" that tends to separate us from the rest of the animal world. Over the past few years, behavioral economists have found in experiments that humans repeatedly show a tendency to share, and they expect others to reciprocate.[7]

Reciprocity can have its benefits, too. Organizations like the Rainforest Alliance, Fair Trade USA, and UTZ Certified have experienced tremendous growth in recent years, certifying that cocoa and coffee is grown by sellers who support sustainable farming and "equitable" prices for poorer farmers worldwide.[8] The result of this trend has allowed certified sellers to earn about $150 a ton more for cocoa than non-certified supplies.

A recent study found that 72% of consumers said they would be more likely to patronize a company with fair prices and a good cause, than a company offering deep discounts but little in the way of charitable or environmental initiative.[9]

Behavioral economists suggest that there is a "civilizing effect" of the marketplace that leads perfect strangers to develop more giving tendencies.[10]

After all, how many times during the day do you deal with complete strangers in the market? Do you know who makes and transports the gasoline you buy? Are you on a first-name basis with your favorite chef or author? When is the last time you had dinner with your grocer or the local movie theater manager?

Dealing daily with strangers in the free market creates a critical level of trust between you and the seller of goods and services. If you drink Budweiser, you have an implicit contract with Anheuser-Busch that the "born on" date that is provided is not a lie and that the beer does not contain laundry soap. Anheuser-Busch trusts you to pay the full price for a six-pack, rather than to steal it off the beer truck. Over time, trust leads all of us to develop a sense of fairness that tells Anheuser-Busch, "If you make me feel good and treat me fairly, I'll make you feel good and treat you fairly." We still may not care about the person who manned the bottling station the day our Bud was born, but we still help him or her get paid by not stealing from their company.

Do you care where this comes from?

All of this leads us back to the original issue of whether or not markets are fair. On one hand we have seen that there seems to be a level of fairness that maintains some quality controls and product reliability. There also seems to be a sense of fair play when it comes to prices.

Oftentimes when hurricanes hit, grocery stores that could easily raise prices do not. Is that because the law prohibits price-gouging, or is it because the grocer does not want to take advantage of people during an emergency?

After September 11th, there was an increased need for vaccines, and that led to severe shortages. The free market would suggest that higher prices were necessary, yet drug companies did not follow the free market and left prices unchanged, all while shipping vaccines to the areas immediately impacted by the terrorist attacks.

On the other hand, we also see examples of things that seem to be unfair. Is it fair that the free market pays Tom Cruise $25 million per movie? Is it fair that teachers and firemen earn less money than bench-warming baseball players? Is it fair that hotel room prices rise in Daytona Beach, Florida, during spring break? How about business travelers? Is it fair that they pay hundreds of dollars more per airplane ticket than vacationers? Is it fair that some people can afford a mansion, while others live in a box? This is not a new debate. As far back as 1805 people were complaining about prices. During that winter, while Lewis & Clark were living in Oregon's Fort Clatsop, they regularly traded with American Indians that lived near by. William Clark once complained in his journal that the Indians, "….never close a bargain except when they think they have the advantage" and that they charged, "immodest prices."[11] Was Clark right?

It depends on whom you ask. Surely, we can all see that fairness is in the eye of the beholder. What is fair to one person − $30 for a steak, for example − might be unfair to the bologna-eater. A fair wage to a Taco Bell cook might be $117 per hour − if you ask him − yet to

the customer of Taco Bell, who would have to pay $39 for a chalupa, the $117 wage might seem excessive.

Some economists have tried to find the answer to this "fairness" issue, but the answer eludes us. The subjectivity of the word makes coming up with a definitive answer impossible.

WHO CONTROLS THE MARKET?

Many people are under the misconception that the market is controlled by consumers through our wants and needs. Others are willing to argue that it is the sellers of goods and services that control our lives. Both of these perceptions are far from reality.

For those of you who are convinced that it is consumer sovereignty that dictates market outcomes, I have a couple of little tests I would like you to perform. First, go down to a local car dealership that is featuring their line of new automobiles.

Tell the salesperson that, as a consumer, you are in control of the car market and that you insist that he sell you a new car for under $2,400. At that time you will be politely escorted out of the dealership and pointed in the direction of the nearest used car lot. When you get to the used car lot, and find a car for under $2,400, tell the salesperson that you insist that your used car be equipped with a satellite navigation system so that you can fall asleep anytime you want to and have your car safely transport you to your final destination. At this time you will be invited to leave the car lot, and you will be directed to the nearest mental institution.

The preceding exercise was designed to help you understand that, as a consumer, you are part of the market process, but not the process itself. Your demands are counterbalanced by the willingness and ability of multitudinous sellers to provide you with goods and services at prices from which they can earn profit. New cars for $2,400 may be purchased in your dreams, but not in reality. By the same token, asking for or demanding features that are

Photo courtesy Jack Chambless

SUGGESTED CLASSROOM DEBATE

This photo was taken near Ely, Minnesota. The guy who sells the wood is never standing near his woodpile. Instead, he has a box (locked) near his wood, his price per bundle on the box, and people can simply pull over, pick up this wood, and put money in the box. Does this system elicit more or less honesty from people who buy firewood? Why?

not technologically feasible or cost-effective at this time will also leave you with no service from your fellow man.

On the other hand, if you believe that evil and greedy businesses are all conspiring to charge whatever price they want and produce whatever product they deem sufficient, you probably also believe in Santa Claus and the Easter Bunny. A wonderful example of the hysteria that markets can create can be found in the gasoline market of 2008.

You may recall that in July of 2008, gasoline prices topped $4 per gallon. This price caused some people to conclude that we are at the mercy of the oil companies and the Organization of Petroleum Exporting Countries (OPEC). After all, isn't gasoline an extreme necessity? Won't we have to pay any price that is charged by the big oil companies?

The answer is a resounding no! If it were true that the oil companies control our lives, why did the price of oil fall from $147 per barrel (when gas prices topped $4) to under $32 per barrel by February 2009, where gas prices fell to under $2 per gallon in much of the country?

Did the executives at BP, Chevron, and ExxonMobil decide to take it easy on us? Were they all economically illiterate during the spring of 2009?

Gas prices – just like any other good or service – change not because sellers decide they should, but because sellers and buyers interact to create a price that is mutually agreed upon. Our increasing consumption of oil – along with more consumption in India and China – lead to the dramatic increase in prices. When the world economy began to slow down in the latter part of 2008 through 2009, there were fewer buyers of oil and thus prices began to fall sharply. This will be clarified in much greater detail in the next chapter.

Suppose that, as you read this chapter, gas prices are $4.79 per gallon. Buying into the idea that the gas suppliers can operate with impunity begs the question of how much more we would pay for gas before their power was undermined.

Would you pay $5.79 per gallon? $8.79? $11.79? If you think about this situation from a sane and dispassionate point of view, you will quickly realize that there is a limit to how much of these price hikes we will stand by and take. At some point you would see a huge increase in the demand for small cars – just as we did in 2008. You would also see more people moving closer to work, commuting with their friends, taking the bus, or riding bicycles. The point is that the sellers may have a great deal of power over price, but they cannot charge whatever price they want. Consumers inevitably have a say in the matter.[12]

Which Comes First, Supply or Demand?

Most students answer by saying, "Both" or "Demand." As it turns out, supply has to appear first. Did consumers line up outside the post offices of America protesting the slow pace of mail delivery – demanding, in essence, that someone ship boxes overnight? Did unhappy moms demand disposable diapers? Did children demonstrate in the streets for novels about wizards? No, no, and no.

Capitalism is the epic search for fixable problems. If you want to become rich, listen to what people are complaining about and fix it – or invent something that people never knew they wanted. Our markets are dependent on entrepreneurs who notice that something is missing or wrong in our economic system, then take the risks of fixing it. This means we have to wait for the supplier to appear first. Fred Smith, the founder of FedEx, got his idea for this company while in college. He turned in a paper proposing an overnight mail delivery business and received a poor grade and criticism by his professor. Oops. Then he turned his vision, into a service. There was *no market* for overnight mail delivery services. He had to turn his comparative advantage and his self-interest into a service, and then supply that service to whoever might be willing and able to purchase it. Only then did then we find out whether, or not, there was a market. This is known as *Say's Law.*

> ➤ **Say's Law – named after the French economist Jean Baptiste Say – states that supply creates demand.**

According to Mr. Say, who was a follower of Adam Smith, the production of goods and services leads to income earned for the producer and the employees of the producer. This *income leads to a demand* for even more production and the production of new goods and services.

CONCEPT CHECK

Psychologists who study markets have found that women who are ovulating tend to spend more money on attractive clothing.[13] Does this mean that during those times the suppliers of this type of clothing are in control of this market? Why, or why not?

Going back to chapter two for a moment, this means that for a free market to work, government must first encourage suppliers to "show up" by not taking and regulating the market too heavily. If government tells suppliers that they can enter the market, make money and keep the bulk of their earnings, the suppliers of everything from dresses to dog food will appear, create jobs and those jobs will create the income that fuels demand in the long run.

We could argue that Fred Smith "knew" that there must be a demand for his product offering and therefore he was simply responding to the guaranteed demand. We can argue this, but we would be incorrect to do so. No supplier ever knows with 100% certainty that demand will be there, or that if demand is there, that demand will be large enough to create a profit.

Which brings us to Harry Potter, or more appropriately, J.K. Rowling – the creator of Harry Potter.

In 2010, Universal Studios Orlando opened the nearly $400 million Wizarding World of Harry Potter attraction.

This attraction was the culmination of an incredible story born out of poverty and imagination – and is proof of Say's Law.

Consider this: when Ms. Rowling began writing her first Harry Potter book, she was living in poverty in England. In 2009, she ranked 709th on the list of the richest people in the world, with a net worth of $1 billion.

No one saw Harry Potter coming except for her. Until she put pen to paper, there were none of the thousands of jobs she helped create. Once she did, think about what happened next. All of the jobs she created or supported in the book publishing and marketing industry. The jobs she created in the movie industry. Then there are the hundreds of people who became employed in the construction of the Universal Studios attraction and the people who now work at the attraction or in hotels that are filling up because of this attraction.[14] Universal Orlando reported that 1 million more people visited this park in 2010 compared to 2009 and that over 1 million mugs of "butterbeer" were sold.[15]

Out of the mind of this entrepreneurial author came one of the greatest examples of the importance of the supplier – and why the most prosperous nations are the ones that attract more people like her.

THE DETERMINANTS OF SUPPLY

Now that we know that we have to wait for suppliers to appear first, let's look at what issues the supplier has to resolve before he or she can offer us goods and services.

What follows is a list of the determinants of supply – the factors that influence the existence of suppliers and the amount of production once suppliers appear.

- Price
- Input costs
- Technology
- The number of sellers serving the market
- The price of other goods that can be produced with inputs that are used or owned by the seller
- Expectations concerning future prices

Price is the most important determinant of supply. The next time you are in a job interview, ask yourself what is the most important aspect of the job you have applied for. Is it the health care plan? The size of your office? The work hours? The morals of the company? All of these things might be important to you, in varying degrees, but chances are money is the main thing you are concerned about. After all, how many people do you know who would be willing to take a big office, a flexible schedule, and a position with a firm that donates money to the "Save the Weasels" campaign, all for the wage of $1.27 per hour? Not many would.

In the labor market, just as in the markets for hybrid cars, shaving cream, and day-old donuts, price is the most important factor in determining whether a person or business will supply a good or service.

Input costs are costs associated with the price of land, labor, capital, and entrepreneurship. Do not discount the importance of this determinant to millions of individual participants in our economy. In an era where global competition and the Internet have dramatically increased the competitive pressure faced by business firms, there has never been greater pressure to control the costs of production. Approximately *70%* of the cost of production in America is associated with labor! This includes wages, salaries, health care costs, pensions and other benefits, lawsuits, workman's compensation claims, and so forth.

Other costs can include rent, materials, debt obligations, and of course government-mandated licenses, taxes, insurance, litigation costs, and regulations. These last two items have become increasingly major factors in determining the ability of firms to stay in business.

In fact, when we look at some of the major forces that can disrupt the supply of goods and services in any country, at or near the top of the list are government regulations.[16] Regulations over wages, work hours and working conditions, and other well-meaning regulations can stifle the production process by raising costs to the point where suppliers question the rationality of being in business.

CONCEPT CHECK

After hurricane Katrina, it cost $60,000 to tow this Bayou La Batre, Alabama shrimp boat. How does that towing bill – and the bills paid to tow hundreds of other boats – impact the supply of shrimp in Alabama?

Photo courtesy Jack Chambless

Technology is the knowledge of how to produce a good or service. Recently, Psychemedics Corporation did parents all over America a huge favor when the company introduced home drug test kits that allow parents to get a sample of their kids' hair to test whether their little one has been hitting the bong lately. Part of what makes Say's Law so powerful is this technology determinant. Without new technology, this product – and others like it – does not get supplied to begin with.

Another factor that determines the overall supply of a good or service is the **number of sellers** serving the market or, put another way, the level of competition. The market for beef cattle has over 1 million producers and is extremely competitive, to the point that no individual rancher has even a modicum of control over prices. The market for professional hockey games in Edmonton is not competitive. The Edmonton Oilers is a virtual monopolist in this market, thus the supply of games is much smaller than if the Oilers had four other teams selling hockey games in the area.

During the early 1990s, the first Bush Administration was very successful in driving down the demand for cocaine in the United States. At one point the price of a kilo of cocaine fetched "only" $20,000. At the same time, the price of heroin was about $200,000 per kilogram. Colombian drug lords soon realized that Colombia's lush mountain valleys were perfectly suited to produce the poppy flower that is used to make heroin. With the runways, planes, and dealer networks already in place, the drug cartels simply shifted away from the production of cocaine and into the production of heroin. This is an illustration

of how the **price of other goods used or owned by the seller** is often a determinant of supply.

More recently, central Kentucky farmers have begun turning their tobacco farms into goat farms, as a result of the growing demand for goat meat and the declining demand for cigarettes. In each case, the supplier will allocate resources based on what market conditions call for.

The last determinant of supply is **expectations concerning future prices**. Often, as hurricanes approach the East Coast of the United States, generator and lumber dealers withhold the supply of their products. Do they do this to avoid shortages? Not exactly. They reduce the available supply in order to get a higher price *after* the storm.

They realize that if prices are going to rise due to the increase in demand for storm necessities, it would be profitable to wait until the storm is over and then offer up these items. Therefore, an expectation of higher prices in the future leads to a reduction in supply today. The opposite is true when businesses expect prices to fall in the future. This is why you see sales on summer clothing before the summer is over. Retailers fear that if they do not make more items available at slightly discounted prices, they may have to practically give the clothes away when cooler weather arrives.

Shutterstock © Heidi Brand, 2011.

CONCEPT CHECK

In 2011, the price of cotton rose to a 140-year high. In response, cotton farmers in China began hoarding cotton and refusing to sell their crop.[17] What supply determinant were Chinese cotton farmers reacting to? With thousands of cotton farmers worldwide, was this a good strategy? Why, or why not?

THE SUPPLY CURVE

We have seen that we can use diagrams to simplify complex economic models. Supply analysis is no different. When we illustrate the behavior of a supplier, we do so with the use of a supply curve.

> ➤ **A supply curve illustrates the relationship between the price of an item and the quantity supplied, ceteris paribus.**
> ➤ **Quantity supplied is the amount of an item sellers are willing and able to sell at a particular price.**

The difference between supply and quantity supplied is that supply measures the relationship between all possible prices and all possible quantities supplied at various prices. Quantity supplied, on the other hand, measures a specific amount that is offered up for sale at a particular price, at some particular moment in time.

Ceteris paribus is a Latin term that means "other things being equal." For our purposes, the supply curve will be drawn under the assumption that input costs, technology, the number of sellers, and the other determinants of supply do not change. While this is not a realistic assumption

to make over a period of time, it is helpful in isolating the specific relationship between price and quantity supplied. Graphs 6.1 and 6.2 will help us understand what is on the mind of the supplier.

Have you ever wondered what it would be like if you could own a device that would record your dreams while you are asleep?

A device like this would almost certainly be a hit with consumers, but alas, Say's Law is in the way. We will have to wait for the technology to show up before the supplier shows up. But for a moment, let's think about what the Acme Dream Recorder Company might do if it is ever possible to supply us with this remarkable item.

In graph 6.1 we see that, at a price of $2,900, Acme offers up 500 recorders per week. However, at a price of $4,400, the company is willing and able to sell 750 per week. Finally, if Acme can get $6,800, quantity supplied increases to 1,500 per week. Why does the company increase production as prices increase? Is this positive relationship between price and quantity supplied an anomaly, or do all suppliers act this way? Does graph 6.2 make more sense for Acme and other suppliers?

The answer is very simple. Graph 6.1 represents one of the most important of all economic laws. It is called the law of supply.

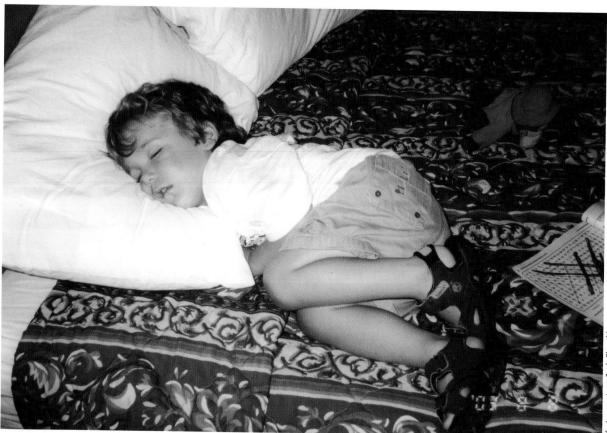

What if his dreams were on DVD?

Photo courtesy Jack Chambless

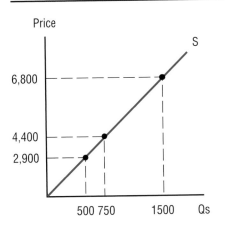

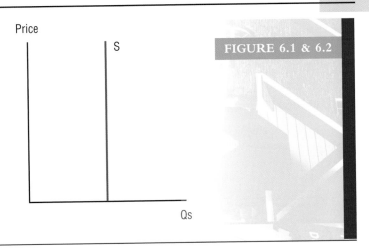

FIGURE 6.1 & 6.2

> ➤ **The law of supply states that, as prices increase, quantity supplied will increase, and as prices decrease, quantity supplied will decrease.**

Why is it a law, rather than a theory? Recall from the chapter on economic modeling that economists often find a cause-and-effect relationship between two variables. This is what has happened here. Ever since markets first appeared, people and businesses have responded to higher prices by increasing production. There are two basic reasons for this positive relationship. The first reason has to do with self-interest and the ability to earn more money at higher rates of output. The second reason has to do with the impact of rising output on total costs.

> ➤ **The total revenue effect shows that, at higher prices, increased production is desirable because it leads to higher total revenue for the supplier.**

Think of it this way: At a price of $2,900, Acme decides to produce 500 dream recorders. Five hundred machines equals the amount the company is willing and able to provide given the costs of production, available technology, and so forth. If we simply multiply $2,900 by 500 machines, we get total revenue of $1.45 million.

At a price of $4,400, the company is willing to increase production to 750. That is because $4,400 x 750 = $3.3 million.

Finally, if the company could get $6,800 per machine, it would be willing to increase output to 1,500. $6,800 x 1,500 = $10.2 million.

At this point you might be wondering who would pay $6,800 – or even $2,900 – for one of these machines. It does not matter. When we are studying what motivates the supplier, we do not take into consideration whether there would be a demand for this machine or how much

of a demand there would be. We are simply looking for what the supplier would do if it could get these prices.

A more realistic way of thinking about the supply curve is to consider what you would do if your fellow economics students offered to pay you for tutoring services. You tell them that you can offer one hour of tutoring for $10 per hour. Suppose the hour has concluded, and they start begging you to stay to help them. They pool their resources and offer you $75 to stay one more hour. What would you do? At the end of that hour, they are still in dire need of help and offer you $380 to stay one more hour. What would you do?

It should be fairly easy to see that, in the real world, few of your classmates would demand your services at $380 per hour. If they offered you $380 for that last hour, you – or someone like you – would agree to stay and prove the existence of the law of supply.

The second reason why there is a positive relationship between price and quantity supplied is because of the total cost effect.

> ➤ **The total cost effect shows that, at higher rates of production, the short-term costs of production tend to increase; therefore, higher prices are necessary to justify the increase in quantity supplied.**

When Acme increases the production of dream recorders, the company has to hire more workers and order more materials. This leads to higher production costs and the need to increase prices to help cover those costs.

The same is true for you in the tutoring example. Staying an extra hour comes at an increasing opportunity cost. Every hour you stay is an hour you cannot devote to the next-best thing you would like to do. At your job, every extra hour you work is more money you have to pay in taxes and perhaps more money spent on driving

CONCEPT CHECK

What does the supply curve look like for 3D television sets? Why?

to work, cleaning your work clothes, tolls, and so forth. Therefore, your employer offers you your wage, plus a little extra, to entice you to hang around a few more hours.

Graph 6.2 represents a minor "exception" to the law of supply. This diagram illustrates a supply curve where – no matter what price is offered – production levels do not change. In 2006 a $20 bill was auctioned off for $25,300. The bill was not even old. What made it unique is the fact that it has a Del Monte sticker on it, with the serial number over the Del Monte sticker.[18] This means before the bill was finished printing, the sticker got on it, then it went on to the next step of the printing process. There is now exactly one of these bills on Earth. Therefore, if the next buyer offers $250,300 there would be no way to increase the quantity supplied from one to two.

Of course, the law of supply is not nullified by this fact. If the government could get a high enough price, it is possible to increase the quantity of dollars supplied that are precise duplicates of the original.

DEMAND

During the next few seconds, think of something you really want to have. A bigger apartment might be nice. How about tickets to the next Daytona 500? Would a year's supply of massage therapy do it? Now think of something you need. A new car? A do-it-yourself tattoo removal kit?

Earlier we looked at how the market serves our wants and needs, but as it turns out, the word "demand" is *not* the same as the words "want" or "need." The problem with wanting to see the next Daytona 500 or needing to remove an inappropriate tattoo is that we may not be able to purchase these things. Our wants and needs are largely irrelevant if we cannot afford to act on them. Therefore, in this section, we will focus on the factors that influence both our willingness and ability to demand certain goods and services.

> ➤ **Demand is the relationship between the price of an item and the quantity demanded, ceteris paribus.**
> ➤ **Quantity demanded is the amount of an item buyers are willing and able to buy, at a particular price, at a particular moment in time.**

Just like supply and quantity supplied, demand is a relationship between all prices and all possible quantities demanded, while quantity demanded is one amount of purchased goods or services at one particular price. If you spent $4.19 per gallon today on nine gallons of gasoline, the quantity demanded equaled nine at the price of $4.19.

THE DETERMINANTS OF DEMAND

Economists have uncovered over time that the following factors are of significant importance in establishing the demand for goods and services.

- Price
- Income
- Wealth
- Tastes and fashion
- The number of buyers in the market
- The price of substitutes
- The price of complements
- Expectations concerning future prices

Price is clearly the most important determinant of demand. It does not matter how much income or wealth you have, if the price is beyond your ability to pay, you have to move on.

Apartments in Boston can easily rent for over $3,000 per month. This is because of the greater level of **income** and **wealth** that exists in that city compared to other areas around the country. Income is important in all demand considerations. In fact, right after a prospective tenant in Boston learns the price of an apartment, the next step will be to figure out whether the individual brings home enough money to make the payments. Wealth – the accumulated value of our assets – is more important for big-ticket items like a new home, a car, or the purchase of an entire apartment building.

Few things change as fast as consumer **tastes and fashion**. One trip to a clothing store will bear this out. In the mid 1980s a typical college student probably wore Levi's 501 jeans, white canvas Nike shoes, an Izod shirt, and a Members Only jacket. In 2011 you could not find many young folks who would be caught dead in these items – but weathered looking t-shirts, baggy jeans and belly rings were abundant.

While it is very difficult, or even impossible, to measure why or when tastes and fashion change, one thing is very clear to businesses. Once male consumers in Japan decided they wanted to wear lipstick, Japanese retailers did not ask "Why?" Their next step was to react to those changes and serve the customers with lipstick – no matter how the buyers decided on what it is they wanted.[19]

India has a much larger population than the United States. Why then does the U.S. consume far more goods and services than India? The answer lies in the **number of buyers** in the respective markets. A buyer is someone who is willing and able to buy.

The U.S. has far more people with the income and wealth to purchase any number of goods and services; therefore, we have a greater demand than the Indians for almost everything. Within the U.S. this determinant can also be found. Just look at the number of Mercedes dealerships in Beverly Hills compared to Jackson, Mississippi. Jackson is a larger city, but it has a lower per capita income and thus, a lower demand for expensive cars.

The **price of substitutes and complements** also matters in many demand decisions.

If the price of beer skyrocketed next summer, you would see a decrease in the overall demand for peanuts. Complements are goods and services that are jointly consumed, while substitutes are goods and services that are rivals in consumption. During the winter of 2005 the price of home heating oil shot up dramatically. This led to an increase in the demand for firewood in Maine and other New England states.[20] Firewood is a substitute for home heating oil. So, if the price of oil increases, people will be more inclined to switch to an alternative source of heat.

Finally, **expectations of future price changes** can also impact demand. If you saw a report on the news tonight that a major explosion at a gasoline refinery had taken place, you might conclude that the price of gasoline was going to increase in the next few days. That expectation would send you – and/or others like you – out looking for gasoline today before the price increase took place. The opposite is also true. If consumers believe prices will fall in the future, demand tends to decrease today.

THE DEMAND CURVE

As you might imagine, self-interested consumers respond very differently to price changes than suppliers do. In fact, our reaction to price changes is the exact opposite of the sellers.

> ➤ **A demand curve illustrates the relationship between the price of an item and the quantity demanded, ceteris paribus.**

Just like the supply curve, a demand curve is drawn under the assumption that all demand determinants – other than price – are held constant. Let's revisit the dream recorder example to see what this means. Figure 6.3 illustrates a typical consumer response to changes in prices.

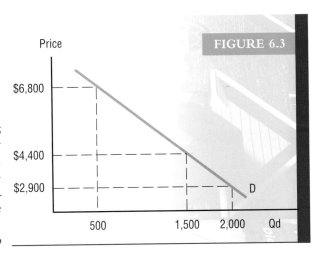

FIGURE 6.3

Notice that at a price of $2,900 the quantity of machines demanded is 2000 per week. If the price were to increase to $4,400, consumers would be willing and able to buy 1500 per week.

Raising prices to $6,800 and higher would continue the downward pressure on quantity demanded. This behavior is typical of how consumers in all markets act. In fact, it does not matter if we are discussing insulin for diabetics, tickets to Oklahoma City Thunder basketball games, or rhubarb pie in British Columbia – every market is ruled by the *law of demand*.

> ➤ **The Law of Demand states that, all things being equal, an increase in prices will lead to a decrease in quantity demanded, while a decrease in prices will lead to an increase in quantity demanded.**

Are there any cases where the law of demand can be challenged?

How many of you did not cut back on the consumption of gasoline as prices increased? If the price of toothpaste increased by $1 a tube, would you walk around with a dirty mouth? If the price of toilet paper increased would you – oh, never mind.

Figure 6.4 illustrates what some students believe to be a valid demand curve for some products that are absolute necessities to our lives. You might be willing to argue that no matter what the price, consumption of certain extreme necessities like electric power and water would never drop. You might make this claim, but you would be wrong to do so.

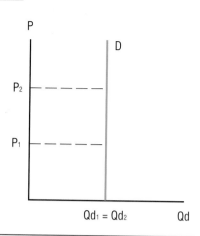

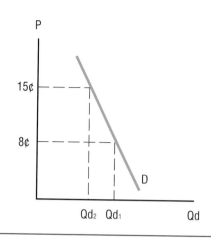

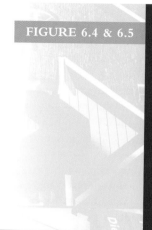

FIGURE 6.4 & 6.5

The more likely demand for electric power looks like figure 6.5, where changes in prices bring about negligible changes in consumption. This is also what the demand for college textbooks, shampoo, soap, car insurance, and other necessities looks like. Notice that, whether prices rise or fall, there is a small change in quantity demanded. This does not mean quantity demanded does not change at all – even for extreme necessities.

The law of demand tells us that consumption levels change as prices change. The law does not tell us when you will change your behavior. If gas prices increased to $9 per gallon, you would alter your driving behavior. Higher electricity or water prices eventually would lead to a more uncomfortable house or a thirstier lifestyle. In some countries in Africa people die because of the law of demand. They cannot afford food. No matter what product or service we are talking about, there is a price where all of us would, at some point, change our behavior. It is just a question of when.

"an invisible hand." This invisible hand is the process of establishing prices and output levels without the formal process of communication – i.e. letters, email, phone calls, riots, and so forth. The invisible hand is a hand guided by self-interested but interdependent parties who realize that each will go without service if a compromise is not sought out.

If the Acme Dream Recorder Company ever becomes a reality, it will face the same problem every company faces when it comes to prices. No one knows exactly what consumers will pay. Businesses have to rely on trial and error to find out what the market will support. Of course, Acme would like to charge $900,000 per machine. Potential customers would like to see a sign that reads "Free Dream Recorders." Neither price is realistic. The moment a price appears on the dream recorder, it will begin a process of creating a mutually agreed-upon price. That price will play at least *four important roles* in our economy.

THE FOUR ROLES PRICES PLAY IN ANY ECONOMY

Now that we understand the forces of supply and demand as separate motivations, let's consider what happens when these opposing forces are thrust together in the market. We will find that Adam Smith was arguably a genius when he discussed the market process as a mechanism driven by

PRICES HELP PREVENT BARTER

While running for a seat as Senator from Nevada, Sue Lowden suggested that "bartering is really good" and that people should "go ahead and barter with your doctor." In a television interview that sought clarification for these comments, she said, "You know, before we all started having health care, in the olden days, our grandparents, they would bring in a chicken to the doctor."[21]

CONCEPT CHECK

During the Irish Potato Famine, some argued that the demand for potatoes actually sloped upward and to the right. Does this make sense? Go online to research this event before you come to your conclusion.

Before coinage, and eventually currency, became widely used to buy goods and services, barter was a major part of the world's economy. *Barter* is the trading of goods and services to meet our wants and needs. The dilemma this poses is clear. Barter, for it to be successful, hinges on the *double coincidence of wants*. That means that you and the person you are trading with have to each want what the other is offering. If you offer your doctor 19 chickens in exchange for a physical, you are going to have a problem if the doctor is a vegetarian or is allergic to chicken feathers.

You should be glad that this is no longer the predominant system that prevails in the United States. You can imagine how long even the most basic transactions would take if every time you ventured into some market you had to bring along a variety of goods in the hope they would be accepted by the seller. By having a system that puts a monetary value on all goods and services, we can easily make a decision on whether or not we will supply or demand anything. After all, your doctor can easily understand your offer of $200 and does not have to inspect your chickens to see how many of them are healthy.

PRICES CONVEY INFORMATION

Let's bring Acme together with potential customers to see how valuable information can be. Figure 6.6 illustrates the possible market conditions that exist for this product.

Notice that, at a price of $2,900, the quantity of recorders supplied by Acme equals 500 per week. Acme isn't saying that this is the *fairest* price possible. Remember, fairness is a subjective evaluation. All we can say is that this is the price Acme wants for one recorder. In this example

Acme has 2,000 people who are willing and able to pay $2,900. Since the quantity of recorders demanded is greater than the quantity supplied, a *shortage* of recorders exists. Does the shortage exist because Acme did not provide enough recorders? No. The shortage exists because the *price is too low.*

This is the first, and often the most difficult, lesson students must learn about markets. When a shortage exists, it means the buyers are telling the seller – through our nonverbal behavior – that the seller could have charged a higher price. We send this information out in an informal manner. Few, if any, of you have ever faced a shortage and explicitly asked the seller to charge you more. Instead, it is the mere fact that there are more people searching for the product than there is product available that signals the seller that they could have charged more.

If people email Acme and ask the company to make more recorders, they are not paying attention to an important lesson from Adam Smith: He reminds us that we do not speak to people about our necessities, but rather about their self-love.[23] If we say, "I need you to make more recorders," Acme can say, "I need you to offer more money to convince me to make more."

What should Acme do now? The company has three *choices.* The first option is to lower prices. This would make no sense whatsoever for Acme's potential customers or for Acme. Lowering prices would decrease the quantity of recorders supplied, because at lower prices Acme has less incentive to build more. At the same time, lower prices would entice some people who were not willing or able to pay $2,900 per machine to come into this market to look for a dream recorder. As a result the shortage would be even worse! In this case Acme would be worse off, and the customers would be worse off because of the lower probability of getting a recorder.

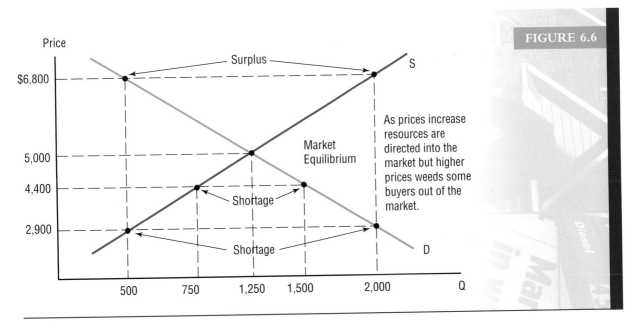

FIGURE 6.6

CONCEPT CHECK

When Microsoft unveiled the XBOX 360 it came at a price of $399. Graphically illustrate and explain why this machine ended up on EBay selling for $2,000.[22]

The second option is to keep prices at $2,900. This is also foolish and inefficient, because leaving the price alone will cause Acme to manufacture more recorders (remember the Law of Supply?) and will not change the number of competing customers.

The only sensible option if Acme wants to be better off while *helping* the customers is to raise prices. Some of you might react by saying, "How is Acme serving people by ripping them off with higher prices!?!" If you think about this option from a rational perspective, you should quickly realize that by raising the price to, say, $4,400, two things would happen. First the resource-directing role of prices will come into effect, and second, the rationing role of prices will appear.

PRICES DIRECT RESOURCES TO THEIR MOST VALUED USE

Let's not romanticize this. Players don't play for little Johnny in the fourth row. A lot of guys who tell you they love this game, wouldn't love it if you didn't pay them $8 million per year.

John Amechi, NBA Basketball Player

What Mr. Amechi can help Acme with is the fact that prices tell us where to put our talents and our resources. You recall that resources are land, labor, capital, and entrepreneurship. As prices increase from $2,900 to $4,400, Acme will be able to cover the costs of producing more machines. This will lead to Acme directing steel, computer chips, and other resources away from less profitable pursuits and into dream recorder production. As a result, the quantity of recorders supplied will increase. In figure 6.6 the output level increases to 750.

It is interesting to note that Acme does not need to know why people would pay $4,400 for a dream recorder. As a *self-interested* company it is instinctively guided to offer more recorders for more money with no other information necessary, just as NBA players are guided to play more years for more money and car manufacturers are persuaded to produce more small cars when gas prices shoot past $4 per gallon.

PRICES RATION SCARCE GOODS

To the average person who tends to be carried through life by emotion, the last role of prices in our free-market economy is the one that is the most upsetting. Figure 6.6 illustrates why. Notice that, as the price of a recorder increased to $4,400, the quantity of recorders demanded fell from 2,000 to 1,500. Five hundred people decided, for whatever reason, that they were not willing and/or not able to pay an extra $1,500 for a dream recorder.

This is the heart of the fairness versus efficiency debate. If you argue that this system is unfair, you are right. It is a totally subjective evaluation that you use to judge unfairness. Those who can afford the dream recorder – or who can't and don't allow emotion to cloud their reasoning – could argue that this change in price is fair. They would be right, too.

What is unquestionable is the fact that this increase in prices is very *efficient*. As prices increase, only those people who are most willing and able to buy will get a dream recorder. Everyone else is weeded out of the market. This is efficient because it has induced Acme to produce more recorders. At the same time, higher prices have also lessened the degree of competition that potential buyers face. This process has thus made the shortage a smaller one and increased the chances of people being served.

CONCEPT CHECK

In 1848 ranchers in Texas were able to sell cattle for $1 per head, while the same cattle fetched $75 per head during the Gold Rush in California.[24] On one graph, illustrate the market supply in each state, the possible market demand in each state and explain how your graph easily illustrates why cattle drives from Texas to railroads in Kansas became commonplace during this time.

CONCEPT CHECK

It could be argued that the free market practices a form of "discrimination" – but not the type of discrimination we are used to reading about. What does this mean in the Oregon oyster market?

Photo courtesy Jack Chambless

What if Acme gets carried away and raises prices to $6,800 per machine? Maybe Acme sees that there is a shortage at $4,400 and miscalculates how much more people would be willing and able to pay for a recorder. At $6,800 the quantity of recorders supplied skyrockets to 2,000 per week. However, the quantity of recorders demanded falls to 500 per week. At this price the quantity supplied exceeds quantity demanded; therefore, a surplus exists. When a *surplus* exists, the information being conveyed by the buyers, is that the price of the product is *too high*.

Once again Acme faces three choices. Raise prices, keep prices where they are, or lower prices. Raising prices would make the surplus even bigger and Acme's profit smaller. Leaving prices alone would guarantee that the surplus continues. Acme will notice the dust gathering on the recorders in the stores and pursue the third option, which is to lower prices. Acme is not lowering prices out of love for its customers, Acme is doing it because of self-love, yet the customers ultimately benefit.

Notice that when the price falls to $5,000 Acme cuts back on production. However, more people come back to look for a recorder. At this price, notice that the quantity of recorders demanded just equals the quantity of recorders supplied. This is known as *market equilibrium*.

> ➤ **Market equilibrium is established when the economic forces of supply and demand have balanced to the point where the quantity buyers are willing and able to buy just equals the quantity sellers are willing and able to sell, at a mutually agreed-upon price.**

At this point there are no angry customers waiting for a chance to record their dreams because of a shortage. Furthermore, at this price, retailers are not standing around with nothing to do while people with dreams to record wait for a sale. For Acme – and the customers left in the market – everyone is satisfied with the result.

APPLICATIONS OF THE INVISIBLE HAND

Now that we have a sound conceptual understanding of how markets work, we can branch out and examine more unusual and analytically challenging examples. So if you are ready to put your mind to work, we will begin.

WHEN IS A SALE NOT A SALE?

The Wall Street Journal once ran an article that examined the practice of discounting products like washing machines and cameras by offering a mail-in rebate.[25] "The whole point behind rebates is to entice purchases and hope (consumers) don't remember to submit" their claims, according to Charles Weil, president of Young America Inc., whose company mails out about 30 million rebate checks a year on behalf of various companies.

With a redemption rate of "only 5–10%," it is obvious how compelling it must be for companies to choose this format to eliminate surpluses. If prices are above equilibrium, and a television company knows that prices will have to fall in order to move the merchandise, why not put the responsibility on the consumer to work for the discount? The consumer sees the ad stating that the set is $150 off the regular price and reacts to that price cut, as the law of demand would predict.

However, when the consumer gets the television home, the hassle of mailing in the rebate form – along with the receipts, UPC symbols, and other items that must accompany the form – makes mailing it in an uneconomic endeavor.

A similar situation exists with coupons that appear in your Sunday paper. How many of you take the time to cut out coupons to save money on deodorant and cat food? If the opportunity cost of cutting out coupons is measured by the value of doing nothing – and doing nothing is more valuable – you will pay full price for cat food, but will at least be well rested when you do.

PROFITS OVER PEOPLE IN AFRICA?

> We are furious at the university's complicity in the denial of access to life-saving medication to poor people across the world. We are disgusted.
>
> Amanda Swarr,
> University of Minnesota graduate student

What was Ms. Swarr talking about? As it turns out, she was complaining about the fact that the University of Minnesota was expected to collect more than $300 million in royalties from its patent on Ziagen, an AIDS drug, sold by GlaxoSmithKline.

The protestors, like the ones at Yale, who were successful in getting Bristol-Myers Squibb Co. to relinquish patent rights for an AIDS drug in South Africa, were up in arms over profit being earned in the Africa market for AIDS medication.

Over 22 million people in Africa[26] – by far more than in any other continent – suffer from AIDS. Making matters worse is the fact that new drug-resistant strains of HIV have been spreading throughout the world, lowering the odds of helping as many people as society would like to see helped.[27]

In response to mounting international pressure, many of the drug companies have lowered the price of AIDS medication – in some cases below the actual cost of manufacturing the drugs.[28] As figure 6.7 illustrates, the price cuts may not be enough to satisfy the AIDS patients or the student activists.

Even with lower prices, the overall quantity demanded has not increased very much, because the income of the average African with AIDS is so low that – even at an average price of $1 per day for some medication – there is still going to be a surplus of unsold treatments.

For the student protestors, only a price of zero would satisfy them. However, we can use market equilibrium analysis to see that, at a price of zero, the quantity demanded would increase, but the incentives to provide medication in Africa would fall dramatically. Maybe some donations would occur to foster goodwill, but the cost of production would far exceed the total revenue ($0), and therefore a massive shortage of medicine would break out. Ultimately, the shortage of medicine would hurt far more Africans then the market price would.

WHAT IS A NEW BABY WORTH?

> I've got championship Rottweilers. I sell them by supply and demand. I raise thoroughbred racehorses. I sell them by supply and demand. I'm not going to let people sell children by supply and demand. What's the difference between that and slavery?
>
> Reverend Ken Hutcherson

What is the reverend talking about? Well, he is talking about the fact that there is a market for children, and the market price is a function of race. Yes, that's right: Children of different races are "worth" different amounts of money in the adoption business.

Reverend Hutcherson is fighting to change the laws of supply and demand from his Redmond, Washington, church. He is upset because in the market for adopted babies, white children routinely "sell" for $35,000. Latino babies go for $10,000, and black babies are sold for $4,000 to their new parents.

The reverend argues that, besides putting a price on children, the practice discriminates against white babies and people who seek to adopt them by charging them more. "I know about discrimination," said Hutcherson, who is black. "Tell me if it was black babies that cost $50,000 and white babies that cost $4,000, people would be screaming their heads off."

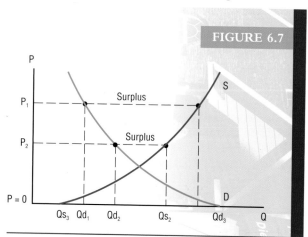

FIGURE 6.7

CONCEPT CHECK

Using three separate diagrams, illustrate and then explain why the prices are different for each group of babies. Would a law creating a uniform price of $10,000 make economic sense? Why or why not?

THE ECONOMICS OF RECYCLING

If you are like many Americans, you want to leave the Earth as clean as you can for your children and grandchildren. This is a noble goal that I share with you, but the economics of recycling does not add up as nicely as we would like for it to.

According to *BioCycle* magazine's annual survey, the United States has over 7,200 curbside recycling programs serving 108 million people. Furthermore, every state in the union has some type of program aimed at recycling. The programs range from diverting large amounts of plastics, aluminum, paper, and cardboard from landfills to sorting facilities, which send them on their way to be reused in manufacture, to simply having state governments buy products containing recycled materials. "It's become a way of life," says Donald Berman, director of solid waste management for Allegheny County, Pennsylvania, which includes Pittsburgh.

But is it a way of life that makes economic and environmental sense? Recently a number of economists and policy analysts have questioned whether the benefits of recycling outweigh the cost of disposing of waste materials in landfills. Critics say that what seems at first to make a great deal of sense doesn't always stand up to a close examination. For instance, some critics argue that collection costs make recycling a bad bargain for many localities because the costs often exceed the prices that the recyclables bring on the open market. They also charge that operating additional trucks to pick up recyclables increases toxic diesel emissions, offsetting any environmental gains.[29]

As figure 6.8 illustrates, in many cities, the government doesn't even pay for paper, cans, and bottles. The recycler – the good citizen – has to pay the government to take the stuff away. This means supply and demand intersect at a *negative* price! Not many markets are characterized by the seller paying the buyer. It appears that in order to keep Earth clean, we have to.

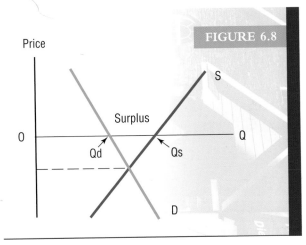

FIGURE 6.8

WHEN FAIRNESS IS AN UNFAIR THING

The following photo is of the Snappy Lunch – a restaurant so famous for its fried pork chop sandwiches that Oprah Winfrey regularly flies all the way to Mt. Airy, North Carolina, to eat here. Why is there a waiting line at this place?

Look at the little boy waiting in the July heat for a sandwich. Should he have to suffer because this restaurant does not comply with the laws of supply and demand? What if he fainted from hunger? The elderly folks in front

SUGGESTED CLASSROOM DEBATE

Go online to conduct research on the business practices of WWII industrialist Oskar Schindler. Then, graphically illustrate and fully explain what the market for Jewish employees looked like for him during the war. Was he benevolent or simply a clever businessman? Why?

of him don't seem to care that he is hungry. Of course, after waiting over an hour for a table, maybe they should tell him that part of life is learning to suffer.

However, we could argue that if the Snappy Lunch raised prices from less than $3 per sandwich to say, $5, then some people who were only marginally interested in a pork chop sandwich would not go in. This would ration the sandwiches to the parents of this little fellow, Oprah Winfrey, and anybody else who were willing and able to pay. The higher price in effect is arguably the fairest price since there would be less wasted time in lines, people who like pork chops – and who

have $5 – would be served, and the Snappy Lunch would earn more money! Now we turn to the government's handling of park entrance fees.

It should not come as any great shock that the United States government has blown it when it comes to pricing a service. After all, since the government is a not-for-profit agency, what reason would it have to let market forces dictate entrance fees to our national parks? You might even agree that the government should not act like Disney World and charge over $65 per day. However, there is an untold part of the story that you need to know.

Waiting lines like the one depicted in the following photograph have caused severe damage to Yellowstone National Park.[30]

With prices well below equilibrium, an artificially high number of cars enter this valuable park each year. This leads to a shortage of space for vacationers to enjoy the mountains, geysers, and wildlife, and – perhaps more troubling – a shortage of quiet, clean air and protection that the animals and the ecosystem need to survive.

Each year, the NPS reports that Yellowstone's infrastructure is crumbling due to too many cars. Each year, the NPS reports that not enough money is available to hire people to protect the animals and animal habitat. And each year, the NPS charges prices that are so far below

the market equilibrium price that these problems only intensify.

What if the NPS charged $100 per car, per week? On one hand you could say, "Unfair! The parks belong to all of us, and $100 fees discriminate against the poor!" On the other hand you could argue that if the poor really care about the long-term health of the park, they will understand the need to raise prices. Then you could argue that, if the poor want to see the parks enough, they will save the extra money needed to visit. Finally, you could argue that there is no guarantee the poor will see Yellowstone at $25 if the NPS ever sets limits on the number of cars that can enter to ration the scarce space.[31]

It should be noted that the cost to drive through the Great Smoky Mountain National Park is $0. Consequently, at popular attractions like Cades Cove, it can take two hours to travel just a few miles and this park has been hit by some of the highest levels of air pollution in the Eastern United States.[32]

What to Do if a Gun Range Opens Near Your Home

Ronald Coase won the Nobel Prize for Economics in 1991. During his lifetime as an economist, he distinguished himself by a paper he published in 1960 that revolutionized the economics profession.[33]

It was in this paper that Mr. Coase argued that, as long as property rights are clearly defined and transaction costs are low, any two people facing a disagreement should be able to use the market system to reach a reasonable accord. Before we explore his views, let's take a brief look at four types of goods and the degree to which each is excludable (one where the supplier of the good can prevent people who refuse to pay from consuming it) or non-excludable (one where the supplier cannot prevent non-payers from using it).

> ➤ **Private goods are goods that are excludable and rival in consumption. Rival in consumption means that the same good cannot be consumed by more than one person at the same time. Examples include airline tickets, underwear, and contact lenses.**
> ➤ **Artificially Scarce Goods: Goods that are excludable, but nonrival in consumption. This means that more than one person can consume the good at a time but some can be excluded. Examples include video games and pay-per-view movies.**
> ➤ **Common Property Resources: Goods that are non-excludable and rival in consumption. Fish from a lake, the air we breathe, and a forest trail come to mind.**
> ➤ **Public Goods: Goods that are non-excludable and nonrival in consumption. National defense is the classic example of a good that everyone gets to enjoy and no one can be turned away.**

The people in eastern Georgia could use Ronald Coase right now. In many rural areas, residents are awakening to an entrepreneurial endeavor that is a bit noisy – and at times that is somewhat inconvenient. What residents are upset about is the opening of a gun range near local farms.

The basic problem in this case is that farmers own their land (a private good, excludable in consumption) – as do the gun range owners – but no one owns the air surrounding the land. The air is *common property*, so the farmers face some difficulty in claiming that they should be guaranteed quiet. It would appear that they have no recourse, unless they understand the Coase Theorem.

> ➤ **The Coase Theorem states that if people can negotiate the purchase and sale of the right to perform activities that cause externalities, they can arrive at efficient solutions to the problems caused by externalities. An externality is any positive or negative spillover effect from the consumption of a good or service.**

In this case the *negative externality* is the noise generated by the rifle range. Suppose the value of quiet to a local farmer is $80 per hour after 5 a.m., while the value of running the rifle range is equal to $60 per hour after 5 p.m. At an official price of zero, the quantity of silence demanded exceeds the quantity of noise supplied. Notice that, at a price equal to zero, the farmer does not expect total silence, but he doesn't want the quantity being supplied either. Therefore, there is a shortage of quiet in his home.

If the *transactions cost* of negotiating with the rifle range equals zero – meaning he doesn't mind approaching the range owner with an offer, or working out an offer – he could consider letting the range owner know that he would be willing to pay $80 per hour – after 5 p.m. – for quiet. Of course, if the farmer is smart, he will attempt to pool the resources of the local farmers so he doesn't have to pay the entire cost.

If the range owner is smart, he will agree, since he was earning $60 per hour after 5 p.m. and the farmers are offering $80 to close down in the evening hours. The farmer could actually approach the range owner and say, "How much would you be willing to take to close down at 5 p.m.?" The range owner might say "$61," in which case both parties are still better off.

Through negotiation the parties have simply changed the air around them from common property to private property.

ENDNOTES

1 Authors note: This is the one area where I envy people with cell phones…

2 See "Phone-Wielding Shoppers Strike Fear into Retailers" by Miguel Bustillo and Ann Zimmerman, *The Wall Street Journal,* December 16, 2010.

3 "The Age of 'Wal-Mart' Airlines Crunches the Biggest Carriers," by Melanie Trottman and Scott McCartney, *The Wall Street Journal,* June 18, 2002.

4 See "Bargain Air Fares Spark Probe" by Melanie Trottman and Stephen Power, *The Wall Street Journal,* April 11, 2002, p. D1.

5 See "Keep it Moving" by Bruce Ingersoll, *The Wall Street Journal,* January 20, 1993.

6 See "Egg-donor business booms on campuses" by Jim Hopkins, *The USA Today,* March 16, 2006; and "Women touting their bodies to sell dream of the perfect child" by James Bone, *The London Times,* March 20, 2006.

7 See "A fair debate: Do human beings possess a genetic drive for fairness?" by Faye Flam, *The Orlando Sentinel,* from Knight Ridder Newspapers, September 24, 2000; and "There's economic theory, and then there's reality" by Steven Pearlstein, *The Orlando Sentinel* from *The Washington Post,* February 10, 2002.

8 See "Selling Candy With a Conscience" by Leslie Josephs, *The Wall Street Journal,* December 24, 2010.

9 See "Charity, hope and consumer faith in both" by Beth Kassab, *The Orlando Sentinel,* December 24, 2010.

10 See "The Civilizing Effect of the Market" by David Wessel, *The Wall Street Journal,* January 24, 2002.

11 Source: Fort Stevens State Park, Oregon.

12 See "In Central Florida, gas prices pump up bike, scooter sales" by Sarah Hale Meitner, *The Orlando Sentinel,* June 8, 2004.

13 See "The psychology of spending" by Gregory Karp, *The Orlando Sentinel,* November 7, 2010; and "Darling, why the urge to buy that sexy dress? Oh…." By Christopher Snowbeck, *The St. Paul Pioneer Press,* August 2010.

14 See "Can Potter Lift Lagging Resort?" by Jason Garcia, *The Orlando Sentinel,* May 30, 2010; and "Potter Works Magic for Hotels" by Sara W. Clarke, *The Orlando Sentinel,* January 21, 2011.

15 See "Universal Draws 46% more visitors" by Jason Garcia, *The Orlando Sentinel,* January 22, 2011.

16 For example, new regulations on the way shrimp can be caught in the Gulf of Mexico has dramatically increased the cost of fishing for shrimp. This has led to the bankruptcy of many shrimpers in the Gulf Coast region and an opening for foreign shrimpers – who do not face the same regulations – to enter the market and take over for the Americans that are now unemployed. See "Sunset for Shrimpers?" by Mark Holan, *The Tampa Tribune,* April 4, 2004.

17 See "Chinese Cotton to Hoarding" by Carolyn Cui, *The Wall Street Journal,* January 29-30, 2011.

18 See "The $25,300 Bill" by Christopher Boyd, *The Orlando Sentinel,* January 7, 2006.

19 See "Asia's Lipstick Lads" by Geoffrey A. Fowler, *The Wall Street Journal,* May 27, 2005.

20 See "With fuel costs up. Firewood prices, sales, soar" *The Orlando Sentinel,* January 2, 2005.

21 See "Chickens for check-ups and a cup of GOP tea" by Eugene Robinson, *The Orlando Sentinel,* May 2, 2010.

22 See "XBOX 360: Stores Sell Out Fast" by Chris Cobbs, *The Orlando Sentinel,* November 23, 2005; and "Why Shortages of Hot Gifts Endure as a Christmas Ritual" by Nick Wingfield and Robert A. Guth, *The Wall Street Journal,* December 2, 2005.

23 See *The Wealth of Nations* by Adam Smith, 1776 Book 1; pg. 14.

24 Source: National Cowboy Hall of Fame and Western Heritage Museum, Oklahoma City, Oklahoma.

25 See "Rebates Secret Appeal to Manufacturers: Few Consumers Actually Redeem Them" by William M. Bulkeley, *The Wall Street Journal,* February 10, 1998.

26 Source: UNAIDS factsheet.

27 See "Student Protestors Target Universities Profiting from AIDS Research" by Rachel Zimmerman, *The Wall Street Journal,* April 12, 2001.

28 See "Drug Resistant Strains of HIV Are Spreading" by Mark Schoops, *The Wall Street Journal,* February 8, 2001.

29 See www.ehpnet1.niehs.nih.gov/docs/1995/103-11/focus2.html.

30 Take a look at www.cnn.com/2000/NATURE/04/05/endangered. parks/ as well as www.yellowstone.net/.

31 Only recently did the NPS raise prices from $20 per week to $25. At the Smoky Mountain National Park – where there is no fee at all – the air pollution that has been generated in places like Cades Cove is among the worst in the entire United States. See "Entrance fees to rise at some national parks" www.cnn.com, September 27, 2005; and "Visitors flock to Smoky Mountains valley, www.cnn.com, September 13, 2005.

32 Source: nps.gov.

33 For more on Coase, see www.nobel.se/economics/laureates/1991/coase-autobio.html. To read his paper, "The Problem of Social Cost," see 3 *Journal of Law & Economics* 1 (1960).

CHAPTER REVIEW

1. What is Say's Law? Does this law apply to medicine, food, and education? Why, or why not?

2. Why do demand curves and supply curves have the slope that they do?

3. Does the law of demand apply to gasoline? Why, or why not? Does the law of supply apply to land? Why, or why not?

4. What are the four key roles prices play in a market? Use the market for steak to explain.

5. Explain how the Coase Theorem could be used to clean up the Earth's oceans.

Chapter Seven

CHANGES *in* SUPPLY *and* DEMAND

Shutterstock © CURAphotography, 2011.

*I*t will not make a difference if Saudi Arabia ships an extra
million or two million barrels of crude oil to the United
States if you cannot refine it. It will not turn into gasoline,
and it will not turn into lower prices.

ADEL AL-JUBEIR, FOREIGN POLICY ADVISOR TO
CROWN PRINCE ABDULLAH OF SAUDI ARABIA

FROM SNAPSHOT TO VIDEO

As your income and age increases, do you think you will eat out at nicer restaurants and wear different clothing than you do now? What will happen to housing and gas prices in your state next year? Does it make sense that the technology associated with producing hybrid cars will change, or that the number of sellers in the video-game market will remain what it is today?

In the last chapter we focused solely on changes in prices and the way price changes impact quantity demanded and quantity supplied. In this chapter we will relax the assumption that the other determinants of demand and supply do not change. We will take an in-depth look at what happens when market equilibrium is disrupted by changes in supply and/or demand. This investigation will put you in a much better position to understand the changing world around us.

CHANGES IN DEMAND VS. CHANGES IN QUANTITY DEMANDED

In the wake of rising gasoline prices in 2008, newspapers around the country reported on the drop in demand for large trucks and SUVs – and the increase in demand for small cars.[1] As the economy weakened during that time we also observed an increase in consumer spending at places like Wal-Mart and Costco, while Target and Kohl's suffered.[2] We also witnessed a huge drop in the demand for real estate agents as the housing market seemed to fall apart.[3]

You might also recall that the price of food increased dramatically during the latter part of this decade – and into the new one. As a result of higher prices at the grocery store, nurseries around the country reported a significant increase in the sales of fruit and vegetable plants.[4]

Did the rise in grocery prices lead to an increase in the demand for nursery plants or and increase in the quantity of nursery plants demanded?

The answer is: demand. Why? Recall from chapter six that, if the price of a good or service changes, there will be a change only in the *quantity demanded* for that good or service. If you went into a nursery and saw a sign that read "Today Only! 46% off all rutabaga plants," you and others like you might be inclined to respond to the price cut by buying one or two more plants than you normally would. Take a minute to draw a demand curve to re-prove the law of demand.

At a price of $3 per plant, perhaps your quantity demanded might equal one per week. At $1.25 per plant you might buy two per week.

Notice that a movement along the demand curve represents the increase from one to two plants. If you can't draw this, go back to chapter six or take a look at figure 7.1.

Notice that as the price changes, only quantity demanded changes. However, this is a *monumentally different* event compared to a change in demand.

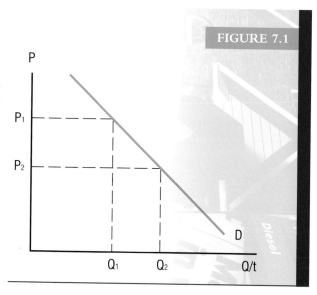

FIGURE 7.1

A change in demand occurs if, and only if, some demand determinant, *other than the price*, changes.

Let's review what those "other" determinants are:

- Income
- Wealth
- Tastes and fashion
- The number of buyers in the market
- The price of substitutes
- The price of complements
- Expectations concerning future prices

In figure 7.2 you can see what happens if the demand for a good or service changes. Suppose rutabaga plants normally sell for $3 per plant. When the price of vegetables increases at the supermarket this creates an interest in nursery plants among many people that did not have anything to do with changes in the price of nursery grown plants! Simply put, the number of buyers in the market for nursery plants increased.

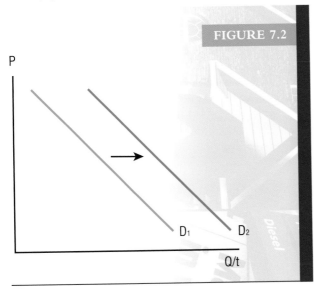

FIGURE 7.2

All of this led to an increase in the overall demand for nursery plants. This can be seen as a rightward shift in the entire demand schedule. In essence, the old demand curve disappeared, and consumers – at all possible prices – were more willing to buy nursery plants.

If any of you get stumped on the difference between changes in demand and changes in quantity demanded, your professor will accurately suggest that you practice the

following analysis and simply keep in mind that a demand curve represents all possible prices and all possible quantities demanded at those prices. Therefore, *any time prices change, the only thing that can happen is a change in quantity demanded*.

CHANGES IN DEMAND AND THE IMPACT ON MARKET EQUILIBRIUM

In order to grasp the impact of a change in demand on a stable market condition, you must be able to work through the *chain of causation* that takes place. The term "chain of causation" means that as one event takes place it will cause the next event to take place. The causal links in demand analysis can be summarized in the following four questions that you must be able to answer:

- What demand determinant or determinants has/have changed or will change, and in what direction?
- What was, or will be, the impact on the demand for the good or service?
- What was, or will be, the impact on the price of the good or service?
- What was, or will be, the impact on the quantity of the good or service supplied?

For most students, the most difficult step in this process of analysis is step one. You may have a hard time at first being able to single out which determinant or determinants are changing. Two helpful tools to manage step one are to commit to memory the determinants of demand and to try to use logic to determine which determinant is changing. A good memory and sense of logic will help you here.

CASE STUDY #1: HAVE YOU HAD YOUR GRASS-FED BEEF TODAY?

As we all know, it seems like every other week someone is on television telling us about the latest and greatest food

CONCEPT CHECK

When the Boston Red Sox won the 2004 World Series, it ended an 86-year period in which they failed to win a championship. During this period between 1918 and 2004, many vendors made a lot of money selling t-shirts and other items suggesting that the Red Sox were cursed.[5] After the 2004 World Series, did the demand for these shirts decrease, or did quantity demanded decrease? How do you know?

or supplement that we should eat more of in order to avoid dying before we are 50.

Dennis and Alicia Stoltzfoos operate Full Circle Farms near Mayo, Florida. Their farm specializes in beef from cattle that has grazed entirely on organically grown grasses. No hormones, steroids, or corn-based feed ever enters the bodies of their cattle. They had a nice business going until the movie Food, Inc. came out. Now they are so busy fielding emails, phone calls, and processing new orders that they normally put in dawn to dusk work hours.[6]

This movie depicted the very difficult lives that cattle, chickens, pigs, and other animals we eat go through in large, commercial operations. Once people got to see how their food is treated, it led to a huge increase in the demand for humanely raised animal products.

Shutterstock © photazz, 2011.

As you can clearly see in figure 7.3, we are depicting an increase in the demand for grass-fed beef. If we refer back to the four questions in the chain of causation, we can see what has occurred in this market.

1. As people have become more health-conscious, there has been an increase in the *number of buyers* in the market for grass-fed beef. There was also an increase in *consumer tastes* for this product.

2. With more buyers in the market – along with an increase in consumer tastes – the *demand* for grass-fed beef has *increased*. In figure 7.3 this is represented by a rightward shift in the entire demand curve.

3. What would have happened if demand had increased, but grass-fed beef suppliers had kept prices constant at P1? At this price you can take one look at where quantity demanded would be on the new demand curve (D2), and you will see that a *shortage* of this product would have emerged. How does the market get rid of shortages? *Prices must increase.* On figure 7.3 you can see that the new price (P2) establishes a new equilibrium condition.

4. What do you suppose beef suppliers did in response to higher prices? If you are guessing that they *increased quantity supplied,* then you are correct. The last step is simply verification of the law of supply. The more money you can make, the more incentives you have to offer grass-fed beef to consumers who are concerned about their health and the humane treatment of animals.

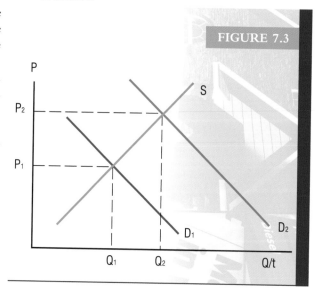

FIGURE 7.3

CONCEPT CHECK

As economic growth heated up in China and India, the overall price of copper used in construction projects increased all over the world.[7] Graphically illustrate and explain why copper prices shot up in 2010 as a result.

THE ECONOMICS OF PRICE-GOUGING

A huge question for debate is whether or not higher prices during wars or natural disasters constitute a form of reprehensible "price-gouging" or a much-needed dose of free-market economics.

When natural disasters strike, hoarding becomes pervasive. Ask any resident of Florida what the 2004–2005 plywood market looked like and they will tell you that it resembled the earliest stages of a riot.

Impending storms creates panic buying that makes the average consumer buy a great deal more plywood, water, ice, etc. than he or she normally would. The demand determinant at work here is *expectations of future prices*. When people think that prices will rise in the future, demand increases significantly.

As demand increases, the natural progression of events suggests that prices will rise. Rising prices lead to a much-needed dose of market-correcting in many ways.

First, as prices rise, hoarding is dramatically reduced. The entire reason people buy enough bread to hold a picnic for some small countries is because the government prohibits grocery stores from raising prices to a level that would slow down the rate at which people stock their shopping carts. If prices are allowed to rise, more of these essential items would be available for more of our fellow shoppers. This is simply the *rationing role of prices* at work. Some would argue that higher prices would mean that poorer people would be shut out of the market. The problem with this argument is that poor people are no better off showing up only to find the shelves are bare. At least with higher prices the poor have a chance of finding a little of what they need.

A second benefit of price-gouging is that it speeds up the rate at which suppliers send products to areas affected by disasters. This is the *resource-directing role of prices*. If the quantity of plywood demanded exceeds the quantity supplied, but prices are not allowed to reflect that, what incentive does a lumber company have to incur the expense of rushing extra plywood into that area? Should the lumber companies operate under the mantra of promoting the moral good of the community? Is this why they are in business?

No. The companies are in business to make money. If, in the process of making a few extra bucks per foot of plywood, they are given the incentives to rush the wood to people who need it, this assures that more of us get plywood.

How much should water cost when the wind is blowing 127 mph?

Photo courtesy Jack Chambless

When my daughter was in the first grade, she came into my office to show me three "books" she had constructed. One was a book about a bat, one was about a cat, and the third one was about a dog. When she asked me if I would like to have one of the books, I jokingly asked, "How much money do you want?" She replied, "Zero dollars for one, $3 for two and $30 for three." When I queried her as to why she wanted such a high price for all three books, she said, "Because if you take all three, Sarah [my wife] and Gehrig [her brother] won't get any."

If a six-year old understands the importance of how prices ration scarce goods, then anyone should be able to.

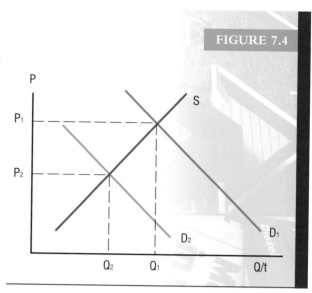

FIGURE 7.4

Case Study #2: Do you mind telling me where those Oysters came from?

This is a question that hundreds of thousands of sea-food loving Americans may have found themselves asking in 2010 and 2011.

That is because people have this really funny aversion to eating oysters that are tainted with petroleum…

The BP oil spill constituted an unmitigated disaster for businesses that deal in wholesale and retail oysters. With the threat of contamination in one of the world's greatest oyster-producing regions, it was not long before dramatic changes took place in this market.

1. As a result of the oil spill in the Gulf of Mexico, *the number of buyers* and consumer *tastes* for Gulf oysters plummeted.[8]
2. As the number of buyers in the market fell, the overall *demand* for Gulf oysters *fell*. Figure 7.4 illustrates a decrease in demand. A decrease in demand means that at all prices, buyers were less willing to buy Gulf oysters than they had been before.
3. As the demand for Gulf oysters fell, a surplus of oysters broke out at the old price (P1). This left many oyster dealers with no other option than to begin to offer lower-priced options, (P2), which is precisely what happened over time.
4. As prices fell, oyster sellers saw that selling Gulf oysters in many locations was not very profitable, so the

overall *quantity supplied decreased* as the less profitable suppliers closed down. After all, why would they maintain the same output if fewer buyers existed?

Why Amish Grocers Enjoy Recessions

Normally, when the economy is strong the demand for most goods and services goes up.

Conversely, when unemployment is rising and people are earning less money, the demand for various products tends to fall. That is not the case when people consider some goods to be *inferior goods*.

> ➤ **An inferior good is a good that people buy more of during bad economic times and less of during times where consumer income and wealth is increasing.**

A lot of college students drive used cars, eat low-quality fast food, and drink cheap beer. However, you might find that as your income goes up over time, your demand for these things will drop because you consider them inferior when compared to new cars, expensive meals, and imported beer.[9]

CONCEPT CHECK

When NFL quarterback, Ben Roethlisberger was accused of inappropriate advances and contact toward more than one woman, he was suspended for the first four games of the 2010 NFL season and the price of his jerseys fell sharply in Pennsylvania. Graphically illustrate and explain why.

When the U.S. economy slid into a recession in 2007 an interesting thing happened in parts of the country where Amish retail shops exist – the demand for goods in these shops actually increased.[10]

With traditional grocery store prices rising, many Americans opted for inferior goods like pesto sauce that was five months past the "best if used by" date; boxes of corn taco shells that had water damage – and were taped up and other expired, dented or questionable items.

CHANGES IN SUPPLY

Now that we know what happens when consumers change their mind about a product – for better or worse – we now turn our attention to how changes in supply determinants (other than price) can impact the market. Recall that, other than price, our supply determinants are:

- Input Costs
- Technology
- The number of sellers serving the market
- The price of other goods that can be produced with inputs used or owned by the seller
- Expectations concerning future prices

If any of these determinants change, there will be a change in the supply of the good or service in question. This is different than a change in quantity supplied. If the price of snowmobiles increases in New Hampshire, the quantity of snowmobiles supplied will increase and vice versa. If the input costs of making snowmobiles change, there will be a new supply curve in the snowmobile market. This is because changes in input costs, technology, or any other determinant of supply alters the willingness and ability of the supplier to provide the good or service. The following questions must be answered in analyzing a change in supply.

- What determinant or determinants of supply has/have changed or will change, and in what direction?
- What was, or will be, the impact on the supply of the good or service?
- What was, or will be, the impact on the price of the good or service?
- What was, or will be, the impact on the quantity of the good or service demanded?

CASE STUDY # 3: ANYONE FOR AN LCD TELEVISION?

Over the past several years the pace of technological change has been staggering. While this can be scary for some, there is no question that our lives have been positively impacted by the emergence of things like computers, cell phones, remote control, DVD players, and satellite dishes.[11] Can you imagine what your life would be like if you had to rely on typewriters, pay phones, and record players?

Not only have we been exposed to an array of new technological goodies to consider buying, the prices of all of these items continues to fall and the products have become better and better at serving us. Is this magic? Yes. It is the magic of the free market. In figure 7.5 we will look at one market – the LCD (liquid crystal display) television market – to find the explanation for why all of the high-tech items we crave have become more powerful and less expensive.

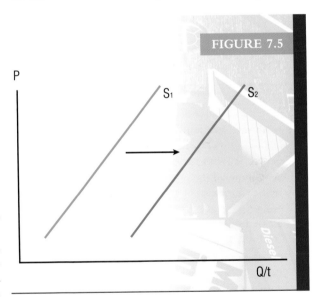

FIGURE 7.5

1. Over the past few years, the *technology* associated with making LCD televisions *has increased* dramatically as manufacturers have learned more and more about how to improve the efficiency of their production processes. As technology has increased, the *input costs* of producing LCD televisions have *fallen*. This is because better technology in the production of liquid-crystal display panels led to economies of scale – cost savings associated with large-scale production. As the input costs of production have fallen, this has led to *more sellers* entering the market for LCD televisions.

2. With more sellers and lower costs of production, the result has been (and will continue to be) an *increase in the supply* (S2) of LCD televisions. An increase in supply means that at all prices sellers are more willing and able to supply than before. If we superimpose figure 7.5 on 7.6 we see that an increase in supply – in the market – is a rightward shift in the entire supply schedule.

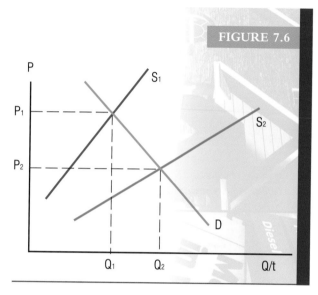

FIGURE 7.6

3. While LCD manufacturers would love to be able to continue charging the $8,990 price that was being fetched for 42-inch models in 2004, they can't. This is because, with heightened competition, an increase in supply with no corresponding cut in prices would lead to surpluses of LCD televisions. At some point one or more companies had to *lower prices* – and still make profit – due to falling costs of production. By 2011 many these sets could be had for under $500.

4. As prices have fallen, self-interested consumers have become more apt to buy an LCD television. As you recall from the law of demand, lower prices will lead to an *increase in the quantity demanded*. This has been precisely the case in all markets where technology is important, from laptop computers to DVD burners.[12]

CASE STUDY # 4: STELLA LIEBECK AND YOUR BIG MAC

Coffee is supposed to be hot.

Jerry Seinfeld

If you are like many other college students, good nutrition constitutes eating cheeseburgers – for breakfast. If you are like all consumers, the price you pay for everything from cheeseburgers to movie theater tickets is impacted greatly by lawsuits and government regulation.

Several years ago, Stella Liebeck – aged 81 years at the time, entered the drive – through window at a McDonald's near her home and ordered a cup of coffee. While removing the lid to add cream and sugar, she spilled the coffee, causing third-degree burns of the groin, inner thighs, and buttocks. Her lawyers argued that the coffee was too hot and therefore defective, and a New Mexico jury awarded her $2.9 million in damages.

More recently, two class-action lawsuits were filed against McDonald's and others charging that the restaurants are responsible for customers becoming obese. The most recent class-action lawsuit was on behalf of some of New York's homeless children, claiming that fast foods were causing a national epidemic of obese children. These lawsuits are causing many people to wonder where the responsibility for obesity lies – in the hands of those who eat the food or those who make it.[14]

Before you jump up and down in celebration over lawsuits that punish "evil" corporations, please bear in mind that lawsuits like these, along with the threat of lawsuits and overt government regulation of businesses, all

Photo courtesy Jack Chambless

CONCEPT CHECK

In the wake of Hurricane Katrina, a surplus of unskilled labor emerged in places like Houston, Texas,[13] while in southern Mississippi many fast-food restaurants had to put up signs like the one seen above. On two graphs, illustrate the labor supply changes that took place in Houston and in Biloxi, Mississippi.

have one thing in common: They lead to higher prices for all of us. Figure 7.7 illustrates this fact.

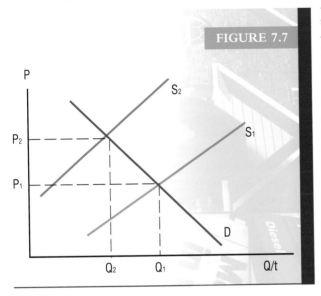

FIGURE 7.7

1. As you can clearly see, when a jury awards staggering damages to the "victims" of "careless" companies, this translates into *higher costs of production* for the company in question. The higher costs may come in the form of the damages paid out, but more likely in the form of rising insurance costs to cover potential lawsuits over fatty hamburgers and hot coffee!

2. As the input costs of production increase, this means sellers are less willing and able to supply their products at the previous price level. The result? *A decrease in the supply of the good or service* (S2). The decrease in supply does not necessarily mean less coffee will be served. It simply means that McDonald's will be less willing and able to supply coffee for the price we used to pay.

3. As supply decreases, *upward pressure is put on prices* (P2) to help recover the higher costs of production.

4. As the prices of these products increase, the *quantity demanded will fall* – forcing consumers who do not spill hot coffee to help pay the price for those who do.

Ms. Liebeck is not alone. In 2005 Roy Pearson took a pair of pants to his drycleaner for a $10.50 alteration. Apparently, the pants were misplaced and Mr. Pearson sued the business for between $54 million and $67 million – plus $2 million for "pain and suffering."[15] This mentality has also led to lawsuits claiming that smokers are the victims of tobacco companies. Tobacco companies recently agreed to pay damages of over $200 billion to settle the suit with states seeking money to pay for the health care needs of smokers. A growing number of metropolitan areas have begun suing the makers of guns, claiming that the gun industry victimizes people by selling guns in an irresponsible manner.[16]

For you readers who enjoy surfing in Florida, you may have noticed a change that has taken place in the surfboard industry. This change has some of you reaching a bit deeper into your wallets, in order to catch a nice wave.

From 1961 to 2005, Gordon Clark ran the Clark Foam company – a business that produced about 80% of the polyurethane foam "blanks" used to produce surf boards.

All of a sudden, Mr. Clark decided he was leaving the business. The reason for his sudden departure was pretty straightforward. He got tired of getting pushed around by people who don't surf.

The lawsuits were not coming from surfers who kept getting hurt. In this case, the lawsuits kept coming from government regulators who were constantly bothering Clark Foam about the environmental implications of the company's production process.

The production of blanks relies on the use of a chemical called Toluene diisocyanate, or TDI, which manufacturers say made Clark's foam core light and sturdy.[17] The government apparently did not care about light or sturdy as much as the effects of this chemical spilling during the production process. Thus, after years of hassling with regulators, Mr. Clark abruptly left the business.

The impact of his departure was felt immediately. With a major supplier gone, the remaining sellers in the market increased their prices substantially. Then, the surf shops, facing higher input costs, increased prices as well.[18]

CONCEPT CHECK

In the wake of the fears stirred up by "Mad Cow Disease," the German government now requires that German pig farmers follow new regulations. The regulations include a rule that a pig should get one square meter of stall space and a straw or soft rubber mat for napping. When it's time to play, the pigs must have chains or chewy toys on hand. Each pig must get at least eight hours of daylight. During the darker, shorter days of winter, farmers must compensate with lamps. Finally, there is the declaration that a farmer or farmhand must spend at least 20 seconds looking at each pig each day – and back up the loving care with paperwork showing he has enough pig-hands to provide quality time.[20] What, do you suppose, this has meant for pork *consumers* in Germany? Why?

By the second half of the last decade prices had fallen slightly – as suppliers from China and other foreign sources stepped in[19] – but for thousands of surfers around the country, a painful lesson in the cost of overzealous regulation and litigation made their sport a bit less enjoyable than before. For the workers at Clark Foam that lost their jobs, the pain was even more pronounced.

The following table represents a summary of the analysis we have undertaken thus far. Keep in mind that this table should serve as a guide to working out any problems you may have with the chain of causation. You would be wise not to simply memorize the contents of the table but to practice the concept checks and make up your own examples as you go along. Any economics professor will concur that by setting up multiple diagrams and problems, you can pick up the skills necessary to master this rather difficult material. Or you can ignore us and fail the upcoming exam.

IF	AND	THEN
Demand increases	Price increases	Quantity supplied increases
Demand decreases	Price decreases	Quantity supplied decreases
Supply increases	Price decreases	Quantity demanded increases
Supply decreases	Price increases	Quantity demanded decreases

SIMULTANEOUS CHANGES IN DEMAND AND SUPPLY

O.K., so we have seen how markets can change over time as demand or supply changes. But what happens if supply and demand changes at the same time? Is that even possible? Given the complexity of the graphs you are about to interpret you will probably wish it was unrealistic for buyers and sellers to alter their behavior simultaneously, but alas, they often do.

CASE STUDY # 5: IT'S GREAT TO BE A CORN FARMER – BUT FOR HOW LONG?

Sometimes it really pays well to work hard every day and wait for your government to do something colossally stupid. In this case, the hard workers are corn farmers who probably get up early and work late on many days out of the year. Now their long work days are translating into huge paychecks thanks to the U.S. Congress and President Bush decision that one-third of the nation's corn crop should be shoved into our gas tanks every time we fill up.

In 2007 President Bush signed legislation that mandated increased usage of biofuels for all American drivers of gasoline-powered cars. The law also required refiners to replace 36 billion gallons of gasoline with biofuel by 2022.[21]

In Brazil, biofuels come from processed sugar cane – which is nearly eight times more energy efficient to use than biofuels from corn and creates between 55 to 90% less air pollution when burned.[22] So why don't we just import this highly efficient and planet-friendlier source of fuel from Brazil?

Because the agricultural lobby in the United States was successful in pressing our government to use an American crop instead.

Since Mr. Bush signed this legislation, the demand for corn has skyrocketed. The initial pressure on the demand for corn meant that shortages broke out and prices increased accordingly.

However, as prices increased not only did we see the normal reaction on the part of existing corn farmers (more corn planted and an increase in quantity supplied), but we ended up with billions of extra bushels of corn being grown from farmers who previously grew wheat, soybeans and other crops.

Figures 7.8-7.10 illustrate the short- and long-run adjustments that are under way in this market. In each market, both the demand for, and supply of corn is increasing. The difference in each case is the *magnitude* of the change in supply and demand.

In figure 7.8 you can see what it would mean to the corn industry if the demand for corn increases by a larger amount than supply increases. If demand increases to D2, but supply increases to S2 (due to the lure of higher profits), the long-run impact will be higher prices (P2) and a higher output level. In this case, prices would increase in the long run – even though supply increased – because demand increased by a larger amount than supply.

For much of 2007–2011, this is what was occurring in much of the country as oil refineries were forced to buy corn. Even with an increase in the number of corn farmers – and an increase in corn supplies to 12.3 billion bushels, it was estimated in 2008 that it would take another 10 *million* acres of harvested corn to meet the expected demand for corn over time.[23]

In figure 7.9 we see that *demand and supply have increased by the same amount*. If this occurs, the equilibrium output level will increase – due to the greater demand and greater supply – but prices in the long run will fall back to where they were. In this case, farmers had better enjoy their good fortune while they can, because higher prices will direct more growers into the market, and increased competition will drive down prices and profits in the long run.

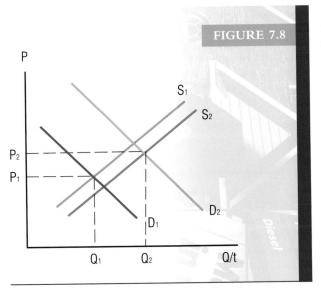

FIGURE 7.8

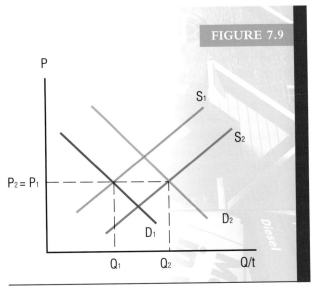

FIGURE 7.9

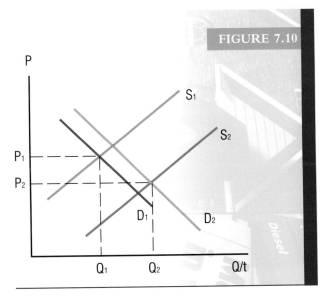

FIGURE 7.10

Figure 7.10 presents the worst-case scenario for farmers and the best-case scenario for consumers. In this instance, the increase in demand – driven by expectations of higher prices and more buyers in the market – has led to a flood of new sellers entering the market. With no ability to foresee what demand growth will exist into the future, there is no way to keep some farmers from taking a chance that they will be successful. *If supply increases by a larger amount than demand increases,* the overall impact will be higher equilibrium output levels, but lower prices!

It would be an irresponsible omission to fail to mention the impact this ethanol legislation has had on food prices in the United States and around the world.

If you recall from chapter one, economists sometimes try to warn policy makers that laws tend to create unintended consequences. In this case the consequences have been seen in grocery stores and food markets all over the world.

With the dramatic movement by farmers toward corn production – and away from other crops – we have seen higher corn prices stemming from greater demand and rising soybean, wheat and other crop prices resulting from a falling supply. As farmers moved away from wheat and soybeans the price of these crops increased. The increase was more than 70%.[24]

Higher corn prices led to an increase in the price of corn syrup, corn-based cereals and the price of feed for animals. Of course, since the price of feed increased, ranchers and processors of pork, chicken and other animals had to raise their prices to cover rising input costs, while bread companies and firms that produce soybean products did the same.

The result was the largest increase in food prices since the 1970s – along with rising gas prices as the price of corn shot up.

As food shortages mounted around the globe riots began to break out in the Caribbean, Mexico, Africa and Europe, prompting European officials to formally announce plans to mandate less use of biofuels in order to free up crops for human consumption instead.[25]

Compounding the problem created by irrational government policies, a massive drought in 2010 led to spiraling wheat, soybean, and corn prices. In the absence of our ethanol laws, the price hikes would have been less severe.[26]

CASE STUDY # 6: THE HOUSING MARKET – A DISASTER OR A NECESSARY CORRECTION?

If you are a typical college student – poor and living in something you do not own – this next section might be a bright spot in your life. At the time this part of the chapter is being finalized housing prices are falling every month by record amounts.[27] By the time you are reading this you might find a house for about the same price as a used SUV. Not really, but it sure seems like it might happen.[28]

It would take three chapters or more to clearly explain everything that has happened in America's housing market over the past few years. Since you have only this case study to work with, we will have to focus on the high – and low points of this evolving marketplace.

In a nutshell, the first decade of this century saw an unprecedented increase in the demand for new and used homes up until 2006. The increase in demand was largely fueled by relatively low home mortgage interest rates, a strong economy with solid wage and salary growth and the combined effects of pressure from the Bush Administration on the home mortgage industry to expand available credit to poorer Americans.[29]

Following a loosening of regulations on the banking industry during the Clinton Administration, banks found greater freedom to loan money in what became known as this "subprime" market. This meant that many people with questionable credit and employment histories and virtually no down payment were encouraged by banks and our government to seek out loans to buy a house.

As demand increased markedly and prices followed, many predictable events followed. First, more and more people – convinced that they could reap unheard of profits – began to put their homes on the market for sale. Investors began buying up undervalued homes, made

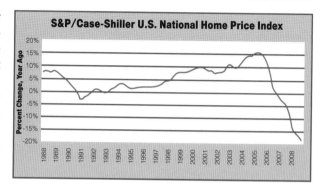

some repairs and/or modifications and began "flipping" those homes. As the profits from this quick turnover began to convey information to other potential investors we saw more and more people borrowing more and more money to jump into this lucrative market.

Other people saw their homes increasing in value and rushed into banks to borrow against the rising equity in their homes so that they could buy swimming pools, new cars and other goodies.

Many Americans – who had questionable credit and employment histories and little or no money for a down payment – were encouraged by the banking industry, and the Bush Administration to run down to their local branch office to borrow money for their first home.

And of course, home builders – seeing this epic surge in demand – began bulldozing every inch of ground they could find to build the latest subdivision with the latest cute name.

How does this impact the price of homes?

It all came to a screeching halt beginning in 2006 when millions of people saw the interest rates on their homes and/or investment properties begin to rise sharply.

Many of the people who bought homes during the boom time did so with mortgages that came at very low initial interest rates, but that called for adjustable rates that would increase over time.

When these interest rates began to rise, hundreds of thousands of homeowners could not make their payments and began to fall behind on their payments. This led to an increase in home foreclosures – and an increase in the supply of homes available on the market.

With more homes on the market a surplus broke out (for practice, draw a graph and show an increase in the supply of homes with no initial change in prices).

The surplus put downward pressure on home prices, causing investors to see the value of their properties fall. This caused the investors who flip houses to panic and thus they tried to dump their houses as fast as they could. This caused supply to increase even more. On top of this was the fact that all of those homebuilders were now building inventory in a market that was seeing bulging supplies – especially in Nevada, Florida, and California.

Then, the banks began to get into trouble as more and more people were unable to pay and were walking away from their homes or losing them outright. Homebuilders began to file for bankruptcy because they had borrowed too much money in a speculative market.

By the fall of 2008 some of the largest banks in the world had filed for bankruptcy. On September 15, 2008 Lehman Brothers, the fourth largest bank in America, filed for bankruptcy. This came after of the collapse of Bear Stearns, Fannie Mae, and Freddie Mac.[30] These major banks had been major investors in the bundled mortgage business – the practice of buying thousands of mortgages bundled together in a single investment portfolio.

As banks were forced by market conditions to tighten their lending practices, more potential home buyers were turned away. This led to a decrease in the demand for homes during this time period.[31] Furthermore, with housing values falling and housing falling out of favor as an investment vehicle we saw not only less demand, but a drop in the supply of subdivisions, custom homes and used homes that were up for sale. Figures 7.11 – 7.13 illustrate the potential impact of a *drop in demand and supply.*

In figure 7.11 we see a scenario where the demand for houses has decreased, along with a decrease in supply. If there is a *larger decrease in supply than the observed decrease in demand*, then we would see higher home prices in the next couple of years and a reduction in the equilibrium quantity of homes in the market.

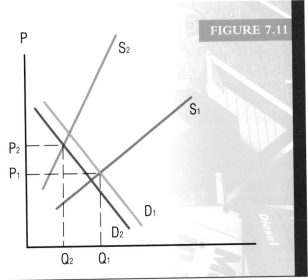

FIGURE 7.11

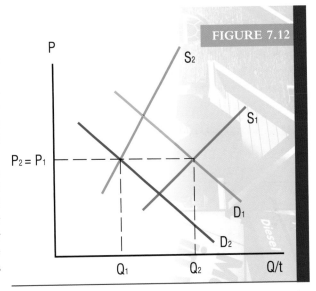

FIGURE 7.12

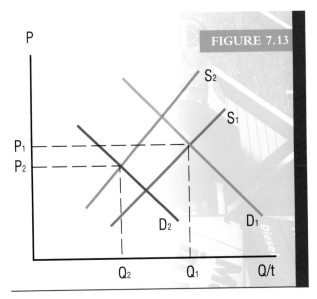

FIGURE 7.13

Since supply decreased by more than demand decreased, the upward pressure on prices from the supply effect offsets the downward pressure on prices from the demand effect.

In figure 7.12 we see a long-run scenario where the *demand for homes falls by the same amount as supply decreases.* In this example, the downward pressure on prices from the decrease in demand is precisely offset by the increase in prices that would come from fewer sellers being left in the market. While the price of houses would remain constant over time, the bad news is pretty obvious – fewer houses in the final equilibrium condition.

In the final diagram (7.13) we see the impact of a *relatively small decrease in the supply* of houses *with a larger decrease in demand.* In this scenario, an ongoing drop in demand that is larger than the drop in supply would lead to some good news – lower long-run prices – but some bad news as well, as the quantity of homes available decreases. For 2011 and possibly the foreseeable future, this appears to be the prevailing trend until the financial sector and consumer confidence rebounds.

CASE STUDY #7: AN INCREASE IN DEMAND AND A DECREASE IN SUPPLY: THE PAINFUL PRICE AT THE PUMP

Anytime you see police officers at a gas station attempting to maintain order, you know things must not be going well. A few days after Hurricane Ike hit, the lines at gas stations all parts of America were long, tempers were short and uniformed officers with guns were standing around to keep the peace. Less than seven years before Katrina hit, gas could be had for under $1 per gallon.

The increase in gas prices from 94 cents per gallon in December 2001 to more than $4 per gallon by July 2008 was just about the easiest change in supply and demand economists have ever predicted.

The following analysis is designed to help you see that while 90-something percent of Americans are convinced that some grand conspiracy was afoot – those 90-something percent were 100 percent wrong…

Petroleum is bought and sold in the commodities market with prices negotiated on the New York Mercantile Exchange every day. Traders on the floor of this exchange represent either companies that wish to purchase oil con-

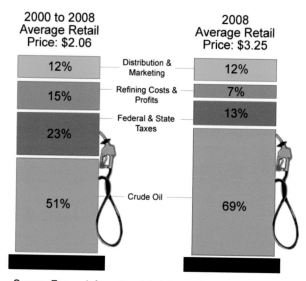

Source: Energy Information Administration.

Shutterstock © Norman Chan, 23011.

CONCEPT CHECK

In the wake of the bank failures that have taken place, there will likely be a drop in the demand for employees in this industry. If, at the same time, more college students decide to avoid majoring in finance, what would be the long run impact on salaries and the equilibrium quantity of banking employees? A graph – as always – will help with your answer.

tracts for future delivery or companies that are looking to sell oil contracts for future delivery. The price you pay for gasoline is determined by these traders in New York weeks before you fill up your car.

As it became increasingly apparent that war with Iraq was imminent, the traders who showed up for work each day became convinced that war would probably disrupt world oil supplies to some degree. This made the traders believe that the price of oil in the future was going to rise. Therefore they began bidding more aggressively on oil contracts to secure the best deal possible for future delivery. As the traders who were buying soon realized, the potential sellers were in no mood to part with oil contracts for, say, $50 per barrel, when everyone thought the future price might be $70 per barrel. The buying traders had to offer up higher and higher bids to get the sellers to part with their contracts. This "shortage psychology" added up to a daily run-up in oil futures contracts – and eventually higher prices at the pump.[32]

How do less of these impact your wallet?

Photo courtesy Jack Chambless

Beginning in 2004 multiple factors combined to push gasoline prices to historic high levels.

Starting with demand, 2004 saw China impact the global energy market in a major way. In 2003 China consumed just over five million barrels of oil per day. That figure was 30% higher than in 2002. China became the world's second-largest consumer of oil in 2004, as the free-market reforms under way in that nation led to an epic increase in demand.[33] Today China consumes more than 6.5 billion barrels of oil per year. In 2010 China announced plans to increase its strategic oil reserves, a move that many experts felt would lead to $100 per barrel oil once again.[34]

In addition to the growing demand from China, we have begun to see much higher demand for cars in India,[35] while in America SUVs became the most popular vehicle of choice by the middle of the decade.

On the supply side of the equation, the declining value of the U.S. dollar in 2004 through much of 2008 led to lower total revenue for OPEC. Since all oil is bought and sold in American dollars, OPEC felt compelled to restrict supply during this time period in order to prop up the cartel's profits. In 2011, the revolt in Libya led to speculation that oil supplies would fall further, which caused prices to rise to over $100 per barrel, and once again, gas prices that shot past $3.50 per gallon.

Moreover, over the past two decades, no new oil refineries have been built in the U.S. Environmental restrictions and lawsuits, combined with some refineries going out of business, have actually led to an overall *decrease in the number of refineries.*[36] The result is straightforward. If demand is increasing and we do not have the refinery capacity to meet demand, shortages will break out and prices will rise.

This is not the end of the story. Adding to the market mayhem was the fact that, to combat air pollution, California and many other states passed laws that require reformulated gasoline to be burned in cars. This process adds to the overall cost of producing gasoline, which reduces supply and drives up prices.[37] Today there are regulatory requirements for 50 different blends of reformulated fuels for individual cities and regions around the country. These regulations add 10-13 cents per gallon to our costs.[38]

In 2006 Congress passed legislation that made "price gouging" a felony. The legislation passed 389-34. The 34 votes against this bill came from politicians who correctly pointed out that federal and state governments add, on average, 59 cents to the price of every gallon of gas in the form of taxes, while gas stations earn, on average, less than 10 cents per gallon in profit.[39] Those politicians also argued that federal bans on where oil can be retrieved in America – by one estimate there are 800 million to two trillion barrels of oil from oil shale in the western U.S. – also causes supply to fall and prices to rise.[40]

Figures 7.14-7.16 provide a look at the impact of a decrease in supply and increase in demand. Figure 7.14 illustrates a situation where the supply of gasoline has decreased a great deal, while the demand has increased

Is Sarah Palin correct that the United States should drill for more oil in Alaska?

slightly. *If supply decreases by more than demand increases,* the net effect will be an increase in prices — after all, both an increase in demand and a decrease in supply cause upward pressure on prices — and a decrease in the equilibrium quantity of available gasoline.

Figure 7.15 shows an offsetting change in supply and demand. When *supply decreases by the same magnitude as demand increases,* prices will rise, but the equilibrium quantity of gasoline will not be any different than it was in the initial equilibrium condition.

Finally, in Figure 7.16 we see the effects of a relatively small decrease in supply and a much larger increase in demand. If this is the case (which is most likely the situation that played out in 2007 and 2008), prices will (and did) rise, but there will be an increase in the overall quantity of gasoline available in the marketplace.

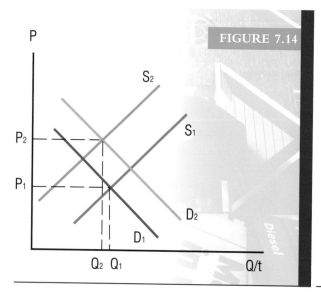

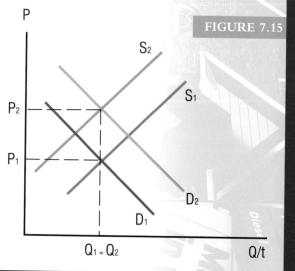

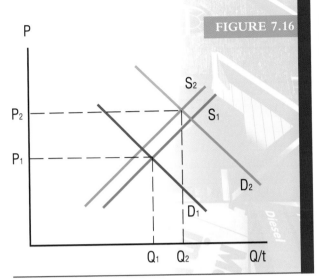

FIGURE 7.16

2009 AND BEYOND – THE SUPPLY SIDE OF THE STORY

> The fundamental laws of supply and demand are at work.
>
> John Hofmeister, Chairman, Shell Oil Co.

Obviously few of us are happy about the changes in supply and demand that have unfolded in the gasoline market. Yet, there are limitations to what can be done about this market in the short run. The long run, on the other hand, is a different story.

First, we should take some comfort in knowing that the forces of supply and demand can still work in our favor. When prices started to shoot past $3 and $4 per gallon in 2007 and 2008 many doomsayers began predicting a new energy crisis. In July 2008 oil prices hit $147 per barrel – leading many to predict that $200 was not far off.

Then a funny thing happened on the way to another flawed prediction. With oil approaching $150 per barrel and gas prices rising to previously unheard of levels, consumers began to show that the law of demand was alive and well.

SUV and truck sales began to plummet, small and hybrid car sales took off and people became generally more sensitive to higher prices. Demand even began to fall in India and China as well. This led to the beginning of lower oil prices and a new "surplus psychology" among commodities dealers. From July through March of 2009 oil prices fell from $147 per barrel to almost $30 per barrel. Traders in New York became convinced that a slowing world economy would put downward pressure on the global demand for oil.

Thus, they began receiving orders to sell their contracts for the best price possible. As more traders were attempting to sell, the buyers began expecting prices to fall even more. This forced the sellers to continually lower their prices in order to find someone willing to take their futures contracts.[41] All of a sudden, the millions of Americans who kept saying that the oil companies were ripping us off and that we were helpless in our struggles against corporate greed were left – mouths agape – wondering why those "mean old oil companies" were suddenly cutting prices by more than $110 per barrel.

It is because the oil companies never did control our lives to begin with.

By 2011 oil prices were back over $100 per barrel as Middle East unrest, strong economic growth in places other than the United States and Western Europe, along with declining refining capacity and greater state-ownership of oil reserves pushed demand up and supply down.[42]

There is also some good news that has come out of higher priced oil. High prices have led to a great global hunt for more oil reserves. You will recall in chapter six that prices direct resources to their most valued use. In Alberta, Canada, the U.S. Department of Energy estimates that 174 billion barrels of oil can be found in the tar sands of this region.[43] With $80 billion worth of development projects underway, Canada stands to move into second place, behind Saudi Arabia, in total oil supplied to the world. And Canada does not have a track record of aiding terrorists....

When it comes to OPEC, we have to bear in mind that this cartel has a long and rich history of causing price fluctuations. In the 1970s gas prices increased tremendously in response to the Arab Oil Embargo of 1973, strikes in the Iranian oil fields, and the Iranian revolution of 1979. At that time OPEC thought that it could get away with "practically anything with respect to price."[44] Soon, high prices acted as a magnet that drew in production form the North Sea and Alaska, which caused an increase in supply, lower prices, and the collapse of oil markets in 1986.

Not only do we still see the temptation to cheat showing up, but we also have the fact that high oil prices has allowed OPEC to invest in new exploration techniques. This expansion in exploration has taken Saudi Arabia alone from 88 billion barrels of proven oil reserves to almost 264 billion barrels.[45]

THE DEMAND SIDE OF THE STORY

The news is mixed when it comes to the future demand for oil. On the negative side, there is the fact that China and India are going to continue to cause us pain as economic growth continues. With over one-third of the world's population, these two countries alone will cause the demand for oil to grow as more of their residents leave poverty behind and seek the mobility that comes from rising levels of wealth.[46]

However, there is some underlying positive news that could not only temper dramatic price increases in the future, but also accomplish some socially-desirable outcomes as well. That news lies within the law of demand and the love of profit.

While gasoline is certainly a necessity in the U.S., where one-fourth the world's oil is consumed, 2008 proved that we are not immune from a negatively-sloped demand curve. If prices start rising towards 2008 levels again, self-interested consumers will rationally respond by engaging in more conservation measures. For some of us it might mean moving closer to work or commuting, or voting for better public transportation. For others it will mean searching out more fuel-efficient vehicles, or vehicles that use alternative sources of energy.

This is where the automakers come into play. Just as people were pretty amazed over a hundred years ago by the site of the first car, many of us are amazed today by the lack of sound coming from all these new hybrid vehicles that are becoming more commonplace.

Given time, and the desire to make money, we can count on Toyota – and others – to supply us with cars that get 60, 70 or maybe even 100 miles per gallon. We can also expect to see the day where the automakers have successfully lowered the overall production cost of cars that don't use petroleum at all. When that happens, the price of alternative-fuel cars will fall, quantity demanded will increase and our energy worries will be a distant memory.

In the meantime, it is worth noting that political remedies for our current pain will not work very well. In the next chapter we will take a detailed look at what happens when politicians place limits on what suppliers can charge. You can probably guess that price ceilings create shortages and long waiting lines – just like in the 1970s when the government, anxious to come to our aid, created a disaster instead.[47] But then again, that is what government is best at creating.

One final thought for Americans who are mad about "high" gas prices. The following table illustrates what consumers in other nations paid to drive around when gasoline hit its 2008 levels. High gas taxes and massive regulations have created these prices. So, the next time you pay $4 per gallon to go to the beach, be glad you are not in the Netherlands or Belgium, where going on a Sunday drive practically requires borrowing money from a bank to fill up your car!

Retail Premium Gasoline Prices (for the week of 6/9/2008)	
Country	U.S. Dollars per Gallon
Netherlands	$9.87
Belgium	$9.00
Germany	$8.83
Italy	$8.82
Finland	$8.77
Denmark	$8.75
Portugal	$8.74
France	$8.63
United Kingdom	$8.60
Sweden	$8.44
Poland	$7.99
Slovakia	$7.89
Austria	$7.87
Czech Republic	$7.84
Luxembourg	$7.69
Hungary	$7.38
Greece	$7.33
Spain	$7.26
Ireland	$7.26
Slovenia	$6.96
Estonia	$6.80
Bulgaria	$6.66
Cyprus	$6.66
Lithuania	$6.63
Latvia	$6.48
Romania	$6.44
Malta	$6.40
United States	**$4.27**

Case Study # 8: Don't Become a Mint Farmer

One of the things you learn early on in business is that the only thing that is certain is uncertainty. Mint farmers have learned this the hard way.

It is pretty rare to see a case where demand is falling while supply increases, but mint farmers in America are in that precise predicament right now.

Over the past few years, the number of foreign sellers serving the mint market has increased dramatically. This has caused an increase in the overall supply of mint oil – used for gum, toothpaste, etc. to increase within the United States.

At the same time, due to the fact that the foreign suppliers provide a cheaper substitute for American-

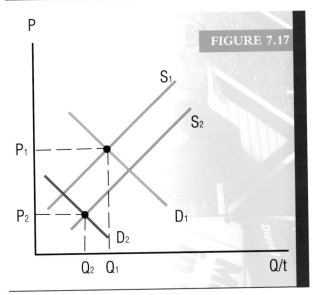

FIGURE 7.17

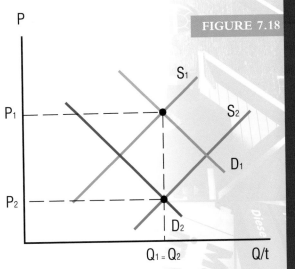

FIGURE 7.18

grown mint, the demand for mint grown by Americans has decreased.[48]

Figures 7.17-7.19 illustrate the long-run adjustment that took place in the market for mint in the last few years.

Figure 7.17 illustrates a market where the supply of mint has increased by a relatively small amount while the demand has decreased by a very large amount. In this case if *supply increases by a smaller amount than demand decreases*, the cumulative effect will be lower prices (from both the increase in supply and decrease in demand) and a much lower equilibrium quantity of mint oil. The lower quantity would come from less profitable mint farms closing down.

Figure 7.18 illustrates a market where the changes in supply and demand offset one another. *If demand decreases by the same amount that supply increases*, prices will still fall, but there will be no change in the equilibrium output level.

In the final diagram (7.19), we see a case where the *demand* for mint oil *falls by a smaller amount than supply increases*. If this occurs the overall price will decrease, but there will be a net increase in the quantity of mint oil available.

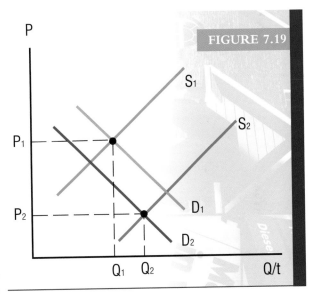

FIGURE 7.19

CONCEPT CHECK

In 2010 the price of cotton at the wholesale level reached its highest level since the year 1870.[49] Suppose by the time you are reading this book, the U.S. economy is growing at a much stronger pace. If cotton prices continue to rise as you are taking this class, graphically illustrate and fully explain what would happen to t-shirt prices as a result of these two realities.

SUMMARY – SIMULTANEOUS CHANGES IN DEMAND AND SUPPLY

The table that follows summarizes all the possible combinations of simultaneous changes in supply and demand and the effect on the market equilibrium price and output level. It is again important to remind you to practice by creating your own examples from the news or newspaper. This is the most efficient way of learning this material.

IF	AND	THEN
Demand increases	Supply increases by less than demand increases	Equilibrium output will increase and price will increase
Demand increases	Supply increases by an equal amount	Equilibrium output will increase and price will not change
Demand increases	Supply increases by more than demand increases	Equilibrium output will increase and price will decrease
Demand decreases	Supply decreases by less than demand	Equilibrium output will decrease and price will decrease
Demand decreases	Supply decreases by the same/equal amount than demand	Equilibrium output will decrease and price will not change
Demand decreases	Supply decreases by more than demand	Equilibrium output will decrease and price will increase
Demand decreases	Supply increases by more than demand	Equilibrium output will increase and price will decrease
Demand decreases	Supply increases by the same/equal amount than demand	Equilibrium output will not change and price will decrease
Demand decreases	Supply increases by less than demand	Equilibrium output will decrease and price will decrease
Demand increases	Supply decreases by more than demand	Equilibrium output will decrease and price will increase
Demand increases	Supply decreases by the same/equal amount than demand	Equilibrium output will not change and price will increase
Demand increases	Supply decreases by less than demand	Equilibrium output will increase and price will increase

ENDNOTES

1 See "Car lots suffering fuel sadly" by Andy Vuong, *The Denver Post*, June 12, 2008; "Local car buyers dream small" by John Gillie, *The News Tribune* (Tacoma, WA), July 13, 2008; and "Used small cars net big bucks" by Tom Krisher, *The Orlando Sentinel*, May 23, 2008.

2 See "A Retail Mixed Bag" by Jackie Crosby, *The Star Tribune* (Minneapolis, MN), August 8, 2008.

3 See "Drop in Home Prices Accelerates to 14.1%" by Sudeep Reddy, *The Wall Street Journal*, May 28, 2008.

4 See "An appetite for edibles" by Laura Gunderson, *The Oregonian*, July 8, 2008.

5 See "Reversal of Fortune: If the Red Sox Win, Curse Industry Loses" by William M. Bulkeley and Mark Maremont, *The Wall Street Journal*, October 25, 2004.

6 Source: December 2010 interview with Dennis Stoltzfoos.

7 See "Copper is in Record Territory Again" by Tatyana Shumsky, *The Wall Street Journal*, December 29, 2010, p. C10.

8 See "Oysters, a New Orleans Staple, Are Latest Victim" by Perry Stein, *The Wall Street Journal*, June 19-20, 2010.

9 See "Sorry, We're Booked: The Restaurant Slump Ends" by Katy McLauglin, *The Wall Street Journal*, March 30, 2004, p. D1.

10 See "Strapped shoppers try Amish Salvage" by Meghan Barr, *The Orlando Sentinel*, May 24, 2008, pg. A17.

11 In fact, by the time you are reading this, you may have already purchased the first $100 laptop. See "$100 Laptop Moves Closer to Reality" by Steve Stecklow, *The Wall Street Journal*, November 14, 2005.

12 See "Cordless Computers Get Affordable" by Nick Wingfield, *The Wall Street Journal*, June 26, 2002, p. D1; and "Is It Time to Get a DVD Burner?" by Anna Wilde Mathews, *The Wall Street Journal*, December 18, 2002, p. D1.

13 See "Job Outpouring For Evacuees Sparks Backlash" by Ilan Brat and Janet Adamy, *The Wall Street Journal*, September 13, 2005, page B1; and "Louisiana Frets About Job Poaching" by Jeff D. Opdyke and Dionne Searcey, *The Wall Street Journal*, September 12, 2005.

14 See "How a Jury Decided That a Coffee Spill is Worth $2.9 million" by Andrea Gerlin, *The Wall Street Journal*, September 1, 1994.

15 See "$67 Million Pants," *The Wall Street Journal*, June 26, 2007.

16 See "When All Else Fails, The American Way is to File a Lawsuit" *The Wall Street Journal*, November 14, 2000; and "Is Food the Next Tobacco?" by Shelly Branch, *The Wall Street Journal*, June 13, 2002.

17 See "Wipeout for Key Player in Surfboard Industry" by Peter Sanders and Stephanie Kang, *The Wall Street Journal*, December 8, 2005.

18 See "To Central Florida surfers, factory closing's a wipeout" by Harry Wessel, *The Orlando Sentinel*, December 8, 2005.

19 See "Surfboard Costs Subside" *The Orlando Sentinel*, February 4, 2006.

20 See "After Mad-Cow Scare, German Pigs, Farmers 'Enjoy' More Quality Time" by Vanessa Furhmans, *The Wall Street Journal*, March 6, 2002.

21 See "Increase ethanol production?" by Lynn Edward Weaver, *The Orlando Sentinel*, June 24, 2007.

22 See "Green Dreams" by Joel K. Bourne Jr., *National Geographic*, October 2007.

23 See "Corn pops back, may be 2nd largest crop" by Sue Kirchhoff, *USA Today*, August 13, 2008, pg. 13.

24 See "Historic Surge in Grain Prices Roils Markets" by Scott Kilman, *The Wall Street Journal*, September 28, 2007.

25 See "Europeans backpedal on switch to biofuels" by James Kanter, *The Oregonian*, July 8, 2008.

26 See "Wheat Prices Surge to a Two-Year High" by Tom Polansek, *The Wall Street Journal*, December 29, 2010, p. C10; and "Prices Soar on South America Drought" by Liam Pleven and Matt Moffett, *The Wall Street Journal*, December 30, 2010.

27 In Orlando, Florida housing prices fell from a peak of over $250,000 in the middle of the last decade to less than $100,000 by 2011.

28 See "Housing Recovery Stalls" by S. Mitra Kalita and Sudeep Reddy, *The Wall Street Journal*, December 29, 2010.

29 See "Rethinking Home Ownership" by David Wessel, *The Wall Street Journal*, June 17, 2010.

30 See "Crisis on Wall Street as Lehman Totters, Merrill is Sold, AIG Seeks to Raise Cash" by Carrick Mollenkamp, Susanne Craig, Serena Ng, and Aaron Lucchetti, *The Wall Street Journal*, September 15, 2008; and "AIG, Lehman Shock Hits World Markets" by Susanne Craig, Jeffrey McCracken, Jon Hilsenrath, and Deborah Soloman, *The Wall Street Journal*, September 16, 2008.

31 See "The United States of Subprime" by Rick Brooks and Constance Mitchell Ford, *The Wall Street Journal*, October 11, 2007.

32 See "A 'shortage psychology' that's keeping oil prices high" by Marilyn Geewax, *The Bulletin* (Bend, Oregon), June 26, 2008.

33 See "China's Growing Thirst for Oil Remakes the Global Market" by Peter Wonacott, Jeanne Whalen, and Bhushan Bahree, *The Wall Street Journal*, December 3, 2003; and "China's thirst for oil poses threat to U.S." by Gal Luft, *The Los Angeles Times* (appearing in *The Orlando Sentinel*), February 9, 2004; and "Oil is Up Because the Dollar is Down" by David T. King, *The Wall Street Journal*

34 See "China May Fuel Move to $100 Oil" by Dan Strumpf, *The Wall Street Journal*, December 30, 2010.

35 Ford reported sales to India were up 41% in 2003-2004. See *The Economic Times*, April 7, 2004.

36 See "Lack of new refining capacity puts pressure on supplies of oil" by Kevin Morrison, *Financial Times*, March 12-13, 2005.

37 See "Pait at the Pump" by Sudeep Reddy, *The Dallas Morning News*, June 6, 2004, pg. 3D.

38 See *Ten Principles of Energy Policy* by Joseph L. Bast, The Heartland Institute 2008.

39 See "The Real Gas Gougers," *The Wall Street Journal*, May 11, 2006.

40 See "Blame Congress for High Oil Prices" by Mackubin Thomas Owens, *The Wall Street Journal*, May 29, 2008, pg. A17.

41 See "Another bubble – commodities - may have burst" by Stevenson Jacobs, *The Star Tribune* (Minneapolis, MN), August 9, 2008, pg. D1.

42 See "Oil at a Two-Year High: $91.86" by Jerry A. DiColo, *The Wall Street Journal*, January 13, 2011; "Refiners ready to cut capacity" by Ronald D. White, *The Orlando Sentinel*, March 12, 2010; and "The Long Shadow of the Visible Hand" by Ian Bremer, *The Wall Street Journal*, May 22-23, 2010.

43 See "A Black-Gold Rush in Alberta" by Tamsin Carlisle, *The Wall Street Journal*, September 15, 2005; and "Tides turn for companies that seek new energy sources" by Paul Luke, *The Edmonton Journal*, July 26, 2008.

44 See *The Prize: The Epic Quest for Oil, Money and Power* by Daniel Yergin, Simon & Schuster, New York, 1992.

45 See "Some Wonder if the Surging Oil Market is Ignoring Supply and Demand" by Simon Romero, *The New York Times*, March 15, 2005; and "The Oil Bubble" *The Wall Street Journal*, October 8-9, 2005.

46 See "Balance of Power" by Josiah R. Baker, *The Orlando Sentinel*, October 16, 2005.

47 See "Fun for Politicians, Legal Nightmare for Gasoline Retailers" by Holman W. Jenkins, Jr., *The Wall Street Journal*, September 14, 2005.

48 See "Mint's Bad Taste" by Ilan Brat, *The Wall Street Journal*, November 3, 2005.

49 See "Flashback to 1870 As Cotton Hits Peak" by Adam Cancryn and Carolyn Cui, *The Wall Street Journal*, October 16-17, 2010; and "Cotton Tale: Apparel Prices Set to Rise" by Elizabeth Holmes and Rachel Dodes, *The Wall Street Journal*, May 19, 2010, p. B8.

CHAPTER REVIEW

1. Graphically illustrate and fully explain what would happen in the market for organic food if the average income of people in America rose by 12% next year.

2. Suppose over the next several years the number of people applying for medical school decreases in the United States. Graphically illustrate and fully explain what this would mean in the market for doctors and health care services.

3. Suppose more and more Americans expect the price of silver to rise in the near future. Illustrate and explain the impact this would have on the demand for and supply of silver bars.

4. Suppose the number of buyers in the market for camping tents increases next year while the input costs associated with making tents decreases. If the impact of falling input costs is greater than the impact of more buyers in the market, what will be the effect on tent prices and the final equilibrium quantity?

Chapter Eight

GOVERNMENT INTERFERENCE *in the* MARKET

Photo courtesy Jack Chambless

*G*overnment's view of the economy could be summed up this way. If it moves, tax it. If it keeps moving, regulate it. If it stops moving, subsidize it.

RONALD REAGAN

THE VISIBLE FOOT

In much of America it is legal to consume cigarettes, but not marijuana. You can visit a strip club, but not a prostitute. You may abort an unborn child, but you cannot kill yourself with the aid of a doctor. You can drive a car over 70 miles per hour, but you cannot bet on National Football League games. You can drink alcohol, but you cannot drive a motorcycle without a helmet. You can sell your house for an unlimited amount of profit, but you cannot sell a ticket to a sporting event for more than $1 above face value. You can buy books on satanic cults, visit a body-piercing establishment, and watch graphic horror movies but you cannot buy wine on Sunday in many cities.

A major question that every market-based economy must answer is, to what extent certain market activities should be regulated, taxed, or banned outright. This is a very difficult issue because it delves into the rights of the individual and our property, versus the rights of the public to go unharmed by negative externalities.

> ➤ **A negative externality exits when the transaction between two parties impacts a third party who was not part of the transaction.**

Who determines the definition of the word "harm"? How much of a negative externality is acceptable? How should negative externalities be dealt with? Consider the following:

THE ECONOMICS OF BILLBOARDS

In 1999 I was traveling on the Florida Turnpike with my daughter, who was six at the time. When we were approximately an hour south of Gainesville, she looked up and saw a billboard advertising an adult entertainment club.

Having learned to read months earlier, she said, "Daddy, what does 'We bare all' mean?"

Naturally, this question caused me to come close to wrapping my car around a tree, but I quickly recovered from the trauma of my little girl's exposure to the "real world." I attempted to explain to her that there are certain things that are difficult for her to understand and that when she is a little older, I would try to clear up the meaning of this billboard.

I have no idea what an expert in child psychology would say about my approach to this sticky situation, but I wonder if I should be allowed to ask what in the world a billboard like that is doing near a public road? After all, isn't it one thing to allow someone the right to visit a strip club, but an entirely different matter to have the advertisement for the strip club imposed upon unwilling drivers who are offended by this industry? The line isn't very clear. First, the billboard was sitting on private property, and the U.S. Constitution is very clear on the rights of the individual to use their property in a manner that does not violate the rights of others. Second, the billboard does not depict naked women.

Nonetheless, if I was (am) offended, do I have the right to argue that the rights of the property owner and the strip club have violated my rights to not be harmed by such a display? Should I find a new route to travel in Florida? Should the billboard be able to show naked women? Should we remove religious billboards that offend atheists? What about billboards featuring fast-food restaurants? Are they offensive to vegetarians and people with weight problems?

What then, is the proper role of government in our economic system? When should our freedom be reined in for the betterment of society? To the extent that freedom has shown to be a valuable tool for helping human beings, most economists suggest that government exercise a great deal of caution when considering what markets to interfere with.

Of course, we have to realize that what makes good economic sense may not get politicians elected! This means that often politicians feel compelled to alter the final market outcome in the name of the public good or some normative definition of fairness. When the government decides to interfere with the natural workings of the free market, it usually takes the form of:

- Forcing prices downward through price ceilings and laws against unfair pricing
- Forcing prices upward through artificial price supports and minimum wages
- Banning the good or service
- Regulating the manner in which the good or service is sold
- Creating regulations or subsidies to impact prices and output

As the following examples will illustrate, when political pressures rather than economic principles determine public policy, some very bizarre, inefficient, and even deadly outcomes can, and do, emerge.

WAL-MART AND THE GERMAN GOVERNMENT

Decades ago, Sam Walton envisioned a time when consumers in small and mid-size towns could have access to the same goods and services as citizens in large towns, without having to pay outrageous prices. His vision led to the creation of today's retail giant known as Wal-Mart. With low prices and large shopping selections, Wal-Mart has put intense competitive pressure on other retail establishments.

This seems to be a good thing for budget-conscious Americans. Just don't tell that to German bureaucrats in that nation's cartel office that ordered Wal-Mart and retailers Aldi Nord and Lidl Stiftung & Company to raise prices on items like milk, sugar, and flour or face fines up to $443,900.[1] Why?

As it turns out, Wal-Mart is just too good at discounting prices. According to the German government, Wal-Mart deliberately discounted prices in Germany in order to hurt smaller competing retail companies. The government felt that, while this practice helped consumers in the short term, it would hurt small and medium-sized rivals that "can't match the lower prices."

Wal-Mart's entry into Germany created 88 super-stores[2] and had, according to *The Wall Street Journal*, "forced rivals to remodel stores, realign prices, and change procurement policies to cut costs." German consumers like Claudia Haemel seemed to like this change. "I have nothing against these prices if it makes basic foods cheaper for the consumer," she says.

The German government seems to believe it knows best what Claudia should pay for food. It doesn't matter much now, because in 2006 Wal-Mart announced that it was closing all of its stores in Germany.

ABORTION? LEGAL. SELLING A KIDNEY? FIVE YEARS IN PRISON...

On Oct. 5, 1983, Al Gore — at the time a representative from Tennessee — sponsored a Senate bill that became the 1984 National Organ Transplant Act. He worked vigorously to get this bill passed. But were his efforts misguided?

If you, a friend or loved one aren't waiting for an organ, you probably aren't familiar with Title III of this law, which makes the selling of any organ a federal crime, an act penalized at a maximum of $50,000 or five years in prison — or both.

The legislation doesn't note that the person selling the organ could benefit because of the monies received, nor is there any mention of how the potential recipient, who may die if a kidney isn't recovered, could benefit from this voluntary transaction. Most importantly, there's no mention that this transaction takes place between two emancipated humans and doesn't deny anyone else the right to life, liberty and the pursuit of happiness.

A nationwide shortage has created a bleak outlook for those who are waiting for a new lease on life. In January 2011, The United Network for Organ Sharing reported that 93,405 individuals were waiting for kidneys; 16,840 for livers; 1,814 for lungs, and 3,187 for hearts.[3] One could easily conclude that there aren't enough organs to go around, but this is far from the truth.

SUGGESTED CLASSROOM DEBATE

Should people be allowed to sell their votes to other voters in a presidential election? Why, or why not?

The National Organ Transplant Act has helped create this shortage by ignoring the fundamentals of the law of supply and instead relying on a system known as non-price rationing.

> ➤ **Non-price rationing is the practice of rationing a good or service through a waiting line, waiting list, or lottery.**

The first consequence of non-price rationing is the *opportunity cost of wasted time*. In essence, without a free market with equilibrium prices, thousands of people are required to wait in their homes, near a hospital, hoping and praying that an organ will become available. If the market were allowed to work, those same people would be able to find an organ much faster and would not have to spend so much time inefficiently.

The second problem with non-price rationing is that the *seller* (or prospective seller in this case) *fails to maximize revenue*. Many people who donate organs would rather earn some money for their valuable resources. Others who refuse to donate, would do so if they could earn cash for themselves or their family. At a price of $0, we are not given the proper incentives, nor receive the maximum reward for supplying these "products."

The final inefficient outcome is that the *buyer who places the highest value on the good or service, does not necessarily get the good or service.* This means that someone who might be on the list who is willing and able to pay $20,000 for a new kidney, might get one ahead of someone who would have paid $200,000 for one. The person who is lucky enough to be next in line might be 71 years old in declining health, while a 33-year old mother of four young children is in an unlucky spot in the line. In this case, the younger person might have been willing to sell their home or borrow the money to stay around for their children, while the older person might not decide (in a market system where the price is set by supply and demand) that a new organ is worth the cost.

WHY ECONOMISTS LOVE AUCTIONS

I have never been to Cuba or North Korea. Like most Americans, I can normally find everything I need when I go shopping. However, sometimes I wish more suppliers would use the tools of economics to help me live a less stressful life.

What is sleeping on this shoreline worth?

Photo courtesy Jack Chambless

One supplier that comes to mind is the Minnesota Department of Natural Resources. It is this government agency that uses a well-meaning approach to rationing camping spaces that almost gave me a heart attack.

A few years ago I was driving down highway 61 along Minnesota's famous Lake Superior shoreline with the intention of camping in the famous Split Rock Lighthouse state park.

When we arrived at the park office to register for a campsite, we were told that almost all the sites were full and that we would have to be added to a waiting list. The ranger also mentioned that four sites would be opening up at 9 a.m. My name was number five on the list.

Rather than leaving, I hung around just in case any of the four people ahead of me did not show up at 9 a.m. when the rangers planned on registering the lucky few.

The next hour dragged on forever. Every time someone walked into the office I panicked, thinking they were one of my competitors.

At 9 a.m. there were four of us waiting for the names to be called. I was tempted to lock the door just in case one of the people in front of me on the list was about to come in.

Fortunately, the other person ahead of me on the list did not show up, we got a spot for the next few nights and had a great time.

Why did it have to come to this? Why couldn't the state of Minnesota opt for a system that would take less time, create less stress, and raise added funds to help count moose and wolves?

The perfect system to ration something that is in short supply is an *auction*. With an auction there could have been 5 or 500 people in the office that day. It would not have mattered. I could have relaxed, had a cup of coffee, and returned at 8:59:59 a.m. At 9 a.m., the ranger could have said, "What am I bid for campsite number ..."

Each of the four sites would have been auctioned off to the highest bidder. Instead of getting $17 per night, the state of Minnesota could have earned $50 a night. For sites closer to Lake Superior, someone might have bid $100 per night.

The bottom line is that an auction could help the market equilibrium appear within seconds; help people who really, really want to sleep in Minnesota's woods

get the site they are willing and able to pay for; encourage those who lose out in the bidding to either work harder or save more money for the next time there is an auction and help Minnesota earn more money from its scarce resources.

THE ECONOMICS OF SUPER BOWL (AND OTHER) TICKETS

In an era where we can go online and find concert and sporting event tickets at the click of a mouse, it is somewhat amazing that in many states, it is still illegal to buy and sell tickets for more than face value.

The day tickets went on sale for the Green Bay Packers – Pittsburgh Steelers Super Bowl game, the face value set by the NFL ranged from $600-$1,200. It did not matter. The cheapest ticket online was over $2,660 and ranged to over $14,000.

This brings us to the question of whether ticket scalping – the practice of charging more than face value – *should* be illegal. If you think carefully about the full magnitude of this type of transaction, you would be hard-pressed to defend the government's intrusion into our entertainment life.[4] Where is the harm? The seller offers a product for a price. The buyer decides that price is what they are willing to pay. The buyer gives the seller money, and neither party has inflicted any measurable damage on a third party.

If we argue that the seller is the owner of the ticket, shouldn't sellers be allowed to do whatever they want with *their* property? If you argue that scalping takes advantage of customers, the question is how?

Photo courtesy Jack Chambless

The customer can walk away, if the price is too high. Attending a concert is not one of life's necessities – nor is there a Constitutional guarantee to cheap tickets. Maybe you think that ticket scalping robs the National Football League of money it could have earned. Maybe the NFL should charge the equilibrium price to begin with and there would be no scalping at all.[5]

Notice in the previous photo something quite funny. Depicted here are ticket scalpers outside of Florida State University's football stadium. On this day, it was still illegal in Florida to do this. However, the owner of the parking lot they are standing in – who normally lets people park their cars free of charge – is charging $20 per car and no police officers chased him around the block.

It is also somewhat ironic that, if scalpers are forced to charge prices that *are below face value* (a common occurrence for events that do not sell out), there is no law against that.

In August of 2005 I was driving into Chicago with plans to take my family to a Chicago Cubs baseball game. My youngest son, a huge Cubs fan, was so excited he could barely contain himself. I kept telling him there was one potential problem. We did not have any tickets.

The Cubs were playing their arch rivals, the St. Louis Cardinals, which normally means a sell-out and huge profits for scalpers. However, that day it was raining when the game started. I put on a rain jacket and staked out near the main entrance waiting for the scalpers to panic.

After a one-hour delay I finally got what I wanted. One scalper, convinced the game would be rained out, sold me tickets only 15 rows from the field for $8.50 each. The face value of the tickets was $46. Had it not been raining, the tickets would have cost over $100 and my son would have had to watch on television.

Why is it that I am assumed to be smart enough to know when I am getting a good deal, but not smart enough to know when I am getting ripped off?

The final argument by the government is that tickets sold on the black market are not taxed. That is easily fixed, too. Legalize ticket scalping and require tickets to be sold from a legitimate brokerage business. The government can then apply sales tax laws to the product and collect whatever money they deem necessary. Or the government could just let the market fix itself.[6]

This is already happening to an extent. In 2008 the NFL's New York Jets announced that the best seats to their new stadium would be auctioned off on eBay.[7] Eager to get in on profits being earned in the secondary market, other professional sports teams have finally wised up and have begun creating websites where season ticket holders can resell tickets they cannot use. Of course, the teams get a percentage of any transaction, but at least everyone wins in this situation. Someone who might get a chance of being close to the action once in a season fills the seat.

The season ticket holder gets some extra money, as does the team. Should this be illegal, too?

The bottom line is that, from the economic perspective, it seems to be a colossal waste of taxpayer money to have the police arresting people for interjecting the lessons of Adam Smith into a market sorely in need of the invisible hand.

THE ECONOMICS OF PRICE CEILINGS

So far, we have seen how the government tries to force prices down by making certain discounts illegal and by outlawing private property exchange. In the case of price ceilings, the government actually enters the market and picks the price for the buyer and seller!

Consider the market for apartments in Santa Monica for a moment. For 20 years, this beautiful city in southern California was home to more than just surfers and sushi bars. It was also home to a great deal of economic illiteracy in the form of rent-controlled apartments. Figure 8.1 illustrates this fact.

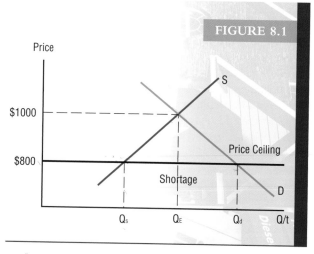

FIGURE 8.1

Back in the 1970s, the Santa Monica government decided that many people – mostly the poor and young – simply could not afford to rent an apartment in this increasingly affluent city. In order to make this market more equitable, the government voted to impose a price ceiling on apartments in this city.

> ➤ **A price ceiling is an artificial limit on what a business can charge for a good or service. Usually, the price ceiling is set below the market equilibrium price.**

Read over the First Amendment to the United States Constitution. It could be argued that rent control laws that prevent buyers and sellers from agreeing to equilibrium prices are tantamount to a violation of our rights to free speech. Fully explain whether this argument has an economic merit.

Suppose that, at the time of this ruling, the average equilibrium price of an apartment was $1400 per month. A price ceiling of $800 per month would, in theory, lead to greater assistance for the targeted groups. In reality, rent control in Santa Monica and other cities that jumped on this bandwagon of good intentions led to an increase in the quantity of apartments demanded, but also a decrease in the quantity of apartments supplied!

Many landlords simply vacated their buildings or turned them into condominiums. In New York City, rent control programs that were started in 1947 prompted some building owners to burn their buildings down to collect insurance, rather than rent them out at unprofitable prices. The result has been major shortage of apartments and no significant help for the very people that the law was intended to assist. Today approximately 70% of New York's apartments have rent control imposed upon them – a total of over 1.08 million units. Fully 35% of the people who live in these apartments have incomes of over $50,000 per year and 87,358 of these "apartments for the poor" have tenants who earn more than $100,000 per year.[8]

It is interesting to note that rent control was eventually lifted in Santa Monica. As expected, rents initially shot up to well over $1,000 per month. At these prices, *The Wall Street Journal* reported that surpluses broke out. Over time, prices began to come back down toward a market equilibrium condition.[9]

1980 was a terrible year in American history. The overall level of unemployment was on the rise, inflation hit a one-year record of 13.5%, and the economy was in a recession. Making matters worse was an ongoing increase in crude oil prices and a hostage crisis in Iran that paralyzed the nation and the presidency of Jimmy Carter.

In the meantime, the Soviet Union was not standing still in its attempts to push the doctrine of communism on the rest of the world. Tremendous inroads were made in Asia, Africa, and Latin America, while the Soviet Union's stranglehold in Eastern Europe and influence in the Middle East remained strong. In 1980 the Soviet Union invaded Afghanistan in a move that stunned the world. On the surface, the Soviet Union looked invincible. But deep inside the economic corridors of the USSR, the foundation of communism was crumbling under the weight of massive shortages.

You may recall in the earlier chapters reading about the implementation of production quotas and price ceilings by Josef Stalin. Under this centrally planned system, the Soviet government hoped to simultaneously prevent the pursuit of profit and hold down prices for consumers. Figure 8.2 illustrates the problems this system created.

You might find yourself wondering whether the shortages were a big deal to the Soviet people. After all, for decades they had accepted the long lines and empty shelves.

HOW PRICE CEILINGS HELPED DESTROY THE SOVIET UNION

The dustbin of history is littered with the remains of those countries which relied on diplomacy to secure their freedom. We must never forget in the final analysis that it is our military, industrial and economic strength that offers the best guarantee of peace for America in times of danger.

Ronald Reagan, address as Governor of California, 1974

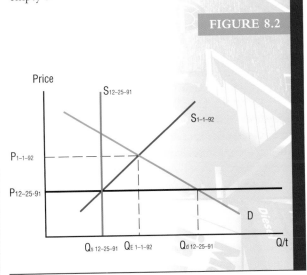

FIGURE 8.2

The Soviet people accepted this condition because to complain about it openly could lead to execution or slave labor camps. It was not until 1981 that the Soviet leadership began to worry about where shortages might lead them.

In 1980, Ronald Reagan easily won the presidency over Jimmy Carter and subsequently pushed for a massive buildup in America's military power. Hundreds of billions of dollars later, the United States was in an accelerated arms race with our Cold War rivals.

Mikhail Gorbachev, the last Soviet leader Reagan would deal with, faced a big problem in trying to keep up with the military spending that was taking place in America. While the United States was enjoying record prosperity during the 1980s, the Soviet Union was floundering.

This came to pass because, in the U.S., the military and the private sector are essentially separate entities. The Reagan administration did not go to the private sector and take away resources to be redirected to military production. The private sector was left alone to provide for the people. In the Soviet Union, the military and private production came from the same source – the government. Therefore, during the 1980s, as the military demanded more and more resources, the people of Russia had to face increasingly long lines for food, clothing, and other necessities.

Realizing that the people were suffering and that dissent was mounting, Gorbachev embarked on a campaign known as perestroika (restructuring) and glasnost (openness). Under these two reforms, Gorbachev sought to allow more private control over the means of production and the profit that might result from it. In addition, he allowed people to be more openly critical of the government – hoping that these changes would ease some of the pressure that was building behind the Iron Curtain. It was too late. As the Soviet Union lost the economic and political ability to maintain power throughout Eastern Europe, one by one those nations that had lived under the shadow of tyranny broke away and pushed for democratic reforms.

In September of 1991, a military coup in the Soviet Union led to the ousting of Gorbachev and the ascension of Boris Yeltsin as the eventual president of Russia.[10]

It is stunning that Gorbachev was not thrown out for violating the basic tenants of communism. He was thrown out because, once people gained a taste of political and economic freedom, there was no amount of moral or military force that could contain their demands to accelerate the march toward democracy and free markets.

On Christmas day of 1991, with the Soviet Union bankrupt, Gorbachev officially dissolved this once-feared and seemingly invincible nation and allowed the individual republics to operate on their own. Six days later, Mr. Yeltsin removed most of the price ceilings and production controls in Russia. The result was mass chaos, as prices increased by *300%* for the most basic goods and services! However, shoppers immediately noticed more of everything in Russian stores. As can be seen in figure 8.2, lifting the ceilings and the production controls meant that Russian suppliers were given the proper incentives to increase production.

Today, Russia is on a journey toward freer markets. It has not been easy. The Russian mafia is a significant problem. Tax collections are sporadic. Abuses of private property and widespread hunger are omnipresent, and the Communists are wrestling to regain power, as the war with neighboring Georgia illustrated. Some economists have expressed concern that Russia has backtracked on protection of private property and wealth accumulation. The arrest of Mikhail Khodorkovsky, the head of the Yukos oil company, is one example of why some are worried about Russia's future.[11]

If Russia makes the final painful turn and beats back the calls for the return of government control, we will all be better off. Overall, Russia seems to be on a path committed to freer trade, flat taxes, and more sound financial management, which has helped the Russian economy see some economic growth.[12]

This painful transition could have been avoided. In 1917, Russia had a choice between two economists – Adam Smith or Karl Marx. They simply picked the wrong one.

WAS RONALD REAGAN SIMPLY IN THE RIGHT PLACE AT THE RIGHT TIME?

The following quotes are from economists prior to the collapse of the Soviet Union.

> The Soviet economy has made great national progress in recent years.
>
> John Kenneth Galbraith, Harvard University

> It is a vulgar mistake to think that most people in Eastern Europe are miserable.
>
> Paul Samuelson, Nobel Laureate

> Can economic command significantly compress and accelerate the growth process? The remarkable performance of the Soviet Union suggests that it can. In 1920 Russia was but a minor figure in the economic councils of the world. Today it is a country whose economic achievements bear comparison with those of the United States.
>
> Lester Thurow, Massachusetts Institute of Technology

Why were the prominent economists wrong? How could Reagan have seen the demise of Marxism nine years before the Soviet Union collapsed? In the early '60s many political and economic experts believed that the United States and the Soviet Union were destined to go to war. The prevailing "wisdom" was that the only way war could be averted was to engage in commerce with the Soviet Union, contain communism where we could, and not engage in acts that were seen by the USSR as provocative. Reagan did not share this view. In 1963 Reagan argued:

> If we relieve the strain on the shaken Russian economy by aiding their enslaved satellites (Eastern Europe and Cuba), thus reducing the danger of uprising and revolution, and if we continue granting concessions which reduce our military strength giving Russia time to improve hers as well as shore up her limping industrial complex—aren't we perhaps adding to the communist belief that their system will through evolution catch up and pass ours?
>
> If we truly believe that our way of life is best aren't the Russians more likely to recognize that fact and modify their stand if we let their economy come unhinged so that contrast is apparent? Inhuman though it may sound, shouldn't we throw the whole burden of feeding the satellites on their slave masters who are having trouble feeding themselves?[13]

Eighteen years later, as president of the United States, Ronald Reagan fully implemented the incredible vision he singularly held in 1963. By halting trade in the area of military equipment and petroleum technologies Reagan ravaged the Russian economy and forced a deep recession in the Soviet Union.

By building up the U.S. military – and simultaneously cutting taxes and deregulating the private sector – Reagan helped launch an economic boom in the United States that created $400 billion in extra revenue for the government.

The Soviet Union tried to keep up, but the centrally planned economy was doomed to failure. It simply could not adapt fast enough. It could not offer its people the proper incentives to produce. It could not offer the average Soviet citizen any reason to believe that working for the government was better than working for one's own self-interest.

In June of 1982, in an address to the British Parliament, Ronald Reagan said,

> In an ironic sense, Karl Marx was right. We are witnessing today a great revolutionary crisis–a crisis where the demands of the economic order are colliding directly with those of the political order. But the crisis is happening not in the free, non-Marxist west, but in the home of Marxism-Leninism, the Soviet Union. What we see here is a political structure that no longer corresponds to its economic base, a society where productive forces are hampered by political ones.

Economists are very bright people. Sometimes we make predictions that are accurate. In the great battle of ideas that pitted the free-market vision of Ronald Reagan against the iron fist of communism, Reagan seemed to see what no one else could see.

The world is indeed fortunate that he had the opportunity to put his vision for our nation – and the world – to a test. That test lasted from 1981 to 1989. In just eight short years, Mr. Reagan managed to undo almost 75 years of Marxist ideology. The people of Eastern Europe and the former Soviet Union have more freedom than at any time in recent history. Estonia has even passed the United States in the rankings of economic freedom.[14]

To say that Reagan was simply in the right place at the right time is not an intellectually honest assessment of his presidency. If the Soviet Union would have eventually failed anyway – as Reagan's critics are quick to argue – the question that must be asked is, how – and due to what forces – would the collapse have taken place? There was no sign that the USSR was ready to collapse until it was *forced* to the brink of bankruptcy.

It should also be noted that the Cold War of 1947-1991 was ended without any Americans dying on Soviet soil. It was ended with zero missiles being fired from the Soviet arsenal of 45,000 nuclear weapons.

In an era when the U.S. is concerned about other nations having weapons of mass destruction, it is all the more impressive that our arch-enemy – an enemy that considered starting WWIII as its economy spiraled downward – never attacked us. The U.S. won the Cold War by destroying an ideology from within the borders of the enemy. We won because of the moral superiority of liberty over tyranny. For this, it could be argued, all of us owe Ronald Reagan a great deal of gratitude.

CONCEPT CHECK

A humanities professor at Valencia College once argued that, "No American should be allowed to earn over $250,000 per year." Graphically illustrate and explain what would happen in U.S. labor markets if his wish became a reality.

THE ECONOMICS OF PRICE FLOORS

In the 1930s, American farmers were ravaged by falling prices for a number of agricultural products. The Great Depression caused a staggering decline in household income, which translated into stagnant demand for food and into bankruptcy for many family farms. In response to this collapse in prices, farmers across the nation appealed to Franklin Roosevelt to do something to save farmers.

The resulting aid — which is still in place today — took the form of *agricultural price supports* as depicted in figure 8.3.

Suppose the price of milk is $2.75 per gallon in its equilibrium state. You might wonder where you could get milk for such a good deal. Don't spend too much time shopping around, because it will be an exercise in futility. Dairy producers in this country have tapped into one of the most lucrative forms of welfare that has ever been conjured up by Washington, D.C.

In this case, dairy farmers (and producers of a number of other commodities) do not have to worry about the price of milk falling to a level that will jeopardize their profits. That is because the government has imposed, on their behalf, a price floor well above the market equilibrium price of milk.

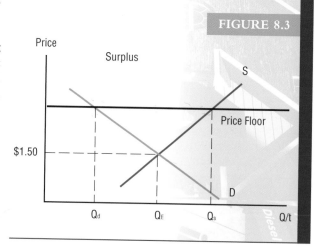

FIGURE 8.3

> ➤ **A price floor is an artificial limit on how far prices can fall in a particular market. Usually, a price floor is set above the market equilibrium price.**

The price floor tells the dairy producer to take his milk to the market and charge whatever he thinks he can get. If consumers do not purchase the milk that is offered up, the federal government will step in and buy the milk from the producer — at the floor price!

Is this cow guilty of plunder?

The result is straightforward and predictable. The quantity of milk demanded comes down due to the higher price. However, the quantity of milk supplied increases. After all, if the government is going to buy up any milk that is not purchased in the open market, wouldn't the dairy farmer be crazy to not increase production? For taxpayers, the result has been less than ideal.[15] Even if prices in the free market are low, some farmers do quite well. Consider this:

- From 2006 to 2007 total farm income increased by 44% to $73 billion.
- From 2009 to 2010 farmland values rose 10% while the residential and commercial real estate values plummeted.[16]
- The average farmer in America had an annual income of $83,194 in 2010.[17]
- Two-thirds of all price support payments are given to the wealthiest 10% of the farmers.
- The average farmer in America has an income that is 30% higher than the average for all other workers.
- The average net worth for an American farmer is over $830,000.[18]

As a result of price floors in agricultural markets, enormous surpluses have sprung up from time to time. Some of the surplus food rots. Some is given away in federal food relief programs overseas. Some is given to poor people in this country. In the past, the government has tried everything from paying farmers to kill their excess cows to paying them not to produce milk![19]

The surpluses end up being paid for by consumers in several ways. First, you pay artificially higher prices at the grocery store, because the farmers send the food to market at prices near the floor level. In 2007 alone, Americans paid $12 billion more for groceries as a result of price supports. Farmers don't care if you buy their products at these inflated prices because whatever you don't buy, the government gets out of your other pocket — using your tax dollars to relieve the plight of corporate farms.

By the way, those milk ads that you sometimes see with celebrities posing with milk mustaches? You helped pay for those, too! Years ago, the dairy industry convinced Congress that they needed help slowing down the decline in milk consumption in the United States. $169 million dollars later, you helped develop — unbeknownst to you — these ads.[20]

It should be comforting for you to know that, after the milk ad campaign began, the consumption *fell* by over 4%. Don't expect to see the ads cancelled, though. According to the milk industry, they need to keep spending your money on the ads, or demand might fall even faster. Only in Washington, D.C., is an ad campaign that fails to boost sales seen as a successful ad campaign.

Perhaps we taxpayers should create our own billboard ad campaign in Washington that shows a perplexed milk consumer asking "Got common sense?"

Does it matter to Uncle Sam that most farmers who receive the subsidies have net incomes of over $100,000 per year? No, not really. After all, it is not the politician's money that is being transferred to farmer Bob. It is your money. In fact, the top 1% of farmers — 24,111 recipients — "raked in $13.5 billion over five years, an average of $558,698 per farmer."[21]

Ted Turner — yes the same billionaire who founded CNN — got some free money, as did at least 20 Fortune 500 companies and 1,200 universities.[27] Other "farmers" getting your money included ExxonMobil, Chevron, International Paper and Caterpillar.

It should also be pointed out that many critics of our farm subsidy programs cite the implicitly racist outcomes that many agricultural price supports create.[28] The peanut program, for example, provides generous subsidies for southern peanut farmers. In order to prevent rampant surpluses from emerging, the government assigned quotas to various peanut farms during the 1930s that limited how much each farm could produce.

These quotas were handed out during a time when most of the farms were white-owned. Black farmers today are often not allowed to participate in the peanut program since they were not farming peanuts when the quota was established. It is a bit ironic that it was a black man — George Washington Carver who was almost solely responsible for discovering all of the various uses for peanuts.

CONCEPT CHECK

U.S. cotton farmers receive some of the most generous subsidies — $3 billion per year[22] Now, because of cotton surpluses, the government subsidizes U.S. companies to encourage them to buy more U.S. cotton.[23] However, much of the surplus cotton gets exported to Africa where African farmers receive no subsidies.[24] Graphically illustrate and explain what this has meant for African farmers and why this policy has also led to some African farmers joining al-Qaeda.[25] Meanwhile, taxpayer-financed sugar subsidies have contributed to pollution in the Everglades[26] and high candy bar prices. How?

MINIMUM WAGE LAWS

A final, but no less disturbing, example of the damage price floors inflict can be found in many inner cities and impoverished rural areas around our country.

Franklin Roosevelt was on a roll in the 1930s when it came to propping up sellers in America. At about the same time the farmers were lining up for their taxpayer-funded aid program, Mr. Roosevelt signed into law the first federal minimum wage. The well-intended law was designed to increase the hourly earnings of poor Americans who were suffering from the Depression.

While the Depression ended in the 1930s, the minimum wage lives on. What few people realize is that the people who were supposed to be helped by this price floor in unskilled labor markets have often fallen victim to government's attempt to repeal the law of demand.

Figures 8.4 and 8.5 illustrate the disparate impact the minimum wage has on entry-level workers.

Suppose the equilibrium wage rate for fast-food workers is $5.25 per hour in Detroit, Michigan. Detroit had an unemployment rate of almost 30% in 2010. Suppose employees in Salt Lake City, Utah – where unemployment was about 7% – can command $7.85 per hour. With the federal government providing a price floor of $7.25 per hour, notice that the overall quantity of labor demanded in Detroit decreases.

This is because many small business owners, who operate on very thin profit margins, are often unable to absorb forced increases in wage rates. If fast-food restaurants were left alone in Detroit wages would fall to $5.25. That would mean more teenagers and unskilled workers finding employment. At the mandated wage of $7.25 the quantity of labor supplied is greater than the quantity demanded. This leads to a surplus of labor services. That is another way of saying unemployment. The empirical evidence also links increases in the minimum wage to higher levels of crime, higher drop-out rates, and poverty.[29]

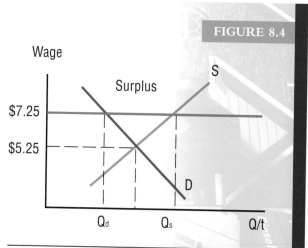

FIGURE 8.4

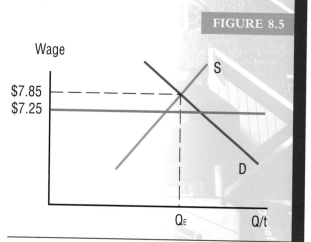

FIGURE 8.5

However, in places like Dallas, Raleigh, and other growing metropolitan areas, the equilibrium wage rate has been pushed up – by the invisible hand – to a level well above the minimum wage.

This means that where the price floor is below equilibrium, the minimum wage had no effect on the unemployment rate. Unfortunately, in other cities, the guarantee of at least $7.25 – or more – per hour has led to a guarantee of zero dollars per hour as the benevolence of the United States Congress destroys jobs.

The most recent increase in the minimum wage could not have come at a worse time for teenagers. In the middle of the 2007-2009 Recession, the unemployment rate for teenagers rose to 27.6%. For black teenagers the numbers were even worse. As employers struggled to cover their costs, the increase in the wage floor led to a 52.2% unemployment rate.[30]

Perhaps Congress – when it comes to regulating the terms in which emancipated human beings can interact with one another – should at least consider the words of Chief Justice John Marshall who in the case of *Ogden v. Saunders* stated:

> Individuals do not derive from government their right to contract, but bring that right with them into society every man retains [the right] to dispose of [his] property according to his own judgment.

DO GOVERNMENT BANS WORK?

What happens when the government tells people they can no longer demand or supply a good or service? The good or service goes away, right? No, it doesn't. That does not mean that government should never try this strategy. Sometimes banning a good or service is precisely what the economy needs to preserve liberty.

When the government made hiring a hit man illegal, this was a very good decision. If we legalized hit men, we would see person A – the person who wants someone rubbed out – hire person B (the hit man) in order to kill person C. The problem is that person C not only did not voluntarily consent to be part of this transaction, but person C's fifth Amendment rights are violated when he or she is shot while mowing the yard one day.

Another example of where attempting to ban something can promote liberty is in the area of child pornography. A recent estimate put the number of children who are trafficked as sex slaves at between 30,000 and 50,000.[32] This horrifying reality definitely fits into the negative externality category since children are not consenting adults.[33]

Clearly, the government can and should play a role in trying to fight the laws of supply and demand where life, liberty, and property rights are in jeopardy. However, the legal system can also seek to ban things that a lot of people want and where it is unclear that measurable negative externalities exist.

THE DRUG WAR

Have you ever used illegal drugs? Perhaps you should not answer out loud. Some of, maybe most of, your classmates have at least experimented with marijuana at some point in their lives. If you know someone who has smoked marijuana, did they engage in violent acts while they were stoned, or did they munch on a bucket of chicken wings while watching *SouthPark* reruns?

Either way, the federal government does not care. The federal government spends almost $20 billion trying to keep drug demanders away from drug suppliers.[36] More than 19,000 state and local police officers work full-time on drug cases.

Approximately 20% of America's prison population is made up of willing buyers and sellers who did not harm anyone in the process of buying and selling. Yet the demand for drugs continues to increase, all while the drug supply is plentiful.

The unintended consequences of the drug war are no laughing matter. In addition to the bloated prison population, we have young people in the inner cities dying in gun battles as drug sellers compete with one another. Drug prices are artificially high, so more people engage in crime to pay for their habits. Police officers are often corrupted by the allure of drug money. The government earns no tax money from the sale of drugs, while the individual rights of people to use drugs – the same as they can cigarettes, alcohol, and Internet pornography – are taken away. In Mexico, the drug war had claimed over 34,000 lives by 2011 and had turned the northern part of that country into one of the most dangerous places on Earth.[37]

HOW THE U.S. HELPED AFGHANISTAN'S OPIUM DEALERS BECOME MORE PROSPEROUS

You may recall that we learned how the principle of comparative advantage is an important function in determining success in the marketplace. This principle applies not only to the individual trying to decide what to produce, but also to an entire nation trying to decide what to produce. In Afghanistan, the land is perfectly suited to grow the poppy flower. Poppy flowers are perfectly suited to produce the powerful drug known as opium.

The problem for poppy farmers was that the Taliban did not like the idea of allowing people to buy and sell drugs. That led to a ban on opium poppies for the brief time that the Taliban was in power. Just like women who are happy to shed their burkhas, poppy farmers in Afghanistan are somewhat thankful that the United States has helped them earn a living once again.[38]

Now that the Taliban is weakened, farmers like Gul Haidar are back in business. In Mr. Haidar's case, he has sown 250 acres of poppies, which will yield about 650 pounds of opium. Mr. Haidar – and farmers like him – produced 75% of the world's supply of opium (3,611 tons) before the Taliban came into power. Production fell to 204 tons by the year 2000.

With the increase in the number of farmers re-entering the market, the overall supply of opium is increasing. Predictably, the increase in the supply of opium has led to lower prices and an increase in quantity demanded. This prompted the Bush Administration to step up its efforts to fight opium production in Afghanistan.

As it turns out, Afghanistan is not the only worry for drug enforcement officials. In 2005 the U.S. put pressure on the Canadian government to arrest Marc Emery – a man accused of being one of the biggest marijuana suppliers to the U.S.[39] Apparently, so many border patrol officers were diverted into the war effort following September 11th that drug dealers from Latin America and Canada found it less risky and less costly to smuggle cocaine and marijuana into the U.S. As the supply of these drugs increased by 25% in Florida alone, the United States found that the laws of supply and demand undermined the war on drugs as the war on terrorism became the priority.[40]

SUGGESTED CLASSROOM DEBATE

If the U.S. legalized drugs, would quantity demanded increase by a large amount or by a small amount? Why? Does the drug war harm young black men in America's cities – as some critics charge – more than young white men?[41] Why, or why not? Should the National Football League and Major League Baseball encourage or discourage steroid use among professional football and baseball players?[42] Why or why not?

MARKET FAILURES

> There are all kinds of reasons why liberal economists say that markets are inefficient and that we must replace the invisible hand with a visible hand.
>
> Jagdish Bhagwati, economics professor, Columbia University

At this point in the semester, you have most certainly detected that this textbook tends to lean heavily on the belief that free markets work very well and government interference in the market often creates more harm than good. Yet sometimes it does not work that way. Every now and then, the free market struggles to provide goods and services in the most efficient quantity or quality or provides goods and services at fraudulent prices. So let's take a look at how the market sometimes fails.

Did you watch in stunned disbelief as bank after bank failed in 2008? Do you remember when some rancher in Washington let a cow inflicted with mad cow disease into the meat supply? Did Toyota's response to questions about its brakes shake your faith in the free enterprise system? Have you ever been ripped off by a company that promised to serve you with high quality and a "low" price?

> ➤ **A market failure takes place when the free market fails to produce an efficient price or market equilibrium outcome, or when one side of the market violates the rights of the other.**

In 2001, three economists – Joseph Stiglitz, George Akerlof, and Michael Spence –shared the $1 million Nobel prize in economics for their work in the area of market failures.[43] Up until these gentlemen won the most prestigious award in economics, the award had routinely been awarded to economists from the University of Chicago, where Adam Smith and the free market are held as sacrosanct. Mr. Stiglitz and his colleagues have spent their careers looking into instances where market failures arise.

What causes market failures? According to the Nobel laureates, market failures typically occur when the problem of asymmetric information or externalities appears.

> ➤ **Asymmetric information occurs when one party in a transaction has perfect information about the price, quality or availability of a good or service and the other party does not.**

Shutterstock © Roypix, 2011.

Consider for a moment the market for used cars. If you have ever been involved in this market as a seller or a buyer, you know how frustrating – if not downright scary – this process can be. How does the seller of a used car that has been beautifully maintained get skeptical potential buyers to believe that they will not be ripped off? In this case, imperfect information might cause the seller to have to settle for less money than the car might actually be worth, because the buyer has no way of verifying the true history of the car. For buyers, how do you know whether the car you are looking at has been taken care of?

If you are in the market for a used car, and the one you settle on for what appears to be a great price was once under water in Iowa, how do you find this information out? Again, the problem of asymmetric information leads to your paying either more than you should have or paying for a total piece of junk.

Stiglitz pointed to the breakdown in security at airports on September 11th as an example of a market failure. "There are certain activities like airport security that should not be in the private sphere. That market is not self-adjusting," he argued.

What he means by the term "self-adjusting," is that the market, in his opinion, does not respond quickly enough or does not have the proper incentives or information necessary to keep us safe when we get on a plane. The pre-September 11th market for flying demanded a quick, relatively unobstructed, process of getting on our airplanes. The free market told private companies that people were more interested in getting checked in and boarding in the least amount of time possible – even if it meant that not everyone got checked who needed to be checked.

Stiglitz and other economists, who do not have as much faith in the efficiency of the market, would suggest that the market failed to recognize that security is actually more valuable than a speedy check-in process, and that the terrorist hijackings of four jets indicate that the market did not know best what consumers really need.

What then, do Stiglitz and others in his camp suggest we do when the market fails to operate efficiently? They believe that where markets fail, government intervention is necessary. In the used car market, they would argue that disclosure laws with respect to odometer readings, previous wrecks, and so forth be strictly enforced with vigorous government oversight of the used car industry, and they would advocate tough penalties for violators of the law.

In the case of airport security, Stiglitz argued strongly in favor of turning over security to the government, with the theory that government – being nonprofit – will not have to worry as much about consumer demands and cost controls. Government uses taxes to provide security, and therefore, has access to a deep pool of money from which to launch increases in security that the private sector might find too costly.

In the case of Toyota and the recent financial crisis, critics of capitalism seemingly had truckloads of ammunition to fire away at the followers of Adam Smith and largely unregulated markets. As *The Wall Street Journal* uncovered, executives at Toyota may have known about braking and acceleration issues with many Toyota cars, long before it became a nationally-discussed issue.[44] Meanwhile, banking executives all over the world, in the face of mounting evidence that the housing bubble was about to burst, kept betting on ever higher prices – only to run for taxpayer aid when the bets did not pay off.

When it comes to the issue of prices, many economists argue that markets sometimes fail to accurately reflect the full cost of certain goods and services. Consider gasoline as an example.

Whatever you paid today for gasoline is not enough, many argue, when you take into account the *marginal social cost* of gasoline.

> ➤ **The marginal social cost is the total cost to society as a whole for producing one further unit, or taking one further action, in an economy. This total cost of producing one extra unit of something is not simply the direct cost borne by the producer, but also must include the costs to the external environment and other stakeholders.**

In the market for gasoline many costs are taken into account – the price of crude oil, marketing, transportation, refining, and so forth. What is not taken into account is the net damage to the environment from creating and burning gasoline, and the net cost to society from the thousands of people who have died in wars to protect the supply of oil, and thus, the relatively low price of fuel.

If we took into account the marginal social cost of the fuel we buy, the total cost would be higher. With higher input costs would come a decrease in supply and higher prices would follow. Higher prices would reduce quantity demanded and thus, reduce not only pollution but the pressure to go to war to secure low gas prices.

IS NON-PRICE RATIONING EVER BENEFICIAL?

We have looked at the argument in favor of government intervention when markets fail to provide good information or don't work as well as capitalists argue they should. We now turn to a defense of government-created shortages through the use of non-price rationing. The idea that shortages, long waits, and mass inconvenience could ever be a good thing might seem odd, but had you been alive during World War II, you might have been happy that the invisible hand was replaced with the government hand.

In 1940, the United States government spent (in today's dollars) just over $17 billion for national defense. That same year Germany spent over $250 billion.[45] Of course, Germany was already one year into World War II, and America was still avoiding military intervention in Europe and Asia.

All that changed with the bombing of Pearl Harbor. Almost overnight, the U.S. economy shifted into high gear to prepare America for entry into WW II in 1942. The problem was that, for much of the 1930s and early 1940s, the U.S. economy had either been in the depths of the Great Depression or attempting to get out of the worst downturn in our history. This meant that there was no vibrant economy from which to draw the necessary resources. That meant that the government had to turn

RATIONING MEANS A FAIR SHARE FOR ALL OF US

Were shortages necessary to win the war?
Source: Minnesota Historical Society

ration books authorizing the purchase of only a certain amount of various products per week. Beginning in April of 1942, sugar was rationed, followed by coffee, meats, butter, canned goods, dried peas and beans, and a variety of other products. In addition to food, consumer products like shoes and clothing were rationed or restricted. Alcohol was not rationed, but it remained in critically short supply and black markets sprung up all over the nation.

In one instance a warehouse in Sugarland, Texas had 22,000,000 pounds of sugar that the refinery refused to offer up to the marketplace. The general manager, M.G. Thompson, cited the inability to earn any profit as the reason for keeping the sugar warehoused.[48]

THE ECONOMICS OF FLORIDA WATER—MARKET FAILURE OR GOVERNMENT FAILURE?

We close this chapter with a blended look at the importance of the market, and the role government can play in cleaning up the problem of asymmetric information, with a detailed examination of a brewing crisis of epic proportions. We are speaking of Florida's growing shortage of water.

Some of you — especially those of you not from Florida — might find yourself saying, "That's absurd. There is water under the ground. We have tons of lakes, the Atlantic Ocean, and just about every afternoon in the summer it rains so hard, I am tempted to build an ark!" Others might say, "Hey, buddy, water is common property. We deserve it. It falls from the sky for free, and it ought to be free when we use it!" Sound familiar? After all, if gasoline and Budweiser fell out of the sky to the tune of 150 billion gallons per year (the annual quantity of Florida rainfall), we might expect to drive and drink free of charge, too.

Let's start with science before we do economics. First, of the 150 billion gallons that drench us, 110 billion gallons evaporate in the sweltering heat.[49] That constitutes 38 out of the 53 inches of annual rainfall. Another 8 inches runs off into lakes, rivers, wetlands, and eventually the ocean, where salt water remains at the bottom of the list of desired beverages. Only 7 of the 53 inches drip down into the aquifer (the underground supply of water that we rely on).

Now to the economics. The overall demand for water has grown exponentially in Florida for several years. The state's population now tops 18.5 million residents, who consume 2.4 billion gallons of water every day. Florida's

to private citizens and ask them to — voluntarily in some cases and through force in other cases — submit to massive rationing of almost all goods and services.

For example, during WW II, there were drives to preserve rubber, scrap metal, rags, paper, and grease.[46] People were asked to plant "victory gardens" and adhere to "meatless" days to stretch the nation's food supply.

Shortages and rationing of various goods became commonplace during the war. Rationing boards were established in every county, with the power to regulate the sale of 90% of all civilian goods. Every man, woman, and child received a ration book, limiting what could be purchased.[47]

In early 1942, rubber became the first item to be rationed by the Federal Government's Office of Price Administration (OPA). Gasoline soon followed, with mandatory rationing becoming effective on December 1, 1942. Citizens were issued A, B, or C stickers, allowing them a specific number of gallons per week, depending on their occupation. Those unfortunates with 'A' stickers were authorized only four gallons per week, a paltry total that was actually decreased to three gallons later in the war. In 1943, gasoline rationing became even more severe, with all forms of "pleasure driving" becoming illegal.

The rationing of food had a great impact on the lives of average Americans. As with gas, the government issued

agricultural industry is the biggest user at 3.2 billion gallons per day. Daily use by industry, power generators, and recreational entities amounts to 1.6 billion gallons. This includes Walt Disney World, which consumes more water in one day than the nation of Somalia (9.1 million people) consumes in a day.[50]

The problem is that the demand for water is growing at a faster rate than nature or God (depending on your view) is supplying it. By now, you have learned enough about economics to knock out a

Shutterstock ©ncn18, 2011.

What if water cost the same amount as gasoline?

diagram in just a few seconds, showing that if demand increases a lot and supply is increasing only a little, a shortage will persist at the prevailing price, and therefore, prices will have to rise to re-equilibrate the market. Problem solved.

Not so fast. That would be true if economics and the free market dictated the price of water. In Florida, politics and the government dictate the price of water. Do you remember the common property problem? In chapter one, we saw that if something is considered to be "owned by all," there is not much of an incentive for any one individual to be conservative in using that product. Water is considered by many to be common property.

As Joseph Stiglitz would say, the market has failed to accurately deliver good information about the amount of water available and the real price of water. As free-market economists would say, the market has not been allowed to convey information about the scarcity of water or the real price of water, because the government has disrupted the invisible hand.

You are probably aware of the fact that Pepsi owns the Aquafina brand of bottled water and Coca-Cola produces Dasani. Pepsi and Coke do not run Florida's water supply. No private company does.[51] Municipal governments control municipal water supplies, and prices are generally established on a monthly basis by those governments.

Since the officials in charge of setting water rates are elected and the public (a) does not know how acute the shortage is and (b) believes abundant, cheap water is our birthright, we end up with (c) prices well below market equilibrium and the virtual guarantee of ongoing shortages.

The government's response to the water shortage in many places like Central Florida has been to resort to Soviet-style rationing, where residents are told they cannot water their lawns during certain days or times of the day. Residents facing such watering restrictions largely ignore the government edicts. Why? Because there is an imbalance between how pretty and green we want our lawns to be and how pretty and green they would be if we listened to the government. Ignoring the government is also the rational thing to do. As long as the expected benefits (pretty green lawn) exceed the expected costs (the chance of getting caught and punished, plus the slight increase in their water bill), the residents will take their chances and water their lawns.

The price of water is set so low by government that about half of all water that goes to homes is used on lawns, and half of that is wasted on inefficient sprinkler systems. How many of you have ever driven down the road and seen badly aimed sprinklers watering the road or sidewalk rather than the grass? How many of you have seen sprinklers running during a rainstorm? Have you ever seen people turn on a garden hose to spray their driveway?

Consider this. Budweiser costs about $5.69 per six-pack. Six beers at 12 ounces each amounts to 72 ounces. One gallon equals 128 ounces. That means that Budweiser – which is 92% water – costs 7.9 cents per ounce or $10.11 per gallon. On February 1, 2011, a gallon of regular unleaded gasoline averaged $3.04 in Winter Garden, Florida – a suburb of Orlando. That same day, the city of Winter Garden charged residential customers $1.03 per 1,000 gallons of water,[52] up to 10,000 gallons. From 10,000-15,000 gallons, the price increased to over $1.27

per thousand gallons. Over 15,000 gallons equals a price of $1.53 per gallon.

The average Floridian consumes between 147 and 180 gallons of water per day. If we conservatively put Winter Garden usage at 147 gallons per person per day, that would be 4,410 gallons per month. Since the city of Winter Garden does not round up to calculate the water bill of its residents, 4,410 gallons would be a bill of $4.54. Specifically, the price of water equals $.000103 per gallon. We have plenty of beer, because the price is set by supply and demand. We are running out of water because our system is modeled after the same planning and rationing that bankrupted the Soviet Union.

SOME FINAL THOUGHTS

Do you remember the movie *Jurassic Park*? In that film, the mathematician tried to explain to the owner of the park that it would be impossible to keep his dinosaurs from breeding because "life finds a way."

The same could be said about the interaction of supply and demand in the face of market failures. In essence we can say, "Markets find a way."

I am sure some of you read the section on used cars and thought, "Hold on a second. Didn't the free market, rather than government, give us Carfax?" Well, yes. Carfax is the online service that allows you to submit the vehicle identification number of the car you are considering purchasing. For a fee, Carfax will give you a detailed vehicle history report that dramatically reduces the asymmetric information problem.

Some of your classmates, while reading about September 11th and the "market failure" surrounding security were saying, "Wait a minute! Before September 11th, the average consumer wanted to get on the airplane as fast as they could with minimal hassles. Therefore the market did not fail on September 11th at all. It was simply bound to happen that if consumers wanted few hassles, some consumers would hijack airplanes." This is a strong argument, too. After all, the government set the standards for screening passengers before the hijackers boarded the planes. Why is it that the market failed when government was ultimately in charge of our safety? Why, after 10 years of government control over airport security, do we still see TSA officials failing its own tests of airport security?[53]

Moreover, any astute observer of our housing market and financial industry would note that it was the government-chartered Fannie Mae and Freddie Mac, along with Bush-era rules that forced taxpayer dollars into the subprime market that helped fuel the overheated market.[54] One could also accurately point out that Toyota – even if

it intentionally covered up any wrong doing – was ultimately held accountable by the millions of customers that it stood to lose to Honda, Ford, and other companies. That threat alone forced Toyota to respond faster than government does, when it fails to inspect our food, bridges, schools, medicines, and other products properly.[55]

This leaves us with an unresolved debate. Do markets ever fail? If they do, is the government or the invisible hand the most efficient correction tool? That is for you to decide over time.

ENDNOTES

1 See "Stores Told to Lift Prices in Germany" by Ernest Beck, *The Wall Street Journal,* September 11, 2000.

2 See http://walmartstores.com/GlobalWMStoresWeb/navigate.do?catg=376&contId=5382 for more on Wal-Mart in Germany.

3 Source: www.unos.org.

4 In one case police arrested a man in Jacksonville, Florida, for selling $34.72 tickets to a Jacksonville Jaguars football game for $35! See "State tosses scalping case over six cents," *The Orlando Sentinel,* November 26, 1998.

5 Apparently, rock stars now realize the error of their ways because ticket prices to many shows have increased significantly over the past few years. See "The show must go on, but at higher prices" by Kati Schardl, *The Tallahassee Democrat,* March 13, 2004.

6 As it has in many cases with websites like www.stubhub.com. See "Need a ticket?" by Kathy Bergen, *The Orlando Sentinel,* September 11, 2005; and "Wait Till Next Year, but Lock in the Ticket Price Now" by Alan B. Krueger, *The New York Times,* February 2, 2006.

7 See "Jets to Auction Seats on eBay" by Matthew Futterman, *The Wall Street Journal,* September 17, 2008.

8 See "Rent Control is the Real New York Scandal" by Eileen Norcross, *The Wall Street Journal,* September 13-14, 2008, pg. A11.

9 "In Santa Monica, Rent Decontrol Brings Surprises" by Stacy Kravetz, *The Wall Street Journal* 1999.

10 See "End of an Empire," *Newsweek,* September 9, 1991.

11 See "Crime and Punishment for Capitalists" by Leon Aron, *The New York Times,* October 30, 2003; and "In Russia, Apathy Dims Democracy" by Steven Lee Myers, *The New York Times,* November 9, 2003.

12 See "Russian economy perks up" by Michael Wines, *The Orlando Sentinel,* November 18, 2001, p. A19.

13 See *Reagan's War,* by Peter Schweizer, Doubleday books, New York, 2002, pp. 35-36.

14 Log on to www.heritage.org/research/features/index/downloads.cfm.

15 In 2002 as part of an election-year campaign, Congress passed a $73.5 billion subsidy bill that added chickpeas, peanuts, and other "second-tier" commodities, to go along with the money that continues to flow to corn, wheat, cotton, and rice. See "Farm Subsidies Blossom Anew, Fertilized by Election Politics" by David Rogers and Jill Carroll, *The Wall Street Journal,* April 2, 2002.

16 See "The Farm Belt Boom," *The Wall Street Journal,* December 9, 2010, p. A22.

17 Source: The USDA.

18 See "Farming for Dollars," *The Wall Street Journal,* July 6, 2007, pg. A8; and "The No Farmer Left Behind Act," *The Wall Street Journal,* November 14, 2007, pg. A16.

19 See *The Farm Fiasco* by James Bovard, ICS Press, San Francisco, 1991.

20 See the December 2, 1998, edition of NBC Nightly News titled "The Fleecing of America."

21 See "Prairie Plutocrats," *The Wall Street Journal,* February 1, 2002, p. A18.

22 See "Farm Aid flows to those not so needy" by John Kelly, *The Orlando Sentinel,* September 10, 2001, p. A5; and "Farm Boondoggle" *The Orlando Sentinel,* April 7, 2002.

23 See "U.S. Loses Latest Appeal on Cotton Subsidies" *The New York Times,* June 3, 2008.

24 See "U.S. Subsidizes Companies to Buy Subsidized Cotton" by Elizabeth Becker, *The New York Times,* November 4, 2003.

25 For more on these issues, see "African Nations Press for an End to Cotton Subsidies in the West" by Elizabeth Becker, *The New York Times,* September 12, 2003, p. A5; "Delegates From Poorer Nations Walk Out of World Trade Talks" by Elizabeth Becker, *The New York Times,* September 15, 2003; "Western Farmers Fear Third-World Challenge to Subsidies" by Elizabeth Becker, *The New York Times* September 9, 2003; and "Cow Politics" *The New York Times,* October 27, 2005.

26 See "US farmers are doing very well, thank you, and feeding al-Qaeda" *The Sydney Morning Herald,* September 26, 2003.

27 See "America's Sugar Daddies," *The New York Times,* November 29, 2003, p. A32; and "...and too many lumps" *The Orlando Sentinel,* April 7, 2002.

28 See "Why Did FDR's New Deal Harm Blacks?" by Jim Powell, *The Cato Institute,* December 3, 2003; and "Black Farmers down to a precious few" by E.G. Vallianatos, *The Seattle-Post Intelligencer,* February 22, 2005.

29 See "Minimum Wage vs. Supply and Demand," *The Wall Street Journal,* April 24, 1996; "Minimum Wage Hikes Help Politicians, Not the Poor" by Bruce Bartlett, *The Wall Street Journal,* May 27, 1999; "The Minimum Wage Law and Youth Crimes: Time–Series Evidence," by Masanori Hashimoto, *The Journal of Law and Economics,* October, 1987; "Higher Minimum Wage, Higher Dropout Rate" by Robert J. Barro, *The Wall Street Journal,* January 11, 1996; and "Job Slayers," *The Wall Street Journal,* August 29, 2005.

30 See "The Lost Wages of Youth," *The Wall Street Journal,* March 5, 2010, p. A20.

31 See "Set floor of $4 a gallon" by Thomas Friedman, *The Orlando Sentinel,* May 31, 2008

32 See "The Girls Next Door" by Peter Landesman, *The New York Times Magazine,* January 25, 2004.

33 On April 16, 2002, the U.S. Supreme Court seemingly weakened the laws against "virtual child-pornography" by ruling that the 1996 Child Pornography Prevention Act violated the first amendment by outlawing computer-generated child pornography. See "High Court strikes down child-pornography law" by David Stout, *The Orlando Sentinel,* April 17, 2002.

34 See "Videogames as Free-Speech Issue" by Jess Bravin, *The Wall Street Journal,* November 1, 2010.

35 *See "Four* Loko controversy brings pile of lawsuits" by Jeff Weiner, *The Orlando Sentinel,* January 27, 2011.

36 ?

37 See "Acapulco staggers under drug war" by Ken Ellingwood, *The Orlando Sentinel,* January 16, 2011.

38 See "War on opium flawed, group says" by Stephen Graham, *The Orlando Sentinel,* February 1, 2005.

39 See "Uncle Sam orchestrates Vancouver pot busts" by Brad Badelt and Amy O'Brian, *The Vancouver Sun,* July 30, 2005.

40 See "Smuggling Drugs? Let Us Count the Ways" by Mary Anastasia O'Grady, *The Wall Street Journal,* August 26, 2005, p. A13.

41 See "How the War on Drugs is Destroying Black America" by John McWhorter, *Cato's Letter,* Winter 2011, Volume 9, Number 1.

42 For more on the ephedra ban and the issue of steroid use, see "Fans of Ephedra rush to stock up" by Paul McLeod, Melinda Fulmer and David Wharton, *The Los Angeles Times* (appearing in *The Orlando Sentinel*), January 4, 2004; and "In Pursuit of Doped Excellence" by Michael Sokolove, *The New York Times Magazine,* January 18, 2004.

43 See "Three Americans Win Nobel for Economics" by Jon E. Hilsenrath, *The Wall Street Journal,* October 11, 2001.

44 See "Secretive Culture Led Toyota Astray" by Kate Linebaugh, Dionne Searcey and Noriiko Shirouzu, *The Wall Street Journal,* February 10, 2010.

45 Source: The National D-Day Museum, New Orleans, Louisiana.

46 Source: The Museum of Florida History and the Florida Department of Veterans' Affairs, Tallahassee, Florida.

47 Source: "Keeping the Home Fires Burning: Florida's WWII Experience" by David J. Coles and the Museum of Florida History, Tallahassee, Florida.

48 Source: *The Oregonian,* June 23, 1942.

49 See "A Drying Oasis" by Debbie Salamone, *The Orlando Sentinel,* March 3, 2002.

50 See "The Human Thirst" by Debbie Salamone, *The Orlando Sentinel,* April 7, 2002.

51 In places where private companies do own the water supply, shortages do not exist and poor people have ample water supplies. See "Water Works" by Luis Alberto Moreno, *The Wall Street Journal,* March 10, 2006.

52 Source: City of Winter Garden, FL.

53 See http://www.msnbc.msn.com/id/11863165/ns/nightly_news-nbc_news_investigates/

54 See "Market Failure or Government Failure?" by Allan H. Meltzer, *The Wall Street Journal,* March 19, 2010, p. A19.

55 See www.freemanonline.org.

CHAPTER REVIEW

1. What is non-price rationing and what are all of the reasons this type of rationing is considered to be inefficient by economists?

2. Fully explain what the market for parking spots would look like at your college if an auction were held each semester.

3. What is the difference between a price ceiling and price floor?

4. What are some reasons why some economists suspect that markets fail from time to time?

Chapter Nine

The PRICE ELASTICITY of DEMAND and SUPPLY

Photo courtesy Jack Chambless

*There's no such thing as supply and demand,
when you don't have a choice.*

BOB BUTTERWORTH, FORMER FLORIDA ATTORNEY GENERAL

THE SEARCH FOR PROFIT

If you have ever flown anywhere, you know that there is a law of flying that is never broken. The law states, "Thou shalt sit next to someone who will annoy you." The next time you find yourself next to someone like this, ask that person what he or she paid for his or her ticket. Then ask the person behind you and maybe the person in the back of the plane and so on and so on. While you are annoying everyone with this question, you might find, to your amazement that in a flight filled with 137 people there might be close to 50 different prices.[1]

Why do senior citizens receive discounts on hotels and other goods and services, when the rest of us do not? Why do bars have ladies' nights? Men have feelings – and limited budgets, too – so why isn't there a men's night? Do you pay out-of-state or in-state tuition? Should there be a difference in tuition when everyone gets the same lectures? Why do some retailers pursue pricing strategies of frequent discounts, while other industries pursue ways to increase prices? The answer to these and other questions surrounding pricing strategies will be uncovered through an in-depth look at what drives profit.

> **Profit = total revenue – total cost**
> **Total revenue = price x quantity sold**

In this chapter we will solve for the first half of the profit equation by examining how businesses look at their pricing strategies in the short run and over longer periods of time. In the next chapter, we will find out how a business firm keeps their total costs of production as low as possible.

In the equation for total revenue, you have probably detected a dilemma that every business in America – or the world, for that matter – faces. Since total revenue equals the price of the good or service in question, multiplied by the quantity sold, there are two ways that total revenue can increase. One way is by raising the price. The other way is to sell more stuff. The problem is that there is only one way that both price and quantity sold can

increase, and that is if the overall demand for your good or service increases. If a business arbitrarily increases prices, quantity demanded will fall.

On the other hand, if the business wants to increase quantity demanded, prices must fall. With that understanding, how does a business know whether it should shoot for the revenue gains that come from higher prices or the revenue gains that come from an increase in quantity demanded?

THE PRICE ELASTICITY OF DEMAND

What do owners of parking garages in Chicago and every gas station in America have in common? Each supplier does not have to worry much about raising prices.

In Chicago, parking spaces can go for as much as $25,000. At every gas station consumers can expect to pay a *few dollars* for each gallon of gasoline. In each case, the owners of the garages and gas stations know that the law of demand is omnipresent. If prices increase, *someone* in the Windy City will balk and not pay to park. *Someone* in Provo or St. Louis will switch to a bicycle. However, in some instances, suppliers have discovered that the demand for their product or service, while not vertical, is very steeply sloped. This translates into a great deal of power to raise prices over time.[2] This reality is not unique to the United States. In December 2010, the Iranian government raised the price of gasoline by 300%. Quantity demanded fell by only 14% as of January 2011.[3]

The rest of the world's suppliers are generally not as fortunate. Global competition has made it increasingly difficult for businesses to push for higher prices. With constant changes in consumer confidence, Internet competition, the threat of terrorism, banking crises, a recent recession, and so forth – along with an unpredictable business climate – the pricing environment in many areas of the economy is anything but favorable. As a result, there is much more uncertainty as to what might be the ideal pricing strategy.

For example, the $580 billion U.S. restaurant industry has discovered that recessions are not kind to those who would cook for us. From 2007-2011, 39% of Americans reported being more "price sensitive" and 33% reported eating at less expensive restaurants. This reality put enormous pressure on restaurants all over the country to pay more attention to prices.[4]

How can any company know which path to pursue in the quest to maximize total revenue? The answer begins with an understanding of the price elasticity of demand.

> ➤ **The price elasticity of demand (Ed) is a number that represents the percentage change in the quantity of a product demanded in response to a 1% change in the price of the product. This number reflects buyer sensitivity to price changes.**

Some of you might be under the impression that we are about to rehash the law of demand. This is not the case. All businesses know that, if prices increase, quantity demanded comes down and vice versa. In this chapter we will focus on how much quantity demanded changes in response to price changes. Businesses that understand the concept of elasticity are much more suited to find greater revenue – even in times of uncertainty. Those that do not pay attention to this important concept tend to increase their chances of extinction.

TYPES OF DEMAND ELASTICITIES

For any given product, there exists the possibility that the demand for the good or service will be inelastic, elastic, or unit elastic at any moment in time.

> ➤ **An inelastic demand means that buyers are not very sensitive to price changes. Therefore if prices change by a certain percentage, quantity demanded will change by a smaller percentage.**
> ➤ **An elastic demand means that buyers are very sensitive to price changes. Therefore, if prices change by a certain percentage, quantity demanded will change by a larger percentage.**
> ➤ **A unit elastic demand means that price and quantity demanded at a given point in time will change by an equal percentage.**

THE CHARACTERISTICS OF AN INELASTIC DEMAND

How much did you pay for this textbook? Would you pay more? What about tuition? If the college you are now attending raised tuition rates by 10%, would you leave? By how much did your consumption of gasoline fall as prices shot up in 2011? If you are honest about your answers they will look something like: "Yes," "No," and "Not much,"

This is because you have a very inelastic demand for all of these items. This book was a requirement for your course. Whatever you paid, you would pay more. *How much more* is a question we will address shortly. Tuition, gasoline, car tag renewals, auto insurance, electric power, toothpaste, deodorant, and soap are a few of the many examples of products that you basically have to have.

The demand for a good or service will be inelastic if any one or more of the following characteristics are in place:

> ➤ **The good or service is a necessity.**

Think of all of the things you buy that fit this description. Many are mentioned above. If a good or service is a necessity to you, it means that if prices increase significantly, you will not cut back much on the consumption of that item. It also means that if prices were to fall significantly, you would not consume a great deal more of it. Does it make sense that if headache medicine prices fell by 45% that you would start listening to loud music or banging your head on the sidewalk to justify consuming more painkillers? No. You buy what you need and are relatively insensitive to price changes.

> ➤ **There are few or no close substitutes for the good or service.**

> We don't think we'll lose business to the postal service.
>
> Rick Campana of UPS

What is Mr. Campana talking about? A few years ago, United Parcel Service and Federal Express pushed through significant price increases – up to 20% in some cases – for their overnight and expedited delivery services. The price changes pushed the price of UPS and FedEx services well above the rates the United States Postal Service charged for similar services, yet UPS and FedEx did not seem too concerned about a mass migration of angry businesses and individuals lining up at post offices around the country, eager to switch to the government-subsidized mail delivery service.[5]

The reason UPS and FedEx didn't have much to worry about is that businesses and individuals alike, who need to have packages arrive in one or two days, undamaged, know that the postal service is not a very good substitute for the for-profit businesses that specialize in fast deliveries. With the post office's track record for being slower and less reliable, FedEx does not face the prospect of a large drop in quantity demanded. The more people believe that other substitutes do not exist the more likely they will be to have an inelastic demand for a particular good or service.

One way businesses try to convince people that products and services offered are necessities or have few or no close substitutes, is to try to create *brand-name loyalty* for that product or service.

> ➤ **Brand-name loyalty exists when a consumer continually opts to purchase an item that is more expensive than others available.**

In advertising there is an old axiom that states, "If the customer believes the products are different – even if they are the same – they're different." This means that there may not be a dramatic difference between different brands of mascara, shaving lotion, or toothpaste. If Revlon, Edge Gel, and Colgate have convinced you that their products are better, you will become brand-name loyal, as long as they maintain a high-quality product.

They may charge more than a store brand of mascara or a generic form of shaving cream or toothpaste, but it does not matter. You become willing to pay a premium for quality. That, of course, imposes a tremendous amount of pressure on names like Under Armour, Microsoft, and Timberland. If they ever shirk on the *implicit contract* they have cultivated with their loyal customers, the reputational damage can be severe.

Many companies have learned the hard way that, once a name reputation is developed, customers expect the same quality and level of service every time. In fact, Toyota and General Motors have suffered recently from product recalls and less than favorable quality reports that have hurt both companies,[6] while Ford and Honda continue to sell cars that are perceived to be of high quality and reliability.

INCOME ISSUES

Would you travel 100 miles to save 10% on a new car? Would you travel 100 miles to save 10% on toilet paper? If you said no to the toilet paper part, then it is most likely due to the fact that toilet paper, chewing gum, salt, paper for your printer, and other items have an inelastic demand. Demand for these items will be inelastic because:

> ➤ **The proportion of buyer's income spent on the good is low.**

Of course, this characteristic depends a great deal on your income. For Larry Page (CEO of Google), an increase in the price of BMW convertibles may not be alarming. For you, as a college student, an increase the price of gasoline may cause you to lose your cool. The smaller the percentage of a person's income it takes to buy a good or service, the more inelastic demand will be.

TIME ISSUES

A few years ago, I was traveling with my family near Richmond, Virginia, around 3:30 in the morning. Finally, I decided that I should stop at a motel, rather than run the risk of launching my family into a river. When I finally found a place, I asked the clerk how much a room would be, for what little time was remaining that night. When he quoted his price, I said, "That seems a little high considering that we would only get a few hours' sleep." His response? "It seems a little low to me, considering it is so late and you seem pretty tired."

I should have praised him for being more aware of the price elasticity of demand than I was at that moment. Maybe it was because I was tired, but he had me. I had very little time left to shop around that night, and he knew it. That meant that he rightfully concluded that the demand for his rooms was inelastic. This fact happens when:

> ➤ **The amount of time buyers have to adjust to price changes is insignificant.**

Have you ever booked an airline flight with just a day's advance notice? What kind of price did you pay? You may have found yourself having paid over $600 for a flight to Philadelphia and sitting next to someone who paid less than half that. You get the same stale pretzels and same uncomfortable seats. The difference was that you called the day before the flight and the other person called a month in advance. The airline knew that the other person had a lot of time to shop around or maybe even drive to Philadelphia. You, on the other hand, might not have been able to take a train, bus, or car to Philadelphia. You might have to fly. They knew it, and therefore they charged you a price that reflects the inelastic nature of the service.

CONCEPT CHECK

As the U.S. economy struggled to recover from "The Great Recession," beer and food suppliers launched a wave of price increases.[7] What assumptions about the price elasticity of demand for beer and food did Anheuser-Busch InBev and Kraft Foods Inc., make in order to justify this move? Which elasticity characteristics suggest that higher prices make sense? Why?

The airline industry is not the only industry that has figured out how time impacts the price elasticity of demand. The funeral home industry is a world-class example of an industry that not only knows that you have no time to "shop around" for a reasonable burial fee when a loved one has died.

The funeral director knows you won't shop around. They are selling a product that is a necessity with no close substitutes. Even though the thousands of dollars you may pay for a burial is a large percentage of your income, the other three characteristics offset this fact.

THE CHARACTERISTICS OF AN ELASTIC DEMAND

What is a good night's sleep worth to you? You do realize that if you live to be 90, it means you will have spent around 30 years of your life lying in bed? Shouldn't that warrant a mattress that is comfortable, therapeutic, and pricey? Would $33,000 for a mattress make sense?

To E.S. Kluft & Co., this is a perfectly reasonable price to sleep on a mattress that is made from Belgian pima cotton jacquard, cashmere, mohair, silk, New Zealand wool, organic cotton felt, and 2,000 hand-laced steel springs supporting over 19 inches of mattress.[8]

From 2008 to 2010 the company sold about 100 of these luxurious mattresses. That means that the rest of our population of 308 million people got by with a less expensive model.

There are many characteristics that make the demand for a good or service elastic. Buyers might consider these mattresses to be an elastic product because:

> ➢ **The good or service is a luxury item.**

A luxury item is something that people do not have to have (like a mattress that costs more than a really nice car). It could be an expensive product like gold watches or high-definition televisions, or something inexpensive that you can live without – like a CD featuring music your parents used to listen to.

The demand for a good or service will be elastic if any of the following characteristics appear.

> ➢ **There are several close substitutes for the good or service.**
> ➢ **If the proportion of buyer's income spent on the good is high.**
> ➢ **If the amount of time buyers have to adjust to price changes is significant.**

When you go to the grocery store, you see countless varieties of cereal, cheese, diapers, and dog food. If you are the type of shopper who cares a great deal more about finding a bargain than being brand-name loyal, you will be very responsive to any price increases or sales. The *more substitutes* an item has, the more elastic will be the demand.

If you read your local newspaper with any frequency, you will often see full-page ads featuring sales on computers, cars, furniture, and appliances. The reason for this strategy is simple. For most Americans, these items consume a very *large portion of their income*. That being the case, we have a relatively elastic demand for these products.

Rarely do you see full-page ads featuring butter or salt. Just as is the case with inelastic products, relative income is important here. As your income increases (hopefully) over time, your personal demand for restaurant meals and nice hotel rooms will go from being very elastic (or nonexistent) now to somewhat inelastic in the future.

Have you ever been out shopping for some particular item and been informed that next week it will go on sale?

CONCEPT CHECK

In Utah, the demand for alcohol is very elastic. Why? In Nebraska, the demand for snow skis is elastic. Why? Use as many elasticity characteristics as you can to justify your answer.

If you went home and waited for seven days to pass, it is because you had an elastic demand for that item at that moment in time. In general, the *more time* we have to find a cheaper alternative, the more elastic the demand for any good or service will be.

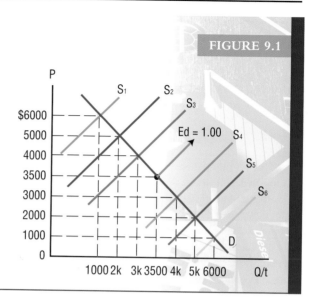

FIGURE 9.1

CALCULATING THE PRICE ELASTICITY OF DEMAND

When high-definition television sets first appeared in Japan, the price per set was $30,000. By the time these sets were starting to enter the United States in 1994, the price averaged $6,000 per set. At this price, the demand for these state-of-the-art sets was most definitely elastic. Is that the case now? The demand for computers, cell phones, and DVD players also started out elastic, but now demand is much more inelastic. How this happens and what it means for the average seller of HDTVs will be examined in this section.

As technology advanced and production costs fell, the price of HDTVs began to fall. Suppose prices for the largest models continue to fall to the $1,000 range. A Kansas City television dealer notices that, as prices have fallen, the following sales and total revenue figures have emerged.

PRICE	QUANTITY DEMANDED	TOTAL REVENUE
$6,000	1,000	$6 million
$5,000	2,000	$10 million
$4,000	3,000	$12 million
$3,000	4,000	$12 million
$2,000	5,000	$10 million
$1,000	6,000	$6 million

The following diagrams represent this market and the accompanying total revenue stream that is earned at each price and output level.

You can see by the law of demand that the lower price causes quantity demanded to increase, but that is not what the dealer is interested in. You also notice that as prices fall, his total revenue rises at first, seems to top off at $12 million and then falls. That should concern him. He wants to charge a price that maximizes revenue. In order to do that he must be able to calculate his price elasticity of demand and apply the answer to his pricing strategy.

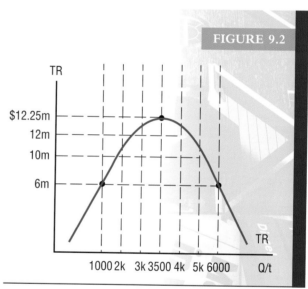

FIGURE 9.2

STEP ONE – CALCULATE THE CHANGE IN PRICE AND THE CHANGE IN QUANTITY DEMANDED

This is the easy part. If we begin by calculating the initial price cut from $6,000 to $5,000, we see that this is a reduction of $1,000. In response, the quantity demanded increased from 1,000 to 2,000 units, an increase of 1,000.

STEP TWO – CALCULATE THE PERCENTAGE CHANGE IN PRICE AND THE PERCENTAGE CHANGE IN QUANTITY DEMANDED

If you have ever been exposed to calculus, you know that if we have the functional relationship between price and quantity demanded along the entire demand curve, we can take the first derivative of price with respect to quantity demanded and know exactly what the price elasticity of demand is at any point on the demand curve. However, since many of you are not well-versed in this branch of mathematics, we can solve for the elasticity between two points. This is known as the *arc price elasticity of demand*. To do this, we rely on *average prices* and *average quantities demanded*.

The percentage change in price equals

$$\left[\frac{\Delta P}{\frac{1}{2}(P_1 + P_2)} \right] \times 100$$

Where; P1 equals the initial price and P2 the price after the change was made. In this case, P1 equals $6,000 and P2 equals $5,000. The Δ symbol means "change."

The percentage change in quantity demanded equals

$$\left[\frac{\Delta Q}{\frac{1}{2}(Q_1 + Q_2)} \right] \times 100$$

Where; Q1 equals the initial quantity demanded and Q2 equals the quantity demanded after the change in consumption takes place. In this case Q1 equals 1,000 and Q2 equals 2,000.

If we plug in the appropriate numbers and solve for each problem, we find that the percentage change in price is −18.18% and the percentage change in quantity demanded is +66.67%.

STEP THREE – CALCULATE THE PRICE ELASTICITY OF DEMAND

The formula for the price elasticity of demand is:

$$Ed = \frac{\%\Delta qd}{\%\Delta price}$$

If we plug in the results from part two, we find that 66.67/−18.18 = −3.67

WHAT YOUR ANSWER MEANS

> *Never, ever calculate a number whose meaning you do not understand.*
>
> David Dickey, Professor of Statistics, North Carolina State University

These are certainly wise words from Dr. Dickey. So what does −3.67 mean? First, it means that along this range of the demand curve, for every 1% change in price, quantity demanded will change by 3.67%. More importantly, it means that the demand for HDTV's at that price range was elastic. The way we know that stems from the following rule:

> ➤ **If Ed > 1 demand is elastic because the percentage change in quantity demanded is greater than the percentage change in price.**
> ➤ **If Ed < 1 demand is inelastic because the percentage change in quantity demanded is less than the percentage change in price.**
> ➤ **If Ed = 1 demand is unit elastic because the percentage change in quantity demanded is equal to the percentage change in price.**

With an answer of −3.67 how can we conclude that the demand is elastic? After all, the negative sign makes the answer less than one. Shouldn't this imply an inelastic demand? No. The answer we get when calculating the price elasticity of demand will always be negative because of the inverse relationship between price and quantity demanded. In order to interpret the elasticity of demand correctly, we must *take the absolute value* of our answer.

When we do this, we see that the answer is 3.67, which is greater than one. This is not a mathematical trick. It is done to reflect the reality of the marketplace. The negative sign is irrelevant to this reality. When prices fell by over 18%, quantity demanded increased by more than 18%. This proved that demand was elastic at that time. If we left the negative sign in, it would appear that consumers had an inelastic demand, which is clearly not the case.

CONCEPT CHECK

In 2010 a drought in Russia caused a huge drop in the supply of corn, wheat, and soybeans. At the same time, farmers in Minnesota experienced a "bumper crop" of these products.[9] Suppose the price of corn rose from $4.11 per bushel to $6.55 per bushel. If the quantity of Minnesota corn demanded fell from 982,219 bushels to 977,368 bushels, what is the price elasticity of demand for Minnesota corn?

THE PRICE ELASTICITY OF DEMAND AND REVENUE MAXIMIZATION

Bear Bryant, the legendary football coach at the University of Alabama, was once asked why he rarely let his quarterbacks throw the football. His answer? "Because when you throw the ball, three things can happen, and two of them ain't good." This summarizes the pressure businesses face in attempting to earn more revenue by changing prices.

If we go back to our HDTV dealership for a moment, we can get a pretty clear picture of what any given business should do in order to squeeze out the highest level of revenue.

Notice that when the firm charged $6,000, total revenue was $6 million. When prices fell to $5,000, revenue increased to $10 million. Revenue increased again when prices fell to $4,000. This is because from $6,000 to $5,000 and from $5,000 to $4,000, the demand for HDTV sets was elastic. The upward pressure on revenue that was created by selling more sets offset the drop in revenue from lowering the price.

RULE # 1: IF DEMAND IS ELASTIC, TO INCREASE REVENUE, LOWER YOUR PRICES.

The firm lost 18.18% of their total revenue from lowering prices from $6,000 to $5,000, but they gained 66.67% more revenue when they sold 1,000 more sets! As long as demand is elastic, keep lowering prices – and of course never raise prices when demand is elastic.

RULE # 2: IF DEMAND IS INELASTIC, TO INCREASE REVENUE, RAISE YOUR PRICES.

Notice that, at a price of $1,000, the firm earned revenue of only $6 million. If they raise prices to $2,000, they will sell fewer sets, but their total revenue actually increases to $10 million! This is also the case when prices rise from $2,000 to $3,000. This is because the demand for HDTV sets is inelastic along this range of the demand curve. The revenue that is lost from selling fewer units is more than offset by the revenue that is gained from raising the price. Therefore, if you ever are selling a product that is a necessity, has few close substitutes, takes a small percentage of your customers' income, and/or is an impulse item, you should raise your prices if you want more cash. *Never lower your prices when demand is inelastic* – unless you don't mind losing money.[10]

RULE # 3: IF DEMAND IS UNIT ELASTIC, DO NOT CHANGE YOUR PRICES.

Should the dealership charge $4,000 or $3,000 in order to maximize revenue? Your calculations show that the price elasticity of demand is 1.00 in this range. However, it is impossible to have two maximum point on this function. Since the elasticity of demand equals 1.00 over this range, it must equal 1.00 in the midpoint of this range. Therefore a price of $3,500 – and output level of 3,500 – is the optimum price. At this price, the firm earns $12.25 million – the maximum amount of revenue. Any change in prices away from this point will lead to less revenue. If they increase prices, they will push the product into the elastic range of the demand curve. If they lower prices, demand will become inelastic and total revenue will fall.

CELL PHONES AND EUROPEAN TUITION ARE TOO CHEAP

One trip to your local theater will prove that life was better when only rich people could afford cellular phones.

Over the last several years the price of cellular phones has plummeted as more sellers have entered this once-lucrative market. It was once lucrative when lower prices led to huge increases in quantity demanded. However, for many suppliers, there is now a struggle to remain profitable. What happened?

As the price of cell phones has decreased, there are fewer and fewer people walking around without one. In fact, I am one of the few people who have such disdain for these devices that a price of one penny would not induce me to buy one. For almost everyone else in America, this is not the case.

And that is precisely the dilemma with which cell phone suppliers are now grappling. With the proliferation of cell phones, lower prices are no longer leading to large increases in quantity demanded. The new reality is that prices are falling along the inelastic range of the cell phone demand curve. So many people consider cell phones a necessity that they have already purchased one. Lower prices might convince some people to upgrade to better quality phones, but overall, the percentage decrease in prices is not leading to a larger percentage increase in consumption. Not surprisingly, total revenues have been falling for many companies as a result of prices that are *too low*.[11]

In the meantime, many European nations have discovered that the longstanding tradition of taxpayer-subsidized tuition is an increasingly bad idea.

At the current level of tuition charged in Great Britain, Germany, and other more socialistic European nations, the demand for college classes is extraordinarily inelastic. Such low tuition means that colleges in Europe do not have sufficient revenues to offer better technology, more professors, and greater course options. This problem prompted former British Prime Minister Tony Blair to propose tripling annual tuition fees for England's universities.

British students immediately took to the streets in protest. Protests also took place in France and Germany, where students argued that German Education Minister Toni Schmid was right when he said, "It is part of the Social Democrat ideology that one of the prime rights of humanity is to have free university education."[12]

Of course, the students might also be wondering why the professor-to-student ratio is 80 or 90 to 1 in Germany.

With such low levels of tuition, overcrowding has been a big concern. If overcrowding diminishes educational quality, one might wonder if European kids will begin to rethink the idea that low tuition is a birthright. Sometimes, you get the quality you pay for.

What would it take to fill these seats?

Photo courtesy Jack Chambless

WHY SPORTS TEAMS DON'T ALWAYS CARE ABOUT SELL-OUTS

If you have ever attended a professional sporting event, you may have noticed that there were many empty seats around you. You may also notice that, over the past few years, the price of attending professional football, baseball, basketball, and hockey games has increased substantially – much to the chagrin of many fans. Before you blame the empty seats on greedy owners who have priced the average fan out of the market, or millionaire players whose rising salaries makes price hikes necessary, perhaps you should give some thought to the role the price elasticity of demand plays in all of this.

Suppose the overall demand for Milwaukee Bucks tickets is inelastic in Wisconsin. This means an increase in prices would certainly reduce attendance, but it would lead to higher revenue. A simple check of basic math tells us that an average price of $42 x 22,000 tickets sold is less revenue than $63 x 18,000 seats sold. The same is true for your local movie theater. Notice that, after a movie has played for a while, you may see only 20 or so people in the theater. As long as the revenue from those 20 people covers the cost of showing the movie, the theater doesn't worry about not selling out.

Sports teams and theater owners realize that, in order to sell out, they might have to lower prices so much that they would actually lose revenue. To sell the entire upper deck at a Bucks game might require prices as low as $7. If cutting prices by 80 or 90% would be necessary to create a relatively small percentage increase in sales – and thus, a full stadium – it would not be worth the trouble. Therefore the owners become willing to accept a lower total fan turnout in order to enjoy maximum total revenue from ticket sales.

PRICE DISCRIMINATION

Have you ever noticed that some businesses seem to be nicer to certain customers than others? I am not talking about the level of service. I am speaking of how different customers are treated in terms of the price they are asked to pay for things like theme park tickets, tuition, hotel rooms, movie theater tickets, haircuts, and even alcoholic beverages. These are some of the multitudinous examples of businesses practicing what economists call price discrimination.

> ➤ **Price discrimination is the practice of charging different customers different prices for the exact same product.**

CONCEPT CHECK

Baseball teams have recently begun charging higher prices when the Boston Red Sox come to town and lower prices when the Pittsburgh Pirates are the opponent.[13] Is this good economics? Why or why not?

Why do women get to drink at bars for less than men? Why do the elderly get discounts on seemingly everything? The answer lies in the fact that business firms have figured out that it is one thing to be able to find a price that corresponds to the unit elastic point of a demand curve. It is a whole different ball game when businesses discover that different customers have different price elasticities of demand.

ECONOMICS AND NATIONAL PARK PRICES

Over the past several years the National Park Service has grappled with a huge dilemma of overcrowding in America's most popular national parks. As we saw earlier,

in Yellowstone, Zion, and Yosemite National Parks, cars, buses, and visitors fill the park with noise and air pollution that has strained the park's infrastructure to the breaking point.[14] One solution that has been proposed is to let the national parks predetermine the number of guests who can visit a park each day and what time the guest can come.[15] What if – rather than relying on non-price rationing – the U.S. National Park Service allowed the various national parks to set their own prices?

If an economist ran Grand Teton National Park in Wyoming, he would recommend that the park charge a relatively low price to residents of Wyoming and a relatively high price to people from other states. Figures 9.3 and 9.4 on the following page illustrate why. As you can see in figure 9.3, residents of Wyoming have a fairly elastic demand for passes to this breathtaking park. The reason is straightforward. For Wyoming residents, visiting Grand Teton is probably something of a luxury – especially if they have been on more than one occasion already.

What is this scene worth?

Photo courtesy Jack Chambless

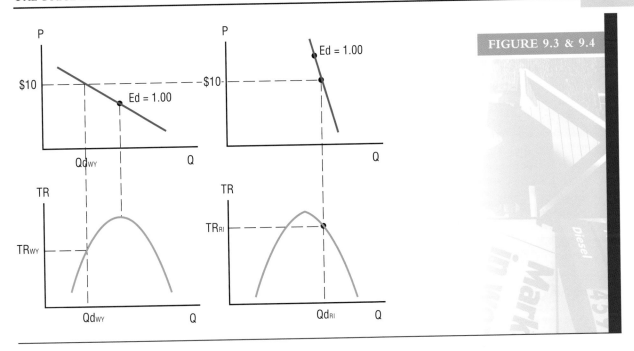

FIGURE 9.3 & 9.4

Wyoming residents have many close substitutes and can wait to visit during off-peak times of the year when it is not so crowded. Therefore, at a price of $10, the state of Wyoming fails to maximize revenue from this group.

On the other hand, residents of Rhode Island vacationing in the state of Wyoming would have a very inelastic demand for admission passes. People from Rhode Island do not get to see sights like this every day. Therefore, once in Wyoming, it would be a necessity for many of these tourists to see Grand Teton. There would be few or no close substitutes and they have virtually no time to wait around for lower prices. A fee of $10 is pretty cheap for Rhode Island residents, and as you can see, this price fails to maximize revenue from this group as well.

The economically sensible thing to do is to separate the customers based on their differing elasticities, where Wyoming residents are charged a lower price ($9 perhaps), while residents of other states would be asked to pay much more ($49?). This way the National Park Service would maximize revenue derived from both consumer groups, and the parks would have more funds to help protect the bears and clean out the bathrooms.

Is price discrimination legal? The Supreme Court has taken up this question on many occasions and seems to have settled on a pretty simple test. If the seller can show *that price differences reflect differences in the cost of delivering the service* (for example out-of-state residents might need more maps and guides, may get lost or injured more, etc.), then it is legal to charge one group more than another.[16]

THE ECONOMICS OF SIN TAXES

If you are like me – pure of heart and without any faults – you probably won't be able to identify much with the following analysis. On the other hand, if you smoke, drink alcohol, or drive a gas-guzzling car you are considered "special" by the United States government. How so, you might ask? You are special in the sense that the government taxes your vices at a much higher rate than a typical local sales tax.

In many places in America there is no tax on food. Taxes on contact lenses, running shoes, and hair coloring products are uniform. However, if you smoke, you should be aware of the fact that the current federal cigarette tax is $1.01 per pack. The federal tax on gasoline is 18.4 cents per gallon. Of course, since states, counties, and cities are independent taxing authorities, local and state taxes can make driving in places like California a much less pleasurable experience. Finally, if you drink beer, wine, or any other alcoholic beverage, the government makes sure you pay up, too. Why?

THE RATIONALE FOR SIN TAXES

Two primary reasons have been offered to explain the existence of "sin" taxes. The first justification offered up by the government is that the goods in question create negative externalities. Second-hand smoke, highway deaths from drunk drivers, and pollution emitted from automobiles are examples of this problem. Therefore, when the government taxes these items, the stated goal is to raise the price enough to reduce consumption and truncate the externality effect to some degree.[17]

The second – and more important reason – is that the demand for cigarettes, alcohol, and gasoline is inelastic. Therefore, if the government imposes a tax on any of these items, consumption will fall by a very small amount.[18] If the consumption decreases only slightly, the government is able to collect enormous sums of tax revenue. When John McCain proposed dropping the gas tax for the summer of 2008 the Tax Policy Center estimated that it would lead to a $9 billion loss in revenue for the federal government.[19]

For our purposes the significant question we want to answer is: *Who bears the burden of these taxes?* The most obvious answer is that consumers do. But sometimes what is obviously true isn't totally true. Figures 9.5 illustrates why.

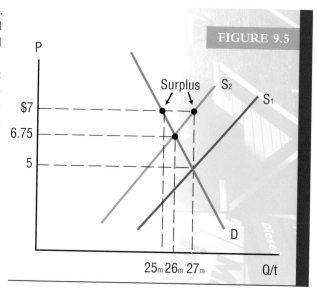

FIGURE 9.5

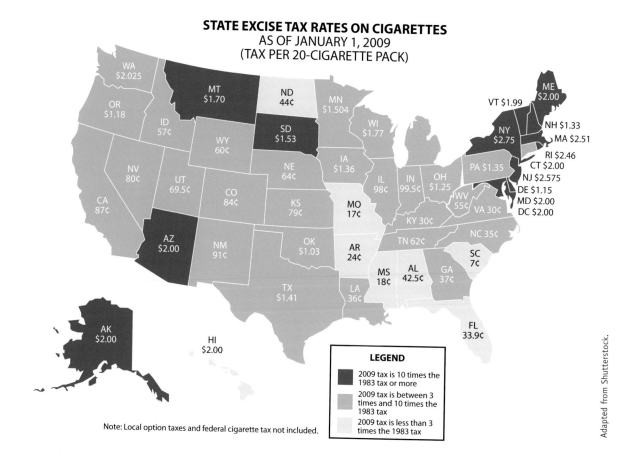

STATE EXCISE TAX RATES ON CIGARETTES
AS OF JANUARY 1, 2009
(TAX PER 20-CIGARETTE PACK)

LEGEND

2009 tax is 10 times the 1983 tax or more

2009 tax is between 3 times and 10 times the 1983 tax

2009 tax is less than 3 times the 1983 tax

Note: Local option taxes and federal cigarette tax not included.

Adapted from Shutterstock.

CONCEPT CHECK

Which state probably has the most cigarette smuggling — New York or Virginia?[20] Why? In Norway, cigarettes are taxed at $5.23 per pack. Do you think demand is inelastic in Norway? Why, or why not?

Figure 9.5 considers what would happen if the government decided to raise the cigarette tax by $2 per pack in an attempt to combat smoking among young people. With respect to cigarettes, we see that the overall demand is inelastic – due largely to the addictive nature of the product. The tax, therefore, would have little impact on their buying behavior. This, of course, is not true for new smokers who would have an easier time quitting. Therefore, if the government imposes a $2 per-pack tax on the supplier of cigarettes, the tax will raise the input costs of producing the product. As we recall from chapter seven, higher input costs would mean a decrease in the supply of cigarettes to S2.

If cigarette makers tried to pass the entire burden of the tax on to smokers, the quantity of cigarettes demanded could fall from 27 million packs per day to 25 million packs per day. Therefore, at a price of $7 per pack, there would be a small surplus of cigarettes. The surplus would force tobacco companies to lower prices slightly – to $6.75 in this example. With the price cut, the quantity of cigarettes demanded increases to the new equilibrium of 26 million packs.

Notice that the net result of the tax is bad for consumers and bad for the tobacco companies, but great for the government.

- Consumers are hurt because the price of cigarettes has increased by $1.75 per pack – from $5 to $6.75.
- Producers are hurt because the after-tax price of cigarettes has fallen by $.25 per pack. They were receiving $5 per pack. Now they take in $6.75 but are forced to send $2 to the government. $6.75–$2.00 equals $4.75, which is $.25 less than before.
- The government is better off after the tax hike. A tax increase of $2 per pack multiplied by 26 million packs sold (the new equilibrium) equals $52 million in new revenue.

Of course, the preceding analysis was constructed purely for the purposes of exposition, so it is important that we do not get bogged down on the exact numbers. The principle, however, should be clear. If demand is inelastic and the government wants to earn more money, a tax on the product is a wise move. However, it is very important to note that if the tax is increased too much, the price of the product will be pushed into the elastic range of the demand curve.

This means that government revenue will decrease over time as black markets emerge and people begin buying untaxed cigarettes. This is precisely what happened in Canada not long ago. High cigarette taxes led Canadians to buy smuggled cigarettes from the United States. The Canadian government lost so much money that the tax hike was eventually repealed.[21]

TAXES AND UNINTENDED CONSEQUENCES

Figure 9.6 illustrates what happened when Congress decided to create a luxury tax in 1990. This tax was levied on boats, planes, furs, jewelry, and expensive cars. The thinking in Washington, D.C., was that the rich could afford to pay more for their toys and that the tax would create enormous revenue gains since rich folks have an inelastic demand for these items. What the politicians learned is that rich people do not get to be rich by being stupid.

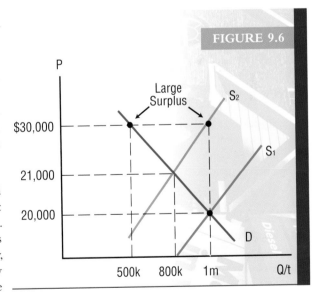

FIGURE 9.6

As you might imagine, the demand for yachts is somewhat elastic – given by the flatter-sloped demand curve on the diagram and logic that tells us that new yachts are a luxury item. When Congress passed the luxury tax, the input costs of producing yachts increased. The supply then decreased, and prices increased. As it turned out, the demand for these luxury goods was extremely elastic. Sales of pleasure boats fell by nearly 90% in south Florida alone in early 1991, as prospective buyers bought boats in the Bahamas to avoid paying the tax. Sales of high-priced cars like Mercedes and Lexus also fell substantially.

This unexpected high elasticity of demand carried two bits of bad news for the economy. First, rather than falling on the wealthy as had been hoped, the burden of the new luxury tax actually ended up falling on the workers and retailers who manufactured and sold these luxury items. Second, the luxury tax raised far less money than had been expected.

The Congressional Budget Office had forecast that the tax would raise about $1.5 billion over five years. But in 1991, it raised only about $30 million. Once the costs of setting up and enforcing the new tax were considered, along with the economic dislocations from higher unemployment, lower sales, and lower profit, the luxury tax most likely led to a net loss in total tax revenue. By one estimate, the tax on boats cost 25,000 employees of boat-builders their jobs.[23]

It is highly unlikely that any of these 25,000 people who were laid off were wealthy enough to buy one of the boats they used to build. It is also terribly ironic that, while Congress's goal was to soak the rich, the unintended consequences were detrimental to people who were not rich. It is also ironic that Congress actually called the tax a "luxury tax."

If yachts and these other items are really luxuries, someone in Congress should have dusted off an old economics book and looked up what happens when the price of a luxury item goes up. They would have discovered that the tax would have little impact on consumers and total revenue but would decimate producers and their employees. With a little research, the U.S. Congress could have avoided ruining the lives of so many people. But then again, economic illiteracy can infect politicians, too. All of this might be why Congress finally woke up and repealed the luxury tax on January 1, 2003. [24]

entered into this lucrative market in search of profits. This would mean lower drug prices and an increase in quantity demanded. The critics are correct. The real issue is *by how much* quantity demanded would increase.

Figure 9.8 illustrates what would happen if the demand for drugs were relatively inelastic. It is easy to see why that might be the case. Intuitively, it makes sense that there would not be a tremendous increase in the quantity of drugs demanded. Addicts are comfortable with their current level of consumption.

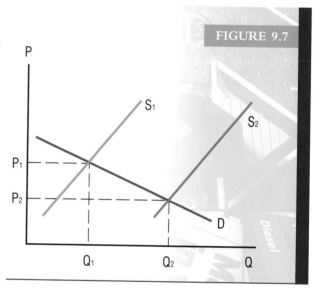

FIGURE 9.7

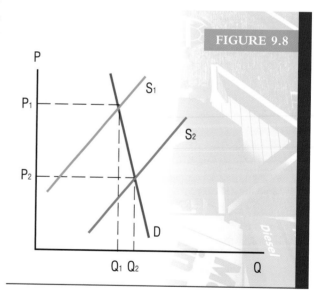

FIGURE 9.8

DRUG LEGALIZATION AND THE PRICE ELASTICITY OF DEMAND

Critics of the push to legalize drugs argue that legalizing drugs would lead to an increase in supply, as more sellers

Casual users would not seek to become addicts – and many, if not most, non-users would stay that way. If prices fall and consumption does not increase that much, we would get all of the benefits of legalizing drugs – less crime, no tax dollars wasted fighting the drug war, more tax revenue, and the promotion of individual liberty – but very little in the way of costs imposed upon society.[25]

If the demand for drugs is elastic (Figure 9.7), a lower price would mean a huge increase in quantity demanded. This would result from casual users becoming addicted and many former non-users jumping into the market. If this occurred, the costs of legalizing drugs, in terms of increased health care costs, lost productivity, and the possibility of more crime, would perhaps offset the benefits of legalizing drugs.

What is the correct answer? In Europe, drug legalization has led to a decrease in the demand for drugs as drug use has become "boring" to young people. Perhaps the same would be true in America.

Photo courtesy Jack Chambless

THE PRICE ELASTICITY OF SUPPLY

Not long ago a survey of America's top high school students found that they would consider engaging in sex with a complete stranger – for a price. Forty-three percent of males surveyed and 25% of the females said they would have sex with "a reasonably attractive stranger" for $1 million. Not surprisingly, as the dollar figure dropped, so did the number of consenting students. Only 19% of men and 3% of women said they would take $1,000 for the same act. Not only does this prove the law of supply, but it also helps introduce the concept of the price elasticity of supply.

> ➤ **The price elasticity of supply is a number that represents the percentage change in quantity supplied with each 1% change in price.**

This number – which is calculated in the same way as the price elasticity of demand, is used to gauge how responsive sellers are to changes in prices. The supply of a good or service is said to be inelastic if sellers are not very responsive to price changes and elastic if sellers are very responsive to price changes. The factors that influence the price elasticity of supply are the *flexibility of inputs*, the *mobility of inputs*, *input costs*, the *substitutability of inputs*, and the amount of *time* sellers have to adjust to price changes.

As more and more Americans have flocked to high-protein, low fat diets, the overall demand for buffalo meat has increased dramatically. Apparently, buffalo meat is one of the best sources of protein available. As demand has

increased, so has quantity supplied. The question is, by how much can quantity supplied increase?

If the resources available to produce buffalo meat are easily accessible, the quantity supplied can increase by a larger amount than prices have been increasing. This depends on how many buffalo ranchers enter the industry, the gestation period of the buffalo, and the success of breeding programs. If it is relatively inexpensive to increase the production of buffalo meat, the increase in demand will lead to an increase in quantity supplied of a more elastic nature. Figure 9.9 illustrates this possibility.

Supply will also be very elastic if you can easily substitute one input for another in the production process, or if the seller has a great deal of time. With time, sellers can easily adjust to price changes. For example, as the demand for cherries increases each summer, orchard owners in

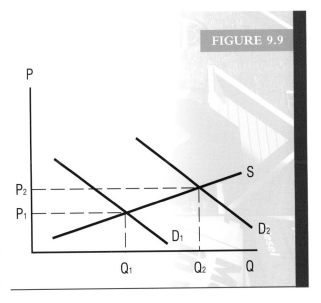

FIGURE 9.9

Oregon are able to meet the increased demand quickly because migrant workers are mobile. Workers respond to the rising demand for labor by moving to Oregon during the summer months.

Orchard owners are also able to substitute between labor and capital for many of the functions involved in getting cherries from the trees to the trucks. It is also true that the orchard owners have time to adjust to the rising demand because they plan for the inevitable increase in demand, by managing their orchards months in advance of the harvest to be ready for the summer buying season.

The supply of a good or service will be very inelastic if there is little flexibility or mobility of inputs, or if the seller cannot easily substitute different inputs in the production process, or if there is little time to adjust to increases in demand, or if there are rapidly rising input costs of production as production increases. The market for National Basketball League players illustrates this point.

If Kevin Durant – a star basketball player for the Oklahoma City Thunder – were to suffer a season-ending injury, the Thunder would be in big trouble. It is not because the Thunder does not have a backup for Mr. Durant. It is because the overall quantity of "starting caliber" NBA players is incredibly small. The problem is that out of a population of 308 million Americans, there are only 150 jobs available as an NBA starting player. Finding someone at an unemployment office, temp agency, or walking along the sidewalk who could play as well as Kevin Durant is impossible.

In a nutshell, the supply of NBA-caliber players is very inelastic, but not perfectly inelastic. It is possible, as demand increases, to find more people who are willing and able to play. The problem is that it takes a lot of time – and a lot of money to develop these players. Therefore, as demand increases over time, salaries increase significantly, but quantity supplied increases by a much smaller amount than the salaries change. Figure 9.10 illustrates this fact.

OTHER TYPES OF ELASTICITIES

We conclude this chapter with a brief look at a couple of elasticity applications that help economists and business people better understand markets. First, there is the concept of the cross-price elasticity of demand.

> ➤ **The cross-price elasticity of demand is a measure of the responsiveness of the demand for a good or service to the price of a substitute or complement.**

For example, if the price of Molson beer increases by 4% and then the demand for Moose Head beer increases by some positive amount, that means Molson and Moose Head are *substitutes* for each other. On the other hand, if the price of car insurance increases by 27% and the demand for sports cars falls, that negative reaction indicates that car insurance and sports cars are *complements*.

> ➤ **The income elasticity of demand is a measure of responsiveness of demand to a change in income.**

If consumer income increases and the demand for a good increases, the good is a *normal good*. If an increase in income leads to a decrease in consumption of some good or service, the good or service in question is an *inferior good*. For example, many of you will stop going to a coin-operated laundry service as your income grows. Buying a washer and dryer indicates that the income elasticity of demand is positive for these latter goods and negative for the coin-operated machines.

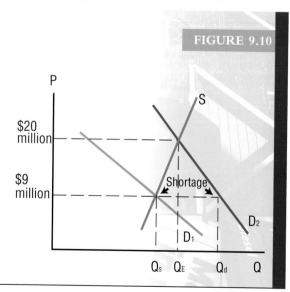

FIGURE 9.10

ENDNOTES

1 For more on how airlines set prices, see "You Paid What for That Flight?" by Scott McCartney, *The Wall Street Journal*, August 26, 2010, p. D1.

2 See "City Drivers pay the price to park" by Charisse Jones, *USA Today*, May 12, 2004; and "You want how much?" by Linda Shrieves, *The Orlando Sentinel*, October 29, 2004.

3 See "Iranians, Given No Choice, Adjust to Soaring Prices" by Farnaz Fassihi, *The Wall Street Journal*, January 20, 2011, p. A10.

4 See "the Burger and Fries Recovery" by Tim and Nina Zagat, *The Wall Street Journal*, January 25, 2011.

5 See "Package Carriers Deliver Bad News to Shippers: Heap of Higher Fees" by Rick Brooks, *The Wall Street Journal*, January 3, 2002, p. B1.

6 See "That sinking feeling," *The Economist*, November 19, 2005; "GM's productivity Growth Does Little for Woes" by Joseph B. White, *The Wall Street Journal*, June 3, 2005; and "U.S. carmakers see Midwest dominance fade" by Sharon Silke Carty, *USA Today*, August 3, 2005.

7 See "Sticky Price Hikes Help Beer Profits" by David Kesmodel, *The Wall Street Journal*, November 3, 2010; and "Food Sellers Grit Teeth,

Raise Prices" by Julie Jargon and Ilan Brat, *The Wall Street Journal,* November 4, 2010.

8 See "What Makes a Mattress Cost $33,000?" by Anjali Athavaley, *The Wall Street Journal,* June 16, 2010.

9 See "Minnesota farmers might be escaping the worst of pricing realities" by Edward Lotterman, *The St. Paul Pioneer Press,* August 5, 2010.

10 Some of you might be thinking that using HDTV is not a good example, because, in reality, changes in technology will keep prices falling. While this is a sound argument, I used this example merely to illustrate the concept. Also, it is not unreasonable to assume that some HDTV dealerships might opt to stop carrying the less-expensive models in order to get a higher amount of revenue from the bigger HDTV sets.

11 See "Pricing Pressure Squeezes Cell phone Makers World-Wide" by Jesse Drucker, David Pringle, and Evan Ramstad, *The Wall Street Journal,* January 15, 2004, p. B1.

12 For more on the tuition controversy in Europe, see "Europe Weighs the Unthinkable: High College Fees" by Sarah Lyall, *The New York Times,* December 25, 2003.

13 See "The Barry Bonds Tax: Teams Raise Prices for Good Games" by Stefan Fatsis, *The Wall Street Journal,* December 3, 2002.

14 See "Popularity could be fatal for our parks" by Alfred Borcover, *The Orlando Sentinel,* May 20, 2001; and "The Forecast? Hazy Skies Continue" by Rob Schultheis, *National Parks,* January/February 2004, p. 26.

15 See "Reaching Capacity" by Glenn E. Hass, *National Parks,* March/April 2001.

16 See generally *Federal Trade Commission v. Morton Salt Company* 334 U.S. 37 (1948).

17 See "Politicians Are Hooked on Cigarette Taxes" by Gordon Fairclough, *The Wall Street Journal,* February 20, 2002.

18 See "Still Smoking in New York City, and Venting About the $8 Pack" by Alan Feuer, *The New York Times,* January 25, 2006.

19 See http://www.taxpolicycenter.org/taxtopics/quick_gastax.cfm.

20 See "Dope Smokers," *The Wall Street Journal,* November 7, 2007.

21 See "Sin Taxes: Inferior Revenue Sources" by Robert A. Sirico, *Budget & Tax News* (The Heartland Institute), July 2004, p.13.

22 See "Federal Tan Tax Burns Some Badly but Keeps Everybody in the Dark" by Janet Adamy, *The Wall Street Journal,* July, 1, 2010; and "Tanning salons fear new tax will drive away customers" by Bob LaMendola, *The Orlando Sentinel,* July 5 - July 11, 2010.

23 See "Good Riddance to the Luxury Tax," *The Wall Street Journal,* January 6, 2003.

24 In 2002 the luxury tax on cars fell to 4% on every $1 over $38,000.

25 For more on this issue, see www.geocities.com/drug_abuse_and_legalization/.

CHAPTER REVIEW

1. What are some of the reasons why sugar and cell phone services tend to have an inelastic demand?

2. Suppose the price of gasoline rises from $4.27 per gallon in 2014 to $4.93 per gallon in 2015. If consumption in the state of New Hampshire falls from 32.17 million gallons to 30.86 million gallons, what is the price elasticity of demand for gasoline in New Hampshire?

3. Suppose the price elasticity of demand for cherries is .71 in Utah, 1.00 in South Dakota and 1.26 in Georgia. A national distributor of cherries should follow what type of pricing strategy in each state? Why?

4. Suppose instead of making it harder to own guns, Congress passes a $23 per bullet tax on sellers of bullets. What would be the impact on bullet producers, consumers, and the government?

5. Why is the price elasticity of supply for ice cream greater than one?

Chapter Ten

PRODUCTIVITY *and* COST ANALYSIS

*U*nbounded morality ultimately becomes counterproductive even in terms of the same moral principles being sought. The law of diminishing returns applies to morality.

THOMAS SOWELL

THE OTHER HALF OF THE PROFIT EQUATION

In the last chapter we learned that half of the formula for profit involves the search for a price that corresponds to unit elasticity. Once this point is found, a firm is able to maximize its total revenue. The other half of the profit equation deals with the simultaneous goal of minimizing the total costs of production. Total costs equal the sum of fixed costs and variable costs.

> ➤ **Fixed costs are costs that do not change as production levels change.**

Examples of fixed costs might include rent on a piece of property, managerial salaries, and perhaps interest payments on fixed-interest loans.

> ➤ **Variable costs are costs that change as output levels change.**

Most types of labor, materials, fuel, and electric power are examples of the types of costs that will vary as a company increases or decreases production.

How can a company minimize its total costs over a period of time? For most businesses in the United States, approximately 70% of the cost of production is associated with labor. Wages, salaries, pensions, health care and other benefit plans, taxes, and so forth make up such a huge portion of the cost of doing business that companies quickly realize (or had better realize) that in order to minimize the total cost of production, they must minimize their labor costs.

How can they do this? By pushing wages down to the lowest level possible? This is a popular but incorrect assumption. As we will see in the international trade chapter, low wages do not always add up to low costs. In order for a firm to minimize its labor costs, one overriding objective must be pursued. The firm must seek to *maximize labor productivity.* This chapter will teach you the various ways that can be done.

PRODUCTION FUNCTIONS AND THE LAW OF DIMINISHING MARGINAL RETURNS

Every business has the economic equivalent of a fingerprint, known as a production function.

> ➤ **A production function is some combination of input services – land, labor, capital, and entrepreneurship that leads to maximum output.**

The question is: What is that combination? You rarely see a restaurant the size of a Target store. You don't see a Target store the size of a gas station, or a gas station the size of a roadside coffee stand. It would also shock you to go into a restaurant and see 7,000 servers running around. Universities never hire high school drop-outs to teach economics and physics. Construction companies rarely use station wagons to haul dirt. You get the idea. For every organization, there are certain types of economic resources and an amount of those resources that must be used in order to maximize total output.

Businesses sometimes rely on "trial and error" to derive the optimal combination of resources. Sometimes, sophisticated industrial engineering models can solve for the optimal theme park or opera house size. However it is done, it is important that the proper combination be found relatively quickly.

As many of you may know, when companies are chronically overstaffed or understaffed, the total output of that company will be reduced. Moreover, outdated equipment, poor organization, and lack of inventory control can reduce profits substantially. Even if a company has found the perfect production function, another problem exists. That is the fact that it will always operate under pressure created by *the law of diminishing marginal returns.*

> **The law of diminishing marginal returns states that as more and more variable inputs – such as labor or capital – are added to the fixed inputs of production, the additional output gained will decline.**

This is an economist's way of saying, "Too many cooks spoil the broth." In other words, we notice that as a company adds more and more workers, at first the additional output from each worker will increase at an increasing rate. Over time, however, each worker added will add less and less to the total production of the company. Eventually, the last worker added would add nothing to total output, and if one more worker is added beyond that point, total output will actually fall.

What is true for labor is true for any input. If this law did not hold true, you could grow the world's entire supply of food on one acre of land by simply adding more and more seeds, water, and fertilizer.

MEASURING PRODUCTIVITY AND COSTS

Gabriel runs a small shoe factory in Malaysia. He is aware of the law of diminishing returns and the concept of the production function. He is also in business to make as much money as he can. He is considering opening a second factory in Uzbekistan, but he is not sure how many workers he should employ from the labor force in that nation. The following table and diagrams will help you understand how critical this decision is.

VARIABLE INPUT # OF WORKERS	TPL	MPL	APL	FC	VC	TC	AFC	AVC	ATC	MC
0	0	0	0	500	0	500	0	0	0	0
1	7	7	7	500	300	800	71.43	42.86	114.29	42.86
2	18	11	9	500	600	1100	27.78	33.33	61.11	27.27
3	33	15	11	500	900	1400	15.15	27.27	42.42	20.00
4	46	13	11.5	500	1200	1700	10.87	26.09	39.96	23.08
5	55	9	11	500	1500	2000	9.09	27.27	36.36	33.33
6	60	5	10	500	1800	2300	8.33	30	38.33	60
7	63	3	9	500	2100	2600	7.94	33.33	41.27	100
8	65	2	8.13	500	2400	2900	7.69	36.92	44.61	150
9	66	1	7.33	500	2700	3200	7.57	40.19	48.48	300
10	66	0	6.6	500	3000	3500	—	—	—	★
11	64	−2	5.82	500	3300	3800	—	—	—	★
12	60	−4	5	500	3600	4100	—	—	—	★

★Undefined

TPL: The total product of labor, also known as total output

MPL: The marginal product of labor (the additional output produced from each additional worker).
   MPL = the change in TPL / the change in labor

APL: The average product of labor. APL = TPL / L

FC: Fixed costs

VC: Variable costs

TC: Total costs. Total costs = FC + VC

AFC: Average fixed costs. AFC = FC / TPL

AVC: Average variable costs. AVC = VC / TPL

ATC: Average total costs. ATC = AFC + AVC or TC/TPL

MC: Marginal cost. MC = The change in TC/MPL: The change in total cost divided by the change in the number of workers.

CONCEPT CHECK

What is the maximum number of workers he should hire? Why?

CONCEPT CHECK

If New York City hires more garbage collectors, will the law of diminishing returns immediately come into effect? Why or why not?

Photo courtesy Jack Chambless

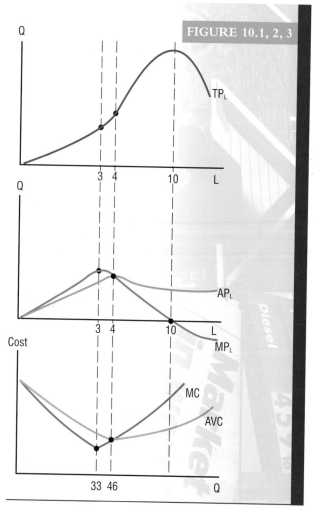
FIGURE 10.1, 2, 3

As can be seen by the preceding table and diagrams, initially, as Gabriel adds more workers (from 0-3 units of labor), his output increases at an increasing rate. This means that each additional worker added contributes more to output than the preceding worker does. Does this mean that each additional worker is smarter, more skilled, or has a better work ethic? Not necessarily. What this most likely means is that one worker running around trying to use all of the available capital and floor space is simply not enough. Giving the first – and then the second – worker some help has increased the total product of labor. Since each worker added contributes more than the preceding worker, the marginal and average product of labor increases as well.

When we look at Gabriel's cost structure we see that, with a fixed cost of $500 and a wage of $300 per week paid to each worker, his average variable and marginal costs of production each fall as he adds the second and third worker. *Average variable cost* is his total variable cost (in this case the total wages paid) divided by the total product of labor. It is easy to see that the first worker was paid $300 and produced seven pairs of shoes. $300/7 = $42.86. Two workers cost her $600 and produced 18 pairs of shoes; therefore his average variable cost fell to $33.33.

Since the *marginal cost* of production is the change in the total cost of production divided by the marginal product of labor, we see that his total costs increase by $300 with each additional worker. Dividing 7, 11, and 15 pairs of shoes (the marginal product of labor for the first, second, and third employees) causes his marginal cost to fall from $42.86 to $27.27 and $20, respectively. The fact that rising productivity leads to lower costs is not a coincidence.

RULE # 1: As long as all three productivity measures are increasing as your variable inputs increase, keep adding variable inputs to the production process. This is because with rising productivity comes lower average variable costs and marginal costs of production.

Notice that things begin to change for Gabriel after he hires the fourth worker. At this point, the total product of labor is still increasing, but by a smaller amount than before. This is because Gabriel has reached the point of diminishing marginal returns. The fourth worker's marginal product of labor was 13 pairs of shoes compared to 15 for the third worker. In this small plant, with a fixed amount of space and equipment, he must come to terms with the fact that output cannot increase at an increasing rate indefinitely. Since the *marginal product of labor is now falling,* this will pull down the average product of labor, just as when it increased the average product of labor increased.

Think of it this way: As long as each test you take yields a score that is higher than the last test, your average grade will rise. If your test scores begin to fall, it will pull down your average grade.

Should he stop at four workers? Not necessarily. There is actually a range of workers (from three to nine) that he could hire and still make a profit. This statement might make little intuitive sense to you, but consider this: What if the current market for the shoes he sells has an equilibrium price of $21? How many workers would he hire? If you said three, you are correct.

Suppose the global economy grows considerably in 2013, leading to an increase in the demand for shoes. An increase in demand would mean an increase in prices. An increase in price creates the ability to cover the rising costs of producing more shoes.

Do you remember the law of supply? *If prices increase to $301 per pair of shoes, he could afford to hire the ninth worker even though that worker produces only one pair of shoes.*

The marginal cost of the ninth worker is $300, but that is fine with Gabriel. If he can sell his shoes for more than the marginal cost of the last worker, that worker will be employed.

Rule # 2: As long as the additional revenue earned from increasing production offsets the additional cost of production, more variable inputs should be added to the production process.

Would Gabriel ever hire ten workers for his plant in Uzbekistan? Notice that the tenth worker added nothing to his total output and the 11th and 12th workers caused total output to fall. This is because eventually he reaches a point where the total product of labor is maximized and the marginal product of labor is zero. He has no more equipment or space to add more employees – in the short run. Unless Gabriel adds more space or equipment over time – or unless this is a government-run factory where productivity would probably not matter as much – he will never add more than nine workers to his plant.

Rule # 3: When the total product of labor has been maximized, do not add any more variable inputs to the production process. Adding any more variable inputs will cause the total product, marginal product, and average product of labor to fall and all costs to increase.

In summary, you should make sure you recognize the "mirror-image" relationship that exists between productivity and costs. *As long as your productivity increases, your costs will fall. When productivity falls, costs will increase.*

THE ECONOMICS OF DOWNSIZING

What if the global economy falls into a deep recession in the 2014 and the demand for Gabriel's shoes falls sharply? What should he do then? If he is like a large number of U.S. firms, he will adopt a widespread, albeit controversial, practice known as *downsizing.*

> ➤ **Downsizing is the practice of laying off workers in an attempt to increase productivity, decrease costs, and increase profit.**

CONCEPT CHECK

A recent trend in retail clothing has been the adoption of computer programs that measure each employee's average sales per hour, units sold and dollars per transaction.[1] With such "performance metrics" in place, clothiers like Ann Taylor and Gap have begun scheduling higher-performing workers in more favorable time slots. In the long run, how could such a system impact the productivity and cost curves for these companies? Can you draw the appropriate graphs that reflect your answer?

For a quick overview of the mechanics of downsizing, refer to figures 10.1–10.3 for a moment. Suppose when the recession hits, Gabriel was operating at the maximum possible output level of 66 pairs of shoes and nine workers. As you know, a drop in the demand for his shoes would mean downward pressure on prices, over time. If prices settled at $61 per pair, he might feel compelled to make the hard choice of laying off three employees. If he cuts back to six workers, this brings his marginal cost of production down to $60 per worker and keeps his in business.

Notice that when times are very good, companies do not worry much about productivity and costs. With a strong economy comes pressure to maximize production, rather than productivity because the demand for products is so high. However, during economic downturns, with people unwilling and unable to buy as much as they did before, companies have less pricing power. They must get costs under control, and they often choose to accomplish this goal by getting rid of workers that are "too expensive." This is precisely what happened in the U.S. in 2007–2009. Keeping workers on board in the face of falling revenue is very difficult to do.

Is downsizing a panacea for struggling firms? It may or may not surprise you to find out that many firms that have used the business strategy have had it backfire on them. The reason is fairly simple to understand. When a downsizing takes place, sometimes the workers who are left employed become mistrustful or resentful toward the company that has let go hundreds or perhaps thousands of employees.

The remaining workers begin wondering if they are next on the list to go. Workers who bear hard feelings toward management, or who are fearful of being laid off, tend not to be the most productive workers. The American Management Association found that in those companies that downsized during the early 1990s, worker productivity fell at 30.1% of those firms while morale fell an astonishing *86%*.[2] This is why a growing number of companies in this century have been attempting to lay off workers in a more caring manner.[3]

Another problem occurs when firms lay off too many people. Even if the remaining workers maintain their morale, there can still be diminished productivity. If too many workers are let go, the remaining workers are required to do even more work than they did before. This can lead to increased stress, fatigue, and inevitably less output.[4] This would be the equivalent to Gabriel dismissing all of his workers but two. Remember, with only two employees he did not have enough people, and productivity was lower than it could be.

CONCEPT CHECK

During the 2007–2011 recession and recovery, productivity in the United States actually increased sharply as many businesses shed workers, closed unprofitable stores, and cut back on everything from R&D to maintenance spending.[5] If the average business has an elastic product demand, what are the implications for total revenue if these decisions prove to be successful in the long run?

ALTERNATIVES TO DOWNSIZING

While the evidence is mixed as to whether downsizing helps the bottom line, historically many American firms have adopted extremely creative ways to maximize labor productivity.

At PepsiCo's headquarters in New York, workers who have personal chores that may keep them preoccupied or on the phone – and not working – are able to use a concierge service that PepsiCo offers. Does PepsiCo do this because this soft-drink giant loves its employees? Maybe, but it could also be because the company simply found that all of life's routine chores were interfering with their employees' ability to work. Therefore, for minimal expense, PepsiCo has increased their profits, while giving the appearance of being a caring corporation.[6]

Other companies like the SAS Institute in Cary, North Carolina, have constructed state-of-the-art child day-care facilities as an employee benefit. Day care is extremely expensive due to the liability insurance costs, but SAS and other companies have found that the increased costs of the facilities are more than offset by higher productivity and better recruitment of young, skilled workers. [7]

That's not all. Have you ever heard of "casual Friday"? This is a concept where workers are allowed to "dress down" one day a week – usually on Fridays – in a move to allow for more comfort and better productivity. Some companies – especially high-tech firms like Google with more free-spirited, younger employees – now allow casual dress every day. Other companies have found that piping in the smell of flowers, or having breakfast, rather than lunch meetings can boost output.[8]

Other firms offer exercise facilities, massage therapy[9] or season tickets to sporting events. One architectural firm in Portland, Oregon, built an ocean-side weekend retreat for its employees. More and more firms like Home Depot offer stock options – which make workers feel that their interests and the company's interests are more closely aligned.

Of course, some of the most obvious ways to improve productivity – flexible or more stable scheduling,[10] better equipment for workers,[11] and treating workers with respect[12] are always worth considering, too. The Lincoln Electric Company in Cleveland, Ohio, has found that offering lifetime job security along with a pay-for-performance model where workers get paid only for what they produce has dramatically improved output and profit over time.[13]

IS TENURE GOOD, OR BAD, FOR COLLEGE STUDENTS?

Students, administrators, and regents from boards around the country have complained for years, that the concept of tenure – the guaranteeing of lifetime jobs for certain college professors – leads to lower productivity in the classroom. Tenure originated in Europe, where centuries ago, universities protected professors who spoke on issues that offended religious institutions. Today the tradition of tenure lives on. Tenure is designed to protect professors who often take on incredibly controversial subjects in a way that generates a great deal of passionate debate.

However, there is an unquestionable tendency for some tenured college professors to take tenure as a license to lower productivity. Knowing it would be very difficult and extremely expensive to fire someone with tenure, some professors use this safety net to insulate themselves from the pressure to be innovative, creative, and motivational in the classroom.

If the costs of shirking are fairly low, and if the professor does not mind a reputation for being unproductive in the classroom, the benefits of shirking will outweigh the costs, and the students will not be effectively served. On the other hand, without tenure it might be very difficult for professors to take on extremely controversial issues without running the risk of their college letting them go for taking academic freedom into areas that make people uneasy.

SUGGESTED CLASSROOM DEBATE

More and more companies are using cameras and other forms of surveillance to monitor employee activity.[14] Is this good, or bad, for productivity? Why?

THE LONG-RUN COSTS OF PRODUCTION

Thus far we have seen how changes in the amount of labor or capital can bring about change in the short-run productivity and cost relationship for any given firm. We now turn to the issue of what the long-run costs of production look like for business firms.

The reason we need to look at this issue is simple. In the short run, some factors of production – the size of a plant or the acreage of a farm – are fixed. In the long run, all inputs in the production process are variable. This means that for any given firm it is possible to achieve *economies of scale* over time.

> ➤ **Economies of scale occur when a firm's per-unit cost of production falls over a long period of time.**

Economies of scale are derived most often from the ability to mass-produce goods and services and through technological advancement. In the early 1900s, Henry Ford pioneered a new way of producing cars that helped revolutionize manufacturing in the United States. Rather than have his workers pick up the parts of the Model-T he produced and walk to some fixed point of production, Ford developed an assembly line that moved the cars past workers, who could remain in one spot and assemble parts of the car as it moved past their location.

This led to a dramatic reduction in Mr. Ford's long-run average fixed, average variable, and average total costs of production. This also put Mr. Ford in a position to lower the price of the Model-T dramatically. Since the demand for his car was very elastic when it was first introduced, lower prices led to huge revenue gains for Mr. Ford over time.

Figure 10.4 illustrates this concept. Notice that at a production level of Q1, the average fixed cost is $850. As production increases over time, the higher level of output

divided into the same total fixed cost will bring average fixed costs down to point A.

Notice that the long-run cost curves begin to turn upward at some point. This is known as the point where diseconomies of scale begin.

> ➤ **Diseconomies of scale occurs when the long-run costs of production increase as a result of bureaucratic inefficiencies, breakdowns in the communication process, conflicts of interest, and cumbersome progress in product development.**

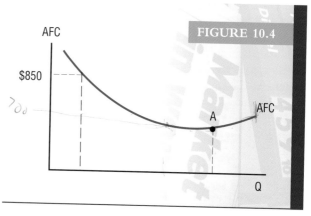

How does robotic technology impact the long-run costs of production?

Over time, with all inputs becoming variable inputs, many companies find as operations get larger, inefficiencies begin to appear. It can take the form of *too many layers of management* that do not effectively communicate with one another. It can result from *divergent goals* between the engineering and management divisions. It can result from a *plant getting too large*, where the spatial considerations make it difficult for resources to move freely from one area to another. *Internal politics* can also create impediments to productivity gains. Finally, some companies find that when they attempt to branch off into areas where they do not have a great deal of expertise, inefficiencies can occur. On figure 10.4, a level of production past point A illustrates this problem.

The recent struggles of General Motors and Toyota – and the constant struggle of government agencies – are representative of all of the aforementioned examples.

ECONOMIES OF SCALE AND THE ECONOMIC HISTORY OF THE BEER INDUSTRY

Ben Franklin once said, "Beer is proof that God loves us and wants us to be happy." While we cannot be entirely sure his theological argument is fundamentally accurate, we can say that the history of the United States suggests that beer is proof that, in a free-market economy, anything can and will happen.

When Christopher Columbus mistakenly landed in America, one of the first things he was offered was a fermented maize beverage. In one of his letters, Columbus said he found the natives produced a fermented beverage similar to beer.

Beer also played a part in the Pilgrims' decision to land at Plymouth Rock. A passenger's journal states that the Mayflower landed at Plymouth because "we could not now take time for further search or consideration, our victuals being spent, especially our beer." Isn't it amazing to consider the founding of our great nation being based in part on a "beer run"?

Many of the founders of our country were either brewers themselves or advocates of beer. George Washington had his own brew house, and Thomas Jefferson brewed beer on special occasions.

For thousands of years, beer was made with top-fermenting yeast. These beers were known as ales. The lager beer (lighter in color and smoother in taste) has been in America for only about 150 years. This is where the story of economics, beer, and economies of scale gets interesting.

When German immigrants began flooding into America in the 1800s, they soon discovered that New York, Boston, and many other eastern cities were too crowded and not conducive to economic opportunity. The Germans migrated west to Ohio, Wisconsin, Minnesota, and North Dakota. No sooner had the Germans arrived than they began brewing the lager beer that had been so popular in Germany for centuries. Soon the beer the Germans loved would be the beer Americans would love.

By 1873 there were 4,131 breweries in the United States. The companies we know so well today – Anheuser-Busch, Coors, and Miller – were all started by German immigrants who sold most of their beer to saloons where men would stop off on the way home from work, and sometimes on the way to work, to have a beer with friends.

The initial stages of the production process were costly and cumbersome in the U.S. For example, the Miller Brewing Company had its workers go out to the frozen lakes in Wisconsin to saw huge blocks of ice. The ice was then transported to vast underground caverns where it was kept cold – but not for long. Because pasteurization had not yet been invented, beer had to be transported and sold almost immediately after it was ready. If not, it would go bad.[15]

Pasteurization made it possible for the beer industry to ship beer much longer distances, which lowered the overall cost of production as sales volume increased significantly. However, it was the invention of the bottle cap that really generated economies of scale.

Before the bottle cap was invented, beer bottles were corked with a wire attachment that kept the cork in place. This was a very costly, time-consuming, labor-intensive exercise that prevented beer producers from gaining efficiencies necessary to lower prices and expand market share. When the bottle cap was invented, the beer industry was once again transformed into a more nationalized industry. But the biggest hit was yet to come.

The beer industry was almost knocked flat by Prohibition from 1919 to 1933. When Congress ratified the 18th Amendment to the U.S. Constitution, the overall supply of beer in America shrank by millions of barrels per year. The only source of supply came from "bootleggers" like the gangster Al Capone, who became a millionaire serving the demands of the people. Capone found that the demand for beer was extremely inelastic during the roaring '20s, which allowed him to charge very high prices for beer and make a fortune doing so.

The major breweries managed to survive prohibition by selling cheese, ceramics, root beer, and other products, all while campaigning to repeal prohibition on the grounds that the Founding Fathers would have never tolerated such a monumental intrusion into the lives of the American people. Seeking election in 1932, Franklin

D. Roosevelt accepted the position that voters should be allowed to drink.

With the 21st Amendment, economic liberty was restored to the American people, and the demand for beer increased sharply. Prohibition had wiped out hundreds of smaller brewers, leaving the major companies to fight for market share. In 1936 Anheuser-Busch found that economies of scale could be achieved by producing beer in cans. The introduction of the steel – and eventually the aluminum – can allowed beer makers to lower their costs of production not only by saving money on the container beer was sold in, but also by being able to fill up as many as 2,000 cans per minute, as opposed to 1,200 bottles per minute in the production process.[16]

Today, the production of beer looks like something out of science fiction. The Jacksonville, Florida, Anheuser-Busch brewery, the facility used to produce beer for distribution in the southeastern part of the U.S., is one million square feet in size, yet you will be hard-pressed to say hello to many workers in this building. It is not because Anheuser-Busch workers are unfriendly, but rather because the brewery relies on state-of-the-art automation that is controlled by computers.

Every process – from the brewing to the bottling, canning, and labeling of the beer – is automated.

Automation is used to construct the boxes used to hold the beer. Automation is used to stack beer and load it onto trucks. What does all of this do to the costs of production?

You guessed it. When you have four floors of computer-controlled storage tanks, it is easy to see how the scale of operation leads to huge reductions in the average variable, fixed, and total costs of production.

Having costs forced down from such massive production allows Anheuser-Busch to use the cost savings for what this company does best – marketing, advertising, acquisition, and product development.

Today, Anheuser-Busch InBev has approximately 50% of the domestic beer market. This St. Louis-based company (which was purchased by Belgium's InBev for $49 billion in 2008) produces over 100 million barrels of beer annually. The nearest rival is SAP-Miller with approximately 19% market share. Coors is the number three company, with about 11% share of the market. All three of these companies have large automated breweries. All count on their lower costs of production to help out in the fight for your business.

There are no longer more than 4,000 breweries in America. While microbreweries have enjoyed continued demand growth, there is no way they will ever compete with the "big three." The reason is lack of economies of scale.

Photo courtesy Jack Chambless

THE ECONOMICS OF DISCRIMINATION

When a Negro girl learns to cook, to wash dishes, to sew, to write a book, or a Negro boy learns to groom horses, or to grow sweet potatoes, or to produce butter, or to build a house, or to be able to practice medicine, as well or better than someone else, they will be rewarded regardless of race or color. In the long run, the world is going to have the best, and any difference in race, religion, or previous history will not long keep the world from what it wants.

I think that the whole future of my race hinges on the question as to whether or not it can make itself of such indispensable value that the people in the town and the state where we reside will feel that our presence is necessary to the happiness and well-being of the community. No man who continues to add something to the material, intellectual, and moral well-being of the place in which he lives is long left without proper reward. This is the great human law which cannot be permanently nullified.

Booker T. Washington, a former slave, speaking on the future of black Americans in 1901

Was Mr. Washington right, or is discrimination an ingrained part of economic systems that will live on and flourish in perpetuity? Should a company that cares about profit ever practice discrimination in the hiring, pay, or promotion of potential or existing workers? Based on what we know about markets and productivity and cost relationships, the answer would appear to be a resounding no. Simply put, discrimination imposes an economic price that many firms cannot afford to pay. Or does it?

Before we plow headlong into one of the most inflammatory and controversial of all economic topics, it is important that we approach this subject in a sane and dispassionate manner.

In other words, we must first break down how economists define and classify discrimination in labor markets.

> ➤ **Labor market discrimination occurs when a company intentionally refuses to hire or promote a person because the person has some non-productivity characteristic that is deemed undesirable by the company. Those characteristics include, but are not limited to, race, religion, national origin, gender, age, disability status, or sexual orientation. Discrimination can also take the form of salary disparities and the willingness to lay off a member of the aforementioned group(s) before a person from a "preferred" classification is laid off.**

As you can see, there is a pretty broad definition of what constitutes discrimination, to economists who study labor markets. We must bear in mind that this definition is a generalization. You may have a company that refuses to hire people who smoke or who wear earrings. The classification of groups that is presented here is designed to illustrate the most common types of groups that face discrimination and the groups that are protected by federal laws against discrimination.[17] Historically, there have *been four major types of discriminatory practices* that a person could suffer from:

> ➤ **Employer-based discrimination is a situation where the employer of a company has some "tastes for discrimination" and acts on those tastes.**

Keep in mind that there is a huge difference between racism, sexism, homophobia, and discrimination. It is legal to be a racist. It is legal to dislike people for their religious beliefs. Employer-based discrimination does not occur until the employer *acts* on his or her disdain for another race or homosexuals or whomever, by denying them economic opportunities that others enjoy.

> ➤ **Employee-based discrimination is a situation where the employer of a company is indifferent as to the makeup of the company's workforce, but the employees have some tastes for discrimination and persuade the employer to act on those tastes.**

A few years ago the National Basketball Association began hiring female referees. Suppose, at the time this decision was announced, that all of the male referees had banded together and informed the NBA owners that they would not work if women were hired. If this happened, and if the NBA owners crumbled under the threat of a labor shortage, this would be a form of employee-based discrimination.

> ➤ **Statistical discrimination exists when a company discriminates against a person who possesses some perceived negative stereotype as a function of that person's membership in a certain group.**

The classic example of this type of discrimination occurs against women of childbearing age and the elderly.[18] One reason for the perception that there is an artificial glass-ceiling that keeps women from being promoted as often as men, is due to the fact that women of child-bearing age are sometimes perceived – rightly or wrongly – to be an expensive risk to some corporations.

The thought process is that if a woman is hired and the company invests a great deal of time and money in training her, childbirth – which removes her from the labor force – imposes very high costs on the company in the form of lost productivity. Therefore, rather than take that chance, some companies simply adopt an implicit policy of denying women access to the top of the corporate ladder. The elderly, on the other hand, are sometimes discriminated against because of a perception that they are not productive enough due to advancing age, or lack of knowledge about ever-changing technologies.

The problem for economists who study discrimination is that the companies that do this have no idea whether the young woman or elderly person will disrupt productivity at all! What if the young woman does not plan on having children? What if she has children but remains in the labor force? What if she leaves the labor force, but returns as productive, or more productive, than before? Without knowing what a person's intentions or abilities are, the company simply gives them a negative label and moves on.

It is worth noting that this form of discrimination has decreased markedly over the past several years. Women now make up a larger part of the labor force than men for the first time in U.S. history. The "baby-boomers" – roughly 25% of America's population are also faring better as employers increasingly have difficulties finding younger qualified workers.

> ➤ **Customer-based discrimination exists when a company practices discrimination under the impression that the customers are discriminatory**

A terrific example of this type of discrimination is shown in the lawsuit where a woman sued Jazzercise, the San Diego-based company that operates over 5,300 fitness centers in 38 countries. Jennifer Portnick filed suit when Jazzercise refused to hire her to teach a work-out class. Jazzercise claimed that Ms. Portnick – who was 5'8" and weighed 240 pounds at the time – would cause a decrease in the demand for the company's fitness class in a San Francisco establishment.[19]

Jazzercise members, in fact, did threaten boycotts if Ms. Portnick was hired, but the company dropped its "lean-look" policy under pressure from obesity-based discrimination laws in San Francisco.

PROVING DISCRIMINATION

Suppose a wetsuit manufacturer in Portland, Oregon, decides to employ only white people between the ages of 18–29. There may be several reasons for this decision. Maybe the owner of the company has strong tastes for discrimination.

Maybe the owner thinks that ethnic minorities and the elderly don't know as much about wetsuits and therefore would be less efficient. Maybe the owner has no preferences, but the young white people who work there are a very cohesive group and make it clear that they do not want anyone working there who does not fit their description. Whatever the reason, economists like Gary Becker have shown that this practice will lead to *less profit* in the long run.[20] Here's how:

Suppose the firm in Portland operates in a very competitive market for wetsuits. Further suppose that the firms that compete with the Oregon-based company do not practice any sort of discrimination. While the discriminating company goes out of its way to employ only the most "desirable" workers, the other profit-seeking firms will search for the most productive workers possible, without regard to race, age, etc. The end result should be clear. Over time, the *non-discriminating companies will have a higher distribution of profit* than the Portland company will – assuming all other variables like demand conditions and other input costs are the same.

The lower distribution of profit for the discriminating firm stems from hiring less productive *and thus, more expensive* workers than their competing firms. If the Portland company employs a white guy – even if he is less qualified – just to make sure that an Asian person is not hired, the company forgoes the most productive

---

SUGGESTED CLASSROOM DEBATE

Not long ago, Abercrombie & Fitch was sued for practicing hiring discrimination against Asian, Hispanic, and black Americans. Supporters of Abercrombie & Fitch argued that if most of the company's customers are young and white, the company should be able to hire mostly young and white sales personnel. Do you agree or disagree? Why? Should the makers of FUBU clothing be prosecuted for discrimination? Why or why not?

labor force possible and therefore forgoes profit. Another point that should make labor market discrimination less appealing to would-be discriminators is the possibility that consumers find out – through the media or word of mouth – that a company does not operate in an equitable manner. Imagine the possible boycotts and cancelled sales that could mount in retaliation for economic stupidity.

As the demographics of the country continue to change, and economic power continues to be disseminated to people who did not have it 30 or 40 years ago, the economic ramifications of practicing discrimination are increasing to the point of making the practice itself absurd. The educational achievement of women and ethnic minorities in America – in particular, Hispanic and African-Americans – is higher than it has ever been. International competition a weakened economy and the Internet are putting increasing pressure on American firms to keep costs down. With all of those factors in place, how could any firm afford to practice discrimination in a labor market that is made up of large numbers of women, qualified minorities and intense competition?

Yet, there is still the possibility that some firms may be willing to forgo maximum profit in order to maintain the "most desired" labor pool. Let's look at what economists look for when a hiring discrimination charge has been brought.

First, we want to know about the qualifications of the individual who has claimed he or she was not hired, based on discrimination. If the person's overall qualifications were lower than other applicants, or did not meet the minimum guidelines for employment, there will be virtually no chance of proving discrimination took place. If the qualifications are identical, is that proof of discrimination? What if, on the day the person in question requested a raise or applied for a new position, that person was not feeling well? What if he or she came across as rude or indifferent? You might wonder what this has to do with hiring a person.

The company might feel that an applicant would not fit in well because he seems to be a jerk. And there is no protection for jerks in the 1964 Civil Rights Act or any other subsequent legislation.

What if the applicant had the same qualifications and came across as very respectful and competent and still didn't get the job? Does that prove his case? For discrimination to be proven, economists look for a *systemic pattern of mistreatment* of some particular group, or groups, of people. There are, believe it or not, instances where 100 people apply for a job for which 10 will be hired. There may be 30 people who could have been hired. You may not get a job some day, not because of discrimination, but perhaps because you did not give a good interview, or were reluctant to accept the travel demands of the job. You were technically "qualified" but on the margin another applicant may have been 1% better that day.

An accusation of discrimination looks like a much stronger claim if, of the 30 that are not hired – who were qualified and had good interviews – almost all of them were part of some particular group. If, upon investigation, it appears that this is a trend at this company, the firm could be in a great deal of trouble. The courts will throw out a discrimination lawsuit if the company can show that the person, who was not hired, for example, was denied employment because he or she did not satisfy the company's *bona fide occupational qualification* (BFOQ).

A BFOQ means that if there are certain attributes a person must possess to do a job; discrimination does not exist if they do not possess those attributes. A disabled person in a wheelchair would lose a lawsuit to play quarterback in the NFL. An American Indian economics professor with no course work in physics would not be able to sue NASA for employment discrimination if he was turned down for work as an astronaut.

THE OUTRAGE OVER OUTSOURCING

Anything that is not nailed to the floor is being considered for outsourcing.

Thea Lee, Chief international economist for the A.F.L.-C.I.O.

SUGGESTED CLASSROOM DEBATE

Starting in January 2011, federal regulations require that the Securities and Exchange Commission, the 12 Federal Reserve Banks, and other financial firms create an Office of Minority and Women Inclusion to improve diversity at these establishments.[21] If far fewer minorities and women major in economics and finance while in college, how could this law impact the productivity of financial firms in America?

The 2008 Presidential election was special for many reasons. One of the areas where it was most special was in the area of jobs – or the rate at which jobs were vanishing. Unemployment topped 6% the day America went to the polls and on the minds of many was the question of why so many jobs were leaving for places like India. When unemployment stayed near 10% in 2011, more and more Americans began clamoring for jobs to come back to the United States.

Why India? As it turns out, India's push for more and more capitalism has led to more companies from around the world having an interest in doing business there. With a highly educated population of English-speaking people, India has long been known for tremendous potential in the area of computer programming and other jobs. However, a bloated bureaucracy, high taxes, and overwhelming government regulations kept most Indians from being able to transfer their skills into meaningful jobs. Not anymore.

American companies – including Home Depot, Delta Airlines, Citibank,[22] IBM, and others – are now tapping into the enormous reservoir of highly productive people and have begun outsourcing jobs in everything from call centers[23] to computer programming and even construction work.[24] The result – on the surface anyway – *appears* to be a hemorrhaging of jobs in America with low-paid Indians being the beneficiaries. That is where reality has separated from fallacy – in this case the *low-wage fallacy*.

> ➤ **The low-wage fallacy is the belief that high-wage nations cannot compete with low-wage nations and thus, will lose jobs to low-wage nations if international competition is allowed.**

Shutterstock © Arvind Balaraman, 2011.

The inherent flaw with this fallacy is that it ignores the most important part of the equation for total cost. That is, it ignores the role of productivity in determining costs.

If low wages are what really matter to all businesses, then I would like to suggest that the Miami Dolphins football team get rid of their starting running back and replace him with me. Most NFL running backs earn more than $1 million per year. I would be willing to play running back for $350,000 per year. I was a very good high school running back in Oklahoma more than 28 years ago and would be all too willing to give up teaching and writing to help my team get to the Super Bowl. There is just one little problem. I am willing, but I am not able. There is not much call for people of my age and size in the NFL. That is because the NFL cares about productivity – as does every other business on Earth. That is why not all jobs are leaving the United States.[25]

THE ECONOMIC BENEFITS OF OUTSOURCING

It makes for wonderful headlines when politicians like bemoan the death of American jobs, but in economic reality, there are many benefits that our country receives when some jobs leave. Among the benefits are *lower prices, increased corporate profits,* and *more jobs for Americans.* Let's take them in order.

The Institute for International Economics found that globalized production had accounted for 10 to 30% of the decline in computer hardware prices during the 1990s.[26] The same is true for the price of software, clothes, food, toys, and many other goods.

It should make intuitive sense that if a company can get productive workers in India or China for a fraction of the wage cost in America, the lower costs would lead to lower consumer prices so the company can remain competitive.

While few people will jump up and down in celebration over higher corporate profits, what corporations do with profit should make you smile. That is because when Dell or Microsoft saves thousands of dollars per person per year in employment costs, these companies see their average variable and average total costs of production decline. As costs decline, profit will naturally increase. Rising profits over time has allowed the companies to invest in new research and development projects, new products and services, and ultimately in new jobs for *Americans.*

This final reality is one you don't hear a lot about because, frankly, the news networks need to make money. What type of program will make more money: one that scares people into believing every job on Earth is heading to Asia or one that explains how skilled workers in America gain jobs in the long run as a result of outsourcing? Fear sells; logic does not.

Over the past several years, as more and more white-collar jobs have left America, the resulting income for American companies has led to even more jobs here in areas where India, China, and other countries cannot effectively compete. Whether the reports come from automobile manufacturing, health and medical services, or banking, the data show that far more jobs are being created in America than we are losing, even with an unemployment rate of over 9%.

America's unemployment rate is a function of many factors. Approximately 4% of our unemployment rate is made up of people who have voluntarily left jobs or are entering or re-entering the labor force, along with people who have lost their jobs as technology or consumer tastes change. The rest can be attributed to the sluggishness in our economy, not outsourcing.[27]

In fact, economists point out that many foreign companies like Honda, Siemens, BMW, and others have left Europe or Japan *for the United States*. If they wanted only low wages, they all could have skipped the U.S. for other poorer nations in the Caribbean. The reason those companies stopped in America is because they know that ultimately the bottom line is enhanced most with productive workers – and America is still one of the most productive nations in the world.

While it is certainly unfortunate and painful when someone loses his or her job, we need to remember that this does not perpetuate the zero-sum game. Job losses are often the fuel to create new small businesses. Job losses can signal the unemployed to adapt to changing economic circumstances so that one's earnings potential can grow in the long run. And of course from a more normative standpoint, every job gained by an Indian is one fewer Indian living in the horrid poverty that nation has for so long experienced. The more Indians who gain employment, the more money Americans can make selling Indians things they cannot produce.

ENDNOTES

1 See "Retailers Reprogram Workers in Efficiency Push" by Vanessa O'Connell, *The Wall Street Journal*, September 10, 2008.

2 See "Some Companies Cut Costs Too Far, Suffer 'Corporate Anorexia'" by Bernard Wysocki Jr., *The Wall Street Journal*.

3 See "The Kinder, Gentler Way to Lay Off Employees" by Kemba J. Dunham, *The Wall Street Journal*, March 13, 2001.

4 See "Recalculating the Cost of Big Layoffs" by Scott Thurm, *The Wall Street Journal*, May 5, 2010.

5 See "Moment of Truth for U.S. Productivity Boom" by Justin Lahart, *The Wall Street Journal*, May 6, 2010; and "Propelling the Profit Comeback" by Scott Thurm and Joe Light, *The Wall Street Journal*, October 4, 2010.

6 See "Undivided Attention: How PepsiCo Gets Work Out of People" by Julie Amparano Lopez, *The Wall Street Journal*, April 1, 1993.

7 See "Westgate Resorts lets workers share time with kids at office" by Christopher Boyd, *The Orlando Sentinel*, February 20-26, 2006; "From Harley Factories to Desert Gold Mines, More Bosses Get It" by Sue Shellenbarger, *The Wall Street Journal*, July 21, 1999; and "An Entrepreneur's Pitch: Day Care for Sick Kids" by Rodney Ho, *The Wall Street Journal*, March 30, 2000.

8 See "Workplace aromas: The scent of productivity" by Lini S. Kadaba, *The Orlando Sentinel*, December 14, 1994; and *Coastal Living*, March-April, 1998, p. 105.

9 See "Working Out Kinks" by Harry Wessel, *The Orlando Sentinel*, April 6, 2005.

10 See "Fairer Flextime: Employers Try New Policies for Alternative Schedules" by Sue Shellenbarger, *The Wall Street Journal*, November 17, 2005; "Flexible Scheduling Works Best if it Serves Both Boss and Worker" by Sue Shellenbarger, *The Wall Street Journal*, January 17, 2001; and "Seeking the New, Slimmed-Down Workday: 9–5" by Kemba J. Dunham, *The Wall Street Journal*, January 17, 2001.

11 See "Sri Lanka Keeps Victoria's Secret" by Jonathan Karp, *The Wall Street Journal*, July 13, 1999.

13 See "Companies Are Finding It Really Pays to be Nice to Employees" by Sue Shellenbarger, *The Wall Street Journal*, July 22, 1998.

14 See "Lincoln Electric," *60 Minutes*, November 8, 1992.

14 See "They are Watching You" by Patricia Kitchen, *The Orlando Sentinel*, March 1, 2006, p.F1.

15 For a detailed look at the economic history of beer, see *The History Channel's* Brewed in America, a one-hour tape that can be purchased at www.historychannel.com/.

16 Source: Anheuser-Busch brewery VIP tour, Jacksonville, Florida.

17 Of all the groups mentioned in the definition, homosexuals are the only ones not protected by federal law from discrimination. However, many cities—like Orlando and San Francisco—have laws that protect homosexuals from discrimination. See "Gays bear witness to prejudice" by Mark Schlueb, *The Orlando Sentinel*, April 14, 2002.

18 Pregnancy-related discrimination lawsuits have increased by 25% since 1992. See "Labor relations" by Tiffini Theisen, *The Orlando Sentinel*, April 17, 2002, p. G1.

19 See "Jazzercise drops lean-look hiring policy" by Yomi S. Wronge, *The Mercury News*, May 7, 2002.

20 See Gary S. Becker, The Economics of Discrimination (2d ed. 1971).

21 See "Diversity law stirs Wall Street" by Julia Love and Jim Puzzanghera, *The Orlando Sentinel*, August 27, 2010.

22 Two separate studies estimated that between 500,000 and 2 million jobs in banking and other financial institutions would be outsourced by 2008. See "And Away They Go" by Richard Burnett, *The Orlando Sentinel*, March 16, 2004, p. C1.

23 See "Press 1 for Delhi, 2 for Dallas" by Jesse Drucker and Ken Brown, *The Wall Street Journal*, March 9, 2004, p. B1.

24 See "IBM to Export Highly Paid Jobs to India, China" by William M. Bulkeley, *The Wall Street Journal*, December 15, 2003, p. B1; and "Bracing for the Blow" by Bob Hebert, *The New York Times*, December 26, 2003.

25 In fact, many companies that have outsourced jobs from the United States to India have since brought the jobs back. See "Lesson in India: Not Every Job Translates Overseas" by Scott Thurm, *The Wall Street Journal*, March 3, 2004.

26 See "The Bright Side of Sending Jobs Overseas" by Eduardo Porter, *The New York Times*, February 15, 2004.

27 See "The Great Outsourcing Scare of 2004" by June Blanchette, *The Freeman*, March 2005 p.12; "Ever Heard of Insourcing" by Walter B. Wriston, *The Wall Street Journal*, March 24, 2004; "Outsourcing is Good for America" by Douglas A. Irwin, *The Wall Street Journal*, January 28, 2004; and "Why Your Job Isn't Moving to Bangalore" by Jagdish Bhagwati, *The New York Times*, February 15, 2004.

CHAPTER REVIEW

1. In 2011 the owners of National Football League teams expressed a desire to increase the number of NFL games from 16 to 18 per season. The NFL players did not like this idea. Where does the idea of the law of diminishing marginal returns enter in to this disagreement?

2. If the total product of labor is increasing at an increasing rate at a factory in Africa, what is happening to the marginal product of labor and the average variable cost of production? Why?

3. What are the various types of discrimination? Which one would disabled people most likely have to contend with?

4. What are the benefits of outsourcing? What are the costs?

Chapter Eleven

LABOR ECONOMICS

Photo courtesy Jack Chambless

*W*e might think of dollars as being "certificates of performance." The better I serve my fellow man and the higher the value he places on that service, the more certificates of performance he gives me. The more certificates I earn, the greater my claim on the goods my fellow man produces. That's the morality of the market.

WALTER WILLIAMS

HOW MUCH IS ENOUGH?

In 2011 Carl Crawford was paid $20 million to play left field for the Boston Red Sox. This was $13 million *less* than Alex Rodriquez was paid by the New York Yankees that year. Alex Rodriquez earned $27 million *less* than boxer Floyd Mayweather Jr. that year.

Former California governor Arnold Schwarzenegger was once paid $30 million to make one movie (*Terminator 3*). Former Disney CEO, Michael Eisner, once received over $500 million, in one year, for his services. All the while, police officers, firefighters, nurses, public school teachers – and just about all the rest of us – went to work knowing that we might not earn in our lifetime what an athlete or actor might make in one year. How does this happen? Why do people who seem to have jobs that do not add much to the social fabric of society make so much, when so many people with dangerous jobs, or jobs critical to education, make so much less?

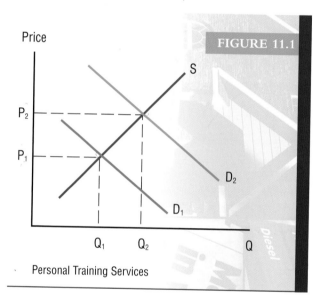

Personal Training Services

THE DEMAND FOR LABOR

In any labor market, the demand for labor is a *derived demand*. This means the demand for a worker comes from the demand for the good or service the worker produces. For example, over the next few decades, the number of elderly people in America is going to increase dramatically as the baby-boomers age and medical breakthroughs continue to prolong our lives. Surely the elderly are going to want to be active and fit as they age. This will translate into a large increase in the demand for personal training services geared toward seniors.[1] As can be seen in Figures 11.1 and 11.2, the increase in the demand for personal training services will lead to an increase in the demand for personal trainers. In each market, the result will be higher prices and an increase in quantity supplied.

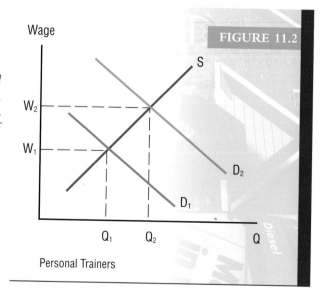

Personal Trainers

CONCEPT CHECK

Who has a greater derived demand – Oprah Winfrey or your economics professor? Why?

THE LABOR SUPPLY

The labor supply is the relationship between the prevailing wage rate in an industry and the quantity of labor hours offered in that industry. The number of people who are willing and able to do a particular job at various wage rates determines the labor supply curve. The willing part is easy. Many of you might be willing to be the starting goalie for the Chicago Blackhawks or play the lead opposite Mark Wahlberg. The hard part is satisfying the *able* part of the equation. As we will see, major differences in wages and salaries in America stem largely from widely divergent labor supply curves, rather than large differences in the demand for labor.

What would you do if, while you were reading this section of the book, your boss called you and offered you $200 per hour to come in to work today? Would you turn down the money in order to keep reading, or would you run every stoplight as you drive like Dale Earnhardt Jr. to get to work? For some of you, it is pretty straightforward: The more money you could make, the more hours you would be willing to work (figure 11.3).

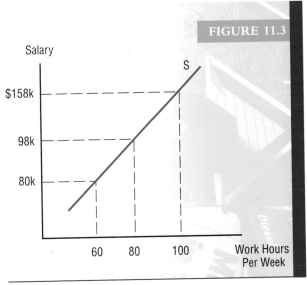

FIGURE 11.3

THE SUBSTITUTION EFFECT

John Allen is a very busy man. As an investment banker and Internet entrepreneur he routinely puts in 90 hours in a single workweek. Why does he do this? Because he is what an economist calls a "substitution effect" person.

Mr. Allen earned his degree in economics from the University of Virginia in 1995. After leaving Virginia where he received "high distinction" from the distinguished majors program, he went to work for Stern Stewart & Co. – a company that specializes in value-based management. By the time he was 28, he was a vice-president. Mr. Allen quickly ascended the corporate ladder and left Stern Stewart's New York office in 1999 to open a similar office in Century City, California.

Today he earns a six-figure salary as a financial executive in Los Angeles, and he does so at the expense of leisure time. Why does he work so hard? "Because I am willing to sacrifice leisure now, in order to gain leisure in the future, and the money to enjoy leisure in the future."

Mr. Allen is a classic example of the tendency of some workers to work a lot of hours, at the expense of relaxation. This substituting of work for leisure reflects their belief that, as their pay rate increases they cannot afford to take time off, because the opportunity cost of each hour of leisure is too great. In essence, leisure becomes too expensive to consume as the price of it – measured in lost income – increases. As a result, Mr. Allen faces an upward sloping supply curve like the one presented in Figure 11.3.

THE INCOME EFFECT

On the other hand, many of you may know people – or may be one of the people – with a *backward-bending* labor supply curve. This curve (as depicted in Figure 11.4) indicates a willingness to forgo higher levels of income, and actually reduce work hours, as income increases. This means that, as income rises, the individual can more easily afford to take time off. In essence, these people choose to purchase more leisure time without being concerned about working less. They feel they have earned enough money, in advance of the cut back in work hours, so leisure is a more desirable pursuit.

Which type of person are you? Before you answer, consider this. The type of labor supply curve that you are inclined to have says a great deal about the type of person you might consider marrying. Mismatching of "income-effect" and "substitution-effect" people has been proven to be a recipe for divorce. If you want to work 103 hours per week and your spouse wants you home, or vice versa, imagine the acrimony this can create. Perhaps before you consider asking or answering "The Question," you should sit down and find out what philosophy you and your loved one have with respect to work hours and money. You may find out that you are better off avoiding marriage – to that person – and the greater probability of disastrous consequences.

UNDERSTANDING EARNINGS DIFFERENCES

Figures 11.5–11.8 illustrate four distinct labor markets – the market for fast-food workers, elementary school teachers, doctors, and professional athletes.

As you can see in each diagram, the derived demand for labor is quite large. This is empirically true for each market. Americans spend more money on fast food, education, health care, and professional sporting events than any nation on Earth. This creates a constantly growing demand for all of these employees. With such a large demand for each, why are salaries that are paid to each type of worker so different? The answer lies with the overall supply of labor in each market.

There are currently approximately 165 million people in America's labor force. Of that number, 165 million have the ability to work as a food preparer at Taco Bell or Burger King. Because of the nature of the job, those relatively unskilled positions can be easily filled by almost anyone looking for gainful employment. This means that

the overall supply of fast-food workers is extremely large. When you combine a relatively large demand for labor with an enormous supply of labor, the result is downward pressure on wages.

The supply of teachers is smaller than the supply of fast-food workers. Elementary school teachers have to spend at least four years of their lives learning how

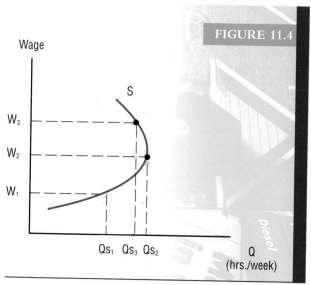

FIGURE 11.4

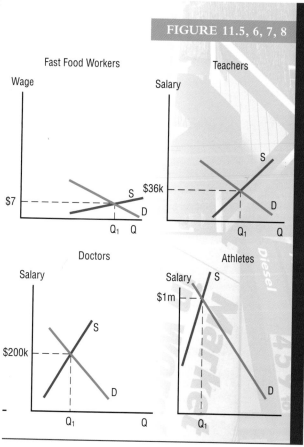

FIGURE 11.5, 6, 7, 8

CONCEPT CHECK

Laborers in Costa Rica earn about $2,800 per year to make baseballs for Major League Baseball.[2] Major league baseball players earn, on average, over $3.3 million per year. On two graphs, illustrate why there is such a large difference in earnings. Are these differences fair? Why, or Why not?

to educate America's youth. This requirement of higher education means that fewer people are willing and able to become teachers. With a smaller supply and a relatively large demand, teachers can always expect to earn more than a fast-food employee.

With respect to the labor market for doctors, the weeding-out process is even more intense. Because of the extremely long commitment to medical school, excruciatingly difficult coursework, long hours, and stressful working conditions, the supply of doctors is much smaller than the supply of teachers. It also helps that the American Medical Association has helped facilitate rules of medical practice that reduce competition for physicians' services. Given a very large demand for doctors and a very small supply of people who can meet the demand, salaries tend to stretch well into six-figures. For specialized fields like neurology and vascular surgery, the compensation can easily reach over $1 million per year.

Speaking of millions per year, the gentlemen in the photo below represent a labor market that for many Americans defies all common sense and rationality. Of course, this is referring to the labor market for professional athletes.

NBA players earned an average of $3.4 million in 2010-2011. Professional baseball and hockey players earn an average over $2 million per year. NFL players earned a median salary of over $750,000 in 2010. During Michael Jordan's last year with the Chicago Bulls, he received *$36 million* for his services. If we attempt to get past the emotional reaction to numbers like these, we can easily understand – and perhaps even accept – the reasoning behind such huge levels of compensation. After all, it is *our fault* athletes make the money they do.

When people plunk down their hard-earned money to be entertained by the skills of professional athletes, they

Photo courtesy Jack Chambless

expect — as the paying customer — to see the highest-quality product available.

That means those of us who attend professional sports events expect, and demand, to see the highest-quality athlete available. No one wants to see Sidney Crosby's gardener playing hockey for the Pittsburgh Penguins or Josh Hamilton's accountant swinging for the fences in Texas.

People pay money to see the best athletes in the world. The problem, if we wish to call it a problem, is that that the overall supply of people who can perform like Kobe Bryant or Peyton Manning is so limited (the able part of willing and able), that the supply of world-class athletes is extraordinarily small.

> People don't know how hard it is to play this game. It's like when Michael Jordan came over to play baseball. I heard guys in this clubhouse say "Yeah, Michael Jordan, he's not much. I could have guarded him in basketball." Michael Jordan! Nobody in the NBA could guard him! And you could? Why hasn't the NBA snapped you up? People are unrealistic.[3]

When we think about this situation analytically, we can see that — with only a small fraction of the world's population capable of satisfying the sports consumer, and a voracious appetite for pro sports in America — salaries naturally rise to the levels they do. In essence, it is not the athlete's fault for earning so much money. They simply charge what the market will bear.

Look at what soccer players in Europe earn compared to the U.S. In America, where soccer is not as popular on the professional level, the derived demand for star soccer players is so low that they make far less here than in Great Britain or Brazil. It is also ironic to point out that athletes are cheaper, for many of you, than teachers! If you never go to a game, never buy a jersey, or do not live in a city that is building stadiums with your tax dollars, it costs you nothing when an athlete earns a big salary. However, you do have to pay your taxes, and your taxes pay for teacher salaries.

The Economics of Labor Unions

In the nineteenth century, workers in America faced a difficult situation when it came to negotiating the terms of labor with business firms. During this time, if a worker wanted more money or better working conditions, the worker had to bargain individually with his or her employer. This put the employee at a tremendous disadvantage, because if the company did not want to pay what the person was asking, the company could say no without fearing repercussions from the disgruntled employee. Things began to change in the late 1800s and the early 1900s as more and more people began to join labor unions.

> **A union is a worker association that bargains with employers over wages and working conditions.**

Today, there are many different types of unions that negotiate wages on behalf of teachers, firemen, steel and auto workers, airline pilots, and electrical workers, to name just a few.

The major objective of each union is to use the collective bargaining process to increase wages and improve working conditions for union members.

> **Collective bargaining is the process by which unions and firms agree on the terms of employment.**

In America, there are two types of unions — the *craft union* and the *industrial union*. A craft union is a group of workers who have a similar range of skills but who work for firms in many different industries and regions. Examples include the carpenters' union and the International Brotherhood of Electrical Workers that represents electrical workers. An industrial union is a group of workers who have a variety of skills and job types but who work for the same firm or industry.

The United Auto Workers and the Steelworkers Union are examples of industrial unions. In 1886 the American Federation of Labor was formed to organize craft unions. In 1938, the Congress of Industrial Organizations was formed to organize industrial unions. Today the AFL-CIO represents millions of workers around the country, although union participation has fallen from a high of 35% of the nonagricultural work force to about 12% today.[5]

CONCEPT CHECK

During the 1920s, oppressive Jim Crow laws led to many black residents moving out of the state of Florida.[4] This movement led to a labor shortage in Florida during that time period. Illustrate and explain why.

HOW UNIONS IMPACT WAGES AND WORK HOURS

Historically, the goal of labor unions has been to restrict the supply of labor and drive up wages and benefits for union members. This is accomplished in three key ways. The first method is for the labor union to restrict the number of people who can join to begin with. With fairly rigorous apprenticeship and training programs and a selective mindset, unions have been successful in controlling the total number of workers that they offer to management in a collective bargaining setting. The second method is to successfully organize labor to become part of the union.

How does this cost you money?

For example, the Farm Labor Organizing Committee once attempted to unionize the farm workers in North Carolina.[6] The more workers a union can get to join, the more bargaining power the union will have in contract negotiations. Of course, the final – and most publicized – way unions attempt to impact wages and working conditions is by threatening a strike if desirable labor terms are not met.

> ➤ **A strike is the organized withdrawal of labor from a firm by a union.**

In 2001, the writers and actors in Hollywood – through the Screen Actors Guild – threatened to go on strike if union members did not receive higher residual payments from commercials and television programs that are rerun. The writers and actors argued that the studios were able to make money each time an episode of *Seinfeld* or a shampoo commercial aired, but that the actors and writers were being paid far too little money from these rebroadcasts.

More recently, labor unions have taken up the fight against the proliferation of Wal-Mart stores, in an attempt to force Wal-Mart to hire more union labor[7] while simultaneously pushing to get more union labor involved in reality television shows.[8]

What is the impact of restrictions on union entry, union organizing efforts, and strikes? Figures 11.9 and 11.10 will help provide an answer to this question. In

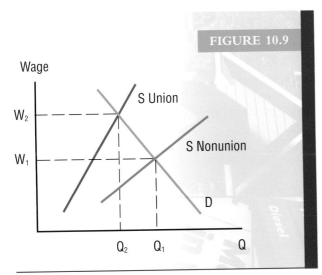

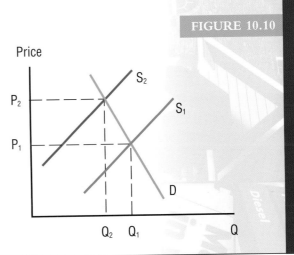

Figure 11.9, we see that, by restricting the supply of labor, unions are able to increase the earnings of their members. However, this practice also means that the quantity of labor hours demanded by the employer will fall – leading to fewer total jobs and work hours.

At the same time, we see in Figure 11.10 that unions cause the input costs of production to increase as a result of higher wages and benefits. For example, the average autoworker in Detroit, working as a member of the UAW, earns over $70 per hour in wages and benefits. This pay structure is one reason why car prices are higher than would be the case if nonunion workers built the cars. In Tennessee and Kentucky, where many nonunion members build Japanese cars, the prices of these cars have been kept down by much lower hourly wages.[9]

ARE UNIONS GOOD OR BAD FOR THE ECONOMY?

Studies show that union members tend to have a higher marginal product than nonunion members do.[10] With higher productivity come lower costs of production. However, unions also help create a reduction in employment opportunities and higher prices for goods and services that union members produce.

The real question for labor economists is whether the productivity differences between union and nonunion labor equals the wage differences. If productivity is 10–25% higher on average but wages are 30% higher – as the research suggests that it is – then nonunion labor makes more sense for employers. Employers that hire union labor face higher long-run costs, lower profits, and the reality of charging uncompetitive prices.[11] The Mackinac Center for Public Policy found that from 1970 to 2000, states with right-to-work laws added 1.43 million manufacturing jobs while heavily unionized states like Michigan, lost 2.18 million jobs due in large part to the widening gap between pay and productivity among union workers.[12]

Recently, President Obama pushed for a new law that would do away with secret ballots used by workers to vote on whether they want a union or not. The regulation was designed to put pressure on more workers to select the union option. Studies show that if the level of unionization in America in this decade reached the same level of the 1970s, employment would fall by 4.5 million and the GDP would be reduced by $500 billion.[13] One study in America even found that union-management problems at Firestone played a role in low productivity and the production of defective tires responsible for more highway deaths.[14]

Finally, the public sector union uprising that took place in Wisconsin in 2011, illustrates some of the economic dilemmas that occur from union labor. In Wisconsin and many other states around the U.S., the rising cost of public sector union pensions has left many states on the brink of financial insolvency. Thus, when Wisconsin's governor tried to rein in union power in this state, the unionized teachers, firefighters, and police officers naturally protested and helped draw attention to the high cost of allowing collective bargaining to take place in many sectors of our economy.

THE ISSUE OF WORTH

Whenever the issue of pay and worth comes up, it can spark a great deal of controversy. At the college where I work, I spent more than two years on a committee that was in charge of coming up with a new salary model for professors. At one point the committee recommended higher salaries for professors who taught in areas where there was a shortage of qualified instructors. One of my colleagues in the science department fired off a memo that stated in part:

The precedent has been established to offer additional compensation to professors in disciplines that are in demand in the marketplace. Does this mean that humanities professors are WORTHLESS?

Obviously, this professor either never took a microeconomics class or has simply forgotten her economics altogether. Of course, not all humanities professors are worthless. Many do wonderful things in the classroom.

SUGGESTED CLASSROOM DEBATE

Increasingly, colleges and universities all over America are trying to measure the economic value of professors.[15] Read the article footnoted here then engage in a debate over how best to measure the value of a professor.

How would you know if you were being paid what you are worth? Should the calculation be based on the earnings of your co-workers? Should it be based on how hard you work compared to others? Labor economists have devised a methodology for determining value. The methodology involves calculating the marginal revenue product of labor.

> ➤ **The marginal revenue product of labor (MRPL) is the extra revenue earned from each additional worker.**

In the previous chapter, we learned that the marginal product of labor is the change in the total product of labor that takes place from the addition of one more worker. The MRPL is simply the marginal product of labor, multiplied by the price of what the employer can charge for the output the worker produces.

Chuck owns a salmon farm in Washington. He can sell each salmon for $11. Chuck wants to know how much each worker he adds to his farm is worth. The table below will help him find out.

As you can see, the value of each worker depends on individual productivity and the price of the product that the worker helps to sell. This means that we look only at the revenue a worker is directly responsible for creating for the employer in determining that worker's economic value. This may seem caustic, but to the extent that economic models cannot measure the quality of a person's character or the value of his or her smile, we must rely on measurable components of worth.

THE LINK BETWEEN PAY AND WORTH

Now that we have a firm understanding of the supply and demand conditions that create differences in pay, as well as an idea of how we measure worth, we turn to the issue of how the level of competition on the demand and supply side of the labor market impacts wages and salaries.

To the extent that workers find themselves operating in markets with disparately competitive conditions, the answer to the question of how pay compares to the MRPL can be uncovered. At any time, a worker can find himself or herself in one of four economic environments. They are:

- A perfectly competitive labor market with respect to supply and demand.
- A perfectly competitive supply side of the labor market and an imperfectly competitive demand condition.
- An imperfectly competitive labor market with respect to supply and demand.
- A perfectly competitive demand side of the labor market and an imperfectly competitive supply condition.

Quantity (L) (Workers)	Total Product of Labor TPL (Salmon Caught Per Hour)		Marginal Product of Labor $MP_L = \Delta TP/\Delta L$ (Salmon Caught Per Worker)	Marginal Revenue Product of Labor $MRP_L = P_X MPL$
0	0	>		
1	5	>	5	$55
2	9	>	4	$44
3	12	>	3	$33
4	14	>	2	$22
5	15	>	1	$11

CONCEPT CHECK

A recent study found that America's 5.4 million stay-at-home parents would earn $131,471 in annual salary, including overtime pay, if they were doing the same work for an employer that they do at home.[16] Does this figure make sense? Why, or why not? Another study found that NFL quarterbacks that are good-looking make more money, ceteris paribus than more homely quarterbacks.[17] Does this make sense? Why, or why not?

THE PERFECTLY COMPETITIVE LABOR MARKET

If you are like thousands of other college students in the United States, you have decided to major in accounting for your degree plan. Of course, you already know that this is a particularly difficult subject, and naturally you expect to be appropriately rewarded for your services in this labor market. There is good news and bad news.

The good news is that there is a very competitive demand condition in this market. In other words, there are a very large number of firms in the U.S. who employ accountants now and will do so in the future. With the tax laws becoming infinitely more complex almost every year, you should feel comfortable knowing that there should be a strong demand for quite some time – especially in the wake of the Enron scandal where auditors have become more important then ever.

The bad news is that you cannot swing a dead cat without hitting someone who either is an accountant or is aspiring to be one. They are all over the place – meaning a very competitive supply side of your market. What will this mean to you in terms of pay versus worth?

Suppose that, upon receiving your degree, you find out that the average salary of a first-year accountant at any given corporation is $39,000. You decide that your hard work and dedication to your field is worth at least $53,000 per year. On your first interview, you inform the human resources manager that you do not really regard $39,000 as the salary commensurate with your skills and that you will require the higher figure to work for them.

Three seconds later, when your interview is over, you will find out the hard way that if the market for accountants is very competitive on each side of the market, you will not be able to get more than the market clearing wage rate. You should take comfort in knowing that the firm will not offer you $24,000 per year either. If a company in this market offers less than the MRPL, you can simply seek employment with any of their competitors for a salary that is equal to $39,000. In a nutshell, *you will be paid what you are worth* due to the mutual *lack of market power* you and prospective employers possess.

A common question at this point in the proceedings is "How do companies make profit if they pay their workers a salary equal to the workers' MRPL?" This is a very good question and one that is easy to answer. If we consider all of the factors that go into the production process – labor, fuel, materials, insurance, and so forth, any given company can expect to pay the market equilibrium price for the inputs of production.

What they do next is *mark up the final price* of the good or service to a level that will help them make profit. Of course, the amount of mark-up depends on several factors like the amount of competition in the product market, location, the ability to keep out new competitors, and luck. The bottom line is that wages are but one part of the cost of doing business, and you must come up with competitive wages and salaries to attract workers.

YOU WILL BE UNDERPAID IF...

Several years ago, the German automaker Daimler-Benz built a factory in Vance, Alabama, where the M-class Mercedes is built.[19] Vance, Alabama? What could this company possibly be thinking building a plant nowhere near Germany or Detroit – where many cars are made? Perhaps the carmaker knows something about a concept that has helped many small towns gain large employers. It is the concept that has driven the labor market for many unskilled and skilled workers alike all over the world. It is even used by professional sports organizations and the NCAA.[20] It is known by economists as the use of *monopsony* power.

As the following analysis (from the July 5, 1994, edition of *The Wall Street Journal*) clearly illustrates, when a monopsony exists and there is a very competitive labor supply to draw from, workers will be paid less than their MRPL. It does not matter how much the employee of the monopsonist earns. Workers can be underpaid even when they earn millions of dollars per year. One study found the existence of monopsony in the market for senior college professors.[21] Monopsony power has also appeared in markets ranging from truck driving,[22] call-center workers,[23] and teaching assistants at major universities.[24]

SUGGESTED CLASSROOM DEBATE

The average CEO's salary in the U.S. is 475 times greater than the average worker's salary. In Japan it is 11 times greater; in France 15 times; in Canada 20 times.[18] Why are the differences so large? Is this good, or bad for our economy? Why?

Poor Underpaid Millionaires

By JACK A. CHAMBLESS

When I was a youngster, I passed many scorching summer days in the air-conditioned confines of my home watching NBC's baseball Game of the Week with my father. Inevitably, at some point during every game we watched, someone would commit a fielding error and my father would cry out, "There is no way in the world that player is worth the hundreds of thousands of dollars he's being paid." After hearing him repeat this assertion year after year, I began to wonder: If the players are not worth the money, why do the owners pay such exorbitant salaries? Are they fiscal illiterates incapable of rational decision making?

As it turns out, the owners are pretty smart. They squeeze more revenues out of ballplayers than they pay out in salaries. And they keep players locked into a form of indentured servitude where the vast majority don't have any control over their future. That's a big reason why ballplayers are likely to walk out sometime this month for the first time since 1985. This prospect may be painful to fans transfixed by Ken Griffey Jr.'s quest for the season home run record of 61 (set in 1961 by Roger Maris), but the players would be justified in striking. Simply put, the bulk of them are underpaid.

I have created a computer model that calculates an individual player's impact on the bottom line. This multiple regression model calculates the impact on total team revenues of such variables as population, unemployment rate, attendance at games, even team colors. According to my model, the most important impact on the bottom line is the number of wins. Every game that a major league team wins increases its revenues by $349,000. It's also possible to determine each player's contribution to a win based on his offensive and defensive statistics; for example, the model has found that every run scored by a player creates .043 wins.

Based on this model, I've found that a few major league players are grossly overpaid. For example, outfielder Darryl Strawberry, who played for the Los Angeles Dodgers last season, earned $3.8 million but produced only $772,088 at the box office. But most players earn less than they should—even the San Francisco Giants' highly paid outfielder Barry Bonds. Mr. Bonds received $4.2 million last season. Yet his play—including 129 runs scored and 29 stolen bases—contributed $9,831,360 to the Giants' bottom line. This is no fluke. My model finds that, on average, professional ballplayers receive only 30% of the revenues they create.

And the ill-treatment of players doesn't stop there. Consider that every year, hundreds of young men ranging in age from 18 to 22 are "drafted" (note the martial term) by the 28 major league baseball teams, most of whom are sent down to the minor leagues. Once a player signs a contract to play professionally, he becomes the exclusive property of the team for seven years, with no right to renegotiate his salary or shop around for other employers. If the player quits, he cannot play for pay in the U.S., unless his team agrees to give him his unconditional release. However, at any time, the owner can fire him.

Ask yourself for a moment: "If, in my chosen profession, I could only work for one company for seven years with no opportunity to negotiate my salary or threaten to leave, would the company pay me what I'm worth?" The answer is pretty obvious.

This phenomenon is known as the use of monopsony power. A monopsonist is the single buyer of some resource. Underpaying workers as a function of monopsony power is very common in small cities where one company is the major employer. The company will pay its workers a wage that is higher than that paid by the local bowling alley or supermarket, but far less than it would pay if the workers could be bid away by a competitor.

Monopsony power over the players extends to both the minor and major leagues. As a major leaguer, a player cannot change teams or renegotiate his pay for three seasons. This means a player could have already put 10 years of his life into one team before being allowed to attempt to recover part of his lost earnings. After three years of service, the player can file for binding arbitration, which means he stays tied to his team but can now have a third party determine his salary once his contract expires. Since the arbitrators cannot "split the difference" between the amount sought by the player and what the owner offers, sometimes the player still isn't guaranteed a salary commensurate with his worth.

If the player is fortunate enough to survive the potential 13 seasons of servitude, only then can he become what each of us is, a free agent. He can sell his services to the team that pays him the salary he desires, located in the city he chooses to live in. This seems to be the type of player my dad used to refer to in his antimillionaire tirades. But as we have seen, even many of these players, like Mr. Bonds, are underpaid.

It is perhaps ironic that the players most likely will strike soon after the nation celebrates Independence Day. I wonder if my father will believe me when I tell him the players are fighting for their own independence from a tyrannical system.

Mr. Chambless is an economics professor at Valencia Community College, Orlando, Fla., and a sports agent who represents minor league baseball players.

THE BILATERAL MONOPOLY

A relatively rare labor market outcome is a situation where one buyer (a monopsonist) and one seller (a monopolist) of labor services interact with one another. This is known as a bilateral monopoly.

A bilateral monopoly occurs where a very strong labor union faces a situation where one major employer is pretty much the union's only option. This is precisely the condition that exists in professional sports. The players in each of the four major sports belong to a union that bargains with the owners of their respective sports franchises over terms such as minimum pay, pensions, conditions for termination, drug testing, and other aspects of the job. Of course, as we saw in the preceding analysis, an athlete is severely underpaid early in his (or her) career, due to the inability to shop his services around. However, the collective bargaining agreements that have been negotiated in football, baseball, basketball, and hockey have provisions allowing for players to become "free agents" after a specified period. There once was a time when this was not the case.

Early in the history of professional sports, the owners of the teams in each league realized that there was a growing demand for entertainment in America — especially the type of entertainment created by athletes. The problem the owners faced is that, with such a small pool of people who could compete at the level that was demanded, players would have the ability to shop their services around to the highest bidder. In major league baseball this is precisely what happened as players routinely "jumped ship" for more lucrative offers, made by other teams. It was this problem that led the owners to institute what was known as a reserve clause.[25]

The reserve system gave a team the exclusive rights to a player while he was under contract with the team and for the next contract year, effectively binding the player to a team for life. From the owner's perspective, this protected the team from interference by richer teams and enabled the team to recoup its investment in the player.[26] By being able to keep players like Lou Gehrig locked up for their entire career, it also helped teams like the New York Yankees win multiple championships in a row.

However, this system effectively made the players indentured servants with no prospects to ever leave a team unless they were summarily fired by the organization that employed them. Of course, the players eventually sued the owners, claiming that this system violated the 1890 Sherman Antitrust Act, which makes artificial restrictions on the movement of resources illegal. However, in a landmark decision, the U.S. Supreme Court ruled that "giving exhibitions of baseball, which are purely state affairs" makes baseball exempt from the federal antitrust laws.[27] This ruling, which has never been overturned, gave the

owners of major league baseball teams a free hand to dictate the terms of employment for players with impunity. Or so it seemed.

By the 1970s the players had had enough, and they enlisted the assistance of Marvin Miller, an attorney and expert in labor economics. Mr. Miller helped the players create a union that would eventually wrestle away the power of the owners to dictate salaries. In 1976 the players successfully fought for the right to become free agents after they had fulfilled a certain number of years with one organization. Today that number is six years. For the first six years of employment, a baseball player cannot leave his team.

After three years, he can file for binding arbitration and let an independent arbitrator decide what his compensation will be. After six years, the player is free to shop his services around to the highest bidder.

You might wonder why the players would not fight for total free agency and the abolishment of any reserve system. The reason is fairly simple. The owners have convinced the players that if a system of total free agency existed, the richest or most successful teams – or the teams in the nicest climates – would be able to raid the rank-and-file members of the best talent.

This monopolization of the available talent would mean that only a few teams would ever be competitive. Over time, the owners argue, the demand for professional sporting events would fall as fans grew tired of the

Should the "reserve clause" be reinstated?

same group of teams dominating the league each year. If demand fell, eventually some teams would go bankrupt and the entire league would be in jeopardy. Imagine, for example, what would have happened if Sam Bradford – the quarterback for the Oklahoma Sooners and former Heisman Trophy winner – would have been able to stand on a stage and let all 32 NFL teams bid on his services (like many economists want[28]) rather than the NFL allowing only the St. Louis Rams the option of his services. Mr. Bradford received tens of millions of dollars from the Rams. An auction would have pushed his compensation closer to $100 million.

Therefore, the owners have been able to convince the players that – in order to ensure the solvency of their leagues – they must be able to control player movement for a certain period of time. With many players now making decisions on where to live based on non-monetary factors – like proximity to family, the playing surface a team uses, climate, and so forth, this argument is a bit questionable.

The current bilateral monopoly situation in sports has created a mutual interdependence between owners and players, where over a player's career he will receive payments close to his MRPL. Owners cannot underpay players forever, and the players cannot hold out for money in excess of their value.

Critics of this system believe that player movement has ruined sports because fans can no longer follow a player throughout his entire career with one team. It is also interesting to note that, on more than one occasion the owners of major league baseball franchises – and other sports – have told city leaders that a new, taxpayer financed, stadium would have to be built in order to keep the team profitable in today's economic climate. The owners have testified before Congress that baseball is a very unprofitable business to be in, all while refusing to open up the financial records of each team to public scrutiny.

The reality is that professional sports is an incredibly lucrative business to be in. When baseball commissioner Bud Selig told Congress that the owners lost $519 million in 2001, he did not address the fact that the Boston Red Sox had recently sold for $700 million and that in all the major sports, the annual appreciation of franchise values makes owning a team an incredible investment.[29]

The owners are also reluctant to tell the public that much of their day-to-day operations are tax write-offs, including private jet flights and player salaries! That's right. When a baseball player signs a contract for $100 million, the owner of the team is allowed to depreciate much of the value of the contract over time, just as if the player were a bulldozer or computer. The tax laws end up shielding the owners from the full financial burden of owning the team. When you combine this fact with the free stadiums many of them play in, you might find yourself in agreement with former Minnesota governor Jesse Ventura,

who also testified before Congress on baseball economics and had this to say:

> Baseball wants us to build a park [for the Minnesota Twins] at public expense. Then they'll come back in five or eight years and say, "This isn't good enough either." If we build a library with public funds, we don't charge people to get in. If the public builds a stadium, the owner charges the public to get into their own stadium.
>
> The owners are not losing the money that they claim. If they were, they wouldn't be paying the salaries they are paying. It's asinine. These people did not get the wealth they have by being stupid.

The Twins got their new stadium in 2010.

It is worth addressing that at the time this chapter was being written, the National Football League was on the verge of a major work stoppage. In March 2011 the collective bargaining agreement between the players and owners expired. The owners wanted the new agreement to lower the percentage of total revenue the players receive and a new 18-game regular season schedule. The players wanted to keep the 16 game-season and their 59% revenue share. Millions of NFL fans waited anxiously for an agreement to take place because this bilateral monopoly does not afford us the opportunity to simply switch over to another high-quality football league to entertain us.

CAN A PERSON EVER BE OVERPAID?

If you have ever worked with a person with the work ethic of a slug, you would adamantly say yes, it is possible for someone to be paid more than their MRPL. However, this question is not meant to elicit examples of people not pulling their weight. Instead, economists want to know if an employer would ever face a labor market condition where a worker would be intentionally paid more than he or she is worth.

> It's like we're living in another galaxy. It seems so unreal that we would make this much.
>
> Tom Cruise

By now you should have a pretty firm footing to help you explain how Mr. Cruise can get a $25 million paycheck for movies like *War of the Worlds*. With a huge demand for his services and only one Tom Cruise on the planet, the laws of supply and demand keep Mr. Cruise relatively happy. If Mr. Cruise were just some "regular" actor with little star appeal, he would make far less. None of us would turn down $25 million to do what we do for a living, so we can't even blame him when studio executives drop boatloads of cash in his lap.

What is a bit curious is the possibility that Mr. Cruise could be overpaid from time to time. It has nothing to do with the fact that some of his films fare poorly at the box office. It has to do with the fact that Mr. Cruise has a monopoly over his name, his looks, and his ability. However, there is not a monopsony situation that faces him when he seeks employment. There is far more than one studio competing for his services. When you have a labor market that is very competitive on the demand side of the equation, coupled with only one seller of some labor service, where does the prospective employee opt to work if they all offer a salary equal to his or her MRPL?

If Mr. Cruise is actually worth only $19 million per film – based on the revenue he specifically creates – why would any studio offer $25 million? It is because, in the bidding for his services, if all studios offer $19 million, no one studio has an advantage over the other. Someone is going to have to increase the offer in order to procure his talent for the next project. This means the studio is already $6 million in the hole before one ticket is purchased. How can this be overcome? All the executives have to do is make sure that Mr. Cruise works with a lot of underpaid actors and actresses!

You must understand that in Hollywood there is a dichotomized labor market. Stars have all of the market power. Struggling no-name performers have none. They face a monopsonistic situation. If a studio offers a young actress $50,000 to be in a film that also features Tom Cruise, would she turn it down? She may very well be worth $500,000 to this film, but for the chance to add a film with a star of Cruise's magnitude to her resumé, she is not going to hold out for more money.[30]

ANOTHER WAY OF LOOKING AT IT

A final way to determine if you overpaid, underpaid, or paid what you are worth, is to simply examine whether the market is in equilibrium or not. If there is a surplus

of labor, it is an indication that wages will have to fall to restore equilibrium and that current employees in that market are paid more than their MRPL.[31] If there is a shortage of labor, it is an indication that wages or salaries will have to increase to reach equilibrium and workers are currently paid less than their MRPL. Such has been the recent case for nurses and airline mechanics.[32] If an equilibrium condition exists (indicated by stable wages or salaries), workers are being paid equal to – or very close to – their MRPL.

OTHER PAY ISSUES

OK, so we have seen that the perception that athletes and actors are overpaid is not necessarily so. However, we have not addressed the issue of whether people who make a lot in the labor market would actually keep working even if their pay were cut – even dramatically cut. This question is part of the economics of labor markets that examines *reservation wages.*

> ➤ **A reservation wage is the lowest wage an individual would be willing to work for in any given market before he or she would opt out of that market.**

People like the Tampa Bay Buccaneers' Mike Alstott – a former running back – have found that it is often better to take a pay cut than to lose their job and be forced out of the league or to a new team in a city that represents their second-best choice. Mr. Alstott agreed to pass up a $2 million bonus he was set to receive in April of 2002. He passed up the bonus when he was informed that it was either that choice or be cut from the team. To Alstott, the decision was not as tough as one might think. "When you build something with the teammates you have, the core teammates, you don't want to leave. ... It's tough to leave. I know it's a business; there's a business side to football and sometimes there's change. But for me to stay here ... it is an honor."

SUGGESTED CLASSROOM DEBATE

The President of the United States receives a salary of $400,000 per year. Would it be good for the country if the salary was $40 million per year? Why, or why not?

CONCEPT CHECK

What is your reservation wage at your current job?

EFFICIENCY WAGES

Suppose your boss approached you today and said, "I fully realize that the market equilibrium wage rate for your particular job is $10 per hour, but I would like to pay you $11.32 per hour and offer you a free membership to the local health club of your choice." After you emerged from your coma, what would you think about such an offer? After all, if we recall the lessons of Adam Smith, why should your boss pay you more than the market requires? Because maybe he or she did think about Adam Smith and reached the conclusion that paying you an "efficiency wage" would make you *more efficient*.

> ➤ **Efficiency wages are above-market wages designed to increase productivity, reduce employee-monitoring costs, and reduce shirking by employees.**

The efficiency wage theory is fairly new to the labor economics literature, although there is a lot of research on this issue.[33] The research finds that employers offer up efficiency wages largely to improve workers' morale in order to reduce absenteeism and labor turnover. It is also done in order to improve the quality of recruitment when quality cannot be directly observed, improve work effort, improve the perception of "fairness" in the labor market, and reduce the costs of monitoring worker effort.

The idea is that, if your employer pays you more than you know the market would suggest, you will be grateful, improving your morale and therefore your productivity. All of this should lead to lower costs of production for your employer, as turnover rates fall and effort rises. The costs of checking up on people should fall as well, since workers getting paid more will not want to lose their jobs.

Why don't all firms pay efficiency wages? From the employee's perspective it seems to make perfect sense — pay me more and I will give you more.

However, the real question is: *How much more* will you give? What if your pay increased by 22% but your productivity increased by 4%? This would translate into higher average variable costs of production for your employer and potential economic losses and even bankruptcy if worker productivity did not increase much across the board.

There is the very real possibility that, for many workers, productivity could fall even after the pay hike. After all, if a person sees an increase in pay for no obvious reasons, but rather the hope that productivity will rise, what incentive does the worker have to work harder? In fact, some might be absent more often or shirk their responsibilities with greater frequency since they are making more money without being first required to improve productivity. There is a reason why, in most labor markets, higher productivity precedes higher pay. Efficiency wages constitutes a risky venture that requires a lot of trust — a trust that may or may not be well founded.

Photo courtesy Jack Chambless

CONCEPT CHECK

When George Vanderbilt set out to construct and maintain the Biltmore House in Asheville, North Carolina, he paid his construction workers and servants a wage that was far greater than the local labor market dictated. Was this a rational strategy?

THE "LIVING WAGE" MOVEMENT

What do Ben Affleck, Jesse Jackson, and the musical group *Rage Against the Machine* have in common? If you say, "They are all rich!" then you are right. If you said, "They all care about janitors at Harvard!" you are right again. If you said, "They need a refresher course on supply and demand!" then you are a genius.

Over the past several years, a movement has spread across America that calls for government to impose city-by-city "living wages" on America's businesses.[34]

> ➤ **A living wage is a wage that would be sufficient for an individual to be able to afford food, clothing, and shelter in the city in which the individual resides.**

This sounds like a great idea, and certainly no economist wants to see people earning pennies per hour before they return "home" to their box under the bridge and their roasted rat dinner. The question for you, the student, is how many labor markets like this are out there, at least in the United States? What market exists where people earn so little money that they are homeless, malnourished, and barely clothed at the end of the day? If you remember the material on reservation wages, you will be able to see the first of many economic flaws in the logic of the living wage movement.

If being on welfare – or even being homeless and panhandling for money – pays more per hour than work, the rational person lacking in skills, education, and training will opt for the more lucrative alternative of avoiding work. How could any business find enough people to carry out day-to-day operations if the business offered $.08 per hour? Very few (no one?) would work for that.

According to Affleck, Reverend Jackson, and others, Harvard University was exploiting the custodial staff by paying less than $10.25 per hour to keep the buildings clean. Reverend Jackson and others recently called upon Harvard to do the "decent" thing and increase the pay rate to a level where custodial staff could earn a dignifying wage that would allow them to have the basic necessities of life.

Maybe Jesse and Ben never took an economics class, but perhaps they should. According to labor economists at the Employment Policies Institute, an artificial increase in the wage rate for the most unskilled Americans would have two harmful effects on those very people Ben and Jesse want to help. First, much like the minimum wage, a forced creation of a living wage would push wages to a level where many janitors would find themselves unemployed and many Harvard kids would find dirtier bathrooms. The second problem is that employers, facing higher wages, would opt to look for people with higher skills to fill those jobs.

Let's say someone in Cambridge is making $9.22 per hour working at a local copier business while the custodians are earning $8.04 per hour. If the living wage is pushed to $10.25, employers are going to want to get more productivity for the extra pay. The person at the copier shop might be responsible not only for fixing copiers but also cleaning the store at night. Harvard might opt to hire someone who can serve the functions not only of a custodian but could also help professors teaching at night who have found the copiers jammed. The result? The custodians who were earning $8.04 per hour would now earn $0 per hour as a result of the misguided efforts of busybody actors and politicians.

Maybe Ben, Jesse, and the rest of this wealthy crowd could help their cause by donating half their annual pay to Harvard custodians. That would push the wage rate to *well above* $10.25 per hour.

NONPECUNIARY WAGES AND COMPENSATING WAGE DIFFERENTIALS

For most of us, money is not the only thing that influences our career choices. For some people flexible scheduling or on-site day care might be important. There is also the concern of how dangerous or distasteful certain work requirements might be. All of these are examples of nonpecuniary wages.

> ➤ **Nonpecuniary wages are the non-monetary benefits or costs of any particular job that must be added to or subtracted from money wages to obtain total compensation per hour of work.**

When nonpecuniary wages exist, it has been observed that some compensating wage differential will also be present.

> ➤ **Compensating wage differential is a difference in money wages necessary to make total compensation for similar jobs equal when nonpecuniary wages are not equal to zero.**

PARK RANGERS AND FIREFIGHTERS – WHO IS BETTER OFF?

If you are ever traveling through southern Montana, you would be well advised to stop at the Little Bighorn National Monument to watch Kurt Brockmann work.

Mr. Brockmann, a native of New Mexico, is a ranger with the National Park Service whose job it is to provide a description of the events that led up to General George Custer's demise at the hand of the Sioux and Northern Cheyenne Indians on June 25, 1876.

Mr. Brockmann provides one of the most entertaining and intellectually stimulating historical accounts of this event that a person could ever hope to hear. As a graduate of the University of New Mexico with a degree in history, Mr. Brockmann could easily earn thousands of dollars a year more than the $9.33–$10.95 per hour that seasonal rangers received when I spoke with him. Why doesn't he bolt for greener pastures?

"Because I love the job and money cannot buy the things that are truly important in life," was his response to this question.

This is a classic sentiment of someone who places a great deal of non-monetary value on a job. The sheer joy of doing his job so well, being outdoors, meeting new people, and being a part of history each and every day, carry significant positive nonpecuniary wages. The problem is that the National Park Service is fully aware that park rangers have these psychological benefits stemming from their jobs with the NPS.

Therefore, the NPS does not need to pay Mr. Brockmann a salary that is commensurate with the money he could command in the private sector. The NPS knows that less can be offered, and there will still be plenty of people willing to work at the Little Bighorn National Monument. When positive nonpecuniary wages exist, a negative compensating wage differential will be present in order to make the total compensation of a job equal to that of others where nonpecuniary wages are not present. In essence, Kurt Brockmann is paying for the *psychological benefits* he receives in the form of reduced monetary compensation.[35]

What if nonpecuniary wages are negative?

After September 11th we heard countless stories of incredible heroism displayed by firefighters in New York City. For months that followed the collapse of the World Trade Center, people argued that firefighters and police officers – the "real heroes" of America – deserve more recognition and more money.

How much more? Firefighters in some markets make a great deal of money. The men and women who put out oil-well fires after the Persian Gulf War were paid a lot. Firefighters who work on oil rigs earn a great deal of money, too.

One reason some firefighters make more money than others do, is the severe negative nonpecuniary wages that they deal with on many days. Sure, there might be many days where there's not much more to do than train, wash the fire trucks, and exercise. But when the call comes to go into a place just hit by two fuel-filled jet airplanes, and then climb as many as 110 stories to save people, the stress of this job can be overwhelming.

Because of the enormously high odds of dying in the line of duty, firefighters in places like New York earn more money on average than firefighters in smaller towns that have few buildings, no skyscrapers, and virtually no chance of being bombed by terrorists. In New York, therefore, a positive compensating wage differential is paid to firefighters to help offset the negative nonpecuniary wages. If positive compensating wage differentials were not paid, there would not only be a shortage of firefighters but a lot more buildings burning to the ground in New York City.

ENDNOTES

1 Personal training is not the only area where senior citizens are expected to be demanding more. See "Marketing Surprise: Older Consumers Buy Stuff, Too" by Kelly Greene, *The Wall Street Journal*, April 6, 2004.

2 See "Low-Wage Costa Ricans Make Baseballs for Millionaires" by Tim Weiner, *The New York Times*, January 25, 2004.

3 Interview with Cal Ripken Jr., former third baseman for the Baltimore Orioles, *Sports Illustrated*, April 24, 2000.

4 Source: Florida Center of Political History and Governance, Tallahassee, Florida.

5 Source: Bureau of Labor Statistics http://www.bls.gov/news.release/union2.nr0.htm.

6 See "Farm Union Takes Aim at a Big Pickle Maker" by Somini Sengupta, *The New York Times*, October 26, 2000.

CONCEPT CHECK

According to economists who study labor markets, working in a toll booth, as a coal miner, or cowboy puts you in some of the worst jobs in America.[36] Why might this be the case? In which of these three occupations would you argue that economists might have missed some of the nonpecuniary wages that might make the job one of the better ones a person could have?

7 See "The War on Wal-Mart" by Steven Malanga, *The Wall Street Journal*, April 7, 2004, page A18.

8 See "Unions Aim to Share in the Success of Reality TV" by Jim Rendon, *The New York Times*, January 25, 2004.

9 See "Auto Workers of the World Unite…" by John B. Schnapp, *The Wall Street Journal*, January 25, 2006.

10 Source: *The Economist*, February 22, 2007.

11 See "Weak Unions Create a Strong Economy" by Bradley R. Schiller, *The Wall Street Journal*, February 19, 2002.

12 See "It Takes a Recession," *The Wall Street Journal*, June 16-17, 2007.

13 See "The Right Way to Raise Wages" by Lee E. O' Hanian, *The Wall Street Journal*, July 8, 2010.

14 See "The Hidden Cost of Labor Strife" by David Wessel, *The Wall Street Journal*, January 10, 2002; and "Labor Disputes Can be Deadly for Consumers," *The New York Times Magazine*, December 14, 2003.

15 See "Putting a Price on Professors" by Stephanie Simon and Stephanie Banchero, *The Wall Street Journal*, October 23-24, 2010, p. C1.

16 See "Stay-at-Home Salary: $131,471" by Pamela Yip, *The Orlando Sentinel* (from *The Dallas Morning News*), Febuary 5, 2006.

17 See "Do Pretty-Boy Quarterbacks Make More Money?" by David J. Berri, *The New York Times*, September 14, 2008.

18 See "Are CEOs Worth Their Weight in Gold?" *The Wall Street Journal*, January 21-22, 2006, p. A7.

19 See "Alabama's Mercedes deal led to jobs, ill will" by Christopher Boyd, *The Orlando Sentinel*, October 19, 2003, p. A16.

20 Many economists who study sports argue that the NCAA uses its power to restrict the earnings of college athletes. This is one reason why some athletes seek to leave college early for the riches of professional sports. See "Free at Last" by Sam Walker, *The Wall Street Journal*, February 13, 2004, p. W6.

21 See "Seniority and Monopsony in the Academic Labor Market" by Michael R. Ransom, *The American Economic Review*, March 1993.

22 See "Truckers From Down Under Find Themselves in Legal Limbo" by Carlos Tejada, *The Wall Street Journal*, April 11, 2000.

23 See "City-Slicker CEO Finds Fun, Profit Home on the Range in North Dakota" by Susan Carey, *The Wall Street Journal*, April 10, 2000.

24 See "Degrees of Academia" by Christina Nifong, *The Raleigh News & Observer*, September 22, 1999.

25 See "Title VII and the Reserve Clause: A Statistical Analysis of Salary Discrimination in Major League Baseball" by Jack F. Williams and Jack A. Chambless, *The University of Miami Law Review*, Volume 52, Number 2, January 1998.

26 See "Labor Relations in Professional Sports: Lessons in Collective Bargaining" by Robert A. McCormick, *Employee Relations Law Journal* 14, 501, 502 (1989).

27 See *Federal Baseball Club of Baltimore v. National League of Professional Baseball Clubs*, 259 U.S. 200 (1922).

28 See "Why the NFL Draft Drives Economists Crazy" by Reed Albergotti, *The Wall Street Journal*, April 22, 2010, p. D8.

29 See "Artful Dodging" by Peter Keating, *ESPN Magazine*, January 7, 2002, p. 93.

30 For more on compensation issues in Hollywood, see "The new age of greed" by Josh Rottenberg, *Entertainment Weekly*, April 22, 2005.

31 See "Getting a Job in the Valley is Easy, if You're Perfect" by Matt Richtel and Laurie J. Flynn, *The New York Times*, November 19, 2003, p. C1.

32 See "Airlines Find Good Mechanics in Short Supply" by Susan Carey, *The Wall Street Journal*, May 10, 2001.

33 For some of this research, see www.bath.ac.uk/~hssdac/macro-2001-2/macro-2001-2-week5-efficiency-wages.htm and greywww.kub.nl:2080/greyfiles/center/1995/doc/31.pdf.

34 See "Effort mounts for 'living wage'" by Jason Garcia, *The Orlando Sentinel*, April 11, 2005.

35 These benefits can also take the form of job security, health care benefits, family leave, and more. Studies show that nonmonetary benefits are increasingly important to U.S. workers. See "The Wages of Prosperity" by Stephen Moore, *The Wall Street Journal*, August 29, 2005, p.A9.

36 See "Working in a Toll Booth is All Change, and None" by Jared Sandberg, *The Wall Street Journal*, April 9, 2003; "Despite dangers, miners keep going underground" by Jay Reeves, *The Orlando Sentinel*, January 8, 2006; and "Cowboy as a Career?" by Perri Capell, *The Wall Street Journal*, June 14, 2005.

CHAPTER REVIEW

1. Why do underwater welders make more money than people who feed gorillas at a zoo? Use two graphs to assist your answer.

2. What is the marginal revenue product of labor? How could an economist use this concept to evaluate the worth of a hairdresser? Could it be used to evaluate the worth of a preacher at a church? Why, or why not?

3. When Lou Gehrig played baseball for the New York Yankees, he was underpaid every year of his career. Why?

4. What is good and bad (economically speaking) about labor unions?

5. Where do nonpecuniary wages enter into the earnings of lifeguards, nature photographers, and military snipers?

The ECONOMICS of INTERNATIONAL TRADE

Photo courtesy Jack Chambless

*I*f a foreign country can supply us with a commodity
cheaper than we ourselves can make it, better buy it of them
with some part of the produce of our own industry, employed
in a way in which we have some advantage.

ADAM SMITH

WHAT IS ALL THE FUSS ABOUT?

Economists joke about how we don't agree on much. In fact, even when two economists are in agreement about some issue, one of them is bound to pretend to disagree just so a good argument can break out.

That is why it is so nice that there is at least one topic where you will get near-universal agreement among professionals in the dismal science. The agreement surrounds our view of the importance of international trade in furthering the progress and happiness of mankind.

You might find yourself wondering how there can be a near-consensus among economists that trade is a wonderful thing when every time there is an international trade conference rioters and protesters take to the streets claiming that trade is so horrible that it must be dramatically reduced in order to save workers and the planet. As it turns out, there is a good reason why the rioters feel this way. It is either because they are stupid or because economists have done a terrible job of educating the masses on the benefits of international commerce.

It is more likely the latter is true. When we consider the fact that an increasing number of Democrats and Republicans (including Tea Party types) think that international trade is doing more harm to the U.S. than good,[1] well, somewhere the economics community has dropped the educational ball...

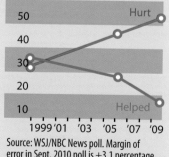

Rising Anxiety

Q: Do you think free-trade agreements have helped or hurt the U.S.?

50 — Hurt
40
30
20
10 — Helped

1999 '01 '03 '05 '07 '09

Source: WSJ/NBC News poll. Margin of error in Sept. 2010 poll is ±3.1 percentage points.

A REFRESHER ON THE PRINCIPLE OF COMPARATIVE ADVANTAGE

Oregon is one of the leading hops-producing states in the U.S. Hops is the plant used to give beer a spicy flavor. Louisiana is one of the largest oil-producing states in America.

What if residents of Oregon decided to boycott oil from Louisiana, and at the same time, brewers in Louisiana began refusing to buy hops from Oregon? Furthermore, suppose Oregon decided to become self-sufficient in oil production, while down on the bayou, an attempt was made to grow hops.

What would it take for each state to become self-sufficient? First, it would require that each state *ignore the concept of opportunity cost*. If Louisiana shifted into high gear on hops production, more and more of the states resources would have to be allocated to growing hops.

The same is true for Oregon. Imagine all of the hops farms that would have to be destroyed as the state cleared the land to make room for petroleum exploration and drilling. More resources devoted to hops growing in Louisiana and oil exploration in Oregon would mean less resources in each state to produce the most efficiently supplied product.

Residents of Oregon would be very upset to read geological reports indicating that there is little, if any, oil in Oregon. People in Louisiana – where the temperatures are not conducive to producing hops – would be equally upset to find out that a beer shortage is imminent because the state can't produce enough – or any – hops.

In the long run, each state will come to realize that, through trade, Oregon will realize a steady flow of high-quality oil from Louisiana while residents of Louisiana will be able to enjoy what might be America's finest hops. This is in addition to the fact that Louisiana and Oregon will enjoy a net increase in total jobs available. This takes place because Louisiana will produce more oil than it needs and simply sell off the excess to states like Oregon, while Oregon will do the same with the hops. Trade, therefore,

Photos courtesy Jack Chambless

is a positive-sum game — not the zero-sum game that enriches one party at the expense of another.

TRADE BETWEEN NATIONS

Since the beginning of human beings, trade has been a natural function of any economy. This is true at the individual level, state to state, and at the international level as well. For this reason, over the past several centuries people have looked outward to meet their wants and needs when their own economy lacked the resources to do so.[2] As far back as the time when people got around on foot, horseback, or small canoes, trading between tribes, villages, and nations has been viewed as the best way to avoid pervasive scarcity.

Today, most people are aware of the fact that it makes sense for Saudi Arabia to export oil and import computers. Honduras has no business trying to catch the United States in jet aircraft production, so Honduras buys jets from us and we buy bananas from Honduras. What is unclear to many students is why, for example, the United States would ever import cars from Japan when we have shown that we can effectively produce them here.

This question is not limited to cars. The mere mention of washers and dryers, televisions, VCRs, DVDs, stereo players, steel, bulldozers, clothing and assorted agricultural products will create an uproar among Americans who recall a time when America dominated the world market in the production of these and other goods and

services. Over time, that dominance has faded to the point where you would be hard-pressed to find an American-made television or DVD player. How America lost these markets and why we are strong in so many new ones, like computer software, energy equipment, medical technology, and movie production is a critical lesson in comparative advantage. Let's look at it.

HOW AMERICA LOST THE AUTOMOBILE MARKET

While the automobile was not invented in America — the Germans actually beat us to it — the United States was the dominant nation in automobile production from the days of Henry Ford's Model T until the early 1970s. Mr. Ford got us off to such a great start by producing a high-quality affordable product on an assembly line that saved his company millions of dollars in production costs.

Over time, General Motors and Chrysler entered the arena — as did others with much less success — until by 1970 the world's automobile market was dominated by the "Big Three." Of course, Germany, Japan, Sweden, and Italy were also factors in the international marketplace, but the majority of cars sold in America were built in the U.S. by one of the three major companies.

In the early 1970s all of that changed. It started with the dramatic increase in oil prices that stemmed from the 1973 Arab Oil Embargo. With gas prices skyrocketing, all of a sudden the very large, gas-drinking cars of the U.S. were not as attractive. Americans had always had a love affair with speed and larger cars. Cheap gas helped fuel this market. However, with the days of inexpensive gas quickly disappearing, Americans began noticing the fact that Honda, Toyota, and other Japanese companies were producing much smaller, fuel-efficient cars.

As the demand for Japanese cars increased, the initial reaction in Detroit was one of indifference and some would say, arrogance. Former Ford and Chrysler Chairman Lee Iacocca even went so far as to say, "A true American will only buy an American-made car." What he and other American executives quickly learned is that a true American has a budget constraint to worry about and will be more loyal to her wallet than the origins of her car.

Eventually, the U.S. automakers woke up and realized that the Japanese were not going to go away. It was during the remaining years of the 1970s that the Americans responded with their own version of small cars. You may have heard of or seen such products as the Ford Pinto, the Chevy Vega, and the Gremlin. Not only were Americans not impressed with the rather hideous look of these cars, but the quality of these automobiles also left a great deal to be desired. As a result, the demand for American cars continued to fall.

Of course, the next response was predictable. With their market share eroding faster than they could fathom, the executives of the Big Three ran straight to Washington, D.C., and begged for protection from this "unfair" intrusion by the Japanese into our markets. It did not hurt that it was less than 40 years since the Japanese had bombed Pearl Harbor. The executives appealed to the consumers' sense of patriotism and residual resentment against our former enemy and Congress's sense of political savvy to help get very restrictive tariffs and quotas placed on the Japanese. At one point during the 1980s, things got so bad that Chrysler filed for bankruptcy.

Not only did the government use our tax dollars to bail out this firm that had been selected for extinction, but then the Reagan administration caved to the mounting pressure for protection and asked the Japanese to "voluntarily" reduce imports. The world "voluntary" actually meant "mandatory," lest the Japanese face even greater punitive measures.

It did not matter. The American consumers kept on buying the superior Japanese product. The Japanese, with the use of "Kan-Ban" or "Just-in-Time" inventory management, continued to turn out better and better cars at terrific prices.

In 1986 oil prices collapsed. As a result, the demand for larger cars began to increase once again. The Japanese

were years ahead of schedule in meeting this change in the market. Figuring that oil prices would not stay high forever and recognizing that Americans prefer bigger cars, the Japanese rolled out such products as the Toyota Camry, the Honda Prelude and Accord, and the Nissan Maxima.

These larger cars proved to be a huge hit with Americans and another blow to the American carmakers that were begging Americans to believe that quality problems were dissipating. The consumers were buying it.

By the late 1980s the American economy was roaring, and consumers had plenty of money to spend. It was then that the Japanese made the final monumental step in their march toward taking over the American car market. Automobiles called Acura, Lexus, and Infiniti appeared in showrooms around the country. These cars, produced by Honda, Toyota, and Nissan, respectively, did not bear the names of the Japanese producers. The Japanese did not want car shoppers to think that these new luxury models were simply slight alterations of the other Japanese cars. They wanted the consumer to perceive them as being like Mercedes-Benz or BMW.

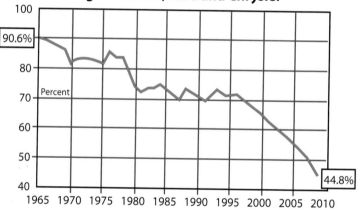

U.S. Vehicle Sales Market Share Big Three: GM, Ford and Chrysler

Today, the Big Three, for the first time in history, sell less than 45% of the vehicles bought in America. In 2008, General Motors saw its stock fall to below $10 per share. Eventually the company filed for bankruptcy and received billions of dollars in taxpayer money to stay afloat.

Foreign automakers who build cars in the United States pay an average of $30 per hour in wages and benefits to non-union workers while U.S. companies pay over $70.[3]

Given what you learned in chapter seven about the impact input costs have on supply and prices, you might be inclined to believe that such a competitive disadvantage in labor costs would lead to higher prices for American

Shutterstock © Orchidflower, 2011.

CONCEPT CHECK

Asia enjoys a tremendous comparative advantage in the shrimp business. Does this mean that Louisiana shrimpers should stop fishing? Should the U.S. government provide protection for American shrimpers? Why or why not?[7]

cars relative to what Japanese producers charge. That is not the case. Japanese cars are actually around *$2,500 more* than comparable American cars and still the American consumer prefers the Japanese brand.[4]

American companies have scrambled to improve the quality of the cars built in this country. The minivan, the SUV, and divergent types of pickup trucks have helped companies like Ford survive — and at times prosper — in the world automobile market, but serious cost pressures and quality issues remain.[5]

While similar events in electronics, steel, and other industries have contributed to the emergence of other nations as world leaders in production, the primary reason why America is not self-sufficient is simple.

Whether it is red wine from France, DVD players from Japan, vodka from Russia, or sugar from Haiti, there are some countries (for reasons associated with climate, technology, years of experience, or perhaps national priority) that do a better job producing certain goods than we

do. However, as the table that follows clearly illustrates, the United States has no reason to worry about being "taken over" by the rest of the world. The good news is that we enjoy a tremendous advantage over the rest of the world in most categories of production.[6]

THE ECONOMICS OF PROTECTIONISM

The problem in a lot of our trade agreements is that the Administration tends to negotiate on behalf of multinational companies instead of on behalf of workers and communities.

Barack Obama

A HEALTHY SHARE OF THE WORLD MARKET SHARES OF
GLOBAL CORPORATE PROFITS AND SALES

	U.S.		JAPAN		EUROPE	
INDUSTRY	PROFITS (%)	SALES (%)	PROFITS (%)	SALES (%)	PROFITS (%)	SALES (%)
Energy equipment and services	99.6	92.7	0.8	1	★−0.4	6.3
Aerospace and military technology	81.6	75.8	0	0.4	18.4	23.8
Data processing and reproduction	65.1	73.2	10.7	22.2	24.2	4.6
Electronic components and instrument	65	61.8	30.5	35.8	4.5	2.4
Beverages and tobacco	63	63.4	3.6	16.4	33.4	20.2
Health and personal care	61.9	48.9	8.2	20.3	29.9	30.8
Leisure and tourism	60.3	45.7	7.4	16.3	32.3	38.1
Forest product and paper	59.7	51	7	17.4	33.3	31.6
Energy source	50.4	45.8	2.3	13.5	47	40.7
Metals-Nonferrous	45.7	30.2	11.9	30.8	42.4	39
Recreation and other consumer goods	44	33.2	46.4	60.7	9.7	6.1
Food and household products	42.6	32.6	7.8	21.7	49.6	45.7
Electrical and electronics	41.1	21.4	25.7	50.7	33.2	27.9
Chemicals	41	28.2	13.3	30.3	45.7	41.5
Industrial components	38.2	24.5	32.5	44.7	29.3	30.8
Automobiles	23.6	37	31	35.3	45.5	27.6
Machinery and engineering	19.2	18.9	34.3	46.3	46.3	34.9
Appliances and household durable	16.5	7.6	74.4	66.6	9.1	25.7
Metals-Steel	2.3	10.1	51.2	57	46.5	32.9
All industries	47.7	37.4	15.5	31.5	36.8	31.1

★Europe's businesses in the sector had a net loss.

Source: Morgan Stanley Captial International and Daniel Strickberger

Despite all of the evidence that trade creates a positive-sum game, there are still those who argue that the best use of public policy is to restrict trade – or even ban it under certain circumstances.[8] Where does this argument come from? Does it garner any support among economists? In this section, we will uncover the historical reasons for tariffs and quotas and whether or not trade restrictions make any economic sense.

> ➤ **A tariff is a tax on an imported good or service.**
> ➤ **A quota is an artificial limit placed on the amount of a good or service that can be legally imported each year**[9.]

If you are wondering how the government decides which products are hit with tariffs and quotas and what formula is used to determine the amount of the tariff, it is very simple. The system used can be found in the invisible manual called *Twilight Zone Economics*. Consider this:

The United States allows Jamaica to sell only 950 gallons of ice cream to hungry Americans each year. Mexico is allowed to export 35,292 bras per year to the U.S. Haiti – the world's most efficient producer of sugar – is allowed to sell only 7,730 tons to the U.S.[10]

Low-priced watch parts are hit with a tariff of 151.2%. Tobacco stem importers pay 458%. Shoe importers pay 67%. Pity the consumer whose watch breaks down the day he decides to take up smoking and cross-training.

If you eat food on occasion, keep in mind that the tariff on grapefruit juice is 41.3%. Carrot and dried prune importers pay 17.5%. Olives, dates, frozen chicken, cucumbers, watermelon, yogurt, garlic, and asparagus all are assessed tariffs of 20% or higher.[11]

Representative Richard Roe once proposed to reduce the 33% tariff on protective garments worn by firefighters. Even though no American companies make this garment, the American Textile Manufacturers Institute objected. ATMI argued that only if the tariff were kept high, would the price of these garments reach a level that *might* encourage some American firms to make this garment. The Bush administration followed the same logic when it imposed import quotas on Chinese brassieres to protect the totally nonexistent U.S. bra industry.[12]

In his second term, Mr. Bush approved billions of dollars in taxpayer-financed subsidies for American farmers. He indicated that unless India took steps to reduce assistance to Indian farmers, the U.S. would consider a tougher trade stance with India.[13]

In 1988, foreign ice cream makers "swamped" the U.S.; 576 gallons came from New Zealand and *12 gallons* from Denmark. With a whopping one-tenth of 1% of the domestic ice cream market dominated by foreigners, the United States government was outraged when Canada – banned from America's ice cream market altogether – imposed a quota on U.S. ice cream.

The first President Bush sent a letter to the U.S. International Trade Commission demanding an ice cream investigation, "telling the ITC to stop everything else and give ice cream imports their highest priority."[14] With over 30 people working on this project, a final report was submitted on August 28, 1989. The details of the report were never revealed for "national security" reasons.[15]

The U.S. recently complained about Australia's 12% tariff on almonds. The U.S. almond tariff is 14.8%. Also receiving criticism was Canada's 12.5% tariff on frozen peaches. The U.S. frozen peach tariff is 20%. We also do not like the 7% tariff Guatemala imposes on soybean oil. The Guatemalans are probably not thrilled with our 22% tariff on this product.[16]

Former U.S. Trade Representative Clayton Yeutter once noted, "The Florida Citrus Industry…believes that removal of Japan's unfair barriers could cut the price of oranges for Japanese consumers by one third." Interestingly enough, the price of orange juice would fall by an even larger amount in America if not for our *60%* tariff on Brazilian oranges.[17]

It is also interesting to note that Congress seems to have a great deal of concern for the plight of America's poor people. Mink furs are tariff-free. Polyester sweaters pay 34.6%. Lobster is duty-free. Baby food pays 17.2%. Orange juice pays 40%, so maybe a poor mom should give her baby Perrier water, which is taxed at 0.8%.

THE HISTORICAL "JUSTIFICATION" FOR TARIFFS AND QUOTAS

No analysis of protectionism would be complete without some exploration into the reason tariffs and quotas are used against our trading partners. The defense of protectionism is vigorous. Therefore, each reason will be fully

addressed, along with what economists think about the justifications offered.

TARIFFS AND QUOTAS PROTECT DOMESTIC JOBS

On July 7, 1999, President Clinton announced that the U.S. would impose stiff new tariffs on lamb imported from Australia and New Zealand. While New Zealand has a population of approximately four million people, the New Zealand sheep population totals sixty million. In contrast, the U.S. has a sheep population of about seven million.

With a tremendous comparative advantage in lamb and wool production, Australia and New Zealand have been able to sell lamb meat and wool to Americans at a much lower price than American producers can. Since the price of foreign lamb and wool is lower (and the quality arguably better), the demand for American-made lamb and wool is fairly low. This means that the derived demand for American workers in this industry is fairly low.

The way Mr. Clinton's tariff was designed to increase employment in this industry is straightforward. The imposition of a 40% tariff forced the Australians and New Zealanders to increase prices in America to cover the higher cost of selling their products. If prices increased enough, the average American consumer would opt to start buying American lamb and wool. As the demand for American lamb and wool increased, the demand for workers in these industries would follow, and voila! Jobs are saved in our country.

This has been the key argument for tariffs in almost every instance tariffs are considered. The only problem is with the research that suggests this argument is largely void of any economic merit.

"…THE SINGLE WORST DECISION OF HIS PRESIDENCY."

That is what the conservative editorial board of *The Wall Street Journal* called Mr. Bush's 2002 decision to dramatically increase the tariff on imported steel.[18]

> Every day we go without expanding trade is another day of missed opportunities to strengthen the economy.
>
> President Bush, April 27, 2002

Not long after these remarks, President Bush imposed a 30% tariff on foreign steel. Not only did the tariff lead to an increase in the price of goods made with steel (during a time when our economy was suffering the lingering effects of a recession), but the tariff led to a loss of $680 billion in national income and the elimination of 200,000 jobs in the steel-using industries![19] In California, 19,392 jobs were lost. Texas saw 15,553 more people lose employment, while Ohio, Michigan, and Illinois each lost nearly 10,000 jobs. The Consuming Industries Trade Action Coalition estimated that the steel tariff had led to a loss of $4 billion in wages.

At least the tariff helped our steel industry, right? Well, no. It did not. While President Bush hoped that the higher tax on foreign steel would buy our steel industry time to improve efficiency and gain market share, the opposite actually occurred.

Steel prices shot up by a much larger amount than the administration had expected. The price for hot-rolled steel increased from $210 a ton to $350 a ton.

Since, in the short run, the demand for steel is fairly inelastic (meaning that it is a necessary good) the higher prices did not lead to a very large drop in quantity demanded around the globe. As a result, foreign steel producers like Brazil, Russia, and Japan increased their production of steel – in some cases by as much as 36%![20] Moreover, the higher prices did not help the U.S. steel industry that much.[21] Old and inefficient, the U.S. steel mills were unable to effectively increase output as much as our more efficient foreign rivals could. The end result was a glut of steel coming in from foreign nations that, even with the tariff, were more cost-effective in their operations and in a better position to absorb the new tax.

Making matters even worse was a World Trade Organization ruling in November 2003 that found the Bush administration's steel tariff illegal under international trade law. The W.T.O. then gave Europe and other regions around the world the authority to impose up to $2 billion in sanctions on everything from U.S.-made orange juice to motor boats and sunglasses.[22]

The fact that our steel industry failed to expand is not surprising. Economists Robert Z. Lawrence and Robert E. Litan surveyed 16 major industries receiving protection from 1950 through 1986. They found that only one industry – bicycle making – expanded. How could this be true? It is very simple, as it turns out.

Suppose the Pittsburgh Pirates baseball team – arguably one of the worst in recent history – struck an agreement with Major League Baseball that allowed the Pirates to pitch to opposing teams from only 10 feet away instead of the normal 60 feet, 6 inches away. Would this encourage the Pirates to try harder at improving their baseball skills, or would it give them a false sense of security, and erode their work ethic and the quality of their product? The answer is pretty obvious, and the applications to protectionism are clear.

Even with protection, industries like steel are in decline because consumers and businesses are not going to flock to the company that has been insolated from the free market. The market makes people and industries work hard or die. When the government protects inferior competitors, the incentive to improve is truncated, demand continues to fall, and jobs vanish.

Another issue that comes up with respect to the protection of domestic jobs is the cost of such protection. Import quotas on Japanese cars during the 1980s cost American car buyers about $4.3 billion. That's nearly *$160,000 per year for each job saved*. According to the Federal Trade Commission study, tariffs cost the American economy $81 for every $1 saved. This should not come as a great surprise.

If you were asked to use your money to help improve the productivity of two students – one who had a 3.93 GPA and studied 30 hours per week or one who had a GPA of 0.93 and smoked crack 30 hours per week – who do you think would be more expensive to help? If you said the crack smoker, go to the head of the class. The ratio of $81 per $1 saved is merely a function of whom we are attempting to help. Microsoft, Nike, and Rolex don't need much help – these companies are good at what they do.

Shutterstock © Scott Richardson, 2011.

CONCEPT CHECK

The United States has a 60% tariff on cement from Mexico.[23] What would happen to the price of construction projects in the U.S. and unemployment in the U.S., if the tariff dropped to 6%? Why?

Protecting sugar producers in Florida costs American taxpayers millions of dollars every year. This is because America does not possess a comparative advantage in sugar growing.[24] Consequently, many American candy makers have left America in order to be able to buy foreign sugar at lower prices. This move has led to thousands of Americans losing their jobs in the candy industry.[25]

All told, tariffs and quotas not only make job protection a very expensive proposition for consumers (the London-based Trade Policy Research Center places the cost at about $1,200 per year, per family), but the gains in terms of total job creation are illusory.

ANOTHER LESSON FROM BASTIAT

You will recall from chapter three that we examined the views of the French economist, Frederic Bastiat in the area of government spending and taxation. Bastiat also held very strong views on the subject of economic liberty as it pertains to trade. What follows is one of his more famous works on the subject.

A PETITION From the Manufacturers of Candles, Tapers, Lanterns, Sticks, Street Lamps, Snuffers, and Extinguishers, and from Producers of Tallow, Oil, Resin, Alcohol, and Generally of Everything Connected with Lighting.

To the Honourable Members of the Chamber of Deputies.

Gentlemen:

You are on the right track. You reject abstract theories and little regard for abundance and low prices. You concern yourselves mainly with the fate of the producer. You wish to free him from foreign competition, that is, to reserve the *domestic market* for *domestic industry*.

We come to offer you a wonderful opportunity for your – what shall we call it? Your theory? No, nothing is more deceptive than theory. Your doctrine? Your system? Your principle? But you dislike doctrines, you have a horror of systems, as for principles, you deny that there are any in political economy; therefore we shall call it your practice -- your practice without theory and without principle.

We are suffering from the ruinous competition of a rival who apparently works under conditions so far superior to our own for the production of light that he is *flooding* the *domestic market* with

it at an incredibly low price; for the moment he appears, our sales cease, all the consumers turn to him, and a branch of French industry whose ramifications are innumerable is all at once reduced to complete stagnation. This rival, which is none other than the sun, is waging war on us so mercilessly we suspect he is being stirred up against us by perfidious Albion (excellent diplomacy nowadays!), particularly because he has for that haughty island a respect that he does not show for us.

We ask you to be so good as to pass a law requiring the closing of all windows, dormers, skylights, inside and outside shutters, curtains, casements, bull's-eyes, deadlights, and blinds -- in short, all openings, holes, chinks, and fissures through which the light of the sun is wont to enter houses, to the detriment of the fair industries with which, we are proud to say, we have endowed the country, a country that cannot, without betraying ingratitude, abandon us today to so unequal a combat.

Be good enough, honourable deputies, to take our request seriously, and do not reject it without at least hearing the reasons that we have to advance in its support.

First, if you shut off as much as possible all access to natural light, and thereby create a need for artificial light, what industry in France will not ultimately be encouraged?

If France consumes more tallow, there will have to be more cattle and sheep, and, consequently, we shall see an increase in cleared fields, meat, wool, leather, and especially manure, the basis of all agricultural wealth.

If France consumes more oil, we shall see an expansion in the cultivation of the poppy, the olive, and rapeseed. These rich yet soil-exhausting plants will come at just the right time to enable us to put to profitable use the increased fertility that the breeding of cattle will impart to the land.

Our moors will be covered with resinous trees. Numerous swarms of bees will gather from our mountains the perfumed treasures that today waste their fragrance, like the flowers from which they emanate. Thus, there is not one branch of agriculture that would not undergo a great expansion. The same holds true of shipping. Thousands of vessels will engage in whaling, and in a short time we shall have a fleet capable of upholding the honour of France and of gratifying the patriotic aspirations of the undersigned petitioners, chandlers, etc.

But what shall we say of the *specialities* of *Parisian manufacture*? Henceforth you will behold gilding, bronze, and crystal in candlesticks, in lamps, in chandeliers, in candelabra sparkling in spacious emporia compared with which those of today are but stalls.

There is no needy resin-collector on the heights of his sand dunes, no poor miner in the depths of his black pit, who will not receive higher wages and enjoy increased prosperity.

It needs but a little reflection, gentlemen, to be convinced that there is perhaps not one Frenchman, from the wealthy stockholder of the Anzin Company to the humblest vendor of matches, whose condition would not be improved by the success of our petition.

We anticipate your objections, gentlemen; but there is not a single one of them that you have not picked up from the musty old books of the advocates of free trade. We defy you to utter a word against us that will not instantly rebound against yourselves and the principle behind all your policy.

Will you tell us that, though we may gain by this protection, France will not gain at all, because the consumer will bear the expense?

We have our answer ready:
You no longer have the right to invoke the interests of the consumer. You have sacrificed him whenever you have found his interests opposed to those of the producer. You have done so in order *to encourage industry and to increase employment*. For the same reason you ought to do so this time too.

Indeed, you yourselves have anticipated this objection. When told that the consumer has a stake in the free entry of iron, coal, sesame, wheat, and textiles, ``Yes,'' you reply, ``but the producer has a stake in their exclusion.'' Very well, surely if consumers have a stake in the admission of natural light, producers have a stake in its interdiction.

``But,'' you may still say, ``the producer and the consumer are one and the same person. If the manufacturer profits by protection, he will make the farmer prosperous. Contrariwise, if agriculture is prosperous, it will open markets for manufactured goods.'' Very well, If you grant us a monopoly over the production of lighting during the day, first of all we shall buy large amounts of tallow, charcoal, oil, resin, wax, alcohol, silver, iron, bronze, and crystal, to supply our industry; and, moreover, we and our numerous suppliers, having become rich, will consume a great deal and spread prosperity into all areas of domestic industry.

Will you say that the light of the sun is a gratuitous gift of Nature, and that to reject such gifts would be to reject wealth itself under the pretext of encouraging the means of acquiring it?

But if you take this position, you strike a mortal blow at your own policy; remember that up to now you have always excluded foreign goods *because* and *in proportion* as they approximate gratuitous gifts. You have only *half* as good a reason for complying with the demands of other monopolists as you have for granting our petition, which is in *complete* accord with your established policy; and to reject our demands precisely because they are *better founded* than anyone else's would be tantamount to accepting the equation: + x + = -; in other words, it would be to heap *absurdity* upon *absurdity*.

Labour and Nature collaborate in varying proportions, depending upon the country and the climate, in the production of a commodity. The part that Nature contributes is always free of charge; it is the part contributed by human labour that constitutes value and is paid for.

If an orange from Lisbon sells for half the price of an orange from Paris, it is because the natural heat of the sun, which is, of course, free of charge, does for the former what the latter owes to artificial heating, which necessarily has to be paid for in the market.

Thus, when an orange reaches us from Portugal, one can say that it is given to us half free of charge, or, in other words, at *half price* as compared with those from Paris.

Now, it is precisely on the basis of its being *semi-gratuitous* (pardon the word) that you maintain it should be barred. You ask: ``How can French labour withstand the competition of foreign labour when the former has to do all the work, whereas the latter has to do only half, the sun taking care of the rest?'' But if the fact that a product is *half* free of charge leads you to exclude it from competition, how can its being *totally* free of charge induce you to admit it into competition? Either you are not consistent, or you should, after excluding what is half free of charge as harmful to our domestic industry, exclude what is totally gratuitous with all the more reason and with twice the zeal.

To take another example: When a product -- coal, iron, wheat, or textiles -- comes to us from abroad, and when we can acquire it for less labour than if we produced it ourselves, the difference is a *gratuitous gift* that is conferred up on us. The size of this gift is proportionate to the extent of this difference. It is a quarter, a half, or three-quarters of the value of the product if the foreigner asks of us only three-quarters, one-half, or one-quarter as high a price. It is as complete as it can be when the donor, like the sun in providing us with light, asks nothing from us. The question, and we pose it formally, is whether what you desire for France is the benefit of consumption free of charge or the alleged advantages of onerous production. Make your choice, but be logical; for as long as you ban, as you do, foreign coal, iron, wheat, and textiles, *in proportion* as their price approaches zero, how inconsistent it would be to admit the light of the sun, whose price is zero all day long!

Jobs and NAFTA

This might come as a huge shock to many of you, but one of the first major economic decisions Bill Clinton made was associated with not telling the whole truth. Fortunately for America, his less-than-honest approach to trade helped America's economy tremendously during the 1990s.

When Mr. Clinton was running for president in 1992, he told union workers and environmental groups that he would not ratify the North American Free Trade Agreement with Mexico and Canada unless there were protections for union workers and adherence to environmental laws.

When he won the election he came into office and ratified NAFTA without any special protections for either group.[26]

Mr. Clinton also did not buy into the argument launched by Ross Perot and others, that NAFTA would kill jobs in America. Their argument was based on the simplistic theory that, since Mexican workers make so much less money than their American counterparts, once tariffs were lifted or even reduced, American companies would no longer be able to compete with the low wages paid to Mexican workers. Perot argued that the next event would be "a giant sucking sound of jobs leaving for Mexico."

When NAFTA was eventually ratified in 1993, America's unemployment rate was 7.5%. By May of 2000, the unemployment rate was 3.9%. While this is not all due to NAFTA, some interesting data has emerged about NAFTA's impact on the American economy.

On July 1, 1997, Congress issued a detailed "report card" covering the first three years of implementation of NAFTA. The data indicated that NAFTA had led to an increase in exports and imports by all three countries involved (U.S. exports to Mexico grew by 37%, to Canada by 33%) and the linkage of 2.3 million jobs in America to this agreement.[27]

By 2010, the data was even better. Trade between the U.S. and Mexico had increased from $40 billion in 1992 to $148 billion, while contributing to a 14.4% *increase* in the earnings of U.S. factory workers.[28]

Why did the dire predictions of net job losses to Mexico go unrealized? As it turns out, Perot is not totally off-base. Free trade has led to devastating job losses for manufacturers of toys, food, and textiles, to name just a few. The perception is that low wages in developing or third-world nations kill our jobs. The reality is that low wages are only a small part of the reason why some people lose jobs when tariffs and quotas are abolished.

Revisiting the Low-Wage Fallacy

Suppose you were the owner of a company that produced the guiding systems for orbiting satellites. You have three choices of where you are going to build your next plant: the United States, Mexico, or Rwanda. Suppose the average salary of a guidance system programmer would be $120,000 per year in America, $48,000 in Mexico, and $19,000 in the impoverished African nation of Rwanda. There is no question: You are going to move to Rwanda, right?

Before you depart, please consider the following questions. Are you concerned about the overall level of skill, education, and training of the Rwandan labor force? Are you concerned about the stability of the government there? Does potential language or cultural problems worry you? What about the quality and reliability of the phone, computer, and electric power delivery systems?

How about the highway system you will use to transport your guidance systems? What about the availability and location of suppliers? Are you starting to see the problem? The reason why most companies in America that employ highly skilled, educated workers do not leave for low-wage nations is because you get what you pay for. Low wages often mean low skills. Low skill means low productivity, and low productivity means very high labor costs.

In reality, it is actually cheaper to build many products in the United States than in nations with very low wages, simply because of the vast differences in labor productivity.[29] In fact, many American companies that left for Mexico when NAFTA passed have since *returned* to the U.S.

When companies do relocate to foreign nations, it is usually for one or more of the following reasons. One is to improve the *productivity-to-wage relationship.*

This means that in Malaysia, workers sitting at a sewing machine making bed sheets are performing a task that requires very little in the way of skill. Since this task can be done in a repetitive manner, the productivity of a 13-year-old girl in Malaysia would come close to that of an adult in a South Carolina textile mill. With the combination of high productivity and low wages, the average cost of the Malaysian worker makes them too cost-effective to keep the South Carolina plant open.

In this case – and others like it – people who oppose free trade have a point. Jobs will continue to be lost in American industries where foreigners have similar productivity but lower wages. This may seem horribly unfair, and certainly the person in South Carolina would have every reason to be angry, but let's consider the alternative.

Would you be willing to pay $15 for a cotton T-shirt made in America if it meant not being able to pay $7 for one from China? What about those Nike shoes you wear? How about a price of $159 rather than $99? You do have a choice.

If enough Americans decided to boycott all companies that use cheap foreign labor, the demand for their products would fall to the point that relocating back to America would be their only viable option. Once here, with the much higher wages being paid, we would then have to pay higher prices. Any takers?

THE REAL COST OF A NIKE SHOE

Suppose you go out to the mall and buy a pair of Nike running shoes for $70. Who gets the money? The answer might surprise you. The table below will help you overcome the belief that Nike earns ridiculously high profits by exploiting people in other countries.

As you can clearly see, the manufacturer, Nike, and the retailer each earn profit, but the retailer earns most of the profit. Nike earned 8.83% profit, the manufacturer earned 1.78% profit, and the retailer earned 12.86% profit out of the $70 price tag.

A second reason U.S. companies relocate to foreign nations is to *reduce their regulatory costs.* It is a fact of life that American companies face much higher regulatory costs than many other nations impose. Regulations stemming from worker safety, environmental protection, child labor, and other laws effectively increase the operating costs of doing business in the states. Moving to Indonesia and not having to worry about complying with thousands of pages of government rules and regulations can be enticing to many corporations.[30]

Increased regulations have also been the reason for many European companies leaving for the U.S. Laws that keep workers from working more than 40 hours (or even less) per week and mandating family leave and extended vacation time has made it very expensive for companies to survive in places like Spain and France.

Avoiding tariffs and quotas is another reason for the migration of U.S. and other nation's companies. If you drive a Japanese-brand car, chances are it was made in the United States.

According to the American International Automobile Dealers Association, over 50,000 American workers are employed in the building of cars like the Honda Accord (Marysville, Ohio) and Civic (East Liberty, Ohio); the Nissan Sentra (Smyrna, Tennessee); the Toyota Camry (Georgetown, Kentucky) and Corolla (Fremont, California); and the M-Class Mercedes-Benz (Vance, Alabama).[31]

A major reason for this proliferation of "foreign" auto production in America, is based on the protectionist legislation that raises the costs of building a car in Japan or Germany, then shipping it to the U.S. as well as the strong productivity of U.S. workers.

Reducing transportation costs and *opening new markets* are also valid justifications for plant location in foreign markets. When PepsiCo built a bottling plant in Vietnam, a big part of the decision to do this was to bring down the costs of shipping Pepsi products to this market and to open up this market that was impenetrable before Bill Clinton lifted the embargo against our former enemy.

MANUFACTURER (ASIA)		NIKE (BEAVERTON, OREGON)		RETAILER (YOURTOWN)	
Materials	$9.00				
Cost of labor	2.75	Cost of shoe to Nike	$20.00	Cost of shoe to retailer	$35.50
Cost of capital	3.00	Sales, distribution, and		Sales clerks' wages	9.50
		administration	5.00		
Profit	1.75	Advertising	4.00	Shop rent	9.00
Shipping	0.50	Research and development	0.25	Retailer's other costs	7.00
Import duties	3.00	Nike's profit	6.25	Retailer's profit	9.00
Total paid by Nike		Total paid by retailer		Price paid by you	70.00
for shoe	20.00	for shoe	35.50		

PUNISHING RIVAL NATIONS FOR CLOSED MARKETS

In more recent times, this argument has been widely used by administrations when imposing tariffs and quotas.

The Clinton Administration once threatened to impose a tariff of 100% on the Japanese in retaliation for not opening up their markets to more American cars and car parts.[32] Japan has also been a target in cases involving cellular phones, citrus, and semiconductors. The U.S. has threatened Canada with tariffs and quotas for perceived unfairness in our market penetration with respect to beer, lumber, and wheat.

This argument for tariffs and quotas is not without merit. For economists the test is very simple. *If* the United States has a comparative advantage in the production of beer, economic reasoning would indicate that Canadians should be allowed to drink our product without having restrictions on the supply or without having to pay artificially high prices. Therefore, if we were to tell the Canadians that we would not import hockey sticks from them until more Calgary residents can drink Bud Light, this would promote efficiency in both markets. The problem is that the United States has often been guilty of world-class hypocrisy when it comes to this argument.

The U.S. once charged Japan with not allowing Motorola to sell as many cellular phones as Motorola argued it should be able to. The only problem was that, at the time, Motorola was trying to sell the Japanese phones that were made for America's frequencies and were useless in Japan!

The first President Bush flew to Japan in the early 1990s to try to open up the Japanese car market to American cars. The Japanese drive cars with the steering column on the right side of the car. The American carmakers kept trying to sell them cars with the steering column on the *left-hand side*. In one of the most egregious examples of corporate arrogance ever, the U.S. carmakers informed the Japanese that building cars with the steering column on the right-hand side would impose higher costs of production on the Americans.

The Japanese were therefore told that when they had purchased enough left-side steering column cars, the Big Three would use that revenue to finance the production of the models with the steering column on the right-hand side…

HOW NOT TO MAKE FRIENDS IN FOREIGN LANDS

In 2001, Congress approved huge increases in agricultural subsidies for U.S. farmers. The average cotton farmer, for example, now earns half his income from government subsidies, rather than from the actual sale of cotton. Moreover, the approximately 25,000 cotton farmers in the U.S. have an average net worth of $800,000. What's the point?

Armed with roughly $3.4 billion in subsidy checks, the U.S. cotton industry produced a record crop of 9.74 billion pounds in 2001.[33] This level of production led to a huge increase in the global supply of cotton, which in turn suppressed cotton prices for vastly poorer cotton farmers in Africa, Asia, and other parts of the world.

Many of the farmers in Mali, and other countries where subsidies do not exist, ended up going out of business because of America's arbitrarily anti-free-market welfare program for wealthy cotton farmers. The U.S. response to the increase in poverty for these farmers was not surprising. To offset the $30 million in losses for Mali farmers, the U.S. government sent them $40 million in foreign aid – paid for by the same taxpayers who were called upon to subsidize U.S. cotton farmers.

For 2002, the $118 billion farm subsidy bill – which assured cotton farmers about 70 cents per pound – did not call for U.S. cotton farmers to leave any land idle, like past agreements had. The result was an even bigger surplus of cotton, even lower global prices, and more poverty for people in those nations.

Cotton is but one example of America's hypocritical stance on trade. From our recent steps to seek punitive damages against nations engaging in "unfair trade"[34] to rules that allowed the Export-Import bank to take U.S. taxpayer money and give it to wealthy corporations to promote trade,[35] America is often looked upon as a nation that believes in trade as long as the rules favor those with power and influence, rather than benefiting those that have a comparative advantage to begin with.

PUNISHING COMPETING NATIONS FOR PREDATORY PRICING, A.K.A. "DUMPING"

In 1997, the United States accused Chile of dumping salmon on American markets. This does not mean that the Chileans were piling up dead fish on our docks. It means we were piling up a rather smelly case against the Chileans for doing a great job of selling fish.

Predatory pricing occurs when a company or industry drops the price of some product below the costs of producing that product in an attempt to run its rival out of business.

In the short run, predatory pricing exacts an economic toll on the predator as prices fall to levels where losses are incurred. In the long run, after the predator's rivals are gone – unable to stay in business due to below-cost prices – the predator will dominate the market.

This allows the predator to raise prices to a level that not only helps them recover their losses from the predatory act, but also confers upon them the ability to take advantage of monopoly power and charge very profitable prices indefinitely.

With constant mild ocean temperatures, lower labor rates, and freedom from burdensome regulations, the Chileans have a comparative advantage in the harvesting of Atlantic salmon, which farmers grow

A threat to our prosperity?

in pens sunk along bays in the ocean.[36] From 1994 to 1997, exports of Chilean salmon increased from $46.5 million to more than $111 million, and Chile captured about 45% of the American market at prices that were up to 25% lower than American companies were charging.

If you are a lover of salmon, you might say "Great, now I can eat more of the product I enjoy." Not so fast. In America, land of the litigious, this price advantage was not left unchallenged by fishermen hurt by the law of demand.

Led by international trade lawyer Michael Coursey, the U.S. charged that Chile had charged prices that were 42% below cost in America and the rest of the world. The solution? A 42% tariff on Chilean salmon.

For economists, this is a curious claim. Let's put on our critical thinking hats for a moment and reflect on what must take place for an industry to pull off a successful predatory pricing scheme.

First, the Chileans would have to *identify their rivals' cost of production*. In salmon fishing or farming, this might be easy to do, but this decision still carries two types of costs. The Chileans would have to willingly spend money to find out what it costs to harvest salmon in America. Without this information, they would not know by how much to lower prices. Spending this money raises their costs of production and therefore, causes profit levels to fall.

The Chileans would also incur an *opportunity cost* from this decision. Spending money on industrial espionage is money that could have been spent on the next-best alternative, like better harvesting techniques, new nets, better marketing campaigns, and so forth.

Let's assume the Chileans are willing to fork over the money for this research. We come to step two. Once your rival's costs of production are identified, you must *lower your prices below their cost of production and keep the price there until they are out of business.* This is a sticky issue. Lowering prices to the point where your rival is gone may take a long time. In the meantime, your rival might merge with another company or be bought outright by a deep-pocketed investor.

The even greater problem is the issue of the Chileans' own profits falling from lowering prices to damagingly low levels. How smart can this strategy be when you have to inflict low profits or losses on your own firm in order to hopefully have long-run success?

Nevertheless, let's just assume the Chileans are willing to incur losses or that they have large profit reserves to support this venture. Step three takes place once your rival is gone. *When your rival is gone, you must increase prices* to a level that recovers your losses from the predatory act and ensures monopoly profit in the long run.

How likely is monopoly profit in the long run? Monopoly means the single seller of some good or service with no close substitutes. To make monopoly profit in the long run, you would have to make sure no one ever entered the industry to challenge your economically enviable position. Is that possible? Could the Chileans patent their salmon? Can they create a cartel like the Colombian drug lords and execute any fisherman who ever ventures out looking for competing salmon? Can they make sure no salmon ever swim anywhere away from Chile?

In reality, the Chileans have as much of a chance of monopolizing the salmon industry as George W. Bush has of being appointed to the United States Supreme Court.

If the Chileans can identify all the costs of production in America, and *if* they can afford to lower their prices, and *if* they can run all of the U.S. fisherman out of the market, there is no way they can keep one or more new firms from entering once they are raking in the profits from being the only country producing salmon. Profits act as a magnet to attract new competitors. This is always the case. This means that *in order to be a successful predator, you have to be willing to be a predator forever.*

It is not surprising that a growing number of economists not only question the merits of predatory pricing claims, but now argue that what appears to be predatory pricing is just good, old-fashioned competition that leads to lower prices for consumers and the rewards for a comparative advantage to the nation accused of wrongdoing.[37]

That is why economists became so fatigued sorting through the dumping claims levied by the Bush Administration against Canada and China.

For our neighbors to the North, the past few years have been frustrating ones. First, there was the accusation by the U.S. that "Mad Cow disease" was a threat from Canada. The U.S. government decided to temporarily create a quota of zero pounds per year in order to make sure now sick cows came in from Alberta and other provinces.[38]

Then we had the argument that the Canadians were dumping softwood lumber in our markets. With a red hot housing market already causing home prices to hit record levels, the 25% tariff on Canadian wood did not help consumers find much in the way of affordable housing in the last decade.[39]

China has not gotten off easy either. After years of protectionist tariffs and quotas on Chinese trousers, skirts, shirts and other clothing, China was finally allowed to export – with no quotas, various textile products. The lifting of the quota took place on January 1, 2005. In that year, exports from China increased by 60%.[40] Not surprisingly, the price of clothing in Wal-Mart and other stores fell as well.[41]

With such a huge increase in supply, many American textile manufacturers, already reeling from years of job losses and declining profit, lobbied the Bush Administration to stem the tide of low-priced imports from China.[42]

Should Canadian beef compete with Longhorns from Texas?

Photo courtesy Jack Chambless

In the end, President Bush approved across the board increases in tariffs on Chinese textiles and the renewal of quotas as well. By some estimates the protection of American textile makers effectively raised taxes by $55 billion on consumers in our country.[43]

In the meantime, China is not standing still. While U.S. companies continue to seek out ways to avoid direct competition with the world's largest emerging market, the Chinese government has embarked on a policy of seeking out alternative countries that might be willing to sign free trade agreements that the U.S. shies away from. In 2003 China had formal free trade pacts with *zero* nations. By 2005 China had agreements with 25 countries – proving that there is more than one way – and one place – to sell underwear.[44]

The three previous "justifications" represent the primary rationale for tariffs and quotas. The last three arguments are not used as much, but from time to time can be a thorn in the side of free traders.

TO PROMOTE HUMAN RIGHTS AND ENVIRONMENTAL PROTECTION

When demonstrators showed up in Miami and Seattle to riot over the issue of trade, a great number of them were there to show their support for human rights in China and other nations and to argue for greater environmental awareness. These are certainly noble and valuable goals. I cannot think of too many people who rejoice over the conditions in which many people in Asian factories work. Not too many people seem to be hoping for the eradication of the sea turtle and the pollution of the oceans, either.

Opponents of trade argue that the globalization of markets has led to companies exploiting workers in slave-like conditions around the world while ravaging the environment in nations that do very little, if anything, to stop them or even slow them down. Let's look at it.

Nike has been at the crux of the firestorm of criticism for employing thousands of Asians at pay rates that Americans would never accept in conditions that OSHA would squash in about 30 seconds. We now know why Nike is in Asia. This Portland-based company feels it is too expensive to make shoes in Oregon and still make profit. Since Nike is a private company, it can produce shoes wherever it can secure the property rights to do so. The question is what would the lives of the Asian workers be like if Nike did move back to Oregon?

Is Nike forcing anyone to work for them in Asia? Are they using slaves held at gunpoint? Do the workers in those factories have alternatives to Nike that pay more? The answer to all of these questions is obvious – and no. If Nike pulled out of Asia, the workers who lost their jobs would have to turn to their next-best choice. As you might imagine, their next best choice is worse than what Nike offers.

We cringe at the thought of working for pennies an hour, but all wages are relative. Recall that actor Ben Affleck cringed at the "low wages" paid to custodians at his alma mater, Harvard.[45] Bill Gates might cringe at the "low pay" Mr. Affleck takes in. Who are we to say that the Asians don't want Nike there? If Nike and other companies continue to set up shop in those developing nations, over time the demand for labor will rise, and so will wages. This has already been observed in China, where more and more factory bosses are lamenting the growing pay rates that workers can command as the Chinese economy continues to grow.[46] With pay rates rising by nearly 20% per year in some cases, companies like Ann Taylor Stores Corp., Guess Inc., and J.C. Penney have been leaving for Vietnam and Bangladesh.[47] Ironically, it was companies like these that helped create rising wages, higher standards of living and economic development that

made China a more expensive place to do business. Thus, what some people call exploitation, is called opportunity by people in Asia.[48]

As for the issue of environmental protection, here is an interesting fact: The dirtiest nations in the world are the *poorest nations* in the world. In northern Bohemia in the Czech Republic, breathing the air is "like smoking 10 cigarettes a day" due to the smog created by antiquated coal-fired power plants.[49] In Mexico City, air pollution is so bad that cars are allotted specific times when they can be driven on the roads. In Africa, the chief source of energy creation is the burning of wood – one of the worst sources of air pollution. In the meantime, the quality of water in India and much of Africa, Asia, and South America would repulse the average American.

How can trade help these problems? As it turns out, trade is a two-edged sword. It is true that with increased trade comes development, and development can damage the environment. However, studies show that as a nation develops, it gains the economic and political resources to emerge as a net protector, rather than damager of the environment.[50]

The United States has cleaner air in many regions than ever before.[51] We have more trees than we did in 1900. Recycling programs flourish while we voluntarily buy environmentally safe products and insist on less pollution emanating from our cars and power plants. The Internet and other high-tech inventions continue to move us away from the old smokestack industries to industries that create virtually no pollution. All of this has been made possible by economic growth.

While it is true that more trade means more wealth, and more wealth can mean more malls and fewer trees – initially, it is a paradoxical truth that if you want to see a nation stay dirty, keep them poor. Poor nations do not care about buying unbleached cotton T-shirts. Nor do they have the money to fund an Environmental Protection Agency or to assist in the fight against global warming. Poor nations are simply trying to survive. That means big trouble when the choice is burning a rainforest to create farmland versus protecting the rainforests so wealthy Americans can go on nice vacations in South America.[52]

SUGGESTED CLASSROOM DEBATE

In 2010 President Obama signed a trade agreement with South Korea that was designed to phase out tariffs on 95% of the trade goods coming into South Korea.[53] Will this agreement hurt South Korea? Will it do anything to help the American economy grow? Why, or why not?

PROMOTING NATIONAL SECURITY

> Without steel, we cannot guarantee our national security. Without steel, we cannot rebuild from our national tragedy.
>
> Senator John Rockefeller, D–West Virginia

Up until September 11th, one of the least-used argument in support of tariffs and quotas was the argument that trade jeopardizes the national security of our nation. The conjecture goes something like this:

Over the past several years the United States has imported approximately 67% of the oil that is used in this country. Suppose in the wake of the most recent increase in oil prices, the domestic petroleum industry begins lobbying Congress to put more restrictive tariffs or quotas on our Middle-Eastern trading partners, in order to be less dependent on foreign oil, and protect America from being hurt by OPEC policies. After all, oil is of vital interest to our national security, so why not protect the domestic suppliers?

The problem with this argument is twofold. *First*, it is not as if we are at the mercy of OPEC. We have reserves in America and access to even more oil in non-OPEC nations like Canada and Mexico. Therefore, a cry for national security tariff protection is a bit spurious if our national security is not actually at stake. *Second*, if we confer this status on oil, what is next? Why can't farmers claim that we cannot afford to lose agriculture to foreign concerns? What about jets, computer software, and toothbrushes? Why can't Boeing, Microsoft, and Oral-B argue that we must protect America from foreign planes, software, and toothbrushes that are not made by people with American teeth?

It is hard for economists to accept the argument that there are industries in our country that are of vital national security and are simultaneously threatened with extinction at the hands of foreign competition.

ONCE AGAIN, STEEL...

> Ask anyone if we should have a steel industry in America, and they will say yes!–unless they're economists.
>
> Anonymous steel lobbyist

For years, the U.S. steel industry has sought protection from imported steel on the grounds that foreign steel makers were unfairly dumping cheap steel in America. From time to time, administrations from Reagan to Clinton bought this argument and provided relief in the form of tariffs and quotas. Yet the domestic steel industry never seemed to do any better in world markets. This led to some initial reluctance on the part of the Bush administration to offer even more protection for this floundering industry. That is, until the steel beams of the World Trade Center melted and sent the icons of American capitalism crumbling into the streets of New York City.

Immediately after September 11th the steel industry junked its call for tariffs on the grounds of predatory pricing and adopted a new strategy for gaining artificial protection from competition. The new argument was simple. Steel is needed to build tanks, guns, and jets, and steel will be needed to rebuild the World Trade Center if that should occur.

If the steel industry in America dies, so say the steel unions and steel executives, Osama bin Laden or some other enemy of America would eventually attempt to disrupt the supply of foreign steel coming to America and the U.S. would be at greater risk of losing the war on terrorism.[54] Thus began the lobbying efforts to impose tariffs on foreign rivals.

Not only that, but the steel industry sought a $12 billion bailout – specifically asking the Bush administration to use taxpayer dollars to take over the retiree pension and health insurance obligations of the major steel producers.[55]

CONCEPT CHECK

Go online and research the "Golden Arches Theory of International Conflict." Does it appear to be a theory that supports free trade? Why, or why not?

President Bush finally caved into the political pressure to do something about the weakened steel industry. With steel-producing states being key battleground states in the 2002 Congressional elections and the 2004 presidential campaign, Mr. Bush felt the politically rational thing to do was capitulate to the calls for help. His help came in the form of the aforementioned 30% increase in the tariff on flat-rolled steel that is used to make cars and appliances. Steel rebar – used in construction and highways – got a 15% tariff, while other products like hot rolled steel, stainless wire, tool steel, stainless flanges, and slab got tariffs ranging from 8% to 24%.[56] Do you remember the law of unintended consequences? This law came into effect about three seconds after the Bush announcement.

What should this cost?

First, the European Union announced the possibility of increased tariffs on U.S. motorcycles, fruit juices, handguns, and textiles. Russia then banned the importation of all U.S. poultry – costing chicken producers over $600 million. Canada then imposed a 71% tariff on U.S. tomatoes. Canada also imposed a tariff on lumber from the U.S. that impacted our $6 billion market[57] and announced that a tariff on U.S. steel was being considered.[58]

Of course, well before President Bush imposed this tariff, steel-using companies and economists howled in protest. The Bureau of Labor Statistics pointed out that while approximately 160,000 people work in the steel industry, over *12 million* people work in steel-consuming jobs. This means companies like Whirlpool, Ford, John Deere and many other giants of industry would face much higher prices for steel. This would translate higher prices on consumers of washing machines, cars bulldozers, and so forth or a push to cut costs somewhere else – like labor hours, wages, benefits, or capital expenditures.[59]

Perhaps the greatest fear in the economics community was summed up by Gary Hufbauer of the Institute for International Economics, who said that the danger of the precedent-setting steel tariff was that, "the first big Faustian bargain on steel will be followed by a lot of mini-Fausts" in order to satisfy various constituencies.

For those of you who are unfamiliar with the famous story by Johann Wolfgang von Goethe, a "Faustian deal" is one where you give up a lot to gain a little. For President Bush, his deal with steel could cause other struggling industries to line up and look for a hand-out instead of looking into ways they can be more competitive in the

global arena. As we saw in the section on job losses, the steel tariff ultimately led to higher prices, less job creation, and a questionable use of taxpayer dollars just as the economy was struggling to rebound from the recession of 2001.

PROTECTING INFANT INDUSTRIES

An infant industry is one in its earliest stages of development. In some countries, this gives rise to the argument for government-induced insulation from competition. To economists, there is some merit to this type of protection under limited circumstances.

If Costa Rica – a nation rich in botanical wildlife – decided to create a biotechnology industry and protect it with tariffs and/or quotas on foreign pharmaceuticals, this would receive tepid support from a good number of economists if Costa Rica could rationally be expected to develop a comparative advantage in this relatively new industry. It would also be important to have some assurances that, once a comparative advantage was acquired and Costa Rican companies could compete head to head with U.S. and European drug companies, that the protectionist measures would be eliminated.

The fact that once support is given it may be lobbied for indefinitely is one reason why most economists would have trouble extending the hand of government to fledgling industries. Temporary support has a way of becoming permanent welfare very quickly.

TO PUNISH CHINA FOR "CURRENCY MANIPULATION"

A significant portion of this book has touched on China's rising economic power – and the factors that have precipitated this amazing occurrence.

What has not been broached is the question concerning the degree to which China has achieved some of this magnificent progress by artificial means. Specifically, many critics of China's economic policies point out the Chinese government places controls on the value of the Yuan – the Chinese currency.

The table below illustrates some of the various exchange rates when converting foreign currency into dollars, and vice versa. This data is from January 28, 2011, but will be useful for our purposes even if the data has changed by the time you are reading this section of the book.

Currency	1 U.S. dollar	in U.S. dollars
Australian Dollar	1.00746	0.992595
Brazilian Real	1.68522	0.593394
British Pound	0.631439	1.58368
Canadian Dollar	0.999	1.001
Chilean Peso	484.481	0.00206406
Chinese Yuan	6.58103	0.151952
Colombian Peso	1863.81	0.000536535
Danish Krone	5.47998	0.182482
Euro	0.734991	1.36056
Hong Kong Dollar	7.79318	0.128317
Hungarian Forint	202.063	0.00494895
Iceland Krona	116.597	0.00857655
Indian Rupee	45.8467	0.0218118

Suppose a citizen of China wanted to buy a GMC Yukon SUV that retailed for $38,000 in the United States. $38,000 x 6.58103 = 250,079.14 Yuan. By the same token, a new king-size bed sheet produced in China and sold for 444.71 Yuan, would mean a customer in a mall in Utah would pay $67.57 (444.71 x .151952).

The value of the dollar is determined by the same forces that create the value of anchovies and parachutes – the forces of supply and demand.

When people around the world are confident in the strength of the U.S economy and the economic policies of our government, the demand for our dollars typically rises. This causes the value of the dollar to rise. When the value of our dollar rises, our products become more expensive to folks in China and other nations; while Chinese, and other foreign goods, become cheaper in America.

Recently, as America has gone deeper into debt and has experienced a lengthy economic slump, the demand for dollars has fallen while government borrowing has increased the supply of dollars. This has lowered the value of the dollar, helping our exporters fare better in international markets while making the price of foreign goods rise in the U.S.

It is widely argued that if China allowed its currency to "float" with the forces of supply and demand, that the price of the Yuan would increase. Now each Yuan would be able to "purchase" fewer dollars. Let's say that a floating exchange rate would mean $1 (U.S) equals 4.24 Yuan. Therefore, each Yuan would now be worth $.235849. That GMC Yukon would now cost only 161,120 Yuan, while the bed sheet would cost $104.88 (444.71 x .235849).

The result, critics charge, would be greater exports of American goods to China, a falling trade deficit with this nation, and more economic growth for American industries that have a comparative advantage but are simply shut out of China's market.[60]

There are some problems with this argument that many economists have pointed out and can be discovered by you, if you are willing to take the time to do proper research.

For example, China has not officially pegged its currency to the dollar since 2005. During that time the value of China's currency has risen, but we continue to buy more from China than China buys from us. Among the many reasons for this reality is rising productivity in China; improvements in technological progress in China that has given it a growing share in world metals and equipment markets; a strong educational system that is turning out far more mathematicians, engineers, and scientists than America; and a continued move toward lower taxes and greater property rights.

While it is certainly possible that China has engaged in "unofficial" limits on the Yuan-to-dollar ratio, our problems with China extend well beyond currency markets. Quite often political realities overcome economic ones, when facing economic realities would get politicians in trouble.

FINAL THOUGHTS

Free and open trade creates new jobs and new income. It lifts the lives of all our people. It spurs the progress of economic and legal reform, and open trade reinforces the habit of liberty and sustains democracy.

President George Bush, speaking during the Summit of the Americas, April 2001

Yes, that was one year before the steel tariff decision. During this semester, you have been exposed to a great number of topics that not all economists agree on. As you can see, not even the president agrees with his own statements from time to time. Hopefully, it is somewhat comforting to end this chapter with a consensus view from the economics community.

The *winners* from international trade are fairly obvious.

Nations with a comparative advantage, skilled workers in America and other developed nations, unskilled workers in developing nations, the environment in the long run, and governments in terms of increased tax revenue and economic prosperity make up the beneficiaries of trade.[61] This is the case even with more and more white-collar jobs being "outsourced" to India, Russia, and China.

As we saw early in the textbook, there are actually more jobs coming in to American than there are going out. India's technology industry employed over 800,000 people in 2006. In America, over 10 million people had similar jobs.[62]

As long as America continues to achieve high levels of productivity, there will always be jobs that pay very well and that stay within our borders. The outsourcing of jobs was inevitable as India opens up to international trade.[63] However, this should be seen as an opportunity for Americans to increase our competitiveness rather than to run into the unproductive hole of protectionism. As the great economist David Ricardo taught us long ago, trade leads to shared gains, not gains for one at the expense of another.

It should also be noted that the United States has benefited from international trade in a less obvious manner – a slower rate of illegal immigration. Increased trade with Mexico has created greater prosperity in Mexico. Greater prosperity has led to a lessened need of many Mexicans to try to enter the U.S. illegally. While 2007 saw a tremendous debate about illegal immigration, there would be even more immigrants if not for NAFTA.

It is also somewhat interesting that as the value of the dollar fell in 2008, the demand for American goods increased dramatically overseas. From 2007 to 2008 exports increased by $115 billion and made up 13.5% of the gross domestic product – the highest level since World War II.[64] 2011 saw further movement upward in America's presence overseas.

Many of the winners during this time frame were small regional economies like Greenville, South Carolina, Waterloo, Iowa, and Kingsport, Tennessee, where the production of everything from turbines and forklifts to tractors and chemicals help propel much of the country forward while housing, banking, and other sectors faltered.

The *losers* from international trade have been many of America's unskilled workers in manufacturing industries, lower-skilled jobs in the technology sector, as well as industries that cannot stand up to the pressure of global competition.

One thing is certain: As technology continues to develop and the goal of economic freedom continues to be embraced around the globe, markets will become ever more interconnected. As that occurs, Adam Smith's treatise on the value of self-interest and liberty will be the standard-bearer for the global economy. As long as people desire more goods and services than can be found in their own nation, free trade will be rationally pursued.[65]

THE FUTURE OF TRADE – RELATIVELY FREE MARKETS?

In 2002, Congress voted to give President Bush five years of greater latitude to pursue expanded free trade opportunities. This agreement did not come without a potentially high price, however. In the narrowly passed legislation, U.S. union members stood to gain $1.2 billion from the newly created Trade Adjustment Assistance Program.

This taxpayer-financed program was designed to provide help to workers who lose their jobs to foreign competition. For example, people over 50 who lose jobs due to trade would qualify for $5,000 a year in "wage insurance" if they end up taking a job that is lower-paying than the one they had before trade eliminated their job.

Farmers also gained – at the expense of taxpayers – by authorizing subsidies of $100 billion over ten years. This particular feature was particularly galling to many of our foreign trading partners that have been trying to crack our agricultural markets for years. The subsidies give American farmers an advantage in global markets and thwart the progress toward more open markets.

During the 2004 presidential campaign, John Kerry moved away from the policy stance of Bill Clinton by advocating a much more interventionist role of government in international trade matters.[66] He advocated overhauling the U.S. tax code to raise taxes on corporations that outsource jobs and indicated that he would take a harder look at trade policies that did not provide more protection for labor union workers but did not advocate getting rid of agreements like NAFTA.[67]

In the 2008 campaign John McCain voiced support for free trade and said he would continue to work toward agreements with Columbia, South Korea, Panama and other nations. Barack Obama did not seem as enthusiastic about free trade – contending that he would renegotiate NAFTA and not pursue new trade agreements without more protections for union workers and the environment.[68] In the Ohio debate between Mr. Obama and Hillary Clinton, Mrs. Clinton repeatedly claimed that

Ohio had suffered greatly because of free trade. When Tim Russert, the debate moderator, produced data showing that Ohio had seen more jobs created because of trade Mrs. Clinton struggled to defend her position that free trade was working to our detriment.[69]

Mr. Obama and Mrs. Clinton are not alone in their reluctance to support the reduction of tariffs and quotas. Former Senator Robert Byrd from West Virginia was successful in getting legislation passed that has hurt the cause of freer trade. Under what is known as the Byrd Amendment, US companies that win anti-dumping and anti-subsidy cases against foreign rivals not only get higher US tariffs imposed on those competitors' goods but they also *receive the revenues* from those tariffs. This has led foreign governments to protest that the law unfairly punishes non-US suppliers not only with tariffs but also with subsidies for US rivals. In 2007 alone, companies received $264 million in compensation for not being an effective competitor.[70]

In this decade, we now face new challenges. As aforementioned, more and more Americans of all political persuasions and income brackets have come to believe that free trade is bad for our country. It is a bit odd that despite all of the things we wear, eat, and use every day from other nations, we still think somehow trade is harming us.

In "The Fatal Conceit" (1988), Friedrich Hayek wrote that, "man's instincts were not made for the kinds of surroundings, and for the numbers, in which he now lives." According to Hayek and modern-day evolutionary psychologists, it is man's natural instincts to believe that the world is a zero-sum world with a fixed number of jobs and a static amount of wealth.[71] Hence, if you get more, I must get less.

Recessions and 10% unemployment rates help magnify what may very well be our natural inclination to believe that one must lose if another person gains. The recent "Great Recession" therefore has quite possibly created a "Great Misunderstanding," that America can only regain her prosperity by closing off products from China and other nations.

Two final notes: First, the last time America bought into the wholesale notion that avoiding trade would rescue our economy, was in 1930 when we let our government pass the Smoot-Hawley Tariff Act. This Act led to enormous increases in the tariffs we required other nations to pay. Retaliation by those nations ensued, world trade collapsed, and the U.S. lurched even closer to entry into World War II.[72]

Second, as the United States continues its war against terrorism, it should be noted that there is a direct cause-and-effect link between open trade and economic wealth. The poorest nations – and the nations most plagued with terrorist activity – are the nations that are the most closed off from the rest of the world.[73]

ENDNOTES

1 See "Americans Sour on Trade" by Sara Murray and Douglas Belkin, *The Wall Street Journal*, October 4, 2010.

2 See "Aid is Good; Trade is Better" by Supachai Panitchpakdi, *The Wall Street Journal*, January 17, 2005; "Progenitor of the Paper Millionaires," *The Wall Street Journal*, July 19, 2000; and "We Want Trade, Not Aid" by Yoweri K. Museveni, *The Wall Street Journal*, November 6, 2003.

3 See "The Decline of Detroit" by John Schnapp, *The Wall Street Journal*, July 14-15, 2007.

4 See "Detroit's automakers lose ground to imports" by Tom Krisher, *The Orlando Sentinel*, August 2, 2007.

5 See "Why Toyota Won" by James P. Womack, *The Wall Street Journal*, February 13, 2006; and "Behind GM's Slide: Bosses Misjudged New Urban Tastes" by Lee Hawkins Jr., *The Wall Street Journal*, March 8, 2006.

6 The last year such comprehensive data was available was 1992. However, individually, the numbers have not changed dramatically from 1992 through 2011.

7 See "Shrimp Gets a Makeover, as Foreign Imports Rise" by Katy McLaughlin, *The Wall Street Journal*, August 19, 2004; and "Trade and Aid Clash over Shrimp Tariffs" by Greg Hitt, *The Wall Street Journal*, April 25, 2005.

8 This is not a new sentiment. During the time he was emperor of France, Napoleon implemented tariffs on farm products to aid French farmers. Source: Museum of Florida History, Tallahassee, Florida.

9 More than 8,000 products have tariffs attached to them when they arrive in the U.S.

10 See "'Fair Trade' is Unfair" by James Bovard, *Newsweek*, December 9, 1991, p.13.

11 See *The Fair Trade Fraud* by James Bovard, St. Martin's Press, 1991.

12 See "The Great Brassiere War," *The Wall Street Journal*, November 19, 2003; and "U.S. Moves to Limit Textile Imports from China" by Edmund L. Andrews, *The New York Times*, November 19, 2003.

13 See "Bush Seeks to Use Backlash on Jobs as Lever in India" by Michael Schroeder and Jay Soloman, *The Wall Street Journal*, March 8, 2004.

14 See "A U.S. History of Trade Hypocrisy" by James Bovard, *The Wall Street Journal*.

15 See "The Great Ice Cream War" by James Bovard, *The Wall Street Journal*, September 14, 1990.

16 See *The Fair Trade Fraud*, Bovard, p. 66.

17 See "U.S. panel order tariffs on Brazilian OJ" *The Orlando Sentinel*, August 18, 2005.

18 See "Steeling Our Wealth," *The Wall Street Journal*, September 23, 2003.

19 See "The Steel Tariffs' Costs," *The Wall Street Journal*, February 25, 2003; "Bush's Steel Opening," *The Wall Street Journal*, November 11, 2003; and "Lessons of Steel," *The Wall Street Journal*, December 2, 2003, p. A18.

20 See "So Far, Steel Tariffs Do Little of What President Envisioned" by Neil King Jr. and Robert Guy, *The Wall Street Journal*, September 13, 2002.

21 Arthur T. Denzau of St. Louis's Washington University found that restrictions on imported steel in the 1980s saved 17,000 jobs in the steel industry and among its suppliers. However, the higher prices that resulted led to the loss of 52,400 jobs in American steel-using industries. For every job saved, three were lost.

22 See "U.S. Tariffs on Steel are Illegal, World Trade Organization Says" by Elizabeth Becker, *The New York Times*, November 11, 2003; and "The White House Steel Trap" *The New York Times*, November 11, 2003.

23 See "U.S. Nears Mexican Cement Pact" by Jim Carlton, *The Wall Street Journal*, August 29, 2005.

24 See "Clinton's Sugar Daddy Games Now Threaten NAFTA's Future" by Mary Anastasia O'Grady, *The Wall Street Journal*, December 20, 2002.

25 See "A Saga of Politics and Candy Canes" by Sean Mussenden, *The Orlando Sentinel*, December 24, 2002.

26 See *The Commanding Heights* by Daniel Yergin and Joseph Stanislaw, Simon & Schuster, 1998.

27 See The Heritage Foundation's: NAFTA's *Three-Year Report Card: An "A" for North America's Economy* by John Sweeney.

28 See "The Triumph of NAFTA," *The Wall Street Journal*, January 12, 2004 p. A14; and "Free Trade Accord at Age 10: The Growing Pains are Clear" by Elizabeth Becker, Clifford Krauss, and Tiem Weiner, *The New York Times,* December 27, 2003.May 16, 1997.

29 See "We're # 1 And It Hurts" by George C. Church, *Time*, October 24, 1994.

30 See "Is Free Trade Immoral?" *The Wall Street Journal*, February 26, 2004, p. A10.

31 Source: http://www.aiada.org/

32 Source: May 16, 1995, edition of the *CBS Evening News.*

33 See "Hanging by a Thread" by Roger Thurow and Scott Kilman, *The Wall Street Journal*, June 26, 2002.

34 See "Come on, America, Play By the Rules!" by Pascal Lamy, *The Wall Street Journal*, March 3, 2003; "Why Can't America Be More Like Us?" by Franz Fischler, *The Wall Street Journal*, February 19, 2004; and "Brave New World" by Supachai Panitchpakdi, *The Wall Street Journal*, February 26, 2004.

35 See "A Guardian of Jobs or a 'Reverse Robin Hood'" by Leslie Wayne, *The New York Times*, September 1, 2002.

36 See "The U.S. Builds a Fishy Case Against Chilean Salmon" by Greg Rushford, *The Wall Street Journal*, September 26, 1997.

37 See "Predation: The Changing View in the Economics and the Law" by James C. Miller III and Paul Paulter, *Journal of Law & Economics,* vol. XXVIII (May 1985); "Not So Fast: The Myth of Predatory Pricing– Exposed" by Rob Norton, *Fortune*, February 7, 2000, p. 49.

38 See "The errors in closing the border to our beef," *The Globe and Mail*, June 27, 2005.

39 See "It looks like it's time to play let's make a deal in the softwood dispute" by Barry McKenna, *The Globe and Mail*, July 26, 2005.

40 See "Deal expected on textile imports," *The Orlando Sentinel*, August 18, 2005.

41 See "Tension rises over textile exports" by Lorrie Grant, *USA Today*, June 1, 2005, p. 5B.

42 See "How the Textile Industry Alone Won Quotas on Chinese Imports" by Greg Hitt, *The Wall Street Journal,* November 10, 2005; and "Bush trade nominee talks tough on China" by Christopher Swann and Edward Alden, *Financial Times*, April 22, 2005.

43 See "Protect Us From Protectionists" by Richard W. Fisher, *The Wall Street Journal*, April 25, 2005.

44 See "China Irks U.S. as It Uses Trade to Embellish Newfound Clout" by Peter Wonacott and Neil King Jr., *The Wall Street Journal*, October 3, 2005.

45 See "Prime Numbers," *The Chronicle of Higher Education*, May 19, 2000, p. A14.

46 See "Rising Wages will Burst China's Bubble" by Peter Tasker, *Financial Times*, January 10, 2011.

47 See "U.S. Apparel Retailers Turn Their Gaze Beyond China" by Elizabeth Holmes, *The Wall Street Journal*, June 15, 2010.

48 See "The Left Should Love Globalization" by Francis Fukuyama, *The Wall Street Journal*, December 1, 1999; and "U.S. Trade Law Gives Africa Hope and Hard Jobs" by Marc Lacy, *The New York Times*, November 14, 2003.

49 See "Czech Republic's air pollution sickens and enrages citizens," *The Orlando Sentinel,* February 15, 1993.

50 See "Does Helping the Planet Hurt the Poor?" by Bjorn Lomborg, *The Wall Street Journal*, January 22-23, 2011, p. C1.

51 Source: The American Lung Association.

52 For more on this issue, see "NAFTA: Part of the Trade-Environment Solution" by Kathryn S. Fuller, *The Wall Street Journal*, July 16, 1993.

53 See "Obama and Trade" *The Wall Street Journal*, December 6, 2010, p. A18.

54 See "Steelmakers Say They Are a Key Component of Security" by Robert Guy Matthews, *The Wall Street Journal*, September 19, 2002, p. B4.

55 See "Big Steel Still Enjoys Outsized Clout on Trade" by David Wessel, *The Wall Street Journal*, December 6, 2001; and "Steel's Shakedown Attempt Will Test Bush's Resolve" by George Melloan, *The Wall Street Journal*, January 22, 2002.

56 See "Imposing Steel Tariffs, Bush Buys Some Time for Troubled Industry" by Robert Guy Matthews and Neil King Jr., *The Wall Street Journal*, March 6, 2002.

57 See "So Far, Bush's Gamble on Steel Tariffs Isn't Paying Off" by Neil King Jr. and Michael M. Phillips, *The Wall Street Journal*, March 27, 2002, p. A20.

58 See "Canada Weighs Imposing Tariffs on Steel," *The Wall Street Journal*, March 28, 2002, p. A2.

59 See "Bush's Steel Trap: Tariff to Aid Producers Anger Users" by Neil King Jr., *The Wall Street Journal*, February 11, 2002, p. A24.

60 See "China Trade and American Jobs" by Daniel Ikenson, *The Wall Street Journal*, April 2, 2010.

61 See "Human Betterment Through Globalization" by Vernon L. Smith, speech before the Foundation for Economic Education, September 2005; and "We Grow, They Grow" by David Malpass, *The Wall Street Journal*, November 3, 2004.

62 See "An Outsourcing Giant Fights Back" by Saritha Rai, *The New York Times*, March 21, 2004.

63 See "Creative Jobs Destruction," *The Wall Street Journal*, January 6, 2004.

64 See "Second Thoughts on Free Trade" by Charles Schumer and Paul Craig Roberts, *The New York Times,* January 6, 2004; and *Open World: The Truth About Globalization* by Philippe Legrain, Ivan R. Dee, 2004.

65 See "Trade Keeps Growing, Despite Stalled Global Talks" by John W. Miller, *The Wall Street Journal*, January 31, 2011.

66 For more on the Clinton administration's trade policies, see "They Support Free Trade, Except in the Case of..." by David E. Rosenbaum, *The New York Times,* November 16, 2003, and *The Commanding Heights: The Battle between Government and the Marketplace that is Remaking the Modern World* by Daniel Yergin and Joseph Stanislaw, Simon & Schuster, 1998.

67 See "Kerry Targets Job Outsourcing With Corporate-Tax Overhaul" by Bob Davis and John Harwood, *The Wall Street Journal*, March 26, 2004; and "Free Trade becomes hot campaign issue" by Tom Raum, *The Associated Press* (appearing in *The Tallahassee Democrat*), February 22, 2004, p. 6A.

68 See "Trade: What Exactly is a Free Trader, Anyway?" *The Wall Street Journal*, August 25, 2008.

69 To see this exchange between Mr. Russert and Mrs. Clinton log on to: http://www.youtube.com/results?search_query=february+26+ohio+debate&search_type=&aq=f

70 See "An expensive Byrd," *The Wall Street Journal*, September 11, 2008, pg. A14.

71 See "The Protectionist Instinct" by Paul H. Rubin, *The Wall Street Journal*, October 7, 2010.

72 See "Goodbye, Free Trade?" by Douglas A Irwin, *The Wall Street Journal*, October 9-10, 2010.

73 See "The Map that Predicted the Terrorist Attacks" by Mark Skousen, *FEE Today,* 2002.

CHAPTER REVIEW

1. What is the principle of comparative advantage? How does this principle explain the benefits of open trade between states and nations?

2. Fully explain four of the major reasons given for tariff protection and what most economists think about the justification given.

3. What are two reasons for tariffs and quotas that economists sometimes support? Why is the support given?

4. What is predatory pricing? Does it work? Why, or why not?

A BIOLOGICAL APPROACH
to the THEORY *of the* FIRM

Photo courtesy Jack Chambless

*T*hose who realize positive profits are the survivors;
those who suffer losses disappear.

ARMEN ALCHIAN

Historically, economics students have been exposed to the concept of profit under the assumption that organizations of widely disparate sizes and structures have the ability to know how to maximize profit.

In this chapter we will take a detailed look at the various types of business firms that exist in our economy and how the concept of profit "maximization" is flawed in the real world of competition. By gaining insight into the true meaning of pursuing profit, you will see that our economy is actually a system – much like an ecosystem – that selects profitable business firms for success and unprofitable ones for extinction.

TYPES OF BUSINESS FIRMS

In our economic system we have three major types of business firms.

THE SOLE PROPRIETORSHIP

A sole proprietorship is a business owned by one person. By far, the most popular form of business organization in the U.S. – accounting for about 70% of all business firms – this type of business has several advantages and disadvantages.

A major *advantage* of the sole proprietorship, of course, is that all profits earned go back to one person. Another significant draw to this type of business is the autonomy: One person makes all of the decisions that impact the business.

Among the *disadvantages* of the sole proprietorship are the strict liability associated with decisions, lower odds of obtaining credit for new ventures, less operating capital, fewer people to disseminate ideas, and higher bankruptcy rates.

THE PARTNERSHIP

A partnership is a business owned by two or more persons, each of whom receives a portion of any profits. Because more than one person is involved, a partnership has more opportunity to expand than a sole proprietorship and greater access to various skills of the individuals who run the business.

However, partnerships can be fraught with difficulties. One of the key problems that can emerge is conflict that arises in the decision-making process. Since no two personalities are guaranteed to mesh at all times, it is a given that partnerships will run into cooperation barriers that result from different perspectives, agendas, or perhaps risk-taking characteristics. Some of these reasons might help explain why a partnership is the least popular type of business arrangement, with approximately 10% of all firms falling into this category.

THE CORPORATION

A corporation is a business legally established under state laws that grant it an identity separate from that of its owners. From the legal standpoint, a corporation is a legal person. By incorporating, owners of a firm create an organization than can legally own property, incur debts, and can be granted many of the other legal rights of a citizen, including the right to engage in litigation. Any group of people can form a corporation by obtaining a corporate charter from one of the 50 states. While corporations represent about 20% of America's business firms, they account for about 90% of total sales revenue!

There are several distinguishing features of the corporation. First, the corporation is owned entirely by its stockholders who have purchased shares of ownership in it. These shares are called *stock*. If you own 100 shares of Google stock, for example, you own a small percentage of Google. The percentage depends on the number of outstanding shares of stock that Google has issued. As a

CONCEPT CHECK

Why do corporations spend more on advertising than sole proprietorships do?

Photo courtesy Jack Chambless

stockholder, you have certain rights. You can vote for the directors of the corporation and on other issues.

A second feature of the corporation is that stockholders are entitled to a share of the corporation's income. The portion of any corporate profits paid to its stockholders is called *dividends*. Dividends are paid to stockholders on a per-share basis. The portion of profit that is not paid out is called *retained earnings*. Retained earnings are usually held to help finance new ventures, expansions, research and development, and so forth.

Third, stockholders cannot be held personally liable for the debts of the corporation. *Limited liability* is a legal provision that protects the owners of a corporation (its stockholders) by putting a ceiling on how much a person can lose if the corporation goes out of business. That ceiling is equal to the amount of money a person has invested in the company. This is an enormous advantage that the corporate form of organization has over the sole proprietorship or partnership. Limited liability makes it much easier for a corporation to raise money.

It is also a tremendous advantage that a stockholder can sell his or her shares of ownership relatively easily. This ability to transfer private property within seconds helps make the corporation a safer investment than other business firms.

There is a downside to this type of firm. One key problem is the fact that there is *separation of owners from managers* in the corporation. This can lead to conflicts of interest. The stockholders in the Disney Corporation might not have approved of Disney's expansion of health care benefits to partners in homosexual relationships. However, stockholders have a limited voice – based on their shares of ownership – in Disney's business plans.

Another problem is the issue of *double-taxation*. The corporate income tax subjects profits earned by the corporation to tax. Whatever is paid out in dividends is then hit with personal income tax. When stocks are sold, the capital gains tax applies. All of this can dilute the value of owning stock. In balance, the market has apparently decided that the benefits of the corporation outweigh the costs, because over 25% of the U.S. labor force is employed by a corporation and the majority of income is earned at this level.

WHAT ECONOMISTS KNOW ABOUT PROFIT

If you have ever taken an accounting class, you know that accountants are great with numbers. If you ask an accountant to define profit, he will say, "Total revenue minus total cost." This sounds very simple, so let's complicate matters a little by looking at how economists think about profit.

The publisher of this book has provided you with this product (with my help) for the purpose of profit. Suppose this book sells 10,000 copies around the country over the next year at an average price of $97. That would mean total revenue of $970,000. If the total cost in terms of royalties, paper, editing, printing, permissions, taxes, etc. comes to $70 per book that would mean a total accounting cost of $700,000. To the accountant, Kendall-Hunt has cleared $270,000 in accounting profit. Not so fast.

Suppose – rather than publishing this book – the publisher had produced an interactive CD-ROM with the same material that is in this book. Suppose the CD-ROM would have generated $118,000 in income for the publisher. To the economist, the economic profit is measured by the difference between total revenue and the sum of the accounting cost, *plus the opportunity cost* of this book.

Total Revenue: $970,000
Accounting Cost: $700,000
Opportunity Cost: $118,000
Accounting + Opportunity Cost = $818,000
Economic Profit = $152,000
(Total revenue – Accounting + Opportunity Cost)

Why does a business need to include opportunity cost in their profit calculations? It is very simple. If a firm ignores the value of the next-best alternative use of their operating funds, they may pass up on opportunities that are more profitable than the path selected.

WHERE TRADITIONAL ECONOMICS GETS IT WRONG

Charlie Trotter is a world-renowned chef and the owner of a restaurant in Chicago's Lincoln Park that bears his name. *Wine Spectator* once voted Mr. Trotter the best chef in America, yet Mr. Trotter has more lofty goals – "to be the best restaurant in the world."[1]

With incredibly creative dishes like African pompano with macadamia nut crust, Bok Choy and spicy coconut emulsion, and oven-roasted rosemary plums with Friar plum sauce, and black sesame seed brittle ice cream, Mr. Trotter has been able to command prices that rise well above $450 for a couple dining out. Does this mean he is maximizing his profit? Would he make more money by opening a few more restaurants around the globe that bear his illustrious name? Could he make more money by lowering his prices just a bit? Would even higher prices do the trick? Should he seek to reduce or increase the salaries he pays his staff? How should he plan for the next recession?

These are just a few of the thousands of questions that Mr. Trotter has to consider over time. To the economics community, Mr. Trotter must seek to charge prices that coincide with unit elasticity, all while making sure his productivity is maximized. This is the theory students have learned for years. The reality of the business world does not fit so neatly into a three-ringed binder or executive summary. The reality of business is that the only thing that is certain is *uncertainty*. Mr. Trotter knows no more about what exact prices to charge to maximize revenue on any given day, or how to extract maximum productivity, than the rest of the business world knows when the next downturn in the business cycle will take place. Welcome to biological economics.

INTRODUCTION TO BIOLOGICAL ECONOMICS

When a great question is first started, there are very few, even of the greatest minds, which suddenly and instinctively comprehend it in all its consequences.

John Adams

For years, *The New York Times* and Anheuser-Busch (now Anheuser-Busch InBev) had something in common that allowed each company to thrive. That "something" was brand-name loyalty that allowed each company to earn profit during good times and bad. After all, during recessions people drink more and search the want ads in the paper. During times of economic prosperity, people drink more and read the paper to see what sporting event or concert is coming. You get the idea.

However, in recent times there has been an environmental shift that has both companies worried. In fact, this shift has almost all newspapers and beer producers concerned.

Over the past couple of years, breweries have noticed a shift in consumer tastes away from beer and more toward wine, liquor and flavored alcoholic beverages.[2] As a result, the overall demand for beer has begun to slump, leaving the major brewers scrambling for answers to this new dilemma.

The picture is even more dire for America's newspapers. In this marketplace there seems to be an unending assault from every direction. Economist Joseph Schumpeter once argued that markets go through a sort of "creative destruction." This means that over time, unexpected changes take place in any market-based system that requires a reaction by participating capitalists in order to continue to prosper. Often that reaction is one that sees businesses destroying old ways of doing things – or having their competitors destroy them – in order to make way for a new – and hopefully superior way of doing business.

For newspapers, Schumpeter's analysis is clear. Today people can get news from the Internet, their phones, constant cable television coverage and more. What sense does it make to wait for the morning paper to arrive with sports scores and the weather when you can simply lift your cell phone off your night stand, turn it on and see the highlights and predicted rain in an instant?

This permanent shift in the market for news was not reacted to soon enough by American's newspapers. Many of them did not see Internet advertising as a major threat to their traditional cut and paste form of marketing. As a result, most papers are struggling, readership is in decline and consolidation has begun to take place – where buyers can be found.[3]

Not surprisingly, newspapers – and the beer industry – have begun to respond to this free market pressure. Smaller market papers in places like Bakersfield, California have not only expanded their web-based advertising options, but have reached out to younger readers with subjects and features that are traditionally not found in daily papers, while the beer industry has seen an increase in the number of mergers and has begun looking for new customers among younger minorities as well as offering new varieties of beers.[4]

These and other examples like them indicate that business firms are not unlike a species that must respond to changes in the environment in order to have a chance to survive.

The economy is like an ecosystem that must endure drought, tornadoes, global warming, and earthquakes. When the ecosystem gradually changes from, say, a slight drop in temperatures, burrowing animals might have to forage for food a little longer. When a blizzard strikes, some of those animals who are strong will survive, while the weak will die. When an ice age comes along, all bets are off as to who will emerge as a survivor.

If this sounds like the theory of natural selection, well, it is. If you are wondering if Darwin knew economics, he did. Let us begin our process of blending what we know about biology with what we know about economics. Since the two subjects are so similar, this would seem like an appropriate thing to do.

CHARLES DARWIN, ECONOMIST?

As a 22-year-old amateur geologist and naturalist, Mr. Darwin began his international journeys believing, like most people, that species were individually designed and placed in their habitats by the Creator. Over time, Darwin became convinced that if the Earth itself undergoes profound changes associated with volcanoes, drought, hurricanes, and so forth, individual species can, and do, also undergo evolutionary changes.[5]

Over the years, Darwin spent countless hours studying the forces that shape biology and geology, along with the social sciences like psychology and economics. It was his research in economics that led him to the writings of Adam Smith. Smith's contention that human beings are led by "an invisible hand" to promote their self-interest, and therefore the long-run interests of mankind, was very influential in the development of Darwin's writings on natural selection. Darwin and Smith shared the view that unguided activities of diverse individuals could generate a coherent overall trend.[6]

However, the turning point in Darwin's evolution as a scientist came with his readings of the works of Thomas Malthus, an economist who had examined the relationship between the population of the Earth and the resources available to sustain it. Malthus argued that if the growth of the population outstrips the available food supply (an event he thought was inevitable), certain members of society – the weaker or poorer ones – would die off, leaving the more affluent or "strong" members of the world to survive.

In 1859, Darwin published *The Origin of Species*, which put forth the concept of "natural selection" as an evolutionary force that creates winners and losers across the globe. Natural selection holds that, because parents tend to produce more offspring than can be supported by the environment's limited resources, and because every individual is genetically different from every other individual, those offspring who are born with physical characteristics giving them even a modest edge in life's competition for food, space, and security stand a better chance than their siblings of surviving long enough to have their own offspring.

Over time, as one generation follows another, the effects of the probabilities accumulate, and nature selects those creatures most suited to their environment.[7] The applications of the concept of natural selection to economics are straightforward and intellectually appealing. Consider how physical attractiveness and athleticism plays a role in determining economic success.

Tom Brady – the quarterback of the New England Patriots is a classic example of the process of natural selection. With good looks and/or athletic ability comes a greater likelihood that the market will select a person for success.[8]

Shutterstock © r.nagy, 2011.

CONCEPT CHECK

Studies show that women from nations with healthier populations prefer men with more feminine-looking features, while women in poorer nations prefer more masculine-looking men.[7] Why might this be the case? Does this make economic sense? Why, or why not?

Social scientists have noticed that beautiful people often are more successful in finding attractive and/or successful mates. Studies also show that the more symmetrical a person's face and body are, the more attractive the person is considered to be. Because Mr. Brady – who routinely appears in magazines advertising clothes and cologne – is considered to be a very attractive man, he had a greater likelihood of attracting other good-looking people. Since looks play a part in the long-term success of a large portion of the population, being good-looking raises the probability that a person will be economically advantaged over time.

It also is plausible to expect Mr. Brady to have sons or daughters who have a good chance of being athletic. Notice that many professional athletes end up having sons who also play professional sports. Clay Matthews of the Green Bay Packers is the third consecutive member of this family to end up in the NFL. With athletic genes comes an enhanced probability of having an athletic progeny.

NATURAL SELECTION AND PROFIT

The preceding examination of the concept of natural selection poses some difficult questions for the traditional textbook evaluation of the business firm, as well as the concept of profit maximization as the determining factor of success or failure. In reality, the goal of maximizing profits is an unrealistic, and in some cases impossible, goal. That is not to say that a business firm should not try to make as much profit as possible. It simply means that to the biological economist, the realization of maximum profit is not a requirement of success.

Think about what would happen if you were backpacking with one of your siblings or friends in the wilds of Wyoming. You stumble across a grizzly bear that is late for breakfast. You, along with everyone on Earth, cannot outrun a grizzly bear. However, being able to outrun the bear is not as important as *being able to outrun your sibling or friend*.

In the real world of business, the same principle holds true. It is a sufficient condition of success to realize a *positive distribution of profit* over time. In other words, in the Darwinian landscape facing business firms, the strongest companies – *relative to their next-best competitor* – are selected for success. There are multitudinous examples of businesses that do not maximize profit, but are still operating successfully because some profit is being earned.

HOW UNCERTAINTY AND EVOLUTION IMPACT SUCCESS

Economists Gerhard Tintner and Armen Alchian argue that business firms are not individual units making decisions that are separate from the economic system. Rather, the business firm is shaped by the adoptive mechanism of the economic system itself. This is to say that each day, hundreds upon thousands of microeconomic decisions are made, and their outcome is totally uncertain. Whether the decision will be a profitable one, or one that may lead to bankruptcy, is entirely dependent on the economic systems' willingness to select that decision for success or failure.

Leaders of business are plagued by two major problems. The first is *uncertainty*.[10] The second problem is that there are *too many variables* that are exogenous (outside of our control) to the profit equation for any one individual firm to be able to make decisions that are immune from the punitive aspects of those variables.[11]

Consider the impact weather has on any number of businesses. A sinkhole beneath a popular recreational lake is one example of how uncertainty can create havoc for a business. Suppose a brand-new jet-ski shop opened up the week before the sinkhole did. How does the owner of this shop predict whether a drought will lead to a sinkhole, which will lead to a black hole, where his investment disappears? From the blizzard that hit the U.S. Midwest in 2011, to flooding in Australia and wildfires in California, some businesses, like airlines and farmers, get hurt, while others, that sell everything from mold removal services to cadaver storage equipment, flourish.[12] There is more....

Who would have predicted that a small Arkansas-based firm that specialized in building large shopping centers in rural areas would become so successful?

Can you imagine what might have happened if Wal-Mart founder Sam Walton would have approached investment bankers 40 years ago pitching the idea that small-town folks like to get good prices and large selections just like their friends in metropolitan areas, and therefore money should be spent serving them with large stores? He would have probably been laughed out of the offices of these bankers who were trained in the traditional economic setting. Now we have Wal-Mart selling everywhere – and everything.

How many banks that were heavily invested in south Florida condominiums actually could see a time when the housing market would collapse? How about Nike? In a major golf tournament, golfer Tiger Woods putted a golf ball that slowly rolled toward the hole. With television cameras panning in toward the ball, it stopped right in front of the hole with a perfect shot of the Nike logo for millions of people to see.[13] How much was that free advertising worth? How much less were Nike golf balls worth when Tiger Woods ended up getting in a lot of marital trouble?

Speaking of trouble, in the wake of the "Great Recession of 2007-2009," many business leaders complained incessantly that the recovery of 2010-2011 was proceeding too slowly because the government was creating uncertainty.

You may recall that as late as December of 2010 with unemployment near 10%, the Obama Administration was pushing for tax increases on every American earning more than $250,000. Most small business owners fall into this category. All corporate leaders do.

With the prospect of rising taxes in the middle of an economic recovery, many business leaders were reluctant to expand, invest and hire new workers because of the uncertainty surrounding how much the government would confiscate from future earnings.[14]

Because of these, and millions of examples like them, Alchian contends that, "Where foresight is uncertain, profit maximization is *meaningless* as a guide to specifiable action." This is certainly a new way of looking at economics. It means that, rather than focusing on some specifiable action that is forecasted to generate some level of maximum profit, business firms must understand that every decision made carries not one potential outcome, but a distribution of outcomes – and therefore a distribution of possible profits.

Therefore, the task at hand is for any company is to make decisions whose "potential outcome distribution is preferable," rather than choosing some profit-maximizing distribution.[15]

PROFIT AND UNCERTAINTY

Since the system a firm operates under dictates whether profit will be made, it is imperative that firms within the system make decisions that increase the probability of realized positive profits. By focusing on earning positive profits over time, rather than making decisions that shoot for a narrowly defined outcome of maximum profit, it is far more likely that the environment will select the firm for success. After all, in an economic system the realization of profit is the basis of success. Those firms who make profit – however large it may be – are the survivors. Those who don't, disappear. Survival hinges on the following endogenous and exogenous factors:

CHANCE

One glance at the newspaper will give you a very clear idea of why life is a random walk with an array of outcomes – good and bad. The idea of chance or "luck" applies to business firms regardless of how efficient a firm is or how careful the decision-making process is. It should be noted that it is not a necessary condition of profit that a firm be particularly adept. Positive profits are conveyed upon firms, who are better than their actual competitors, "even if the participants are ignorant, intelligent, skillful, etc."[17] Natural selection dictates that it is one's aggregate position relative to real competitors, rather than theoretical competitors that matters. This reality is why "luck" can sometimes make the difference between success and failure.

The makers of Gatorade set out to provide a drink that would help the University of Florida football team avoid fatigue. What they found was a formula that not only helped the Gator football players but athletes of all types as well. The scientists probably did not have fore-

CONCEPT CHECK

For years, Blockbuster Video was a dominant firm in the video-rental business. By 2011 Blockbuster was on the verge of bankruptcy while its rival, Netflix, flourished.[16] Where does the process of natural selection and the concept of uncertainty enter in to the evolving business of renting movies?

knowledge that the product would be a commercial hit.[18] Neither did the marine biology instructor who drew the figure that became SpongeBob SquarePants.[19] It is also unlikely that New Orleans mayor, Ray Nagin could have known how many prospective business owners he turned away when he said his desire was for New Orleans to become a "chocolate city."[20]

September 11th and the banking crisis of 2008 are perfect testaments to the random walk that all businesses take. On any given day the economic environment might pick you for success beyond your wildest dreams or for extinction, even if you are following every textbook definition of how to run a successful business.

When uncertainty exists in the business world, a portion of success or failure is always attributed to chance. The key for the business firm is make decisions in a manner that minimizes the possibility that chance will work against the firm. However, even if these steps are taken, we do not know whether the decisions are viable ones until the economic system – made up of competitors, consumers, and the government – have their say.

MUTATION

In nature, a mutation occurs when a member of a species creates an offspring that is significantly different than the common characteristics of the species. Years ago, in a forest in England, it was observed that a population of black moths had replaced the entire population of white moths. Scientists initially believed that the moths had adapted to the incessant smog created by local factories and had become black.

When they were white, birds had trouble spotting them on the white ash trees of the forest. When the pollution made the trees darker, perhaps the moths had to become darker to avoid detection. Later discoveries revealed that at some point two white moths had created a black mutant offspring that was better suited to avoid detection by birds. As the black moths mated, they created other black moths until predators had eliminated the white moths, leaving the black moths as the dominant group.

In business, mutation occurs when a company within an industry comes up with an entirely new product or way of doing business that is not in response to some change in the economic system. The invention of strips of plastic that will whiten your teeth and the introduction of diapers for chickens will help illustrate the concept of economic mutation.

THE ECONOMICS OF VANITY AND SILLINESS

When is the last time you were attracted to someone with black teeth? Enough said.

Crest – and other toothpaste manufacturers – know that we all want to look nice for our mates, or prospective mates. It also helps to have a nice smile at work. With this in mind, the toothpaste companies have been busy mutating their core product line in order to capitalize on our fear of being hideous. This has led to a dizzying array of gels, pastes, foams, and strips designed to whiten teeth. In particular, the makers of Crest White Strips have seen that people seem to prefer a strip of whitening gel to a brush-on paste.

With a wildly successful product, the makers of Crest White Strips took their product a step further by introducing Night Strips – a product that could be worn for up to 14 consecutive hours. Then another version of White Strips came out with the promise of dramatically whiter teeth in only seven days.

At this rate, we might someday see a product that will turn your teeth as white as snow instantaneously!

Predictably, the successful mutation of the teeth-whitening business by Crest has led to similar products by other toothpaste manufacturers.

Photo courtesy Jack Chambless

CONCEPT CHECK

More and more young boys are being placed in very competitive "travel leagues" in baseball, hockey and other sports. These leagues have almost daily practices and extremely long schedules. How much of a role does the average salary of an NHL goalie play in parent's decisions to place their sons in travel leagues? Should probability theory play a greater role? Why, or why not?

CONCEPT CHECK

In 2002 ChickenDiapers.com was formed to help people who keep chickens as house pets have a cleaner home. The company offers diapers for chickens since these birds cannot be trained to be housebroken.[21] Is this type of mutation one that stands a greater or lower chance of success? Why?

As Alchian put it:

> Wherever successful enterprises are observed, the elements common to these observable successes will be associated with success and copied by others in their pursuit of profits or success. What would otherwise appear to be merely customary, orthodox, nonrational rules of behavior, turns out to be codified imitations of observed success.

It should be noted that Alchian also points out that "Those who are different and successful become innovators, while those who fail become reckless violators of tried-and true rules." Simple mutation is not enough to guarantee profits.

TRIAL AND ERROR

The problem of uncertainty means that there are so many variables coming into play that a great idea one day (opening a hotel in New Orleans on August 1, 2005) is a terrible idea on another day (August 30, 2005). This is where the issue of trial and error becomes so important to the economic system in which any business operates.

Most of the time, in the world of business, you gather all the information you can about the probability a new idea or company will be successful, then you launch a trial. The trial either meets with success (positive profit) or failure (extinction of the idea or company). Consider these recent trials:

If you are a vertically challenged male in America, you might consider Gary Anders one of the greatest humans who ever lived. That is because he has offered up a mutated version of a men's clothing store in Chicago and Milwaukee. Mr. Anders – who is five feet, five inches tall – spent years wearing ill-fitting clothes purchased in department stores that cater to the "average" male or to the adolescent male. Either way, Mr. Anders felt that the market for men's clothing was in need of a new type of store that would feature a bright yellow sign on the door, five feet and eight inches off the ground, reading, "If you are taller than this line, the clothing will not fit you. Our store is exclusively for men 5'8" and under." Thus was born Napoleon's Tailor Shop in each of these Midwestern cities.[22]

So far Mr. Anders has managed to earn a nice profit from each of these stores, but he has noticed that fewer men frequent his establishment than one might expect. "Give me 10% of that market," says Mr. Anders, "and, man, I'd be living on a beach somewhere." The reason he is not yet at 10% of the height-deprived man's clothing market seems to have more to do with the embarrassment men face into walking in his store than the lack of a high-quality line of clothing. In his ads, he consciously avoids words like "small" and "short" in an effort to draw more men in. Only time will tell if this mutation in the world of retail will come up short of expectations.

With the issue of uncertainty surrounding any business idea or change in direction, all business firms must experiment with new concepts – bleach in detergent, side air bags, smoothies, voice recognition computers, and so forth – to find out what the economic landscape will tolerate. Of course, some trials end up as permanent features of the marketplace. Others, like disco music and bell-bottom jeans, are more cyclical. Trials like alcoholic beverages with caffeine and belly rings may be more fleeting and temporary, while some never get off the ground.

What is important is that businesses realize that a necessary condition for success is experimentation. Just like the lion in Africa that sometimes must leave his territory in search of more fertile feeding grounds, entrepreneurs must deviate from the status quo to find new avenues to profit.

CONCEPT CHECK

Do spinning rims make economic sense? Where will the poker craze end up? Will *Dancing with the Stars* be around 10 years from now?

HEREDITY

In biology, natural selection dictates that successful genetic characteristics are passed down from generation to generation. As a matter of fact, stronger members of a species tend to mate with other members who also possess good genes in order to increase the chances that the species will survive. The same is true in economics.

When Sam Walton (the founder of Wal-Mart) and J.C. Penney passed away, their companies did not go out of business. Had Messrs. Walton and Penney died in the earliest stages of their respective companies' development, it would have most likely spelled the end of their businesses. Instead, all of these firms survived. You may have noticed that in 2007, the Indianapolis Colts won the Super Bowl with Peyton Manning as the quarterback. One year later, the New York Giants won with Peyton's brother, Eli Manning playing quarterback. Sitting in a luxury box for both games was Archie Manning – the father of these men – who, you guessed it, played quarterback for the New Orleans Saints!

Just as Sam Walton and James Cash Penney passed on a successful way of doing business and a brand-name following that increased the chances of survival, Mr. Manning passed on his genes and experiences to Peyton and Eli, which increased their chances of playing quarterback in the NFL.

One reason so many new restaurants die in the first year is that there is no brand-name identity, or successfully tested model. Chains like Red Lobster and the Olive Garden can undergo difficult times and come out alive because there are enough strong business "genes" in their framework to overcome a great deal of adversity.

Heredity means that when terrorists crash jet airplanes into buildings or housing prices collapse those airlines and construction companies that have developed a strong set of business genes will be more likely to survive a dramatic downturn in air travel or home construction, or even be able to turn down taxpayer assistance. Such was the case of Southwest Airlines. This company has long exhibited the tendency to pursue – and be rewarded for – mutative behavior.

In its 30-plus-year history, Southwest has emerged as the most profitable airline in the United States by offering low fares, no-frill service, and a higher on-time arrival record to go along with fewer customer complaints and lost bags than other major carriers.

With a high level of efficiency and profit, Southwest was the only airline that did not lay off any workers in the wake of September 11th and actually went ahead with expansion plans, all while refusing to take part in the taxpayer-financed government bailout of the airline industry. You may have also noticed that in 2011, Southwest launched a series of commercials that mocked and criticized other airlines for baggage fees and surcharges for changing flights. This mutation from what has become "normal" in the airline industry was very cleaver and potentially profitable.

ADAPTATION

Do the plants in your home turn toward the sunny side of the room because of a conscious attempt to survive or because the leaves on the sunny side grow faster than those that are exposed to limited sunlight? Do business firms that make profit do so because of some *a priori* knowledge of what the market wants, or does the market force businesses to adapt to the system that is in place? If you remember your biology lessons, you know that business firms must adapt or face a greater likelihood of dying.[24]

Adaptation takes place when the economic environment undergoes some change and participants in that system change the way they do business in an attempt to be selected by the new environment as a successful adapter.

Adapting to changes in the environment has been the reason for an increase in the demand for larger-size lingerie. It has also led to the resurgence of Harley-Davidson. As America has become "larger," more women have clamored for lingerie that accommodates changes in body sizes.[25] As demand has grown, existing lingerie makers would not be wise to question why more women need larger-size lingerie. If suppliers care about profits, they will adapt to the change and ride it out until the demand for lingerie changes again.

SUGGESTED CLASSROOM DEBATE

In September of 2008, the Bush Administration authorized a $700,000,000,000 bailout of financial institutions in the United States.[23] Will bailing out the banks who participated in the historic collapse of the housing market lead to a stronger, or weaker banking and housing sector in the future?

CONCEPT CHECK

When wolves were first reintroduced to Yellowstone National Park, the elk and moose in the park did not know what wolves were. This led to a short run and long run adjustment in this ecosystem.[27] In many ways, Google's entry into the market for Internet services — and Microsoft's initial reaction to Google — mirrors what happened in Yellowstone. Fully explain. What will be Microsoft's long-run adjustment? Why?

Shutterstock © Daniel Korzeniewsi, 2011.

Harley-Davidson, after years of slumping sales — brought on by a huge increase in sales of cheaper Japanese models — finally got the message. With market share falling, Harley-Davidson changed the way it made motorcycles, by streamlining the production and inventory management systems and by updating its product to match the popular features of the Japanese bikes. After nearing bankruptcy, one of America's great institutions is once again making profit and having a hard time keeping motorcycles in the showrooms.[26]

Of course, adaptation is not a sufficient condition for success. Some adapters are selected for failure. Years ago, PepsiCo thought that the wave of clear products hitting the market (deodorant, gasoline, and so forth) meant that the time was right to come out with ClearPepsi. The environment hated that idea and selected this product for extinction.

The collapse of Lehman Brothers, AIG, and Bear Stearns is a classic example of adaptive behavior that went array. When housing prices began to increase exponentially, these firms — under pressure from the federal government and under pressure to maximize profits — jumped into the market to invest in bundled mortgages. These firms were simply adapting to what was seen as a new way to make money quickly.

The economic environment is now signaling banking firms that changes in investment strategies would be necessary to assure survival.

The way AIG and Lehman Brothers went about getting into this position is now very useful information — economic fertilizer, if you will — to other firms about how not to die or get sick. The nature of business is to observe successful firms and emulate their methodology, while watching those who failed and learning from their mistakes. Now that the federal government is playing a huge role in how these firms are run, future bank executives — assuming they don't want to be managed by the government — will have to run their affairs in a manner that is more accepted by the free market.

Adding It All Up

To the biological economist, the search for the accomplishment of maximum profit is a noble but relatively unrealistic goal. As it turns out, business firms know this already. This is why, when the demand for snow blowers falls during the winter, prices don't always fall to an equilibrium level. Sometimes surpluses are tolerated.

SUGGESTED CLASSROOM DEBATE

Over the past few decades, the overall popularity of baseball has fallen in the United States.[28] What environmental changes may have led to this reality? How can Major League Baseball adapt to this trend in order to increase the chances of profit in the future? Did banning steroids hurt or help baseball's desire for profit? Why?

This is because, if prices fall, an expectation of some permanence in low prices could be built into the consumer's mind. Companies might be willing to earn less profit, and live with surpluses, rather than deal with wild fluctuations in prices.

For the same reason, it is possible that maximizing productivity might be an elusive or even irrelevant proposition. How else can you explain why some companies seem perpetually understaffed or overstaffed? There are even corporate leaders, like the Google executives that are willing to forgo maximum profits in the name of practicing strong moral convictions. As long as profits are positive, any number of factors can be inconsistent with the profit maximization goal but not lead to the bankruptcy of the firm or industry in question.

DOES GOVERNMENT PROMOTE SURVIVAL OF THE UNFIT?

What do tariffs and quotas, price ceilings, price floors, affirmative action programs, welfare programs, and progressive taxes have in common? They all would make Charles Darwin roll over in his grave.

Often the government decides that markets are not working very well and that markets need be altered in order to bring about a fairer outcome. How well does this fairness goal go along with the principle of biological economics? For example, if the market price of rice decreases due to expanded supply, and rice farmers begin to suffer, the biological response would be to let them suffer.

The biological economist would argue that, by creating artificial price supports and welfare payments to farmers, the wrong signals are being sent. In essence, the government becomes a force that has the ability to insulate rice farmers from the deleterious changes in the economic environment. If some rice growers go under, only those rice farmers that were most efficient or best suited to adapt or mutate the way they do business would survive. This would give consumers lower rice prices and would signal future rice farmers that efficiency, rather than taxpayer-financed handouts, will be the key to survival.

The same is true for labor markets. Affirmative action programs that set aside job openings for protected classes – even when the protected person may not be the most qualified applicant – have the potential of forcing businesses to hire some people who may have lower productivity, while at the same time the protected person may be sent the signal that job qualifications are less important than being a member of the "right" group. Over time, businesses lose by having higher costs imposed upon them, while the protected group loses by having less incentive to be as competitive as possible.

Human beings are the only species on Earth that exerts valuable resources to prop up the weakest members of the species. This is done because we have compassion for our fellow man, but when compassion leads to gross inefficiencies in the economic system, the result can be negative for the people who are being protected, as well as for the individuals who have to provide the protection.

ENDNOTES

1 See "The Wizard of Ahs" by Jonathan Black, *Chicago*, September 1997, p. 109.

2 See "Vintners cheer growing taste for wine" by Tim Barker, *The Orlando Sentinel*, February 5, 2006.

3 See "The Future in Black and White" *The Wall Street Journal*, March 14, 2006; "Brave News World," by Gary Pruitt, *The Wall Street Journal*, March 16, 2006; "For Sale – Mostly Second-Rate Newspapers" by John Ellis, *The Wall Street Journal*, November 19-20, 2005; and "Hey, Buddy, Wanna Buy a Newspaper? How About a Dozen?" by Joseph T. Hallinan, *The Wall Street Journal*, March 14, 2006.

4 See "As Market Shifts, Newspapers Try to Lure New, Young Readers" by Julia Angwin and Joe Hagan, *The Wall Street Journal*, March 22, 2006; "Cervaza, Si' o No?" by Miriam Jordan, *The Wall Street Journal*, March 29, 2006; and "The Search for Fresh Beer" by G. Bruce Knecht, *The Wall Street Journal*, January 28-29, 2006.

5 See *Bionomics* by Michael Rothschild, Owl Books, 1990, pp. 37-38.

6 Rothschild at p. 39.

7 Rothschild at p. 39.

8 See "Good looks may mean better pay" by Jim Salter, *The Orlando Sentinel*, April 8, 2005; and "The Hunk Differential" by Hal Varian, *The New York Times*, August 28, 2003.

9 See "The Masculine Mystique" by Jena Pincott, *The Wall Street Journal*, March 27-28, 2010.

10 See "The Theory of Choice Under Subjective Risk and Uncertainty" by Gerhard Tintner, 9 *Econometrica* 298–304 (1941); and "Uncertainty, Evolution and Economic Theory" by Armen Alchian, in *Economic Forces at Work* 15–35, (1950).

11 For more on this, see "Uncertainty is an essential ingredient of progress" by Virginia Postrel, *The Wall Street Journal*, January 1, 2000, p. R16.

12 See "Disasters' Silver Lining: Green" by Sarah E. Needleman, *The Wall Street Journal*, June 17, 2010.

13 See "Product placement" by David Haugh, *The Orlando Sentinel*, April 13, 2005, p.C1.

14 See "Uncertainty and the Slow Recovery" by Gary S. Becker, Steven J. Davis and Kevin M. Murphy, *The Wall Street Journal*, January 4, 2010, p.A17.

15 Alchian at p. 18.

16 See "Netflix Sees Surge in Subscribers" by Nick Wingfield, *The Wall Street Journal*, January 27, 2011.

17 Alchian at p. 20.

18 See "Gator-Made" by Michael McLeod, *The Orlando Sentinel*, August 14, 2005.

19 See "Inspiration: Where Does it Come From?" by Arthur Lubow, *The New York Times Magazine*, November 30, 2003.

20 Mr. Nagin meant that he wanted New Orleans to be a predominantly African-American city. See "Livable city preferable to chocolate city" by Leonard Pitts, *The Orlando Sentinel*, January 22, 2006.

21 See "Fowl Fans See Golden Eggs in Catering to Pet-Chicken Market" by Sarah E. Needleman, *The Wall Street Journal*, July 8, 2010.

22 See "Napoleon's Tailor Has This Little Problem: Short Guys in Denial" by Jonathan Eig, *The Wall Street Journal*, January 18, 2002.

21 See "Lawmakers Battle Over Wall Street Rescue Plan" by Greg Hitt, Damian Paletta and Deborah Soloman, *The Wall Street Journal*, September 22, 2008.

22 For more on this concept, see "New corporate philosophy: Adapt or die" by Steve Kaufman, *The Orlando Sentinel*, January 8, 1995, p. H-6.

23 See "Fashion's New Frontier: Racy Lingerie for the Larger-Size Woman" by Rebecca Quick, *The Wall Street Journal*, February 3, 2000, p. B1.

24 See "Message to American companies: Rebuild from scratch" by Jon Van, *The Orlando Sentinel*, December 8, 1991, p. F-12.

25 See "The Decade of the Wolf" by Jena Ball, *Backpacker*, December 20, 2005.

26 See "Our Fading National Pastime" by John R. Miller, *The Wall Street Journal*, April 6, 2010, p. A17.

CHAPTER REVIEW

1. What is the difference between accounting profit and economic profit? Why do partnerships typically earn less profit than corporations?

2. What role does uncertainty, heredity, and natural selection play in determining whether a Minnesota-based canoe manufacturer will earn profit next year?

3. What is the difference between economic adaptation and mutation? Give some examples of each.

4. What would a biological economist say about the government's decision to force carmakers to raise fuel efficiency standards? How could we get higher fuel economy without government interference?

PURE COMPETITION

Photo courtesy Jack Chambless

*T*he natural price, or the price of free competition...is the lowest which can be taken, not upon every occasion indeed, but for any considerable time together...[It] is the lowest which the sellers can commonly afford to take, and at the same time continue their business.

ADAM SMITH

THINGS WE CANNOT CONTROL...

In the previous chapter, we learned that firms operating in our economic environment make decisions that may or may not lead to the goal of "maximum profits." Since the sufficient condition for survival for any business is the realization of positive profits, we must dispense with the notion that all factors that influence the success, or failure, of a company are controlled *by* the company.

Many factors are exogenous and thus must be factored into the decision-making process. A huge part of the exogenous influence is the degree of competition that any given company might face. As you will quickly see, the more competition that exists, the less control over the environment any one business has.

THE CHARACTERISTICS OF PURE COMPETITION

Mark Scott is a cattle rancher near Hugo, Oklahoma. On most days he is up at the crack of dawn working to maintain his herd of cattle. Mr. Scott has long understood that, for all practical purposes, he operates in a purely competitive market for beef. A market is classified as purely competitive if – and only if – the following conditions apply to that market:

> ➤ **There are many sellers in the market competing to sell a product to many buyers.**

According to the NASS (National Agriculture Statistics Service), Mr. Scott operates in a market with 950,000 cattle ranchers nationwide. There are, of course, over 308 million people in the United States – many of whom eat beef.

> ➤ **The products sold in the market are homogeneous, which means that each seller's product is identical to that of other sellers.**

For the average consumer of beef, cauliflower, broccoli, wheat, and other agricultural commodities, there is little, if any, difference in the products that are offered in the market by various agricultural concerns. Mr. Scott knows that for the great majority of Americans "beef is beef." We do not care if it comes from Hugo, Oklahoma, or Hugo, Colorado. To many of us, it is all the same.

> ➤ **No individual firm will ever advertise their product.**

Since beef is a homogenous product to most consumers, it would do Mr. Scott no good to run a nationwide, statewide, or citywide campaign trumpeting his beef as superior to all other types of beef. He knows that the consumer would not be very likely to believe that there is much of a difference in his product from any other rancher's product, and therefore would be less likely to pay extra (for the cost of advertising) to find out.

> ➤ **Each firm has a very small market share of total sales. Market share is a single seller's percentage of total sales over any period. Generally, in a purely competitive market, no seller's market share exceeds 1%.**

With a very small operation, Mr. Scott's ranch does not serve 1% of Oklahoma, much less the United States.

> ➤ **No seller in the market regards competing sellers as a threat to its market share. Firms are therefore unconcerned about their competitor's marketing or production decisions.**

Mark Scott does not need to worry about a rancher in Wyoming or Texas who is attempting to gain more market share by a special marketing technique or method of lowering feed costs. With so many ranchers, no one rancher is in a position to take over the U.S. cattle market.

> ➤ **Information is freely available on prices, technology, and profit opportunities.**

Mark Scott, like all other ranchers, finds out what price his cattle will fetch on the open market when he takes his cattle to auction markets in Oklahoma and Texas. Once the auction market determines the price, there is nothing he can do about it. If he does not like the price, he cannot refuse to sell his cattle in the hopes of affecting the market supply. Nor can he threaten to flood the market with cattle and reduce prices even more to punctuate his frustration. Mr. Scott, like all other ranchers, is a *price taker.* He must take whatever price the market will give him.

Photo courtesy Tonya Scott

While information on prices is freely available, so is information on technology and profit opportunities. By keeping up with information published by industry newsletters, Mr. Scott can alter the way he runs his ranch – if necessary – and extract maximum value for his beef. The problem, of course, is that all other ranchers have access to this information as well. Therefore, if one rancher learns about a new vaccine for cattle or some technique for increasing weight gain, all other ranchers will soon adopt these practices, negating any opportunity for one rancher to gain an advantage. This is a problem that affects all agricultural operations.

> ➤ **There is freedom of entry into and exit out of the industry. This means that there are no barriers to entry if a new ranching operation wants to enter the market. Nor is there any artificial protection to keep him from leaving the industry should economic losses mount.**

Mr. Scott knows that if the year 2013 sees a huge increase in the demand for beef and more profit in his industry, more ranchers would enter the market for beef. In the long run, he knows that this increase in supply would reduce prices and wipe out any short-run profits he was able to enjoy.

In essence, Mr. Scott is at the mercy of the economic system his ranch operates in. This system picks survivors and failures based on which ranchers happen to be making the best decisions – or are having the best luck – at the time. He cannot persuade more Americans to eat red meat any more than he can prevent the Europeans from boycotting his beef over the use of growth hormones. If the economic system is favorable – and if he is operating his ranch in a productive manner – he will be selected for success. If the system is unfavorable (recessions, fears of mad cow disease, drought, and so forth), he knows that he could go under at any time.

In fact, I visited Mr. Scott in October 2010 while he was at a cattle auction looking to enhance his herd. I asked him how the recent recession had impacted his operations. He indicated that leading up to 2007 his ranch was doing quite well. Rising feed prices and the economic slump changed that quickly. He summarized his view of his chosen profession very succinctly:

> "I have been broke before and I will be broke again someday."

THE DEMAND CURVE AND PRICE FOR THE PURELY COMPETITIVE FIRM

As mentioned before, Mr. Scott is a price taker. Whatever the system offers is what he will sell his beef for. Figures 14. 1 and 14.2 illustrate what this means.

Once the market has set the price of beef (14.1), every rancher takes that price. Since the beef market is homogeneous, the demand for Mr. Scott's beef is *perfectly elastic* – a horizontal line. If Mr. Scott raises the price of beef above what the auction market dictates, he will sell nothing. Lowering the price makes no sense, either. He can sell all of his beef at the market price, so why offer it for anything less?

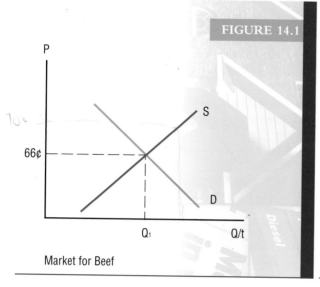

Market for Beef

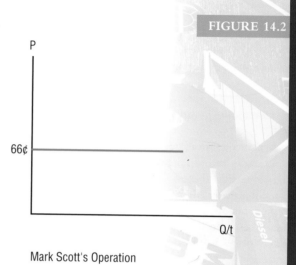

Mark Scott's Operation

CONCEPT CHECK

Could Mr. Scott increase the price of beef by reducing output?

THE OUTPUT DECISION FOR THE PURELY COMPETITIVE FIRM

Once the market sets the price, the question Mr. Scott and other ranchers must answer is, "How much beef should I produce?" This question is answered by comparing the marginal revenue of beef production with the marginal cost.

> ➤ **Marginal revenue is the additional revenue a firm earns from each additional unit of production.**
> ➤ **Marginal cost is the additional cost a firm incurs from each additional unit of production.**

Figure 14.3 illustrates the decision-making process, associated with determining the output level that he hopes will lead to maximum profit.

Suppose the market price of beef in September 2014 is 66 cents per pound. At this price, how many pounds of beef should Mr. Scott offer to the market?

If he produces 1,000 pounds (point A), his marginal cost is 45 cents. However, his marginal revenue is 66 cents. If you ran a business, and at your current price, the marginal revenue you were earning was greater than the marginal cost, what would you do? You really have only one rational choice, and that is to expand output.

Notice that when he increases beef output to 2,000 pounds (point B), his marginal cost rises to 58 cents. The reason for the rising marginal costs, you will recall, is the

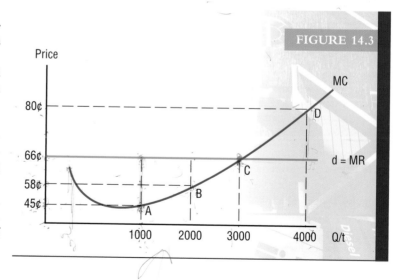

Why not stop at 2,999 pounds of beef production?

law of diminishing marginal returns. His marginal revenue is still 66 cents, so at this price he would be able to cover the additional cost of producing beef. Since he is still taking in more revenue than he is incurring cost, he should continue to expand his level of production.

Many of you will be inclined to argue that Mr. Scott should not expand output to 3,000 pounds (point C). This belief is based on the idea that at 3,000 pounds marginal revenue equals marginal cost therefore no profit is being earned. This is not the case. Look at the region between 2,000 and 3,000 pounds. Would he make a profit at 2,500 pounds? 2,800 pounds? 2,999 pounds?

As you can see, at every point up to point C, Mr. Scott's marginal revenue of 66 cents is greater than his marginal cost. His goal is to extract every dollar of possible profit. Even the movement from 2,999 to 3,000 squeezes out a little more profit; therefore, the purely competitive firm will always seek to operate where marginal revenue equals marginal cost.

a firm's average total cost equals total cost divided by output. Therefore, total cost must equal average total cost multiplied by total output.

> **Average total cost = TC/Q so: Total cost = ATC x Q**

We have already solved for Mr. Scott's total revenue. He produces 3,000 pounds of beef at a price of 66 cents. Therefore his total revenue equals $1,980. If his average total cost looked like the curve in Figure 14.4, we would find that he is incurring $1,740 in costs (58 cents x 3000 pounds).

Whatever the source of his good fortune — a strong economy, low feed costs, or just the right amount of rain — he had better enjoy it while it lasts, because it will not last for long.

SHORT-RUN PROFITS IN PURE COMPETITION

Now that you have an understanding of where the price and output decision comes from, the issue we must now resolve is how to determine whether the purely competitive firm is making a profit. Figure 14.4 should help with this question.

For Mr. Scott, and the 950,000 or so ranchers, profit is calculated by examining the difference between total revenue (price x quantity) and total cost. You will recall from the productivity and cost chapter that

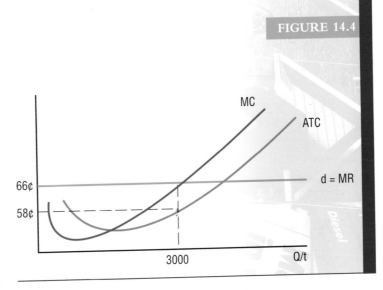

FIGURE 14.4

In January 2011 the U.S. cattle herd shrunk to its lowest level since 1958.[1] Rising feed costs and increasing prices for young cattle were the primary factors that contributed to this situation. What should have been the reaction to this event by ranchers like Mr. Scott? Why?

LONG-RUN PROFITS

Recall the discussion in the last chapter on how an economic system constantly changes. Short-term profit can be a reason for such changes. If profit is being earned in any industry, this acts as a signal for other potential competitors to join the fun. Figures 14.5 and 14.6 illustrate the consequences of profit in the long run.

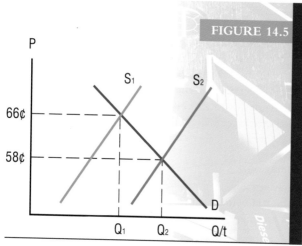

FIGURE 14.5

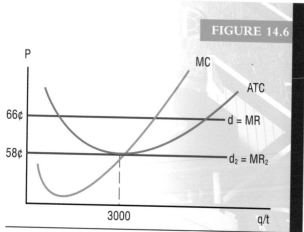

FIGURE 14.6

Since information about profit is symmetrical, there will be an increase in the number of ranchers willing and able to serve the market. As the *market supply of beef* increases to S2, the market price of beef will fall. If prices fall to 58 cents, Mr. Scott and the other ranchers who had been enjoying life will find themselves in a more common position of just breaking even.

Notice that when we calculate his total revenue, it has fallen to $1,740. Since his costs of production have not changed, we see that he is now breaking even. *Breaking even* in the economic sense means that he is covering his accounting, or out-of-pocket costs, *plus* the opportunity cost of being in that business. Mr. Scott is an accomplished

welder. For him to say he is breaking even would mean he has covered the cost of being in ranching plus the lost wages from not being a welder.

This is where accountants and economists disagree on the definition of profit. To the accountant, opportunity cost is not considered part of the bottom line. To an economist, it is. We simply believe that second-best choices are weighed – or should be weighed – in determining whether a good decision has been made.

For the purely competitive firm, the long-run position they can always expect to be in is the break-even position. Markets simply adjust too fast to help them carve out profit for very long.

ECONOMIC LOSSES

On Christmas Day 2003, Mr. Scott woke up to find that a rancher somewhere in Washington had allowed a steer with mad cow disease to be sold into the beef market.[2] The consequences for Mr. Scott and other ranchers were severe. Figures 14.7 and 14.8 illustrate what this meant for many ranchers.

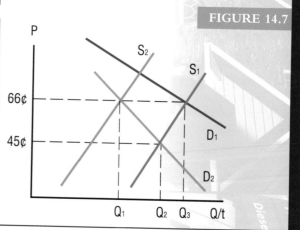

FIGURE 14.7

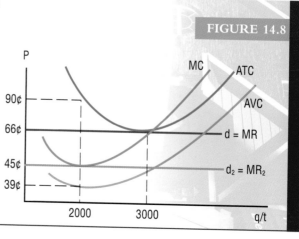

FIGURE 14.8

The outbreak of this disease – and subsequent boycott by some foreign nations – lead to a decrease in the demand for American beef. As demand in the market fell, prices fell for all American ranchers.[3] Notice that if the price falls to 45 cents per pound, the rancher is now incurring losses and will curtail his output to 2,000 pounds of beef, where marginal cost equals his new marginal revenue. Should he have gone out of business? That depends on his average variable cost of production.

If he decides to shut down, he must still pay his fixed cost of production. The bank does not care about Japanese people eating less American steak. The bank cares about receiving the rancher's loan payment. If he shuts down, he will have no revenue coming in to pay for any of these fixed costs. Therefore, his decision will hinge on whether or not he can cover the only costs he can control – his variable costs of production.

In Figure 14.8 we can see that, while he is incurring losses, his total variable cost of production (AVC x Q) is equal to $780. Multiplying his output of 2,000 pounds by the 39-cent average variable cost of production gave us this figure. Since his total revenue of $900 (45 cents x 2,000 pounds of beef) is greater than this total variable cost, he can pay all of his variable costs and still have $120 left over to pay part of his fixed costs. Therefore, in this case, he should stay in business. Going bankrupt will wipe out his revenue and leave him with all of his fixed costs to pay.

If fears of mad cow disease linger, it would behoove the ranchers who are in dire straits to try to reduce their costs of production, if possible, in order to survive. This may entail refinancing a loan or trying to get better leasing terms. After all, if the rancher goes out of business, the bank may not recover its money. On the other hand, you may have seen the television commercials trumpeting beef as "Real Food for Real People." This is a collective attempt on the part of the ranchers of America to promote the demand for their product.

If the drop in demand continued long enough to drive prices down to 36 cents, the ranchers would be in big trouble. In this case, the revenue earned at the 36-cent price would be less than his variable cost

of production. In this case, the individual rancher is not only failing to pay for any of his fixed costs, but he cannot pay all of his variable costs either. Therefore, he can minimize his losses by shutting down.

In a purely competitive market structure, *a firm will shut down at the point where the price falls below the minimum point on the average variable cost curve.* As some ranchers shut down in this example, the overall supply of beef fell (S2 on Figure 14.7). As supply fell, the price of beef would increase back to the point where the firms that have been selected for survival are breaking even again.

> ➢ **The shutdown point is the minimum point on the average variable cost curve. If prices fall below this point the firm can no longer cover any of their fixed costs and only part of their variable costs. Shutting down helps minimize total losses.**

For the purely competitive firm, this means that the supply curve is the marginal cost curve above the shutdown point. This is where businesses find out what their price and quantity supplied will be over time.

It is important to note that it is not just changes in demand that can lead to profit in the short run, or bankruptcy in the long run. Changes in the cost of production can alter the profitability of the purely competitive firm as well.

In 2005 and 2006 a severe drought hit northeastern Texas and Southeastern Oklahoma. In fact, the area where Mr. Scott lives had the worst drought of any region in the United States.[4]

To stave off extinction, should Kentucky tobacco farmers advertise?

The drought effectively wiped out much of the pasture land that cattle in Oklahoma graze on. Without the low-cost grasses, many ranchers had to resort to purchasing hay, which is much more expensive over time.

The hay purchases dramatically increased the average variable cost of production for Mark Scott and others. With higher average variable costs, any previous profit reserves began to fall for many ranchers and some even faced mounting economic losses. By 2008-2011 the rising price of corn – a key ingredient in cattle feed – had increased as the ethanol legislation and other weather-related factors came into play. These factors are one reason why the number of ranching operations has fallen from 1,046,883 several years ago to the 950,000 mark in 2011.[5]

Such is the nature of any business that relies on the uncertainty of rain, government legislation, and other environmental factors.

Photo courtesy Jack Chambless

TAXPAYERS AND THE ECONOMICS OF PINE TREE FARMING

Florida has a long and rich history as one of the nation's leading producers of pine trees and pine tree-related products.[7] Among the products these trees have brought to consumers is turpentine, pine tar, and, of course, lumber for the production of paper and furniture products.

For all practical purposes, the Florida pine tree business is purely competitive. Ostensibly, a pine tree is a pine tree. You won't see many brand names posted on the pine tree farms as you drive along the highways of central and northern Florida. Many of the farms are thousands of acres of manicured properties. Some of them are only a few acres. All of the farmers of pine trees must hope for good market conditions, and they are all subject to a controversial law that has helped insulate pine tree farmers from the rigors of pure competition.

The law in question dates back to 1959, when rapid economic growth in Florida pushed up the value of real estate to the point where many farmers were unable to pay the property taxes on their land. The state of Florida, in an attempt to save farming, created a tax break for farmers known as the greenbelt exemption.[8] Under this exemption, farmland would be taxed at a far lower rate than the actual market value of the land.

Welcome to the law of unintended consequences. No sooner than the ink had dried on the new law, real estate developers and other corporations found a way to use the law to save millions of dollars in taxes. The Walt Disney Corporation, for example has maintained pine tree farms near Disney World for years. Land near the theme park can sell for more than $1 million per acre, yet for tax purposes is assessed at a value of $320 per acre.[9]

Disney is not alone. Real estate developers in Orlando and other cities have found that one of the greatest ways to save money is to buy a piece of land, spend the average cost of $35 per acre planting pine tree seedlings, and then wait until that land is ready to be turned into a mall

CONCEPT CHECK

As a result of high energy costs and the declining demand for newspapers, the Montreal-based Abitibi-Consolidated Inc. announced that some of its paper mills would close in Canada.[6] Graphically illustrate and explain what is going on in the Canadian paper industry. Is there anything this industry can do to adapt to the changing economic landscape? Why, or why not?

CONCEPT CHECK

Graphically illustrate and fully explain how the greenbelt exemption led to increased profits for pine tree farmers in the short run and an artificially high number of pine tree farmers in the long run. For the debate, what do you suppose Alchian would say about the efficacy of this law? Would he support it? Why or why not? Do you support this law? Why or why not?

or apartment complex. Since it takes about 15 years for pine trees to be ready for harvest, oftentimes the developer never actually engages in any farming. When the area to be developed becomes worth more as a mall than as a pine tree farm, the bulldozers come out and the trees go away – all while as much as $500 million in annual tax revenue is lost in the state of Florida to the greenbelt exemption.

quality and availability among the various suppliers. This means that not only will prices and services offered be relatively uniform, but we also have a larger number of drug dealers, prostitutes, and online pornography businesses than would exist in a more monopolistic market structure. Thus, the negative externalities associated with these industries arguably make pure competition the least desired market structure in some instances.

ADDING IT ALL UP

On the surface, perfectly competitive markets would seem to be the ideal market structure to achieve efficiency, low prices, and the optimal product selection for consumers. Alas, what often appears to be so, is not so.

In pure competition, firms tend to just break even in the long run. Without economic profits to draw from, where is the money necessary for new technologies and products? Typically research and development take place among less competitive markets since those markets can most afford to take these risks. Therefore, what appears to be ideal – low prices and limited profit – leads to less product choice and less innovation over time.

Then there is the issue of whether or not pure competition is most desirable for the economic, social, and even moral well-being of the nation. The market for drugs, prostitution, and Internet pornography (where more than 400,000 sites exist) tends to approximate pure competition.[10]

Consumers of these products and services can – with relative ease – obtain information about prices, product

ENDNOTES

1 See "Smaller Herds Spell Pricier Beef" by Lester Aldrich, *The Wall Street Journal,* January 29-30, 2011, p. B11.
2 See "Many Stocks Linked to Beef Continue Fall" by Jennifer Bayot, *The New York Times,* December 27, 2003; and "Beleaguered Cattle Farmers Prepare to Weather Another Blow" by Sarah Kershaw, *The New York Times,* December 25, 2003.
3 See "Some Atkins Fans Will Switch; Others Plan to Remain Steadfast" by Daniel J. Wakin, *The New York Times,* December 25, 2003.
4 See "No rain in sight as drought plagues Texas, Oklahoma" by Scott Gold, *The Orlando Sentinel,* January 1, 2006 and "Drought endangers crops and herds in Oklahoma" by Kelly Kurt, *The Orlando Sentinel,* January 17, 2006, p. A4.
5 Source: The National Agriculture Statistics Service.
6 See "Abitibi announces shutdowns as forestry slump drags on" by Bertrand Marotte, *The Globe and Mail,* July 28, 2005.
7 For some of this history see www.maritime.org/conf/conf-kaye-tar.htm.
8 See "State tax break on farmland a cash crop for developers" by Lawrence J. Lebowitz, *The Orlando Sentinel,* July 19, 1992.
9 See "Measure makes pine trees look greener to developers" by Lawrence J. Lebowitz and Robin Benedick, *The Orlando Sentinel,* July 19, 1992.
10 For one economist's research on the Internet pornography industry as it relates to pure competition, see www.americanacademy.de/fellows/Alumni/Fall_01/freeman/body_freeman.html.

CHAPTER REVIEW

1. What are the major characteristics of pure competition? How does the rutabaga market fit this description?

2. Graphically illustrate and explain what short run profits look like in the purely competitive wheat market for the firm and the industry.

3. Graphically illustrate and explain what the long run adjustment looks like if profits are being earned in a purely competitive industry.

4. What is the shutdown point for the purely competitive firm? Why?

Chapter Fifteen

MONOPOLY

Photo courtesy Jack Chambless

*T*he exclusive right to invention [is] given not of natural right, but for the benefit of society, the right to a monopoly to exploit a new idea," he argued, "isn't the same as the right to life, liberty and the pursuit of happiness.

THOMAS JEFFERSON

MONOPOLY – A DIRTY WORD

On November 7, 1999, U.S. District Judge Thomas Penfield Jackson, in a scathing ruling against the Microsoft Corporation, stated:

> …Microsoft's interactions with Netscape, IBM, Intel, Apple, and RealNetworks all reveal Microsoft's business strategy of directing its monopoly power toward inducing other companies to abandon projects that threaten Microsoft and toward punishing those companies that resist.[1]

Monopoly means *the single seller of a product with no close substitutes.* If you have ever played the board game version of this term, you know that the objective of the game is to crush your opponents, then charge them outrageous prices to partake of your services.

However, the real world is not a board game and in the real world, monopolies are very rare.

In fact, your economics professor will be hard-pressed to illustrate even one case of a business that is totally immune from competitive pressure. Having a monopoly would be a great thing. It would be like a large animal that gets to eat all of the food in its environment without fear of any predator or competitor. In reality, there is always another animal – or computer software company – waiting to take on the strongest member of the species.

THE CHARACTERISTICS OF MONOPOLY

Even though monopolies – in the purest sense of the word – are hard to find, we study what a system would look like if a monopoly existed or if tremendous monopoly power were present in order to delve into the more realistic market structures of oligopoly and monopolistic competition in the next chapter.

For the single seller of a product with "no substitutes," the best substitute a monopolist faces is the refusal to use its product if prices get too high. Cable television had a monopoly until satellite dishes became smaller and less expensive. A small-town gas station owner, in the mountains of Montana, miles from any other station, cannot charge any price he desires. If the price got too high, there would be some reduction in consumption.

This could happen as word got out that the station owner charged exorbitant prices. Some people would then make sure they had enough gas before they ventured into his monopolistic market. In short, any monopolist has to worry some about new firms entering the market or consumers avoiding their good or service altogether. The monopolist might dominate the economic system, but the fruits of that dominance lead to other firms wanting to share in the bounty.

CONCEPT CHECK

During the Alaska gold rush, a woman baked several pies, walked to the top of a mountain where prospectors were coming by, and sold the pies for far greater prices than they paid at the bottom of the mountain. Did she have a monopoly? Why, or why not?

DEMAND AND MARGINAL REVENUE FOR A MONOPOLIST

With around 91% of the computer operating systems market, suppose, for a moment, that Microsoft is, for all practical purposes, a monopolist in this market. What would this mean, in terms of the demand curve Microsoft would face and the price that could be charged? For a monopolist, since there is effectively no competition, the market demand curve is the monopolist's demand curve. This also means that the marginal revenue condition facing a monopolist will be different than the purely competitive firm.

Suppose Microsoft charged $99 per box for its latest software upgrades. At this price, suppose 10 million boxes are sold for total revenue of $990 million. How does Microsoft ensure increased sales of this product? The answer is by lowering the price. Notice, however,

that as the price falls to $89, $79, and $69 and so on, the marginal revenue of Microsoft falls. This is because, to sell each additional unit, the company must not only lower the price on the last unit sold but on all of the preceding units as well. Therefore, the marginal revenue continues to fall until it equals zero at the point where total revenue is maximized. (This, as you should recall, is where the price elasticity of demand equals one.)

THE PRICE AND OUTPUT DECISION UNDER MONOPOLY

Contrary to popular belief, a monopolist, even if it faces no competition, will not charge any price it wants to. To find out how much output will be produced and at what price, look at Figure 15.2.

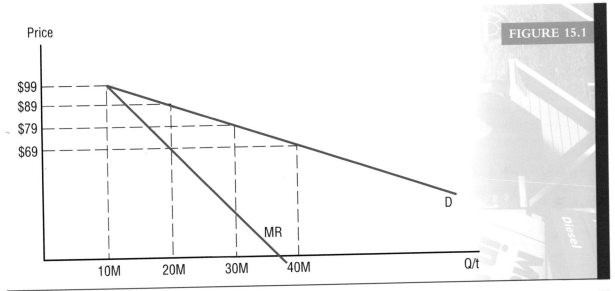

FIGURE 15.1

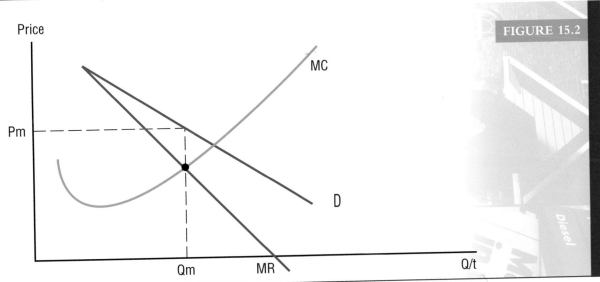

FIGURE 15.2

CONCEPT CHECK

In the movie, *Flash of Genius*, an inventor fights with Ford over the rights to his invention. Do unique inventions confer monopoly power on the inventors? Why, or why not?

As you can see, the output decision of Microsoft is exactly the same as it was for Mark Scott's ranching operation. If Microsoft produces at an output level lower than the point where marginal revenue equals marginal cost, profit that could be earned from expanding production is lost. If output is above the point where MR = MC occurs, Microsoft would lose money. Therefore, Microsoft will produce where MR = MC. From there, Microsoft, being a *price maker*, rather than price taker, simply picks the price (Pm) on its demand curve that corresponds to the profit maximizing output level (Qm).

There are two interesting facts concerning monopoly. First, a monopolist will produce an output level that is lower than the output that would occur in pure competition. Why? Because it can! The monopolist knows that by restricting output, prices increase.

Second, it is *impossible* for a monopolist to ever charge a price that maximizes total revenue. Total revenue is maximized at the point where the price corresponds to a unit elastic demand. Where total revenue is maximized, marginal revenue equals zero. Since the firm must produce where marginal revenue equals marginal cost, and because *marginal cost can never equal zero*, it becomes an economic impossibility to ever maximize revenue. The monopolist ends up charging a price along the elastic range of the demand curve – even though there are no close substitutes for the good!

As you might imagine, it would be very, very unusual for a monopolist to incur losses. Maybe an electric blanket dealership in Arizona in July would incur losses, but not many other monopolists do – with the exception of the U.S. Postal Service.[2] Figure 15.3 illustrates the fact that most monopolists earn profit by charging a price that lies above average total cost.

The real issue, for the monopolist, is not whether profits will pour in, but for *how long* profits will pour in. In order to make sure profits stay positive, indefinitely, the monopolist must erect and maintain *barriers to entry*.

TYPES OF ENTRY BARRIERS

A barrier to entry is any natural, or artificial force that prevents new firms from entering a monopolized market (or one where monopoly power is present), when profits are being earned. There are many potential entry barriers that a business might pursue. We will find that, just because an entry barrier exists, that does not mean consumers will be hurt. There are some significant benefits – to the consumer – from entry barriers.[3]

PATENTS

There are two types of patents granted by The U.S. Patent and Trademark Office in Washington, D.C. A *utility patent* grants the right to be the exclusive seller of a good for 20 years. For example, recently, MIT graduate student, Anmol Madan invented a product called the Jerk-O-Meter.[4] This hand-held device has software that allows a person to analyze speech patterns and voice tones and rate people on how engaged they are in a conversation. Can you imagine how useful this could be to help all of us avoid conflict – or annoying people?

This type of product – if patented – would allow Mr. Madan to avoid competition for two decades. While that might seem excessive, the U.S. Constitution provides for patent protection in order to encourage the development of such products and to reward the inventor with reasonable profits over time.

A *design patent* allows a manufacturer to have exclusive rights to some particular feature of a product, but not

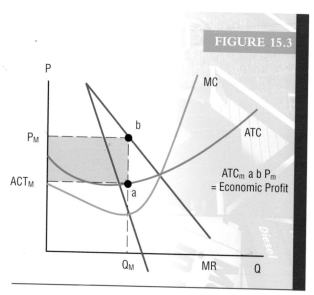

FIGURE 15.3

ATC_m a b P_m = Economic Profit

the product itself. If you look at the back of your calculator you might notice that it has several patents. This means that anyone can produce a calculator, but there are certain features of your calculator that cannot be copied. Design patents last for 14 years.

In order to obtain a utility patent, you have to prove that the product is unique, marketable, and not the logical extension of some existing product. A device that recorded the thoughts of people you are talking to would satisfy all three criteria. A DVD recorder that automatically deleted commercials might not. This recorder could be viewed as a logical extension of existing DVD recorders. However, a design patent – protecting that feature – would probably be allowed.

WHY PATENTS ARE IMPORTANT

In the 1950s, one of the most innovative and exciting products developed was the instant-picture camera, developed by Polaroid. This camera – able to develop photos in one minute – was an immediate sensation. As the holder of the patents over this camera, Polaroid was able to monopolize the market for instant cameras.

In 1976, some of Polaroid's patents expired, and so, apparently, did its monopoly on instant-picture cameras. After the patents expired, Eastman Kodak entered the market with its own instant cameras and film. By the mid-1980s, Kodak accounted for 25% of the annual sales of instant-picture cameras.[5]

Polaroid was not pleased. Claiming Kodak had infringed on its remaining patents, Polaroid sued, seeking to block Kodak from selling any more instant cameras.

In 1985 a federal judge ruled in favor of Polaroid, finding that Kodak had infringed on seven of Polaroid's patents. In 1986, Kodak was ordered to cease manufacturing both the cameras and the film.

Since customers with cameras made by Kodak were no longer able to get film for them, Kodak offered to exchange the cameras for other Kodak products, certificates to buy Kodak products, or Kodak stock. But the bad

news was not over. Kodak had estimated that the shutdown in production and buy-backs would cost the company $200 million.

In October 1990, a U.S. district judge order Kodak to pay $909.5 million in damages to Polaroid. This cemented Polaroid's monopoly over the instant camera market and made Kodak cameras visual reminders of why patent violations are serious business – that is, if you are infringing on an invention that is protected.

THE DEMISE OF THE BRUSHMASTER BAIT COMPANY

In 1974, a man was fishing in a bass tournament at Millwood Lake in southern Arkansas when he made a discovery that almost made him rich. While relaxing by a campfire, after a day of angling for large-mouth bass, he took out a pocketknife and began cutting a multi-angled shape out of an aluminum can. At the time, he was a fledgling entrepreneur in the artificial fishing lure business. The design he cut out of the can, and subsequently bent into an abstract shape, gave him the idea of putting the device on the shaft of a spinner bait fishing lure. With a pair of pliers, he fastened this configuration to the shaft of one of his lures, and the next day, he tossed it into the water. What happened next changed the history of the fishing lure business.

When this bait was pulled through the water, it made a peculiar buzzing sound that made bass practically jump into the boat. Obviously encouraged by this good

Photo courtesy Jack Chambless

Should she be allowed to keep using this camera?

fortune, he took the device to a materials producer to make thousands of copies for his new invention. Next, he took the bait to Bentonville, Arkansas – headquarters of Wal-Mart – and secured a contract to sell the lure in stores in southeastern Oklahoma and northeastern Texas.

By all indications, the new Brushmaster Bait Company was being selected for success by the economic environment. That is, until a local fishing guide near the entrepreneur's hometown discovered this incredible lure. The guide not only earned money by taking people out to find the best places to haul in bass, but he was also a representative of a major fishing lure company. Realizing that nowhere on the Brushmaster packaging were the words "Patent No." or "Patent Pending," the guide rushed back to the company's headquarters with his fortuitous discovery. Very soon there was a patent on the "Buzz Bait" – but my father (yes, my father) was not the owner of it. The corporation was. The corporation's lawyers informed my dad that he was to cease making the bait at once or risk being sued.

How could this happen? My dad had made the mistake of not pursuing a patent on his bait before he put it in the public domain. The other company changed the bait enough so that it was considered a unique product and effectively put my father out of business – and kept me from driving a Porsche at the age of 16!

The lesson to be learned from these cases is that patents are designed to protect consumers and reward innovation. Patents protect consumers to the extent that innovation is encouraged. If patents did not exist, few – if any – new inventions would come about. Who would want to take the risk of creating something new, just to have another company come along and steal the idea at virtually no cost?

With the laws in place, we do pay more for protected items, but we get more items coming out every year as a result.[6] The second point to emphasize is that if you ever invent something that you think might be worthy of a patent, do not hesitate. Contact a patent lawyer or the U.S. Patent and Trademark office immediately. There are also online sites where you can begin the patent process. Even if your idea is eventually rejected, you are protected from competition until this office decides your fate.

COPYRIGHTS

> Do we want a society where every thought, every expression, every story is owned by someone?
>
> Michael Agee, agent for Hal Roach Studios

A copyright (designated with the © symbol), gives the author of original works of authorship the right to sell items like movies, books, songs, computer programs, maps, photographs, and so forth without fear of the work being illegally copied. *Copyrights typically last for 70-120 years.* This book, for example, is copyrighted and will be as long as I am alive plus another 95 years. That means that no one else can reproduce this book and sell it as if the book was their product. Disney is allowed to keep other firms from using the likeness of the characters from *The Aristocats.* Tim McGraw gets to protect his lyrics from copycat artists and so forth.

This is good for consumers to the extent that, by protecting the books, images, movies, music, maps, and so forth, you do not have to worry about inferior movies using Disney's images to defraud you, or lousy country singers pretending to be Tim McGraw. If copyrights did not exist, fewer artists and authors would have the incentive to create new products to serve us.

This brings us to the issue of movie piracy. For the past few years, the movie industry has been trying to avoid the same disastrous results that plagued the music industry when it first became possible to download music with the click of a mouse. Part of the fight has taken the form of direct mailing of DVDs by companies like Netflix, while others have tried using the courts to punish people.[7]

TRADEMARKS

If you have ever seen the TM or ® symbol on a product, it means that item has some trademark protection. A trade-

---

SUGGESTED CLASSROOM DEBATE

Should it be legal to download movies at no charge if the movie studios are too slow in responding to consumer demand for instant home use of their product? Should people to whom you rent your home be allowed to sublet it to others without asking you? If you loan your neighbor your car, should she be allowed to loan it out to 10 other people? Why or why not?

mark is any word, name, symbol, or device, or combination thereof, adopted by a manufacturer to identify and distinguish its goods from others. While any soft drink company can use the name Cola in describing their drink, they cannot use Coca or Pepsi in front of Cola.

Should the company in the following picture be sued for trademark infringement? Notice how long this company has been around. The courts would not force Amazon.com to change its name – even though this Orlando-based company came first – because there is little possibility that a reasonable consumer would confuse the two companies as being one. A hose and rubber company is probably not going to branch out into the book market. Consumers would probably recognize this fact easily.

On the other hand, there are some names that are so common that companies have to rely on changing logos, fonts, or slogans to differentiate their product. For example, a tire company with the name Ford could cause confusion. So could a toothpaste company started by sisters with the last name Johnson. Therefore, the tire company and the Johnson sisters would have to have markedly different looks to their name to keep people from thinking that the Ford Motor Company and Johnson & Johnson

were now in these markets. This is an issue because, if the tire or toothpaste companies sell a lousy product, it could impact the demand for Ford cars and baby soap produced by this trusted name.

TRADE SECRETS

A trade secret occurs if a company has some particular formula, blueprint, design, or customer list that it keeps out of the public domain. The secret formula for Coca-Cola is a great example of this type of barrier. As long as

Entitled to federal protection?

Shutterstock © Daniel Rajszczak, 2011.

Photo courtesy Jack Chambless

Al Johnson's Swedish Restaurant in Sister Bay, Wisconsin features goats eating on grass that grows on the roof of his restaurant. In 1973 Mr. Johnson trademarked the right to put goats on a roof to attract customers but now many places around North America have the same attraction.[8] Should his trademark be enforced or is this an example of government extending protection where it is not appropriate to do so?

Coca-Cola has this legal trade secret, no other company will be able to successfully duplicate the taste of this product, and therefore Coca-Cola maintains an entry barrier in this market.

OWNERSHIP OF AN ENTIRE SUPPLY OF A RESOURCE, LOCATION AND PROPERTY RIGHTS

Albert Pujols of baseball's St. Louis Cardinals enjoys this type of entry barrier. The Chinese government does, too.

Mr. Pujols is the sole owner of his rare baseball skills that have produced a highly successful career. As a monopolist over his skills, Mr. Pujol's services are priced at a very high level. If anyone could play baseball like he does, Mr. Pujols would not command $30 million per year.

China can understand the power Mr. Pujols has. More than 90% of the world's supply of "rare-earth" minerals like cerium, used in pollution-control equipment; terbium, used in energy-efficient light bulbs; and thulium, which is used in x-ray devices, comes from China. All told, China has a huge market share in 17 rare-earth elements, many of which are critical in the production of military products and energy generation.[9] It is pretty easy to keep other competitors from entering the market when you have the recognition of international borders and property rights on your side...

FRANCHISES AND LICENSES

In New York City, not anyone can paint their car yellow and call it a taxi. In order to legally operate a taxi, you must buy a medallion that costs $766,000 *per car*. The government claims that this hefty fee makes sure only reputable companies will provide taxi services.[10] In reality, it has led to an enormous entry barrier, as few people are willing and able to pay this fee. With this barrier intact, patrons of cabs in New York City often feel as though they are being "taken for a ride" while they are being taken for a ride!

Professional sports organizations also enjoy this type of entry barrier. Suppose you wanted to start a professional hockey franchise in Minneapolis and call your team the Minnesota Marmots.

You build a state-of-the-art stadium complete with luxury boxes and all the amenities that hockey fans expect to see. Before the puck gets dropped on the Marmots inaugural season, you will find yourself in court, and your team will never take one shot. That is because the National Hockey League – and the rest of the major sports organizations – have exclusive rights to create new franchises.

Photo courtesy Jack Chambless

How does the right to franchise impact the price this pitcher's jersey?

Just as Taco Bell and Burger King are allowed to regulate the number of restaurants, and where they will be located, sports owners regulate the number of teams and the cities in which games will take place. This can prove to be very costly for fans in many ways. Since the Minnesota Wild has a virtual monopoly over the market for hockey games in this central Minnesota (assuming that The University of Minnesota or local high school and colleges are weaker substitutes), the owner of this team can charge much higher prices than if there were two or three teams in the area.

The Wild owner can also play an economic game of "chicken" that has become very popular over the past few years. That game entails the owner of a team offering direct or veiled threats to move the team to a new city if a brand-new stadium is not constructed. This has worked for numerous owners to bilk taxpayers out of hundreds of millions of dollars for places like the new stadiums for the Dallas Cowboys and New York Yankees.

In the meantime, with a monopoly in place, the owners are able to negotiate huge television contracts with the networks and charge very high prices ($800 million for the Washington Redskins) for the right to be a part of the league. All of this has led to a very lucrative market for the owners and, ironically, some major *benefits* for fans.

If anyone could start a new NHL, NFL, NBA or Major League Baseball franchise, there would be a tremendous decrease in the overall quality of play as dozens of new teams entered the market. There are only so many world-class athletes available to compete in these leagues. The more teams you add, the more you dilute the talent pool and the overall integrity of the product. In a bizarre twist, the owners' monopoly power provides consumers with a better product, albeit at a higher price, than a purely competitive market would.

CONCEPT CHECK

Can violence – as an entry barrier – be good for society?

VIOLENCE

In the days of prohibition, when it was illegal to buy and sell alcohol in the United States, gangsters like Al Capone took full advantage of the fact that as long as there is a demand for something, someone will supply it. Mr. Capone's problem was that if he earned profit selling alcohol in and around Chicago, he could not use any legal means to erect a barrier to entry. After all, the government would not have been very pleased with an advertisement trumpeting his liquor during a time when no one was supposed to be drinking.

Mr. Capone understood that the only way he could effectively keep out new competitors was to let them know that if they entered his market, they would exit the planet. This barrier is used today to keep profits from drugs extremely high. Of course, this entry barrier has been the key to the drug trade's ability to flourish and has led to countless innocent victims being gunned down in the global drug war.

ECONOMIC FORBEARANCE

This is the practice of buying up the distribution points of your product to prevent competing firms from being able to enter a particular market. A classic example of this is when Pepsi purchased Pizza Hut, Taco Bell, and Kentucky Fried Chicken many years ago. By purchasing these distribution points, Pepsi was able to guarantee that Coca-Cola would never sell in any of those establishments. While this had the effect of raising the price of soft drinks in those restaurants, it also led to price wars, and increased variety, in the very competitive market for fast food.

BRAND NAME LOYALTY

When you hear the names Lexus, Vera Bradley, Armani, Apple, and Rolex, the word "quality" would probably come to mind. These companies, and others like them, have invested millions in producing a product to which people have come to be brand-name loyal. This occurs by making sure that the product provides a great deal of consumer satisfaction every time it is purchased. The barrier occurs when a new company with no brand-name following attempts to carve out a market niche and realizes it cannot, because consumers are willing to pay more money for the established product.

PATH DEPENDENCE

A relatively new debate has emerged concerning the extent to which consumers, facing high transaction costs of finding better products, are willing to stick with a product that is not living up to expectations or is inferior to some new product. The question is, if a product or company is not meeting its obligation to you, or if a new product comes along that might be better, will you leave that product or company? Is it possible that the cost of leaving, measured by the time and money you have to spend searching for a better product, is too great?

If it is, you may find yourself becoming *path dependent* – dependent on a particular good that is actually worse than what you could find somewhere else. This is a very interesting concept. The barrier, of course, comes in the form of the inferior company knowing many customers won't incur the cost of leaving. With path dependency in place, no incentives exist to make a better product or deliver better service.

Economists Steve Margolis of North Carolina State University and Stan Liebowitz of the University of Texas at Dallas argue that, over time, the issue of path dependence is a *non-issue*. According to these distinguished economists, eventually the market finds those ineffective restaurants or car repair shops or magazines and selects them for extinction – or far lower profit than companies that provide a good product, good prices, or superior service. It is simply too hard for inferiority to remain hidden, and consumers eventually are willing to incur the cost of searching for a better product.[11]

MARKET PACKING

This is the practice of packing the market with every conceivable variety of a product to prevent new firms from finding a niche in that market. The diaper, pet food, canned soup, and cereal aisles of your local supermarket illustrate this practice. Think about the countless varieties of cereal that exist. A quick glance at who manufactures these items will reveal that they are produced by only a handful of firms.

Photo courtesy Jack Chambless

For a major cereal company, the fear is that if every niche is not plugged, a new company will come along with a successful product, gain a brand-name following, and end up expanding – diluting the monopoly power of existing cereal makers. To an extent, this barrier is bad for consumers, because it can be very confusing sorting out the endless varieties and claims made by various companies. Nevertheless, defenders of the market will contend – and have a good point doing so – that consumers are made better off by an ever-increasing variety of products, to serve our diverse tastes.[12]

ENTRY LIMIT PRICING

This is the practice of charging a price that is just high enough to earn profits, but not high enough to induce entry by new competitors. This barrier is fascinating because it requires a company to overcome the age-old problem of greed. The logic is simple: If a firm that has monopoly power charges a price that generates positive profit, but not maximum profit, that firm may be able to forestall entry for a long period of time. Potential entrants, realizing that they must incur the high costs of starting up, only to be faced with relatively low prices, decide it is not worth their while to enter the market.

This was another argument against Microsoft – the claims that low prices were a ruse to mask their goal of forestalling competitive pressure.

Some economists argue that we should not care about low prices – for any reason. Nevertheless, we still see many examples of low prices getting blueberry growers in Maine, paper companies in South Carolina and insurance companies in Alabama and Pennsylvania – too list a few – getting in trouble with the government for discounting goods and services.

The government's concern is that low prices now, leads to monopolization of these industries – and higher prices later.[13]

GOVERNMENT LICENSES

Suppose you got tired of having to pay for postage stamps and relatively low-quality service at the post office. Suppose at the same time you grow weary of the long lines at the tag office or driver's license office. Furthermore, you have become fed up with the low performance levels of the local government school system. In response, you decide to start your own company that delivers first-class mail and sells car tags and driver's licenses. You also decide to pull your kids out of the local public school and send them to a different public school that is more productive. When you are arrested, make sure you bring lots of bail money.

In the United States of America it is illegal to compete with the government-run postal service in the market for first-class postage. UPS and Federal Express are OK, since they deal in parcels. If you start mailing envelopes for less than $.50, look out. The same is true for selling car tags and driver's licenses. In your state, the government provides these services, and unless this function has been privatized, the government has a monopoly over the terms under which you get a tag or license.

If you cannot afford private school tuition, or you do not home-school your child, you are in the unenviable position of having no choice but to send your little tyke to the public school in your district. Critics of this system (see chapter five) argue that with no choice, public school teachers and administrators — along with postal workers, and officials at the Department of Motor Vehicles — have no incentive to provide a high-quality product, and that the product that is provided becomes more and more expensive every year.[14]

ASYMMETRIC INFORMATION

You might recall that asymmetric information exists when one party to a market transaction has good information concerning the price, availability, level of competition, and so forth, but the other party does not.

When the seller of a good or service is the possessor of such information, and the potential buyers are not, monopoly power can exist in everything from the market for strawberries to newspapers.

CAN A MONOPOLY BE BENEVOLENT?

Fran Long owns a stand near Otter Creek, Florida, that offers up a large variety of strawberries and other fruit. Her stand is located on Highway 19 between Crystal River and Chiefland. Over that approximately 45-mile stretch of road, you will find one strawberry stand — hers. What if you did not know that? Welcome to the problem of asymmetric information.

Mrs. Long is in the enviable position of having a monopoly over a homogenous product, due to her location and the lack of information that drivers have about the possible location of other stands. Even if a driver approaching her Otter Creek stand was willing to bet that another stand might exist further down the road, asymmetric information still exists. If there is another stand, will it be open? If it is open, will it have any strawberries? If it has strawberries, will they be as good as the ones in Otter Creek? If they are as good, will they be more expensive?

For these reasons, Mrs. Long never seems to lack a steady stream of customers. In fact, she seems to be pretty busy all of the time. Yet, she charges "only" $10 for a flat of strawberries. Anybody who is a strawberry lover knows that $10 is pretty cheap. Mrs. Long knows that it is cheap, too, yet she *deliberately* charges relatively low prices. "My mark-up suits me just fine," she told me as I devoured her "Sweet Charlie" strawberries.

Photo courtesy Jack Chambless

A monopoly ahead?

When asked why she would pass up the chance to make more profit without risking offending her customers, her reply was, "Sharing and caring never hurt anybody."

What a nice monopolist.

Thousands of miles away, another sector of the economy is benefiting from monopoly power that stems from location and asymmetric information. That sector is the small-town newspaper business.

This book has chronicled the plight of large newspapers in some detail. Yet, when one looks at what is taking place in places like Bismarck, North Dakota and Casper, Wyoming, we don't see economic losses and downsizing. Instead, the evidence is suggesting that profits can be made selling traditional news formats.[15]

What newspapers in smaller towns have going for them is simple to understand. With fewer people using the Internet, less high-speed service, insufficient cell phone towers and no competition from other newspapers for hundreds of miles in some cases, it is possible for these publishers to realize positive profits.

Smaller newspapers should be able to avoid the trend toward declining demand as long as their customers do not have good information about the alternatives that are available to them. However, this could also change as technology continues to bring faster outlets to mid-size cities.

This would seem to be an entry barrier that will not hold up over time.

Photo courtesy Jack Chambless

ECONOMIES OF SCALE

You will recall that when a firm enjoys cost savings through large-scale production, economies of scale are created. This is very common for companies that rely on high levels of technology, such as computer software and the delivery of electric power. This creates a natural entry barrier by making it very difficult for a new company to enter – knowing that the established firm already has built-in cost advantages, and thus the ability to charge lower prices, than the new firm. This creates a situation called a "natural monopoly" that will be addressed in the last section of this chapter.

TYING CONTRACTS

Suppose that before you could by a Ford car, you had to agree to buy tires only from Goodyear. This illegal practice is called tying, and it is an entry barrier, to the extent that Ford and Goodyear would be able to prevent another tire company from serving this enormous market for Ford cars. Defenders of this practice suggest that tying creates a certain synergy among products or companies that increases efficiency. If Microsoft's software can be tied to Internet Explorer, the consumer – it is suggested – is better off by being able to work with each system simultaneously.

ADDING IT ALL UP

It is pretty clear that it would be nice to have a monopoly over the good or service that you sell. That would mean higher prices and the opportunity not to worry as much about quality or innovation. What is not clear is whether this situation ever really exists in its purest form. After all, email and electronic banking are great examples of how markets correct for a monopoly outcome. Home-schooling is on the rise, and the Internet has transferred a tremendous amount of power from producers to consumers.

Moreover, even where monopoly power exists, when we look at some of the benefits we get from the entry barriers that help companies maintain profit, we see that a lot of entry barriers serve to help us live better lives. Therefore, before we jump at the chance to castigate firms that seek to erect and maintain entry barriers, maybe we should consider the full scope of what market power does. In many cases, market power creates sufficient profit – above that which would exist in a purely competitive market – to finance innovative efforts that lead to new and better products.

THE LIFE AND TIMES OF JOHN D. ROCKEFELLER, WILLIAM GATES, AND ....LARRY PAGE?

Finding someone with an opinion on the government's case against Microsoft is like finding ants at a picnic. They are everywhere. On one side you have the United States Department of Justice that believes Bill Gates and his compatriots have harmed us all. On the other hand are consumers, business executives, and economists who are struggling to find out what all of the ruckus is about.

At the core of this issue is whether Microsoft violated an 1890 law designed to protect consumers, and markets from the perceived ruinous outgrowth of overt monopoly power. The Sherman Antitrust Act is very clear: Companies that contract, conspire, or combine to restrain free trade or fix prices have violated the law. This law was used to break up John D. Rockefeller's Standard Oil Company in 1911.

For years the very essence of monopoly – in the minds of Americans – was Mr. Rockefeller. Let's start with him to see why Bill Gates was lumped into the same negative category as the deceased oil tycoon – and why Google CEO Larry Page might be next.

Up until 1859, the principal sources of fuel used for illumination were candles and whale oil. However, whales were common property, so over-hunting them led to huge whale oil shortages and a great hunt for alternative sources of fuel. It was around this time that petroleum was discovered in Pennsylvania. When it was found that oil could be used as a fuel and light source, there was a mad rush of men and equipment to this region. Soon, oil derricks sprang up seemingly everywhere and entrepreneurs in this new industry pumped oil out of the ground as fast as they could. The dilemma was that – while a person might have had a private property claim on the land where the oil was being pumped – no one owned the oil beneath the ground.

As common property the *"rule of capture"* dominated this market. The rule of capture meant that you had to suck the oil out of the ground quickly, lest your neighbor beat you to it.

With the inevitable glut of oil that developed in the market, oil prices collapsed. Eventually, a new player in this market entered the scene with a different mindset. John D. Rockefeller believed that, at the rate oil was being extracted, it would be gone very soon and the entire market would vanish. Rockefeller abhorred the wasteful means of production and sought more stability in this market. Therefore, as his wealth increased, he began buying out competing producers. At the same time, he secured very favorable rates with the railroads to ship his oil.

His pitch, to the carrier of his oil, was that they could ship small quantities provided by small companies or large quantities shipped by his company. Of course, the railroads felt they would be better served by catering to Rockefeller, so they secretly negotiated lower rates with his firm. This gave Rockefeller a huge competitive advantage over his rivals and the power to increase the pressure he mounted on them to sell out. Rockefeller used the practice of charging very low prices in areas where producers refused to sell, to run them out of business. Once they were facing bankruptcy, he would offer to buy them out – sometimes for stock in his company.

By the late 1800s, Rockefeller controlled more than 90% of the domestic oil market. As a firm with tremendous monopoly power – derived from built-in cost advantages – he was able to restrict the supply of oil and manage the growth of this industry. In the purest form of biological success, the invention of the internal combustion engine and gas-powered automobiles increased the demand for oil (and his wealth) to astronomical levels. This good fortune did not last. Ida Tarbell, a reporter whose father had been a victim of Rockefeller's predatory tactics, uncovered the secrets of Standard Oil's grand plan – including the secret deals with the railroads – and published a series of scathing articles about Rockefeller. As public outrage grew, it became politically popular for the government to move in and break up the company into several smaller concerns.

About 75 years after the break-up of Standard Oil, a young college dropout named William Gates founded the Microsoft Corporation – a computer software company based in Redmond, Washington. Along with friends Steve Ballmer (now CEO of Microsoft) and Paul Allen, Gates got the company off to a strong start with the development of its MS-DOS operating system. This system allowed computer makers like IBM to offer a much more efficient way of working with computers than had previously existed. Ironically, it was IBM that accidentally made Mr. Gates the richest man in the world.

Gates offered to license MS-DOS exclusively with IBM. IBM – in one of the great screw-ups in modern economic history – allowed Gates to sell his operating software to whomever he wanted. This opened the door for Microsoft to penetrate every facet of the computer business and quickly made the company rise into the echelons of the most powerful entities in the world. This is where the story gets a little muddy. Some argue that Bill Gates used his tremendous power to artificially crush potential competitors.

They cite Gates' offering his software to computer makers only if they also accepted his web browser, as an example of illegally tying his products together.

The argument is that no computer maker in their right mind would turn down the Windows product just because they were not excited about the web browser Microsoft offers. With over 90% of the computer operating system market (sound familiar?) going to Microsoft, the company was able to "force" companies to take other Microsoft products. In essence, some suggest that Bill Gates created an implicit form of path dependence by being able to sell a lower quality product (Internet Explorer) than other companies provided by threatening to withhold the superior product (Windows).

Competitors, not customers, of Mr. Gates also argued that offering his web browser for "free" constituted an illegal practice of *predatory pricing*. Predatory pricing, you will recall, is the practice of lowering your prices below your rivals' cost of production in order to run them out of business and secure long-term monopoly power.

Defenders of Microsoft point out that the Sherman Antitrust Act was designed to protect consumers from the high prices, lower output, and stagnant technological development that monopolies create. If you look hard at Microsoft and the computer software industry, you will find that prices in this highly fluid industry have fallen, the number of computer software companies has increased, quality has improved, and the rate of technological development has been astounding.

This has left many asking whether or not the Sherman Antitrust Act is out of touch with modern developments in markets or whether Microsoft is guilty of anything more than being a better competitor that is more in touch with consumer demand than less competitive companies are.[16] Of course, the response to this argument is that even if Microsoft has done all of these wonderful things, the rate of technological change would have been even greater and prices even lower if the company had not engaged in such aggressive or illegal maneuvers.[17]

An entire book could be written and an entire semester devoted to sorting out the details of why both sides believe they are more accurate. What is clear is that the future is unclear for this software behemoth.

Some argued that the company should be broken up – as the government originally suggested might be the case.[18] Other suggested remedies should require Microsoft to bundle competing products with its products, or give away the source code to Windows software. Fines, government regulation, and combinations of these penalties were also examined.[19]

The second Bush Administration had reached a settlement agreement with Microsoft that originally included giving away software to public school children, but this agreement was rejected. Many saw that solution as going too soft on Microsoft.[20]

In the meantime, Mr. Gates has not stood still. He is actively trying to compete with Google and other companies like RealNetworks even in the face of questions of whether we get enough innovation from Microsoft and in the midst of legal judgments like the $613 million fine levied by the European Union.[21]

However, this could be only the beginning of a new dynamic in our country where in the face of superior competitors, companies don't adapt or don't mutate – but rather sue for the government to change the economic environment in such a way that inferiority is no longer punished, but rescued by the United States Justice Department.

Which brings us to Larry Page. This young entrepreneur, along with Sergey Brin, started Google and was named CEO of this mammoth company in 2011. Maybe too mammoth is the word on the antitrust street today…

I, like most of you, would not know what to do without Google. I know that in the old days (1990s), I had to tell my students to go to the library and use the Dewey Decimal System to look up information that proved I was not lying to them. Today, they can Google my statements on the way out of the classroom door and within seconds find out if I am prone to big fibs.

Now that Google has a 70% market share of search engine advertising, the U.S. Justice Department has begun sniffing around to determine whether Messrs. Page and Brin are really a couple of bad dudes who are hurting all of us (or 70% of us…).

The accusation is straightforward: Google, critics charge, rigs clicks by lowering competing search engines rankings on Google pages and the company also locks up critical content, like video and books, so that rival search engines cannot provide their users with access to that content.[22]

Google has denied these charges and contends that there is not only plenty of search engine competition but that the company places websites on its page based on what the consumer is most likely wanting, as we begin typing in words like "canoeing in British Columbia," "Thai restaurants," or "Bronko Nagurski jersey," rather than on some rigged system designed to help with advertising dollars.[23]

PUBLIC UTILITY ECONOMICS

A final issue to consider in this discussion of monopoly is what to do about natural monopolies. A natural monopoly is a monopoly that emerges as a result of significant economies of scale. The electric utility industry has long been considered a prime example of this type of monopoly.

This type of monopoly has gone through serious examination in the last 25 years or so, beginning with the deregulation of natural gas pipelines in the United States. Today, there is a serious question as to whether or not the situation illustrated in Figure 15.4 is reality or fiction in an age where technological advances have changed the way electric power is transmitted to households and business firms. For now, where you find a natural monopoly, you will find government regulation over the prices, output, and costs of production.

The basic problem with the natural monopoly is that competition – even if invited – is not economically possible. Once an established firm enters the market and achieves economies of scale, entry by even a second firm is pointless.

Consider the cost of constructing a new hydroelectric power plant located in the mountains of North Carolina. Once the hundreds of millions of dollars of construction costs are incurred and the transmission lines, grids, and physical connections to homes and businesses are complete, the electric company must produce a very large amount of power in order to lower the average fixed, average variable, and average total cost of production. This

Photo courtesy Jack Chambless

gives a tremendous advantage to the first company that enters the market. Once that company is established and has achieved economies of scale, no other company could feasibly enter the market.

With a natural monopoly in place, the established firm would be able to operate with impunity and charge very high prices (Pm) without worrying about new competitors emerging. Making matters worse is the case of electric power. Electric power is not like the market for donuts. If a donut monopoly emerged, we could live without donuts. We cannot live in total darkness taking cold showers and eating spoiled food!

More than a century ago, state and local governments (dealing with railroads at the time) felt that if a firm has a significant impact on the safety and well-being of the community – and if it enjoys a natural monopoly position – the most desirable means of dealing with that firm is to *regulate* the price and output level.[24]

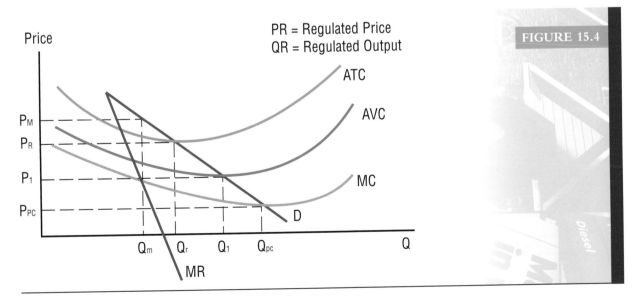

FIGURE 15.4

Regulation means not allowing the firm to charge a monopoly price, but it also means not forcing a price so low as to eliminate the incentive to provide the product to begin with. Notice that if the regulators forced the monopolist to act like a purely competitive firm, the price would equal *Ppc* and output would equal *Qpc*. *Marginal cost pricing* would lead to a bankrupt electric utility and an increase in candle sales in your town.

If the regulators allow the utility to charge a price that lets the utility just cover the *average variable cost* of production, the utility will be operating right at the shutdown point. Where would money for innovation or pollution-reduction technology come from if the company cannot cover its fixed costs of production?

The regulators end up settling on an average total cost-pricing model. Under this model, the utility is allowed to cover their fixed and variable costs of production, plus earn a set profit that is hopefully high enough to attract investors and provide safe and effective service as well as new technologies. The formula for this type of *average cost pricing* is:

$$RR = 0 + T + (V\text{-}D)\ r$$

Where RR is the revenue requirement, 0 is the operating expenses of the utility, T equals taxes paid by the utility, V equals the value of the current plant in service, D equals accumulated depreciation on the plant in service, and r equals a rate of return on the plant in service. Once the revenue requirement is set, the commission divides this amount of money by the projected kilowatt hours demanded to set the per-kilowatt-hour charge you see on your electric bill.

PROBLEMS WITH UTILITY REGULATION

Did you visit California in 2000? Did you take along some flashlights and fresh batteries? In one of the most bizarre economic catastrophes in recent memory, the state of California focused America's attention on an industry people never thought much of in the past. In the "good ol'

days" we flipped a switch and the lights came on. People were not taking that for granted as much as they used to, thanks to a deregulation model gone awry. Before we get to that problem, we will address other inefficiencies that plague the utility industry.

GOLD PLATING

One of the major criticisms of public utility regulation is that if utilities are allowed to submit expenses to a body of elected regulators, the utility will have every incentive to inflate expenses in order to be allowed a higher rate charged to its customers. Moreover, some charge that utilities have an incentive to offer gifts to regulators to curry favor in the attempt to get better rates. This is known as "gold-plating" the rate base, and was very common in the 1970s, before skyrocketing oil prices made regulators pay more attention to the costs of providing electricity.

THE LACK OF RESEARCH AND DEVELOPMENT

In August of 2003 I was in Central Park playing with my children, when all of a sudden I saw what appeared to be every human on Earth walking in the streets of Manhattan. The great blackout of 2003 caused Congress, consumers, businesses, and probably your neighbor's dog to scream for the government to do something to help with energy conservation, new energy sources, and improvements in the technology associated with energy use.

The problem is that most of this research has been traditionally attempted by utilities, but utility regulators are concerned about keeping rates low so voters will keep them in office. How can a utility incur costs associated with research and development without these costs being rejected in a rate hearing? This is a very real problem.

One study found that one of the major reasons the United States has failed to successfully develop alternatives to highly polluting energy sources like coal and oil is that utility regulators often refuse to allow research and

SUGGESTED CLASSROOM DEBATE

While he was campaigning for the presidency, John McCain advocated increasing the number of nuclear power plants this country utilizes. Is this a good — or bad — idea? Why?

development expenditures to be passed on to rate-payers. The commissioners appear to be afraid to raise rates on current consumers with the hope that the R&D will lead to a long-run improvement in service and thus a long-run reduction in prices.[25] This myopic view has meant that the United States continues to trail the rest of the world in alternative fuel research that could help clean up the environment while saving rate-payers' money.[26]

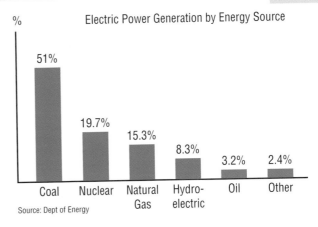

Electric Power Generation by Energy Source

Coal: 51%
Nuclear: 19.7%
Natural Gas: 15.3%
Hydro-electric: 8.3%
Oil: 3.2%
Other: 2.4%

Source: Dept of Energy

THE NUCLEAR SCARE

Watch an episode of *The Simpsons* and you will know all you need to know about why Americans are afraid of nuclear power. In our economically — and often technologically — illiterate nation, people believe that the use of nuclear power means that we will end up glowing in the dark, with strange new limbs protruding from our bodies. This can be attributed to an accident that took place on Three Mile Island in Pennsylvania in 1979 and the meltdown of the Soviet Union's Chernobyl plant in the mid-1980s, as well as the recent catastrophe in Japan. Since 1973 there has not been one nuclear plant application in the United States.[27]

As you can see in the next table, the United States relies primarily on coal for power generation. France, on the other hand, uses nuclear power for about 80% of the power generated in that nation.[28]

What does France know that we don't? France knows that in terms of pollution, coal and oil generate far greater damage to the environment than nuclear power.

Besides contaminating the environment with toxic sulfur and nitrogen oxides (18 million tons in one recent year), arsenic, mercury, fluorine, and lead, coal plants release about 100 times as much radioactivity, megawatt for megawatt, as nuclear systems. This is because coal contains radioactive uranium and thorium that is concentrated by burning.[29] By contrast, nuclear power plants release no significant pollutants into the environment. A 1,000-megawatt power plant generates about 20 cubic meters of waste per year. This is enough waste to fill two SUVs. A similar size coal power plant creates 500,000 tons of sold waste, while a natural gas plant creates 200,000 tons of waste.

The sulfur dioxide emissions from coal-fired power plants in the eastern half of the United States have been responsible for smog, acid rain, and the devastation of forests ranging from Smoky Mountain National Park to Maine. Even with scrubber technology that allows power plants to reduce airborne pollutants, coal is a less desirable energy source in comparison to nuclear power.[30] France also knows that nuclear power is relatively cheap, safe, and reliable. In fact, if we look at other forms of power generation like wind and water, we find that, while wind and hydropower are fairly nonpolluting, the British Thermal Unit cost comparison to nuclear makes nuclear an economically superior form of power generation.[31]

With millions of pages of regulations that govern nuclear power generation, the chances of America having a Chernobyl-type accident are extremely low. In fact, more people have died as a result of pollution from other sources of energy than the sum of every person who has ever died from the blast of a nuclear bomb or the meltdown of a nuclear reactor. If rational thought, rather than hysteria, governed America's energy policy, we would see many more nuclear plants built and a possible resolution for many of our energy problems.[32]

Would it be better to rely on wind power?

Photo courtesy Jack Chambless

Is Help on the Way?

As we have seen in the previous chapters, when the economic environment undergoes sudden changes, we tend to see adaptive responses to those changes. Some adaptive behavior works while other trials end in error. Most often we see the adaptive behavior take place in the private sector. In the case of electricity markets, the United States government might actually have some sensible plans.

Many economists have been arguing for years that electric power was moving away from being a natural monopoly and toward a market similar to long-distance telephone service where more than one carrier could feasibly provide safe and reliable service.

In March of 2002, the Federal Energy Regulatory Commission announced plans to create mandatory universal rules for the nation's electricity markets.[33] Under this plan, the utilities will be encouraged to surrender control of their high-voltage transmission lines to independent organizations. The idea is to stimulate investment in transmission lines and substations that currently impede the flow of electricity and raise wholesale prices.

In theory, the increased investment would lead to greater economies of scale and lower prices in the future — especially since those utilities that do not voluntarily give up their lines will still have to operate under the new rules for transmitting power.

More recently, in 2009 President Obama proposed spending $3.4 billion for 100 projects aimed at modernizing the power grid. The projects include installing "smart" electric meters in homes, automating utility substations, and installing thousands of new digital transformers and grid sensors.[34]

Given the age and state of disrepair in the nation's power grid, such discussions by the President are timely and appropriate. Whether his proposal is the right one to implement remains to be seen.

Endnotes

1 See "Microsoft is Found to be a Predatory Monopolist" by John R. Wilke and David Bank, *The Wall Street Journal*, November 8, 1999.

2 See "Postal Service Eyes Closing Thousands of Post Offices" by Jennifer Levitz, *The Wall Street Journal*, January 24, 2011.

3 See "Barriers to Entry" by Harold Demsetz, *The American Economic Review*, Volume 72, No. 1, March 1982.

4 See "Beware the Jerk-O-Meter" by Michael Kunelman, *The Courier-Journal*, August 12, 2005.

5 See David N. Hyman, Economics, 3rd edition, Irwin 1994, p. 284.

6 For more on the importance of patents, see "In India, a High-Tech Outpost for U.S. Patents" by Saritha Rai, *The New York Times*, December 15, 2003; and "Patents" by Sabra Crawford, *The New York Times*, December 29, 2003.

7 See "Movie Industry Steps Up Drive Against Pirates" by Sarah McBride and Bruce Orwell, *The Wall Street Journal*, January 27, 2004, p. B1; and "Copyfight," *The Wall Street Journal*, November 26-27, 2005.

8 See "Lars Johnson Has Goats on His Roof and a Stable of Lawyers to Prove It" by Justin Scheck and Stu Woo, *The Wall Street Journal*, September 17, 2010.

9 See "China Denies Halting Rare-Earth Exports to Japan" by James T. Areddy, David Fickling and Norihiko, *The Wall Street Journal*, September 23, 2010.

10 See "A Lender Hopes to Profit from the New Taxi Math" by Tim Gray, *The New York Times*, January 25, 2004.

11 See "QWERTY Spells a Saga of Market Economics" by Lee Gomes, *The Wall Street Journal*, February 25, 1998; and "The Beta-VHS Battle Offers Some Insights Into Coming DVD War" by Lee Gomes, *The Wall Street Journal*, 2006.

12 See "Move Over, Coke" by Gwendolyn Bounds, *The Wall Street Journal*, January 30, 2006, p. R1.

13 See "How Driving Prices Lower Can Violate Antitrust Statutes" by John R. Wilke, *The Wall Street Journal*, January 27, 1975, p. A1.

14 This may be why many nations have privatized the postal service. See "39 reasons to privatize mail system" by Sam Ryan, *The Orlando Sentinel*, January 8, 2006.

15 See "Unlike Big Dailies, A Paper Prospers in Bismarck, N.D." by Joseph T. Hallinan, *The Wall Street Journal*, February 8, 2006.

16 See "On Microsoft, Standard Oil and Trustbusters" by Holman W. Jenkins Jr., *The Wall Street Journal*, May 20, 1998; "Is Microsoft a Natural Monopoly?" by Ted Lewis, *The Scientific American*, February 1998; and "Government against business" by Walter Williams, *Jewish World Review*, April 12, 2000.

17 See "Why Bill Gates is Wrong" by James F. Rill, *The Wall Street Journal*, November 20, 1997.

18 See "Why the Case for a Breakup Breaks Down" by Richard B. McKenzie and William F. Shugart III, *The Wall Street Journal*, April 25, 2000.

19 See "That's Some Fine Mess You've Made, Mr. Gates" by Michael A. Cusumano, *The Wall Street Journal*, 2000; and "Microsoft Judge Faces Demands of Market and of Monopoly Law" by John R. Wilke, Rebecca Buckman, and David P. Hamilton, *The Wall Street Journal*, April 4, 2000.

20 See "U.S. Settlement With Microsoft is Opposed by Top Economists" by Nicholas Kulish, *The Wall Street Journal*, January 28, 2002.

21 See "The Coming Search Wars" by John Markoff, *The New York Times*, February 1, 2004; "Musical Chairs with the Big Boys" by Steve Lohr, *The New York Times*, March 21, 2004; "Do We Get Enough in Innovation for What we Give to Microsoft" by Lee Gomes, *The Wall Street Journal*, March 8, 2004, p. B1; and "Defeat" by Jube Shiver Jr., *The Los Angeles Times* (appearing in *The Orlando Sentinel*), March 25, 2004, p. C1.

22 See "Trust Us Isn't an Answer" by Charles F. Rule, *The Wall Street Journal*, September 17, 2010.

23 See "Competition in an Instant" by Amit Singhal, *The Wall Street Journal*, September 17, 2010.

24 To read about the earliest case of public utility regulation (Munn v. Illinois, 1877), see *Public Utility Economics and Finance* by Keith M. Howe & Eugene F. Rasmussen, Prentice-Hall, 1982.

25 See "An R&D Policy for Regulated Natural Gas and Electric Utilities" by Donald Murry, Barnet Groten, and Jack A. Chambless, *The Public Utilities Fortnightly*, February 1991.

26 See "U.S. Power grid still at risk" by William McCall, *The Orlando Sentinel*, November 27, 2005.

27 See "Nuclear Power: Revival or Relapse?" by Rebecca Smith, *The Wall Street Journal*, May 2, 2001.

28 See "The French Idea" by Michael Rival, *The Boston Globe*, February 3, 2002, p. C8; and "With a Big Nuclear Push, France Transforms Its Energy Equation" by Jeffrey Ball, *The Wall Street Journal*, March 28, 2006.

29 See "A nuclear new age" by Richard Rhodes, *The Boston Globe*, February 3, 2002, p. C8.

30 For more on this, see www.pw1.netcom.com/~res95/energy/nuclear.html.

31 See "Nuclear Power Making Worldwide Comeback" by H. Sterling Burnett, *Environment & Climate News* (The Heartland Institute), May 2005, p.6.

32 See "A Nuclear Renaissance?" by Vijay V. Vaitheeswaran, *The Wall Street Journal*, March 30, 2004.

33 See "FERC Plans Rules for Electricity Markets" by Rebecca Smith, *The Wall Street Journal*, March 14, 2002.

34 See "Obama putting $3.4B toward 'smart' power grid" by H. Josef Hebert, *The Associated Press*, October 27, 2009.

CHAPTER REVIEW

1. How does the monopoly demand and marginal revenue curve differ from that of a purely competitive firm?

2. Why can a monopolist never charge a price that maximizes total revenue?

3. List four barriers of entry, how they work, and what good might come out of them.

4. What is a natural monopoly? Is this common in our economy? Why, or why not?

5. What are antitrust laws? Are they necessary? Why, or why not?

Chapter Sixteen

OLIGOPOLY *and* MONOPOLISTIC COMPETITION

*P*eople of the same trade seldom meet together, even for merriment and diversion, but the conversation ends in a conspiracy against the public, or in some contrivance to raise prices.

ADAM SMITH

HOW THE REAL WORLD LOOKS

In the previous two chapters we explored market structures that are very rare in the real world. The purpose of examining such relatively abstract structures is to better understand how industry is actually organized between the purely competitive, or monopoly, cases. These more realistic and very common industries are known as oligopoly and monopolistic competition.

OLIGOPOLY

Oligopoly is a market structure in which a few sellers dominate the sales of a product that may be standardized, or differentiated, and where entry of new sellers is difficult or impossible.

For example, according to the American Meat Institute, four beef packing companies process nearly 70% of the cattle slaughtered in the United States. This is an example of an oligopoly providing a *standardized* service. Oligopolistic industries in the U.S. include the oil, tobacco, aircraft, health insurance, military equipment, and motor vehicle industries.

The market for college textbooks, a *differentiated* industry, has three companies – Pearson, Thomson, and McGraw-Hill – that control over 60% of sales. Five companies sell over 70% of all cellular phones, and in the beer industry, the top three corporations sell over 80% of the beer.[1]

Whether the product sold is standardized or differentiated, every firm in an oligopolistic market is interdependent. Therefore pricing, output, and marketing decisions are always made with the possible reaction of other competitors in mind.

For example, Anheuser-Busch InBev agreed to spend $1.2 billion from 2011 through the 2016 National Football League season, to make Bud Light the "official" beer of the NFL.[2] Anheuser-Busch InBev, the number-one brewer in the United States, entered into this agreement well aware of the fact that the NFL is a huge arena from which to market beer. Anheuser-Busch InBev executives also knew that Molson-Coors and SAP-Miller would not sit still and allow their market share to fall. A reaction by your rivals is always imminent in the oligopoly arena.

HOW OLIGOPOLIES ARISE

Historically, oligopolies have arisen as the result of price wars, innovation, economies of scale, the achievement of brand-name loyalty, and mergers. We will address each of these.

ECONOMIES OF SCALE

You should recall from the chapter on productivity and costs that economies of scale are cost savings associated with large-scale production. Consider for a moment what it would cost for a brand-new company to enter the market for cars at this point in time. The cost would be in the billions of dollars by the time all of the plants were built and the equipment purchased.

Now that Ford, Toyota, Honda, and General Motors have been in the market for decades, the plant and equipment used to build cars has largely been paid for by mass-producing automobiles. This means that these companies have much lower costs than any new company could hope to have from the outset. As a result, the major companies do not have to fend off 20 or 100 new rivals per year like restaurants do. New companies from China have emerged as a long-term threat but the major producers still enjoy a large share of the market.

INNOVATION

One of the negatives of a purely competitive market is the fact that brutal competition leaves no economic profit with which firms can innovate. This is not the case within an oligopolistic market structure.

Over the past few years, American consumers have been deluged with a dizzying array of sandwich choices. Back "in the day," there were so few choices offered up by restaurants that one could have easily argued that this market structure sold a standardized product. Not anymore.

One stop at a sandwich shop today will reveal two facts: First, while there are many competing firms all over the country, there are only a handful that are selling most of the sandwiches. Worldwide, Subway has over 33,000 stores. Quiznos has over 3,500 and Blimpie has over 2,000 outlets. No other chain has even 300 stores.

The intense competition among these three dominant oligopolists has led to constant innovation. Whether the innovation has come in the form of toasted, or more varied breads, unusual sauces or cheeses, soups or wraps, American consumers have experienced firsthand what economists have known for a long time. That is the fact that sometimes you only need two or three profit-seeking firms to have incredible competition.

BRAND-NAME LOYALTY

People in this country are often fiercely loyal to brand names like Sony, Wrangler, Budweiser, and Harley-Davidson. These brands enjoy significant power, which makes it very difficult for new companies to carve out market share. When market packing is factored in, it can be almost impossible for a new firm to be successful. Gatorade, for example, has relied on extensive marketing, scientific research, advertising, and celebrity endorsements to maintain an 80% market share in the market for sports drinks from 2000-2010.[3]

PRICE WARS

A price war occurs when rival firms engage in a series of price cuts that results in prices falling below the cost of production for some firms that end up exiting the market, leaving the rest of the market to the few surviving companies. The classic example of a price war is the ongoing battle in the airline industry. Almost every year – sometimes several times a year – rival carriers embark on a campaign of price-cutting.

This price-cutting is initially designed to take advantage of the elastic demand for air travel that any one company faces. By cutting prices, quantity demanded increases and revenue increases – for a while.

The problem starts when rival carriers begin slashing rates to beat their competitors' price cuts. Over time, prices fall so much that the demand for air travel becomes inelastic. This means that fares keep dropping, but not enough new passengers buy tickets to offset the price cuts. This leads to falling revenue and economic losses. For some companies that has smaller profit reserves or higher costs of production, the fare reductions end up putting them out of business. As a result, a few major carriers, able to survive this temporary war, end up dominating the market.

As revenue begins to drop, why don't the firms simply call off the price war and increase prices? This would seem to make sense, but it is not as easy at is sounds: Someone has to go first. In this economic game of "chicken" the first firm to raise prices runs the risk of losing market share at a faster rate than their rivals.

MERGERS

One of the most pervasive mechanisms used today to move markets toward oligopoly status is the current wave of mergers in the United States. In banking, telecommunications, auto production, beer, oil, and entertainment, companies are being swallowed up at a record pace. What

SUGGESTED CLASSROOM DEBATE

Over the past few years Starbucks, Dunkin' Donuts, McDonald's, and other firms have competed intensely for coffee-drinkers' business. This competition has created a dizzying array of coffees. Does this help, or hurt consumers in the long run? Why?

does this mean for consumers and the economy in general? The answer to that question is likely to be found years down the road.

TYPES OF MERGERS

In our economy, there are three types of mergers – vertical mergers, conglomerate mergers, and horizontal mergers.

VERTICAL MERGER

This is a merger among firms that are interdependent in the stages of production. For example, if Restoration Hardware (a home-furnishing company) purchased a tropical wood plantation in Indonesia, this would be a vertical merger. The rationale for such a merger would be to *assure the supply* of tropical wood and thus lower the long-run input cost of manufacturing furniture. Another reason would be to create some economies of scale associated with shared business strategies and inventory control. In 2005 Federal Express acquired Kinko's in an attempt to give Federal Express faster access to small businesses.[4]

Vertical integration was one of the major reasons why John D. Rockefeller enjoyed such a large market share. By combining the recovery, transportation, refining, and marketing of petroleum, he ensured the supply of oil for American consumers and ensured enormous efficiencies in production for Standard Oil.

CONGLOMERATE MERGER

This is a merger among non-competing firms. A great example of a conglomerate merger is Disney's acquisition of the American Broadcasting Company (ABC). A conglomerate merger is usually designed to help a company *enter new markets* and *diversify their operations*, in order to reduce the risk of having their entire income stream be based on one good or service.

By acquiring ABC, Disney was able to be more aggressive with the sports-related endeavors it has undertaken. ABC owned ESPN – the all-sports channel – and the broadcast rights to football, baseball, and basketball games. With this merger Disney has been able to penetrate these markets to help stimulate the demand for its sports-related goods and services.

HORIZONTAL MERGER

This is a merger among competing firms. The Exxon-Mobil, Ford-Volvo, and SAP-Miller Brewing Company[5] mergers are each examples of a horizontal merger. There are several

reasons for this type of merger. One might be to *penetrate new markets* that otherwise would be difficult to enter.

In 2006 appliance manufacturers Whirlpool and Maytag sought a merger. By merging with one another the two companies would be able to share technology, and blend the marketing styles, making it more likely that one strong company – rather than two – could compete with Korea, China, and the European appliance makers.

A second reason for this type of merger is to achieve *economies of scale*. Sometimes the synergy gained from avoiding the duplication of goods and services can lead to cost savings in the long run. For example, a typical semiconductor fabrication plant costs between $2 billion and $3 billion, compared to about $1 billion in the late 1990s. A maker of basic computer chips must sell far more chips to justify this huge fixed-cost investment, which is why Micron Technology Inc. sought to purchase the chip-making assets of South Korea's Hynix Semiconductor Inc. This proposed merger would have lead to four chip makers dominating 83% of the market – compared to the top four having 46% of the chip market in the mid-1990s.

The biggest reason for these types of mergers, however, is to *reduce competition*. In July of 2008 the Belgian beer company, InBev paid $49.91 billion for rival Anheuser-Busch. As the beer industry continues to go through a wave of consolidation InBev's executives felt that this merger would put it in a better position to compete against Molson-Coors and SAP-Miller and other craft beer suppliers. With one less competitor to deal with, the probability of profit is increased.

MERGERS AND TEXTBOOK PRICES

Many of you may be under the impression that textbook prices take up such a large part of your budget because you usually have only one store selling books. Since Borders must face daily competition from Amazon, eBay, Barnes & Noble, and others, Borders will sell you a thicker book than this one for less money. In the textbook market, it is not always the bookstore – and it is certainly *not the authors* – who are the culprits behind rising prices. Whom, or more accurately what, is to blame?

As it turns out, you can assign much of the blame on the United States Justice Department. This government agency must evaluate every proposed merger of a horizontal nature in the United States for the possible ill effects the merger might have on consumers and economic efficiency. If the Justice Department believes that a merger will substantially lessen competition, dramatically increase prices, and reduce innovation in a given industry, the merger will most likely not be allowed.

In the textbook market, the pace of merger activity has been extraordinary. A few years ago, Thomson, the second-largest publisher, bid for the college textbook line of Harcourt General Inc., which was number four in the market at that time. Charles James, the Justice Department's assistant attorney general for antitrust initially objected to the merger, warning that competition would be lessened and that students would pay higher prices.[6] Some of you who pay more than $200 per book, might be saying, "No kidding!" Hold on. It gets better.

The Justice Department allowed the merger, and now three companies control about 62% of the entire college textbook market. According to the textbook publishers, students will *actually be better off* as a result of the greater oligopoly power of the publishers.

The conjecture here is that sales representatives can now be more specialized and therefore know more about the various books they are offering to professors since they don't have as many books to examine. With greater specialization *could* come a better matching of the needs of your professor with the books available, and thus, a more efficient classroom experience for you.

Critics of this argument suggest that, in the long run, the mergers will reduce the incentives the textbook publishers have to take risks associated with offering books that may not appeal to the masses, but only to certain niches.

If there were hundreds of publishers, we could see more attention focused on a niche' book like the one in your hand. With the market becoming less and less competitive, there is a real concern that the publishers will play it safe and not branch out into more innovative books.

THE LEGALITY OF HORIZONTAL MERGERS

The following table represents the domestic cable television industry not so long ago. Since the time this data was made available, the cable industry has undergone significant merger activity.[7] Let's take a look at one possible merger to see if the Justice Department would allow or disallow the acquisition to take place.

COMPANY	SUBSCRIBERS	MARKET SHARE (%)	CUMULATIVE SHARE (%)
Tele-Communications	13,724,000	23.1	23.1
Time Warner Cable	11,715,000	19.8	42.9
Continental Cablevision, Inc.	4,191,000	7.1	50.0
Comcast Corporation	3,408,000	5.7	55.7
Cox Communications	3,249,000	5.5	61.2
Cablevision Systems Corporation	2,725,00	4.6	65.8
Adelphia Communications	1,654,000	2.8	68.6
Jones Intercable, Inc.	1,390,00	2.3	70.9
Marcus Cable	1,250,00	2.1	73.0
Viacom Cable	1,180,000	2.0	75.0
Falcon Cable TV	1,171,000	2.0	77.0
Century Communications Corp.	1,093,000	1.8	78.9
Charter Communications	1,079,000	1.8	80.7
Scripps Howard Cable	766,000	1.3	82.0
Lenfest Group	759,000	1.3	83.2
Prime Cable	651,000	1.1	84.3
TKR Cabel	646,000	1.1	85.4
TCA Cable TV, Inc.	612,000	1.0	86.5
InterMedia Partners	571,000	1.0	87.4
MediaOne, Inc.	528,000	0.9	88.3
Post-Newsweek Cable, Inc.	518,000	0.9	89.2
Industry Total	59,288,526		
Herfindahl-Hirschman Index (HHI)	**1107**		

Sources: National Cable Television Associations, from Paul Kagan Associates, Inc., 1995, and Warren Publishing.

Suppose Time-Warner Communications (now Bright House Networks) had decided to merge with Cox Communications a few years ago. The test the government would use to determine whether this – or any other – horizontal merger would be allowed is based on the following questions:

WHAT IS THE RELEVANT MARKET?

This question will center on the *geographic* market and *product* market. If the government defines the geographic market narrowly – for example, if the market is confined to the U.S., rather than North America – the merger might not be allowed.

In essence, the government would want to know if consumers have choices from outside the U.S. for cable television. If they effectively do not, the market would be defined as just the U.S. The product market definition would center on whether or not there are viable substitutes for cable television.

If the government defines the market in a broad sense – that is considering satellite dishes and cell phones as a competitor – the merger has a better chance of being allowed, because consumers would stand a lower chance of facing few choices and dramatically higher prices. If, on the other hand, the government defines the market narrowly – just cable television – the merger could be in trouble.

IS THE FIRM TO BE ACQUIRED A FAILING FIRM?

If Cox Communications had been facing bankruptcy, or were already bankrupt, this merger would have a much greater chance of being allowed. That is because the government would view the merger as a rescue of the failing firm. This rescue could lead to jobs being saved and increased income for the economy.

IS THERE EASE OF ENTRY INTO THE MARKET?

If the government determines that it is not very difficult for new firms to enter the market for cable television, the merger has a better chance of being allowed. This is because the government would feel that even if the merger pushed up prices, the higher prices would draw in new firms and push prices back down in the long run. The government does not want to stand in the way of mergers that may actually save or create more jobs, in the long run, than might be destroyed in the short run, as the merged companies shed duplicated services and jobs.

WILL THE MERGER LEAD TO INCREASED EFFICIENCIES?

If this merger led to economies of scale or some synergy in marketing and distributing cable services, it would have a good chance of being allowed under the assumption that such increased efficiencies, in the long run, will benefit the consumer.

HOW IS THE COMPETITIVE BALANCE OF THE INDUSTRY AFFECTED?

To answer this question, the government relies on something called the *Herfindahl-Hirschman Index* (HHI). This index is a number that represents the relative competitiveness of any given market. The test here is simple. Time Warner had a 19.8% market share. Cox Communications had a 5.5% market share. Squaring the market share of each firm and adding it up derives the HHI for the entire cable industry. Notice that the HHI for cable television is 1107.

The squared market share for Time Warner is 392.04. The squared market share for Cox Communications is 30.25. If the companies merge and become one company, combined they would have a market share of 25.3%, and a squared market share of 640.9.

If we take the original HHI of 1107 and subtract 392.04 and 30.25 (to account for the disappearance of Time Warner and Cox as separate companies), we are left with:

$$1107 - 392.04 - 30.25 = 684.71$$

If we then add the new squared market share of the combined firms we get:

684.71 + 640.9 = 1325.61, which means the difference between the original HHI and the post-merger HHI is: 1325.61 - 1107 = 218.6

What does this mean? The government has a simple final test for whether or not a merger among competing firms will be allowed.

> ➤ If the pre-merger HHI is more than 1800, a merger that increases the HHI by more than 50–100 points will be challenged.
> ➤ If the pre-merger HHI is 1000–1800 a merger that increases the HHI by more than 100 points will be challenged.
> ➤ If the pre-merger HHI is below 1000, there will be no challenge.

In this case, the merger would most likely be challenged because the HHI increased by such a large amount. The government would use this information, in addition to the answers to the previous questions, to determine whether the merger would be allowed.

RANK	BREWER	SHARE (%)	VOLUME (MILLIONS OF BARRELS)
1.	Anheuser-Busch	48.4	98.3
2.	SAP-Miller	20.9	41.6
3.	Molson-Coors	11.5	23.0
4.	Pabst	5.3	10.5
5.	Genesee	0.6	1.4
6.	Boston Beer Co.	0.6	1.2
7.	Latrobe Brewing	0.6	1.1
8.	D.G. Yuengling	0.5	0.9
9.	Sierrra Nevada	0.3	0.5
10.	Minnesota Brewing	0.2	0.4

CONCEPT CHECK

Would a merger between Pabst and Minnesota Brewing be allowed? Is the HHI still a relevant tool, or should the antitrust laws be changed to reflect global competition? Why, or why not? In the wake of the investment banking crisis in 2008, should banks be allowed to merge without getting permission from antitrust authorities? Why, or why not?

HOW OLIGOPOLIES ARE MAINTAINED

It goes without saying that maintaining market power is of paramount concern to the oligopolist. Refer to the previous chapter (where barriers to entry were addressed) in order to gain an appreciation for how oligopolists in the real world keep profits rolling in. However, there are two other major ways firms with market power keep that power: That is through price leadership and cartels.

> ➤ **Price leadership occurs when one dominant firm in an industry sets its price and all of the other firms in the industry respond by charging the same, or virtually identical, price.**

The theme park industry in Orlando, Florida, is a classic example of how oligopolies operate. Disney World is considered the dominant theme park in this area. Universal Studios of Florida and Sea World make up the other major parks.

Every time Disney announces a change in prices, shortly afterwards, Universal Studios and Sea World respond by setting prices that are eerily similar to Disney.[8] Is this tacit collusion or just smart business? The debate could go either way. The real question is what would happen if the other parks did *not* follow Disney's lead?

With much higher profit reserves, Disney could potentially punish Universal and Sea World by initiating a damaging price war to *encourage* the other parks to be more cooperative. Sea World and Universal Studios could ill-afford a prolonged battle with Disney, so consumers should not be surprised if prices do not vary much over time.

A second way an oligopoly can be maintained over time is when firms in an industry form a cartel.

> ➤ **A cartel is a group of firms acting together to coordinate output decisions and control prices, as if they were a single monopoly.**

Cartels are illegal in the United States under the Sherman Antitrust Act. However, some economists have suggested that they do exist in the U.S., as we will see in a moment. They certainly exist abroad. The most famous is the Organization of Petroleum Exporting Countries (OPEC).

FORMING A CARTEL

The Rawlings Sporting Goods Company is facing uncertain times. This baseball glove maker for over 120 years is currently facing a serious challenge from Wilson Sporting

Goods and Nike in a market that Rawlings has dominated since before the days of the automobile.[9]

The problem that Rawlings faces is twofold. First, baseball is far less popular among young people than it used to be. Second, among those young people who are buying new baseball gloves, they now prefer Nike's gloves that offer protection from sweat and a wide array of colors, to the traditional (old-fashioned?) black and brown.

Suppose that, rather than fight Nike, Wilson, and others, Rawlings executives get together with the other glove makers in a smoke-filled room and attempt to create a baseball glove cartel. The purpose of the cartel would be to help each firm avoid ruinous competition, and thus earn greater profits over time. If the companies decided to collude, rather than compete, the following steps would be necessary:

> ➤ **Make sure that a barrier to entry prevents other firms from selling baseball gloves after the price of baseball gloves is increased.**

If free entry were possible, an increase in price would attract new baseball glove manufacturers. The supply of gloves would increase, prices would fall, and profits would once again be eradicated. The barrier in this case would most likely be economies of scale and brand-name loyalty.

> ➤ **Organize a meeting of all glove makers to establish a target level of output.**

At this meeting, the Rawlings, Nike, and others would compare the output level that was produced when intense competition existed with the monopoly output level necessary to make profit. Once this output level is determined, the cartel members would:

> ➤ **Set up quotas for the members of the glove cartel and divide the agreed-upon cartel output among the firms.**

In this step, the largest member of the cartel – Rawlings in this case (28-30% market share) – would be allowed to produce the largest part of the target output.

The output level is divided up along these lines until every member knows exactly how much output they are allowed to supply.

> ➤ **Make sure no one exceeds the quota!**

Of all the steps necessary to have a successful cartel, this is the most onerous. Setting monopoly price and output is relatively easy. It may even be easy to get the members to agree on the quota. But due to the age-old problem of greed, each member of the cartel has a *built-in incentive to cheat*.

Cheating usually takes the form of one or more companies deciding that it won't hurt the cartel as a whole if they produce "a few more gloves" than the allowed quota. The problem is that every company is thinking the exact same thing! Once the cheating starts, and a lot more gloves begins to appear on the market, mistrust leads each member to think that if they don't sell all the gloves they can now, the price is going to plummet from the cheating that is taking place. Of course, this only magnifies the over-supplying of the product, and pushes prices down even more.

A CARTEL THAT IS DOING JUST FINE...

A classic example of a cartel that actually works well is the National Collegiate Athletic Association (NCAA) and other major sports industries in the U.S. The NCAA has a barrier to entry that stems from the brand-name loyalty high school athletes have for the elite schools. If an athlete coming out of high school wants to increase the likelihood of making it to the NBA or NFL, he will most likely attend college at some place like The University of Alabama rather than a place like Kansas Wesleyan – a small NAIA school in Salina, Kansas.

Alabama is on television quite frequently and faces top-level competition. Few people even know where Salina, Kansas, is. Another barrier the NCAA cartel possesses is ownership of virtually the entire supply of their

---

SUGGESTED CLASSROOM DEBATE

Sam Bradford, the former starting quarterback at The University of Oklahoma earned as much money playing for the Sooners as little boys earn playing in their backyard. Should the NCAA be abolished by the antitrust authorities? Should college athletes be paid a salary while they are in school?

CONCEPT CHECK

In 2010, the U.S. Supreme Court ruled that the National Football League is not a single entity but rather 32 separate organizations. The ruling allowed American Needle Inc. to sue the NFL for its exclusive contract with Reebok to provide uniforms and apparel.[12] Does the NFL have any of the characteristics of a cartel? Why, or why not?

key resource – the players! In one of the great schemes of all-time, the NCAA is able to procure top talent for *zero salary.*

The players are not allowed to be paid as employees of the college. They can only accept scholarships to attend school. Having virtually free labor is one of the great ways the NCAA makes a fortune – about $300 million for the executive office alone out of total annual revenues of approximately $3 billion. This has prompted some athletes to consider forming a union to seek greater benefits and insurance from the NCAA cartel.[10]

Each year the NCAA sets up the number of games that will be played (the target output) and does not allow, for example, Oregon State University to play Notre Dame for extra money. The NCAA also negotiates television contracts and determines the number of post-season games.

The NCAA also makes sure no one cheats on the quota of games, or on the rules, by having stiff fines and sanctions for violators.[11] As a matter of fact, the NCAA rarely has to worry about revenue shortfalls since taxpayers pay for a lot of the athletics funding at public universities.

OPEC: A STABLE CARTEL?

The members of OPEC can only wish they were as successful in maintaining a cartel arrangement as the NCAA. Formed in 1960, this cartel has gone through economic highs and lows that are of shocking proportions.

From 1960 until 1973, OPEC did not flex its economic muscle as a world power in the market for oil. It was not until the autumn of 1973 when the United States

supported Israel during its war with Syria and Egypt that OPEC decided to act on its market power.

OPEC's response to American support of Israel was to launch the Arab-Oil Embargo. This embargo led to a dramatic reduction in the supply of oil to the United States and much higher oil and gas prices. All of a sudden, OPEC realized just how inelastic the demand for oil was. With this realization came dramatic increases in prices throughout the 1970s – culminating with a price escalation following the Iranian Revolution in 1979. With prices hovering around $40 per barrel, OPEC felt it could

Photo courtesy Jack Chambless

SUGGESTED CLASSROOM DEBATE

As the price of gasoline increases, oil rigs like this one in northern Oklahoma tend to be brought back into production. Should America attempt to become more energy independent – even if OPEC nations have a comparative advantage? Why, or why not?

wield its economic might with impunity against the West. This belief was severely myopic.

Once prices rose to that level and stayed there, there was a great global search by American and other foreign companies for alternatives to Middle-East oil. That search turned up vast reserves of oil in Alaska and the North Sea. These ventures would have been uneconomic when oil prices were low, due to the enormous cost of getting the oil out of these regions. However, with prices at all-time highs, these new sellers saw an opportunity to actually make profit from these new fields. Once Alaskan and North Sea production was under way, it was not very long until economies of scale were realized.

With this increase in supply – that OPEC had invited – the price of oil eventually collapsed to under $10 per barrel in 1986. In March of that year I filled up my car in Paris, Texas, with regular unleaded gasoline selling for 59 cents per gallon.

Since that time, OPEC has tried – unsuccessfully – to restore prices to the levels seen in 1979 and 1980. The problem is the same each time. There is the ongoing incentive to cheat on any agreed-upon quota, and there is too much competition from the rest of the world. In fact, during the summer of 2008, as gas prices shot past $4 per gallon, OPEC production was significantly higher than it was "supposed" to be. OPEC has maintained almost fully capacity production levels for the past few years. The reason prices stayed high during that time was an increasing demand for oil, combined with concerns over production from Nigeria, Venezuela, and Iran.

As a result, U.S. consumers should get accustomed to price fluctuations that will sometimes work to our benefit and other times to our detriment. As long as this cartel and the problem of greed exist, there is no way of accurately gauging which direction oil and gas prices will go.

HOW TO CHALLENGE AN OLIGOPOLIST

What do McDonald's and Burger King have in common? They each have oligopoly power; they each sell hamburgers, and they are both facing serious challenges to the market share that took so long to acquire.

In the case of the burger giants, the challenge has come in the form of *higher-priced* alternatives to hamburgers. One might think that if McDonald's and Burger King have established a long history of appealing to the budget-conscious consumer with fast food and low prices that this loyalty would be hard to combat, unless the two corporations started poisoning people. It did not take a downturn in consumer satisfaction to hurt the fast-food chains. It took the Frontega Chicken Panini.

Over the past couple of years or so, you may have noticed something new in the restaurant business – the fancy sandwich with higher prices. These sandwiches – produced by chains like Panera Bread, the Corner Bakery Café Cosi, and Briazz have nothing in common with hamburgers and everything in common with a market that is adapting to the changing demographics of the American population.

Fast hamburgers traditionally appeal to children up to college-age students. This part of the population is expected to grow by about 5% over the next decade, while the 45- to 64-year-old crowd is expected to see its ranks swell by 30%.

It does not take an economist to point out that people in this latter age bracket have more money and are more health-conscious. This has led to an increase in the demand for a higher-quality fast food. Having established a market niche in burgers, McDonald's and Burger King were not poised to make the step into sandwiches that feature smoked and pulled white-meat chicken, red onion, mozzarella, tomato, chopped basil, and chipotle mayonnaise on rosemary focaccia bread.[13] Yet, McDonald's has successfully adapted to this changing market by incorporating a much more varied menu and has recently seen profits increase as a result.

MONOPOLISTIC COMPETITION

Doug Lieb runs a successful landscaping business near Knoxville, Tennessee. With professionally designed landscapes and a keen eye for detail, he has managed to make a name for himself in the most common type of industry outcome in the U.S. – the monopolistically competitive market structure.

CHARACTERISTICS OF MONOPOLISTIC COMPETITION

Monopolistic competition exists when many sellers compete to sell a differentiated product in a market into which entry of new sellers is possible. In a monopolistically competitive market, these conditions will prevail:

There are relatively large numbers of firms, each satisfying a small, but not microscopic, share of the market demand for a similar, but not identical, product. The market share of each landscaping business in Knoxville is generally larger than it would have been under pure competition, but it is unlikely that any one business satisfies more than 20% of market demand.

The product of each firm is not a perfect substitute for the products of competing firms. Each landscaping business in eastern Tennessee has unique characteristics that cause some buyers to prefer one firm over another. Some companies might offer Sunday planting services while others might specialize in harder-to-obtain trees and shrubs. With a four-year degree from The University of Florida in this field, Mr. Lieb has been able to offer up computerized schematics for his potential customers rather than simply relying on verbal descriptions.

While the services of each business are differentiated, similarities exist. Marketing decisions, therefore, are based largely on highlighting those differences, however slight they may be.

The firms in the market don't consider the reaction of their rivals when choosing their product prices or annual sales targets. Although Mr. Lieb competes against more than 50 other landscapers, he makes decisions independently of what other companies might do. This is because it is understood that his actions can't significantly reduce the market share of his rivals. In the market he works in, he does not have the time, money, or flow of information necessary to gauge how one of his competitors might react to his marketing or sales pitches. He simply focuses on his comparative advantage without regard to who might be pilfering his business strategies.

Relative freedom of entry and exit by new firms exists in monopolistically competitive markets. It is relatively easy to set up a new landscaping business in Knoxville or other cities. Entry may not be quite as easy as it is under pure competition because new firms with new brands or names or services may initially have difficulty in establishing their reputations. When he started his business a few years ago Mr. Lieb did so under the realization that other companies had a brand-name following.

Mr. Lieb had to work extremely hard at providing unique and high-quality services to attract new customers. Of course, once the customers are in the door, the pressure this monopolistically competitive company faces is to keep the clients loyal to his company. This is done by never breaking the *implicit contract* of good customer service.

While it is fairly difficult to generate the necessary cash to be a major participant in the landscaping market, with the right connections, investors can be found to help defray costs. It is also hard – but not impossible – to learn the laws with respect to landscaping in Tennessee, as well as the economics of selling such services. Mr. Lieb does not have a monopoly on the information or financial capital necessary to keep other firms from entering the market.

Neither the opportunity nor the incentive exists for firms in the market to cooperate in ways that decrease competition. Not only does Mr. Lieb understand that it is against the law to attempt to collude with competitors to fix prices, he also understands that this would be a fruitless practice. There are simply too many landscaping companies to coordinate into some sort of cartel arrangement, and entry of new companies cannot be prevented. There is no significant barrier to entry.

MARKET OUTCOMES UNDER MONOPOLISTIC COMPETITION

As can be seen in the diagram below, the demand curve facing Mr. Lieb and other Knoxville landscapers is downward-sloping.

Notice that the slope of the demand curve is not as steep as the monopoly firm. This is because there are several substitutes for any one landscaper's services – making the demand for each landscaper's services relatively *elastic.*

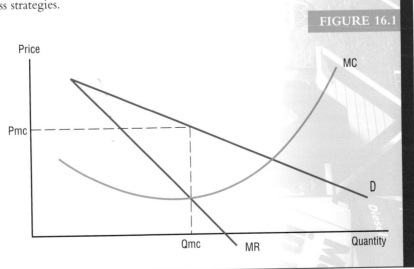

FIGURE 16.1

However, demand is not perfectly elastic because of the differentiated nature of the service provided. If Mr. Lieb raises prices by 17% to cover the rising cost of gasoline, there will still be enough brand loyalty on the part of existing customers that he would not lose significant revenue.

Marginal revenue is less than price for any given output, as in the case of a pure monopoly. Notice, also, that the profit-maximizing output level corresponds to the point where marginal revenue equals marginal cost. Mr. Lieb does not offer to plant trees 24 hours per day. However he also realizes that if he stops working at noon every day, the marginal revenue that could be earned by working a few more hours would be much greater than the marginal cost of working in the afternoon.

However, if he offered to work until 2:30 in the morning, because virtually no one would want to have him making noise out in their yard after midnight, the marginal cost of working that late would be greater than the marginal revenue derived from one or two more customers. Therefore, the profit-maximizing output level (or number of available planting or designing hours) occurs where marginal revenue equals marginal cost.

Once the number of operating hours (output) is set, Mr. Lieb sets his price according to the demand for his services. This price is higher than the price that would occur if there were 10,000 landscapers in Knoxville, but is lower than the price he would charge if the nearest competing landscaper was in Nashville or Charlotte.

SHORT-RUN AND LONG-RUN PROFIT

Of all of the market structures, the one that maintains the greatest fluctuations in profit is the monopolistically competitive market. The problem is very simple. Suppose, at the current average price being charged for landscaping services, firms in Knoxville are making economic profit. With the only barrier to entry being brand-name loyalty, each landscaping company realizes that virtually anyone could enter the market and offer landscaping services. In the long run, profit – like in any other market – attracts new firms, each believing there is room for "one more firm." This means that downward pressure on prices will exist, and profits will be squeezed.

The only way a monopolistically competitive firm can make profit on a continual basis, in the long run, is to constantly strive to *maintain brand-name loyalty* and seek new ways to *differentiate their good or service*.[14] To this extent the monopolistically competitive firm best illustrates the theory of biological economics. There is tremendous pressure on these firms to adapt, mutate, and create a successful way of doing business that will help them survive when times are tough.

Times were very tough in 2007. The Southeastern part of the United States was hit by the worst drought since 1895 – the year rainfall records were first kept. Combined with high gas prices, Mr. Lieb faced a marked downturn in the demand for his services but much higher costs of doing business.

Mr. Lieb has to worry about these cyclical fluctuations in the economy that might erode demand from time to time, but an even bigger problem is that – while Mr. Lieb is busy planning new strategies to separate his business from the rest – the other landscaping companies are doing the exact same thing! He can never be complacent. One missed opportunity could be the difference between being selected by the economic environment for success or selected for extinction.

This is why Mr. Lieb chose to sell off some of his equipment and many of his luxuries while drawing down on his savings to ride out the 2009 economic storm. By 2011 he was flourishing once again. Not cheating on his implicit contract but rather denying his desire for some of life's toys, helped maintain his reputation so that when the recession ended, the people of Knoxville would start calling him again.

GAME THEORY

At a Christmas Eve dinner party in 1997, actor Robert De Niro pulled singer Tony Bennett aside and told him he wanted Mr. Bennett to sing in an upcoming movie. He was referring to the project that became the 1999 Warner Brothers hit comedy Analyze This, in which Mr. De Niro plays a mob boss who is a big fan of Tony Bennett.

For almost a year, Bennett did not hear a word about the project. Then he was offered $15,000 to sing "Got the World on a String" in the movie's final scene. As Danny

CONCEPT CHECK

In 2009 the demand for Mr. Lieb's services – along with the demand for his competitor's services – fell dramatically as the U.S. economy continued to stumble. What would be a rational response by a monopolistically competitive firm to an economic downturn? Why?

Bennett – Tony's son and financial manager – described the conversation, "they made a fatal mistake. They told me they had already shot the film. So I'm like: 'Hey, they shot the whole film around Tony being the end gag and they're offering me $15,000?'"[15]

Warner Brothers ended up paying *$200,000* for Mr. Bennett's performance. Oops – and welcome to the world of economic games. The people at Warner Brothers learned a great deal about the timing of negotiations. In economics, we have learned that much of what people – and companies – do is based on the theory of games.

This means that one person's or business' behavior is predicated on what he, she, or it thinks their rival will do. Oftentimes, our strategy becomes not one of maximizing our well-being, but rather one of *minimizing our worst-case outcome*. Consider a hypothetical case of two men who are arrested for smoking marijuana one evening while watching *Sanford & Son* reruns. The table below illustrates their dilemma – sometimes called the prisoner's dilemma.

RUFUS

JETHRO		Confess	Remain Silent
	Confess	5 Years for Each	0 Years for Jethro 20 Years for Rufus
	Remain Silent	20 Years for Jethro 0 Years for Rufus	1 year for Each

Upon being arrested Rufus and Jethro are sent to separate cells. Given the fact that each man smokes enough marijuana to keep Mexico out of a recession, they are in serious trouble from being found with a Hefty bag full of grass.

The prosecutor has only enough hard evidence to convict them of a minor offense – since the bag was in their back yard, rather than in their house. Each prisoner is told that if one confesses, while the other remains silent, the confessor will go scot-free and the other will spend 20 years fending off new friends in a federal prison. If both confess, they will get an intermediate sentence of five years. Through their tears of remorse, Rufus and Jethro ask to speak to each other and are told that is out of the question. What should each man do? Does either man have a dominant strategy?

> ➤ **A dominant strategy is one that yields a higher payoff no matter what the other players in the game choose.**

In this game, the dominant strategy is for each man to confess. Given the problem of uncertainty, no matter what Jethro does, Rufus will get a lighter sentence from confessing.

If both Rufus and Jethro confess, each man gets 5 years instead of 20. Why not remain silent? Remember, if Jethro remains silent but Rufus confesses, Jethro gets 20 years and vice versa. The temptation to "cheat" on each other becomes so overwhelming that the dilemma of remaining silent, and trusting the other man to do the same, is not overcome. How does this apply to business firms in competition with one another?

In 2009 Amador Cantu opened Taco Palenque, a Mexican Express taco restaurant in Winter Garden, Florida. With home-made flour tortillas, a wide variety of meats, and an unbelievable salsa bar, this small restaurant quickly became a hit in Central Florida – even as the economy struggled and the highway in front of his restaurant went through an ugly widening campaign.

Photo courtesy Jack Chambless

Mr. Cantu went out of his way to avoid providing some of the other traditional Mexican dishes that take longer to prepare, in order to capitalize on consumers who want their food within a few minutes. Let's take a look at what might happen if he decided to move in the direction of more traditional Mexican menus. He would have to consider the reaction of his rival. Here are four possible scenarios:

TACO PALENQUE

RIVAL		Don't Change Menu	Change Menu
	Don't Change Menu	$100K, $100K	$50K, $120K
	Change Menu	$120K, $50K	$80K, $80K

CONCEPT CHECK

The Lighthouse restaurant in Old Town, Florida is famous for its Key lime pie. The Rustic Inn in Castle Danger, Minnesota is famous for its Raspberry-Rhubarb pie. Should each establishment use game theory to compete with one another? Why, or why not?

In this game, no matter what his rivals do, Mr. Cantu will do better to change product line, so mutating is a dominant strategy for Taco Palenque. If neither Mr. Cantu nor his rival change their menu, both will earn $100,000 in profit. If either Mr. Cantu or his rival decides to spend the $30,000 required to change their menu, it will take away $50,000 in profit from the other and the net profit will be $120,000, leaving $50,000 for the other restaurant. If both change their menu, each has incurred higher costs but their profit has grown by a small amount. Profits in this case would be $80,000 for each restaurant.

If neither Mr. Cantu nor his rival has good information about the decision of the other, the equilibrium condition is that both will change their menu and both will earn $80,000 in profits.

At this point we have achieved Nash equilibrium (named after the Nobel Laureate John Nash who developed this concept in the 1950s).

> ➤ **Nash equilibrium is any combination of strategies in which each player's strategy is his or her best choice, given the other players' strategies.**

ADDING IT ALL UP

In the past four chapters you have seen that the problem of uncertainty, combined with market structures that any business might operate under, makes it very difficult to suggest that profit maximization is a realistic – or even attainable goal.

Nonetheless, it remains true that whether a business faces two or two million competitors, the business firm must keep a constant focus on all of the variables that may impact the price elasticity of demand, productivity, and costs. Those business firms like Godiva Chocolates, Lincoln Electric, and Revlon that strive to recognize these environmental changes tend to survive over long periods of time – even in uncertain times, like the times we live in now.

ENDNOTES

1 Source: Simba Information; Legg Mason; Ad Media Partners; Gartner Dataquest; Forrester Research and *The Wall Street Journal.*

2 See "Bud Light to become NFL's Official Beer" by Matthew Futterman, *The Wall Street Journal,* May 4, 2010.

3 See "Gatorade's Formula For Staying on Top: A Blitz of Research" by Jonathan Eig, *The Wall Street Journal,* May 5, 2000.

4 See "A Purple Reign" by Mark Chediak, *The Orlando Sentinel,* October 14, 2005.

5 See "Miller lites 150 birthday candles" *Edmonton Journal,* July 26, 2005, p. F3.

6 See "Why the Sudden Rise in the Urge to Merge and Form Oligopolies" by Yochi J. Dreazen, Greg Ip, and Nicholas Kulish, *The Wall Street Journal,* February 25, 2002.

7 See "Comcast Deal Cements Rise of an Oligopoly in the Cable Business," *The Wall Street Journal,* December 21, 2001.

8 An exception to this practice took place in 2001, when Sea World took the lead in becoming the first theme park in Orlando to top the $50-per-day mark. See "Sea World greets new year with $50 tickets" by Tim Barker, *The Orlando Sentinel,* January 4, 2001.

9 See "'I've Got It!' Rawlings Rushes to Wave Off Other Glove Makers" by Jonathan Eig, *The Wall Street Journal,* April 1, 2002.

10 See "Norma Rae at UCLA" by Stefan Fatsis, *The Wall Street Journal,* May 18, 2001.

11 For more on the NCAA cartel, see "Amateur Athletes Are Worth Millions – to NCAA" by Allan Barra, *The Wall Street Journal.*

12 See "Court Makes NFL Play Defense" by Jess Bravin and Matthew Futterman, *The Wall Street Journal,* May 25, 2010.

13 See "Fast-Food Chains Vie to Carve Out Empire in Pricey Sandwiches" by Shirley Leung, *The Wall Street Journal,* February 5, 2002.

14 For more on this issue, you can read about Procter & Gamble's attempts to redefine their Oil of Olay product in the article entitled, "P&G Tries to Hide Wrinkles in Aging Beauty Fluid" by Emily Nelson, *The Wall Street Journal,* May 16, 2000.

15 As quoted by Geraldine Fabrikant, "Talking Money with Tony Bennett," *The New York Times,* May 2, 1999.

CHAPTER REVIEW

1. What are the major differences between oligopoly and monopolistic competition?

2. What are the various types of mergers? Which type gets the most scrutiny from the federal government? Why?

3. How is a cartel structured and how do they maintain market power? What are the biggest challenges to cartel profits?

4. Use game theory to explain why the National Football League players and NFL owners took such a long time to reach a new collective bargaining agreement.

Chapter Seventeen

HEALTH CARE ECONOMICS

*H*ealth care is a right, not a privilege.

JOHN KERRY

THE DEFINING ECONOMIC "CRISIS" OR NOT?

One of the most pressing issues our country has faced in the past two decades is the issue of rising health care costs and the loss of health insurance coverage that millions of Americans have faced. By some estimates, over 50.7 million Americans have no health insurance – including millions of children – while health care costs are rising at a faster rate than any other good or service.[1]

During the 2008 presidential election – and the elections of 2012, 2016, and so forth – health care coverage and costs took (and will continue to take) center stage.

Should the health care market be left to the forces of supply and demand to determine price and access, or should the government – through the use of tax dollars – correct for the "failure" of the market and provide "affordable care" for all Americans?

THE FUNDAMENTAL PROBLEM WITH HEALTH CARE

In 2010 the U.S. health care system comprised roughly 17.3% of the gross domestic product ($2.5 trillion) of the United States.[2] Moreover, for the past several years, the cost of health care has increased faster than the core rate of inflation.

In 2011, health insurance premiums increased by 9% – the largest jump in five years.[3] As costs have accelerated, more and more Americans have come face to face with a key problem associated with scarce financial resources. It is for this reason that President Obama and lawmakers face a very difficult task in figuring out how to increase access to health care, while decreasing the cost of health care. The irony is that the major reason why health care is so expensive, is that in many cases it is partially to totally free.

In early January 2000, I flew with my family to Boston to present a paper at an economics conference. On the one day I had off, I traveled to the Cranmore Resort in North Conway, New Hampshire, for a day of snow skiing. My wife, a native Floridian, had never seen snow, much less traveled 50 miles per hour on it, and was very excited to partake in this winter sport. On the way, I convinced her that she did not need a skiing lesson and that she would be fine swooshing down the slopes. Sure enough, on her last run of the day, she wiped out, and ended up with a concussion from the fall. When the first-aid team got her to the bottom of the mountain, she had quite a headache, but was aware of where she was, who I was, and what had happened.

Since I knew I was in bad trouble for talking her out of taking skiing lessons – and because I am a wonderful husband – I took her to the local hospital where she was admitted into the emergency room (cost: $254). The attending physician told us that she had a slight concussion and that she needed to rest for several days. When we told him that we had to fly from Boston back to Orlando the next day, he ordered an MRI and CT-Scan just to make sure nothing more serious might be wrong with her (cost: $1,162). Fortunately, the wonders of medical technology revealed that she was safe to travel, and the next day we were on our way, having completed a very expensive skiing trip.

Many of you probably see this bill of $1,416 as an outrageous example of a health care system that gouges people in their most critical time of need. After all, how would I have looked if I had queried the doctor as to the cost of such procedures upon hearing the recommendation for further testing? I would have come across as an uncaring husband who was concerned only with money – even though it was my wife's fault for listening to me when I told her to skip the skiing lessons. What you will learn is that the $1,416 bill is simply the *effect* of a health care system plagued with unusual problems. The *cause* of that effect is what you need to be concerned with.

COST-SHIFTING

Suppose, on the very day my wife bonked her noggin on the slopes, several other people who did not have any insurance or any ability to pay for their care, had been admitted to the emergency room. If this were a grocery or hardware store, the lack of ability to pay would mean a quick exit out the door, with no service provided.

However, in the health care industry it is *illegal* for public hospitals to turn away emergency-room patients for lack of money. This means in many, many cases that people with little or no economic resources get "free" health care. The hospital simply has to absorb the cost of providing care to those who cannot pay. Moreover, there are also many individuals who are on the taxpayer-funded Medicaid or Medicare programs. Typically, Medicaid and Medicare reimburse hospitals for about half the cost of delivering a service.[4]

This leaves U.S. hospitals with literally millions of dollars in unpaid or partially paid health care bills each year. The solution? Obviously, the hospitals are not going to stand by and go bankrupt providing charity. Instead, the hospitals play an economic game of *cost-shifting*.

> ➤ **Cost-shifting is the practice of shifting the cost of those patients who can only partially pay their health care bills – or pay nothing at all – to those people who are fully insured by a health care provider.**

This means exactly what you think it means. When we walked through the door, before we were even asked what the problem was, we were asked for our insurance card. When I pulled it out, the hospital, in essence, shifted the cost of much of that "free" health care to my bill.

Is this legal? It most certainly is. Did I freak out over this huge bill? Absolutely not. The reason? Because I am part of the problem of cost-shifting as well.

When the doctor, who I guessed had about 25 years of medical experience, recommended an MRI and CT-Scan, I knew that my insurance would pick up a very large portion of the tab. Knowing that a *third party* would help offset the full cost of my wife's health care needs, I did not feel pressured to make a tough financial decision.

Suppose I did not have insurance at that time and the hospital asked me to write a check for over $1,000 for these tests. I may have very well turned to my wife and said, "Honey, you look like you are recovering nicely. Let's walk gently back to the car, go back home, and rest awhile."

When we are asked to be fully responsible for the cost of our decisions, it is amazing how much more judicious we are with our money. But as long as a third party is paying, why not order up more from the health care menu?

The cost shifting does not end with my shifting her bill to my insurance carrier. When my carrier gets the inflated bill for the services rendered, along with inflated bills from other policy holders, the company simply shifts the burden to all policyholders – typically our employers – in the form of *rising annual premiums*.

What do employers do as their premiums rise? You guessed it! They also participate in the cost-shifting dance by spreading the pain out to consumers in the form of *rising prices* and to employees in the form of *smaller salary gains* and *fewer full-time job opportunities*.[5]

In addition, more and more companies have opted to hire people on a part-time or temporary basis in order to avoid paying for health care benefits. Of course, we blame the employers, but the real culprit is the "welfare mentality" people have as they overuse the services of our health care industry. The following table summarizes the problem of cost-shifting.

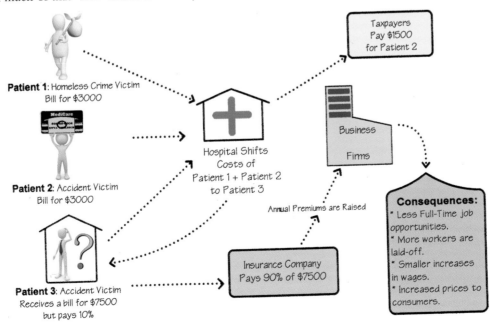

Patient 1: Homeless Crime Victim
Bill for $3000

Patient 2: Accident Victim
Bill for $3000

Patient 3: Accident Victim
Receives a bill for $7500
but pays 10%

Hospital Shifts Costs of Patient 1 + Patient 2 to Patient 3

Taxpayers Pay $1500 for Patient 2

Business Firms

Annual Premiums are Raised

Insurance Company Pays 90% of $7500

Consequences:
* Less Full-Time job opportunities.
* More workers are laid-off.
* Smaller increases in wages.
* Increased prices to consumers.

THE REST OF THE STORY

Cost-shifting is just one reason for ballooning health care costs. There are many other culprits that must be exposed as well.

THE AGING POPULATION

As a direct result of advances in medical technology and greater awareness about the risk factors that can lead to an early demise, life expectancies in the U.S. are increasing annually. In addition, there are approximately 76 million Americans known as the "baby boomers," whom have now begun retiring from the labor force and will continue to do so for the next 15-plus years.

Our aging population is putting mounting pressure on the demand for health care. This situation will only get worse in the future. Many of the baby boomers will flood into the tax-funded Medicare system. Fully *40% of all federal expenditures* go toward retirement and health care benefits for the elderly. Now that senior citizens have a new $8.7 trillion prescription drug benefit plan,[6] the federal government will see a total bill of over $107 trillion in unfunded Medicare and Social Security obligations the not-so-distant future.

To cover that burden, the tax burden of the average American – who now pays 33% of their income in combined taxes, would have to rise by 81% – translating into an average tax burden of almost 60% of our income.[7]

Moreover, the existence of Medicare has been shown to dramatically increase the demand for the services of specialists, even when they are not medically necessary.[8] The cumulative effect of this natural increase in the demand for health care – plus the artificial increase stemming from the perception that care is free – will be upward pressure on prices for all of us. In fact, as much as *40% of our lifetime health care bill* will come in the *last month* of our lives, which adds significantly to the cost-shifting problem.[9]

TECHNOLOGY

When my wife and I went back to Cranmore in February 2003, I got a chance to shift my irresponsible behavior to you. That's right, I got hurt at the same resort she did. I tried to jump over a snow-packed ramp to "catch some air" late in the day and missed the ramp. I hit a wall of ice and snow that allowed me to catch some air and also catch a cracked rib, bruised lungs, and a bruised ego. Total cost? Over $1,500. This is not only because I am a big baby and thought I was dying, but because I wanted Mercedes-Benz quality care while I was in pain.

In this respect I am no different than any of the millions of Americans who expect the highest quality health care when we are beset by illness or injury. The problem – if we wish to call it a problem – is that Mercedes-Benz quality care comes at Mercedes-Benz prices. This is largely due to a medical arms race that pits competing hospitals against one another for paying patients.

By the very nature of the business, life-saving (or enhancing) equipment, drugs, and procedures are very expensive. For example, a Computed Tomography Scanner can cost $3.5 million. The average MRI machine costs between $1 million and $3 million. This equipment must be paid for. Therefore, when we demand its use, part of our bill reflects the enormity of the expense in acquiring the machine to begin with.

COMPETITION – AND THE LACK OF IT...

Unlike any other industry, competition in health care actually leads to higher rather than lower prices. Suppose you need a heart bypass operation some day. You have plenty of time to shop around for the hospital you feel most comfortable with, so you visit all of them in your area that offer this service.

During the search process, you discover that all of the hospitals, with one exception, have equipment that is two years old. The exception has brand-new equipment. Who are you most likely to go with? If you are like most patients with insurance, you will seek the services of the hospital with the most up-to-date technology. This is not because two-year-old equipment would be obsolete, but rather because you think "the newer the better." Since a third party will pick up part of the tab, choosing the newest equipment makes economic sense.

This reality is not lost on hospitals around the country. Administrators realize that if it does not have the latest and greatest equipment the hospital will lose paying customers to their next-best competitor. In essence, hospitals rarely have a chance for any of their equipment to generate economies of scale that might bring down the cost of health care.

If the equipment were used for say, five or six years, over that time it would pay for itself, and the hospital would realize lower costs of providing heart by-pass surgery. Lower costs could conceivably lead to lower prices. Instead of cost savings, hospitals face pressure to constantly update whether it is technically necessary or not. This means that hospitals make new equipment purchases on a more frequent basis, so duplication of technology across hospitals takes place, which leads to rising, – rather than falling – health care bills for all of us.

Unfortunately, there is also a situation that has contributed to rising health care costs that has to do with the lack of competition.

If you live in Alabama – and seek health insurance – you are probably going to end up using BlueCross BlueShield. The reason is simple. This company controls 93% of the health insurance market in this state. Preferred Health Systems has 81% of the Wichita, Kansas market. In 359 metropolitan areas located in 46 states, only two insurers had a combined market share of 70% in over 60% of those areas.[10]

Suppose this was the case in the market for cellular phones. Would you pay more with only two firms competing? More than likely you would. And certainly you would if it was illegal for you to shop for a cellular phone in another state. That is the case for health insurance as this book went to press.

That's right – in our quasi-free market economy, if you live in Alabama, you are not allowed to shop for insurance in Mississippi. For that matter, if you live in any of the 50 states, you can only shop for insurance from companies in your state. That means higher premiums for everyone who has insurance.

MERGERS

In 1890 Congress passed the Sherman Antitrust Act. Section 2 of this Act states:

> Every person who shall monopolize, or attempt to monopolize, or combine or conspire with any other person or persons to monopolize any part of trade or commerce among the several states, or with foreign nations, shall be guilty of a misdemeanor.

The law has been applied to every industry from oil to computer software.[11] The intent of the law is to promote competition, increase quality, and lower prices. However, the law has actually contributed to increasing, rather than decreasing, health care costs.

Several years ago, three hospitals in Rockford, Illinois, attempted to merge and gain efficiencies by sharing equipment. The U.S. Department of Justice blocked that merger, claiming it would monopolize the local market.[12] Since the hospitals were forced to compete, the pressure to buy more and more equipment went unabated, and prices continued to rise in Rockford, just as they have in other markets around the country.

This perceived flaw in the antitrust laws led to a philosophical change in courts during the Clinton administration. The courts – over the objections of the Clinton Justice Department – began allowing more mergers – more than 700 in all from 1996 to 2000.

In cities like Houston, Texas; Richmond, Virginia; and Cleveland, Ohio, mergers have led to an explosion in health care costs. For example, in Houston, HCA Inc. operated five hospitals in 1995. HCA now owns 10 hospitals, or 22% of the market. In Richmond, HCA has a 41% market share. In Cleveland, only two hospital systems dominate 68% of the hospital market. This greater concentration of market power has given HCA and other companies greater control over the prices charged to commercial insurance companies. In 2000 HCA charged an average price of $8,465 for treating a patient with chest pains. This was 47% more than was charged in 1996.[13]

Hospitals argue that consolidation has been economically necessary for many reasons. Among them has been the increase in Medicare claims as the population gets older. Hospitals nationwide have lost over *$76 billion* in reimbursements that did not meet the full cost of providing care.

The hospitals contend that these mergers will eventually lead to increased cost-savings and lower prices for consumers, and that the market simply has not yet generated those cost-savings. So far, the courts agree, having ruled in more than one case that mergers will not lead to long-run anti-competitive behavior since hospitals tend to compete over a wider geographic area than the government has claimed they do. For now though, consumers are feeling the pinch of the rise of oligopoly power.

ASYMMETRIC INFORMATION

Would you ever buy a new car or house without first asking the price? Maybe if you won the lottery, but in any other case you expect information about prices, services, etc. to flow evenly, or symmetrically, from the seller to the buyer. This is how virtually every other market, other than health care, functions.

Suppose you were attacked by a wolverine while hiking in Alaska. When you got to the emergency room, do you suppose you would ask about the price of emergency room care before it was served? Does anybody ask? Probably very few would. Perhaps it is because it is considered to be bad form to ask those who are saving our lives what the bill will be. Maybe we don't ask because we don't want to upset the doctor before she sews our arm back on.

Of course, the third-party payment system might make us reluctant to ask. Finally, there is the fact that even if we did ask, and found out that repairing injuries sustained from a brawl with a wolverine will run into the thousands of dollars, we would probably not ask to be transported to another hospital that might offer a better deal. All these factors lead to asymmetric information – the hospitals know what will be charged, but we don't.

Ask yourself what you might adopt as a pricing policy if customers came to you as spur-of-the-moment shoppers and did not ask about the price before you served them. Would you charge more than if they did ask and did shop around?

Ironically, the managed-care system that was supposed to help contain costs has actually exacerbated the problem of asymmetric information and has contributed to higher health care costs.[14] When health maintenance organizations (HMOs) entered the health care arena, employees were thrilled with the idea of co-payments as low as $5–10 for office visits and drugs.

As anyone familiar with the law of unintended consequences could have predicted, these artificially low prices not only encouraged more office visits for minor ailments, but consumers were not encouraged to shop around for the best prices for drugs or to choose generic drugs over the more expensive name-brand products.

Naturally, this led to a distortion in the flow of information from the health care system to the consumer. People thought drugs were cheap, since the co-payments were cheap. When people see something as inexpensive, they will not be judicious in their purchases. The result has been an increase in the demand for medical treatment and name-brand drugs and an increase in health costs for employers.

Employers are now combating this problem by trying to bring about more symmetrical information between health care providers and customers. This has come in the form of increased co-payments and "tier-pricing," where generic drugs come at the lowest price (tier one), common name-brand drugs are a little more expensive (tier two), more expensive name-brand drugs are even more expensive (tier three), and "lifestyle" drugs like anti-baldness drugs, or rare or experimental drugs (fourth tier) require the highest co-payment of all.[15]

CRIME

Hardly a day goes by without a news report about a drive-by shooting, a drug overdose, an assault, or some other type of violent crime. When crime victims are taken to emergency rooms, how many of them do you suppose have insurance? Most victims of violent crimes are relatively poor. Many of them are uninsured.

It is also highly unlikely that criminals are covered by some insurance plan when they are shot or stabbed during the course of carrying out their occupational requirements. The last time I checked, the Crack Dealers Association of America did not offer group health care coverage in case one of its members encounters a bullet or knife blade.

As you can clearly surmise, with crime comes an intensification of the cost-shifting problem. Criminals and crime victims crowd inner-city emergency rooms, often requiring very expensive care. By one recent estimate, crime-related health care costs total $574 billion in the form of 72,000 deaths and 2.5 million injuries per year.[16] Who pays this astronomical bill for crime-related health care? All of us do – in the form of higher prices and taxes.

UNHEALTHY LIFESTYLES

If you are one of the millions of Americans who is overweight, smokes, drinks to excess, practices unsafe sex, or uses illegal drugs, you are part of a multi-billion-dollar problem that the rest of us who live pure and virtuous lives have to pay for. Consider these numbers:

Sixty-three percent of Americans are overweight or obese, adding $147 billion a year to our nation's health care bill in 2008 alone.[17] Since 1996 the number of men who are morbidly obese (100 pounds or more overweight) increased by 50%. The number of women in this category has increased by 67%. Researchers at Johns Hopkins recently projected that by 2015, 75% of Americans would be overweight or obese.[18]

Doctors are now even worried about children and heart disease. The number of kids who are overweight today has increased by 15% compared to 20 years ago.[19] Moreover, hospitals are facing increasing pressure to build facilities with extra-large rooms, expensive scales, extra-wide wheelchairs, and larger beds.[20] Finally, weight-based discrimination lawsuits continue to impose added costs on hospital finances.[21]

SUGGESTED CLASSROOM DEBATE

This photograph is of a package of cigarettes purchased in Canada. The Canadian government requires such advertising of all companies that sell tobacco products. Would this type of advertising – if forced upon cigarettes sold in the U.S. – lower the cost of health care in the U.S.? Why, or why not?

Photo courtesy Jack Chambless

The American Heart Association estimates that 23.5% of men, 20.6% of women, and 4.1 million teenagers smoke – which is a 73% increase since 1988.[22] By one estimate, smoking adds $100 billion per year to our health care costs.[23]

The National Institute on Drug Abuse reports that alcohol and drug abuse imposed a $215 billion cost on the economy in 2008 alone.[24] This cost reflected treatment and prevention as well as health care costs.

The American Social Health Association found that one out of every five people has had a sexually transmitted disease – adding $8 billion per year to U.S. health care costs. Many of these individuals – including the 65 million with viral STDs[25] – have no health insurance or are only partially covered by Medicare or Medicaid. When their vices lead to health problems for them, or people around them, the cost of delivering care is often shifted to taxpayers and insured patients. Even people with private insurance who get sick more often, due to smoking or drinking, add to the demand for care, and thus, the price that we all have to pay.

THE MEDICAL MONOPOLY

You recall that a monopoly is the single seller of some good or service that has few or no close substitutes. If a person or business or organization has monopoly power, this means they have some power over prices and output in that industry. Historically, monopolies have been vilified for providing poor service (cable television) and/or charging much higher prices than competitive institutions. This problem is pervasive in the health care industry.

For starters, there is the licensing process that people who practice medicine go through. You might find yourself thinking, "You better believe we should license doctors! I don't want some unemployed carpenter off the street telling people he is a neurosurgeon just because he is good with a saw!"

Before you get too carried away, you should know that this process – according to many economists who study health care markets – is not always done with your best interest in mind. Instead, the licensing process is a way for the medical establishment to *artificially control the supply* of caregivers and thus artificially hold up health care prices.[26]

In fact, the American Medical Association established, as a primary reason for licensure, the desire to restrict entry into the profession and thereby secure a more stable financial climate for physicians. As a result of the desire to maintain market power in health care, the AMA helped facilitate a decline in the number of medical schools from 160 at the turn of the nineteenth century to 76 by 1930.[27]

Today there are other ways the medical community restricts the supply of practitioners. One way is to have competitors' services ruled illegal. This has been a common practice to reduce the demand for midwives, who often practice alternative child delivery techniques, at an average savings of $3000 compared to the standard obstetrician fee.[28] Another mechanism is to restrict or limit substitute providers' services from payment by government health programs.

For example, Medicare regulations prohibit reimbursement to chiropractors for services they are licensed to perform in all 50 states.

To many economists, the fact that the AMA has been allowed to manipulate the market for health care in the name of "consumer protection" is a less-than-convincing claim. From restricting entry into medical schools for non-academic reasons to limiting the ability of competing practitioners to enter the market and succeed, the AMA has contributed billions of dollars to our health care bills for reasons unrelated to our health. It should be noted that these restrictions are allowed despite the fact that U.S. taxpayers pay over $10 billion a year in subsidies to help train the very doctors who operate in this restricted market.

Then, there are the lawyers…

THE LAWYER EFFECT

> No one has ever been healed by a frivolous lawsuit.
>
> President Bush, January 28, 2003

You have probably heard of cases where a doctor has made a mistake that led to the loss of a human life or some permanent injury. This is known as medical malpractice. Many of you may have been pleased when you heard about a jury awarding millions of dollars to the malpractice victim. After all, we do not go to the doctor expecting to end up worse off, or dead. Before you rejoice over the perception that justice is served by enormous damage awards, you should consider the following:

In 2009 the average ob/gyn in Dade County Florida paid $238,728 in medical malpractice premiums – the highest in the United States.[29] Across the states, it was not much better for those who deliver babies. Doctors in Utah paid $95,213 per year. In Nassau and Suffolk counties (New York), it was $194,935. In Los Angeles county, where malpractice lawsuits have a cap on the damage awards, it still cost $86,348 to carry insurance and $51,812 to practice general surgery.

What do you suppose such high premiums mean to our health care bills? Of course, it means we have to pay more to receive care. If you were a doctor in Florida, would you charge just enough to cover your insurance bills? If you were insane, maybe you would.

Malpractice awards have led to higher prices, stemming from rising premiums, but also rising fees that result from doctors having to add larger and larger staffs of employees who do nothing more than move piles of paperwork that provide a detailed track record of the doctor's every move. These staff members have to have salaries, so you pay more for that, too. In addition, doctors often order up services that they may not believe are 100% medically necessary, but that are very much *legally necessary* in order to create a paper trail that, doctors hope, keeps the lawyers at bay.

All of these factors have led to dramatic increases in the input costs of providing care to all of us. Nationwide, 1 out of every 12 doctors gets sued each year. In Florida it is one out of six. Keep in mind that whenever a doctor is exposed to a massive lawsuit – whether he or she is guilty of malpractice or not – this leads to insurance companies raising malpractice insurance premiums. In addition to rising premiums, the extra paperwork, less time spent with patients, and the pressure to order up too much care just to be on the safe side, all lead to rising prices.

What should "justice" look like in the health care market?

Compounding matters is the fact that in most cases there is no cap on the amount of money someone can win in a malpractice suit. It should not come as any great shock that doctors in many states have gone on strike, threatened to leave in large numbers, or stopped carrying insurance altogether.[30] With lawyers getting very large portions of such suits, it is no wonder that malpractice lawsuits have become so pervasive and expensive for doctors, patients, and taxpayers.[31]

THE FDA APPROVAL PROCESS

If you are like millions of Americans, you implicitly trust the government to use the money that is taken from you each year in a wise and judicious manner. How silly of you. A glaring example of your government at work is the process that the Food and Drug Administration uses to approve new drugs and medical equipment. Have you ever seen a snail crawl along the ground? The snail looks like Usain Bolt compared to the FDA.

Since its inception in 1938, the FDA's regulation of the medical device and drug industry has increased in scope, detail, and cost to the American people. You may be of the opinion that we need the FDA to make sure products and drugs do not harm or kill large (or even small) portions of the country. You should consider two things. First, at what cost should the people of this country be made safe from faulty medical equipment or drugs? As television reporter John Stossel has noted, when the FDA announces that it has finally approved a drug that will save 14,000 lives, that means the year before – when emancipated adult human beings were not allowed to buy the drug – 14,000 lives were *lost*.[32]

Second, could it be suggested that profit is enough of a motivator to keep drug and equipment companies from harming us? After all, if we haven't forgotten the lessons of Adam Smith, self-interested equipment and drug companies may not care about us at all, but they do care about money. Ask yourself how much money these companies would make if they sold us products that made us sicker or even dead. The last time I checked, killing people is not exactly an industry that is thriving in this country. This is not to suggest that private companies never make mistakes.

It does suggest that cost-benefit analysis and the concept of self-interest keeps us very safe from faulty drugs and equipment. With or without the FDA, profit-seeking companies would strive for this outcome.

Yet, we do have government oversight, so let's look at what the government is doing for us. The government has decided that herbal products – an industry that has seen its revenue climb dramatically over the past few years – are so dangerous that without FDA approval, herb makers cannot make claims that their products have specific medicinal value. The problem is that getting herbal remedies through the drug-approval process is unrealistic. Botanicals are naturally occurring and therefore cannot be patented.

Therefore, the companies that make herbal treatments have to ask themselves if it is worth even attempting to incur the average cost of *$400 million* and the average wait *of 15 years* to have a new drug approved by the government. Medical equipment manufacturers also face a daunting task. In the wake of the silicone breast implant and defective heart valve cases, the FDA has stepped up the amount of paperwork and regulatory loopholes that firms must go through. This does not even take into account the number of drugs that are taken off the market because a fairly small portion of the population had a bad reaction to some pill.[33]

The result has been a dramatic slowdown in the number of devices that are approved and an increase in the number of Americans who are suffering or dying while waiting for life-saving or enhancing equipment to reach the market.[34] In the meantime, the new regulations have added millions of dollars to the budgets of health care companies and have led to companies raising prices[35] while some companies have moved overseas – where drugs are approved much faster to control regulatory costs.[36] For example, the only medicine known for treating the rare and fatal lung disease known as idiopathic pulmonary fibrosis, has been used in Japan since 2008 and was approved in Europe in 2010. It is illegal in the United States – even if the person with this disease is willing to take their chances with the medicine.[37]

Finally, consider this: In May 2007, a new treatment for prostate cancer was announced and rejected by the FDA. Three years later, the FDA approved the drug with the exact same clinical trial results that the company had submitted three years earlier. Eighty-thousand men died of prostate cancer during that time span.[38]

THE ORPHAN DRUG LAW

An orphan drug is a drug developed under the U.S. Orphan Drug Act (1983) to treat a disease that affects a relatively small number of people. The terms of the orphan drug law offer tax breaks and a seven-year monopoly on drug sales to induce companies to undertake development and manufacturing of such drugs, which otherwise might not be profitable. The cancer-fighting drug Taxol is an example of the type of drug that was covered by this law.

Critics of the law point out the fact that drugs developed and protected for seven years come at a very high price to consumers, and that often the government uses tax dollars to assist in the development of life-saving drugs and then gives the selling rights away. This leads to double-charging for these drugs – first in the form of taxes and second in the form of monopoly pricing.[39]

RE-UNDERWRITING OF HEALTH INSURANCE POLICIES

From the April 9, 2002, edition of *The Wall Street Journal*:

> Shaneen and Tom Wahl were paying $417 a month for health insurance when Mrs. Wahl was diagnosed with breast cancer in 1996. The premiums began rising steadily, and by August 2000, the Wahls were told their new rate would be $1,881 per month.[40]

Up until the 1950s, health insurance policies were a lot like car and homeowner's policies. If you wrecked your car, or received tickets frequently, or if you kept burning your house down, your insurance premiums increased. The same was true for health insurance. If you got sick more often, you paid more. This practice began to fade away, in part due to regulatory pressure from many state governments. But now the practice of "re-underwriting" of health insurance policies is making a comeback. Here's how it works:

Companies that provide health insurance, like American Medical Group Inc., will place their customers into one of three groups – preferred, manual, or substandard. The preferred customer is the healthiest and thus, least costly person to insure. The manual customer is one who is less healthy than the preferred customer but who does not suffer from any chronic expensive maladies. The substandard (their words, not mine) customer is one like Mrs. Wahl who suffers from an ongoing disease or illness that is very expensive to cover.

American Medical Group conducts an annual review of their customers before classifying a person. If you did not get sick in 2011, you would see your premiums increase only enough to cover the cost of living (the rate of inflation) in your area. For every dollar of insurance provided to someone in this group, the company pays out $.21 in claims.

For the manual patient – for example, someone who may have suffered a broken leg that mended normally – the premium increase for 2012 might be 5% on top of the cost-of-living increase. A manual customer costs American Medical Group $.48 for every $1 of insurance provided.

The substandard customer is likely to face an increase of as much as 37% on top of the rate of medical inflation. According to American Medical Group, this customer costs $1.71 for every $1 of insurance and thus, must pay more to help cover the added cost. In economics, we learn that "price discrimination" is the practice of charging different customers different prices for the same product.

Price discrimination is legal in most states – and at the federal level – as long as the price differences reflect differences in the cost of service. This appears to be the case with Mrs. Wahl and other people around the United States, who are finding out the hard way that the insurance companies are no longer providing one evaluation of a person at the time the policy is underwritten and then letting the customer go on with their lives.

With cost-shifting becoming a growing problem in America, the insurance companies are trying to shift the burden of rising costs to those customers who are the most expensive to serve. The goal is to keep costs from rising too much for the healthier patients, while using the price mechanism to encourage people to change their lifestyles where possible.

ADDING IT ALL UP

As you can clearly see, the issue of health care reform is not an easy one. There are simply too many variables working together to drive up costs and decrease access. That does not mean individual components of the problem could not be addressed. It also does not mean that we cannot improve the overall picture. What it does mean is that any attempt to "fix" health care in an economically pragmatic way, has to take into account the benefits and costs of every proposal.

OPTION ONE: "OBAMACARE"

Unless you have been hiding under a rock for the past couple of years, you know about legislation that was signed by President Obama in 2010. The legislation set off a firestorm of protests and celebrations over the perceived costs and benefits of this historic reach into the health care market.

Here are some of key provisions that the law established:[41]

> ➤ **Starting in 2010, insurance companies would no longer be allowed to place a lifetime dollar cap on how much coverage would be provided. Furthermore, health insurance providers were required to allow parents of dependent children to continue coverage for their offspring until the child was 26 years old.**
> ➤ **Starting in 2013, Medicare payroll taxes on couples earning more than $250,000 and individuals earning $200,000 were increased. The law also added a 3.8% tax to investment income.**
> ➤ **Starting in 2014, insurers will be prohibited from denying or limiting coverage based on pre-existing conditions; Medicaid expands to cover people up to 133% of the poverty line; citizens and legal residents have to have insurance or pay a fine; and employers with more than 50 workers must offer insurance or face a penalty.**

The first 10 years of this plan were projected to cost $2.7 trillion.[42] Aside from that price tag, many questions have been raised that need to be addressed here. It should first be noted that in 2010, a federal judge in Virginia ruled that the requirement of all Americans to purchase insurance was a violation of Article One, Section Eight, Clause Three of the United States Constitution.[43] In 2011, a judge in Florida ruled the *entire* legislation Unconstitutional.[44] We will cover these rulings in the pages that follow.

For now, the economics of the law is important to dissect.

Starting with the 2010 provisions, the requirement that insurers cover dependent children until the age of 26 had the immediate impact of leading insurance companies to drop "child only" policies.[45] Before the law, many parents – especially during the "Great Recession" – opted to cover only their children while forgoing insurance for themselves.

When the legislation passed, Aetna, Cigna, Humana, and other companies told parents that if they wanted their children to be covered, they (the parents) would have to purchase insurance as well – 2.4 million children were potentially impacted by this business decision.[46] Furthermore, in 2010, with insurers now required to cover people well into adulthood, many companies began raising their insurance premiums. Compounding the rate hikes was the mandate that the companies could no longer place a lifetime maximum on how much health care they would provide.[47] Therefore, the benefit that many thought they were going to receive (more coverage over their life and expanded coverage for older kids) ended up coming with the cost of higher monthly premiums.

As for the 2013 tax increases, you will recall from chapter five that more often than not, tax increases on wealthier Americans leads to less revenue for government as people attempt to shield their private property from the IRS. When investment income taxes fell under Bill Clinton and George W. Bush, tax revenue increased markedly.[48] When income tax rates fell dramatically under John F. Kennedy; under Ronald Reagan, tax revenues shot up.[49] Many economists openly questioned the wisdom of attempting to extract health care revenue from people who not only already pay most of the nation's taxes, but who are needed to provide jobs in the wake of the historically severe recession.[50] If history is any guide, Mr. Obama will be sitting in meetings in 2014 asking his advisors why the revenue projections from the 2013 tax hike were so far off the mark.

This brings us to 2014.

According to President Obama, the problem of cost-shifting can be efficiently reduced if every American is required to purchase health care. Economically, this argument would seem to have some merit. After all, if you are not insured and go to the hospital following a car wreck, either the taxpayers have to pick up the tab (Medicaid or Medicare) or people with insurance have to pay more once your bill is passed on to some other person with insurance. If everyone without insurance is forced into the pool of paying customers (see car insurance), the amount of dollars available to treat people goes up, while the average cost per person treated goes down.

However, there are some potential dilemmas that could emerge in 2014.

First, the year before, people living at least 33% above the poverty line will be added to Medicaid. That would mean that for a family of four, you could make about

Is he misguided?

unemployment and economic recovery is a concern? Is the government unwittingly causing businesses to pick between paying a fine instead of providing health insurance?

President Obama said many times in 2010, that if we like our insurance we can keep it. However, he did not tell us what to do if we like our insurance but our businesses do not. By telling American companies to provide health insurance or pay a fine, he immediately set in motion a huge cost-benefit calculation that has led many companies to forecast that it will be cheaper to pay the fine than to continue to pay for increasingly expensive health insurance.[51]

Finally, there is the question of what do to with the estimated 23 million people – illegal immigrants and people who pay the fine rather than buy health insurance.[52] If we go from 50 million people to 23 million without insurance – at a cost of $2.7 trillion in just 10 years, is that enough of a benefit to justify the cost?

Shutterstock © Lou Oates, 2011.

$30,000 or slightly more, per year, and qualify for taxpayer assistance when you get sick. Potentially millions of Americans would be added to the list of non-paying patients, which would exacerbate the cost-shifting problem.

Second, by forcing people to pay for insurance or face an IRS-levied fine, the government creates more economic hardship for people who are healthy and need the money to pay for housing, food, college expenses, and other necessities. Moreover is the issue of allowing government to force us to engage in commerce. If you do not drive a car, you do not have to buy car insurance. The federal government, before 2010, never passed a law saying to all of us, "We have selected a business that we are going to force you to purchase something from." One might ask the question, if government can force us to buy insurance, does this mean that a precedent has been set that allows government to force us to buy other things that might "be good for us?"

Third, by making it illegal for businesses with 50 or more workers to not offer insurance, do we run the risk of raising the cost of doing business at a time when

HEALTH CARE REFORM AND THE CONSTITUTION

During the 2008 presidential campaign, Barack Obama called health care a "right." In 2004 George W. Bush signed into law the biggest single expansion of health care benefits in U.S. history. What does each of these men have in common?

They both recognize the *political rationality* of making health care more available. With the elderly and their baby-boomer children representing a very large and active voting group, it would be irrational for each candidate to ignore the economic burden health care has become for older Americans. The benefit of any of these proposals – to the candidates – is increased votes.

Should Messrs. Obama and Bush form their views of health care under the guidance of the U.S. Constitution? Recall that Article One, Section Eight, Clause One reads:

> The Congress shall have the power to lay and collect taxes, duties, imposts and excises, to pay the debts and provide for the common defense and general welfare of the United States; but all duties, imposts and excises shall be uniform throughout the United States.

Photo courtesy Sarah Chambless

SUGGESTED CLASSROOM DEBATE

Should 42 year-old men who play tackle football with no pads be covered under the new health care legislation?

If you were to take a close look at this rulebook for public officials, you would not find one reference to the government's role in providing for free health care. You may recall from chapter three that the founder's view of the enumerated clauses were clear, but the Supreme Court sided with Alexander Hamilton as to the true interpretation of the words, general welfare. Whom would you side with regarding the question over health care and this clause? Before you answer, consider this:

In February 2009, I severely sprained my left ankle while playing football in my back yard. In August 2010, I sprained the right one while portaging a canoe in Northern Minnesota. Between the multiple sets of X-Rays, MRIs, walking boots (two different types), and rehabilitation, I probably rang up several thousand dollars in doctor bills. If I did not have insurance, should you be forced to help my ankles get better? Should I be asked to help you if you smoke too much or don't eat right?

Well before the Patient Protection and Affordable Care Act was passed, legal and economic scholars were questioning whether the law would ultimately prevail.[53] When the 2,700 page health care legislation was passed, then Speaker of the House, Nancy Pelosi was asked about the bill's constitutionality. "Are you serious?" was her reply.[54]

As it turns out, Ms. Pelosi may have been a bit too optimistic that the bill she acknowledged not having read, would stand up to legal challenges.

When U.S. District Court Judge, Roger Vinson struck down the entire law as a violation of our Constitutional rights, he argued that the mandate requiring all of us to engage in commerce could not be "severed" from the rest of the law, and so the entire law must be struck down.[55]

At the time this book was going to print, the U.S. Supreme Court had not yet said what our rights were under the guise of health care reform.

Turning over the entire health care system to elected officials and a system of socialistic rationing may sound appealing, but ask yourself why so many foreigners come to the U.S. when serious health concerns must be addressed. Why is there now a *waiting list to get on the waiting list* for health care in Great Britain – a nation where dirty hospitals and botched care are not uncommon?[57] Why has the life expectancy of Canadian women actually fallen over the years? Is there a rational reason why Canadians face an average wait of 17.7 weeks to see a general practitioner, or 18.2 weeks for surgery?[58] Why do half of all Canadians want a different health care model?[59] Why has cervical cancer doubled in Cuba, at the same time patients are now required to bring their own syringes, towels, and bed sheets to hospitals where doctors make $25 per month?[60]

It is because in those nations – and others where the government runs health care – the people have traded in the freedom to navigate through health care markets for the security of having taxpayers pick up the tab. In these nations, taxpayers pay for the care of everyone. Government then sets a budget for hospitals and fixes prices below the equilibrium level on doctors' fees, drugs, medicine, and other forms of care. The low fees are designed to keep people from being "exploited" by higher prices.

However, since the prices are set artificially low, the governments that use taxpayer money to provide care must set budgets; otherwise, people would try to use much more care than they need. This may sound good, but the result has been very hard on the very people who traded in their economic liberty.

In February of 2010, citizens of Ottawa faced the following situation in the market for surgeries:

THE COST OF "FREE" HEALTH CARE

For many, the health care system is so fundamentally flawed that the argument of turning over the entire system to the government is appealing.[56] For those folks, the health care legislation signed by President Obama did not go far enough in dealing with our health care situation. Fortunately, history is a wonderful guide to understanding the future.

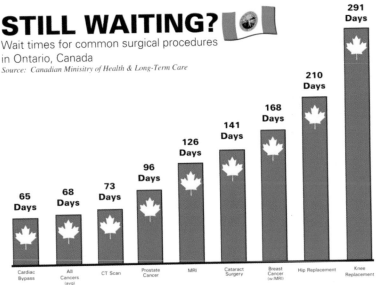

STILL WAITING?
Wait times for common surgical procedures in Ontario, Canada
Source: Canadian Ministry of Health & Long-Term Care

Procedure	Days
Cardiac Bypass	65 Days
All Cancers (avg)	68 Days
CT Scan	73 Days
Prostate Cancer	96 Days
MRI	126 Days
Cataract Surgery	141 Days
Breast Cancer (w/MRI)	168 Days
Hip Replacement	210 Days
Knee Replacement	291 Days

CONCEPT CHECK

Conduct research online to learn more about something called "RomneyCare."[65] Has Mitt Romney provided a solution to our health care condition that could work for the entire country? Why, or why not?

Delays in getting treatment associated with government cost controls, having hospitals that run out of money and close their doors, elective surgeries postponed for months (if not years), and the tax burdens to pay for it all make national health care a highly questionable objective by any measure. That might be why many doctors in Canada continue to lobby for privatization of the Canadian health care system – while others illegally operate for-profit health clinics.[61]

Furthermore, while Americans have become enticed by the prospect of finding cheaper drugs in Canada, the Canadian pharmaceutical industry has come under fire for lax safety standards and inefficient production processes.[62]

And if you are a healthy person in Canada – and other countries with socialized medicine – you arguably get the worst deal of all – because you pay for a service you don't use.

The United States is not immune to this problem. Since the 1960s, the federal government has run a form of socialized medicine in this country known as Medicaid and Medicare. Medicaid is a taxpayer-financed health program for poor people. Medicare is the taxpayer-financed health care system for older Americans – including the 76 million Americans who are about to become old…

States all over the U.S. are increasingly faced with the age-old problem of opportunity cost in the face of scarce resources. The scarce resources in this case involve tax dollars. After all, there is only so much money governments can squeeze out of people to pay for anything. The dilemma that we face is that as the demand for "free" health care grows each year, the supply of money to match this demand is not keeping pace.[63]

This means that officials at the state and federal level are facing budget crisis after budget crisis associated with paying for health care – often at the expense of roads, education, and other items the voters expect to see funded.[64]

CAN THE FREE MARKET SOLVE THE "PROBLEM"?

If we apply a free-market approach to rising health care costs and declining access, we would conclude that the most efficacious policy would be to allow market forces to correct as much of the problem as possible. After all, the U.S. health care system, by many objective measures, is the best in the world.

In the past 50 years, death from cardiac arrest has fallen by 67%. The Nobel Prizes in medicine and physiology have been awarded to more Americans than to researchers in all other countries *combined*. Eight of the top ten selling drugs in the world come from the U.S., while we rank first or second in the world in kidney transplants, liver transplants, heart transplants, total knee replacements, coronary artery bypass, and percutaneous coronary interventions – all while have the shortest wait time for surgeries in the world.[66]

The best cars in the world cost a lot of money. So does the best food and the best World Series tickets. Can everyone afford a Rolls Royce, lobster, and box seats at Fenway Park?

If we think of health care as just another service, why should anything be done about rising costs? We have seen numerous cases where the free market has acted to control the growth of health care costs. Look at HMOs and health clinics that you find inside malls and other shopping centers.

What about generic drugs and nontraditional medical approaches? Doesn't the free market cause these examples of cost-containment?

With respect to declining access, should we not ask how many of the 50 million people do not have insurance not because they cannot afford it, but rather because *they have decided to spend the money on something else?* Isn't this their right in an economy where liberty is valued? Does anyone force you to buy extra auto or life insurance?

One free-market response to rising health care costs has been the new trend of consumers negotiating health care prices with doctors and hospitals.[67] What would have seemed like an absurd notion not so long ago is gaining momentum. The key to negotiation seems to be driven by consumers who are willing to pay their bill up front in exchange for a discounted price and employers who have changed their health insurance policies to a "lump sum" plan, where workers are given a certain amount of money to spend on health care each year. With a budget constraint now in place, workers have an incentive to negotiate lower prices.

With cost-shifting leading to so many unpaid bills, doctors and hospitals are increasingly willing to take less money in exchange for the guarantee that the bill will be paid at the time services are rendered.

The free market has also led to more and more consumers buying drugs from India (where drugs are less expensive) or switching from brand-name drugs to generics in order to save money.[68] The movement toward generics has not only led to a significant drop in the profits of major drug companies, but has forced the drug companies to resort to greater advertising to try to regain market share.

The Internet has begun to play a role in dealing with the problem of asymmetric information. If you ever need surgery, you may want to log onto to the Internet to see if your state has a system where a person can find comparisons of hospitals for prices, length of stay, and many other facts that previously you could not ascertain.[69] The Leapfrog Group has even gone so far as to rate hospitals on the issue of safety.[70]

Finally, the free market has revealed some rather creative ways to fight health care inflation in some obvious – and not so obvious places.

Wal-Mart and other stores have begun opening health care clinics that typically charge between $25 – 60 per visit. This price is far below what many poorer people would have to pay to visit a doctor elsewhere.[71]

More and more companies are now adopting policies that ban smoking and discourage unhealthy people from applying for jobs in order to lower health care costs. This type of reaction to rising health care premiums is a natural one – and one that could bring about more rational decisions by prospective employees as it pertains to drugs, sex, and alcohol.[72]

Insurance companies have also discovered the same thing the automobile industry did years ago. That is the fact that poor people can be profitable customers, too.

Increasingly, many of the 50 million uninsured are gaining some access to insurance plans that are targeted at college students, retirees and others that are often turned off by the high deductibles that traditional insurance requires.[73] This is now being threatened by one provision of the 2010 health care law that caps how much insurers can spend on expenses and take for profits. In response, many insurers have called into question the economic rationality of offering these riskier policies.[74]

Finally, there is a more traditional way the free market has lowered costs. Over the last several years as the technology associated with LASIK eye surgery has increased, the costs of such surgery has fallen and thus, prices have come down considerably. What used to cost thousands of dollars now costs hundreds in some cases, as the free market has acted the same way it does in HDTVs, cell phones, and other areas of our lives.

As these trends continue, and as the flow of information improves, competition that currently does not exist among hospitals and doctors – on the issue of price and quality – should intensify, leading to time and money being saved by patients all over the country.[75]

OTHER "SOLUTIONS"

If solving what ails us in the health care market seems like an exercise in futility, there might be some alternatives for the U.S. to consider that in the long run could at least help to slow the rate of health care inflation and increase the number of people who have access to health care services.

Among the solutions that have been offered are health savings accounts, tax credits for living wills, higher taxes on products that create health care problems, Medicare and Medicaid reform, the legalization of euthanasia, privatization of the FDA, malpractice litigation reform, and modification of the antitrust laws. Let's look at some of these ideas.

HEALTH SAVINGS ACCOUNTS

The concept of health savings accounts is gaining popularity as a quasi-free-market approach to increasing access to health care.[76] During his State of the Union address in 2006, President Bush made this idea a centerpiece of his health care reform proposal.[77] The idea is that a person would be allowed to put a certain amount of money into an interest-bearing account, much like a savings account in a bank that would be tax-deductible and available to them only for medical purposes.

The appeal of this idea is straightforward. Rather than have Americans buy insurance or run the risk of going without insurance, the government would create an economic incentive for people to save money (the tax deduction) while at the same time reducing the number of Americans who have no money available to pay for health care needs.

Of course, the unanswered question is whether Americans would respond to the incentive by saving. We Americans are already notoriously lousy savers for our retirement and our children's educational needs, so saving for the possibility of a health problem might not be at the top of our list of priorities. The incentive might have to be quite large to induce the behavioral response needed.

However, we do see companies like Whole Foods and Safeway offering HSAs with a great deal of success. These companies have insurance plans with high deductibles.[78] You might have to pay for the first $1,000 of your care before insurance kicks in. However, the company gives you money – in the case of Whole Foods, about $1,500 per year – to put into an account. If you do not use the money, it rolls over to the next year so that a worker can actually build up cash over time, to pay for their health care needs.

The result has been more price-conscientiousness by the workers, lower costs for Whole Foods, and a lessening of the third-party payer problem.[79]

THE LIVING WILL TAX CREDIT

The average American will spend almost half of his or her lifetime expenditure on health care in the last month of life. This is a staggering statistic born out of our innate desire to prolong life as long as possible. The problem for many elderly Americans is that when the end is near, they are incapable of making this decision.

Such a painful dilemma often leads the relatives of the dying to ignore the medical experts and opt for any and all technology that can give their loved one a few more chances. This reality leads to an incredible increase in the cost of providing health care and adds billions to the collective bill each year. As baby boomers age, this dilemma will get even worse.[80]

A living will gives a person the opportunity – while alive and coherent – to legally put into place the parameters for extending or saving his or her own life.[81]

These parameters could include "do not resuscitate" provisions or statements that remove the life-ending decision from family members. The problem is, that living wills cost money to create, and few of us are willing to take on this responsibility. If a tax credit (my suggestion) were made available for this expense, it would lower the cost of obtaining such a will. For just a few hundred dollars of tax relief, the government could save millions, if not billions, of dollars over time in Medicare costs from patients who have no chance to live, but have no incentive to say "enough" when someone else will see the bill.

SIN TAX INCREASES

Currently, the federal government taxes cigarettes and alcohol in order to deal with the negative externalities and raise revenue. Should these taxes be even higher?

One proposal that Congress briefly considered called for the government to create a progressive tax on the saturated fat content of food, in order to raise revenue to fight heart disease brought on by bad diets.[82] Based on the current price elasticity of demand for high-fat foods, it was estimated that such a tax would generate just over $20 billion annually.

MEDICARE AND MEDICAID REFORM

Medicaid and Medicare are taxpayer-funded health care programs that cost hundreds of billions of dollars per year. The problem is that many of those billions of dollars are fraudulently spent. Here are some examples from Justice Department records: The supplier who went door-to-door, promising beneficiaries' free milk, and then billed Medicare for expensive nutritional supplements.

Then there was the lab that encouraged physicians to order free tests, as part of a testing panel, and then billed Medicare separately for these unnecessary tests. The durable medical equipment supplier who billed Medicare for canes, wheelchairs, and other items allegedly supplied from his offices on the sixth floor of a five-story building. The guy down in Florida who was billing Medicare for oxygen and supplies for a number of beneficiaries, and when the staff got to his office for a site visit, they found lots of neat souvenirs, like stuffed alligators.[83] By some estimates, Medicare fraud alone costs taxpayers $60 billion per year.[84]

This means any discussion of reducing health care costs must look at these and other examples of wasted taxpayer money.

ELIMINATION OF THE FDA

As we have seen, the FDA approval process has added years and millions of dollars to the development of new drugs. This has prompted some economists to call for the elimination of the FDA.[85] Would the free market do a better job of regulating new drugs and medical equipment?

If the FDA disappeared tomorrow, and if no one were in control of determining the safeness and effectiveness of drugs and medical technology, would it be disconcerting to most Americans? Of course it would be. Disconcerted consumers are seen as potential customers of entrepreneurs. Shortly after the dissolution of the FDA, one or more private companies would jump into the market – as the argument goes – specializing in examining drugs and equipment to determine if they are safe and effective. Just like Underwriters Laboratories has made a reputation for assuring homebuilders that wiring is safe, these new entrepreneurs would know that they would have to gain the trust of the American consumer.

If the new companies put their "seal of approval" on a new drug and people end up dead, or worse off, from taking the drug, how long will it take for that company to go out of business? If the FDA does the same thing, will it go out of business? As long as the FDA is funded with your tax dollars, if it makes a mistake, no matter how bad the mistake is, you will still have to see your taxes go to the FDA. The private business does not work that way. It knows that you can voluntarily refuse to buy anything with its name on it, so in order to make profit the private business has to be diligent, resourceful, and effective in delivering the service.

This also means that the private business would have to be efficient with your money. Long delays would push up costs and prices, and would therefore lower the amount of the drugs or equipment consumed. The private research company would be faster than the FDA but would not be able to simply rush drugs through for fear of making a mistake that could cost lives and profits.

If you recall the concept of self-interest and what self-interest tends to accomplish, it makes a great deal of sense to speculate that drug prices would be lower and drugs and equipment would get to people faster if the FDA did not exist.

MALPRACTICE LITIGATION REFORM

We have seen that lawsuits cause health care costs to rise for several reasons. Lawsuits cost money. Higher insurance premiums and unnecessary tests stemming from fear of lawyers, all drive health care costs up. Some solutions to this problem could be caps on damage awards, the "loser

pays" scenario that is common in Great Britain, and more economic analysis of what damages were caused by the doctor, as opposed to hysterical damage awards driven by emotional juries.

Capping damage awards means just that. For a lost leg, death, or whatever, there would be a limit as to how much someone could get in an award. *Forensic economics* – the use of economics to determine the value of life and body parts – could be used to set the awards. For example, if a right-handed economics professor and a left-handed major league baseball player each had rotator cuff surgery on their left shoulders, and the surgeon blew the operation, resulting in the amputation of each man's arm, a forensic economist would measure the total projected earnings lost by each person and conclude that the pitcher should get a far larger award.

Currently, we have economists do this type of analysis and testimony, but juries often disregard statistics in favor of some normative evaluation of damages. A stricter criterion based on forensic modeling could reduce jury awards to a more rational level and help bring down health care costs.

SOME FINAL THOUGHTS

At the beginning of this book, you learned how the perpetual problem of scarcity forces all of us to make decisions using cost-benefit analysis. Depending on your perspective, the lack of cost-benefit analysis utilized in the health care market is a good thing or a bad thing.

For you, it might be a good thing that the government provides some basic level of health care. Even groups that have seen health care costs explode and understand the problem of cost-shifting still feel that any government reforms of the system should come with some guarantee of basic health care for all.[86] Yet, without some basic level of care, would people die in the streets, or would families and charities provide the needed assistance? It is hard to imagine that we as a society would let our fellow citizens suffer without any aid.

On the other hand, it is easy to understand why so many of you might be furious with your experiences with the health care system. Like many of you, I have waited hours outside of an emergency room wondering how many people ahead of me in line were there for reasons associated with texting while driving, drugs, alcohol, or other bad choices (not skiing or backyard football…), or were there without any real emergency at all.

You might say, "I think people should pay their bills, and if they can't, make them work it off!" Maybe that is not such a bad idea. What if they are too ill to work? Who pays for the administrative and monitoring costs to make sure they do the work? It is not as simple as it sounds.

Nonetheless, one salient fact emerges from this health care mess. That is that no one really seems to know how to fix a system that began unraveling after World War II.

Before the war, if you got sick, you paid your bill and left. During the war, it was illegal for businesses to offer higher wages to entice workers to move from job to job, so businesses instead began offering health insurance as a non-monetary form of compensation.[87]

Once the third party entered the picture, all incentives on everybody's part – patients, doctors, hospitals, insurance companies, lawyers, the government, and so forth – flew right out the window. More than 70 years later, we are on the verge of an epic budgetary meltdown when the children born right after World War II begin demanding their medical entitlement. When that happens, all bets are off as to what the health care market – and the proposed "fixes" for the market – will look like.

ENDNOTES

1 See "Recession Swells Number of Uninsured to 50.7 Million" by Avery Johnson, *The Wall Street Journal*, September 17, 2010.

2 Source: CBS Interactive Business Network.

3 Source: Reuters.

4 See "Do Some Pay Too Little for Health Care?" by David E. Rosenbaum, *The New York Times*, October 26, 2003.

5 See "Shifting Burden Helps Employers Cut Health Costs" by Vanessa Fuhrmans, *The Wall Street Journal*, December 8, 2003, p. B1.

6 Source: The Heritage Foundation.

7 See: "The 81% Tax Increase" by Bruce Bartlett, *Forbes*, May 15, 2009.

8 See "Patients in Florida Lining Up For All That Medicare Covers" by Gina Kolata, *The New York Times*, September 13, 2003.

9 See www.pbs.org/wnet/bid/sb-howmuch.html.

10 See "In some areas, few health insurers to choose from" by Linda Shrieves, *The Orlando Sentinel*, February 8, 2011.

11 For more on the Sherman Antitrust Act, see *The Economics of Antitrust* by Don E. Waldman, Little Brown, 1986, or *Antitrust Law and Economics in a Nutshell* by Ernest Gellhorn, West Publishing Co., 1990.

12 See The Brokaw Report: America's Health Care: Going Broke in Style, *NBC*, December 30, 1992.

13 See "With New Muscle, Hospitals Squeeze Insurers on Rates" by Barbara Martinez, *The Wall Street Journal*, April 12, 2002.

14 See "Uncertainty Inside Emergency Rooms" by Michelle Andrews, *The New York Times*, September 21, 2003.

15 See "Workers swallow bitter pill" by Greg Groeller, *The Orlando Sentinel*, April 28, 2002.

16 See www.economics.about.com/money/economics/library/weekly/aa041300.html.

17 Source: WebMD and "Our Big Problem" by Theodore Dalrymple, *The Wall Street Journal*, May 1-2, 2010.

18 Source: Reuters July19, 2007.

19 See "Heart Disease Hits the Preschool Set" by Ron Winslow, *The Wall Street Journal*, March 18, 2003.

20 See "As Obesity Rises, So Do Indignities in Health Care" by Richard Perez-Pena and Grant Glickson, *The New York Times*, November 29, 2003.

21 See "Obesity's Hidden Costs" by Rhonda L. Rundle, *The Wall Street Journal*, May 1, 2002.

22 See www.americanheart.org/Heart_and_Stroke_A_Z_Guide/cigs.html.

23 Source: Science Progress and the Congressional Budget Office.

24 The U.S. Department of Justice.

25 Source: The Guttmacher Institute.

26 See "The Politics of Health Legislation: An Economic Perspective" by Paul J. Feldstein, (Ann Arbor: Health Administration Press, 1988), p. 81; and "Birth Choices, the Law, and Medicine: Balancing Individual Freedoms and Protection of the Public's Health" by Chris Hafner-Eaton and Laurie Pearce, *Journal of Health Politics, Policy and Law* 19 (Winter 1994): 815.

27 See the Final Report on the Commission on Medical Education (New York: Association of American Medical Colleges, 1932), pp. 151–153, by A. Lawrence Lowell.

28 See "Federal Acute Back Pain Guideline Recommends Medication, Spinal Manipulation, and Exercise: Most Patients Can Safely Defer Specialized Diagnostic Testing," by Mark L. Schoene, *Back Letter* 10 (January 1995) 1.

29 Source: mymedicalmalpracticeinsurance.com.

30 See "So Sue Me: Doctors Without Insurance" by Rachel Emma Silverman, *The Wall Street Journal*, January 28, 2004, p. D1.

31 For more on the nationwide malpractice crisis, see "Legal Malpractice" by Philip K. Howard, *The Wall Street Journal*, January 27, 2003, p. A16; "Health care remains critical" by Ronald Brownstein, *The Orlando Sentinel*, January 5, 2003; "Insurers Missteps Helped Provoke Malpractice 'Crisis'" by Rachel Zimmerman and Christopher Oster, *The Wall Street Journal*, June 24, 2002; and "Flaws riddle state's trauma system" by Greg Groeller and Stephanie Erickson, *The Orlando Sentinel,* March 30, 2003.

32 See *Give me a Break* by John Stossel, Harper Collins, 2004, pp.43-47.

33 See "Paternalism Costs Lives" by Henry I. Miller, *The Wall Street Journal*, March 2, 2006.

34 Policy Analysis No. 235, August 7, 1995, "Wrecking Ball: FDA Regulation of Medical Devices" by Robert Higgs, The Cato Institute.

35 See "High U.S. Drug Prices May Give Pharmaceutical Makers a Migraine" by Laurie McGinley and Rachel Zimmerman, *The Wall Street Journal*, July 21, 2000.

36 For more on how the free market works faster–and creates lower prices–than the FDA, see "Drug makers feel squeeze" by Don Lee and Ronald D. White, *The Orlando Sentinel*, August 18, 2002; and "Rush to Fill Void in Menopause-Drug Market" by Gina Kolata, *The New York Times*, September 1, 2002.

37 See "The FDA is Evading the Law" by Scott Gottlieb, *The Wall Street Journal*, December 23, 2010.

38 See "The FDA vs. Bone Cancer Patients" by Mark Thornton, *The Wall Street Journal*, May 7, 2010.

39 See the April 13, 1998, segment of *NBC Nightly News* titled, "The Fleecing of America."

40 See "Insurer's Tactic: If You Get Sick, The Premium Rises" by Chad Terhune, *The Wall Street Journal*, April 9, 2002.

41 Sources: The Kaiser Family Foundation, House Energy Subcommittee, AP and Tribune Newspapers reporting.

42 See "The Real Impact of the New Health Care Law" by Michael D. Tanner, *Cato's Letter*, Fall 2010, Volume 8, Number 4.

43 See "Ruling likely puts health law into extended legal morass" by Noam N. Levey and David G. Savage, *The Orlando Sentinel*, December 14, 2010.

44 See "Judge Rejects Health Law" by Janet Adamy, *The Wall Street Journal*, February 1, 2011.

45 See "Kids 0, Insurance 0," *The Wall Street Journal*, September 25-26, 2010.

46 See "No thanks to Obama's deal on health care" by Austin White, *The Orlando Sentinel*, November 27, 2010.

47 See "Health Insurers Plan Hikes" by Janet Adamy, *The Wall Street Journal*, September 8, 2010.

48 See "ObamaCare's Worst Tax Hike" *The Wall Street Journal*, March 17, 2010, p. A20.

49 See "The Rich Can't Pay for ObamaCare" by Alan Reynolds, *The Wall Street Journal*, March 30, 2010.

50 See "The $31 Billion Revenue Fantasy," *The Wall Street Journal*, August 28-29, 2010.

51 See "Documents reveal AT&T, Verizon, others, thought about dropping employer-sponsored benefits" by Shawn Tully, *CNNMoney.com*, May 6, 2010; and "Goodbye, Employer-Sponsored Insurance" by John C. Goodman, *The Wall Street Journal*, May 21, 2010.

52 See "Obamacare: Reality versus the rhetoric" by David Moreland, *The Orlando Sentinel*, July 3, 2010.

53 See "ObamaCare and the General Welfare Clause" by Randy E. Barnett and David G. Oedel, *The Wall Street Journal*, December 27, 2010; and "Why the ObamaCare Tax Penalty is Unconstitutional" by J. Kenneth Blackwell and Kenneth A. Klukowski, *The Wall Street Journal*, July 22, 2010.

54 See Congress's Montrous Legacy" by Kimberly A. Strassel, *The Wall Street Journal*, December 24, 2010.

55 See "The Nuts and Bolts of the ObamaCare Ruling" by Randy E. Barnett and Elizabeth Price Foley, *The Wall Street Journal*, February 2, 2011, p. A17.

56 In 2004 the National Academy of Sciences recommended that the government find a way to provide coverage for all Americans. See "Panel urges health coverage for all" by Rob Stein, *The Washington Post*, January 15, 2004.

57 See "Britain's Prescription for Health Care: Take a Seat" by Sarah Lyall, *The New York Times*, April 18, 1999; and "The Health care Wars Are Only Beginning" by Fred Barnes, *The Wall Street Journal*, March 18, 2010.

58 See "Waits for Canadian Health Care Shorten a Bit" *The Wall Street Journal*, October 19, 2005; and *Waiting Your Turn: Wait Times for Health Care in Canada* by Mark Rovere.

59 See "Woe, Canada," *The Wall Street Journal*, September 8, 2002, p. A20; and "Why not buy American health care?" by Anthony Westell, *The Globe and Mail*, August 2, 2005, p. A13.

60 See "Dr. Berwick and That Fabulous Cuban Health Care" by Bret Stephens, *The Wall Street Journal*, July 13, 2010.

61 See "Doctors to argue for private health system" by Gloria Galloway, *The Globe and Mail*, July 27, 2005; and "Sick in America: Whose Body is it, Anyway" John Stossel reporting, *ABC News* 2007.

62 See "Canadian Pharmacies Flunk Inspections" by Conrad F. Meier, *Health Care News* (The Heartland Institute), Volume 4, Number 5, May 2004.

63 See "Governors Chop Spending" by Conor Dougherty and Amy Merrick, *The Wall Street Journal*, February 7, 2011.

64 See "Surging Costs for Medicaid Ravage State, Federal Budgets" by Sarah Lueck, *The Wall Street Journal*, February 7, 2005; "How to Ride the Medicaid Tidal Wave" by James Frogue, *Budget & Tax News* (The Heartland Institute) February 2005; and "Maine's State-Run Health Plan Faltering" by Tarren Bragdon, *Health Care News* (The Heartland Institute), January 2006.

65 See "The Failure of RomneyCare" by Grace-Marie Turner, *The Wall Street Journal*, March 17, 2010.

66 See "Where U.S. Health Care Ranks Number One" by Mark B. Constantian, *The Wall Street Journal*, January 7, 2010.

67 See "Can We Talk Price?" *The Wall Street Journal*, February 8, 2002.

68 See "For Drug Makers, Good Times Yield to a New Profit Crunch" by Gardiner Harris, *The Wall Street Journal*, April 18, 2002; "How Drug Makers Use Pharmacies to Push Pricey Pills" by Ann Zimmerman and David Armstrong, *The Wall Street Journal*, May 1, 2002; and "Generic Drugs From India Prompting Turf Battles" by Saritha Rai, *The New York Times*, December 26, 2003.

69 See "New Ratings Let Patients Shop for Hospitals" by Bernard Wysocki Jr. *The Wall Street Journal*, May 1, 2002.

70 See "Report Card to Rank Hospitals on Safety" by Laura Landro, *The Wall Street Journal*, April 22, 2004, p. D1.

71 See "Getting Your Health Care at Wal-Mart" by Jane Spencer, *The Wall Street Journal*, October 5, 2005.

72 See "Can Employers Alter Hiring Policies to Cut Health Costs?" by Ann Zimmerman, Robert Guy Matthews, and Kris Hudson, *The Wall Street Journal*, October 27, 2005.

73 See "Health Insurer's New Target" by Vanessa Fuhrmans, *The Wall Street Journal*, May 31, 2005.

74 See "No, You Can't Keep Your Health Plan" by Scott Gottlieb, *The Wall Street Journal*, May 18, 2010.

75 See "Trust the Customer!" by Vernon L. Smith, *The Wall Street Journal*, March 8, 2006.

76 For more on health savings accounts, see www.americanhealthvalue.com/

77 See "President Proposes 'Impressive' Health Reforms in State of Union Address" by Susan Konig, *Health Care News* (The Heartland Institute), March 2006.

78 See "How Safeway is Cutting Health Care Costs" by Stephen A. Burd, *The Wall Street Journal*, June 12, 2009.

79 "Sick in America: Whose Body is it, Anyway," John Stossel reporting, *ABC News* 2007.

80 Increasingly, hospitals are attempting to save money by simultaneously denying care that does not raise the chances of living, while providing special palliative-care units that seek to provide comfort for dying patients. See "Unlikely Way to Cut Hospital Costs: Comfort the Dying" by Gautam Naik, *The Wall Street Journal*, March 10, 2004.

81 See "Demand for living wills surges on fears of agony" by Sandra Pedicini, *The Orlando Sentinel*, March 24, 2005.

82 See "Eating with Impunity" by Jack A. Chambless and Sarah C. McAlister, *The Orlando Sentinel*, December 22, 1996.

83 See www.hcfa.gov/medicare/fraud/transcr7.htm

84 See http://www.cbsnews.com/stories/2009/10/23/60minutes/main5414390.shtml

85 See www.aei.org/cs/cs5581.htm

86 See "Health Debate Emerges As Costs Rise Again" by Ron Winslow, *The Wall Street Journal*, December 17, 2001.

87 See "A Way Out of Soviet-Style Health Care" by Milton Friedman, *The Wall Street Journal*, March 20, 2010.

CHAPTER REVIEW

1. Fully explain how a car accident involving a person with no health insurance, can lead all the way to higher prices for your next cup of coffee.

2. What are four of the major reasons for rising health care costs in America? Explain each in detail.

3. What did the legislation signed by President Obama say about how health care markets would work in the future? Give specifics.

4. What is the difference between the Obama plan and what goes on in Canada?

5. What are five free-market based recommendations for dealing with American health care? Which one is the most likely to be politically acceptable to voters? Why?

20ᵀᴴ (*and* 21ˢᵀ) CENTURY ECONOMIC THOUGHT

Shutterstock © Kurhan, 2011.

*T*he problem is not that people are taxed too little;
the problem is that government spends too much.

RONALD REAGAN

THE ECONOMICS OF DISAGREEMENT

We close out the book with a look at the major debate that has framed economic analysis for the last 100 years – and will most likely do so in the future. Looking back, you have read about many economists – Adam Smith, Frederic Bastiat, Jean Baptiste Say, Karl Marx, and more, with varying approaches to economic thought and diverse contributions to this important social science.

During the 20th century the world witnessed the birth – and death – of communism, the collapse of faith in capitalism in the 1930s, renewed faith in markets by the 1980s, and ongoing experiments with how to make markets work for people that are often disadvantaged from birth or geography.

This debate continues today. As we have seen, the United States is currently on a course that calls into question how long we will be able to call America a largely capitalistic nation. In China and Russia – still called communist by many – capitalism is being embraced at a pace that few could have fathomed.

During the last century, the divergent opinions on economics dovetailed into two major schools of thought. While many of you will go on to read about this debate in macroeconomics, it is important for those of you who are terminating your economics studies this semester to gain an appreciation for the transition the United States – and the world has gone through. That transition took us from faith in the Classical School of Thought from 1776-1933 to support for more government involvement in the economy from 1933-1980, and then back to the Classical approach at the end of the 20th century. Of course it would be irresponsible to leave out the current century, so an examination of some of the more recent economic theories will take place to cover the first decade of the 21st century.

What follows is an examination of this evolutionary change.

THE CLASSICAL SCHOOL OF THOUGHT

The Classical School has its roots in the works of Adam Smith, who, as you will recall, believed very deeply in the power of uncontrolled markets to bring about desirable economic outcomes. Smith and the other Classical thinkers of the day – like Say, David Ricardo, and Bastiat – argued that the proper role of government was to protect individual liberties and property rights, and to provide goods and services, like national defense, that the private sector could not provide efficiently.

Other than that, the Classical economists believed that individuals make better decisions than governments do, and should be left alone to pursue their self-interest as long as the rights of others were not violated. The timing of Smith's famous book could not have been better. It was, of course, in that same year that the United States declared its independence from Great Britain and embarked on the great experiment of political and economic freedom. From 1776 until 1933, the Classical ideology of limited government involvement in the economy was largely embraced as the model for the United States.

FROM ADAM SMITH TO FRIEDRICH HAYEK

F. A. Hayek was a Nobel-winning Austrian economist renowned for both his popular arguments against collectivism in *The Road to Serfdom* and his scholarly work on the business cycle, the function of prices, and the nature of spontaneously emerging social orders. Hayek studied economics at the University of Vienna under Ludwig Von Mises and at the Institute for Business Cycle Research, which he helped Mises found.

Hayek's key insights included the recognition that, because knowledge is dispersed and depends on time, place, and context, no central authority could acquire all the knowledge required to plan an economy. For Hayek, market competition generates a particular kind of order – an order that is the product "of human action but not human design."

This "spontaneous order" is a system that comes about through the independent actions of many individuals, and produces overall benefits unintended and mostly unforeseen by those whose actions bring it about. Given the lack of perfect foresight, or perfect people, Hayek argued that any economic system must be allowed to mimic nature, where self-interested individuals are allowed to chart the course of their own lives – whether times are good or bad.

THE CLASSICAL SOLUTION FOR ECONOMIC DOWNTURNS

Based on what you have read thus far on Smith and Hayek, the following policy prescription for a recession should not come as much of a shock. A *recession* occurs when there is a general decrease in the demand for virtually all goods and services throughout the economy. During recessions people lose their jobs and national income tends to fall.

Smith, Hayek, and other Classical economists believed that if the economy goes into a recession, eventually wages and other input costs of production will fall, leading to an increase in the overall supply of goods and services. This "aggregate" supply will continue to increase until the economy's health has been restored.

From 1776-1932 there were virtually no government programs of any kind. If the economy went into the tank, workers faced the choice of losing their jobs or taking a pay cut.

The same was true for suppliers. If the demand for their products or services dropped, they could not turn to the government for relief. They had to lower prices or lose business. When workers and suppliers lowered their wages and prices, it led to lower production costs for American businesses. Recall that production costs are a key determinant of supply. Once these costs come down, it is possible for the recession to end and jobs to be restored.

What would have been the harm of limited government involvement designed to speed up the recovery process? To a Classical economist, the major problem with government is the way decisions are made. Politicians often make decisions based more on *political exigencies* than on sound economics.

That being the case, there is no guarantee that the government would ever or could ever target the areas of the economy that needed to be assisted and provide the assistance in an economically prudent way. Therefore, the government would be far more likely to spend money in ways that please voters, but not necessarily in ways that promote economic growth. Special "earmarks" or "pork" projects designed to funnel money into a politician's district – regardless of whether or not cost-benefit analysis would support the funding – is a logical outgrowth of government involvement.

Moreover, there is the Constitutional question of the proper role of the government in the economy. Many scholars argue that when the government intervenes in a way that does not promote the general welfare of the nation – issuing food stamps, for example – that this type of charitable spending is not a proper function of government.

The bailout of General Motors, of the financial sector, and homeowners facing foreclosure in 2008-2011, is an example of the difference between the private sector response and government response. In a purely Classical model, the banks, GM, and homeowners would be allowed to fail – or fix the problem. Those banks that made good decisions and were solvent during the crisis would survive and probably prosper as competitors failed. The failed banks would provide a sort of "economic fertilizer" for the economy at large. The fertilizer would come in the form of information on how *not* to run a bank.

THE CLASSICAL SOLUTION FOR RISING PRICES

In 1927 the economy was roaring. People were enjoying prosperity of historic proportions and spending money like never before. As a result of this spending, the nations' demand increased enough to create inflationary pressure in the U.S. economy. *Inflation* occurs when prices for most goods and services increase over time.

For the Classical School, inflation is dealt with by the same *self-correcting mechanism* we addressed when a recession was under way. However, in this case, the opposite occurs in labor and factor markets.

When "aggregate" demand increases enough to cause inflation, wages and other input costs will begin to rise. Wages and input costs increase, you will recall, because an acceleration of aggregate demand leads to labor and capital shortages. These shortages are corrected by increasing wages and prices paid to suppliers. Since input costs are now rising, the total supply of goods and services begins to fall until full employment is restored at higher price levels. Workers are not worse off, however, because wages have increased along with the cost of living.

Many Classical economists – and a few politicians like Ron Paul – would also point out that often inflation is a byproduct of failed government decisions.

Mr. Paul, whose Classical views have become quite popular on YouTube, was a vocal critic of the Federal Reserve Bank's role in creating the housing inflation of

2004-2006. Mr. Paul and other disciples of Smith and Hayek pointed out that by maintaining policies of keeping interest rates artificially low, the Federal Reserve had encouraged irresponsible borrowing and lending, and thus, triggered a false explosion in the demand for homes and real estate that was bound to end in disaster.

THE KEYNESIAN SCHOOL OF THOUGHT

> We in America today are nearer to the final triumph over poverty than ever before in the history of any land. The poorhouse is vanishing from among us.

These were the words of President Herbert Hoover in August 1928 – 15 months before the largest economic collapse in America's history.

For 156 years, the United States had operated under the teachings of economists like Adam Smith, Jean Baptiste Say, and Friedrich Hayek. By 1930, Karl Marx and John Maynard Keynes had come to the forefront of economic thought. What happened?

THE GREAT DEPRESSION

Throughout the 1920s, the U.S. enjoyed record levels of prosperity. With rising incomes and personal wealth came increased consumer goods like the automobile and radio. People were dancing the Charleston and watching Babe Ruth crush home runs in the newly built Yankee Stadium. The stock and real estate markets also enjoyed double-digit gains year after year, as billions of dollars of speculative investments flowed freely into these high-risk markets. To some, the days of recession seemed to be over. But unforeseen – or perhaps ignored – warnings of trouble were omnipresent.

First, there was the crisis in agriculture that was ravaging farmers throughout the land. Overproduction in some instances and the "Dust Bowl" that had led to the collapse of farming in the Midwest, had put many Americans into poverty. In February 1928, stock prices began a steady climb that continued, with only a few interruptions, until September of 1929. During this period, stock prices climbed by over 40%. Trading on the New York Stock Exchange went from two to three million shares per day to 10 to 12 million shares as more and more investors jumped at the chance of "easy money."

Compounding this "problem" was the fact that investors were required to put only 10% of the value of one

share of stock to gain control of that share. This margin buying led to a good number of people, who were not well-versed in the workings of securities investing, to enter the market.

By October 1929, the speculative bubble began to burst. On October 21, and again on October 24, there were alarming declines in stock prices. But on October 29, 1929, the market collapsed. A total of 16 million shares traded hands that day, as investors panicked and dumped stock at virtually any price they could get. The problem, of course, was that as brokerage firms began to make margin calls – calls for investors to pay up the remaining 90% of the price of the stock purchased – many investors did not have the money. Those who did have the money, often had it tied up in banks that had contributed to the overvalued real estate and stock markets, by being all too eager to float loans to speculators.

When people realized that much of the money in America's banks had been loaned out in markets that were collapsing, and that 0% of the deposits in any bank were insured, a series of bank runs began – massive withdrawals of money that inevitably caused widespread bank failures and the beginning of the depression.

Making matters worse was the tight monetary policy of the Federal Reserve Bank during the early 1930s. In spite of the fact that banks were failing all over the United States, the Federal Reserve Bank, perhaps reluctant to encourage borrowing when few could repay loans, allowed the money supply to drop dramatically. The money supply fell 27% from 1929 to 1933, and real economic output fell 29% accordingly. The drop in the money supply kept interest rates at damagingly high levels, and prevented consumption and investment from increasing enough to stimulate demand. The Federal Reserve Bank even increased rates in 1931 in an attempt to shore up the value of the dollar.

The final blow to the American economy came at the hands of Congress in 1930. In an attempt to protect American businesses from foreign competition and promote consumption of domestic goods and services, Congress passed the Smoot-Hawley Tariff Act. This Act increased tariffs by approximately 60% on the nation's trading partners. Many economists believe that it was this act, more than the stock market crash and the mistakes of the Federal Reserve Bank, that caused the decade-long economic collapse.

Some have even made the inferential leap of connecting the Smoot-Hawley Tariff Act to the rise of Adolf Hitler and the onslaught of World War II. The argument is that without this act, the entire world might have never seen the Great Depression and thus, the rise of fascism and, eventually, World War II.

Finally, under the political thinking of the day, the federal government decided it was morally prudent to pursue a balanced budget. As tax revenue was plummeting along with economic activity in the period from 1929 to 1932, it was only natural to raise taxes to cover the rising federal budget deficit.

In 1932, Republican president Herbert Hoover, with the support of the newly elected Democratic majority in the House of Representatives, passed the largest peacetime tax increase in the history of the United States. Marginal income tax rates were raised from 1.5 to 4% at the low end and from 25 to 63% at the top of the scale. This was a huge tax increase by any measure.

The timing for this couldn't have been worse, because tax increases generally lead to decreases in the demand for goods and services and the incentive to earn.

THE EMERGENCE OF JOHN MAYNARD KEYNES

It was during this time that the American people lost faith in the free market's ability to bring about an end to economic crises. In fact, during the 1930s, the Communist party of the United States saw a surge in new members, as many Americans believed Karl Marx had been proven right: Capitalism was a model doomed to failure. Under Herbert Hoover, attempts to pull the country out of the Great Depression were limited.

As mistrust of Herbert Hoover grew, more and more Americans began to demand that the government do something to ease their plight. Sharing this opinion was a British economist named John Maynard Keynes.

SUGGESTED CLASSROOM DEBATE

In the wake of the largest financial crisis since the Great Depression, is it possible that another Great Depression could take place in our nation? Why, or why not?

CONCEPT CHECK

During the "Great Recession" of 2007-2009 and its aftermath, wages and salaries fell sharply in the United States.[1] Is this one of the reasons why unemployment started to fall by 2011?

John Maynard Keynes was one of the preeminent economists of all time. At a very young age, he wrote a book, *Economic Consequences of Peace* that claimed that the Treaty of Versailles would lead to instability in Europe, due in large part to the huge financial strain it placed on Germany. While this work was certainly prophetic, it was another book – *The General Theory of Employment, Interest and Money* – that brought him worldwide acclaim. Written during the Great Depression, it relied on very sophisticated mathematical models to tackle a problem that seemed to be above the heads of Classical economists. That problem was what to do about chronic unemployment and a stagnating economy.

By the time his work was done, he had not only influenced a massive change in economic policy in the United States, but also caught the attention of Adolf Hitler, who eventually resorted to Keynesian economics to build up Germany's military-industrial complex. Keynes had observed at close hand how Hjalmar Schacht, Adolph Hitler's chief economic adviser, had turned around the German economy by fully applying Keynes' theories there. As economist John Kenneth Galbraith later wrote, Hitler "was the true protagonist of the Keynesian idea."

Keynes was convinced that the drop in the nation's income from $104 billion in 1929 to $76.4 billion in 1932, and an increase in the unemployment rate to 24.9% by 1933, was magnified by the government's near refusal to come to the aid of the citizenry. Keynes conjectured that during the Great Depression, the Classical model was plagued by two enormous problems: *downward wage rigidity* and *socioeconomic problems* that prevented the self-correcting mechanism from working.

DOWNWARD-WAGE RIGIDITY

Recall that for the Classical model to work, as demand falls, wages must drop by a large enough amount to cause an increased supply. If wages are not flexible enough, the Classical model will not work quickly. Although influence of labor unions declined during the 1930s, they were still part of a labor market that did not take the demands for lower wages without some resistance.

During the Great Depression, wages simply did not respond to downward pressure by a large enough amount to restore full employment. According to Keynes, during the Great Depression, wages did not fall fast enough for the Classical self-correcting mechanism to restore full employment.

SOCIOECONOMIC PROBLEMS

During prolonged recessions, crime, suicide, drug and alcohol abuse, divorce, malnutrition, and depression all increase. In the downturn of 2007-2009, domestic abuse shelters around the country filled up at alarming rates. In addition, more people drop out of school to meet immediate economic needs, when times are bad. These and other socioeconomic problems lead to a reduction in productivity and the inability of the nation's supply to increase. As a result of these two realities, when asked if the economy self-corrects in the long run, Keynes said, "Yes, but in the long run we are all dead!"

THE KEYNESIAN SOLUTION FOR FALLING DEMAND

According to Keynes, when the economy goes into a recession as a result of a decrease in aggregate demand, downward wage rigidity and socioeconomic problems generally prevent the economy from self-correcting, as the Classical economists predict it will. Since the private sector is unable to restore full employment, it becomes necessary to introduce government into the economy.

According to Keynes, the government should first announce its intention to spend money on a massive *infrastructure building* campaign. Infrastructure is made up of the roads, bridges, dams, power lines, water systems, etc. that are the foundation of the productive capacity of the economy. Once the announcement is made, consumer confidence will increase, and as a result, autonomous purchases will rise. Autonomous purchases are purchases

In October of 2008, the amount of credit available to businesses and individuals fell dramatically during the banking crisis. Is this proof that the Classical self-correcting mechanism failed? Is it proof that government was needed to restore the economy? Why, or why not?

based on future expected income, rather than current disposable income. As autonomous purchases increase, demand will begin to slowly increase.

The next step is for the government to borrow money from the banking system (this is called deficit financing) or simply to print the money necessary to begin spending. It is necessary to borrow the money in this instance, because recessions erode the tax base, and any further tax increases to pay for infrastructure spending would be counterproductive.

Once the government begins spending, the "multiplier effect" will kick in. The Keynesian demand multiplier effect is the belief that for every increase in government spending by $1, real GDP will increase by more than $1. This is because once the government gives a company a contract to do work, the company and its workers spend this money. This money ends up being circulated through the economy many times, enabling the government to restore full employment quickly.

Under the New Deal formulated by Franklin D. Roosevelt, the government created work programs such as the Works Progress Administration and the Civilian Conservation Corps and set out to build up America's infrastructure – like the Golden Gate Bridge in San Francisco.

KEYNES, BASTIAT, AND THE CASE OF 43,600 BROKEN WINDOWS

What would John Maynard Keynes say about September 11th – and specifically, the issue of rebuilding the World Trade Center towers? While no one can say with 100%

certainty what he would propose, one can reasonably assume he would contend that rebuilding the towers would generate a multiplier effect for the city of New York and thus, the nation as a whole. Frederic Bastiat would disagree.

Bastiat, you may recall, was a French economist who lived long before the Great Depression. Bastiat was the first economist to draw attention to the "broken-window fallacy." Consider a scenario where a vandal throws a rock through a Chicago landlord's window.

If one looked only at what is seen, one could understand, he said, the common reaction to a landlord's window broken by vandals: "At least it creates work for the glazier." The landlord's misfortune is quickly transformed into a benefit for the city of Chicago because it makes money circulate and "creates" work.

However, Bastiat argued, if the landlord is forced to spend $125 to replace her window, that is $125 she can now no longer spend on the new microwave oven that she wanted to put in an apartment. And she had a perfectly good window before it was broken. Far from the broken window creating a social benefit, it is, in fact, a tiny social calamity.

The $125 has been spent employing the glazier, it is true, but only at a net loss to the community as a whole. Before, the shopkeeper had a window and $125. Now, she has exactly what she had before (a sound window), but not her $125, and so she cannot buy her oven. Both she and the community have been impoverished, not enriched.

From this intellectually intuitive example, one can see the inherent problem with arguing that fixing the 43,600

CONCEPT CHECK

In 2011 the largest blizzard in Oklahoma's history buried the state in snow.[2] Did the rescues, cleanup, and power line repairs stimulate the economy?

Photo courtesy Anna Chambless

windows that were smashed when the World Trade Center was destroyed, will cause a multiplier effect. If one is to take Keynes's argument literally, then we could say that not only were the attacks in New York City and at the Pentagon beneficial because of all the debris removal and construction jobs that were created, but that another attack during our recession would have been helpful to speed recovery and create growth.

HAYEK VS. KEYNES

It is necessary now to state the unpalatable truth that it is Germany whose fate we are in danger of repeating.

Friedrich Hayek,
as quoted in *The Road to Serfdom*

Hayek's lamentations on repeating the mistakes of Nazi Germany did not come after WW II, but rather *during* WW II. In 1944 Hayek argued that Germany's problem began before Adolf Hitler, with the idea that the government should own the means of production and determine output, employment, and price levels.

For Hayek, nations that attempted to control the commanding heights of the economy – e.g. coal, steel, railroads, and heavy industry – were doing so at the great risk of destroying their economy over time and turning over the economic decisions to political bodies who might not be efficient, or worse, evil.

THE KEYNESIAN SOLUTION
FOR RISING PRICES

While much of his professional life was devoted to the problem of recessions, Keynes did have some strong thoughts on the problem of too much demand. In a nutshell, Keynes believed that if a nation's demand increased to the point where inflation was a problem, the solution should be an *increase in taxes* levied on businesses and households.

Higher taxes, according to Keynes, would have two effects. First, greater taxation would mean less money to spend or invest, therefore aggregate demand would be cooled off and full employment restored.

Second, Keynes was concerned that inflation was the result of people having too much money and time on their hands to spend money in a conspicuous manner.

He argued that with rising income and wealth, people become less productive and more prone to engage in wasteful activities, rather than pursuits that create long-run economic growth.

Therefore, Keynes believed that higher taxes would keep people from making too much money, keeping them thrifty and hard-working. This was a major justification for tax increases during World War II.

In late 1943, Treasury Secretary Henry Morgenthau asked Congress for another tax increase. He framed his appeal, in large part, as an anti-inflation effort. The new act, he argued, must help stop inflation. "Nothing in the economic field can interfere with the war effort as much as an uncontrolled rise in prices," he told the House Ways and Means Committee. "An inflationary price rise is a source of grave social injustice. It undermines morale and impedes war production. It strikes at random without consideration of equity or ability to bear the hardships, which it imposes. Once it has acquired momentum, inflation is extremely difficult to control, and leaves a heritage of post-war stresses and strains that will haunt us for decades."

This was the mindset of Washington, D.C. as income tax rates rose to as high as 94% during the 1940s and 1950s, and remained as high as 70% until 1981.

THE CLASSICAL RESPONSE
TO TAX INCREASES

By 1979, a new group of economists, called "supply-side" or neo-classical economists, had begun to step to the front of the stage in the economics community. The term "neo" means new. Supply-side economists are basically classical economists who argue that the massive scale of government is here to stay but that government's size should be reduced.

With that supposition in mind, the supply-side economist concentrated his or her analysis on getting the government out of the economy as much as possible. Why was 1979 the rebirth of classical thinking?

With marginal tax rates topping out at 70% and massive government regulations imposed upon the economy, the United States had entered a period of economic stagnation during the 1970s that had not been seen since the Great Depression.

This new group of economists argued that the government was the source of, rather than the solution for, economic misery. To the supply-siders, the only way the economy would ever be strong again would be to unshackle free enterprise from the benevolent grip of government and allow individuals and businesses to operate in a less-intrusive and lower-taxed environment.

Recall that the major focus of the Keynesian school of thought revolves around changes in demand. Yet whenever demand changes, there is always a tradeoff between unemployment and inflation. By 1979, a growing number of economists became convinced that policymakers should forget about aggregate demand and concentrate on ways to stimulate aggregate supply. One of those economists was a young professor at the University of Southern California named Arthur Laffer.

Laffer believed that the 1970s – where unemployment and inflation were increasing simultaneously – had as much, if not more, to do with excessive government regulation and high taxes than high oil prices had. Laffer's argument was straightforward: The more money the government takes from people's paychecks, the less incentive people have to work and maximize the productivity of their capital or labor. He argued that less taxation and less-burdensome regulation would lead to an increase in the productivity of workers and businesses alike. They would now reap the rewards of extra education, training, or investments in new technology or capital equipment.

If workers and businesses were permitted to keep the bulk of the fruits of their labor, Laffer insisted, economic output would increase, and as a result, the government would get more tax revenue from less taxation. On what might be the most famous cocktail napkin in history, Mr. Laffer drew his basic theory over lunch with friends one day.

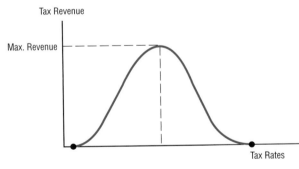

In 1980, the Republican candidate for president, Ronald Reagan, shared Laffer's theory. Reagan had long embraced the concept of lower taxes leading to better productivity. In his autobiography *An American Life,* Mr. Reagan states:

> At the peak of my career at Warner Bros., I was in the 94% tax bracket; that meant that after a certain point, I received only six cents of each dollar I earned and the government got the rest. The IRS took such a big chunk of my earnings that after a while I began asking myself whether it was worth it to keep on taking work. Something was wrong with a system like that. When you have to give up

such a large percentage of your income in taxes incentive to work goes down. When government confiscates half or more of a corporation's profit, the motivation to maximize profits goes down, and owners and managers make decisions based disproportionately on a desire to avoid taxes, they begin looking for tax shelters and loopholes that contribute nothing to the growth of our economy. Their companies don't grow as fast, they invest less in new plants and equipment, and they hire fewer people.

According to Reagan:

> Any system that penalizes success and accomplishment is wrong. Any system that discourages work, discourages productivity, discourages economic progress is wrong. If on the other hand, you reduce taxes and allow people to spend or save more of what they earn, they'll be more industrious; they'll have more incentive to work hard, and money they earn will add fuel to the great economic machine that energizes our national progress. The result is more prosperity for all–and more revenue for government. A few economists call this principle supply-side economics. I just call it common sense.

When Ronald Reagan was elected president in 1980, the unemployment rate in the U.S. was over 7%. Inflation was over 13% and for the year, total production fell by 0.3%. Recall that when he came into office, there were 14 tax brackets, the highest of which was 70%. Reagan immediately began to act on his philosophy of lower taxes and less regulation of business and individuals. The result of his push to get the government out of the marketplace was a $750 billion tax cut, passed in 1981, followed by another tax cut in 1986. When he left office in 1989, there were two tax brackets – 15 and 28%.

WHAT DID THE REAGAN TAX CUTS DO?

For nearly 30 years, economists have wrestled with one of the most argued-about topics in recent economic history. The debate centers on the extent to which Reagan's tax cutting caused, contributed to, or had nothing to do with the boom of the 1980s and 1990s. On one end of the fence you have economists like Laura D'Andrea Tyson who once stated,

> In direct contradiction to 12 years of Republican ideology, there is no relationship between the taxes a nation pays and its economic performance.

On the other hand are economists who claim that much, if not most, of the credit for our unprecedented economic prosperity stems from the technology gains created by the "new" economy and the greater level of economic freedom from confiscatory taxes that took place under Reagan's watch. During the eight years he was in office, while tax rates were falling, the unemployment rate in America fell from 7.6% in 1981 to 5.3% in 1989.

The rate of inflation was 10.3% in 1981 (13.5% in 1980). In every year he was in office, inflation rates fell – eventually to 4.8% in 1989. Productivity of American workers fell by 0.3% in 1980, but increased throughout the rest of the 1980s. Even Laffer's prediction of increased federal revenue came true. The government collected just over $599 billion from taxpayers in 1981. By 1989 the amount was over $990 billion. This was not an uncommon result. When marginal rates were cut in the 1920s from a top rate of 73 to 25%, government revenue grew from $719 million to $1.1 billion, and the economy expanded by 59%.

Due, in large part, to the massive tax cuts and a move to continue the deregulation of industry that began during the Carter administration, the U.S. experienced unprecedented growth during the 1980s. Reagan's plan was aided significantly by the collapse of OPEC and oil prices in 1986 and the emergence of new technologies, but the bottom line was indisputable: Greater economic freedom from burdensome tax rates led to much of the good fortune we had from 1982 through the 1990s. This occurred as a result of expanded productivity, greater labor force participation rates – especially for women – and less tax avoidance.

Since that time, much of the world has increasingly moved away from the Keynesian orthodoxy to the Classical, or Neo-Classical approach. In Chile, Hong Kong, China, Germany, Ireland, Russia, and even Iraq, more and more governments are adopting the classical approach to trade, taxes, regulations, and government intervention in the economy.

Not surprisingly, those nations that have maintained a Keynesian approach to markets – France, Sweden, Venezuela, and other European nations are struggling, while the citizens of nations that are pursuing freer markets are increasingly wealthy.

The real question for the 21st century appears to be, will the United States – the first experimenter with the idea of liberty and free markets – continue on this course, or will we succumb to the Keynesian pressures to provide more security?

This is not a theoretical question. During the 2008 election, a growing number of voters indicated that it would be beneficial for America to move in a direction that provided more health care from government, greater protection from the job losses that stem from international trade, and higher taxes imposed on richer Americans.

In 2003 John McCain voted against income tax cuts, arguing that the cuts favored the rich too much. In 2008 he and his running mate, Sarah Palin, voiced outrage over the "greed" that was, in their opinion, pervasive on Wall Street. Mr. McCain supported increased government spending on health care and global warming, and he supported the original $700 billion bailout of the banking system.

Barack Obama was also against the 2003 tax cuts and only grudgingly passed legislation that kept the rates down through 2012. As examined earlier, he, too, campaigned on the idea that greed was sweeping through corporations, that government should secure us from the lack of health insurance, and more.

Whether populist candidates like Messrs. McCain and Obama continue to gain the support of those whose views run against free markets and Classical economic thinking remains to be seen.

ENDNOTES

1 See "Downturn's Ugly Trademark: Steep, Lasting Drop in Wages" by Sudeep Reddy, *The Wall Street Journal*, January 11, 2011.
2 See "Winter Storm cripples two-thirds of country" by Richard Simon, Geraldine Baum and Abby Sewell, *The Orlando Sentinel*, February 2011.

CHAPTER REVIEW

1. What is the Classical view of how to fix a recession? What potential problems can occur with this model?

2. What is the Keynesian perspective on fixing recessions and inflation? What criticisms do the Classical economists offer for this model?

3. What caused the Great Depression? Fully explain.

4. What was the view of Ronald Reagan on how to promote economic growth? Be specific.

The United States Constitution

We the People of the United States, in Order to form a more perfect Union, establish Justice, insure domestic Tranquility, provide for the common defence, promote the general Welfare, and secure the Blessings of Liberty to ourselves and our Posterity, do ordain and establish this Constitution for the United States of America.

ARTICLE I

SECTION 1

All legislative Powers herein granted shall be vested in a Congress of the United States, which shall consist of a Senate and House of Representatives.

SECTION 2

CLAUSE 1: The House of Representatives shall be composed of Members chosen every second Year by the People of the several States, and the Electors in each State shall have the Qualifications requisite for Electors of the most numerous Branch of the State Legislature.

CLAUSE 2: No Person shall be a Representative who shall not have attained to the Age of twenty five Years, and been seven Years a Citizen of the United States, and who shall not, when elected, be an Inhabitant of that State in which he shall be chosen.

CLAUSE 3: Representatives and direct Taxes shall be apportioned among the several States which may be included within this Union, according to their respective Numbers, which shall be determined by adding to the whole Number of free Persons, including those bound to Service for a Term of Years, and excluding Indians not taxed, three fifths of all other Persons. The actual Enumeration shall be made within three Years after the first Meeting of the Congress of the United States, and within every subsequent Term of ten Years, in such Manner as they shall by Law direct. The Number of Representatives shall not exceed one for every thirty Thousand, but each State shall have at Least one Representative; and until such enumeration shall be made, the State of New Hampshire shall be entitled to choose three, Massachusetts eight, Rhode-Island and Providence Plantations one, Connecticut five, New-York six, New Jersey four, Pennsylvania eight, Delaware one, Maryland six, Virginia ten, North Carolina five, South Carolina five, and Georgia three.

CLAUSE 4: When vacancies happen in the Representation from any State, the Executive Authority thereof shall issue Writs of Election to fill such Vacancies.

CLAUSE 5: The House of Representatives shall chuse their Speaker and other Officers; and shall have the sole Power of Impeachment.

SECTION 3

CLAUSE 1: The Senate of the United States shall be composed of two Senators from each State, chosen by the Legislature thereof for six Years; and each Senator shall have one Vote.

CLAUSE 2: Immediately after they shall be assembled in Consequence of the first Election, they shall be divided as equally as may be into three Classes. The Seats of the Senators of the first Class shall be vacated at the Expiration of the second Year, of the second Class at the Expiration of the fourth Year, and of the third Class at the Expiration of the sixth Year, so that one third may be chosen every second Year; and if Vacancies happen by Resignation, or otherwise, during the Recess of the Legislature of any State, the Executive thereof may make temporary Appointments until the next Meeting of the Legislature, which shall then fill such Vacancies.

CLAUSE 3: No Person shall be a Senator who shall not have attained to the Age of thirty Years, and been nine Years a Citizen of the United States, and who shall not, when elected, be an Inhabitant of that State for which he shall be chosen.

CLAUSE 4: The Vice President of the United States shall be President of the Senate, but shall have no Vote, unless they be equally divided.

CLAUSE 5: The Senate shall chuse their other Officers, and also a President pro tempore, in the Absence of the Vice President, or when he shall exercise the Office of President of the United States.

CLAUSE 6: The Senate shall have the sole Power to try all Impeachments. When sitting for that Purpose, they shall be on Oath or Affirmation. When the President of the United States is tried, the Chief Justice shall preside: And no Person shall be convicted without the Concurrence of two thirds of the Members present.

CLAUSE 7: Judgment in Cases of Impeachment shall not extend further than to removal from Office, and disqualification to hold and enjoy any Office of honor, Trust or Profit under the United States: but the Party convicted shall nevertheless be liable and subject to Indictment, Trial, Judgment and Punishment, according to Law.

SECTION 4

CLAUSE 1: The Times, Places and Manner of holding Elections for Senators and Representatives, shall be prescribed in each State by the Legislature thereof; but the Congress may at any time by Law make or alter such Regulations, except as to the Places of chusing Senators.

CLAUSE 2: The Congress shall assemble at least once in every Year, and such Meeting shall be on the first Monday in December, unless they shall by Law appoint a different Day.

SECTION 5

CLAUSE 1: Each House shall be the Judge of the Elections, Returns and Qualifications of its own Members, and a Majority of each shall constitute a Quorum to do Business; but a smaller Number may adjourn from day to day, and may be authorized to compel the Attendance of absent Members, in such Manner, and under such Penalties as each House may provide.

CLAUSE 2: Each House may determine the Rules of its Proceedings, punish its Members for disorderly Behaviour, and, with the Concurrence of two thirds, expel a Member.

CLAUSE 3: Each House shall keep a Journal of its Proceedings, and from time to time publish the same,

excepting such Parts as may in their Judgment require Secrecy; and the Yeas and Nays of the Members of either House on any question shall, at the Desire of one fifth of those Present, be entered on the Journal.

CLAUSE 4: Neither House, during the Session of Congress, shall, without the Consent of the other, adjourn for more than three days, nor to any other Place than that in which the two Houses shall be sitting.

SECTION 6

CLAUSE 1: The Senators and Representatives shall receive a Compensation for their Services, to be ascertained by Law, and paid out of the Treasury of the United States. They shall in all Cases, except Treason, Felony and Breach of the Peace, beprivileged from Arrest during their Attendance at the Session of their respective Houses, and in going to and returning from the same; and for any Speech or Debate in either House, they shall not be questioned in any other Place.

CLAUSE 2: No Senator or Representative shall, during the Time for which he was elected, be appointed to any civil Office under the Authority of the United States, which shall have been created, or the Emoluments whereof shall have been encreased during such time; and no Person holding any Office under the United States, shall be a Member of either House during his Continuance in Office.

SECTION 7

CLAUSE 1: All Bills for raising Revenue shall originate in the House of Representatives; but the Senate may propose or concur with Amendments as on other Bills.

CLAUSE 2: Every Bill which shall have passed the House of Representatives and the Senate, shall, before it become a Law, be presented to the President of the United States; If he approve he shall sign it, but if not he shall return it, with his Objections to that House in which it shall have originated, who shall enter the Objections at large on their Journal, and proceed to reconsider it. If after such Reconsideration two thirds of that House shall agree to pass the Bill, it shall be sent, together with the Objections, to the other House, by which it shall likewise be reconsidered, and if approved by two thirds of that House, it shall become a Law. But in all such Cases the Votes of both Houses shall be determined by yeas and Nays, and the Names of the Persons voting for and against the Bill shall be entered on the Journal of each House respectively. If any Bill shall not be returned by the President within ten Days (Sundays excepted) after it shall have been presented to him, the Same shall be a Law, in like Manner as if he had signed it, unless the Congress by their Adjournment prevent its Return, in which Case it shall not be a Law.

CLAUSE 3: Every Order, Resolution, or Vote to which the Concurrence of the Senate and House of Representatives may be necessary (except on a question of Adjournment) shall be presented to the President of the United States; and before the Same shall take Effect, shall be approved by him, or being disapproved by him, shall be repassed by two thirds of the Senate and House of Representatives, according to the Rules and Limitations prescribed in the Case of a Bill.

SECTION 8

CLAUSE 1: The Congress shall have Power To lay and collect Taxes, Duties, Imposts and Excises, to pay the Debts and provide for the common Defence and general Welfare of the United States; but all Duties, Imposts and Excises shall be uniform throughout the United States;

CLAUSE 2: To borrow Money on the credit of the United States;

CLAUSE 3: To regulate Commerce with foreign Nations, and among the several States, and with the Indian Tribes;

CLAUSE 4: To establish an uniform Rule of Naturalization, and uniform Laws on the subject of Bankruptcies throughout the United States;

CLAUSE 5: To coin Money, regulate the Value thereof, and of foreign Coin, and fix the Standard of Weights and Measures;

CLAUSE 6: To provide for the Punishment of counterfeiting the Securities and current Coin of the United States;

CLAUSE 7: To establish Post Offices and post Roads;

CLAUSE 8: To promote the Progress of Science and useful Arts, by securing for limited Times to Authors and Inventors the exclusive Right to their respective Writings and Discoveries;

CLAUSE 9: To constitute Tribunals inferior to the supreme Court;

CLAUSE 10: To define and punish Piracies and Felonies committed on the high Seas, and Offences against the Law of Nations;

CLAUSE 11: To declare War, grant Letters of Marque and Reprisal, and make Rules concerning Captures on Land and Water;

CLAUSE 12: To raise and support Armies, but no Appropriation of Money to that Use shall be for a longer Term than two Years;

CLAUSE 13: To provide and maintain a Navy;

CLAUSE 14: To make Rules for the Government and Regulation of the land and naval Forces;

CLAUSE 15: To provide for calling forth the Militia to execute the Laws of the Union, suppress Insurrections and repel Invasions;

CLAUSE 16: To provide for organizing, arming, and disciplining, the Militia, and for governing such Part of them as may be employed in the Service of the United States, reserving to the States respectively, the Appointment of the Officers, and the Authority of training the Militia according to the discipline prescribed by Congress;

CLAUSE 17: To exercise exclusive Legislation in all Cases whatsoever, over such District (not exceeding ten Miles square) as may, byCession of particular States, and the Acceptance of Congress, become the Seat of the Government of the United States, and to exercise like Authority over all Places purchased by the Consent of the Legislature of the State in which the Same shall be, for the Erection of Forts, Magazines, Arsenals, dock-Yards, and other needful Buildings;—And

CLAUSE 18: To make all Laws which shall be necessary and proper for carrying into Execution the foregoing Powers, and all other Powers vested by this Constitution in the Government of the United States, or in any Department or Officer thereof.

SECTION 9

CLAUSE 1: The Migration or Importation of such Persons as any of the States now existing shall think proper to admit, shall not be prohibited by the Congress prior to the Year one thousand eight hundred and eight, but a Tax or duty may be imposed on such Importation, not exceeding ten dollars for each Person.

CLAUSE 2: The Privilege of the Writ of Habeas Corpus shall not be suspended, unless when in Cases of Rebellion or Invasion the public Safety may require it.

CLAUSE 3: No Bill of Attainder or ex post facto Law shall be passed.

CLAUSE 4: No Capitation, or other direct, Tax shall be laid, unless in Proportion to the Census or Enumeration herein before directed to be taken.

CLAUSE 5: No Tax or Duty shall be laid on Articles exported from any State.

CLAUSE 6: No Preference shall be given by any Regulation of Commerce or Revenue to the Ports of one State over those of another: nor shall Vessels bound to, or from, one State, be obliged to enter, clear, or pay Duties in another.

CLAUSE 7: No Money shall be drawn from the Treasury, but in Consequence of Appropriations made by Law; and a regular Statement and Account of the Receipts and Expenditures of all public Money shall be published from time to time.

CLAUSE 8: No Title of Nobility shall be granted by the United States: And no Person holding any Office of Profit or Trust under them, shall, without the Consent of the Congress, accept of any present, Emolument, Office, or Title, of any kind whatever, from any King, Prince, or foreign State.

SECTION 10

CLAUSE 1: No State shall enter into any Treaty, Alliance, or Confederation; grant Letters of Marque and Reprisal; coin Money; emit Bills of Credit; make any Thing but gold and silver Coin a Tender in Payment of Debts; pass any Bill of Attainder, ex post facto Law, or Law impairing the Obligation of Contracts, or grant any Title of Nobility.

CLAUSE 2: No State shall, without the Consent of the Congress, lay any Imposts or Duties on Imports or Exports, except what may be absolutely necessary for executing it's inspection Laws: and the net Produce of all Duties and Imposts, laid by any State on Imports or Exports, shall be for the Use of the Treasury of the United States; and all such Laws shall be subject to the Revision and Controul of the Congress.

CLAUSE 3: No State shall, without the Consent of Congress, lay any Duty of Tonnage, keep Troops, or Ships of War in time of Peace, enter into any Agreement or Compact with another State, or with a foreign Power, or engage in War, unless actually invaded, or in such imminent Danger as will not admit of delay.

ARTICLE II

SECTION 1

CLAUSE 1: The executive Power shall be vested in a President of the United States of America. He shall hold his Office during the Term of four Years, and, together with the Vice President, chosen for the same Term, be elected, as follows.

CLAUSE 2: Each State shall appoint, in such Manner as the Legislature thereof may direct, a Number of Electors, equal to the whole Number of Senators and Representatives to which the State may be entitled in the Congress: but no Senator or Representative, or Person holding an Office of Trust or Profit under the United States, shall be appointed an Elector.

CLAUSE 3: The Electors shall meet in their respective States, and vote by Ballot for two Persons, of whom one at least shall not be an Inhabitant of the same State with themselves. And they shall make a List of all the Persons voted for, and of the Number of Votes for each; which List they shall sign and certify, and transmit sealed to the Seat of the Government of the United States, directed to the President of the Senate. The President of the Senate shall, in the Presence of the Senate and House of Representatives, open all the Certificates, and the Votes shall then be counted. The Person having the greatest Number of Votes shall be the President, if such Number be a Majority of the whole Number of Electors appointed; and if there be more than one who have such Majority, and have an equal Number of Votes, then the House of Representatives shall immediately chuse by Ballot one of them for President; and if no Person have a Majority, then from the five highest on the List the said House shall in like Manner chuse the President. But in chusing the President, the Votes shall be taken by States, the Representation from each State having one Vote; A quorum for this Purpose shall consist of a Member or Members from two thirds of the States, and a Majority of all the States shall be necessary to a Choice. In every Case, after the Choice of the President, the Person having the greatest Number of Votes of the Electors shall be the Vice President. But if there should remain two or more who have equal Votes, the Senate shall chuse from them by Ballot the Vice President.

CLAUSE 4: The Congress may determine the Time of chusing the Electors, and the Day on which they shall give their Votes; which Day shall be the same throughout the United States.

CLAUSE 5: No Person except a natural born Citizen, or a Citizen of the United States, at the time of the Adoption of this Constitution, shall be eligible to the Office of President; neither shall any Person be eligible to that Office who shall not have attained to the Age of thirty five Years, and been fourteen Years a Resident within the United States.

CLAUSE 6: In Case of the Removal of the President from Office, or of his Death, Resignation, or Inability to discharge the Powers and Duties of the said Office, the Same shall devolve on the VicePresident, and the Congress may by Law provide for the Case of Removal, Death, Resignation or Inability, both of the President and Vice President, declaring what Officer shall then act as President, and such Officer shall act accordingly, until the Disability be removed, or a President shall be elected.

CLAUSE 7: The President shall, at stated Times, receive for his Services, a Compensation, which shall neither be encreased nor diminished during the Period for which he shall have been elected, and he shall not receive within that Period any other Emolument from the United States, or any of them.

CLAUSE 8: Before he enter on the Execution of his Office, he shall take the following Oath or Affirmation:—"I do solemnly swear (or affirm) that I will faithfully execute the Office of President of the United States, and will to the best of my Ability, preserve, protect and defend the Constitution of the United States."

SECTION 2

CLAUSE 1: The President shall be Commander in Chief of the Army and Navy of the United States, and of the Militia of the several States, when called into the actual Service of the United States; he may require the Opinion, in writing, of the principal Officer in each of the executive Departments, upon any Subject relating to the Duties of their respective Offices, and he shall have Power to grant Reprieves and Pardons for Offences against the United States, except in Cases of Impeachment.

CLAUSE 2: He shall have Power, by and with the Advice and Consent of the Senate, to make Treaties, provided two thirds of the Senators present concur; and he shall nominate, and by and with the Advice and Consent of the Senate, shall appoint Ambassadors, other public Ministers and Consuls, Judges of the supreme Court, and all other Officers of the United States, whose Appointments are not herein otherwise provided for, and which shall be established by Law: but the Congress may by Law vest the Appointment of such inferior Officers, as they think proper, in the President alone, in the Courts of Law, or in the Heads of Departments.

CLAUSE 3: The President shall have Power to fill up all Vacancies that may happen during the Recess of the Senate, by granting Commissions which shall expire at the End of their next Session.

SECTION 3

He shall from time to time give to the Congress Information of the State of the Union, and recommend to their Consideration such Measures as he shall judge necessary and expedient; he may, on extraordinary Occasions, convene both Houses, or either of them, and in Case of Disagreement between them, with Respect to the Time of Adjournment, he may adjourn them to such Time as he shall think proper; he shall receive Ambassadors and other public Ministers; he shall take Care that the Laws be faithfully executed, and shall Commission all the Officers of the United States.

SECTION 4

The President, Vice President and all civil Officers of the United States, shall be removed from Office on Impeachment for, and Conviction of, Treason, Bribery, or other high Crimes and Misdemeanors.

ARTICLE III

SECTION 1

The judicial Power of the United States, shall be vested in one supreme Court, and in such inferior Courts as the Congress may from time to time ordain and establish. The Judges, both of the supreme and inferior Courts, shall hold their Offices during good Behaviour, and shall, at stated Times, receive for their Services, a Compensation, which shall not be diminished during their Continuance in Office.

SECTION 2

CLAUSE 1: The judicial Power shall extend to all Cases, in Law and Equity, arising under this Constitution, the Laws of the United States, and Treaties made, or which shall be made, under their Authority;—to all Cases affecting Ambassadors, other public Ministers and Consuls;—to all Cases of admiralty and maritime Jurisdiction;—to Controversies to which the United States shall be a Party;—to Controversies between two or more States;—between a State and Citizens of another State; between Citizens of different States,—between Citizens of the same State claiming Lands under Grants of different States, and between a State, or the Citizens thereof, and foreign States, Citizens or Subjects.

CLAUSE 2: In all Cases affecting Ambassadors, other public Ministers and Consuls, and those in which a State shall be Party, the supreme Court shall have original Jurisdiction. In all the other Cases before mentioned, the supreme Court shall have appellate Jurisdiction, both as to Law and Fact, with such Exceptions, and under such Regulations as the Congress shall make.

CLAUSE 3: The Trial of all Crimes, except in Cases of Impeachment, shall be by Jury; and such Trial shall be held in the State where the said Crimes shall have been committed; but when not committed within any State, the Trial shall be at such Place or Places as the Congress may by Law have directed.

SECTION 3

CLAUSE 1: Treason against the United States, shall consist only in levying War against them, or in adhering to their Enemies, giving them Aid and Comfort. No Person shall be convicted of Treason unless on the Testimony of two Witnesses to the same overt Act, or on Confession in open Court.

CLAUSE 2: The Congress shall have Power to declare the Punishment of Treason, but no Attainder of Treason shall work Corruption of Blood, or Forfeiture except during the Life of the Person attainted.

CLAUSE 3: No Person held to Service or Labour in one State, under the Laws thereof, escaping into another, shall, in Consequence of any Law or Regulation therein, be discharged from such Service or Labour, but shall be delivered up on Claim of the Party to whom such Service or Labour may be due.

SECTION 3

CLAUSE 1: New States may be admitted by the Congress into this Union; but no new State shall be formed or erected within the Jurisdiction of any other State; nor any State be formed by the Junction of two or more States, or Parts of States, without the Consent of the Legislatures of the States concerned as well as of the Congress.

CLAUSE 2: The Congress shall have Power to dispose of and make all needful Rules and Regulations respecting the Territory or other Property belonging to the United States; and nothing in this Constitution shall be so construed as to Prejudice any Claims of the United States, or of any particular State.

SECTION 4

The United States shall guarantee to every State in this Union a Republican Form of Government, and shall protect each of them against Invasion; and on Application of the Legislature, or of the Executive (when the Legislature cannot be convened) against domestic Violence.

ARTICLE IV

SECTION 1

Full Faith and Credit shall be given in each State to the public Acts, Records, and judicial Proceedings of every other State. And the Congress may by general Laws prescribe the Manner in which such Acts, Records and Proceedings shall be proved, and the Effect thereof.

SECTION 2

CLAUSE 1: The Citizens of each State shall be entitled to all Privileges and Immunities of Citizens in the several States.

CLAUSE 2: A Person charged in any State with Treason, Felony, or other Crime, who shall flee from Justice, and be found in another State, shall on Demand of the executive Authority of the State from which he fled, be delivered up, to be removed to the State having Jurisdiction of the Crime.

ARTICLE V

The Congress, whenever two thirds of both Houses shall deem it necessary, shall propose Amendments to this Constitution, or, on the Application of the Legislatures of two thirds of the several States, shall call a Convention for proposing Amendments, which, in either Case, shall be valid to all Intents and Purposes, as Part of this Constitution, when ratified by the Legislatures of three fourths of the several States, or by Conventions in three fourths thereof, as the one or the other Mode of Ratification may be proposed by the Congress; Provided that no Amendment which may be made prior to the Year One thousand eight hundred and eight shall in any Manner affect the first and fourth Clauses in the Ninth Section of the first Article; and that no State, without its Consent, shall be deprived of its equal Suffrage in the Senate.

ARTICLE VI

CLAUSE 1: All Debts contracted and Engagements entered into, before the Adoption of this Constitution, shall be as valid against the United States under this Constitution, as under the Confederation.

CLAUSE 2: This Constitution, and the Laws of the United States which shall be made in Pursuance thereof; and all Treaties made, or which shall be made, under the Authority of the United States, shall be the supreme Law of the Land; and the Judges in every State shall be bound thereby, any Thing in the Constitution or Laws of any State to the Contrary notwithstanding.

CLAUSE 3: The Senators and Representatives before mentioned, and the Members of the several State Legislatures, and all executive and judicial Officers, both of the United States and of the several States, shall be bound by Oath or Affirmation, to support this Constitution; but no religious Test shall ever be required as a Qualification to any Office or public Trust under the United States.

ARTICLE VII

The Ratification of the Conventions of nine States, shall be sufficient for the Establishment of this Constitution between the States so ratifying the Same.

Amendments to the United States Constitution

AMENDMENT I

Congress shall make no law respecting an establishment of religion, or prohibiting the free exercise thereof; or abridging the freedom of speech, or of the press; or the right of the people peaceably to assemble, and to petition the government for a redress of grievances.

AMENDMENT II

A well regulated militia, being necessary to the security of a free state, the right of the people to keep and bear arms, shall not be infringed.

AMENDMENT III

No soldier shall, in time of peace be quartered in any house, without the consent of the owner, nor in time of war, but in a manner to be prescribed by law.

AMENDMENT IV

The right of the people to be secure in their persons, houses, papers, and effects, against unreasonable searches and seizures, shall not be violated, and no warrants shall issue, but upon probable cause, supported by oath or affirmation, and particularly describing the place to be searched, and the persons or things to be seized.

AMENDMENT V

No person shall be held to answer for a capital, or otherwise infamous crime, unless on a presentment or indictment of a grand jury, except in cases arising in the land or naval forces, or in the militia, when in actual service in time of war or public danger; nor shall any person be subject for the same offense to be twice put in jeopardy of life or limb; nor shall be compelled in any criminal case to be a witness against himself, nor be deprived of life, liberty, or property, without due process of law; nor shall private property be taken for public use, without just compensation.

Amendment VI

In all criminal prosecutions, the accused shall enjoy the right to a speedy and public trial, by an impartial jury of the state and district wherein the crime shall have been committed, which district shall have been previously ascertained by law, and to be informed of the nature and cause of the accusation; to be confronted with the witnesses against him; to have compulsory process for obtaining witnesses in his favor, and to have the assistance of counsel for his defense.

Amendment VII

In suits at common law, where the value in controversy shall exceed twenty dollars, the right of trial by jury shall be preserved, and no fact tried by a jury, shall be otherwise reexamined in any court of the United States, than according to the rules of the common law.

Amendment VIII

Excessive bail shall not be required, nor excessive fines imposed, nor cruel and unusual punishments inflicted.

Amendment IX

The enumeration in the Constitution, of certain rights, shall not be construed to deny or disparage others retained by the people.

Amendment X

The powers not delegated to the United States by the Constitution, nor prohibited by it to the states, are reserved to the states respectively, or to the people.

Amendment XI

The judicial power of the United States shall not be construed to extend to any suit in law or equity, commenced or prosecuted against one of the United States by citizens of another state, or by citizens or subjects of any foreign state.

Amendment XII

The electors shall meet in their respective states and vote by ballot for President and Vice-President, one of whom, at least, shall not be an inhabitant of the same state with themselves; they shall name in their ballots the person voted for as President, and in distinct ballots the person voted for as Vice-President, and they shall make distinct lists of all persons voted for as President, and of all persons voted for as Vice-President, and of the number of votes for each, which lists they shall sign and certify, and transmit sealed to the seat of the government of the United States, directed to the President of the Senate;—The President of the Senate shall, in the presence of the Senate and House of Representatives, open all the certificates and the votes shall then be counted;—the person having the greatest number of votes for President, shall be the President, if such number be a majority of the whole number of electors appointed; and if no person have such majority, then from the persons having the highest numbers not exceeding three on the list of those voted for as President, the House of Representatives shall choose immediately, by ballot, the President. But in choosing the President, the votes shall be taken by states, the representation from each state having one vote; a quorum for this purpose shall consist of a member or members from two-thirds of the states, and a majority of all the states shall be necessary to a choice. And if the House of Representatives shall not choose a President whenever the right of choice shall devolve upon them, before the fourth day of March next following, then the Vice-President shall act as President, as in the case of the death or other constitutional disability of the President. The person having the greatest number of votes as Vice-President, shall be the Vice-President, if such number be a majority of the whole number of electors appointed, and if no person have a majority, then from the two highest numbers on the list, the Senate shall choose the Vice-President; a quorum for the purpose shall consist of two-thirds of the whole number of Senators, and a majority of the whole number shall be necessary to a choice. But no person constitutionally ineligible to the office of President shall be eligible to that of Vice-President of the United States.

AMENDMENT XIII

SECTION 1. Neither slavery nor involuntary servitude, except as a punishment for crime whereof the party shall have been duly convicted, shall exist within the United States, or any place subject to their jurisdiction.

SECTION 2. Congress shall have power to enforce this article by appropriate legislation.

AMENDMENT XIV

SECTION 1. All persons born or naturalized in the United States, and subject to the jurisdiction thereof, are citizens of the United States and of the state wherein they reside. No state shall make or enforce any law which shall abridge the privileges or immunities of citizens of the United States; nor shall any state deprive any person of life, liberty, or property, without due process of law; nor deny to any person within its jurisdiction the equal protection of the laws.

SECTION 2. Representatives shall be apportioned among the several states according to their respective numbers, counting the whole number of persons in each state, excluding Indians not taxed. But when the right to vote at any election for the choice of electors for President and Vice President of the United States, Representatives in Congress, the executive and judicial officers of a state, or the members of the legislature thereof, is denied to any of the male inhabitants of such state, being twenty-one years of age, and citizens of the United States, or in any way abridged, except for participation in rebellion, or other crime, the basis of representation therein shall be reduced in the proportion which the number of such male citizens shall bear to the whole number of male citizens twenty-one years of age in such state.

SECTION 3. No person shall be a Senator or Representative in Congress, or elector of President and Vice President, or hold any office, civil or military, under the United States, or under any state, who, having previously taken an oath, as a member of Congress, or as an officer of the United States, or as a member of any state legislature, or as an executive or judicial officer of any state, to support the Constitution of the United States, shall have engaged in insurrection or rebellion against the same, or given aid or comfort to the enemies thereof. But Congress may by a vote of two-thirds of each House, remove such disability.

SECTION 4. The validity of the public debt of the United States, authorized by law, including debts incurred for payment of pensions and bounties for services in suppressing insurrection or rebellion, shall not be questioned. But neither the United States nor any state shall assume or pay any debt or obligation incurred in aid of insurrection or rebellion against the United States, or any claim for the loss or emancipation of any slave; but all such debts, obligations and claims shall be held illegal and void.

SECTION 5. The Congress shall have power to enforce, by appropriate legislation, the provisions of this article.

AMENDMENT XV

SECTION 1. The right of citizens of the United States to vote shall not be denied or abridged by the United States or by any state on account of race, color, or previous condition of servitude.

SECTION 2. The Congress shall have power to enforce this article by appropriate legislation.

AMENDMENT XVI

The Congress shall have power to lay and collect taxes on incomes, from whatever source derived, without apportionment among the several states, and without regard to any census or enumeration.

AMENDMENT XVII

The Senate of the United States shall be composed of two Senators from each state, elected by the people thereof, for six years; and each Senator shall have one vote. The electors in each state shall have the qualifications requisite for electors of the most numerous branch of the state legislatures.

When vacancies happen in the representation of any state in the Senate, the executive authority of such state shall issue writs of election to fill such vacancies: Provided, that the legislature of any state may empower the executive thereof to make temporary appointments until the people fill the vacancies by election as the legislature may direct.

This amendment shall not be so construed as to affect the election or term of any Senator chosen before it becomes valid as part of the Constitution.

AMENDMENT XVIII

SECTION 1. After one year from the ratification of this article the manufacture, sale, or transportation of intoxicating liquors within, the importation thereof into, or the exportation thereof from the United States and all territory subject to the jurisdiction thereof for beverage purposes is hereby prohibited.

SECTION 2. The Congress and the several states shall have concurrent power to enforce this article by appropriate legislation.

SECTION 3. This article shall be inoperative unless it shall have been ratified as an amendment to the Constitution by the legislatures of the several states, as provided in the Constitution, within seven years from the date of the submission hereof to the states by the Congress.

AMENDMENT XIX

The right of citizens of the United States to vote shall not be denied or abridged by the United States or by any state on account of sex.

Congress shall have power to enforce this article by appropriate legislation.

AMENDMENT XX

SECTION 1. The terms of the President and Vice President shall end at noon on the 20th day of January, and the terms of Senators and Representatives at noon on the 3d

day of January, of the years in which such terms would have ended if this article had not been ratified; and the terms of their successors shall then begin.

SECTION 2. The Congress shall assemble at least once in every year, and such meeting shall begin at noon on the 3d day of January, unless they shall by law appoint a different day.

SECTION 3. If, at the time fixed for the beginning of the term of the President, the President elect shall have died, the Vice President elect shall become President. If a President shall not have been chosen before the time fixed for the beginning of his term, or if the President elect shall have failed to qualify, then the Vice President elect shall act as President until a President shall have qualified; and the Congress may by law provide for the case wherein neither a President elect nor a Vice President elect shall have qualified, declaring who shall then act as President, or the manner in which one who is to act shall be selected, and such person shall act accordingly until a President or Vice President shall have qualified.

SECTION 4. The Congress may by law provide for the case of the death of any of the persons from whom the House of Representatives may choose a President whenever the right of choice shall have devolved upon them, and for the case of the death of any of the persons from whom the Senate may choose a Vice President whenever the right of choice shall have devolved upon them.

SECTION 5. Sections 1 and 2 shall take effect on the 15th day of October following the ratification of this article.

SECTION 6. This article shall be inoperative unless it shall have been ratified as an amendment to the Constitution by the legislatures of three-fourths of the several states within seven years from the date of its submission.

AMENDMENT XXI

SECTION 1. The eighteenth article of amendment to the Constitution of the United States is hereby repealed.

SECTION 2. The transportation or importation into any state, territory, or possession of the United States for delivery or use therein of intoxicating liquors, in violation of the laws thereof, is hereby prohibited.

SECTION 3. This article shall be inoperative unless it shall have been ratified as an amendment to the Constitution by conventions in the several states, as provided in the Constitution, within seven years from the date of the submission hereof to the states by the Congress.

AMENDMENT XXII

SECTION 1. No person shall be elected to the office of the President more than twice, and no person who has held the office of President, or acted as President, for more than two years of a term to which some other person was elected President shall be elected to the office of the President more than once. But this article shall not apply to any person holding the office of President when this article was proposed by the Congress, and shall not prevent any person who may be holding the office of President, or acting as President, during the term within which this article becomes operative from holding the office of President or acting as President during the remainder of such term.

SECTION 2. This article shall be inoperative unless it shall have been ratified as an amendment to the Constitution by the legislatures of three-fourths of the several states within seven years from the date of its submission to the states by the Congress.

AMENDMENT XXIII

SECTION 1. The District constituting the seat of government of the United States shall appoint in such manner as the Congress may direct:

A number of electors of President and Vice President equal to the whole number of Senators and Representatives in Congress to which the District would be entitled if it were a state, but in no event more than the least populous state; they shall be in addition to those appointed by the states, but they shall be considered, for the purposes of the election of President and Vice President, to be electors appointed by a state; and they shall meet in the District and perform such duties as provided by the twelfth article of amendment.

SECTION 2. The Congress shall have power to enforce this article by appropriate legislation.

AMENDMENT XXIV

SECTION 1. The right of citizens of the United States to vote in any primary or other election for President or Vice President, for electors for President or Vice President, or for Senator or Representative in Congress, shall not be denied or abridged by the United States or any state by reason of failure to pay any poll tax or other tax.

SECTION 2. The Congress shall have power to enforce this article by appropriate legislation.

AMENDMENT XXV

SECTION 1. In case of the removal of the President from office or of his death or resignation, the Vice President shall become President.

SECTION 2. Whenever there is a vacancy in the office of the Vice President, the President shall nominate a Vice President who shall take office upon confirmation by a majority vote of both Houses of Congress.

SECTION 3. Whenever the President transmits to the President pro tempore of the Senate and the Speaker of the House of Representatives his written declaration that he is unable to discharge the powers and duties of his office, and until he transmits to them a written declaration to the contrary, such powers and duties shall be discharged by the Vice President as Acting President.

SECTION 4. Whenever the Vice President and a majority of either the principal officers of the executive departments or of such other body as Congress may by law provide, transmit to the President pro tempore of the Senate and the Speaker of the House of Representatives their written declaration that the President is unable to discharge the powers and duties of his office, the Vice President shall immediately assume the powers and duties of the office as Acting President.

Thereafter, when the President transmits to the President pro tempore of the Senate and the Speaker of the House of Representatives his written declaration that no inability exists, he shall resume the powers and duties of his office unless the Vice President and a majority of either the principal officers of the executive department or of such other body as Congress may by law provide, transmit within four days to the President pro tempore of the Senate and the Speaker of the House of Representatives their written declaration that the President is unable to discharge the powers and duties of his office. Thereupon Congress shall decide the issue, assembling within forty-eight hours for that purpose if not in session. If the Congress, within twenty-one days after receipt of the latter written declaration, or, if Congress is not in session, within twenty-one days after Congress is required to assemble, determines by two-thirds vote of both Houses that the President is unable to discharge the powers and duties of his office, the Vice President shall continue to discharge the same as Acting President; otherwise, the President shall resume the powers and duties of his office.

AMENDMENT XXVI

SECTION 1. The right of citizens of the United States, who are 18 years of age or older, to vote, shall not be denied or abridged by the United States or any state on account of age.

SECTION 2. The Congress shall have the power to enforce this article by appropriate legislation.

AMENDMENT XXVII

No law, varying the compensation for the services of the Senators and Representatives, shall take effect, until an election of Representatives shall have intervened.

Index

NOTE: Page numbers in *italics* represent figures and tables.